S

S

# Medieval German Literature

GARLAND REFERENCE LIBRARY OF THE HUMANITIES
VOLUME 1774

Fol. 125$^r$ of the Manesse (Heidelberg) manuscript (slightly reduced/partial?). Text of the poem: *Ich saz ûf eime steine ...* by Walther von der Vogelweide, with permission of Insel Verlag.

# Medieval German Literature
## A Companion

Marion E. Gibbs
Sidney M. Johnson

Garland Publishing, Inc.
New York and London
1997

Copyright © 1997 by Marion E. Gibbs and Sidney M. Johnson
All rights reserved

Library of Congress Cataloging-in-Publication Data

Gibbs, Marion E. (Marion Elizabeth), 1940–
    Medieval German literature : a companion / by Marion E. Gibbs and
Sidney M. Johnson.
        p.    cm. — (Garland reference library of the humanities ; vol. 1774)
    Includes bibliographical references.
    ISBN 0-8153-1450-7 (alk. paper)
    1. German literature—Old High German, 750–1050—History and criti-
cism.    2. German literature—Middle High German, 1050–1500—History
and criticism.    I. Johnson, Sidney M.    II. Title.    III. Series.
PT175.G53    1997
830.9'002—dc21                                                         97-14299
                                                                          CIP

Cover illustration: miniature of Kaiser Heinrich (slightly reduced) from the
Manesse (Heidelberg) manuscript, fol. 6ʳ, with permission of Insel Verlag.

Printed on acid-free, 250-year-life paper
Manufactured in the United States of America

# Table of Contents

# Preface

This book is intended to serve as a source of information for those who are interested in the study of Medieval German literature. It can be used as a reference book or read straight through for an overview. The arrangement of the book may appear at first as somewhat unorthodox, but we feel that it supports our concept. After a brief discussion of what is meant by the "Middle Ages," there follows a short discussion of the history of the German language, so that readers will have some idea of what is meant, for example, by OHG, EMHG, etc. when they come across such terms later in the book. Next comes a section on the many resources available for the study of medieval German literature. Here some very useful tools are listed for various topics of importance to such study.

The authors recognize that only a few major literary works of the classical period of Middle High German have reached a wider public. We have attempted therefore to present them in the context of German literature from its beginnings to 1400 and its historical background. The structure of our book is thus basically chronological, but it is also generic. We make no claims to comprehensive coverage nor to uniform depth on all the works we treat, yet we hope to enable our readers to attain both if they wish or to be judiciously selective in areas of special interest. The material presented here follows the traditional canon.

In planning our book we asked ourselves the following questions: What do people really have to know for the study of medieval German literature? What are the important works? What do they deal with? Why are they significant? What is characteristic about them? What is their historical and cultural background? And above all, how can one find out more about them? Though they lay no claim to completeness, our answers to these questions will be found, we hope, on the following pages. We should like to think of this volume not only as a source of essential information about medieval German literature as a whole but also as a handy reference work for those in other areas or periods of Medieval Studies who need some knowledge of specific areas of early German literature.

Although our treatment of individual works varies according to their particular qualities and demands, we have tried to provide broadly similar types of information for each one in addition to answers to the questions above: something about the manuscript tradition; available editions, translations, facsimiles; the problems that scholars have encountered and tried to solve; and a short bibliography of pertinent secondary literature. The bibliographical references have been chosen with an eye towards ready availability, relative currency, and significance. When the contents or importance of a book or article did not seem to emerge clearly from the title, we have provided a line or two of explanatory description. For one important group of our intended readers, we have tried wherever possible to include a high proportion of works in English in the secondary literature, and we have provided English translations for all German quotations.

Instead of a traditional index we have included at the end of the book a chronological table of the more important works we have discussed, indicating page numbers in the text. Because of the difficulty of dating medieval German works precisely, the position of the various works and authors in the table is only approximate. We believe that this table, plus the table of contents, will not only make it easy for the reader to locate the information sought but will also provide an interesting visual comparative chronology of the whole period from the rudimentary beginnings to the relatively brief but intense flourishing of the classical period in the decades around 1200 to the gradual movement away from traditional medieval ideas and the broadening of literature towards the close of the Middle Ages in the later 13th and 14th centuries.

M.E.G.
S.M.J.

# Abbreviations Used in Bibliographies in Text

*AbäG* - *Amsterdamer Beiträge zur älteren Germanistik*

*Ahd. Gl.* - v. Steinmeyer, Elias, and Eduard Sievers, eds. *Die althochdeutschen Glossen.* Berlin, 1879-1922. 5 Vols.

*Ahd. Lb.* - Braune, Wilhelm, ed. *Althochdeutsches Lesebuch.* Tübingen: Niemeyer, [14]1962, rev. by Ernst A. Ebbinghaus.

*ATB* - Altdeutsche Textbibliothek.

*Curschmann/Glier* - Curschmann, Michael, and Ingeborg Glier, eds. and trans. *Deutsche Dichtung des Mittelalters.* Vol. I: Von den Anfängen bis zum hohen Mittelalter. München/Wien, 1980.

*Diemer, Dt. Gedichte* - Diemer, Joseph, ed. *Deutsche Gedichte des XI. unf XII. Jahrhunderts. Aufgefunden im regulierten Chorherrenstifte zu Vorau in der Steiermark und zum ersten Male mit einer Einleitung und Anmerkungen heraus gegeben.* Vienna: Braumüller, 1849. lxii + 532 pp. Repr. Darmstadt, 1968.

*DNL* - *Deutsche National-Literatur*

*DTM* - *Deutsche Texte des Mittelalters*

*DVjs* - *Deutsche Vierteljahrsschrift für Literaturwissenschaft und Geistesgeschichte*

*Euph.* - *Euphorion. Zeitschrift für Literaturgeschichte.*

*FMLS* - *Forum for Modern Language Study*

*GAG* - *Göppinger Arbeiten zur Germanistik*

*GLG* - *Grundlagen der Germanistik*

*GLL* - *German Life and Letters*

*GLML* - *Garland Library of Medieval Literature*

*GR* - *The Germanic Review*

*GRM* - *Germanisch-Romanische Monatsschrift*

*Handbook* - Bostock, J. Knight. *A Handbook on Old High German Literature.* Oxford, London, et al.: Oxford Univ. Press, [2]1976, rev. by K. C. King and D. R. McLintock.

*Haug/Vollmann* - Haug, Walter, and Benedikt Vollmann, eds. and trans, *Frühe deutsche Literatur und Lateinische Literatur in Deutschland, 800-1150.* Frankfurt am Main: Deutscher Klassiker Verlag, 1991 (=Bibliothek des Mittelalters, I).

*Henschel/Pretzel* - Henschel, Erich, and Ulrich Pretzel, eds. *Die kleinen Denkmäler der Vorauer Handschrift.* Tübingen: Niemeyer, 1963.

*JEGPh* - *Journal of English and Germanic Philology.*

*Kl. ahd. Sprdmr.* - v. Steinmeyer, Elias, ed. *Kleinere althochdeutsche Sprachdenkmäler.* Berlin, 1916. Repr. 1971.

*Maurer* - Maurer, Friedrich, ed. *Die religiösen Dichtungen des 11. und 12. Jahrhunderts.* Nach ihren Formen besprochen und hrsg. 3 Vols., Tübingen: Niemeyer, 1964-70.

*MLN* - *Modern Language news*

*MLR* - *Modern Language Review*

*MHG* - *Monumenta Germaniae historica*

*MSD* - ("Müllenhoffs und Scherers Denkmäler"). Müllenhoff, Karl, and Wilhelm Scherer, eds. *Denkmäler Deutscher Poesie und Prosa aus dem VIII.-XII. Jh.* Berlin, [3]1892 by Elias v. Steinmeyer.

*Neophil.* - *Neophilologus*

*Neuphil.Mitt.* - *Neuphilologische Mitteilungen*

*PBB* - ("Pauls und Braunes Beiträge") *Beiträge zur Geschichte der deutschen Sprache und Literatur.*

*PMLA* - *Publications of the Modern Language Association*

*PSuQ* - *Philologische Studien und Quellen.*

*QF* - *Quellen und Forschungen zur Kulturgeschichte der germanischen Völker.*

*Schlosser* - Schlosser, Horst Dieter, ed. and trans. *Althochdeutsche Literatur.* Ausgewählte Texte mit Übertragungen. Frankfurt/M: Fischer Taschenbuch Verlag, 1970. Erweiterte Neuausgabe, 1989. (=Fischer Taschenbuch, 6889).

*Schrifttafeln* - Fischer, Hanns, ed. *Schrifttafeln zum ahd. Lesebuch.* Tübingen: Niemeyer, 1966.

*UB* - *Reclams Universalbibliothek*

*VL* - *Die deutsche Literatur des Mittelalters. Verfasserlexikon.* 1933-1955.

*VL*[2] - *Die Deutsche Literatur des Mittelalters. Verfasserlexikon.* [2]1978 et seq.

*Waag/Schröder* - Waag, Albert, ed. *Kleinere deutsche Gedichte des XI. und XII. Jahrhunderts.* Halle (Saale): Niemeyer, [1]1890, [2]1916. (=ATB, 10). New ed. by Werner Schröder. 2 Vols., Tübingen: Niemeyer, 1972. (=ATB, 71 and 72).

*WdF* - *Wege der Forschung*

*Wehrli* - Wehrli, Max, ed. and trans. *Deutsche Lyrik des Mittelalters. Aus- wahl und Übersetzung.* Zürich, 1955.

*Wilhelm* - Wilhelm, Friedrich, ed. *Denkmäler deutscher Prosa des 11. und 12. Jahrhunderts.* Munich: Huber, 1960.(=Germanistische Bücherei, 3).

*ZfdA* - *Zeitschrift für deutsches Altertum und deutsche Literatur.*

*ZfdPh* - *Zeitschrift für deutsche Philologie.*

# Introduction

## THE MIDDLE AGES

It is an oversimplification but perhaps a helpful guide to divide the Middle Ages, as is sometimes done, according to social groupings: thus, the Early Middle Ages is described as the period of the monks, the High (middle period) as the period of the knights, and the Late as the period of the townsmen. Such a view of the centuries usually called, though again not uncontentiously, "the Middle Ages" may provoke scholarly objections, but it does provide some kind of focus and assist in the attempt to define the principal influences which colored the whole period. It does, however, raise another vexing question, for it implies, quite erroneously, that there is a degree of unanimity about the chronological division of a timespan of six or seven centuries.

The focus of this volume is the literature of the so-called classical Middle High German period, the last decade of the twelfth century and the ensuing twenty or thirty years. This brief flowering is in itself a remarkable phenomenon, and we hope to demonstrate the quality and nature of the literature of these decades, both intrinsically and in relation to its social and historical context. These are complex issues, and all we can hope to do is present some of the salient facts and point the way to closer study of individual factors. When it comes to the literary context, the position is if anything even more complex, since it is not altogether possible to see the literature of the *Blütezeit* as part of a continuum: rather does it stand to a large extent in isolation, arising—if not exactly out of a void—often without obvious precursors and with few distinct resonances in the centuries which followed.

Precisely this phenomenon of a single splendid peak of literary achievement has dictated our decision to take this volume back to the beginnings of German literature, in the monuments of Old High German, to lead up through the various developments of the eleventh and twelfth centuries to the products of the turn of the twelfth and thirteenth which truly merit the designation "classical." If medieval German literature never again attained that towering stature, nevertheless what followed commands considerable interest for its variety and originality as well as for the echoes which can be identified of that earlier age.

Historians may argue about where exactly one can place the end of the Middle Ages, and this question has obviously arisen for us too. We have chosen to conclude our discussion at 1400, a date which, though somewhat arbitrary, has an explanation both historical and literary. The date of the deposition of the Emperor Wenzel, who continued until 1419 as King of Bohemia, is not a turning point of any moment, but it happens to coincide with the commonly accepted approximate date for the composition of *Der*

*Ackermann aus Böhmen*, a work which can be seen as a literary turning point of some significance, with its roots in the Late Middle Ages yet in many respects a product of the new intellectual attitudes of the early modern period.

## A WORD ABOUT THE HISTORY OF THE GERMAN LANGUAGE

Some understanding of the historical development of the German language is important for work in medieval German literature. We shall not attempt to present a complete picture of that development; that is a task for historical linguists and beyond the scope of this book. Nevertheless, we should speak briefly about the history of the language for those who may be unfamiliar with it. There are three general periods that can be defined by certain developments that occurred over the course of time in the phonology, morphology, and syntax of the language. Naturally such changes did not happen from one day to the next, but the evidence shows that by a certain date a particular change must have taken place. It is probably safe to say, for example, that by the year 500 A.D. the language, or group of languages that was eventually to evolve into modern German had already undergone significant changes which distinguished it from other Germanic languages. These changes are called the "second sound shift" (*zweite Lautverschiebung*) or the "High German sound shift" in contrast to the earlier "first sound shift" (*erste Lautverschiebung*), or "Germanic sound shift," which distinguished the Germanic family of languages from the general Indo-European.

The resulting language, or group of dialects, is called "Old High German" (*Althochdeutsch*) and abbreviated as OHG (*AHD*). The term "old" refers to chronology: the period of roughly 750-1050 A.D., and the term "high" refers to geography: the area of the southern two-thirds of the German-speaking area, in contrast to the northern one-third in which the second sound shift did *not* take place. That northern area encompasses the North German Plain and is geographically "lower" than the southern parts, which rise gradually toward the alpine regions. Hence, the languages of the north are called "Low German," the most important of which in this early period is "Old Saxon."

It is easy to talk about Old High German as if it were a single language, and scholars used to speak of it that way, but in reality Old High German is a group of dialects that share many common elements but also have important differences. In the first place, there is a difference between the language of the central third of the German-speaking area and the southern third. To be sure, both are "High German," as opposed to "Low German" (*Niederdeutsch*, e.g. *Old Saxon*), but we call the languages of the highest region "Upper German" (*Oberdeutsch*) in contrast to "Middle German" (*Mitteldeutsch*). Furthermore, the terms "Middle German" and "Upper German," convenient as they are for many purposes, do not tell the whole story. Within each region various Germanic tribes had settled, each with its own particular dialect, so that we must subdivide the two High German areas further. Starting in the south and working northward we find the following dialects:

High German - Upper German (*Oberdeutsch*):
Alemannic (*Alemannisch*)

Bavarian (*Bairisch*)
Usually also: East Franconian (*Ostfränkisch*), although it has some Middle German features.

High German - Middle German (*Mitteldeutsch*):
South Rhein Franconian (*Südrheinfränkisch*)
Rhein Franconian (*Rheinfränkisch*)
Moselle Franconian (*Moselfränkisch*)
Ripuarian (*Ripuarisch*)
Thuringian (*Thüringisch*)

Low German (*Niederdeutsch*):
Old Saxon (*Altsächsisch*)
Old Low Franconian (*Altniederfränkisch*)
Probably also: Frisian (*Friesisch*), although there are no monuments until the 13th century.

Since it is impossible to draw boundaries of the dialect areas for the 8th century because of the paucity of documents and their relative concentration in a few scriptoria, we have used the more ample evidence of the 13th century to chart the boundaries. However, it is more than likely that with a few exceptions it is a fair picture of the dialect distribution in the earlier period. Interestingly enough, a dialect map of modern Germany would be almost identical. (See map p. 4).

Our knowledge of these dialects is based largely on surviving literary monuments which were usually written in the scriptoria of monasteries. The scribes who were schooled in Latin used various spellings to record German words, the sounds of which did not always correspond exactly to Latin, so that it is difficult to determine whether the German spellings reflect the spoken language of the area, the spelling conventions of a particular monastery, or an attempt at normalized spellings that would be understood more widely. The question of orthography is further complicated by the fact that some documents are obviously translations from one dialect into another, sometimes done quite mechanically.

Middle High German (*Mittelhochdeutsch*), abbreviated as MHG (*MHD*), is what we call the language of the second stage in the development towards modern German, the period from 1050-1350, again defined by certain linguistic changes that occurred gradually and with roughly the same dialect areas as in OHG. In addition, just as there was considerable lexical influence by Latin on OHG, MHG shows influence from French, particularly in the language of courtly literature. Some scholars feel that a separate category should be made for Early Middle High German (*Frühmittelhochdeutsch*), abbreviated EMHG (*Frühmhd.* or *FMHD*), as a transitional stage between OHG and the more or less standard MHG of the period around 1200, but that is not necessary for our purposes here. However, we should mention that there is some indication that poets of the High Middle Ages, the several decades around 1200, adopted a literary language by using only words in rhymes that would still be rhymes in almost any other dialect.

Early New High German (*Frühneuhochdeutsch*), abbreviated ENHG (*FNHD*), is the third period in the history of the German language of importance to medieval scholars.

Just how important depends on where one dates the end of the Middle Ages, and there is little agreement on that. Some linguists feel the need for a Late Middle High German classification (1250-1350), but certainly by 1350 the changes that allow us to speak of Early New High German had already taken place. They are the structural and phonetic features that have remained constant as German developed over the centuries into the Standard German of today.

In concluding this very brief overview, we should like to stress again the fact that linguistic change is a gradual process and that within an admittedly arbitrarily defined period, several stages of the process of change may be evident at any given point in time. Furthermore, the variations of dialect tend to complicate the picture, but we hope that the

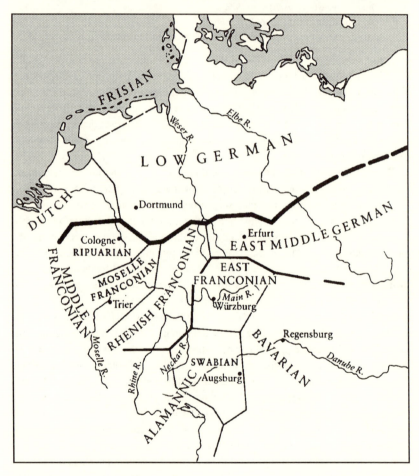

Middle High German literary dialects in the 13th century A.D. (After Paul and Mitzka [1966: Abb. 1] and Orrin Robinson [1992: Map 8], by permission.)

reader will have become acquainted with the general development of the language in the Middle Ages and familiar with some of the terms we shall use in discussing the various texts. Those wishing more information are referred to the following:

## Language—Bibliography

Bach, Adolf. *Geschichte der deutschen Sprache*. Heidelberg: Winter, [9]1971.

A standard, comprehensive German work on the subject, not for the casual reader.

Bergmann, Rolf, Heinrich Tiefenbach, and Lothar Voetz, eds. *Althochdeutsch. Bd.I: Grammatik. Glossen und Texte; Bd. II: Wörter und Namen. Forschungsgechichte*. Heidelberg: Carl Winter, 1987 (= Germanische Bibliothek. 3. Reihe: Untersuchungen).

This immense work attempts to present the state of OHG scholarship as of 1987 in phonology, morphology, word formation, syntax, glosses, Stabreimtexte, Endreimtexte, prose texts, vocabulary, names, history of scholarship. It is not an overview, rather a series of exemplary articles by well-known scholars on the subjects listed.

Chambers, W. Walker, and John R. Wilkie. *A Short History of the German Language*. London: Methuen & Co. Ltd., 1970. Repr. 1973.

A general description of the history of the German language, the development of vocabulary, and changes in phonology, morphology and syntax.

Eggers, Hans. *Deutsche Sprachgeschichte I: Das Althochdeutsche*. Reinbek bei Hamburg: Rowohlt, 1963.

Discussion of Old High German with special attention to the vocabulary. Sample excerpts in an appendix.

_____. *Deutsche Sprachgeschichte II: Das Mittelhochdeutsche*. Reinbek bei Hamburg: Rowohlt, 1965.

Presentation of the language of various types of MHG texts from an historical perspective, with sample excerpts in an appendix.

_____. *Deutsche Sprachgeschichte III: Das Frühneuhochdeutsche*. Reinbek bei Hamburg: Rowohlt, 1969.

A brief cultural and linguistic history of Early NHG language with emphasis on the influence of the Reformation and Humanism. Excerpts from representative texts in an appendix.

Keller, R. E. *The German Language*. London: Faber & Faber, 1978.

A very thorough, comprehensive presentation of the German language from an historical perspective from Indo-European to modern times. The medieval sections cover the first 335 of the over 600 pages.

Lockwood, William B. *An Informal History of the German Language*. Cambridge: W. Heffer, 1965. New edition: London, 1976.

Also has chapters on Dutch and Afrikaans, Frisian, and Yiddish.

Maurer, Friedrich. *Nordgermanen und Alemannen. Studien zur germanischen und frühdeutschen Sprachgeschichte, Stammes- und Volkskunde*. Bern, München: A. Francke Verlag, Leo Lehnen Verlag, 1942. [3]1952 (= Bibliotheca Germanica).

_____, and Heinz Rupp. *Deutsche Wortgeschichte*. Berlin: de Gruyter, [3]1974.

Moser, Hugo. *Deutsche Sprachgeschichte: Mit einer Einführung in die Fragen der Sprachbetrachtung.* Tübingen: Niemeyer, [9]1969.

Penzl, Herbert. *Althochdeutsch.* Bern: Peter Lang, 1986 (= Germanistische Lehrbuchsammlung, 7).

Introduction to OHG with linguistic analysis of illustrative texts.

____. *Mittelhochdeutsch.* Bern: Peter Lang, 1989 (= Germanistische Lehrbuchsammlung, 8).

Introduction to MHG grammar and syntax on the basis of analysis of selected texts.

Priebsch, Robert, and William E. Collinson. *The German Language.* London, [6]1966.

For many years the standard work in English.

Robinson, Orrin W. *Old English and Its Closest Relatives. A Survey of the Earliest Germanic Languages.* Stanford, CA: Stanford UP, 1992.

Although aimed at Old English, it covers Indo-European, Proto-Germanic, Gothic, OHG, OS, Old Frisian, ON, Old Low Franconian. Excellent brief histories of the various Germanic tribes. Informative maps showing geographical distribution and migrations.

Schmidt, Wilhelm. *Geschichte der deutschen Sprache.* Ed. by Helmut Langner. Stuttgart: S. Hirzel, [6]1993.

This history is intended as a text for the linguistic education of Germanists, not simply for linguists. Therefore it is a comprehensive work, including the pre-history as well as the history of the German language.

Schmitt, Ludwig Erich, ed. *Kurzer Grundriß der germanischen Philologie bis 1500.* Berlin: Erich Schmidt, 1970. 2 vols.

Stefan Sonderegger on OHG, pp. 288-346; Gabriele Schieb on MHG, pp. 347-385; and Johannes Erben on ENHG, pp. 386-440.

von Polenz, Peter. *Geschichte der deutschen Sprache.* Berlin: de Gruyter, [9]1978 (= Sammlung Göschen, 915, 915a).

An inexpensive, thorough, but concise treatment of the subject. The period of the Middle Ages is covered on roughly the first 100 pages.

Waterman, John T. *A History of the German Language. Revised Edition.* Seattle: Univ. of Washington, 1976. Reissued 1991 by Waveland Press, Prospect Heights, IL.

A very readable presentation intended for advanced undergraduates and graduate students.


## RESOURCES FOR THE STUDY OF MEDIEVAL GERMAN LITERATURE

We have made the somewhat unusual decision of placing a large section of bibliographical material first. We did this because we felt it important to introduce the reader at the outset to the many aids to the study of medieval German Literature which provide the framework, background, and perspective to what we are trying to do in this book. On some of the more general background issues we have been very selective, but we have tried to indicate some of the major resources and have borne in mind likely availability.

From time to time in the course of the book we shall be referring to these more general works, but there are also specific bibliographies in each section. Where we felt it to be appropriate we have repeated items of particular relevance for the benefit of those readers who may be referring to specific parts of the book, even though its broadly chronological design means that we hope it will be useful for those wishing to read it straight through. Within the specific bibliographies, which inevitably vary in length and type depending on the nature of the topic, we have included principal editions, translations, and facsimiles, along with a selection of secondary literature. We have tried also to indicate the nature or importance of an item with a few words when the title does not tell the reader very much about the work in question.

However, the study of medieval literature involves more than texts, editions, and pertinent secondary literature. One must know what resources there are to find additional information. The resources listed below attempt to provide that: useful reference works, histories of literature, dictionaries, and all the bibliographical aids of various sorts. The wealth of resources is really quite impressive, and the works we present here are a significant part of it.

## Medieval Studies

Powell, James M., ed. *Medieval Studies. An Introduction*. Syracuse: Syracuse UP, [2]1992.

A series of essays that, taken together, define Medieval Studies today by treating all aspects of the discipline.

Weddige, Hilkert. *Einführung in die germanistische Mediävistik*. Munich: Beck, 1987.

A general introduction to Medieval Studies with emphasis on German literature. Tends to be rather theoretical.

Meissburger, Gerhard. *Einführung in die mediävistische Germanistik*. Ed. By Trude Ehlert. Göppingen: Kümmerle, 1983 (= GAG, 369).

Based on Meissburger's lectures, notes, and drafts, expanded and edited posthumously by Trude Ehlert.

## Useful Reference Works

Bächtold-Stäubli, Hanns, ed. *Handwörterbuch des deutschen Aberglaubens*. Berlin: de Gruyter, 1927-42.

Buchberger, M., ed. *Lexikon für Theologie und Kirche*. Freiburg: Herder, [2]1957. Ed. by Josef Hofer and Karl Rahner. [3]1993. Ed. by Walter Kasper with Konrad Baumgartner. 10 vols.

Chandler, Frank W., comp. *A Catalogue of Names of Persons in the German Court Epics: An Examination of Literary Sources and Dissemination, together with Notes on the Etymologies of the More Important Names*. Ed. with an introduction and appendix by Martin H. Jones. London: King's College London, Centre for Late Antique and Medieval Studies, 1992.

Cross, F. L., ed. *The Oxford Dictionary of the Christian Church*. Oxford: Oxford UP, 1957. [2]1974. Ed. by F. L. Cross and E. A. Livingstone.

Hoops, Johannes, ed. *Reallexikon der germanischen Altertumskunde*. Berlin, 1911-19. 4 vols. Berlin: de Gruyter, [2]1968-. Ed. by Herbert Jankuhn, et al.; [2]1973-. Ed. by Heinrich Beck. With supplementary volumes beginning 1986-.

A good source of information about éarly Germanic culture and civilization.

Kohlschmidt, Werner, and Wolfgang Mohr, eds. *Reallexikon der deutschen Literaturgeschichte*. Berlin: de Gruyter, [2]1958 [i.e. 1955]-88. 5 vols. (Vol. 4-5 ed. by Klaus Kanzog and Achim Masser.

First edition by Paul Merker and Wolfgang Stammler, 1925-31, therefore sometimes referred to as "Merker-Stammler." A general literary lexicon, not specifically medieval but a useful reference work.

Schmitt, Ludwig Erich, ed. *Kurzer Grundriß der germanischen Philologie bis 1500*. 2 vols. Berlin: de Gruyter, 1970.

Similar to Stammler (1957-69, below) with articles by various specialists, but much more concise. Vol. I deals with the history of the language, Vol. II with the history of literature.

Stammler, Wolfgang, and Karl Langosch. *Die deutsche Literatur des Mittelalters. Verfasserlexikon*. Berlin: de Gruyter, 1933-55. 5 vols. (4 vols. + supplementary vol.).

The first place to look for basic information on works and authors: biography, dating, mss., editions, brief history of scholarship, main problems, bibliography. Be sure to look up the author's name rather than the title of the work (In the case of medieval works this will usually be the author's *first* name). We have not always listed the relevant lexicon article in our text, unless it is outstandingly good, or where very little else is available, but it is always worth looking there at an early stage. (*VL*). Completely rev. edition by Kurt Ruh, [2]1978-1995. Vols. 1-9 have appeared so far; contents organized alphabetically: A to Sle-Ulr (vol. 9). (*VL*[2]).

_____, ed. *Deutsche Philologie im Aufriß*. Berlin: Erich Schmidt, [2]1957-69 (rev.). Repr. 1978-79. 4 vols.

This huge work is packed with information. It contains articles on all aspects of German philology by eminent scholars. The first volume generally deals with the Germanic languages, the second with German literature, and the third with German in relation to other areas of study, e.g. music. The fourth volume is an index. While the work is not primarily on medieval topics, they occupy a prominent place, hence very valuable here. Although it was compiled over 30 years ago, it is still extremely useful as a source for concise information.

### Histories of Medieval German Literature

Bäuml, Franz. "Mittelalter." In: Bahr, Erhard, ed. *Geschichte der deutschen Literatur*. I: Vom Mittelalter bis zum Barock. Tübingen: Francke, 1987 (= Uni-Taschenbücher, 1436). Pp. 1-244.

A compact literary history, placing German literature in the framework of the European, with due attention to the problems of literary historiography.

Bertau, Karl. *Deutsche Literatur im europäischen Mittelalter*. Band I: 800-1197. Munich: Beck, 1972. Band II: 1195-1220. 1973. 85 illustr. at end of Vol. II.

A very different kind of literary history, it stresses the historical events and places the literary works in that framework. There are more pages devoted to history than to literature. An extensive index of all the dates mentioned in the text (7000 B.C.-1972 A.D.!) takes up almost 100 pp. in Vol. II. (*Bertau*)

de Boor, Helmut, and Richard Newald. *Geschichte der deutschen Literatur.* Band I von Helmut de Boor. *Die deutsche Literatur von Karl dem Großen bis zum Beginn der höfischen Dichtung (770-1170).* Munich: Beck, [9]1979 (rev. by Herbert Kolb); Band II von Helmut de Boor. *Die höfische Literatur. Vorbereitung, Blüte, Ausklang (1170-1250).* [10]1979 (rev. by Ursula Hennig); Band III. *Die deutsche Literatur im späten Mittelalter. Zerfall und Neubeginn.* 1. Teil von Helmut de Boor. *Epik, Lyrik, Didaktik, geistliche und historische Dichtung.* [5]1987 (rev. by Johannes Janota); 2. Teil hrsg. von Ingeborg Glier. *Reimpaargedichte, Drama, Prosa.* 1987.

This history of literature, the first ([1]1949) to appear after World War II, was for many years the standard work of its kind. Repeated revisions have kept it relatively up to date in terms of bibliography. It can be recommended as an objective account, centered on the works themselves, with some regard for cultural history but little for social and political influences. (*de Boor Litgesch*)

Bostock, J. Knight. *A Handbook on Old High German Literature.* Oxford: Clarendon Press, 1955. [2]1976 (rev. by K. C. King and D. R. McLintock).

Good as the first edition was, the second is even better. Both present the many problems in OHG literature fairly and stress particularly the linguistic ones. The second edition does an outstanding job of describing the historical background of the works. In fact, historical events are the framework of the book. The maps and genealogies in the appendix are very helpful. (*Handbook*)

Burger, Heinz Otto, ed. *Annalen der deutschen Literatur.* Stuttgart: Metzler, 1952. Rev. [2]1971.

A collaborative effort by numerous eminent scholars of the day to present German literature from the beginnings to ca. 1900. Separate sections by individual scholars. Sections covering the Middle Ages, pp. 1-286.

Ehrismann, Gustav. *Geschichte der deutschen Literatur bis zum Ausgang des Mittelalters.* Erster Teil: Die althochdeutsche Literatur. Munich: Beck, [2]1932; Zweiter Teil: Die mittelhochdeutsche Literatur. 1. Abschnitt: Frühmittelhochdeutsche Zeit. 1922; 2. Abschnitt: Blütezeit. 1. Hälfte. 1927; Schlußband (Blütezeit. 2. Hälfte; Spätmittelhochdeutsche Literatur. 14. und 15. Jahrhundert). 1935.

Although this work is now very much out of date, it is still quite useful for the wealth of information it provides, especially in respect to sources and summaries of contents. Some of Ehrismann's judgments should be taken with caution, but it is a remarkably comprehensive work. It was reprinted in 1954. (*Ehrismann*)

Frey, Winfried, Walter Raitz, Dieter Seitz, et al. *Einführung in die deutsche Literatur des 12. bis 16. Jahrhunderts.* Bd. 1: *Adel und Hof—12./13. Jahrhundert.* Opladen: Westdeutscher Verlag, 1979 (= Grundkurs Literaturgeschichte).

An introduction to the literature of the period based on interpretations of the most important texts in relationship to their historical reality.

Glaser, Horst Albert, ed. *Deutsche Literatur: Eine Sozialgeschichte*, Vol. I: ed. by Ursula Liebertz-Grün. *Aus der Mündlichkeit in die Schriftlichkeit: Höfische und andere Literatur*. Reinbeck bei Hamburg: Rowohlt, 1988.

Another outstanding, inexpensive social history of medieval German literature, it is a series of articles by noted scholars, including one by the editor. Vast bibliography (over 700 items!) and convenient chronological table.

Heinzle, Joachim, ed. *Geschichte der deutschen Literatur von den Anfängen bis zum Beginn der Neuzeit*. Band I: Von den Anfängen zum hohen Mittelalter. Teil 1 von Wolfgang Haubrichs: Die Anfänge: Versuche volkssprachiger Schriftlichkeit im frühen Mittelalter (ca. 700-1050/60). Königstein/Ts.: Athenäum, 1988; Teil 2 von Gisela Vollmann-Profe: Wiederbeginn volkssprachiger Schriftlichkeit im hohen Mittelalter (1050/60-1160/70). 1986; Band II: Vom hohen zum späten Mittelalter. Teil II von Joachim Heinzle: Wandlungen und Neuansätze im 13. Jahrhundert (1220/30-1280/90). 1984. (It is our understanding that this series is now being continued by Niemeyer: Tübingen and revised volumes will also be published there).

A very readable, relatively recent literary history which strives to present the literature embedded in the socio-historical matrix of the various periods. Vol. II/1 by L. Peter Johnson, Vol. III/1 by Johannes Janota, and Vol. III/2 by Johannes Janota and Joel Lefebvre are in preparation. (*Haubrichs/Vollmann-Profe/Heinzle Litgesch*)

Kartschoke/Bumke/Cramer. *Geschichte der deutschen Literatur im Mittelalter*. Munich: DTV, 1990. 3 Vols.: Geschichte der deutschen Literatur im frühen Mittelalter (= dtv 4551). Von Dieter Kartschoke; Geschichte der deutschen Literatur im hohen Mittelalter (= dtv 4552). Von Joachim Bumke; Geschichte der deutschen Literatur im späten Mittelalter (= dtv 4553). Von Thomas Cramer.

Excellent, concise, inexpensive (paperback) literary history by three distinguished scholars. Emphasis on factual aspects and background of the literary works. (*Kartschoke/Bumke/Cramer Geschichte*)

Nusser, Peter. *Deutsche Literatur im Mittelalter: Lebensformen, Wertvorstellungen und literarische Entwicklungen*. Stuttgart: Kröner, 1992 (= Kröner Taschenausgabe, 480).

A convenient handbook which covers literature from the OHG period to the late Middle Ages. Quite comprehensive, written in a somewhat dense style.

Salmon, Paul B. *Literature in Medieval Germany*. New York: Barnes & Noble, 1967 (= Introductions to German Literature, ed. by August Closs 1).

A concise historical introduction aimed at the general reader and the serious student. Almost 100 pages of the text are devoted to bibliography. English translations of quotations from the works under discussion. Dated now, of course. (*Salmon*)

Schneider, Hermann. *Heldendichtung, Geistlichendichtung, Ritterdichtung*. Heidelberg: Winter, 1925 (= Geschichte der deutschen Literatur, I).

An interesting older approach to the literature based on the social classes of the authors and/or intended audience.

Schwietering, Julius. *Die deutsche Dichtung des Mittelalters*. Potsdam: Akad. Verlagsges. Athenaion, 1932 (= Handbuch der Literaturwissenschaft, ed. by Oskar Walzel). Repr. Darmstadt: Hermann Gentner, 1957.

A profusely illustrated literary history (some hand-tipped color plates in the original edition) by a scholar who stressed the relationship of the visual and the literary arts. Somewhat dated now, of course, but still interesting and informative reading.

von See, Klaus, ed. *Neues Handbuch der Literaturwissenschaft*. Frankfurt/M, Akad. Verlagsges. Athenaion, 1972-. Vols. publ. after 1983 in Wiesbaden: AULA-Verlag. Of 25 planned volumes, only 1-3, 6, 8-13, 15, 17-23 have appeared.

Of interest here is Vol. 6: *Europäisches Mittelalter*, ed. by Klaus von See. This is another collection of articles by various scholars and is very good for the European perspective on literature of the Middle Ages.

Walshe, Maurice O'C. *Medieval German Literature. A Survey*. Cambridge: Harvard Univ. Press, 1962.

A most readable history, presenting the literature in its historical setting, it is an excellent work, not only for those lacking German (all quotations are translated!). The section on Old High German is not so detailed, but for that period we have Bostock (see above). Very good explanation of metrics. (*Walshe MedGerLit*)

Wapnewski, Peter. *Deutsche Literatur des Mittelalters. Ein Abriß*. Göttingen: Vandenhoeck & Ruprecht, 1960.

A very concise history, by an outstanding scholar, shorter by far than Wehrli (below), outlining the main trends (in paperback). (*Wapnewski 1960*)

Wehrli, Max, *Geschichte der deutschen Literatur vom frühen Mittelalter bis zum Ende des 16. Jahrhunderts*. Stuttgart: Reclam, 1980 (= Geschichte der deutschen Literatur von den Anfängen bis zur Gegenwart 1, UB 10294).

A concise, one-volume (paperback) history by a distinguished medieval Germanist. (*Wehrli Geschichte*)

## Dictionaries
### (Listed in Chronological Order)

Benecke, Georg Friedrich, Wilhelm Müller, and Friedrich Zarncke, comps. *Mittelhochdeutsches Wörterbuch*. Mit Benutzung des Nachlasses von Georg Friedrich Benecke ausgearbeitet von Wilhelm Müller und Friedrich Zarncke. Leipzig: S. Hirzel, 1854-61. 3 vols. in 4.

Müller was actually the prime mover behind this dictionary, using the glossary and other material that Benecke had assembled for a dictionary before his death, revising and supplementing that, and persuading Zarncke to work up M-R (vol. 2, part 1). Nevertheless, it is still known as "*BMZ*." Individual words are not listed alphabetically but rather etymologically under "stems," which *are* ordered alphabetically. However, the "stem" is not always readily apparent, e.g., the verb *jehen* is listed under *ich gihe* (N.B.: all verbs are given in the 1st pers. sing.!), so that it takes some practice to use *BMZ* easily. Still, it is a remarkable achievement.

Lexer, Matthias, comp. *Mittelhochdeutsches Handwörterbuch, zugleich als Supplement und alphabetischer Index zum mhd. Wörterbuch von Benecke-Müller-Zarncke.* Leipzig: S. Hirzel, 1872-78. 3 vols. Repr. Stuttgart: S. Hirzel, 1979

As the extended title indicates, Lexer arranged the words alphabetically and gave references in *BMZ* for them. It was so much easier to use that it quickly became the standard MHG dictionary.

_____, comp. *Mittelhochdeutsches Taschenwörterbuch.* Leipzig: S. Hirzel, 1879. 1 vol. Corrected and supplemented, [19]1930; appendix added, [29]1959 and supplemented, [34]1974; most recent edition, [37]1983. Editions after WWII publ. Stuttgart: S. Hirzel.

This has its limitations but for most general users is quite adequate. Also convenient in price and size, especially as it is available in a small paperback (though too big for the normal pocket!).

Bachofer, Wolfgang, Walther von Hahn, and Dieter Mohn, eds. *Rückläufiges Wörterbuch der mhd. Sprache: auf der Grundlage von Matthias Lexers Mhd. Handwörterbuch und Taschenwörterbuch.* Stuttgart: S. Hirzel, 1984.

This is organized on the basis of word endings and is used especially as a dictionary of rhymes or possible ones for words missing or unintelligible in mss.

Koller, Erwin, Werner Wegstein, and Norbert Richard Wolf, comps. *Mhd. Wörterbuch. Alphabetischer Index.* Stuttgart: S. Hirzel, 1990.

This alphabetical index helps to find your way around in *BMZ*.

_____, et al., comps. *Neuhochdeutscher Index zum mhd. Wortschatz.* Stuttgart: S. Hirzel, 1990.

Based on the 37th edition of Lexer's *Taschenwörterbuch*, it lists modern German words with their MHG equivalents.

Gärtner, Kurt, et al., comps. *Findebuch zum mhd. Wortschatz mit einem rückläufigen Index.* Stuttgart: S. Hirzel, 1992.

A kind of supplement to Lexer's *Handwörterbuch*, but *not* a dictionary, it is based on glossaries, word-lists, and indexes for texts edited *after* 1878. The "backward" index is at the end.

Hennig, Beate, comp. *Kleines mhd. Wörterbuch.* Tübingen: Niemeyer, 1993.

This dictionary is derived from a corpus of MHG works treated more than five times in lectures and seminars at German universities during the course of eleven semesters, thus making it very appropriate for students.

Schützeichel, Rudolf, comp. *Althochdeutsches Wörterbuch.* Tübingen: Niemeyer, [5]1995

Revised and expanded edition of the OHG Dictionary on the basis of numerous texts, comprehensive bibliography.

## Anthologies

de Boor, Helmut, et al. eds. *Die deutsche Literatur: Texte und Zeugnisse.* 6 vols. Munich: Beck, 1963-83.

Comprehensive anthology of important works and/or selections from the beginnings to 1933. Vol. I/1 & I/2 (1965, ed. by de Boor) cover the Middle Ages; Vol. II/1 & II/2 (1975-78, ed. by Hedwig Heger) cover late Middle Ages, Humanism and Renaissance.

Braune, Wilhelm, ed. *Althochdeutsches Lesebuch.* Tübingen: Niemeyer, [17]1994. Revised by Ernst A. Ebbinghaus.

This is the best source for OHG literature. It has most of the shorter OHG prose and poetic monuments and excerpts from the longer ones. With bibliography and a dictionary. (*Ahd.Lb.*)

Curschmann, Michael, and Ingeborg Glier, eds. & trans. *Deutsche Dichtung des Mittelalters.* 3 vols. Munich: Hanser, 1980-81.

Excellent selection of texts with mod. Ger. trans. Vol. I is especially useful for OHG and EMHG texts. Vol. II has texts of the High and Vol. III of the Late Middle Ages. Valuable notes and commentary, especially for a broader reading audience. (*Curschmann/Glier*)

Maurer, Friedrich (ed.). *Die religiösen Dichtungen des 11. und 12. Jahrhunderts.* Nach ihren Formen besprochen und herausgegeben. 3 Vols., Tübingen: Niemeyer, 1964-70.

Standard anthology of EMHG religious texts, edited somewhat idiosyncratically by Maurer. (*Maurer*)

Schlosser, Horst Dieter, ed. and trans. *Althochdeutsche Literatur: Mit Proben aus dem Altniederdeutschen.* Frankfurt/M.: Fischer Taschenbuch, 1989.

Inexpensive sel. with mod. Germ. trans., notes, and glossary. (*Schlosser*)

Waag, Albert (ed.). *Kleinere deutsche Gedichte des XI. und XII. Jahrhunderts.* Halle (Saale): Niemeyer, 1890, [2]1916. (= ATB, 10). New ed. by Werner Schröder. 2 Vols., Tübingen: Niemeyer, 1972. (= ATB, 71 and 72).

A handy collection of important EMHG religious texts, edited conservatively. (*Waag/Schröder*)

Wipf, K. A., ed. and trans. *Althochdeutsche poetische Texte: Althochdeutsch/Neuhochdeutsch.* Stuttgart: Reclam, 1992 (= UB, 8709).

Anthology of sel. with mod. Germ. trans. in paperback. (*Wipf*)

### Medieval German History

Barraclough, Geoffrey. *The Origins of Modern Germany.* Oxford: Blackwell, 1972.

A standard text on the subject.

____, trans. *Medieval Germany 911-1250. Essays by German Historians.* Oxford: Blackwell, 1938.

Haverkamp, Alfred. *Medieval Germany, 1056-1273.* Trans. by Helga Braun and Richard Mortimer. New York: Oxford UP, [2]1992. (Engl. version of his *Aufbruch und Gestaltung. Deutschland, 1056-1273.* Munich: Beck, 1988)).

An engaging, vivid, comprehensive portrayal of Germany in its European context during the period. Selected, but more than ample bibliography, genealogical table, index, map.

Holmes, George, ed. *The Oxford Illustrated History of Medieval Europe.* Oxford: Oxford UP, 1988.

A lavishly illustrated history of Europe from 400-1500, intended for a general audience, with chapters written by various scholars, excellent maps, chronology of events.

Hooper, Nicholas, and Matthew Bennett. *The Cambridge Illustrated Atlas of Warfare. The Middle Ages, 768-1478.* Cambridge: Cambridge UP, 1996.

Keen, Maurice. *A History of Medieval Europe.* London: Routledge & Kegan Paul, 1967.
A useful introduction, covering the period 800-1460, written with the non-specialist in mind.

McKitterick, Rosamond, ed. *The New Cambridge Medieval History. Vol. 2: c.700-900.* Cambridge: Cambridge UP, 1995.
A collaborative effort with noted contributors. Excellent for the early period covered in our volume.

Stubbs, William. *Germany in the Early Middle Ages, 476-1250.* And: *Germany in the Later Middle Ages, 1200-1500.* London: Longmans, Green & Co., 1908.
These are standard text-books of a much earlier generation, sound on facts, but old-fashioned in language and approach.

## Medieval Culture and Society

Bäuml, Franz H. *Medieval Civilization in Germany 800-1273.* London: Thames & Hudson, 1969.
A helpful book, very much to the point, with some useful illustrations and particularly maps.

Bloch, Marc. *Feudal Society.* London: Routledge and Kegan Paul, 1961. Trans. by L. A. Manyon from *La Société féodale.* 2 vols. Paris: Michel, 1941.

Fehring, Günter P. *Einführung in die Archäologie des Mittelalters.* Darmstadt: Wiss. Buchges., 1987. Engl. trans. by Ross Samson, *The Archaeology of Medieval Germany. An Introduction.* London: Routledge, 1991.
An introduction to a relatively new discipline which affords important insights into the daily life of medieval Germany. Copiously illustrated.

Painter, Sidney. *Medieval Society.* Ithaca: Cornell UP, 1951.
A useful little book, often reprinted; really an essay on life in the Middle Ages in Europe.

Southern, R. W. *The Making of the Middle Ages.* New Haven: Yale UP, 1953. [12]1966.
This is a classic of its kind, a lengthy essay on the formation of medieval society.

## Courtly Culture

Bumke, Joachim. *Studien zum Ritterbegriff im 12. und 13. Jahrhundert.* Heidelberg: Winter, 1964. [2]1977 (mit einem Anhang: Zum Stand der Forschung 1976). Engl.: *The Concept of Knighthood in the Middle Ages.* Trans. by W. T. H. Jackson and E. Jackson, New York: AMS Press, 1982.
A seminal work on the subject. (***Bumke Ritterbegriff***)

____. *Höfische Kultur. Literatur und Gesellschaft im hohen Mittelalter.* 2 vols. Munich: DTV, 1986. Engl. trans. by Thomas Dunlap: *Courtly Culture: Literature and Society in the High Middle Ages.* Berkeley, CA: Univ.of Cal. Press, 1991.
This remarkable handbook, published in two paperback volumes, gives a detailed and fascinating picture of medieval life, with information on every conceivable aspect of courtly society at this time and copious illustrations from German literature.

It is an indispensable aid to the serious study of Middle High German literature and to anyone wishing to build up a picture of the medieval courtly background. (**Bumke Kultur**)

Jaeger, C. Stephen. *The Origins of Courtliness. Civilizing Trends and the Formation of Courtly Ideals. 939-1210.* Philadelphia: Univ. of Pennsylvania Press, 1985.

The courtier class and its classical education for court service provided the background for the ideal of a courtly, chivalric society that developed in the second half of the 12th century.

Keen, Maurice. *Chivalry.* New Haven: Yale UP, 1984.

An exhaustive study on the topic, based on all available sources.

Schultz, Alwin. *Das höfische Leben zur Zeit der Minnesinger.* 2 vols. Leipzig: S. Hirzel, 1879-80.

One of those great collections of enormous amounts of information made in the 19th century. It is based largely on Lat., OF, and MHG literary sources and profusely illustrated, covering all aspects of courtly life. Though its evaluations may be questioned, it is still a valuable study.

Readers wishing to extend their understanding of the circumstances in which the literature arose and was transmitted will want to look at the following:

Bumke, Joachim. *Mäzene im Mittelalter.* Munich: Beck, 1979.

In his usual meticulous way, Joachim Bumke here examines the important question of the patronage of medieval German literature 1150-1300. Along the way he adds enormously to our understanding of the circumstances of the works. Excellent documentation. (**Bumke Mäzene**)

Chickering, Howell, and Thomas Seiler, eds. *The Study of Chivalry.* Kalamazoo, MI: Medieval Institute Publications, 1988.

A collaborative effort by numerous scholars concentrating on approaches to the study of chivalry and the teaching of chivalric literature.

Fechter, Werner. *Das Publikum der mittelhochdeutschen Dichtung.* Darmstadt: Wiss. Buchges., 1966.

This is a photographic reprint of the original in the series Deutsche Forschungen, 28, Frankfurt, 1935. For a long time the standard work on the subject of the contemporary reception of MHG literature, it remains an interesting account, though largely superseded.

Green, Dennis H. *Medieval Listening and Reading. The Primary Reception of German Literature 800-1300.* Cambridge: UP, 1994.

The approach makes this very much a book for the specialist, although the subject itself—*how* the works will have been received—is an intriguing one for the nonspecialist too.

### Bibliographical Sources

*Bibliographien zur deutschen Literatur des Mittelalters.* Ed. by Wolfgang Bachofer. Berlin: Schmidt, 1966-.

A series of eleven bibliographies on individual authors or works, initiated by Ulrich Pretzel and compiled by various scholars. They are immensely useful, as far as they go chronologically, but only one has been continued with a supplement for a period after its initial publication.

Eppelsheimer, Hanns, et al., comps. *Bibliographie der deutschen Literaturwissenschaft.* 31 vols. Frankfurt/M: Klostermann, 1957 et seq.

Comprehensive bibliography of all areas of German literature, not just medieval, that strives for completeness. Vol. 1 (1957) covers 1945-53. Latest vol. (1993) covers 1991.

*Germanistik. Internationales Referatenorgan mit bibliographischen Hinweisen.* Tübingen: Niemeyer, 1960-.

This quarterly is probably the best running bibliographical source available, at least for the period of each number (quarterly). It covers much more than just the Middle Ages and usually lists books and articles within a year after their appearance. Brief summaries of the books are included, but articles are simply listed. It includes subject-matter cross-listings and is truly international in scope. Latest volume is 1996,1.

*PMLA Annual Bibliography.* The *Publications of the Modern Language Association* included an "American Bibliography" of books and articles on language and literature in the modern foreign languages in its quarterly journal from 1919-55. For the years 1956-62 it became the "Annual Bibliography," and from 1963-68 it became the "MLA International Bibliography." Beginning in 1969 the bibliography was issued as a separate volume. From 1981- in two volumes, one for English and one for other modern languages, it strove to be complete. An on-line computer data base, updated regularly is available in most major libraries in two sections: 1969-80 and 1981-.

Although the bibliographies sponsored by the MLA have been very important for German scholars in the past, *Germanistik* (see above) has superseded them. However, the on-line MLA data base is more current and therefore still important for the latest books and articles on German language and literature. Since *PMLA*, the journal of the MLA, publishes few articles on German literature, let alone on medieval German literature, we have not included it in our list of useful periodicals.

Stapf, Paul, ed. *Handbuch der deutschen Literaturgeschichte.* II. Abt.: Bibliographien. Vol. I, Frühes Mittelalter, by Henry Kratz. Vol. II, Hohes Mittelalter, by Michel Batts. Vol. III, Spätes Mittelalter, by George F. Jones. Bern: Francke, 1970 (Vol I), 1969 (Vol. II), 1971 (Vol. III).

Lists the most important editions and studies from early 19th century to approximate date of publication. One of the few reference works to combine both older and more recent primary and secondary literature.

Other computer data bases, aside from the *MLA Bibliography*, are the *OCLC World-Cat* and the *RLIN/Eureka (National Bibliography Database)*.

# Periodicals

This list of periodicals represents only those journals in which one is likely to find a significant number of articles on medieval German literature.

*Amsterdamer Beiträge zur älteren Germanistik.* Amsterdam: Rodopi, 1972-. Ed. by Cola Minis.

> Articles are in German and English. Volumes appear irregularly but usually comprise ca. 200 pages. Some volumes concentrate on a single topic. Covers all aspects of Germanic philology. Also offers some reviews.

*Arbitrium. Zeitschrift für Rezensionen zur germanistischen Literaturwissenschaft.* Ed. by Wolfgang Frühwald and Wolfgang Harms. Munich: Beck, 1982-.

> Journal of high quality book reviews.

*Beiträge zur Geschichte der deutschen Sprache und Literatur.* Ed. by Hermann Paul and Wilhelm Braune. Halle (Saale): Niemeyer, 1874-.

> This renowned periodical continued in Halle until Vol. 100 (1979) when it changed its title to *Beiträge zur Erforschung der deutschen Sprache* and moved to VEB Verlag Enzyklopädie: Leipzig. In 1955 the Max Niemeyer Verlag, having been expropriated and having moved to Tübingen after WWII, resumed publishing the *Beiträge* and continued the original volume numbers so that from 1955 (vol. 77) to 1979 (vol. 100) there existed two versions of the periodical with different contents that had to be identified by the place of publication: Halle/Tübingen, or sometimes Ost/West. The *Beiträge*, frequently abbreviated *PBB*, but also *Beitr.* or *BGDSL*, is still one of the premier journals in the field. It includes book reviews.

*Colloquia Germanica. Internationale Zeitschrift für germanische Sprach- und Literaturwissenschaft.* Bern: Francke, 1968-.

> Published by the Department of Germanic and Classical Languages and Literatures, Univ. of Kentucky. Has frequently published articles on medieval literature as well as book reviews. (***Colloq. Germ.***)

*Deutsche Vierteljahrsschrift für Literaturwissenschaft und Geistesgeschichte.* Ed. by Paul Kluckhohn and Erich Rothacker. Halle (Saale): Niemeyer, 1923-.

> Publishes a great variety of articles, but there is something medieval in every issue. Some very important studies have appeared here. No book reviews. (***DVjs***)

*Euphorion. Zeitschrift für Literaturgeschichte.* Bamberg: Buchner, 1894-1933. Ed. by August Sauer. Stuttgart: Metzler, 1934. Ed. by Julius Petersen and Hermann Pongs, with title: *Dichtung und Volkstum. Neue Folge des Euphorion* (vols. 34-45). Returned to original title, *Euphorion. Dritte Folge.* Marburg/Lahn, Simons Verlag, 1950. Ed. by Hans Pyritz und Hans Neumann (vol. 45). Heidelberg: Winter, 1952-. Vol. 46 ff. With various editors.

> Although this periodical covers many areas of literary study, it always has had a significant number of important articles on medieval literature. Some reviews but not very many. (***Euph.***)

*The German Quarterly.* Ed. by Elijah Williams Bagster-Collins. Philadelphia, etc.: American Association of Teachers of German, 1928-.

Frequent changes in editorship. Articles on all areas of Germanic Studies, with a representative number of articles on medieval topics. Large book review section though reviews tend to be shorter and descriptive rather than analytical. (*GQ*)

*The Germanic Review*. New York: Department of Germanic Languages, Columbia University, 1926-.

Covers the whole field of Germanic languages and literatures, hence relatively few on medieval works. Modest number of reviews. (*GR*)

*The Journal of English and Germanic Philology*. Urbana, IL; Univ. of Illinois, 1906-. Vol. 6-. (Originally: *Journal of Germanic Philology*. Bloomington, IN, 1897-1902. Vols. 1-4; Vol. 5 in Evanston, IL, 1903-05).

This is one of the premier American philological journals. Many important articles, numerous reviews of moderate length. (*JEGPh*)

*Modern Language Review*. Belfast, etc.: Modern Humanities Research Association, 1905-. Ed. by J. G. Robertson and successors.

The outstanding British research journal, with a good share of articles on medieval German literature. Critical reviews. (*MLR*)

*Monatshefte*. Madison, WI: Univ. of Wisc. Press, 1946-.

Originally a pedagogical monthly for German teachers, 1899-, it evolved over the years into a scholarly quarterly with a representative number of aricles on medieval German literature. Numerous, but short reviews.

*Oxford German Studies*. Oxford: Clarendon Press, 1966-.

This is an annual with a proportionate number of articles on medieval German topics. (*OGS*)

*Seminar. A Journal of Germanic Studies*. Toronto: Univ. of Totonto Press. 1965. Quarterly since 1974.

Sponsored by the Canadian Association of University Teachers of German and the Germanic Section of the Australasian Universities Language and Literature Association. Some articles on medieval subjects. Small number of reviews.

*Speculum. A Journal of Medieval Studies*. Cambridge, MA: The Medieval Academy, 1926-.

Here again the articles are not predominantly on German literature by any means, rather more on history or English, but it is an excellent journal and has numerous longer reviews of major books and monographs.

*Zeitschrift für deutsches Altertum*. Ed. by Moritz Haupt. Leipzig: Weidmannische Buchhandlung, 1841-.

In 1876 the *Anzeiger für deutsches Altertum*, ed. by Elias Steinmeyer, began appearing with *ZfdA* but with its own volume numbers and pagination. This contained only book reviews, whereas *ZfdA* had only articles. It continued appearing with *ZfdA* until *AfdA* 100 (1989) after which it lost its separate identity and was absorbed into *ZfdA* 119 (1990) as a review section. Articles tend to be lengthy, and reviews (also lengthy) are limited in number and to major works. The "grandfather" of all germanistic periodicals. (*ZfdA*) (*AfdA*)

*Zeitschrift für deutsche Philologie.* Ed. Ernst Höpfner and Julius Zacher. Halle: Waisenhaus, 1869-.

Since 1954 (vol. 73) published in Berlin: Erich Schmidt. Not restricted to articles on the Middle Ages, it tends to represent an earlier, broader definition of "philology." Numerous reviews. Highly respected in the field. (*ZfdPh*)

## Serial Publications

Altdeutsche Textbibliothek. Halle: Niemeyer, 1882- (Tübingen: Niemeyer, 1955-).

A relatively inexpensive series of texts that have frequently become standards. Many have been regularly revised. Most are printed with just one column of text, leaving ample room for marginal notes. (*ATB*)

Deutsche Texte des Mittelalters. Berlin: Akademie Verlag, 1904-.

Started in reaction against the dominant practice of the day of producing edited texts based on postulated stemmata, this series offered only diplomatic editions of specific manuscripts. Modern editorial practice continues increasingly in this direction. (*DTM*)

Göppinger Arbeiten zur Germanistik. Göppingen: Kümmerle, 1968-.

A series of monographs, texts, and diverse other works. Frequently dissertations but also collected essays. Originally produced from camera-ready typewritten copy, they vary greatly in quality. The series has made it possible for many works to be published that otherwise would not be commercially viable. Over 600 have been published to date. (*GAG*)

Grundlagen der Germanistik. Berlin: Erich Schmidt, 1966-.

A series of concise handbooks as introductions to individual areas of expertise within "Germanistik." We include it here because it has several valuable works for the medieval period. (*GLG*)

Litterae. Göppingen: Kümmerle, 1971-.

This is a series of black and white facsimiles of manuscripts or parts thereof, usually with transcriptions. Inexpensive yet very helpful when the originals are not available. (*Litterae*)

Münchener Texte und Untersuchungen. Munich: Artemis, 1961. Later publ. by Beck.

Publishes worthy dissertations and "Habilitationsschriften" along with other monographs. (*MTU*)

Philologische Studien und Quellen. Berlin: Erich Schmidt, 1956-.

A distinguished monograph series, published irregularly. (*PSuQ*)

Reclams Universal-Bibliothek. Leipzig/Stuttgart: Reclam.

This is a very old series of texts and translations on a variety of literary topics for the educated public. Very inexpensive paperbacks and very popular. (*UB*)

Sammlung Metzler. Stuttgart: Metzler, 1961-.

A series of "Realienbücher" on specific topics or authors. Very handy, inexpensive, and concise. Unfortunately they have not always been kept up to date. (*Sammlung Metzler*)

Twayne's World Authors. Boston: Twayne.

This is one of several series of authors (English, American) published by Twayne. The "World Authors" series is made up of monographs in English on various non-English writers or works. For several German authors/works, esp. medieval, these are the only studies available in English. (*TWAS*)

Wolfram Studien. Berlin: Erich Schmidt, 1970-.

An annual volume of studies on Wolfram von Eschenbach and the entire German, French, and Middle Latin literature of the High Middle Ages. It was the organ of the newly reconstituted Wolfram von Eschenbach-Gesellschaft and has included since 1986 (vol. 10) a Wolfram-Bibliography. Papers presented at meetings of the Wolfram von Eschenbach-Gesellschaft are usually included.

### Paleography

Bischoff, Bernhard. *Latin Palaeography: Antiquity and the Middle Ages*. Trans. by Daibhi o Croinin and David Ganz. Cambridge: Cambridge UP, 1990, of *Paläographie des römischen Altertums und des abendländischen Mittelalters*. Berlin: Erich Schmidt, 1979, [2]1986.

Probably the best all-around treatment of this important field. Certainly a good starting place, regardless of vernacular interests.

\_\_\_\_. *Manuscripts and Libraries in the Age of Charlemagne*. Trans. by Michael M. Gorman. Cambridge: Cambridge UP, 1994.

Seven of Bischoff's classic essays on aspects of 8th- and 9th-century culture.

Eis, Gerhard. *Altdeutsche Handschriften*. Munich: Beck, 1949.

Facsimiles of 41 texts from runic inscriptions to a sample of Luther's handwriting with transcriptions and notes.

Kirchner, Joachim. *Germanistische Handschriftenpraxis*. Munich: Beck, [2]1967.

All you need to know about German manuscripts and how to deal with them, written especially for students of German philology.

### Medieval Rhetoric

Murphy, James J., ed. *Medieval Eloquence. Studies in the Theory and Practice of Medieval Rhetoric*. Berkeley: Univ. of California Press, 1978.

Miller, Joseph M., et al., eds. *Readings in Medieval Rhetoric*. Bloomington, IN: Indiana UP, 1973.

Translations of important medieval rhetorical texts. Good choices provide an overview of the tradition.

# Old High German Literature 750-1050

## HISTORICAL BACKGROUND

Long before the beginning of the Old High German period ancestors of the Germanic tribes inhabited the shores of the Baltic Sea, modern Denmark, southern Sweden, and the areas between the lower Elbe and Ems rivers. Archaeological evidence indicates that people had lived there even before the Northern Bronze Age (ca. 1700-450 B.C.). They buried their dead in communal graves constructed of very large pieces of stone, or megaliths, but later were influenced by people from the south who dug single graves for their dead and introduced, among other things, a particular kind of pottery known as corded ware because of the designs produced by pressing cords into the damp clay. The mingling of these groups may well have produced the early culture of the Germanic tribes. During the Northern Bronze Age there was a flourishing of culture throughout much of what is today western Europe, but the peoples in the north were eventually outstripped, possibly as a result of climatic change, by the developing civilization of the Hallstatt provinces to the south and later by the emergence and expansion of the Celts across central and western Europe during the subsequent Iron Age.

There is also linguistic evidence to indicate that certain phonological changes which distinguish the Germanic dialects from other Indo-European languages (the so-called first sound shift or Grimm's Law) probably had taken place by about 500 B.C. In the 3rd century B.C. we find the first references to these peoples in the writings of Greek historians. Scholars usually divide the Germanic tribes into five general groups: the North Germanic in Scandinavia; the East Germanic in the area between the Oder and the Vistula; and, using names that the later Roman historian Tacitus records, the Ingvaeones or North Sea group; the Istvaeones or Weser-Rhine peoples; and the Irminones or the Elbe group. The latter three groupings are frequently lumped together as West Germanic.

During the 3rd century B.C. the period of the great migrations (*Völkerwanderungen*) of the Germanic tribes began and extended into the 6th century A.D. Although the North Germanic group remained in Scandinavia, the other groups moved generally southward and spread out to the east and west. The Goths, Vandals, and Burgundians (East Germanic) moved to the east, then west and south to Bulgaria, Italy, Spain, and North Africa. The Alamanni, Marcomanni, and Langobardi (Irminones) settled in southern Germany and Italy, and another group in the area of modern Thuringia. A third group (Istvaeones) pushed into the Netherlands, northern France, the Rhineland, and Hesse, ultimately forming the kingdom of the Franks, and some of the tribes from the North Sea group, the Angles and Frisians, eventually settled in Britain.

Before and even after the first Christian emperor, Constantine, had relocated the seat of the Roman empire to his newly established city of Constantinople in 330 A.D., an ever-increasing power vacuum was developing in the western regions of the empire. Pressure by the Germanic tribes on the Roman territories had been growing for several centuries as Rome gradually lost control of the western provinces. In fact, the Roman army itself had become largely Germanicized. Many Germanic troops were incorporated into the Roman legions and larger contingents were pacified by grants of land which the Germanic peoples occupied in return for their military support of Rome as *foederati*. By the 5th century A.D. Roman forces had withdrawn from Britain, Gaul, and Germany, and the fortified Roman *limes* which had connected the Rhine-Danube frontiers had been breached as the Franks and the Burgundians pushed across the Rhine into northern and southern Gaul, respectively.

Italy had been invaded and Rome sacked in 403 and 410 by the Vandals, who subsequently moved on to Spain and north Africa. They were followed by the Visigoths who established a kingdom in southern Gaul and Spain. Next came the Huns under Attila, attacking across central Europe into Italy and central Gaul before they were defeated by the Romans, Burgundians, and Franks at the battle of the Catalaunian Plains in 451. In 455 the Vandals invaded Italy again from their north African kingdom, and in 476 the Roman army chose its general Odovacer to be king in Italy. But the empire in the east was not yet ready to abandon its western territories. In 488 the Ostrogothic leader Theodorich was commissioned by the eastern Emperor Zeno to regain Italy on behalf of the Empire. Although technically a subject-king to the emperor in Byzantium, Theodorich defeated Odovacer in 493 and established an independent Ostrogothic kingdom in Italy with its capital in Ravenna, not Rome. However, after the death of Theodorich in 526, the Ostrogothic kingdom did not last long, and in 533 the Byzantine emperor Justinian undertook to reconquer as much of the old Roman empire of the west as he could. He was successful in regaining control of Italy, Sicily and North Africa, but the success was only temporary, and the Lombards soon crossed the Alps and conquered northern Italy and parts of the south ca. 572.

Both the Ostrogoths and the Lombards were Arian Christians, hence heretics in the eyes of Rome and Byzantium, but the Merovingian Frankish king Clovis had adopted Roman Catholicism, the faith of his Burgundian wife. This proved to be a significant event because the Franks were the only Germanic peoples to become Roman Catholics at that time. It created a link between the Frankish kingdom and Rome that led eventually to the "renewal" of the Roman empire in the west at the time of Charlemagne and involved the empire in the affairs of Rome and Italy for centuries, not infrequently to the detriment of the empire.

The Germanic tribes left few, if any, written records during the time of the migrations, but Latin and Greek sources do tell us quite a bit about their culture. Even a brief summation of the available information would be impossible here, but, since our interest is primarily literary, suffice it to say that the Germanic peoples apparently had an oral tradition of heroic songs that persisted for centuries. Considerable evidence of such poetry is to be found in later German and Old Norse literature, and fascinating attempts have been made to recapture the oral heroic poetry and reconstruct a literary history of it. The Germanic peoples also developed a system of writing, using their so-called runic alphabet to make inscriptions on stones, weapons and other utensils. Presumably such inscriptions had magical or ritual significance to ward off evil, to destroy enemies, to celebrate certain occasions or places, or to be used in religious ceremonies.

As the Germanic tribes moved into the Roman Empire, sometimes as *foederati* of the Romans, or perhaps attracted by the higher standard of living there, or driven there by the incursion of the Huns, they took over the Roman territories, mingled with the inhabitants, settled down, and became Christianized. Not all, of course, but certainly many did, especially among those who settled in the area of Constantinople. The process of Christianization there was furthered by the work of the Gothic Bishop Ulfilas (or Wulfila). Born in the Crimea in 311 A.D., he translated the Bible into Gothic, from which substantial portions of the New Testament have survived in the so-called *Codex argenteus* (silver codex) now in Uppsala, Sweden. To make his remarkable translation Ulfilas used Greek uncials to represent the phonemes of his native Gothic, supplying runes for Gothic sounds that did not occur in Greek. This is the first extant translation of Christian writing into a Germanic language and provides evidence of the state of those languages after the first sound shift and before the second. It is important to emphasize here that Ulfilas's translation, as great an achievement as it may be, is Gothic, not German. It had little influence on the development of German literature, in part because the Goths were Arian Christians but also because of the ultimate absorption of the Goths into the Graeco-Roman world—the effective end of the Goths as a separate people.

## History—Bibliography

Boudriot, Wilhelm. *Die altgermanische Religion in der amtlichen kirchlichen Literatur des Abendlandes vom 5. bis 11. Jahrhundert.* 1928. Darmstadt, 1964.

Brown, Peter. *The World of Late Antiquity.* London: Thames and Hudson, 1971. 1989 (also: New York: Harcourt Brace Jovanovich, 1971, and W. W. Norton, 1989).

Excellent short account of the Late Roman Empire.

Capelle, Wilhelm. *Das alte Germanien.* Jena: Eugen Diederichs Verlag, 1937.

Translations of accounts of the Germanic tribes from Greek and Latin sources.

Fleckenstein, Josef. *Early Medieval Germany.* Amsterdam: North-Holland, 1978.

Heather, Peter J. *Goths and Romans AD 332-489.* London: Oxford UP, 1992. (= Oxford Historical Monographs).

Fascinating study of the entry of the Goths into the Roman empire and their migrations.

Kellermann, Volkmar. *Germanische Altertumskunde. Einführung in das Studium einer Kulturgeschichte der Vor- und Frühzeit.* Berlin: E. Schmidt, 1966. (= GLG).

Lot, Ferdinand. *The End of the Ancient World and the Beginnings of the Middle Ages.* Trans. Philip and Mariette Leon. 1931. New York: Harper & Brothers, 1961. (= Harper Torchbooks. The Academy Library).

A comprehensive account of the decline of the Roman empire from the 3rd cent. (Constantine) to the 6th cent. (the Frankish kingdom under the Merovingians).

Maurer, Friedrich. *Nordgermanen und Alemannen. Studien zur germanischen und frühdeutschen Sprachgeschichte, Stammes- und Volkskunde.* 1942. Bern and Munich: A. Francke AG. Verlag/ Leo Lehnen Verlag GMBH., ³1952. (= Bibliotheca Germanica).

McEvedy, Colin. *The Penguin Atlas of Medieval History.* Harmondsworth: Penguin Books, 1961.

An annotated atlas of European history from 326—1478 A.D. Concise summaries of events depicted in each map, religion, language, ethnography, economics.

Musset, Lucien. *The Germanic Invasions: The Making of Europe, A.D. 400-600.* Trans. E. and C. James. University Park, PA: Pennsylvania State UP, 1975.

Naumann, Hans. "Die Zeugnisse der antiken und frühmittelalterlichen Autoren zur germanischen Poesie." *GRM* 15 (1927): 258-73.

Owen, Francis. *The Germanic People.* New York: Bookman, 1960.

Rice, David Talbot, ed. *The Dark Ages. The Making of European Civilization.* London: Thames and Hudson, 1965.

Sections written by distinguished scholars. History of Europe from the fall of Rome to ca. 1000 A.D. Profusely illustrated. Excellent sections on the Germanic tribes.

Robinson, Orrin W. *Old English and Its Closest Relatives. A Survey of the Earliest Germanic Languages.* Stanford, CA: Stanford UP, 1992.

Although aimed at Old English, it covers Indo-European, Proto-Germanic, Gothic, OHG, Old Saxon, Old Frisian, Old Norse, Old Low Franconian. Excellent brief histories of the various Germanic tribes. Informative maps showing geographical distribution and migrations.

Schutz, Herbert. *The Prehistory of Germanic Europe.* New Haven: Yale UP, 1983.

Schwarz, Ernst. *Germanische Stammeskunde.* Heidelberg: Winter, 1956.

Thompson, E. A. *The Early Germans.* Oxford: Clarendon, 1965.

_____. *The Visigoths in the Time of Ulfila.* Oxford: Clarendon, 1966.

## The Franks and the Beginning of the Carolingian Dynasty

The Franks under the Merovingian king Clovis, on the other hand, eventually became Roman Catholics after Clovis's baptism on Christmas Day, 496. They subjugated or dominated most of the other Germanic tribes in Gaul and the region east of the Rhine. When Clovis died in 511 his kingdom was divided among his four sons who, acting separately, continued expanding their territory. Clovis's last surviving son, Chlothar, reunited the kingdom in 558, but upon his death in 561, the kingdom was again partitioned, this time among Chlothar's heirs. The traditional partitioning of the realm also produced rivalries, jealousies, and internecine conflict and effectively broke up what had been a unified kingdom for many years.

As the Merovingian line became less and less able to rule, the real power devolved upon the "Mayors of the Palace," noblemen responsible for the administration of the three main regions of Neustria in the west, Austrasia in the northeast, and Burgundy in the south. One of the noble families, that of Pippin, mayor of Austrasia, eventually came to assume control over the entire realm. Pippin's great-grandson, Charles Martel, was able to strengthen the control that his forefathers had achieved and expand it to the south against the incursions of the Saracens (Battle of Poitiers, 732) and to the north against the Frisians. Charles's son, Pippin the Short, put an end to the Merovingian rule and assumed the kingship of the Franks, thus establishing the Carolingian dynasty. His son, Charlemagne, was to become the ruler of the Roman Empire of the West, which was seen as a *renovatio* of ancient Roman rule, when he was crowned by the Pope in Rome on Christmas Day, 800.

During the reign of Charlemagne, we find the beginnings of vernacular German writings in connection with Charles's continuing efforts to regulate the training of the clergy (cf. his *Admonitio generalis* of 789) and to complete the conversion of the Germanic peoples that had begun earlier in the 8th century by Irish and Anglo-Saxon missionaries. Under Charles's orders every monastery was to maintain a school as part of it. He instituted reform in the monasteries, insisting on strict observance of the Rule of St. Benedict. All people in his kingdom were to learn the confession of faith and know the Lord's Prayer by heart and in their own language. All priests were to preach and instruct their parishioners by their sermons and in a language that the people could understand. Charles's court became a center of classical learning. He gathered many of the leading intellectuals of the day to his court, among them Alcuin of York, Paul the Deacon from Lombardy, and Theodulf from Spain, later Bishop of Orleans. They assisted him in his efforts to advance Christianity among the people by encouraging translations from Latin sources and by regulating worship according to the Roman model. He even went so far as to standardize handwriting in the scriptoria by introducing what has become known as "Carolingian minuscule." Many of the Latin and German literary monuments from the period and even later are undoubtedly to be traced to Charles's religious reform policies. According to his biographer Einhard, Charles had heroic poems collected (*barbara et antiquissima carmina*), although it is not clear whether these were poems in the vernacular or not. In any case, the collection has not survived. Nevertheless, there is ample evidence to suggest that songs in the vernacular were popular even if they were denigrated by most of the men of the Church.

Upon Charlemagne's death in 814, his kingdom was inherited by his son Louis the Pious, who was unable to exert the authority that his father had exercised. Although he did continue the monastic reforms of Charles among the Franks, he did not succeed in keeping political control over the entire realm. Even during his lifetime his rebellious sons managed to dethrone him temporarily, and upon his death the younger brothers, Charles (Charles the Bald) and Louis (Louis the German), opposed the oldest son, Lothaire, who had inherited the throne, and defeated him. In the so-called "Strasbourg Oaths" of 842, they confirmed their combined opposition to Lothaire by pledging support to each other against Lothaire and swearing not to enter into any agreement with Lothaire that could harm the other. Interestingly enough from a cultural point of view, the oaths were made by each in both the Romance tongue and German so that their assembled men would all be able to understand them, clearly showing how quickly the language had developed into two separate entities. A year later, by the treaty of Verdun (843), peace was made with Lothaire and the kingdom divided: Charles ruled the western part of the kingdom, Lothaire the middle, and Louis the eastern region. Upon Lothaire's death in 855, the middle kingdom was divided between Charles and Louis, and Lothaire's heirs were left essentially with the Italian part of Lotharingia. However, Charles and Louis still contended for control of the regions north of the Alps, but with the death of Lothaire's heirs and after considerable armed conflict, Charles and Louis negotiated the partition of Meersen in 870, which effectively divided the German- from the French-speaking areas, i.e. Charles the Bald acquired Burgundy and the western part of Austrasia, while Louis the German took the eastern part of Austrasia and Frisia, territory along the lower Rhine, and Alsace.

### The Franks—Bibliography

Gregory of Tours. *The History of the Franks*. Trans. and with an introduction by O. M. Dalton. Oxford: Clarendon, 1972.

Haug, Walter. "Schriftlichkeit und Reflexion. Zur Entstehung und Entwicklung eines deutschsprachigen Schrifttums in Mittelalter." In: *Schrift und Gedächtnis*. Ed. by Assmann, Aleida and Jan, and Christof Hardmeier. Munich: Wilhelm Fink Verlag, 1983. Pp. 141-57.

Also published in his *Strukturen als Schlüssel zur Welt*. 1989. Pp. 51-66.

Lasko, Peter. *The Kingdom of the Franks: North-West Europe before Charlemagne*. New York: McGraw-Hill, 1971.

## OLD HIGH GERMAN LITERATURE

Although we may often speak of OHG as if it were a unified literature during the OHG period, there are two main reasons why we should not. In the first place, although we can call it High German because most of the monuments come from the southern two-thirds of the German-speaking area, there was no common language in that area, only the dialects of the various German tribes living there. This is the region where the influence of Christian monasteries was strongest, where a written literature could have been most easily produced and preserved. To be sure, certain monasteries had their own scribal conventions, and it is sometimes difficult to know the regional limits of such practices, but there was no common written German language. For the literature of the OHG period we should perhaps not think so much of spoken dialects as of the scribal practices of the various scriptoria even within a single dialect area. Furthermore, the influence of the writing conventions of insular scribes through Irish and Anglo-Saxon missionary activity must frequently be taken into account.

In the second place, one can hardly call most OHG writing "literature." Little of it is creative literature in the modern sense of the term. The majority of the documents reflect the efforts to express the Christian faith in German terms. Most people who could read were familiar with Christian concepts expressed in Latin. After all, one learned to read by learning Latin, and many of the German writings are aids to that end, so that we can think of OHG literature with a few notable exceptions as largely literature in the service of Latin Christianity and the Christianization of the German peoples. Much of what still exists today seems to have done so quite by accident. We can only speculate on what might have been lost, but we should never forget that the majority of literary works of the Middle Ages by far were written in Latin.

Nevertheless, while keeping the relative paucity of OHG literary monuments in mind, we can categorize what we do have:

1. Translations and works related to translating.
2. Works written down from oral traditions.
3. Christian biblical and church literature.
4. Lay literature.
5. Latin literature on German subjects.

We shall treat these works by category rather than chronologically and trust that the relative chronology will become apparent within the categories. See also the chronological table at the end of this volume.

### Translations and Works Related to Translating

Knowledge of Latin was the *sine qua non* for participation in the religious and intellectual life of the Middle Ages. Hence the acquisition of the ability to read and write the language of the church was basic to the Christianization of the Germanic tribes. As we have said, many of the earliest monuments are practical aids to learning Latin, such as vocabulary lists, glosses, and translations of Latin texts into German. This involved creating German equivalents not only to further the study of Latin but also to explain Christian verities to the people in their own dialects and to educate people in the faith. Literal translation of Latin words and texts, frequently following Latin word order slavishly, was of prime importance.

The German *Abrogans* contains German glosses on a vocabulary list of Latin synonyms, which may have come from Langobardic Italy in the middle of the 7th century. Although it exists in three manuscripts, Pa, Ra, and K, and seven fragments, the archetype with the German glosses was probably written in Bavaria around the middle of the 8th century. Pa is Bavarian in a folio of the late 8th-early 9th centuries; Ra is Alemmanic, possibly from the early 9th century; and K, the oldest, stemming from the late 8th century, is Alemmanic with influence of Franconian dialect. This distribution would indicate a fairly rapid spread from east to west and northwest.

It is called *Abrogans* from the first Latin word in the alphabetical list, translated along with the synonym "humilis" as "aotmoat, samftmoati," with the German glosses inserted above the Latin text. The Latin text itself is not always accurate, and there are also a number of misreadings by the German glossator. However, at least some of the errors may be scribal and attributed to the copying process. *Abrogans* is important because it is the oldest extant writing in German.

Text:
*Ahd. Gl.* 1,2-270.

*Ahd. Lb.* I,1 pp. 1-2 (Sel.).
*Schlosser* (1989), pp. 308 f. (Sel.; with mod. Ger. trans.).

Facsimile:
*Schrifttafeln* Ia.
Bischoff, Bernhard, Johannes Duft, and Stefan Sonderegger, eds. *Die 'Abrogans'-Hand-schrift der Stiftsbibliothek St. Gallen. Im Facsimile hrsg. und beschrieben von B. B., J. D. und S. S. Mit Transkription des Glossars und des althochdeutschen Anhangs von S. S.* St. Gallen, 1977.

**Vocabularius Sancti Galli.** This is another example of German glosses on Latin vocabulary lists, in this case arranged according to subject. It is preserved as part of a manuscript in the monastery of St. Gall, although it may not have been written there. It contains lists of words for parts of the body, various animals, human qualities, practical topics like the house, natural phenomena, etc. It was obviously very useful as a learning tool, and the condition of the manuscript indicates that it had been subject to hard use. The source of the *Vocabularius* is thought to be the *Hermaneumata*, a Greek-Latin glossary of the 3rd century that circulated widely in the Middle Ages. *Hermeneumata* means "interpretations," i.e., a compendium of many types of information with theological commentary. The *Vocabularius* is thought to have been written at Murbach ca. 790. No other copies are extant.

Text:
*Ahd. Gl.* 3,1-8.
*Ahd. Lb.* I,2 pp. 2-3 (Sel.).

Facsimile:
*Schrifttafeln* 1b.

**Glosses.** Not all glosses were for lists of words like the two mentioned above. There are also glosses that translate entire texts: psalms, hymns, and other religious material. The standard collection of glosses, *Die althochdeutschen Glossen*, was produced by Steinmeyer and Sievers (5 vols., 1879-1922), but there may still be more to be found. Some glosses like the ones for the vocabularies above are interlinear glosses, i.e., written between the lines of the Latin text. Others are found in the margins of manuscripts, or in parallel Latin-German columns, and still others are entered by the scribe within a continuous Latin text, producing an alternating Latin-German mixture. Characteristic of most glosses is the very literal rendering of the Latin text into German. The "Rule of St. Benedict," the "Old High German Isidor," and the later works of Notker are examples of such translations.

The **Benediktinerregel** (Rule of St. Benedict) laid out the rules governing life in Benedictine monasteries from the founding of the first monastery by St. Benedict in Montecassino, Italy, in 529. Charlemagne, who was interested in reforming monastic life as part of his general church reforms, had a copy of the original Latin manuscript made in Aachen in 817 and then sent to the librarian at Reichenau. MS St. Gall 914 is thought to be that very manuscript. Subsequently at Reichenau, or possibly at St. Gall, a German translation was added in interlinear form to a copy of the "Rule." This is now found in

MS St. Gall 916. The translation was made independently of the Latin text to which it was added; i.e., it was copied into the text from another German manuscript. It is not a complete translation. Only the prologue and the first 14 chapters of the 73 are translated fully, then gaps appear in the translation, growing wider until finally only occasional words and phrases are translated. The translation is the work of one man, although the copy of the translation was done by several scribes. The dialect is Alemannic, and the translation is extremely literal, even following the Latin word order. There exist seven other fragments of the translation in mss. from the 9th, 11th, and 14th centuries.

Text:
*Kl. ahd. Sprdmr.* XXXVI.
Daab, Ursula, ed. *Die althochdeutschen Benediktinerregel des Cod. Sang. 916.* Tübingen: Niemeyer, 1959. (= ATB 50).
*Ahd. Lb.* VII, pp. 12-5.
*Schlosser* (1989), pp. 36 f.; 294-9 (Sel.; with Ger. transl.).

Facsimile:
*Schrifttafeln* 3.

The *OHG Isidor* is a translation of the tract "De fide catholica ex veteri et novo testamento contra Judeos" of Bishop Isidor of Seville (ca. 570-636). It argues for the essential unity of Christ in the Trinity with God the Father based on scriptural evidence and against heretical adoptionist views. The translation is truly remarkable in that it is a polished German translation of sophisticated theological material. It is no longer a translation intended to assist in learning Latin, rather it is a rendering of Isidor's text in German by a writer who was thoroughly at home in Latin and had the ability to express himself fluently in German.

The "Isidor" manuscript is Cod. 2328 of the Bibliothèque nationale in Paris. The Latin and German texts are in parallel columns, both written by the same scribe. Unfortunately, the first chapter is missing from both texts, and the German text stops suddenly on fol. 22$^r$. Blank spaces have been left for it on fols. 22$^v$-33$^v$, but then the Latin text continues in both columns until the end. It is very difficult to determine where the manuscript was written or, indeed, what the dialect might be. Some aspects of the orthography would seem to indicate that it was written at the end of the 8th or very early in the 9th century, but others point to a later date. Fragments of another copy have been found in some leaves from what was a collection (*Sammelhandschrift*) now at Monsee, near Salzburg, and some others in Vienna from the same lost collection. They are referred to as the "Monsee-Vienna Fragments." However, they do not help very much to answer our questions. The most recent opinion tends to place the provenance of the "Isidor" in Lotharingia, possibly the monastery of Murbach, and to describe the dialect as West Franconian. The "Isidor" may also attest to the educational reforms instigated by Charlemagne, who reportedly favored translations into the vernacular as part of his general cultural policies. The anti-adoptionist view of the tract may reflect the thinking of Charlemagne's court, specifically the views of Alcuin of York, who wrote his "De trinitate" in 802 defending consubstantiality. Certainly, the adoptionist question was debated (and rejected) repeatedly at about this time.

In any case, the "OHG Isidor" is a most important monument. It shows an apparently sudden development of the German language to the stage that it can be used to discuss theological topics, something that would appear to be quite singular in monastic culture, dominated as it was by its Latin heritage and with little reason to express itself in the vernacular.

Text:
Eggers, Hans, ed. *Der althochdeutsche Isidor. Nach der Pariser Handschrift und den Monseer Fragmenten neu herausgegeben.* Tübingen: Niemeyer, 1964 (= ATB 63).
*Ahd. Lb.* VIII "Isidor," pp. 13-22; IX "Monsee-Wiener Fragmente," pp. 23-7 (Sel.).
*Schlosser* (1989), "Isidor," pp. 58-79; "Monsee-Wiener Fragmente," pp. 132-41; 192 f. (Sel.; with mod. Ger. trans.).

Facsimile:
*Schrifttafeln* 4.

**OHG Tatian** is the name given to a German translation of a Latin diatessaron, or "gospel harmony" (*Evangelienharmonie*), a blending of the synoptic gospels into a single account of the life and teachings of Christ. Tatian, a Christian Syrian of the 2nd century A.D., compiled his "harmony" in Syriac (or Greek?) about 170 A.D. This text, now lost, was then translated into Old Latin, also into Greek and Arabic, and in 546 Bishop Victor of Capua redacted the Old Latin version that he had found to make it conform to the Vulgate Latin of St. Jerome. A copy of Victor of Capua's version found its way to the Abbey of Fulda at the time of St. Boniface (8th century), where it still resides today (Codex Fuldensis Bonifatius I, or F). About the middle of the 9th century at Fulda (?) a "harmony" was copied and a German translation entered side by side with the Latin text. This one complete manuscript of the "Tatian" is now in the library at St. Gall (Codex Sangallensis 56, or G). The Latin texts of F and G are not identical, and questions were raised as to which one was used for the German translation. Recently it has been demonstrated that the German text is not a translation of either F or G, but presumably of another version and was simply added to the Latin text of G by the six copyists who worked on the manuscript.

The "Tatian" is the most extensive extant OHG text before Otfrid (see below), and its East Franconian dialect, a Middle German dialect as opposed to High German, has long been used as "standard" OHG in textbooks. The translation is of somewhat mixed quality, ranging from strictly literal rendering of the Latin to a certain amount of freer translation. A reliable evaluation of the translation is difficult because we do not know the precise wording of its Latin source. There is some evidence of other German "Tatian" translations but not enough to be certain. Of additional importance is the fact that a "Tatian" must have been the source for the *Heliand*, the Old Saxon poetic version of the Gospels (see below).

Text:
Sievers, Eduard, ed. *Tatian. Lateinisch und altdeutsch mit ausführlichem Glossar.* Paderborn, 1872; rev. and enlarged edn. 1892; repr. 1960.
*Ahd. Lb.* XX, pp. 46-56.
*Schlosser* (1989), 82 f.; 86-9; 96-9; 104 f.; 124 f.; 222 f. (Sel.; with Ger. transl.).
Masser, Achim, ed. *Tatian: Die lateinisch-deutsche Tatianbilingue Stiftsbibliothek St.*

Gallen Cod. 65 unter Mitarbeit von Elisabeth De Felip-Jaud hrsg. v. Achim Masser. Göttingen: Vandenhoeck & Ruprecht, 1994 (= Studien zum Althochdeutschen, 25). (Diplomatic edition with critical notes).

Facsimile:
*Schrifttafeln 9.*

***Notker of St. Gall*** is the first German writer we know by name. He is the third Notker and was called "Notker Labeo" because of a large lip but also "Notker Teutonicus" because of his extensive German writings. The first Notker, called "Balbulus," ("Stammerer"), was very well known for his Latin sequences. He also wrote a history of Charlemagne (*Gesta Karoli*). Notker II was called "Piperis Granum" ("Peppercorn") for his fiery temper and was a noted physician. Our Notker III was above all a teacher, loved and respected by his pupils, one of whom, Ekkehard IV, composed a memorial poem after Notker's death. We also know some details about Notker's life from monastery records and from a letter that Notker wrote not long before his death to his friend Bishop Hugo of Sitten, in which he gives a listing of the works that he had written and those he had translated. Notker was born in 950, entered the monastery school in St. Gall, spent his life as a teacher there, and died of the plague on 22 June 1022.

Notker was a highly educated scholar. The writings mentioned in his letter cover almost the entire trivium and quadrivium of medieval education, authors commonly read in the schools, and theological and biblical writings:

"De arte rhetorica"—written in Latin, but with comments and illustrations in German (rhetoric).

"De partibus logicae"—written in Latin, but with German proverbs and expressions as examples (dialectic).

"De definitione"—fragment in Latin (dialectic).

Boethius's Latin translations of Aristotle's "De categoriis" and "Peri hermeneias"— German translations (dialectic).

"Principia arithmeticae"—lost (arithmetic).

"De musica"—written in German (music).

"Novus computus" — in Latin (astronomy).

"Disticha Catonis"—German translation, lost.

"Bucolica" of Vergil—German translation, lost.

"Andria" of Terence—German translation, lost.

"De nuptiis philologiae et Mercurii" of Martianus Capella—German translation, only Books I and II extant.

"De consolatione philosophiae" of Boethius—German translation.

"De sancta trinitate" of Boethius or a commentary on it—German translation, lost.

"Moralia in Hiob" of Gregory the Great—German translation, lost.

A German translation and commentary on the psalter.

All of Notker's works were aimed at instructing his pupils. The German translations are more than just that, they are explanations and commentaries as well. In form, they are text-glosses, i.e., a Latin sentence or phrase is given, followed immediately by a German equivalent or comment, then another Latin section, its German translation, and so on. Occasionally the translations are almost a mixture of Latin and German with a Latin expression thrown into the middle of a German sentence. Notker possessed not only a superb mastery of Latin, but he was also very sensitive to the nuances of his own language. He uses a variety of synonyms for Latin words and demonstrates a remarkable ability to choose or invent just the right words for any particular Latin passage. In this respect he is similar to the translator of the "Isidor." His German is generally a much freer translation and gives the impression of being more like the spoken word rather than a translation, even though the influence of Latin is still apparent.

In addition to his ability as translator and pedagogue, Notker shows a keen awareness of phonetic distinctions. He insisted that long and short vowels be marked with different accents when stressed, and he followed a definite practice in the orthography of the initial consonants b, d, g, and p, t, k, depending on what preceded them (*Notkers Anlautgesetz*), using the unvoiced consonants (p, t, k) at the beginning of a sentence and following a word that ends in an unvoiced consonant; the voiced consonants (b, d, g) are used in words following a voiced consonant (e.g., *Ter bruoder* but *unde des pruoder*).

Text:
Piper, Paul, ed. *Die Schriften Notkers und seiner Schule.* 3 vols. Freiburg/Tübingen, 1882-3.
Sehrt, E. H., and Taylor Starck, eds. *Notkers des Deutschen Werke.* Tübingen: Niemeyer, 1933 (= ATB 32-4); 1935 (= ATB 37); 1952-5 (= ATB 40, 42, 43); cont'd by James C. King and Petrus W. Tax 1972 (= ATB 72); King 1975 (= ATB 81) and 1979 (= ATB 87); Tax 1979-83 (= ATB 84, 91, 93); King 1986 (= ATB 98); Tax 1986-90 (= ATB 94, 100, 101).
*Ahd. Lb.* XXIII, pp. 61-75 (Sel.).
*Schlosser* (1989), pp. 44-51; 196-9; 314-29; 332 f. (Sel.; with Ger. transl.).

Facsimile:
*Schrifttafeln* 11, a and b.

## Translations/Translating—Bibliography

Bergmann, Rolf, comp. *Verzeichnis der althochdeutschen und altsächsischen Glossenhandschriften. Mit Bibliographie der Glosseneditionen, der Handschriftenbeschreibungen und der Dialektbestimmungen.* Berlin: de Gruyter, 1973.

Eggers, Hans, comp. *Vollständiges lateinisch-althochdeutsches Wörterbuch zur althochdeutschen Isidor-Übersetzung.* Berlin, 1960.
Useful Latin-OHG glossary to the text.

Haubrichs, Wolfgang. "Zum Stand der Isidorforschung." *ZfdPh* 94 (1975): 1-15.
Helpful review of Isidor-research.

Matzel, Klaus. *Untersuchungen zur Verfasserschaft, Sprache und Herkunft der althochdeutschen Übersetzungen der Isidor-Sippe.* Bonn, 1970 (= Rheinisches Archiv).
Valuable study of the Isidor and other related texts.

Sehrt, E. H., comp. *Notker-Glossar.* Tübingen: Niemeyer, 1962.
Useful glossary to Notker's work but without text references.

Sehrt, E. H. and W. K. Legner, comps. *Notker-Wortschatz.* Halle, 1955.
Full lexicon of Notker's language based on Piper's edition.

Steinmeyer, Elias von, and Eduard Sievers, eds. *Die althochdeutschen Glossen. Gesammelt und bearbeitet von Elias von Steinmeyer u. Eduard Sievers.* Berlin, 1879-1922. Repr. Dublin, Zürich 1968/69. 5 vols.
Still the standard source on glosses.

## Works Written Down from Oral Tradition

As we have mentioned previously, there must have been an extensive poetic literature among the Germanic peoples which was transmitted orally. Not only are there some tantalizing fragments that did get written down, but references to such oral literature are made by historians who had observed or who knew of the Germanic tribes and their practices. Furthermore, there is abundant evidence in Old Norse literature (poetic Edda, after 1220) of the survival of such poetry. Much of the subject matter of the oral songs was undoubtedly heroic in nature, ranging from songs in praise of leaders or other heroes to stories of battles, but there were surely also songs about the gods and mythological-religious events. The material was pre-Christian and there are admonitions from Christian writers warning people against such songs. Nevertheless, even in some Christian quarters there was apparently a lively interest in this native tradition, and we can also assume that the oral tradition continued well after the Christianization of the Germanic peoples. Certainly, the subject matter of many of the oral tales eventually did appear in written form, e.g., *Nibelungenlied* and the Dietrich-epics.

As for the fragments that do exist, there are always many problems that defy answers. Since they were written down presumably by clerics or monks, it is difficult to judge whether or not there is some influence of Christianity on the extant texts, whether perhaps the originally heathen material was used for Christian purposes, or whether it continued to be alive among the people despite their conversion to Christianity. Aside from the subject matter, there are also problems of form. The traditional alliterative verse used in the oral literature was subsequently used in Christian poetry, and many of the characteristics, such as repetition through variation, were taken over as well. Can one reconstruct the original poetic forms from that?

Alliterative verse (*Stabreim*) is typically found in "long lines" that divide into half-lines with a caesura between them. Alliteration occurs in the initial consonants in stressed syllables (or the initial consonants of stressed parts of compounds or after unstressed prefixes). All initial vowels may alliterate with one another. There are usually two alliterative elements in the first half-line and at least one, frequently two, in the second half-line. There is a variable number of unstressed syllables between the stresses. The following line from *Hildebrandslied* will serve as an example:

Welaga nû, waltant got, [quad Hiltibrant] wêwurt skihit.

(Alas, almighty God! [said Hiltibrant] Something terrible is going to happen!)

The two "Merseburg Charms" (*Merseburger Zaubersprüche*) are examples of pagan poetic material that has survived. Written down in the 10th century on a blank page in a theological manuscript of the 9th century the charms get their name from the place where they were found and where they are still preserved, the library of the cathedral in Merseburg. The manuscript itself is part of a collection of manuscripts bound together, and the charms are on folio 85$^r$ of the page preceding fragments of a Latin evangelary. On the same page, but by another hand, is a Latin liturgical prayer. Thus the heathen charms, written in a Middle German dialect (Fulda?), are embedded in Christian surroundings.

The basic structure of the charms describes first a situation in narrative form, then the words of the magic charm itself are pronounced. The idea seems to be that, in a situation similar to the one described, one need only to recall that event, say the magic words, and the desired result will follow. The charms are in alliterative verse. The situation in the first charm appears to describe three groups of women, the first two tying up enemy prisoners and hampering the enemy, the third group freeing prisoners. Just who the women are is unclear and attempts have been made to find different interpretations, including even some Christian ones. The charm itself states: "Leap from the fetters, escape from the foes." The second charm is for curing a sprain, and the given situation is the occurrence of a sprain of a horse's leg during the ride of several mythological figures through the woods. Several pagan deities then treat the horse's leg and the saying used is: "Be it sprain of bone, be it sprain of blood, be it sprain of the limb: Bone to bone, blood to blood, limb to limbs, as if they were stuck together." This type of charm is found frequently in other Germanic languages and even in the languages of India, so that a chief difficulty lies in determining just how this one fits in with all the rest. Another one is the identification of some of the figures involved. In any event, the charm is unique in German and undoubtedly a very old one. There are also quite a few charms and blessings that show a more clearly Christian influence.

Text:
*MSD* IV.
*Kl. ahd. Sprdmr.* LXII.
*Ahd. Lb.* XXXI, 1a and b, p. 89.
*Handbook*, pp. 27-30 (with Engl. trans.).
*Schlosser* (1989), pp. 252-5 (with Ger. trans.).

Facsimile:
*Schrifttafeln* 16a.

The **Hildebrandslied**, or "Lay of Hildebrand," is the oldest literary work in German. It may be a written recording of orally transmitted heroic poetry, unless, of course, it was written down by a poet who composed it in the tradition of oral poetry. It consists of 68 lines of *Stabreim*, written on the first and last leaves of a Latin codex containing biblical and patristic texts. Since two scribes can be identified, it seems likely that it was copied from some written source. The orthography, in contrast to the insular minuscule of the main part of the codex, is mainly Carolingian minuscule. The manuscript is thought to have been copied during the fourth decade of the 9th century in the scriptorium of the monastery at Fulda, but the codex is now in the Landesbibliothek in Kassel (MS. theol. 54), where it had been since the early 17th century. At the end of World War II, the codex with the text of the *Hildebrandslied* had disappeared from its storage place, but it was subsequently found in New York and returned to Kassel in 1955. However, the first leaf with the beginning of the *Hildebrandslied* was missing. Fortunately, it was later located in a museum in Philadelphia and returned to Kassel in 1972.

The basic tale is one common to several Indo-European literatures: a father returns home after an extended absence to meet his son, who does not recognize him; the father seeks to identify himself, but the son, suspecting a trick, forces the father into combat with him. The ending varies; in some versions the son kills the father, in others the reverse occurs. In the *Hildebrandslied* the ending is missing. Hildebrand returns after an absence of 30 years. He had accompanied Dietrich von Bern (the Ostrogothic King Theoderich) to the court of Attila the Hun. In a reversal of historical events, Dietrich is said to have fled from Otacher (Odovacer, the first Germanic "king" of Italy). Hildebrand as a vassal of Dietrich has returned and now confronts his son, Hadubrand, between two armies. Hadubrand, in response to Hildebrand's request, names himself and his father, whose death had been reported. Hildebrand realizes then that his son is standing before him, hints that they are related, and attempts to give his son an arm-ring, offering it to him on the tip of his spear. Hadubrand, believing his father dead, suspects treachery and insolently refuses the gift, calling Hildebrand an old Hun and insisting that it is all a trick. Hildebrand then laments his fate: either his son will kill him or he will have to kill his son. The duel will decide. The battle is joined—and the text breaks off. It seems likely, however, on the basis of an Old Norse source that the poem ended tragically with the father killing his son and thus obliterating the line. It would also end tragically if the reverse were true or if both the father and son died. Some have even argued that the poem is not a fragment but rather is complete just as it is. Perhaps the tale was so well known that the audience would surely have known how it ended and that the emphasis, or the point of the lay, was in the tragic situation itself.

Although most scholars would probably agree on the general description of the events as we have narrated them, there is considerable uncertainty about many of the particulars. Like many heroic poems, the *Hildebrandslied* depends on dramatic dialogue to tell the story. There is very little narrative description in what Andreas Heusler called "ein doppelseitiges Ereignislied" (lit.: "a two-sided lay about an event"), yet in the text it is sometimes difficult to decide which "side" or person is speaking and which, or how many lines belong to which speaker, even though the text repeatedly identifies the speakers. The antecedents of some of the pronouns or possessives are open to question, and several words in the poem occur only here, therefore their precise meanings are debatable. Other problems include the two armies: are the two men "champions" or "challengers"? Are the armies troops of the father and of the son, or of Dietrich and Otacher? How can one explain the revision of historical events, not only the relationship of Dietrich and Otacher, but also the fact that Attila died before the historical Dietrich was born? Some scholars have perceived gaps in the text and have argued that a number of lines must have been lost or at least are missing in the extant text that would have been expected to explain parts of the action that is hard to follow logically. If it is an old Germanic heroic poem with the idea of the hero standing firm in the face of an unavoidable tragic fate and enduring it even to death, how can we account for Hildebrand's calling on God twice in a way that clearly refers to the Christian God (v. 30: irmingot . . .

obana ab heuane = "the great God . . . from heaven above" and v. 49: waltant got = "almighty God")? Is this a Christianized version of an older pagan lay? Is it by any means connected with Charlemagne's reported interest in *barbara et antiquissima carmina* and/or his attempts to convert the Saxons?

Finally, the language of the *Hildebrandslied* is a curious mixture of Langobardic, Old High German, Upper German, and Old Low German. The Low German forms appear to have resulted from an attempt by the scribe to transliterate some High German forms more or less mechanically into Low German. However, not all High German forms have been transliterated, there are some clearly Upper German spellings, and the Longobardic influence appears at least in the spelling of the names. In view of the phonology and the connection of Dietrich and Otacher with northern Italy, the scholarly consensus is that the *Hildebrandslied* originated in Lombardy, crossed the Alps to Upper Germany, and eventually made its way to Fulda, a center of missionary activity, where the extant version was copied. It may even have been a scribal exercise, for it is impossible to say when and where specific changes were made, but such a transmission could account for the unusual orthography.

With all its problems, the *Hildebrandslied* is a fascinating monument. Along with the Old English "Beowulf," the "Finsburg" and "Waldere" fragments, it is one of the very few relics of what must have been an extensive oral heroic poetry among the Germanic peoples.

Text:
*MSD* II.
*Kl. ahd. Sprdmr.* I.
*Ahd. Lb.* XXVIII, pp. 84 f.
*Handbook*, pp. 44-47 (Engl. trans.).
*Schlosser* (1989), 264-7 (with Ger. trans.).

Facsimile:
*Schrifttafeln* 12-13.
*Hildebrandlied. Faksimile der Kasseler Handschrift mit einer Einführung von Hartmut Broszinski.* Kassel: Johannes Stauda Verlag, [2]1985 (with Ger., Engl., Fr., Span., and Russ. trans.).

The "Wessobrunn Prayer" (***Das Wessobrunner Gebet***) is found in a Latin codex that was discovered in the monastery of Wessobrunn in Upper Bavaria. It is now in the Bavarian State Library in Munich (Cod. lat. 22053). The codex itself contains material on the trivium and quadrivium and may be dated to the beginning of the 9th century. The "Wessobrunner Gebet" is found at the end of a section which deals with arithmetic, with the calculation of time. Like the other sections of the codex, the prayer is introduced by a title, in this instance "De poeta." The language is clearly Bavarian, but the orthography shows an abbreviation and a runic letter that could be signs of Old Saxon or Old English influence. There are actually two parts to the monument: nine lines of verse describing the absence of all things before the Creation, followed by the prayer itself in prose. The verse is alliterative long lines (*Stabreim*), but there are two half-lines apparently missing in the first five lines. The prayer to God the Creator is a request for faith in God's mercies and for the power to resist devils and avoid evils.

The title "De poeta" has been thought to mean "by the/a poet" to point to the fact that what follows immediately is in verse, although the text itself is continuous. Alternatively, it might be a Latinization of the Greek "poietes" meaning "about the creator." In either case, the description of the absence of everything before Creation is similar to the depiction of that same state of the world found in the Old Icelandic *Voluspa* (The Sybil's Prophecy), and this could go back to early Germanic ideas, unless, of course, there is Christian influence in the Old Icelandic poem. It has also been pointed out, however, that the Biblical account in Genesis may be the only source needed and that the "Wessobrunner Gebet" is Christian rather than heathen. It is difficult to determine whether the poetic lines can be said to come from oral tradition.

Text:
*MSD* I.
*Kl. ahd. Sprdmr.* II.
*Ahd. Lb.* XXIX, pp. 85 f.
*Handbook*, pp. 129 f. (Engl. trans.).
*Schlosser* (1989), pp. 28 f. (with Ger. trans.).

Facsimile:
*Schrifttafeln* 14.

*Muspilli* is the name given by the first editor to a poetic text concerning the end of things. The name occurs in line 57 of the poem, and the meaning is not at all clear: "there no kinsman may aid another in the face of the Muspilli." The word occurs twice in the Old Saxon *Heliand* as the fire that will destroy the world on Judgment Day, and it exists also in Old Norse as the name of a giant from the land of fire. Although the beginning and ending of the poem are lacking, "Muspilli" deals with the fate of the individual soul after death: the fire and darkness of hell, the splendors of heaven; and then the final judgment, beginning with the fight of Elijah with the Antichrist, followed by the conflagration of the world and a description of the Last Judgment, in which the administration of proper justice on earth and the proper way to live is related to what one will experience when called to account, a theme in vernacular literature that continues through EMHG literature and beyond.

The "Muspilli" text is found on the empty pages and margins of the second part of a Latin codex from the Monastery of St. Emmeram in Regensburg, now in the Bavarian State Library in Munich (Cod. lat. 14098). The second part of the codex is a sermon falsely ascribed to St. Augustine, "De symbolo contra Iudaeos." According to a Latin dedicatory inscription, the book was presented to Duke Louis of Bavaria (later King Louis the German) by Bishop Adalram of Salzburg (821-836). The beginning and the end of the poem are now missing, and the text was written by a later, much less elegant hand than the Latin sermon, about the middle of the 9th century. The language is a mixture of Franconian and Bavarian dialects with both older and younger forms. The 103 extant lines are predominantly in alliterative verse, but the "Stabreim" is far from perfect, and in a number of instances there are rhyming lines and lines with no apparent rhyme at all. Scholars have puzzled over not only the metrics and the language but also over the structure, which seems to have gaps and interpolations, producing the effect of a montage. Questions have also been raised about the source(s) of the poem and the degree of pre-Christian influence, but there is little scholarly consensus on this and the many other problems presented by the poem.

Nevertheless, "Muspilli" is an important, intriguing work. In subject matter it may not stem from oral poetic tradition, but it contains indications of contemporary legal problems, attitudes, and procedures in connection with the description of the Last Judgment and, like much apocalyptic literature, portrays life after death and the end of the world. In this sense it is a counterpart to the "Wessobrunner Gebet," which deals with the creation. (See above).

Text:
*MSD* III.
*Kl. ahd. Sprdmr.* XIV.
*Ahd. Lb.* XXX, pp. 86-88.
*Schlosser* (1989), pp. 200-5 (with Ger. trans.).

Facsimile:
*Schrifttafeln* 15.

## Oral Tradition—Bibliography

Ebbinghaus, Ernst A. "The End of the Lay of Hiltibrant and Hadubrant." In: *Althochdeutsch, Bd. I. Ed. by R. Bergmann, et al.* Heidelberg: Carl Winter, 1987. Pp. 670-76.

Argues for an ending in which Hadubrant overcomes Hiltibrant, then recognizes him as his father and laments, cf. Persian model of Rustam and Sohrab.

Groseclose, J. Sidney, and Brian O. Murdoch. *Die althochdeutschen poetischen Denkmäler.* Stuttgart: Metzler, 1976 (= Sammlung Metzler, 140).

Concise treatment of OHG literary monuments with bibliography.

Heusler, Andreas. *Die altgermanische Dichtung.* Handbuch der Literaturwissenschaft. Berlin-Neubabelsberg: Akademische Verlagsgesellschaft Athenaion, 1923.

A remarkable attempt at a description of old Germanic (oral) poetry on the basis of extant tangible evidence from various sources.

Lühr, Rosemarie. *Studien zur Sprache des Hildebrandliedes. Teil 1: Herkunft und Sprache, Teil 2: Kommentar.* Frankfurt/M.: Lang, 1982 (= Regensburger Beiträge zur deutschen Sprach- und Literaturwissenschaft. Reihe B: Untersuchungen, 22).

A recent, highly-regarded study of the *Hildebrandslied.*

McDonald, William C. " 'Too Softly a Gift of Treasure': A Rereading of the Old High German *Hildebrandslied." Euph.* 78 (1984): 1-16.

An excellent treatment of why Hildebrand and Hadubrand end up fighting. Special reference to OE sources and a very thorough evaluation of the secondary literature.

Schneider, Karl. "Zum Hildebrandslied 37/38 und 49." In: *Althochdeutsch, Bd. I. Ed. by R. Bergmann, et al.* Heidelberg: Carl Winter, 1987. Pp. 655-69.

Interpretation of these two much-discussed passages; sees the first as lack of communication between father and son and the second as an appeal to the Germanic (not Christian) god. Excellent review of pertinent scholarship.

Wipf, Karl A., trans. and ed. *Althochdeutsche poetische Texte. Althochdeutsch/Neu-hochdeutsch. Ausgew., übers. und kommentiert von Karl A. Wipf.* Stuttgart: Reclam, 1992 (= UB, 8709).
Recent edition of all OHG poetic texts except Otfrid's Evangelienbuch and translations of poetry from Notker's Boethius based on available mss. Translations in mod. Ger. prose.

## Christian Biblical and Church Literature

In some respects there is little difference between the works listed in this section and those in the preceding category. There we had attempted to show the influence of Germanic verse forms from the oral tradition in works that may have some evidence of the heathen past, even though they were undoubtedly written down, possibly composed, by Christian writers. In this section the emphasis is on the rendering of biblical materials into the vernacular, on creative works that tell the life of Christ, the gospels, Genesis, and certain stories from the Bible as well as other religious subjects related to worship and the church. Some of these poems are major attempts to "translate" parts of the Bible into a language that most people without a knowledge of Latin could understand. These are not translations in the modern sense of the term, they are rather re-tellings or re-workings of Christian materials in verse form in Germanic dialects.

The Old Saxon *Heliand* (Saviour) should perhaps not even be included in this section of Old High German literature since it is written in an Old Low German dialect. However, it is generally treated in literary histories of this period and is indeed a major literary work of almost 6,000 lines. It describes the life of Christ on earth and was given the title *Heliand* by its first modern editor, J. A. Schmeller, in his edition of 1830. The *Heliand* may be viewed as being in the tradition of bible poetry, i.e., verse re-tellings of events from the Old and New Testaments. Latin bible poetry (*sacra poesis*) comes from late antiquity when poets in the 4th to 6th centuries began to write poetry on various subjects ranging from the creation of the world to the stories of the apostles, using the style of classical authors such as Virgil, Ovid, and Lucan. Judging from the number of extant manuscripts, such poetry was very popular and became part of the basic education in monasteries and cathedral schools. Foremost among the Latin poets were Juvencus, Alcimus Avitus, Sedulius, Arator, and Prudentius. There is also a tradition of vernacular bible poetry in Anglo-Saxon, and the Old Saxon *Heliand* may be involved in that (see under *Genesis*, below).

Two major manuscripts of the *Heliand* exist: Cgm 25 or M in Munich, and Cotton Caligula A VII in the British Library in London. Although C is more complete than M, it is younger (10th century as opposed to 9th), and its language is closer to Franconian dialects than that of M, which is Saxon. The ending is missing in both manuscripts. Two fragments, a single leaf in the University Library in Prague (P), and Codex Palatinus Latinus 1447 or V in the Vatican Library, which also contains three fragments of the OS *Genesis*, complete the manuscript tradition. M and C stem from the same archetype, but P and C have different sources, not identical with the archetype of M and C. Two prefaces in Latin, one in prose, the other in verse, are thought to have been prefaces to the

*Heliand.* There are no manuscript sources for the prologues. We have them only in a printed version of 1562 in the second edition of Matthias Flacius Illyricus's *Catalogus testium veritatis*, a collection of excerpts attesting to a long tradition on the need for reform of the church. In the prose preface reference is made to a "Ludovicus piissimus Augustus," who had commissioned a Saxon to write the stories of the Old and New Testaments in the Germanic language so that people could understand them better. A case can be made to support either Louis the Pious (778-840), the son of Charlemagne, or Louis the German (804-76), Charlemagne's grandson, as the "Ludovicus" in question. The fact that the prose is in Carolingian Latin makes the authenticity of the preface likely. Furthermore, reference is made to the division of the poem into "vitteas," a word corresponding to OE "fit" = "song" or "poem" and "fittan" = "to sing." Manuscript C has numbered divisions (= "vitteas"?), and this has been adduced as further evidence that the prologue does indeed refer to the *Heliand.* The poetic preface, which seems to be in Humanistic Latin, describes the inspiration of the poet in a manner reminiscent of the calling of Caedmon, a simple farmer who was suddenly inspired by Divine Grace to write verse, in Bede's *Historia ecclesiastica gentis Anglorum.* Flacius Illyricus does not state his source, nor has his source been identified, so that we cannot be sure of the authenticity of the prologues. Nevertheless, aside from the dating of the manuscripts themselves, the prose prologue in particular may assist in determining the date of composition. If "Ludovicus" is Louis the Pious, as earlier scholarship believed, we would have to assume a date of some time after 814; if Louis the German, as has been suggested more recently, sometime after 840 when he became king, unless, of course, he commissioned it earlier while he was still Duke of Bavaria.

Sources for the *Heliand* poet were undoubtedly the Latin bible poetry mentioned above, the gospel harmony of Tatian, and the gospel commentaries of Bede, Alcuin, and Hrabanus Maurus. Much has been made of the poet's purported attempt to "Germanicize" the gospels so that Christianity would be more readily understood by the Saxons, who had recently been converted by Charlemagne. There is something to be said on this score: the use of indigenous alliterative poetry with its traditional repetition in variation, the description of Christ's disciples as his "retinue," the stress on the nobility of Jesus's lineage, Jesus is called "Chieftain" or "Protector of People," the shepherds in the fields are guards tending horses, Bethlehem becomes *Bethlehemaburg* ("Fort Bethlehem"), etc., all seem to indicate at least some interest in adapting the events of Jesus's life to the experiential horizon of the Saxons so that the gospel story would be intelligible to them. It is important to remember, however, that despite the Saxon elements the basic tenets of the Christian faith remain largely unchanged and in accordance with the accepted ideas of the Carolingian period. The narrator seldom injects himself or his own ideas into the story, he merely describes the events of Jesus's life without resorting to allegorical interpretation. He begins with an account of how the gospel was written, follows that up with the story of Zachary and the birth of John, the annunciation to Mary and the birth of Jesus, continues with his life and teachings, his crucifixion and resurrection, and ends with his appearance to the disciples on the road to Emmaus.

The *Old Saxon Genesis*. In 1875, on the basis of linguistic and stylistic features, Eduard Sievers advanced the thesis that the Anglo-Saxon (Old English) *Genesis B* was an interpolation of a translation from the Old Saxon. Nineteen years later in 1894 Karl Zangenmeister, the Director of the Heidelberg Library, discovered three fragments of an OS *Genesis* in the Vatican Library, and that new find (Codex Palatinus Latinus 1447, see above under *Heliand*) substantiated Sievers's thesis splendidly. Indeed, 26 verses of the Anglo-Saxon *Genesis* were found to correspond to the same number of lines in the OS fragment and had obviously been translated from that source. The first fragment in V contains Adam's lament at the loss of paradise (v. 1-26); the second is the story of Cain's fratricide and enumerates Adam's genealogy down to Enoch and mentions the coming struggle of Enoch with the Antichrist (v. 27-150; see also "Muspilli," above), and the third (v. 151-337) recounts the destruction of Sodom and ends where Lot's wife is turned into a pillar of salt.

The OE *Genesis* begins with a hymn of praise to God followed by an account of Lucifer's fall. Next comes the story of creation up to the third day, and, after a gap, the creation of Adam and Eve in the Garden of Eden. This is the OE *Genesis A*. At verse 235 the interpolation known as *Genesis B* begins with God's prohibition against the eating of the fruit of the Tree of Knowledge. Then comes a partial recapitulation of Lucifer's fall and the events leading up to the expulsion of Adam and Eve from Eden. It is at this point in *Genesis B* that the 26 overlapping verses are to be found. Verses 235-851, i.e., 617 verses, of *Genesis B* and the 337 verses of the OS fragments minus the overlapping verses allow us to assume the existence of an OS *Genesis* poem of at least 928 lines.

It has been suggested that the source of *Genesis* may have been a Latin poetic version by Avitus (see above) or some source based on Avitus. There are at least several correspondences with Avitus's poem in *Genesis* that do not follow the story of creation in the vulgate Bible, but no scholarly consensus exists. Stylistically the OS *Genesis* is quite similar to *Heliand*, using indigenous alliterative verse with variation as a rhetorical device. In the three extant fragments the theme of disobedience—Lucifer's rebellion and fall through overweening pride (*superbia*), and various other transgressions against the established order (Cain, Sodom)—appears to be central. It has been suggested that this may have been part of the continuing effort to subdue and Christianize the Saxons and particularly in reaction to the last large-scale rebellion in 842. Mainz is thought to be the likely place of provenance of the manuscript, which is dated to the first half of the 9th century.

The OS *Heliand* and *Genesis* are the only specimens of OS poetry to have survived. In fact, vernacular poetry disappears markedly in the north, but it must be viewed as part of the richer and older tradition of Anglo-Saxon bible poems in England.

Texts:
Behagel, Otto, ed. *Heliand und Genesis*. Tübingen: Niemeyer, [8]1965, revised by Walther Mitzka. (= ATB 4).
*Ahd. Lb.* XLIV, pp. 151-8 (Sel.).
Holthausen, F. *Altsächsisches Elementarbuch*. Heidelberg: Winter, 1921. Pp. 206-22 (Sel.). (= Germanische Bibliothek, I,5).
Sievers, Eduard, ed. *Heliand*. Halle, [2]1935, repr. with an appendix by Eduard Schröder

containing the *Genesis*-fragments. (= Germanistische Handbibliothek, IV).

*Schlosser* (1989), *Heliand* pp. 98-103; 130 f.; 142-7; 164-75 (Sel.; with Ger. trans.).

Doane, Alger N., ed. *The Saxon Genesis: An Edition of the West Saxon Genesis B and the Old Saxon Vatican Genesis.* Madison: Univ. of Wisconsin Press, 1991.

Translations:
Scott, Mariana, trans. *The Heliand. Translated from the Old Saxon.* Chapel Hill: Univ. of North Carolina Press, 1966.

Murphy, G. Ronald, S. J., trans. *The Heliand. The Saxon Gospel.* New York, Oxford: Oxford UP, 1992. xviii+238 p. (Engl. trans. with commentary).

For *Genesis* see Ute Schwab in BIBLICAL AND CHURCH LITERATURE—BIBLIOG-RAPHY (below).

Facsimiles:
*Heliand*: *Schrifttafeln* 17.
*Genesis*: see Ute Schwab (below).

The *Liber evangeliorum* (*Evangelienbuch*) by the monk Otfrid von Weissenburg (Alsace) is a major poetic work of 7,106 long lines, relating the life of Christ in a single version based on selected passages from the four gospels. Unlike the OHG "Tatian" or the OS *Heliand*, it does not attempt to "harmonize" the Gospels, following now this gospel, now that. Furthermore, Otfrid does not merely describe the events of Christ's life and his teachings, he also provides an interpretive commentary which explains their frequently allegorical significance. Some chapters have the headings *mystice, moraliter, spiritaliter*, and in those sections Otfrid provides exegesis according to the sense indicated by the heading. Consequently there is in part a sermonizing tone, but Otfrid also provides paraphrases of the biblical text, meditative passages, lyrical hymns of praise, personal prayers, and other expressions of Christian piety in his work. There is also some indication that he has consciously used number symbolism in the composition of the *Evangelienbuch*. It is obvious that Otfrid, although perhaps not himself an original thinker, was a man of great erudition, and he incorporates much material from theological commentaries and other learned sources available to him into his work.

Although writing in German, Otfrid is an innovator. He does not use traditional alliterative verse (cf. *Heliand* and *Genesis*) in his long lines. He rather has the syllable at the end of the first half-line, i.e., at the caesura, rhyme with the syllable at the end of the second half-line, in effect breaking the long line into a rhymed couplet. Two long lines then form a strophe. This may be seen in the following example from the beginning of the dedicatory poem to King Louis:

**Lu**dowig ther snello, thes wisduames follo
er ostarrichi rihtit **al**, so Frankono kunig sca . . . **L**;

(Louis, the brave, full of wisdom,
he rules the Eastern Kingdom as a Frankish king should)

As indicated by the highlighted syllables above, each half-line contains four stresses. How Otfrid came to use this verse form has been the subject of much scholarly debate. The question is whether he derived it from leonine (rhymed) hexameters, from Latin hymns, or from some other source. Most scholars consider the Latin hymns the likely source because of the similarity in the rhythmical patterns. At any rate, rhymed couplets eventually become the preferred verse form for narrative poetry in German, and alliterative verse disappears very quickly after Otfrid.

The *Evangelienbuch* begins with a dedicatory poem to Louis the German. The superscript: *Ludovvico orientalium regnorum regi sit salus aeterna*, describes the content succinctly. It is a hymn of praise to Louis, in which Otfrid wishes him eternal prosperity and salvation. Interesting is the comparison of Louis with David, the biblical model for the perfect king by the grace of God. Although the poem is in German the letters of the Latin superscript form an acrostic using the initial letters of the *first* long lines of the 48 two-line strophes of the poem. The same letters are used to form the same message in a telestic using the *last* letters of both parts of the *second* long lines (note the "Ls" in the quotation above).

The second prefatory piece is a Latin prose letter to Liutbert, Archbishop of Mainz, requesting his approval of the work and stating why Otfrid had undertaken to write it. He had been encouraged to do so by his fellow monks and especially by a certain lady named Judith (not otherwise identified) as a counter to the objectionable worldly songs of the laity. It is also intended to provide a poetic monument in Frankish that would do for people who did not know Latin what classical Latin poetry or Latin bible poetry do for those schooled in Latin. He goes on to discuss the organization of his work and the difficulties he encountered in using the uncultivated Frankish language for such a lofty subject. It is a fascinating letter, revealing much about Otfrid himself and the culture of mid-9th century Germany.

Bishop Salomo I of Konstanz is the addressee of the third preface, a poem in German similar in form to the one to King Louis the German. It is shorter, with only 24 strophes, and the acrostic and telestic each form the legend: *Salomoni episcopo Otfridus*. In it Otfrid expresses his gratitude for the instruction he had received from Salomo, and he presents the book to him with his wishes for eternal salvation.

At this point the actual *Evangelienbuch* begins—but not quite: first comes a list (in Latin) of the contents of the first book; then in I,1 a disquisition in German verse on the topic, *Cur scriptor hunc librum theotisce dictaverit*. The answer is that the Franks deserve to have a national literature of high quality in their own tongue. They are as brave, mighty, and prosperous as any other nation, e.g., the Greeks or the Romans, but the Franks alone lack literary works in praise of God in their own language. Otfrid is obviously very proud of his people and their talents and hopes to fill a great need with his poetry. After this, Otfrid inserts his prayer to God (I,2), and finally begins his story with Jesus's family tree, going back to David (I,3)

The *Evangelienbuch* is organized into five books, with 28, 24, 24, 37, and 25 chapters, respectively. Heading each book is a list of chapter titles in Latin. Book I covers the annunciation and birth of Christ, his childhood, his baptism by John. Book II begins with the presentation of the Logos from the Gospel of John, followed by the temptation of Christ, the calling of the disciples, the marriage at Cana, the story of the Samaritan woman, and the sermon on the mount. In Book III we find the teachings and miracles of Jesus and his examination by the priests and Pharisees. Book IV continues with Christ's passion and burial in the sepulcher, and Book V describes the resurrection, Jesus's later appearances, his ascension, and Judgment Day. At the end, Chapter 24 is a prayer and Chapter 25 an epilogue for the entire poem.

Following the epilogue there is one more dedicatory poem in German addressed to Hartmut and Werinbert, two monks in the monastery of St. Gall, apparently personal friends of Otfrid. The poem is in verse like the dedication to Louis the German and the one to Bishop Salomo I of Mainz. It is complete with acrostic and telestic in its 83 stanzas: *Otfridus Uuizanbergensis monachus Hartmuate et Uuerimberto sancti Galli monasterii monachis*. It deals to a large extent with figures and events in the Old Testament in which service and obedience to God are the defining traits. Otfrid is obviously encouraging Hartmut and Werinbert to follow such models in their lives.

The text of the *Evangelienbuch* exists in three manuscripts and some fragments of a fourth:

> V = Codex Vindobonensis 2678. Theol. 345 in the Austrian National Library in Vienna. It dates from the 9th century, was written by five different hands, but may well have been corrected, even edited by Otfrid himself. It is the oldest and best, with four illustrations (the first illustrated German book!).
>
> P = Codex Palatinus No. 52 in the Heidelberg University Library. It is thought to have been copied from V, also from the 9th century. Some pages are missing.
>
> F = Cgm. 14 of the Bavarian State Library in Munich, formerly in the Cathedral Library of Freising. It is a copy from V and P, but the scribe has used some Bavarian forms for Otfrid's Franconian ones. It can be dated with considerable accuracy since there is a note by the scribe Sigihart, stating that Bishop Waldo of Freising had commissioned the copy. Waldo was archbishop of Freising from 884 to 906.
>
> D = Codex Discissus, i.e. a codex that had been cut up. Only fragments of this 10th century codex remain, in Berlin, Wolfenbüttel, and Bonn, but they attest to the continued interest in Otfrid's work well after his lifetime and at a time when literature written in German is notably lacking.

Otfrid von Weissenburg is the first German poet we know by name to write in the vernacular, and it has been possible to reconstruct some of the stages of his life from the clues to be found in the dedicatory letters and verses in his *Evangelienbuch*, as well as from other sources. Otfrid was born ca. 800, entered the monastery of Weissenburg ca. 807, became a monk between 812 and 819, a sub-deacon ca. 821, deacon ca. 825, and priest ca. 830. He was then sent to the monastery at Fulda, between 832/33 to 842 for advanced study. He may also have been at the court of Louis the German as a scribe for a short while and may there have met Salomo, the later Bishop of Konstanz. In Fulda he studied under Hrabanus Maurus. Upon his return to Weissenburg, Otfrid was probably responsible for the development and expansion of the monastery library and undoubtedly was on familiar terms with leading figures in other monasteries of the region. His *Evangelienbuch* must have been finished between 863, the year in which Liutbert became archbishop, and 871, the year in which Salomo I died. Otfrid himself may have died about 867.

Otfrid's *Evangelienbuch* is a significant achievement in many respects. It is first of all a book, meant to be read, either privately or to an audience. It may even have been intended to be sung or chanted (there are neumes in Ms. P), we cannot be sure. It produced a systematic written language for Otfrid's native Franconian. It introduced a new way of writing poetry in the vernacular—the use of end-rhyme—and it shows the genius of a highly cultivated, theologically sophisticated, poetically and linguistically gifted man of 9th-century Germany. "He was a bold innovator, both as a teacher and a writer, a nationalist and a churchman, progressive in every respect according to the ideas of his age, and also a sensitive craftsman, conscious of the problems of his art" (*Handbook*, p. 212).

Text:
Erdmann, Oskar, ed. *Otfrids Evangelienbuch. Textabdruck mit Quellenangaben und Wörterbuch*. Tübingen: Niemeyer, [7]1973 rev. by Ludwig Wolff. (= ATB 49).
Vollmann-Profe, Gisela, ed. and trans. *Otfrid von Weissenburg. Evangelienbuch. Auswahl. Althochdeutsch/Neuhochdeutsch*. Stuttgart: Reclam, 1987. 272 p. (= UB, 8384). Excellent mod. Ger. trans. of selections: all dedications, representative chapters from all books, commentary, and informative afterword.
*Ahd. Lb*. XXXII, pp. 92-130 (Sel.).
*Schlosser* (1989), pp. 16-27; 82-5; 88-95; 106-20; 124-9; 148-51; 158-61; 176-9; 182-7; 310-3 (Sel.; with Ger. trans.).

Translations:
See Vollmann-Profe and Schlosser (above) for mod. Ger. trans.

Facsimile:
*Schrifttafeln* 18.
Otfrid von Weissenburg. *Evangelienharmonie. Vollständige Faksimileausgabe des Codex Vindobonensis 2687*. Graz, 1972.

***Christ and the Samaritan Woman* (*Christus und die Samariterin*)** is the title given to an incomplete 31-line poem about Christ and the Samaritan woman from Chapter 4 of the Gospel of John. The fragment was copied onto a blank page (fol. 5[r]) of a manuscript containing the annals of the monastery at Lorsch covering the years 794-803, now in the Austrian National Library in Vienna (Cod. 515). It was probably copied from a Franconian source by an Alemannic scribe, quite possibly on the island of Reichenau in the early 10th century. The poem was written in Otfrid's end-rhyme, but the text is continuous without strophic arrangement.

In contrast to Otfrid, the poem follows the wording of the vulgate text quite closely, gives no interpretation, and uses formulaic fillers to complete the rhymes. The first six lines give the setting for the meeting, and the rest of the poem is dialogue between Christ and the Samaritan woman with no formal indication of who is speaking. In that respect it has a certain balladesque quality. The poem breaks off at the end of line 20 in the vulgate where the woman says that Jesus must be a prophet and then speaks about her ancestors worshipping God on the mountain and not in Jerusalem. It is a stylistically rather simple poem with none of the lengthy sermonizing found in Otfrid's version.

Text:
*MSD* X.

*Kl. ahd. Sprdmr.* VII.
*Ahd. Lb.* XXXIV, p. 136.
*Schlosser* (1989) pp. 120-3 (with mod. Ger. trans.).

Facsimile:
*Schrifttafeln* 21.

***Psalm 138*** (in the Vulgate, Psalm 139 in the Revised Standard) is a free re-working of this psalm of David in Bavarian dialect from the early 10th century. It is found on folio 69$^r$ and 69$^v$ of Cod. 1609 in the Austrian National Library in Vienna. There are 38 lines of end-rhyme verse in the manner of Otfrid, divided into 2- and 3-line strophes, with majuscule initials jutting out into the margin in the first line of each strophe. It is difficult to say whether the scribe was copying from a source or whether the poem is an original creation based on the Vulgate text alone, or possibly even from the scribe's memory of the Latin version of the psalm.

The popularity of psalters in the Middle Ages is well known, as is their use for moral instruction, meditation, and prayer. This German version of Psalm 138 seems intended for similar purposes. It begins with an invitation to the reader/listener to hear the secret thoughts of David and how he addressed his Lord. Unlike the Psalmist, however, the emphasis of the translator appears to lie on David, the exemplary ruler, and his relationship to God, not so much on the omniscience and omnipresence of God. Although God/Christ is everywhere and David remains in his protection, the central part of the psalm is a confession and promise on David's part to keep all evil doers and enemies of God away from his rule and a request for God's protection everywhere and in all things, a sort of new covenant with God. In that respect the translation may well have been intended for the moral instruction of kings and other rulers to follow David's example. At any rate the language and imagery are that of the feudal court of the time.

Text:
*MSD* XIII.
*Kl. ahd. Sprdmr.* XXII.
*Ahd. Lb.* XXXVIII, pp. 138 f.
*Schlosser* (1989), pp. 42 f. (with mod. Ger. trans.).

Facsimile:
*Schrifttafeln* 23.

The ***Georgslied*** (***Lay of St. George***) was entered on the empty final leaves of the Heidelberg manuscript (P) of Otfrid's *Evangelienbuch* at the end of the 10th century. It is an incomplete text of about 60 long lines with end-rhyme, many of them now scarcely legible but written continuously without regard for strophic form. At the end there is the notation: *ihn nequeo Vuisolf* (I, Wisolf, can't go on). In addition, the orthography is quite puzzling, so that much ingenuity has gone into reconstructing what the text was intended to be. The *Ahd. Lb.* gives two texts, one according to Zarncke, the other according to Kögel, plus a diplomatic rendering of the manuscript. The language appears to be Alemannic, but it may be an Alemannic copy of a Franconian source, although it is also possible that the source itself may have been written in an intentionally arcane writing system.

The St. George whose life is recorded here is indeed the dragon slayer we immediately think of, but there is no mention of dragons in the poem. That aspect of St. George's life is not found in western Europe until the time of the Crusades. Instead we have the story of a military officer, a margrave from Palestine, who comes before a tyrant, who had been persecuting Christians, and steadfastly declares his Christian faith. For this George is imprisoned, and he prays to God for help and performs miracles before being put to death. However, he is resurrected, does more wonderful deeds, is executed again and brought back to life again. Thereupon George raises a dead man to life, goes to the royal palace and teaches the queen to accept Christianity. Finally, George is about to go into the pit with the hound of Hell, Apollyon, when the fragment breaks off. St. George is one of the "megalomartyrs" whose firm faith could serve as a model for all Christians and who could be counted on to help people in distress. The poem with its several refrains presents a lively short narrative about a popular saint, who was repeatedly returned to life by divine help.

Text:
*MSD* XVII.
*Kl. ahd. Sprdmr.* XIX.
*Ahd. Lb.* XXXV, pp. 132-5.
*Handbook*, pp. 223 f. (Engl. trans.).
*Schlosser* (1989), pp. 242-7 (with mod. Ger. trans.).

Facsimile:
*Schrifttafeln* 19.


The **Petruslied** (**Petition to St. Peter**) is a short song consisting of three two-line Otfridian strophes, each one followed by the refrain: *Kyrie eleison, Christe eleison*. It was written at the end of a manuscript of Hrabanus Maurus's "Commentary on Genesis," probably in Freising at the turn of the 9th-10th centuries. The manuscript is Clm. 6260 in the Bavarian State Library in Munich, and the song is on folio 158$^v$. The dialect is Bavarian with some Franconian influence. Musical notation in the form of neumes accompanies the text.

The *Petruslied* was probably sung in religious processions or on pilgrimages. It is the oldest church hymn in German and for that reason at least notable. The first two strophes describe the power given to St. Peter by Christ, the "keys to the kingdom" (Matt. 16,19), to give or deny admission to Heaven, and the third strophe asks people to pray that St. Peter will be merciful to sinners. The fact that l.8 is almost identical to Otfrid I. 7. 28 has given rise to inconclusive speculation, either that it was lifted from Otfrid or vice versa or that both may be traced to a common source. There has been considerable interest in the neumes from musicologists but without definitive results.

Text:
*MSD* IX.
*KL. ahd. Sprdmr.* XXI.
*Ahd. Lb.* XXXIII, p. 131.
*Schlosser* (1989), pp. 246 f. (with mod. Ger. trans.).

Facsimile:
*Schrifttafeln* 20.

The *Augsburg Prayer* (*Augsburger Gebet*), sometimes called *Rhenish-Franconian Prayer* (*Rheinfränkisches Gebet*), is a four-line verse translation of a preceding Latin prayer on folio 1$^r$ of Clm. 3851, *Liber poenitentialis*, now in the Bavarian State Library in Munich, formerly in Augsburg. The dialect is Rhenish-Franconian, and it was probably entered into the manuscript around the end of the 9th century. The prayer is an appeal to God's mercy for release from the bonds of sin that bind man.

Text:
*MSD* XIV.
*Kl. ahd. Sprdmr.* XVIII.
*Ahd. Lb.* XXXVII, 1, p. 131.
*Handbook*, p. 214, note 4 (Engl. trans.).
*Schlosser* (1989), pp. 226 f. (with mod. Ger. trans.).

**Bamberg Creed and Confession (*Bamberger Glaube und Beichte*).** There are several of these confessions, more or less detailed and probably not of particular significance. However, because the *Bamberger Glaube und Beichte* is among the most extensive and has received the most attention, we have included it here, first, as an example of this type of literature and, second, as interesting in its own right. It is to be found in a *Sammelhandschrift*, Cod. lat. 4460, in the Bavarian State Library in Munich, formerly in the Dominican monastery in Bamberg. The *Bamberger Glaube und Beichte*, along with the description *Himmel und Hölle* (Heaven and Hell, see below), form the second and third parts of the *Sammelhandschrift*, folios 103$^r$-111$^v$ and 111$^v$-114$^r$ respectively. Both works are in prose, and the dialect is East Franconian. The manuscript is from the 12th century, but the source is probably from the second half of the 11th century.

The creed makes up the first part under the heading "Vera Fides." Beginning with a short forswearing of the devil and all his works and a plea for grace and help in believing, there follows a lengthy description of all tenets of the Christian faith from belief in the Trinity through the birth, life and crucifixion of Christ to his Second Coming. The second part under the heading of "Pura Confessio" is a descriptive catalogue of the nine (!) deadly sins, all of which the author admits to having committed, followed by a negative listing of the virtues, all of which he has failed to practice. The distinctions between the sins and virtues that the author makes through his vocabulary is a notable feature of the work. The confession closes with a prayer for mercy and forgiveness. It has been suggested that the work was intended as a confessional *speculum* for father confessors in monasteries or other religious congregations. Interestingly enough, there also exists a shorter, fragmentary, parallel piece, the *Wessobrunner Glauben und Beichte I*, in the Vienna manuscript of Notker's psalter, in which the confession of sins is rendered by a woman.

Text:
*MSD* XCI (Bamberg), XC (Wessobrunn).
*Kl. ahd. Sprdmr.* XXVIII (parallel texts of Bamberg and Wessobrunn).

***Heaven and Hell*** (***Himmel und Hölle***) is found in the same manuscript as the "Bamberg Creed and Confession" (see above) and was written by the same scribe. It is difficult to call it a literary "type," although similar themes are found in *Heliand, Genesis, Muspilli* and Otfrid. It is a work based at least in part on the Biblical account of the New Jerusalem in Revelations 21 and written in rather creative prose with remarkable variation. As the title suggests, the first part describes the delights and splendors of Heaven, the second the terrors and pains of Hell. The depiction of Hell is achieved in essentially one very long sentence, with image after image connected paratactically.

Text: *MSD* XXX.
*Kl. ahd. Sprdmr.* XXIX.
*Wilhelm*, VIII, pp. 31-33.

***Othlo's Prayer*** (***Othlos Gebet***) is included here as an example of prayers written in the vernacular, of which many were composed during the 11th century, a time of monastic reform and revival of piety not only in monasteries but among the laity as well. In fact, collections of prayers became increasingly common during the 11th and 12th centuries. Othlo was a Bavarian, born around 1010, who entered the monastery of St. Emmeram in Regensburg in 1032. There he directed the monastery school, but in 1062 after a dispute with the bishop and the abbot over the reform movement (Othlo favored it), he left Regensburg for Fulda and Amorbach, returning after five years. He died shortly thereafter around 1070. Othlo was the author of a number of Latin theological writings, in some of which he made autobiographical references, hence we have more information about his life than usual.

His German prayer is found in Cod. lat. 14490 in the Bavarian State Library in Munich. This codex, originally from St. Emmeram, contains Othlo's Latin works and was written and corrected by Othlo himself. His German prayer is on folios 161$^v$-163$^v$ near the end of the codex. The superscript above the prayer directs the reader to the Latin prayer immediately above. The German version is similar in content, but it is not a translation of the Latin prayer nor of any of the three other extant versions of the Latin prayer. Othlo's prayer begins on a personal note with pleas for assistance and spiritual strength in living a proper Christian life in the midst of all the trials and tribulations of everyday life. He continues by naming a large number of saints and martyrs and calling on them to intercede for him. Finally, he prays for his monastery that had been destroyed by fire, for all the congregations of the city, for his relatives, his deceased cloister brethren, and then he commends himself to God. The language is Bavarian, in prose, and interspersed with occasional Latin phrases and expressions.

Text:
*MSD* LXXXIII.
*Kl. ahd. Sprmdr.* XXXV (Latin version printed in parallel).
*Ahd. Lb.* XXVI, pp. 80-82.
*Wilhelm* I, pp. 1-3 (Latin version in commentary section).

### Biblical and Church Literature—Bibliography

Andersson, Theodore M. "The Caedmon Fiction in the Heliand Preface." *PMLA* 89 (1974): 278-84.

Discussion of the Heliand preface, arguing that at least parts of the preface are of Renaisance origin.

Belkin, Johanna, and Jürgen Meier. *Bibliographie zu Otfried von Weißenburg und zur altsächsischen Bibeldichtung.* Berlin: Erich Schmidt Verlag, 1975 (= Bibliog. zur dt. Lit. d. Mas, 7).

Eichhoff, Jürgen, and Irmengard Rauch, eds. *Der Heliand.* Darmstadt: Wiss. Buchges., 1973 (= WdF, 5400).

A collection of important scholarly articles on the *Heliand.*

Gottzmann, Carola L. "Das Wessobrunner Gebet. Ein Zeugnis des Kulturumbruchs vom heidnischen Germanentum zum Christentum." In: *Althochdeutsch, Bd. I. Ed. by R. Bergmann, et al.* Heidelberg: Winter, 1987. Pp. 637-54.

Considers "Wessobrunner Gebet" to be an example of missionary literature, subtly seeking to convince heathens instead of forcing them to become Christians.

Green, Dennis H. "Zur primären Rezeption von Otfrids Evangelienbuch." In: *Althochdeutsch. Bd. I. Ed. by Rolf Bergmann, et al.* Pp. 737-71.

Detailed study of how Otfrid's *Evangelienbuch* may have been received by his audience(s), i.e. by reading, listening to it being read, hearing it being chanted or sung. Problems of literacy in OHG period.

Groseclose, J. Sidney, and Brian O. Murdoch. *Die althochdeutschen poetischen Denkmäler.* Stuttgart: Metzler, 1976 (= Sammlung Metzler, 140).

Haubrichs, Wolfgang. "Eine prosopographische Skizze zu Otfrid von Weissenburg." In: *Otfrid von Weissenburg. Ed. by Wolfgang Kleiber.* 1978. Pp. 397-413 (see below).

This sketch of Otfrid's life is a summary of several more detailed studies on Otfrid's life and the cultural background of his times. Concise, but most informative.

____. *Georgslied und Georgslegende im frühen Mittelalter. Text und Rekonstruktion.* Königstein/Ts: Scriptor, 1979.

Haug, Walter. "Schriftlichkeit und Reflexion. Zur Entstehung und Entwicklung eines deutschsprachigen Schrifttums in Mittelalter." In: *Schrift und Gedächtnis.* Ed. by Assmann, Aleida and Jan, and Christof Hardmeier. Munich: Wilhelm Fink Verlag, 1983. Pp. 141-57. Also published in his *Strukturen als Schlüssel zur Welt.* Tübingen: Niemeyer, 1989. Pp. 51-66.

Kartschoke, Dieter. *Altdeutsche Bibeldichtung.* Stuttgart: Metzler, 1975 (= Sammlung Metzler, 135).

____. *Bibeldichtung: Studien zur Geschichte der epischen Bibelparaphrase von Juvencus bis Otfried von Weißenburg.* Munich: Wilhelm Fink Verlag, 1975.

Kleiber, Wolfgang, ed. *Otfrid von Weissenburg.* Darmstadt: Wiss. Buchges., 1978 (= WdF, 419).

A selection of significant articles on Otfrid from Trithemius (1494) to Wolfgang Haubrichs (1978), the vast majority since 1950.

Krogmann, Willy. *Der althochdeutsche 138. Psalm. Forschungsgeschichtlicher Überblick und Urfassung.* Hamburg: F. Wittig, 1973 (= Deutsches Bibel-Archiv, 5).

Ludwig, O. "Der althochdeutsche und der biblische Psalm 138. Ein Vergleich." *Euph.* 56 (1962): 402-9.

Magoun, Francis P. "Otfrid's 'Ad Liutbertum'." *PMLA* 58 (1943): 869-90.
A translation and commentary on the Latin dedicatory letter to Archbishop Liutbert of Mainz. Also published in German in: Kleiber, Wolfgang (above). Pp. 74-105.

Masser, Achim. *Bibel- und Legendenepik des deutschen Mittelalters.* Berlin: Erich Schmidt, 1976 (= GLG, 19).

Murphy, G. Ronald, SJ. *The Saxon Saviour: The Germanic Transformation of the Gospel in the Ninth-Century Heliand.* New York: Oxford UP, 1989.

Priebsch, Robert. *The Heliand Manuscript. Cotton Caligula A. VII in the British Museum. A Study.* Oxford: Clarendon, 1925.
Description of ms. C.

Schwab, Ute, ed. and trans. *Die Bruchstücke der altsächsischen Genesis und ihrer altenglischen Übertragung. Einführung, Textwiedergaben und Übersetzungen, Abbildungen der gesamten Überlieferung. Hrsg. von Ute Schwab. Mit Beiträgen von Ludwig Schuba und Hartmut Kugler.* Göppingen: Kümmerle, 1991 (= Litterae, 29).
Edition and translation into modern German of the OS and the OE *Genesis*, making a comparison of the parts translated from the OS into OE version readily available. Photographs of all ms. parts and contributions on the illustrations in the codex (Vat. Palat. lat. 1447) containing the OS fragments by L. Schuba and H. Kugler.

Sehrt, E. H. *Vollständiges Wörterbuch zum Heliand und zur altsächischen Genesis.* Göttingen/Baltimore, 1925 (= Hesperia, 14).
Important reference work.

Stavenhagen, L. "Das 'Petruslied.' Sein Alter und seine Herkunft." *Wirkendes Wort* 17 (1967): 21-8.

Vollmann-Profe, Gisela. *Kommentar zu Otfrids Evangelienbuch. Teil I: Widmungen, Buch I, 1-11.* Bonn: Habelt, 1976.

Wipf, Karl A., ed. and trans. *Althochdeutsche poetische Texte. Althochdeutsch/Neuhochdeutsch. Ausgew., übers. und kommentiert von Karl A.Wipf.* Stuttgart: Reclam, 1992. 359 p. (= UB, 8709).
Recent edition of all OHG poetic texts except Otfrid's *Evangelienbuch*, with mod. Germ. prose trans.

**Lay Literature**

Under this heading we shall consider a number of diverse OHG works that could be secular rather than religious in nature. The relative paucity of such literature is not surprising when one considers the fact that writing was effectively under the control of the church or at least of those educated primarily for religious purposes. Literature of the laity was still oral literature and seldom was written down. Of course, as we have seen, creative literature for those who had no Latin did exist but presumably had to be read aloud in order to be received by an illiterate public. Such works, e.g., Bible poetry, were generally intended to spread Christian ideology. Even the few poetic works from the oral tradition that have survived, e.g., *Hildebrandslied*, may show influence of the Christian background of those who recorded them. The works treated in this section, however, were probably not written down from an older oral tradition, although some influence of oral genres may be evident. They deal instead with more recent events of current interest or perhaps topics of a more general concern. Their rarity may also be attributed to the fact that there are so few German texts from the 10th and early 11th centuries, the period of the 'Ottonian Renaissance,' in which practically all surviving writing is in Latin.

The *Ludwigslied* (Lay of Louis III) is a princely encomium, not merely a general hymn of praise for a beneficent ruler, but rather a poem in praise of a king who had performed mightily in defeating a dangerous enemy force in a specific battle. The occasion was the defeat of the Norsemen by the West Frankish King Louis III at Saucourt in Northern France on 3 August 881. The date of composition is quite certain because Louis is referred to in the poem as being alive, although the poem must have been written down after his death in 882 since the Latin superscription indicates that it is a memorial poem ("Rithmus teutonicus de piae memoriae Hludovico . . ."). The poem is found on what was originally a blank page near the end of a manuscript containing religious material, (No. 143) of the public library in Valenciennes in Flanders, and came from the near-by monastery of St. Armand sur l'Elnon. The manuscript is from the late 9th century and, interestingly enough from a linguistic and cultural standpoint, contains the text of the oldest surviving Old French poem, the "Sequence of St. Eulalia," immediately preceding the "Ludwigslied," and written by the same hand. The language of the "Ludwigslied" is Rhenish-Franconian, but the scribe must have been bilingual, since both the OF and the OHG poems are inscribed with almost no errors. The poet uses the long lines of Otfrid with internal rhyme and strophes of two or three long lines.

The *Ludwigslied* begins with a short account of the life of Louis, who was orphaned at an early age, was taken and guarded by God and put upon the throne which he shared with his brother Carloman. Then God sent the Norsemen as a test for Louis and also to remind the Franks of their sins. Louis, however, was far away, yet God called him back to help His people against the Norsemen (v. 23: *"Hliudwig, kuning min, hilph minan liutin!"*—"Ludwig, my king, help my people!"). Louis agrees to help but first calls his council together and addresses the lords, asking them to follow him on his God-given mission and promising them rewards. Louis sings a holy song while riding into battle, and his men sing "Kyrie eleison." The battle itself is described briefly but vividly, and the poem ends with praise to God, acclaim for Louis, and the wish for Louis's salvation.

There have been various opinions about the *Ludwigslied*. Earlier scholars considered it to be in the tradition of the old Germanic *Preislied* (hymn of praise), or following the model of Otfrid's dedicatory poem to Louis the German. Some have seen Germanic custom in the idea that God took young Louis under his wing and trained him. However, it seems more likely that Latin songs of praise to a ruler may have been in the poet's mind and that the Biblical figure of David as the ideal king following God's behest could have been the model. Louis is depicted as in the tradition of an Old Testament warrior king but also as the exemplary Christian ruler. Certainly the Christian setting for the lay subject matter could indicate a kind of early crusading spirit, the Christians with God on their side fighting against the heathens; an example of "Christian heroic poetry," as has been suggested, to be found in the later *chansons de geste*.

Text:
*MSD* XI.
*Kl. ahd. Sprdmr.* XVI.
*Ahd. Lb.* XXXVI, pp. 136-8.
*Handbook*, pp. 239-41 (Eng. trans.).
*Schlosser* (1989), pp. 274-7 (with mod. Ger. trans.).

Facsimile:
*Schrifttafeln* 22.

The fragmentary poem *De Heinrico* (About Henry) is a curious piece of work in that its Otfridian long lines are for the most part in Latin in the first half-line and German in the second, yet the text of twenty-seven lines is continuous, divided into three- and four-line strophes. It is to be found in Ms. Gg. V. 35 of the Cambridge University Library, a collection of forty-seven Latin poems commonly known as *The Cambridge Songs,* which were copied in England from a German source in the first half of the 11th century. *De Heinrico* is number nineteen. The dialect of the source is difficult to ascertain and still open to question.

The text of the poem itself is also problematical. Beginning with a prayer to Christ for assistance in telling his tale, the poet describes a meeting between a certain Duke Henry of Bavaria with Kaiser Otto. After the reception Otto and Henry go to church for prayer, then Otto invites Henry to join his council. There Henry receives great honors, and Otto confers on Henry everything he has except his royal power, which Henry did not want. Henry becomes head of the council and also administers the royal decrees that he helps fashion. Many suggestions have been made as to which Henry and which Otto are intended. Three Saxon Ottos and four Henrys of Bavaria may come into consideration, but there are problems with most combinations and difficulties with the text as well. Perhaps the best guess is that the poem deals with Kaiser Otto III and Duke Henry II of Bavaria, whose son Henry IV of Bavaria became the last of the Saxon emperors in 1002, as Henry II. At any rate, the poem seems to be a song of praise to Duke Henry II, possibly after his death. He is depicted as a noble figure, loyal to the emperor, and as a just counselor and exemplary executive.

Text:
*MSD* XVIII.
*Kl. ahd. Sprdmr.* XXVIII.
*Ahd. Lb.* XXXIX, p. 139.
*Handbook*, p. 253 (Eng. trans.).
*Schlosser* (1989), pp. 278 f. (with mod. Ger. trans.).
Strecker, Karl, ed. *Die Cambridger Lieder.* Berlin, [2]1955 (= MGH 40).

*Cleric and Nun* (*Kleriker und Nonne* or *Suavissima Nonna*) is the other part-Latin, part-German poetic fragment from the *Cambridge Songs* (see *De Heinrico*, above). It appears to be the remnant of a love poem, possibly censored by erasure especially at the end of the fragment, but in any case damaged by chemical treatment in attempts to make it legible. The original text is therefore difficult to read. Like *De Heinrico* it is written in long lines, which form eleven two-line stanzas. The dialect is probably North Rhine-

Franconian or Thuringian, and the poem may be dated from the end of the 10th to the beginning of the 11th century.

The fragment depicts a conversation between a man, thought to be a cleric, and a nun, during which the man attempts to persuade the nun to love him. However, the nun remains steadfast; she has chosen Christ and is interested only in divine love in heaven. Attempts at seduction are a frequent topic in Latin poetry—the Latin poem immediately preceding *Kleriker und Nonne* in the *Cambridge Songs* is such a poem, as are various songs in the *Carmina Burana*. Some have thought of this poem as the earliest German love song, but this seems unlikely in view of the strong classical tradition which it follows in the initial invocation of nature, springtime, and bird song. It is also possible that the nun converts her would-be lover to virtue, but then one wonders why the ending of the poem was erased. Nevertheless, it is important as precursor of the later German *Minnesang*(see p. 224 ff.).

Text:
See Strecker (above).
Dronke, Peter. *Medieval Latin and the Rise of the European Love-Lyric*. Oxford, [2]1968. Vol. II, pp. 353-6 (with reconstruction of text and Eng. trans.).

Facsimile:
Breuel, K. *The Cambridge Songs*. Cambridge, 1915. Pp. 16 f.

**Stag and Doe (*Hirsch und Hinde*)** may also be a fragment of a love poem, although that is not at all certain. It does seem to be written in end-rhyme, but the fragment is so small that it is difficult to say. The text is as follows (*Handbook*, p. 257):

Hirez runeta hintun in das ora
"uildu noh, hinta. . . ?"

(A hart murmured in the ear of a hind: "Wilt thou yet, hind. . . ?")

The poem could have been an animal allegory (*Tierdichtung*) of a story of seduction. The whispering in the ear is found in later love poetry, and the suggestion has been made that the poem could have been a warning against succumbing to passion, i.e. a moral lesson, such as the description of the autula in the German *Physiologus*, a horned animal whose horns get entangled while playing with twigs at the Euphrates river and falls prey to the hunter (the devil).

The manuscript is in the Royal Library in Brussels, and the verses are in the margin of Ms. 8862, folio 15. Date: 11th century.

### Lay Literature—Bibliography

Andersson, Theodore M. "Blood on the Battlefield: A Note on the *Ludwigslied* v. 49." *Neophil.* 56 (172): 12-17.
Dittrich, Maria-Luise. "De Heinrico." *ZfdA* 84 (1952/3): 274-308.
Makes a reasonable argument for Henry II of Bavaria as the Duke Henry of the poem.
Ehlert, Trude. "Literatur und Wirklichkeit—Exegese und Politik. Zur Deutung des *Ludwigslieds*." *Saeculum* 32 (1981): 31-42.

Groseclose, J. Sidney, and Brian O. Murdoch. *Die althochdeutschen poetischen Denkmäler.* Stuttgart: Metzler, 1976 (= Sammlung Metzler, 140).

Jungandreas, W. "De Heinrico." *Leuvense Bijdragen* 57 (1968): 75-91.

Müller, Robert. "Der historische Hintergrund des ahd. *Ludwigslieds.*" *DVjs* 62 (1988): 221-226.

Trost, Pavel. "Zwei lateinisch-althochdeutsche Mischgedichte." In: *Althochdeutsch, Vol. 1.* Ed. by R. Bergmann et al. Pp. 807 f. (see LANGUAGE—BIBLIOGRAPHY). Short article on *De Heinrico* and *Kleriker und Nonne*, theorizing on possible reasons for the mixed language.

## Latin Literature on German Subjects

For a period of almost 150 years, from the beginning of the 10th to the middle of the 11th centuries, very little literature written in German is to be found. Many reasons have been advanced for the absence of vernacular literature during this period after such substantial beginnings under the Carolingians, but it is difficult to explain adequately. Some literary histories note the gap and move on to the 11th century, others attempt to fill the void by discussing Latin poetic works that deal with material from Germanic heroic poetry or other works in Latin of a more popular orientation. We shall note several of such works briefly here.

*Waltharius manu fortis.* (*Waltharilied* or "Lay of Walther"), an epic poem of almost 1,500 Latin dactylic hexameters, appears at first glance to be a Latin version of a Germanic heroic poem. It deals with people whose names are known from other heroic materials: Attila, Gibicho, Gunther, Hagen, Walther, and Hiltgunt. They occur variously in the OHG *Hildebrandslied* (see p. 34), the MHG *Nibelungenlied* (see p. 205 ff.), *Biterolf und Dietleib* (see p. 397) and *Walther und Hildegunde* (see p. 398), the ON *Thidrekssage,* and the OE "Waldere"-fragments, but it is impossible to identify a common original story, although many attempts have been made to explain the relationship of the various works in question. Authorship and dating of *Waltharius* have also been in dispute, with three possibilities: Ekkehard I of St. Gall (901/910-973); Geraldus (died 970-75), a monk (of St. Gall?) who names himself in a prefatory letter to Bishop Erchambald of Strasbourg (965-93); and Ekkehard IV of St. Gall (980-1057). Whoever the author may have been, he obviously had some knowledge of Germanic heroic tales and could well have made up the story himself, since we cannot determine his source. A dating in the 10th century, probably the second half, is likely.

> The story itself begins with the approach of the Huns under Attila to western Europe. The Frankish King Gibicho offers his vassal Hagano as a hostage to obtain peace. The Burgundian King Hererícus sends his daughter Hiltgunde, and the King of Aquitaine, Alphere, gives up his son Waltharius for the same purpose, despite the fact that Waltharius and Hiltgunde are already betrothed. The three hostages are raised at Attila's court in Pannonia and eventually gain high positions there, especially Waltharius as a warrior and army leader and Hiltgunde as an influential member of the queen's retinue. Upon the death of Gibicho, his son Guntharius becomes king and denounces his father's pact with Attila. When Hagano learns of this, he flees from Attila's court by night and returns home. Even-

tually Waltharius and Hiltgunde follow suit, after first securing a substantial amount of the queen's treasure, some provisions, and survival equipment for their journey home. The Huns do not pursue the fugitives, but when Waltharius and Hiltgunde come into Frankish territory, Guntharius demands the treasure from them. They refuse, and Guntharius, despite Hagano's advice to the contrary, attempts to take the treasure from them by force. He sends ten vassals one after the other against Waltharius, who is holed up in an easily defended mountainous region so that he is able to kill each one. Finally, on the following day, Guntharius himself and Hagen, who is torn by his allegiance to his lord and his friendship for Waltharius, fall upon Waltharius together as he comes out into the open, believing that he would not be attacked. In the ensuing battle, Guntharius loses a leg, Waltharius his right hand, and Hagano one of his eyes. They then make peace, Hiltgunde bandages their wounds, Hagano and Guntharius return to Worms, and Waltharius and Hiltgunde travel on to Aquitaine where they are married and reign for thirty years.

The main characters are stock figures of heroic poetry: Waltharius, the superb fighter with high ideals; Hagano, his friend with a conflict of obligations, whom we know from the *Nibelungenlied*; Guntharius, the weak, avaricious king, also in the *Nibelungenlied*; and Hiltgunde, with the usual qualities of the loyal wife. Yet Christian virtues are also present—e.g., Waltharius prays before and after the battle—and Guntharius's sinful greed is punished in the end. The poem does not end with the tragic death of the hero in the face of relentless fate. There is a kind of reconciliation at the conclusion. Furthermore, scholars have been able to trace the influence of classical Latin epic poetry on the language and composition of *Waltharius*.

There are ten manuscripts and/or fragments of the poem from the 11th, 12th, 13th, and 15th centuries, indicating a wide distribution of the poem and lasting popularity.

Text:
K. Strecker. *Monumenta Germaniae Historica*. Poetae VI. 1951. Pp. 1 ff.
*Haug/Vollmann*, VII.

Translations:
Karl Langosch. *Waltharius, Ruodlieb, Märchenepen. Lateinische Epik des Mittelalters mit deutschen Versen*. Darmstadt: Wiss. Buchges., [2]1960. Pp. 6-83 (Strecker's text with mod. German verse trans.).
Felix Genzmer. *Das Waltharilied und die Waldere-Bruchstücke*. Übertragen, eingeleitet und erläutert von F. G. Stuttgart: Reclam, 1957. 54 pp. (= UB, 4174). Mod. Ger. verse trans. New edition: Vogt-Spira, U., ed. and trans. *Waltharius*. Latin text with mod. Ger. trans. In appendix: *Waldere*. English with mod. Ger. trans. by U. Schaefer. Stuttgart: Reclam, 19 (= UB, 4174).
*Haug/Vollmann*, VII. Mod. Ger. prose trans.

**Ruodlieb** is a fragmentary Latin poem in leonine (rhymed at caesura and end) hexameters, which was probably written in the second quarter of the 11th century. The fragments are found on 36 leaves of a manuscript now in Munich (M) but quite possibly from Tegernsee, and two leaves of a later manuscript from St. Florian (F). Some portions of the manuscripts are illegible and there is a discontinuity among the fragments so that it is difficult to reconstruct the story line. Nevertheless, *Ruodlieb* seems to be the story of a young knight who is forced into exile and seeks his fortune at the court of a good king, a model of the just and peaceful ruler, where he is well rewarded for his services. Eventually he returns home, having several adventures along the way, and celebrates a reunion with his mother. The next step is to choose a wife, and in this he is apparently unsuccessful. Finally, there is the episode in which Ruodlieb traps a dwarf, who, in exchange for his freedom, offers to tell Ruodlieb where a great treasure is to be found, and who prophesies that Ruodlieb will win the hand of Heriburg after killing her father and brother.

In many respects, *Ruodlieb* has some of the characteristics of Germanic heroic poetry—adventure, plus a certain didactic element dealing with the proper way to lead one's life, based in part on advice given to the hero but also in his reaction to the circumstances in which he finds himself. The poem is notable for its portrayal of everyday life at court, and Ruodlieb proves to be quite successful there. We are also given a good look at many aspects of common life of the period. Ruodlieb is no supernatural hero, rather a survivor who may make mistakes, but is in the end able to choose the right path. The poem seems to be a precursor of the *Spielmannsepos*, or even courtly literature (see below), and portrays life in Germany before the influence of French courtliness. It is an important cultural document, and for that reason we have included it here.

Text:
Seiler, Friedrich, ed. *Ruodlieb, der älteste Roman des Mittelalters nebst Epigrammen.* Mit Einleitung, Anmerkungen und Glossar hrsg. von F.S. Halle, 1882.
Knapp, Fritz Peter, ed. and trans. *Ruodlieb.* Mittellateinisch und Deutsch. Übertragung, Kommentar und Nachwort. Stuttgart: Reclam, 1977 (= UB ).
Langosch, Karl. (see above under *Waltharius*), pp. 86-215.
Zeydel, Edwin H., ed. and trans. *Ruodlieb. The Earliest Courtly Novel (after 1050). Introduction, Text, Translation, Commentary and Textual Notes.* New York: AMS Press, [3]1969.
*Haug/Vollmann,* IX 2.
Ford, Gordon B., Jr., ed. *The "Ruodlieb." Linguistic Introduction, Latin Text, and Glossary.* Leiden: E. J. Brill, 1966.
Grocock, C. W., ed. and trans. *The "Ruodlieb," Edited with Translation and Notes.* Warminster: Aris and Phillips, and Chicago: Belchazy-Carducci, 1985.

Translations:
Heyne, Moriz, trans. *Ruodlieb. Übertragung des ältesten deutschen Heldenromans von M. H.* Leipzig, 1897.
See Langosch (above). Mod. Ger. verse trans.
See Knapp (above). Mod. Ger. prose trans.
See Zeydel (above). Engl. prose trans.
See *Haug/Vollmann* (above). Mod. Ger. prose trans.
See Grocock (above). Engl. prose trans.

Facsimile:
*Ruodlieb.* Faksimile-Ausgabe des Codex Latinus Monacensis 19486 der Bayerischen Staatsbibliothek München und der Fragmente von St. Florian. Bd. I,1: Einleitung von Walter Haug. Bd. I,2: Tafeln. Wiesbaden, 1974. Bd. II,1: Kritischer Text von Benedikt Konrad Vollmann. Wiesbaden, 1985.

**Ecbasis cuiusdam captivi per tropologiam** (*Ecbasis captivi* or "Flight of the Prisoner"). This is a poem of slightly over 1,200 lines in leonine hexameters, consisting of a prologue, followed by a beast epic/ animal fable (*Tierepos/-fabel*) which frames another animal tale, i.e., a story within a story. There are two manuscripts, A and B, in the

Burgundian Library in Brussels, dating from the end of the 11th to the beginning of the 12th century. The poem was apparently composed by a young monk in the monastery of St. Evre in the Lotharingia-Luxembourg area ca. 930-940.

In the prologue the monk laments his lack of talent in formal composition in school, but he hopes to entertain his readers with the story he will tell. He is writing under arrest in the monastery, is not allowed to work outside in the fields with the other monks and feels like a young calf tied to a stake. His story is of the young calf which gets loose and ends up in a wolf's cave, where it is to be eaten the next day. But the loss of the calf is discovered, and the other animals, led by the steer, eventually find the wolf's lair. There the wolf is telling his vassals, an otter and a hedgehog, the interior story. This is the story of the healing of the lion by the fox, the well-known Aesop's fable. There is much confusion when the other animals arrive, and the calf manages to escape and returns home. The steer ties the wolf to a tree.

Animal fables are usually symbolic, with the animals assuming human roles. Here the outer frame-story uses the parable of the lost sheep, or the good shepherd. It is pointedly allegorical (*per tropologiam*) and describes the fleeing of a monk from the ascetic life of his cloister and succumbing to worldly delights, from which he is retrieved by his monastic brothers and again set on the correct moral path to salvation. There are at least some aspects of the work that are specifically German, but many of them are obscure today. Nevertheless, it does give some indication of the intellectual atmosphere in a German monastery of the time.

Text:
Ernst Voigt, ed. *Ecbasis Captivi. Das älteste Tierepos des Mittelalters.* 1875. (= QF, 8).
*Haug/Vollmann*, IX 1.
Zeydel, Edwin H. *Ecbasis cuiusdem captivi per tropologiam. Escape of a Certain Captive Told in a Figurative Manner.* New York: AMS Press, 1966. Intro., text, Engl. trans., commentary and appendix.

Translation:
Gressler, Emil, trans. *Ecbasis captivi, Die Flucht eines Gefangenen. Das älteste Tierepos des Mittelalters.* 1910.
*Haug/Vollmann*, IX 1. Mod. Ger. prose trans.
See also Zeydel (above).

## Latin Literature—Bibliography

The texts and translations of *Waltharius*, *Ruodlieb*, and *Ecbasis captivi* in *Haug/Vollmann* are accompanied by excellent introductions, notes to the texts, and bibliographies in the "Kommentar"-section of that edition; *Waltharius*, pp. 1169-1222; *Ruodlieb*, pp. 1306-1406; *Ecbasis captivi*, pp. 1250-1305.

Dronke, Peter. "*Waltharius* and the *Vita Waltharii*." *PBB* 106 (1984): 390-402.

_____. *Ruodlieb. The Emergence of Romance.* In: P. D., *Poetic Individuality in the Middle Ages. New Departures in Poetry 1110-1150.* London: Westfield College, Univ. of London, Committee for Medieval Studies, [2]1986.

Götte, Christian. *Das Menschen- und Herrscherbild des Rex minor im "Ruodlieb."* *Studien zur Ethik und Anthropologie im "Ruodlieb."* Munich: Wilhelm Fink Verlag, 1981.

Howlett, D. R. "The Structure of the *Ecbasis Captivi.*" *Studia Neophilologica* 47 (1975): 3-6.

Knapp, Fritz P. *Das lateinische Tierepos.* Darmstadt: Wiss. Buchges., 1979 (= Erträge der Forschung, 121).
Research summary on Beast Epics in Latin. Check here for literature on *Ecbasis Captivi.*

Kratz, Dennis M. *Mocking Epic. "Waltharius," "Alexandreis" and the Problem of Christian Heroism.* Madrid: J. Porrua Turanzas, 1980.

Norman, Frederick. "The Evidence for the Germanic Walther Lay." *Acta Germanica* 3 (1968): 21-35.

Vollmann, Benedikt K. *Ruodlieb.* Darmstadt: Wiss. Buchges., 1993 (= Erträge der Forschung, 283).
A narrative summary of *Ruodlieb*-research and the current status of the scholarship. Excellent place to start.

# Early Middle High German Literature 1050-1170

## HISTORICAL BACKGROUND

### The Saxon and Salian Dynasties (1046-1150)

Even before the Treaty of Meersen (870), which effectively formalized the split of the old Carolingian realm into a western, Gallo-Frankish speaking kingdom and an eastern kingdom of German dialects, a third force, this time from the north, made itself felt in the coastal and estuarial regions of northern Europe. Norsemen, mainly Danes and Norwegians, attacked the shores and sailed up the rivers plundering cities and towns. Some, in fact, even settled down in Neustria, where they eventually assimilated with the local population, and gave their name to the territory which later became Normandy. The incursions of the Norsemen presented difficult problems for both Charles the Bald and Louis the German in maintaining control of their kingdoms.

Charles the Bald died in 877 and was succeeded by his son Louis the Stammerer (Louis II of France), who died after a two-year reign. Louis was succeeded by his two sons, Louis III, who took the northern part of the realm, and Carloman, who ruled in the southern half, i.e., Burgundy and Aquitaine. It is Louis III's victory over the Norsemen at Saucourt in 881 that is celebrated in the "Ludwigslied" (see above, p. 52).

Louis the German died in 876, and two of his three sons, Carloman, King of Bavaria, and Louis the Saxon (also known as Louis the Younger), died soon thereafter. The kingship thus devolved on Louis the German's third son, Charles the Fat, King of Swabia, who proved to be quite incompetent, especially in dealing with the attacks of the Norsemen. Charles was soon forced by the German nobles to abdicate, and he was replaced by Arnulf, Duke of Carinthia, an illegitimate son of Louis the German. Arnulf was successful in defeating the Danes and became Emperor in 896. However, he died in 899 and was succeeded as King of Germany by his son, Louis the Child. Upon Louis's death without heir in 911, the Carolingian dynasty (if one includes the illegitimate Arnulf and his son) in the East Frankish realm, i.e., Germany, came to an end, and a Frankish count, Conrad, was named king by the German nobles. Their squabbling among themselves, however, made Conrad's reign (911-18) difficult, but the very fact that the powerful nobles chose their king became an important political factor for the future of kingship in Germany and in the empire. Here, more so than in the West Frankish territories, election by the powerful nobles was to be the constitutive force behind the realm. It eventually became no longer solely a question of succession or dividing the kingdom among heirs but of the responsibility of the leaders of the various "peoples" in the realm to choose their ruler, despite the divergence of particular and imperial interests.

As emperor, Conrad struggled to assert the interests of the empire against those of the nobles but was ultimately unsuccessful. At his death he yielded the kingship to Henry the Fowler, Duke of Saxony, who became Henry I of Germany and was the first ruler of the Saxon, or Liudolfing, dynasty. Henry was able to stabilize the kingdom by skillfully negotiating with the dukes, allowing them a certain amount of independence in their lands in return for their support of the crown. He suppressed rebellion by force when necessary and successfully defended his realm against the Danes in the north and the Wends, Slavs, and Hungarians in the east. Through family political marriages, he gained recognition and better relations with neighboring states, and fairly soon in his reign he designated his oldest son, Otto, as his successor, relying on the support of the powerful nobility as electors.

Despite claims of other family members for their rights, Otto assumed the throne upon his father's death in 936. As Otto I, also called Otto the Great, he strove to strengthen the royal power in various ways. He installed family members in high ecclesiastical positions, e.g. the archbishoprics of Mainz and Cologne. Incipient rebellions were crushed or relatives assuaged by grants of peripheral dukedoms in the east or advantageous marriages in adjacent lands. In 951, in a successful attempt to forestall the plans of his brother Henry, Duke of Bavaria, and his son Liudolf, Duke of Swabia, Otto invaded Italy and married Adelheid, the Queen of Italy, the Anglo-Saxon princess Edith, his first wife, having died earlier. To extend his control of the eastern borders, he created new bishoprics in the east.

In 960, Otto again invaded Italy when Pope John XII asked for his aid, and Otto was successful in gaining control of Rome. In 962 he was crowned emperor, but once he had left Italy his authority was challenged. Thus began a fateful pattern for German emperors: the success of their attempts to exert their rule in Italy lasted just as long as their personal presence and force were there. They were repeatedly drawn into the quagmire of Italian politics, and this distracted them from their other obligations at home.

Otto's coronation as emperor and his claim of suzerainty over all of Italy and Sicily raised again the problem of two emperors, Rome in the West and Byzantium in the East. Otto attempted to establish cordial relations with the eastern ruler, but found no great willingness to reciprocate there. Eventually, he did manage to arrange a marriage for his son Otto with Theophano, the niece of the newly crowned emperor in Byzantium. They were married in Rome in 972. One year later Otto I died, and his eighteen-year-old son became Emperor Otto II with Theophano the Empress.

The reign of Otto II lasted only ten years, and it was in no wise as successful as his father's. He had to use military force to assert his control in the north and east of the realm against rebellious nobles. In the west, King Lothaire III tried to establish control over Lotharingia and had to be countered, and in southern Italy the Greeks and the Saracens actually defeated Otto's forces. He was able, however, just before his death, to have his three-year-old son, also named Otto, elected Emperor.

A regency under his mother Theophano was set up for Otto III until he should attain his majority. During that time the efforts that Otto II had made to secure his realm were continued, and challenges to Otto III's rule, notably that by his relative, Henry the Quarrelsome of Bavaria, were put down by force. In 996 Otto went to Rome and was crowned Emperor by Pope Gregory V. In collaboration with the papacy, Otto wanted to renew the empire with Rome as capital, hence spent much of his time in Rome and elsewhere in Italy. His concentration on Italy aroused dissatisfaction and unrest at home, and he was troubled also by conflicting interests in Italy, where he died of malaria at the age of twenty-two in 1002.

Henry the Quarrelsome of Bavaria eventually was reconciled with Otto III, and Henry's son became Henry II, King of Germany, after Otto's death. Henry worked hard to reestablish the royal power in the German territories. He depended even more than his predecessors on the church for support in worldly matters. To that end he claimed the right to install bishops, and he furthered monastic and church reform. He, too, could not completely ignore Italy. On his first visit there in 1004, he was crowned King of Italy; on his second visit in 1014, Pope Benedict VIII crowned him Emperor, and on his third visit in 1024 he died of the plague in Apulia.

The Salian, Conrad II, a great-grandson of a son-in-law of Otto I, was elected Henry II's successor by the leaders of the nobility, again an election, but one still based on familial relationships. The Saxon nobility was not enthusiastic about the election of Conrad. His territories were in the area of Mainz on the Middle Rhine. Conrad continued the policy of investing his own bishops, controlling the imperial monasteries, and installing relatives in duchies as they became vacant. Yet he still had much opposition from the nobility to overcome, not only at home but also in Italy. He was crowned Emperor in Italy in 1027 and was eventually able to control the three kingdoms of Germany, Italy, and Burgundy. He ensured that his young son Henry would be his successor and managed to strengthen the idea of the Empire as a corporate union in which the Emperor, the princes, and the people all had their individual roles to play. He sought to administer his lands by appointing *ministeriales*, fiefholders in his service, to do the job. Such fiefholders gradually became more and more powerful by virtue of their land holdings and served as an imperial counter to the free landed nobility. Conrad continued the monastic reforms of his predecessors, but the reformers in the church began to resent the imperial influence on monastic and church affairs, and this led ultimately to the "investiture controversy" (see below).

Conrad's son, Henry III, succeeded him in 1039 and continued to experience troubles with the church when elected bishops, as a result of the church reforms, began to refuse to take the oath of allegiance to the king. However, when three popes were contending for the papal seat, Henry went to Rome, deposed all three and seated his own choice, the former Bishop of Bamberg, as Pope Clement II at the synods of Sutri and Rome in 1046, whereupon he was crowned Emperor. Despite his decisive action and success, the resentment of the church continued.

The era of the Saxon and Salian emperors is sometimes referred to as the "Ottonian renaissance," in analogy to the earlier "Carolingian renaissance," but it is difficult to discern what exactly was reborn. One thinks first, perhaps, of the influence of classical learning in the monasteries and cathedral schools (see, e.g, the translations of Notker, above p. 31 f.), but while there may have been a revival of learning, there was little, if any, creative writing. As we have seen, virtually no literature in the vernacular has survived from this period, and writing in Latin merely continued the historiography of the earlier period, except for works such as *Waltharius* and *Ruodlieb* (see p. 55 ff.) and the remarkable book-dramas (plays for reading rather than acting) of the nun, Hroswitha von Gandersheim (see p. 431). To be sure, it was a period of expansion, increase in population, improvement in agriculture, growth of cities and towns, and the rise of markets and use of money. There were also advances in architecture, and art—particularly book illustrations—where Byzantine influence may be seen. Most importantly, however, monastic reform under the leadership of Cluny and Gorze and church reform in general resulted in the power struggle between the empire and the papacy. As a result of the reform movement, there was indeed a revival of religiosity, not only in monastic circles but even among the laity, where lay religious orders were formed. When this occurred, about the middle of the 11th century, the language used was not only Latin, but once again German.

## The Investiture Controversy

During the latter half of the 11th century, the monastic reform movement which began at Cluny and Hirsau developed into a reform of the church, including the papacy. It took the form initially of reaction to two practices that had long prevailed in the church: the non-observance of celibacy by the clergy (nicolaitism) and the awarding of church and monastic offices in return for monetary or other considerations (simony). Celibacy was generally observed in monastic life, and the drive to return to strict practice of the Rule of St. Benedict in the reform monasteries only underlined that requirement. But the demand of celibacy was not always obeyed even in the church hierarchy, let alone among the local clergy. That was an internal problem for the church. The problem of simony, however, had much more extensive social and especially political ramifications.

The church controlled a good portion of the wealth of the empire in the form of property and the income from it. Monasteries, bishoprics, and other church holdings placed significant political-economic power in the hands of whoever controlled such properties. In fact, much of the political power of the Ottonians and the Salians derived from their direct or indirect control of ecclesiastical lands. The naming of a bishop, therefore, was very important for the king/emperor. He traditionally had the right to install and also to remove such church officials, just as he could lay rulers who were subject to him for their lands. Yet the church, especially the reformers, began to claim the right of investiture, and thus the history of the empire became inextricably entangled with that of the papacy.

At the time of Henry III, the empire was still ruled theocratically, i.e., the emperor had sacral as well as lay powers as defender of the church. He had the right to invest bishops throughout the empire with crosier and ring and to accept their oath of fealty to him in return. Only then were they confirmed in office by the pope. It is obvious that simony probably was involved in such investiture or at least some expectation of a quid pro quo. Bishops and other clerics, frequently from noble families, played an important role in the administration of the empire as well as in the church and had the political and economic power to rival many a duke.

The nomination and election of a pope at this time was a matter of the backing of a candidate by highly influential parties or persons, and strong rivalries existed, particularly among noble Roman families. In some instances, rival popes were elected, causing disorder and confusion not only in the church but in the empire as well. Such was the situation that Henry III faced in 1046, as we have noted above. His intervention in affairs of the papacy resolved the immediate problem, but it was clearly not in accordance with canon law. Nevertheless, it demonstrates the immense power of the emperor at that time.

After the death of Pope Clement II two years later and of Damasus II one year after that, Leo IX (1049-1054), became the first of a series of popes to work for reform in the church administration, the curia, and the college of cardinals. He travelled widely and held a series of synods throughout the empire, spending only a scant six months in Rome during his tenure of office. His reforms were directed towards assuring free church elections and the moral renewal of the clergy, stressing celibacy. Leo's desire for free church elections not only attacked simony but was also an important step towards the eventual power struggle between empire and papacy. However, Leo himself seems not to have made an open challenge to royal prerogatives.

Henry III was a deeply religious man, yet very conscious of his royal position as a servant of God. As such he expected unquestioning obedience to his will. He was scrupulous in refusing any gifts for the ecclesiastical appointments he made, and his reign was a relatively stable period. There were the inevitable problems, of course. Conspirators in Bavaria and Carinthia wanted to overthrow Henry, but these were successfully eliminated. The Billungs in Saxony opposed Henry, but he was able to neutralize them with ecclesiastical support. In general, he relied on building up his ministeriales and ecclesiastical appointments as a counter to the princes, whose support he found increasingly difficult to command.

Henry III died in 1056, during the short papacy of Victor II (1055-57), leaving his six-year old son, Henry IV, whom he had designated as his successor three years before. Victor II was able to persuade the princes to accept Henry IV as king and to recognize his mother Agnes as regent during his minority. Agnes, a very pious woman, was a reluctant regent, and as a result of her policies, or lack thereof, the monarchy was weakened. In the absence of a strong imperial court the reformers in Rome sought political and military backing wherever they could, and the struggle for reform against the conservatives in Rome and in the empire was marked by the naming of a series of popes and anti-popes by the opposing parties over a number of years.

During the papacy of Nicholas II reform of the process for electing a pope was made at the Lateran synod of 1059. It was decreed that the bishop of Rome was to be elected by the cardinals of the city upon nomination of the candidate by the cardinal bishops.

There was also pro forma acknowledgement of the royal prerogatives without precisely stating what they were. A further decree prohibited any layman from investing a cleric either freely or for money. Politically, in view of the weakness of the German king, Nicholas sought to gain support from the Normans, who had been settling in southern Italy and Sicily for some time.

After the death of Nicholas II in 1061, Alexander II became pope with the support of the powerful northern Italian cities and the reform circles in Rome. The election was challenged, however, by the conservative opposition, which elected Honorius II as antipope, but he was never consecrated and was rejected as a schismatic in 1064. Under Alexander II the reform movement intensified as papal legates were sent on missions throughout Europe to further the primacy of Rome.

In Germany Henry IV had many problems to deal with. He no longer controlled the southern duchies of Swabia, Bavaria, and Carinthia, not to mention royal lands in Italy. The Saxons still opposed the crown, and Henry's family lands were not always at his disposal, but he began exerting royal control in the crown lands of Thuringia and eastern Saxony by building castles there. He eventually reached an accommodation with the Saxon nobility, and by 1075 he had managed to recover control of most of the crown lands despite having lost support from many of the dukes.

Meanwhile, Hildebrand, a monk who had become increasingly influential at the papal court, became Pope Gregory VII upon the death of Alexander II in 1073. He was elected and confirmed almost spontaneously with no regard for the election procedures established in 1059. Historians may not agree in their views of Gregory VII, but it seems clear that he was a man of very strong will, fixity of purpose, intolerance, and the "deep conviction that as Peter's successor he alone bore the responsibility for the salvation of the whole church" (Fuhrmann, p. 60). It is not surprising then that he would clash with Henry IV, a man who had developed a deep distrust of advisors from early in his life. He felt that he could not rely on the princes of the realm and wanted to make decisions by himself. He was well aware of his royal position. Lamprecht of Hersfeld wrote of him: "That man, born and bred to be a ruler, always showed . . . whatever misfortunes befell him a royal cast of mind; he would sooner die than accept defeat" (Fuhrmann, p. 61).

Gregory had already excommunicated some of Henry's counselors in 1073 for simony when a disagreement between Henry and Gregory over the investiture of a new bishop for the city of Milan produced the spark that set off an open struggle. Gregory took further steps against the counselors and charged three other imperial bishops with either simony or disobedience in 1075. In response, Henry held an imperial assembly and synod early in 1076 in Worms at which a letter to Gregory was drawn up, demanding his resignation from the papacy. When Gregory received the letter at his Lenten synod that February, he immediately deposed and excommunicated Henry. It was an unheard-of, shocking step to take. In October the princes opposed to Henry met to decide what to do about the situation. Henry agreed to release his excommunicated counselors and to give the pope a letter with a written promise of obedience and penance. It was further agreed separately with the princes that they would no longer consider him their king if he had not freed himself from his excommunication within a year of its inception. A meeting was set for February 1077, the deadline, in Augsburg to which Gregory was invited to mediate between the princes and Henry.

There did not seem to be much chance that Henry could get his excommunication lifted in such a short time. Gregory was in Italy, Henry in Germany, the passes through the Alps were barred by Henry's opposition in South Germany, and with the coming of winter there was hardly any likelihood that Henry could do the penance he had offered to perform to remove excommunication. But Henry outsmarted his enemies by outflanking them. He travelled with his wife and small son through Burgundy, crossing the Alps over the Mt. Cenis Pass, west of Turin, miraculously surviving the difficult terrain in the snow and extreme cold. News of Henry's presence in Italy spread. He was thought to have come with an army. Consequently, Gregory, who was already on his way to Augsburg, drew back to the security of Canossa to await events. Henry appeared dramatically before the castle gate at Canossa, barefooted and dressed in the sack cloth of a penitent. After three days of negotiations Gregory was persuaded to accept Henry's penance and lift the excommunication. He raised Henry, who had prostrated himself with arms outstretched in the form of a cross before the pope, and celebrated communion with Henry and his companions. Henry had promised in writing to submit to the pope's judgment and to allow him freedom to travel across the mountains and elsewhere.

It was an immediate, brilliant success for Henry and a defeat for his opponents, but the price for his penance was the subordination of royal power to the power and authority of the church. Henry's princely opposition was unhappy, feeling betrayed by Gregory. Some of them met in Forchheim in Franconia and elected Rudolf of Rheinfelden as king of Germany, thereby raising an anti-king for the first time. However, Henry continued to dispose of church property despite Gregory's prohibition of lay investiture in 1078. In 1080 Gregory again excommunicated and deposed Henry and declared Rudolf of Rheinfelden the legitimate king. Unfortunately for Henry's opponents, Rudolf died shortly thereafter, and although they elected Hermann of Salm as Henry's successor, he was unable to win adequate support, and the anti-king movement collapsed upon Hermann's death in 1088.

Henry was able to rally support against Gregory, especially among the powerful German archbishops so that the church in Germany was split along royalist and papalist lines with rival bishops at times holding the same office. Henry struck back by having Wibert of Ravenna named Pope Clement III and by attempting to install him in Rome by force. He finally succeeded in 1084. Gregory fled to Castel Sant'Angelo, and Clement, the anti-pope, was installed in St. Peter's on Palm Sunday. He crowned Henry and Bertha as emperor and empress on Easter Monday. But Gregory was rescued when the Normans attacked Rome to save their papal lord. Nevertheless, Gregory had to flee with the withdrawing Normans and died in 1085 in Salerno. Henry had his son Conrad crowned king of Germany in 1087.

The reform party elected Urban II to the papal throne in 1088, and he proved to be quite skillful in advancing the papal cause in opposition to the crown. The political situation in Italy deteriorated rapidly for Henry after he had again come to Rome in 1090, and he was forced to stay in a castle near Verona for seven years, in danger of being taken prisoner. His son Conrad renounced Henry in 1093, and the opposition to Henry increased. Meanwhile, in November 1095, Urban II at the close of the Council of Clermont issued his momentous call to the assembled crowd for a crusade to free the Holy Sepulcher from Saracen control. The first crusade began in 1096, but few German knights were involved, the main force having been supplied by the Franks (i.e., French) and Normans.

Henry IV returned to Germany after negotiations with the powerful Welf IV of Bavaria. He made concessions to Welf and also reached an accommodation with the Zähringen and Staufen dukes in Swabia, who had previously opposed him. Finally, he replaced his son Conrad with his still-underage son Henry, who was crowned king in Aachen in 1099 after agreeing not to interfere in the affairs of the kingdom during his father's lifetime. Paschal II (1099-1118) followed Urban II as pope and refused to lift Henry's excommunication; in fact, he renewed it in 1102. Then Henry's son Henry V started an uprising against his father. Paschal II and many old opponents of Henry IV supported Henry V, and in January 1106, Henry V accepted the imperial insignia in Mainz, and the many princes in attendance swore allegiance to him. His father still refused to accept his dethronement, but his death in 1106 ended the struggle.

Despite his political support of Henry V, Paschal II continued to insist on prohibiting investiture by laymen, and the dispute between spiritual and temporal power remained unresolved. In 1111, when Henry travelled to Italy, discussions between the king's representatives and the pope became intense. Henry still insisted on the monarch's right of investiture. Paschal offered to give back to the king all royal lands and other *regalia* that had been given over to the church if Henry would renounce his right of investiture. Henry agreed to the proposal and to renounce all claims to investiture at his imperial coronation. Paschal would force the prelates to return the *regalia* under threat of excommunication. The reading out of the agreement at the coronation caused an uproar. The bishops and abbots protested, as did the lay nobility which held fiefs from the church. After all, an immense amount of property, wealth, and privileges was at stake. In the ensuing tumult the coronation could not proceed. Henry reverted to his earlier claims, and Paschal refused to crown him, whereupon Henry took the pope prisoner. In time, Henry compelled Paschal to recognize his rights and to agree not to excommunicate him. The coronation was then carried out quickly, and Henry returned to Germany.

Upon his second trip to Italy in 1116, Henry remained deadlocked with the curia in the matter of investiture. When Paschal II died in 1118, Henry, with Roman backing, installed his own pope, Gregory VIII. But Paschal's backers chose Gelasius II as pope and after his death Calixtus II in January, 1119. Henry abandoned Gregory VIII and began negotiations with Calixtus, who fortunately was a very pragmatic man. Although the discussions between the representatives of the emperor and the pope were initially unsuccessful, a compromise based on a distinction between spiritual and temporal powers was arranged that eventually led to the Concordat of Worms in 1122.

The Concordat recognized that the ring and the staff were symbols of spiritual office. Therefore, Henry renounced this type of investiture and agreed to use only a scepter. He promised to allow canonical elections and consecration and to return properties and *regalia* alienated from the Roman and other churches. Calixtus agreed that elections of bishops and abbots of the German kingdom were to take place in Henry's presence "without simony or violence." In the case of a divided election, the king would give his help and agreement to "the wiser party" (*sanior pars*). The elected candidate was to receive the *regalia* by investiture with scepter before consecration. There was an inference that the invested candidate would pledge fealty to the king, but it was not specifically spelled out. Both sides could benefit from the compromise: the church got the assurance of canonical elections with free consecration and no investiture by the king with the spiritual symbols. Henry was allowed investiture of the *regalia* by scepter before consecration, and he could undoubtedly have influence on the election since it was to take place in his presence. The bishops and abbots thus elected and invested remained bound to the king through the *regalia* and became "ecclesiastical princes of the empire."

Three years after the Concordat, Henry died at age thirty-nine, leaving no children. As Fuhrmann concludes: "With Henry V's death the Salian dynasty became extinct in the direct male line, and it also meant if not the end of an age at least the end of a form of government which went back to archaic times, based on the participation of ecclesiastics in politics and government and the active participation of the laity in the life of the church" (p. 94).

Lothar of Supplinburg, Duke of Saxony, was elected Lothar III by the princes of the realm in 1125 in Mainz under the influence of Archbishop Adalbert I. This meant that the prerogative of lineage was not followed—Henry V with no direct male heir had wished to be succeeded by his nephew, the Staufen Duke Frederick II of Swabia. Apparently a deal was arranged with the powerful Welf Bavarian Duke Henry the Proud to support the election of Lothar, and the papacy favored Lothar as well. It caused a fateful split between the two South German families. In 1127, the Swabian and Franconian princes chose the Staufen Duke Conrad of Franconia as king. He was excommunicated by Archbishop Adalbert of Mainz and later by Pope Honorius II. Nevertheless, he went to Italy in 1128 and was crowned king by the Archbishop of Milan, but his anti-kingship never became strong enough to survive.

Upon the death of Pope Honorius II in 1130, there were again two rival popes: Anacletus II, favored by the majority of the college of cardinals, and Innocent II, who was supported by the German bishops and Lothar III. Lothar gathered a small army and headed for Italy in 1132, but he could not drive Anacletus from the city. Nevertheless, Lothar was crowned emperor in the Lateran basilica by Innocent II. After returning to Germany and eventually becoming reconciled with his Staufen opposition, Lothar returned to Italy in 1136 to wage war against the Norman King Roger II, who had driven Innocent out of Rome and had received his crown from the anti-pope Anacletus. Lothar had considerable military success against Roger, forcing him to retreat from Southern Italy to Sicily, but the German army opposed any continuation of the war, and thus Lothar was obliged to return to Germany. He died on the way home in December 1137.

Anacletus died in 1138, leaving Innocent II uncontested, but Innocent eventually had to come to terms with Roger II, whom he had excommunicated in 1139. In Germany and in Italy, the Welf Duke Henry the Proud had become the dominant power. He was therefore opposed by the other German princes and Innocent II, who had arranged for the election and coronation of none other than the Staufen Duke Conrad, the former anti-king, in 1138. Conrad gained general recognition as king, even from Duke Henry the Proud, who handed over the imperial insignia, but when Conrad ruled that no duke could hold two duchies, Henry refused to obey. He would have had to give up either Bavaria or Saxony. As a result Henry was outlawed and lost both his duchies, but the Welf family continued to resist Conrad. In 1142 a compromise was reached: Henry the Lion received Saxony in return for renouncing his family claim to Bavaria, which was given in turn to the Babenberger Henry Jasomirgott.

After Innocent II died in 1143, there were again two popes, Celestine II and Lucius II, during the short period 1143-5. Then Eugenius III was elected to the papacy, but he had to flee to France because of the anti-papal sentiments of the Roman population. The crowds had been encouraged by the radicalism of Arnold of Brescia who advocated clerical poverty and preached against the greed of the church. Pope Eugenius excommunicated him and his clerical followers, but Arnold's movement was difficult to deal with. At about that time the last of the four crusader states in Palestine fell to the Saracens, causing renewed interest in a crusade. Bernard of Clairvaux became responsible for preaching the crusade, and he did it very effectively. The French king, Louis VII, and Conrad III of Germany, both took the cross and led armies to participate in this, the second crusade. In short, the results were disastrous; the Arabs prevailed, and the tenuous co-existence of Arabs and Christians in Palestine was destroyed. Furthermore, the Normans attacked Greece and occupied part of the Peloponesus, while the Byzantine troops had been pulled out of the area.

Eugenius III was still having trouble with the people of Rome, who had offered Conrad III the imperial crown in 1149. Conrad refused the offer out of deference to the pope, who was ultimately forced to leave Rome. Conrad III died in early 1152 before he could come to the aid of Eugenius, who died himself in 1153. Conrad had designated Duke Frederick of Swabia, who became known as Barbarossa, as his successor.

The period of the investiture controversy was a time of great change. As we have indicated above, the relationship between the empire and the papacy was fundamentally changed by the clear distinction between *regalia* and *spiritualia* that was established through the Concordat of Worms. In effect, a feudal relationship arose between the empire and the church. The emperor was conceded authority in temporal matters, i.e., enfeoffment of the church in property and privileges, but investiture in ecclesiastical office, i.e., spiritual matters, was recognized as the province of the church. It was also a time of social mobility. A new social class, the ministeriales, became established. These were people who were in the service of royalty, of the landed nobility, and even of the church. Although they were subservient, they were not serfs and frequently reached positions of power to rival the old aristocracy. The land under their control often eventually came to be hereditary. Other ministeriales performed military service as knights and as courtly retainers. Land-holdings were, however, the main basis of feudal lordship, whether allods (estates held in absolute ownership) or fiefs. Families became identified by the land they owned or controlled, or by a major castle, built to dominate a territory and especially necessary in uncertain times of civil strife. Acquiring more land by clearing or settlement was also important, a process called "territorialization," and carried out extensively in the colonization of the eastern provinces. Cities continued to develop in importance both economically and politically, and the growth of the northern Italian communes increased their influence on church and empire.

We have pointed earlier to an increase in spirituality in this period. It has also been called the "Age of Bernard of Clairvaux," that leading figure of mystical theology as opposed to a more rational early scholastic approach to knowledge of God. The reform of the monasteries did not stop with the Cluniac reforms and the founding of daughter monasteries of Cluny. With a desire to lead a spiritual life, laymen formed communal living groups as canons regular, often attached to a church or cathedral, to live lives not cut off from the world as in a monastery but to follow the rule of St. Benedict *in* the world. In addition, new monastic orders were founded in opposition to the Cluniac system. The Cistercians (ca. 1110), who followed the rule of St. Benedict but included manual labor to support their existence, were effective colonizers and missionaries, and the movement spread very rapidly. Each Cistercian monastery was headed by its own abbot and was not a part of any hierarchical system. Bernard of Clairvaux, famous for his preaching and writings, was himself a Cistercian abbot.

The Premonstratensian order was founded in 1120 by Norbert of Xanten, a cathedral canon and wandering preacher. Its emphasis was, like the canons, on communal living while preaching and performing missionary service in the world, especially in the period of colonization in the East. In contrast to the Cistercians and Premonstratensians, the Carthusians under their founder (1084) Bruno advocated the renunciation of the world and a strict contemplative life with the vow of silence in a combination of Benedictine monasticism and eremitical asceticism. Finally, we should not forget the Templars, or "Knights Templar," founded in 1118 in the Holy Land as a military order to protect pilgrims.

This is the period of early scholasticism and a flourishing of the intellectual life. We have already mentioned Bernard of Clairvaux (1090-1153), but we should also mention a few of the other noted figures: Peter Abelard (1079-1142), the famous dialectician, rhetorician, and teacher; the theologian and historian Rupert of Deutz (ca. 1075-1139); Honorius of Autun (early 12th cent.), writer of commentaries and surveys of Christian doctrine; and Hugh of St. Victor (ca. 1140-1200), grammarian, geometrician, biblical commentator, and author of a guide to the study of the *artes* and theology. There were two outstanding women writers of the period: Hildegard of Bingen (1098-1179), a Benedictine nun, who wrote of her many visions, corresponded widely, and authored a number of theological and scientific works; and Herrad of Landsberg (died 1195) noted for her encyclopedic *Hortus deliciarum* with the portraits of all the nuns of her convent.

### History (1050-1170)—Bibliography

Blumenthal, Uta-Renate. *The Investiture Controversy. Church, and Monarchy from the Ninth to the Twelfth Century.* Trans. by the author. Philadelphia: Univ. of Pennsylvania Press, 1988 (Engl. version of her *Der Investiturstreit.* Stuttgart: Kohlhammer, 1982).

A succinct description of the investiture controversy in the context of monastic reform, papal power, and imperial politics with a survey of recent scholarship. Excellent maps, topical bibliographies at the end of each chapter.

Fried, Johannes. *Die Formierung Europas. 849-1046.* Munich: R. Oldenbourg Verlag, 1991 (= Oldenbourg Grundriss der Geschichte, Bd. 6).

An excellent, concise history of the cultural background and events of the period, with discussion of the basic problems and the tendencies of current research, and with a copious bibliography (1454 items!), chronological and genealogical tables.

Fuhrmann, Horst. *Germany in the High Middle Ages, c. 1050-1200.* Trans. by Timothy Reuter. Cambridge: Cambridge UP, 1986 (Engl. version of his *Deutsche Geschichte im hohen Mittelalter*).

Excellent, very readable description of events against the changing social, economic, and cultural background. Bibliography limited to works in English on German and imperial history of the period with brief comments on the items listed, index.

Haverkamp, Alfred. *Medieval Germany, 1056-1273.* Trans. by Helga Braun and Richard Mortimer. New York: Oxford UP, [2]1992. (Engl. version of his *Aufbruch und Gestaltung. Deutschland, 1056-1273.* Munich: Beck, 1988).

An engaging, vivid, comprehensive portrayal of Germany in its European context during the period. Selected, but more than ample bibliography, genealogical table, index, map.

Jakobs, Hermann. *Kirchenreform und Hochmittelalter, 1046-1215.* Munich, Vienna: Oldenbourg, 1984 (= Oldenbourg Grundriß der Geschichte, 7).

Concise outline of events plus detailed discussion of the basic problems and state of research. Exhaustive bibliography (1,054 items!), genealogies, chronological table, index.

## INTRODUCTION TO EMHG LITERATURE

Whereas the vernacular literature of the Old High German period was concerned largely with educating people about the principles of the Christian faith and the gospel stories, not to mention usage of the vernacular in the practical learning of Latin, the literature of the Early Middle High German period seems to reach out to a larger, popular audience, to present more detailed biblical materials for the instruction of the laity, to inform people of somewhat more sophisticated theological and moral matters, and to give expression to personal religious experience. It is probably not far wrong to think of the literature of this period as reflecting the desire of the church to influence the thinking of the people at large in what developed into a bitter power struggle between the church and the empire for political dominance (the "investiture controversy"—see above). Add to this the increasing interest in religious experience on the part of the laity and the growing importance of the cathedrals in urban life as opposed to reformed monasticism, and the basis for the spread of vernacular religious literature is laid. We must always remember, however, that Latin writings still dominated intellectual life, and it is difficult to say with any certainty how much effect literature in German had on the general populace, given the low rate of literacy, but the didactic nature of EMHG literature is undeniable.

We have used linguistic change as the basis for periodization (see section on language), but we should also remember that linguistic change is a gradual process. The EMHG works we shall discuss here do show the transition from OHG to MHG, but perhaps just as important for classification is the gradual change in subject matter, or genre, if one can speak of that at this stage. Therefore, we have divided EMHG literature into four general categories: Biblical narrative, theological-didactic poetry, poetry of personal religious experience, and historical poetry. It will not be possible to comment more than cursorily on the individual works, but we shall attempt at least to treat the outstanding or typical ones and characterize the rest. The works will be discussed in roughly chronological order within each category, but they may also be grouped together thematically on occasion. They are listed here in outline form for the purpose of an overview.

1. Biblical Prose and Poetry
2. Theological-Didactic Poetry
   a. Natural Science
   b. Salvation History
   c. The Proper Life
3. Personal Religious Experience
4. Historical Poetry

**Early Middle High German Literature—Bibliography**

**General Studies:**

Ehlert, Trude. "Literatur und Wirklichkeit—Exegese und Politik. Zur Deutung des *Ludwigslieds.*" *Saeculum* 32 (1981): 31-42.

Freytag, Hartmut. *Die Theorie der allegorischen Schriftdeutung und die Allegorie in deutschen Texten besonders des 11. und 12. Jahrhunderts.* Bern/Munich: Francke, 1982 (= Bibliotheca Germanica, 24).

Exhaustive exposition of this characteristic aspect of EMHG literature.

Gentry, Francis G. "The Turn toward the World: The Religious and Social Upheaval of the 11th Century and EMHG Literature." In: *Gesellschaftsgeschichte. Fschr. für Karl Bosl zum 80. Geburtstag.* Bd. I. Munich: Oldenbourg, 1988. Pp. 45-51.

____. *Bibliographie zur frühmittelhochdeutschen geistlichen Dichtung.* Berlin: Erich Schmidt, 1992. 278 pp. (= Bibliog. z. dt. Lit. d. Mas., 11).

Indispensable reference work, essentially complete to 1986, with some additions to 1990.

Haug, Walter. "Allegorese und Entscheidung: Literaturtheoretische Positionen in fmhd. Zeit." In his: *Literaturtheorie im deutschen Mittelalter.* Darmstadt: Wiss. Buchges., 1985. Pp. 46-74.

EMHG literature involves allegorical interpretation but also the eschatological view of world history.

Rupp Heinz. *Deutsche religiöse Dichtungen des 11. und 12. Jahrhunderts.* Bern : Francke, [2]1971.

Originally published in 1958, this book of studies of the main monuments seems to have spurred interest in the religious poetry of the period. It is still a valuable source for study.

Soeteman, Cornelius. *Deutsche geistliche Dichtung des 11. und 12. Jahrhunderts.* Stuttgart: Metzler, 1964 ([2]1971). (= Sammlung Metzler, 33).

Concise, informative handbook.

Sowinski, Bernhard. *Lehrhafte Dichtung des Mittelalters.* Stuttgart: Metzler, 1971. (= Sammlung Metzler, 103).

Of somewhat larger scope than Soetemann (above) but of a similar character.


## BIBLICAL PROSE AND POETRY

All the works in this group treat biblical subjects. They are no longer the major epic gospel works of the OHG period, such as Otfrid or the *Heliand*, rather they tend to re-tell books of the Bible or individual episodes, with a definite didactic emphasis on how these biblical stories can be understood and used in life.

*Song of Songs.* There are two versions or exegeses of the "Song of Songs": ***Willirams Paraphrase des Hohenliedes*** (Williram's Paraphrase of the Song of Songs) and the ***St. Trudpeter Hohes Lied***. Williram, Abbot of Ebersberg in Bavaria, wrote his paraphrase about 1060, and the St. Trudpert version, so named after the source of the oldest complete manuscript, was completed about 100 years later by an unknown author. Both are written in prose but have different emphases, even though the younger version uses Williram's translation of the biblical text. Williram begins his work with a Latin preface, after which follows the main text in three columns: the vulgate Latin text in the middle, a Latin interpretation in leonine hexameters on the left, and a German translation with a prose version of the interpretation on the right. The German text is liberally larded with Latin words, phrases, even sentences, so that it is somewhat reminiscent of Notker's translations (see p. 31 f.). In fact, the German is such EMHG that Williram's paraphrase is sometimes included in the OHG period, as, for example, the selections in *Ahd. Lb.* (pp. 75-78). Williram follows the interpretation of the Song of Songs as dialogue between Christ (the bridegroom) and the Church (the bride), whereas in the St. Trudpert version the dialogue is between the Holy Spirit and the Virgin Mary, prefiguring the individual soul, thus representing the more personal, mystical approach of a later period, as opposed to the institutional emphasis of Williram's day, the period of church and monastic reform and the developing investiture controversy. Both works must have attained considerable popularity in view of the number of extant manuscripts and fragments, especially Williram's with over 22. For St. Trudpert there are about six.

Texts:

Bartelmez, Erminnie H., ed. *The "Expositio in Cantica Canticorum" of Williram, Abbot of Ebersberg (1048-1085). A Critical Edition.* Philadelphia: American Philosophical Society, 1967 (= Memoirs of the American Philosophical Society, Vol. 69).

Sanders, Willy, ed. *(Expositio) Willirami Ebersbergensis Abbatis in Canticis Canticorum. Die Leidener Handschrift.* Munich: Fink, 1971 (= Kl. dt. Prosadenkmäler des MAs, H.9).

Seemüller, Joseph, ed. *Willirams Deutsche Paraphrase des Hohen Liedes.* Strasbourg: Trübner, 1878 (= QF XXVIII).

Menhardt, Hermann, ed. *Das St. Trudperter Hohe Lied. Kritische Ausgabe.* Halle (Saale): Niemeyer, 1934.

There are three important *Sammelhandschriften* containing biblical poetry from this early period: Codex 2721 of the Austrian National Library (W = *Wiener Handschrift*); Geschichtsverein Manuscript 6/19 of the Kärntner Landesarchiv in Klagenfurt, Austria (M = *Millstätter* or *Klagenfurter Handschrift*); and Sammelhandschrift 276 of the Augustiner-Chorherrenstift in Vorau, Austria (V = *Vorauer Handschrift*). W is the oldest and dates from the mid-12th century; M is from the last quarter of that century, and V from the last decade. The works contained in them are, of course, from various earlier dates.

Facsimiles:

W—Papp, Edgar, ed. *Codex Vindobonensis 2721: Frühmittelhochdeutsche Sammelhandschrift der Österreichischen Nationalbibliothek in Wien. "Genesis"—"Physiologus"—"Exodus."* Göppingen: Kümmerle, 1980 (= Litterae, 19).

M—Kracher, Alfred, ed. *Sammelhandschrift 6/19 des Geschichtsvereins für Kärnten im Kärntner Landesarchiv, Klagenfurt.* Graz: Akademische Druck- und Verlagsanstalt, 1967 (= Codices Selecti, Vol. 10).

V—Polheim, Karl Konrad, ed. *Die deutschen Gedichte der Vorauer Handschrift.(Kodex 276—II.Teil). Faksimile= Ausgabe des Chorherrenstiftes Vorau.* Graz: Akademische Druck-und Verlagsanstalt, 1958.

The so-called *Altdeutsche Genesis* and *Altdeutsche Exodus* in W and M are among the earliest EMHG literary monuments. The Genesis version in W dates from 1060-80, while the text in M is a re-working of that in W, although W itself was probably not the immediate source. They each follow a manuscript of the same type. The younger M-Genesis has "modernized" the language in comparison to W and can be dated some time before 1122. Both W and M have long lines with internal rhyme (cf. Otfrid, p. 42) and space was left in the text for illustrations, of which only the first seven were completed in W, while M has sixty-one. The text itself is a paraphrase with interpretation of the Genesis story. In narrating the creation of man, for example, the function of each finger is interpreted, the little finger being used to dig in the ear so that one may hear properly. Almost two-thirds of the over 6,000 lines are devoted to the stories of Jacob and Joseph. The exegetical information provided comes from various sources. It is certainly not original with the unknown author, rather it represents traditional theological knowledge. The author was surely a cleric, but there is considerable scholarly disagreement over whether the poem was intended for a lay or clerical audience. The *Altdeutsche Exodus* is younger than the *Genesis*, having been written in the first decade of the 12th century. The version in W is incomplete, in contrast to the full text in M (some 3,300 lines). In form and intent,

*Exodus* is similar to *Genesis*, although there seems to be less exegesis. Nor does it cover all the material in the book of Exodus, stopping after the first fifteen chapters. The Vorau manuscript (V) also has a section called traditionally **Vorauer Bücher Moses**. In it can be found the **Vorauer Genesis**, a section on Joseph in Egypt, the **Vorauer Moses**, a praise to Mary, and a story about Balaam. The latter two sections do not interest us here, but the first three comprise another Genesis and Exodus. The *Genesis* in V (818 lines) is different from that in W/M, although the author undoubtedly knew that version, because the Joseph section that follows (1,735 lines) is taken almost verbatim from W/M. The *Vorauer Moses"* section (1,077+ lines) does not follow the W/M *Exodus*. It has a different source and covers not only the departure from Egypt but the arrival in the Promised Land and the death of Moses, the latter narrated briefly in Latin. The text of V is continuous, but written in two columns per page rather than covering the whole page as in W and M. There are no illustrations.

Texts:
W—Dollmayer, Viktor, ed. *Die altdeutsche Genesis. Nach der Wiener Handschrift.* Halle (Saale): Niemeyer, Niemeyer, 1932 (= ATB, 31).
Smits, Kathryn, ed. *Die frühmittelhochdeutsche Wiener Genesis.* Kritische Ausgabe mit einem einleitenden Kommentar zur Überlieferung. Berlin: Erich Schmidt, 1972 (= PSuQ, 59).
M—Diemer, Joseph, ed. *Genesis und Exodus nach der Milstätter Handschrift.* Bd. 1 (Einleitung und Text); Bd. 2 (Anmerkungen und Wörterbuch). Vienna, 1862; Repr. 1971.
Papp, Edgar, ed. *Der altdeutsche Exodus. Untersuchungen und kritischer Text.* Munich, 1968 (= Medium aevum, 16).
_____. *Der altdeutsche Exodus.* Munich, 1969 (= Altdeutsche Texte in kritischen Ausgaben, 2).
V—*Diemer, Dt. Gedichte,* 1-90.

Two other Old Testament stories are also to be found in V: **Die drei Jünglinge im Feuerofen** (The Three Youths in the Fiery Furnace) and two versions of the apocryphal Book of Judith, **Die ältere Judith** (Older Version of Judith) and **Die jüngere Judith** (Younger Version of Judith). The "Three Youths" is the familiar story from the Book of Daniel (Chapter 3) in which the three young men refuse to bow down to Nebuchadnezzar's golden idol, are thrown into the fiery furnace, but are saved from harm by an angel. The poem is short (84 verses), concise, dramatic, with a ballad-like quality, ending in the recognition by the heathens of God's power. Immediately following the "Three Youths" in V, almost without interruption, comes the *Ältere Judith.* This is an abbreviated story of Judith's slaying of Holofernes, Nebuchadnezzar's general, in his own tent. The ensuing relief of the siege of the Israelites in Bethulia is not narrated, leading to the assumption that this version is fragmentary. The determination of Judith to save her people, who had almost given up hope of salvation from God, and her courage to go into the enemy camp and decapitate Holofernes are evidence of God's working through a woman to save His chosen people. The poem comprises only 136 rhymed verses. However, the "Younger Version of Judith" that follows in V is considerably longer (1821 verses) and is almost a rhymed translation of the biblical Book of Judith, which starts with the events leading up to the siege of Bethulia and ends with the release of the Israelites after Judith's heroic deed. A hint of incipient courtly behavior may be seen in the scenes at Holofernes's camp. There is little overt exegesis in any of these three poems. They are direct examples of divine power working through people of steadfast faith, and the moral interpretation is obvious. All three poems are probably from the first half of the 12th century.

One additional fragmentary poem, based on the apochryphal Old Testament Book of Tobit, but not in V, is the *Tobias* of Pfaffe Lamprecht, the author of the German *Alexander* (see below). Only 272 verses of the first part of what must have been a much larger poem existed in a manscript that has since vanished. Fortunately, a copy of it was published in 1916 and an edition in 1923. Here again we find a clerical author creating a narrative of piety and obedience to God, with little interpretation, although he frequently makes informative reference to biblical events.

The Vorau manuscript also provides the text for a cycle of poems by the first woman whose works in German have survived. She names herself as "Frau Ava," mother of two sons, one of whom has died. She may well have been a recluse, i.e., a woman who late in life renounced the world and spent the remainder of her life as a member of a lay religious sect attached to a church, cathedral, or other religious institution, without taking vows, but leading an ascetic life. She attributes her knowledge of holy scripture to her sons and asks people to pray for her son and for her. There is evidence to believe that she is the *Ava inclusa* who died in 1127, mentioned in the annals of Melk and other monasteries. Her most important work is the *Leben Jesu* (Life of Jesus). It is somewhat comparable to the earlier gospel literature, but it concentrates on the outward events of Christ's life, rather than on his message. Based on the four gospels but strongly indebted to the Gospel of John, her *Leben Jesu* narrates in verse the entire life of Christ from the annunciation to the resurrection. Frau Ava is no theologian. She claims inspiration from her sons for her theological knowledge and is much more concerned with the events of Christ's life than with any sort of allegorical or moral exegesis. Her poem reflects what was generally known by a lay audience about the circumstances of Christ's life. At the end of her *Leben Jesu* there is a section on the seven gifts of the Holy Spirit. She also composed a life of John the Baptist (not in V) to precede the "Life of Jesus" and an "Antichrist" and a "Last Judgment" to follow. She refers to her personal situation in an epilogue to the "Last Judgment." The *Leben Jesu* is from the first two decades of the 12th century.

Priester Wernher's *Driu liet von der maget* (Three Songs on the Virgin) are not religious songs *to* Mary but rather epic songs *about* Mary, i.e., they tell first about the life of Mary's parents and her birth, then about her marriage to Joseph and the Annunciation, and finally the birth of Jesus and events in his life through the death of Herod and the return of the Holy Family from Egypt. Of course, there is also ample praise *of* Mary and appreciation of her role in salvation history as mother of Christ and as helper of people in distress. The poem is divided into three books (the three "songs") and may be dated quite accurately to the year 1172, when according to the author a certain Priest Manigold invited the author to his house and would not allow him to leave before he had finished the poem (Ms. A, 4809-4850). The patron was probably the Provost and later Abbot of the Benedictine Abbey of Sts. Ulrich and Afra in Augsburg. Two extant complete manuscripts of the "Songs," one of which is notable for its colored illuminations, and five fragments attest to the popularity of Wernher's work. His source was probably the Latin Pseudo-Matthew Gospel which may be traced back to the 5th century. It is difficult to determine the length of the original poem. The two complete manuscripts A and D have approximately 5,000 lines each, but the ending is lacking in D, and both manuscripts have numerous gaps. The poem is written in rhymed couplets. The "Songs" is the first of many later lives of the Virgin, a very popular genre from the 13th century on (see p. 90 f. and p. 422 ff.).

Texts:
*Drei Jünglinge* and *Ältere Judith*:
    *Henschel/Pretzel*, No. 7.
    *Maurer* I, No. 15.
    *Waag/Schröder* I, No.4.
    *Diemer. Dt. Gedichte*, 115-123.
    *Curschmann/Glier*, 176-191 (with German trans.).
    *Haug/Vollmann*, 718-727 (with German trans.).
*Jüngere Judith*:
    Monecke, Hiltgunt, ed. *Die jüngere Judith aus der Vorauer Handschrift*. Tübingen: Niemeyer, 1964 (= ATB, 61).
    *Maurer* II, No. 31.
    *Diemer, Dt. Gedichte*, 127-180.
*Tobias*:
    *Maurer* II, No. 44.
    Müller, H. E., ed. *Die Werke des Pfaffen Lamprecht nach der ältesten Überlieferung*. Munich, 1923. (= Münchner Texte, 12).
*Frau Ava*:
    *Maurer*, II, No. 40-43.
    Maurer, Friedrich, ed. *Die Dichtungen der Frau Ava*. Tübingen: Niemeyer, 1966 (= ATB, 66).
    Schacks, Kurt, ed. *Die Dichtungen der Frau Ava*. Graz: Akademische Druck- und Verlags-Anstalt, 1986.
    *Diemer, Dt. Gedichte*, 229-292 (Text of V).
*Driu liet von der maget*:
    Wesle, C., ed. *Prester Wernhers Maria. Bruckstücke und Umarbeitungen*. Halle, 1927 (also as ATB, 26); [2]1969, ed. by Hans Fromm.

Translation:
Degering, Hermann, trans. *Des Priesters Wernher drei Lieder von der Magd. Nach der Fassung der Handschrift der Preußischen Staatsbibliothek* (Ms. D). Berlin, n.d. (German verse translation).

## Biblical Prose and Poetry—Bibliography

Egert, Eugene. "The Curse of the Serpent in the MHG 'Genesis' Poems." *ABäG* 24 (1986): 29-37.

Eßer, Josef. *Die Schöpfungsgeschichte in der "Altdeutschen Genesis" (Wiener Genesis V. 1-123). Kommentar und Interpretation*. Göppingen: Kümmerle, 1987 (= GAG, 455).

Freytag, Wiebke. "Geistliches Leben und christliche Bildung. Hrotsvit und andere Autorinnen des frühen Mittelalters." In: *Deutsche Literatur von Frauen. Band I. Vom Mittelalter bis zum Ende des 18. Jahrhunderts.* Ed. by Gisela Brinker-Gabler. Munich: Beck, 1988. Pp. 65-76.

Concise summary of female writers and their roles in the period.

Fromm, Hans. *Untersuchungen zum Marienleben des Priesters Wernher.* Turku: Turun Yliopiston Kustantama, 1995 (= Annales Universitatis Turkuensis, 52).

Green, Dennis H. *The Millstätter Exodus. A Crusading Epic.* Cambridge: Cambridge UP, 1966.

An original, fascinating approach to the "Exodus" but not widely accepted.

Groseclose, John S. "Passion Prefigurations: Typological Style and the Problem of Genre in German Romanesque Poetry." *Monatshefte* 67 (1975): 5-15.

Hintz, Ernst Ralf. "Frau Ava." In: *Semper idem et novus. Festschr. for Frank Banta.* Göppingen: Kümmerle, 1988. Pp. 209-230 (= GAG, 481).

Discussion (in English) of Frau Ava's pedagogical and rhetorical strategies in all her works. For *Leben Jesu,* see esp. pp. 212-216.

Lenger, Gabriele. *Virgo-Mater-Mediatrix. Untersuchungen zu Priester Wernhers "Driu liet von der maget."* Frankfurt/M.: Lang, 1980 (= Europäische Hochschulschriften, 351).

Wernher's poem seen against the theological background of his time.

Ohly, Friedrich. *Hohelied-Studien. Grundzüge einer Geschichte der Hoheliedauslegung des Abendlandes bis um 1200.* Wiesbaden, 1958 (= Schriften der Wissenschaftlichen Gesellschaft der J. W. Goethe-Universität Frankfurt a. M., Geisteswiss. Reihe 1).

Major study of the interpretation of the "Song of Songs" throughout the centuries.

Schupp, Volker. *Studien zu Williram von Ebersberg.* Bern: Francke, 1978 (= Biblioteca Germanica, 21).

Studies on many aspects of Williram and his life, his sources, problems of genre of his work, and the tradition that it represents.

Wells, David A. *The Vorauer "Moses" and "Balaam." A Study of Their Relationship to Exegetical Tradition.* Cambridge: Cambridge UP, 1970.

Wisbey, Roy, comp. *Vollständige Verskonkordanz zur Wiener Genesis. Mit einem rückläufigen Wörterbuch zum Formbestand.* Berlin: Erich Schmidt, 1967.

The first computer-generated concordance, very useful for lexical study.

For literature on *Die drei Jünglinge* and the *Ältere Judith* see the article by Werner Schröder in $VL^2$ 1 (1978): 288-294. For the *Jüngere Judith* see Werner Schröder's article in $VL^2$ 4, (1983): 923-926. For Lamprecht's *Tobias* see another article by Werner Schröder in $VL^2$ 5 (1985): 494-497.

## THEOLOGICAL-DIDACTIC POETRY

### Natural Science

*Physiologus*. The first subgroup of this type has to do with medieval "natural science," but it is part of a lengthy tradition that goes back to Latin and Greek sources. There are at least two German versions of the *Physiologus*, an older and a younger one. *Der ältere Physiologus*, an 11th century prose translation of a Latin source, is a fragment and exists in only one manuscript, a Vienna codex W 223 (fol. 31ʳ - 33ʳ). *Der jüngere Physiologus* may be found in two *Sammelhandschriften* (see above, p. 75), between the *Wiener Genesis* and *Exodus* (fol. 129ᵛ - 158ʳ, in prose) and the *Millstätter Genesis* and *Exodus* (fol. 84ᵛ -101ʳ, in verse), from ca. 1120. The *Physiologus* contains a description of various animals and their characteristics (the Millstatt version has illustrations) and then interprets them on the basis of biblical and theological traditions. For example, the lion has several traits that may be referred to in passages in the bible. One of such traits is that the lioness bears her young in an apparently lifeless state. After three days, the lion comes and roars at his son, thereby awakening him to life. In just such a way did God awaken his son, Jesus Christ, from death after the crucifixion. In other words, the lion, king of the beasts, symbolizes Christ. Twenty-nine animals and birds are described in the "Younger Physiologus," over half of which are exotic creatures, like the phoenix, or at least not native to Western Europe, like elephants and apes. In addition to biblically related typology, moral examples for human beings are embodied in some of the creatures, thus providing a didactic slant to natural science.

*Merigarto* (lit.: land surrounded by water) is the title given to two fragments of a poem discovered and published by Hoffmann von Fallersleben in 1834. They are on a double leaf now in Donaueschingen and may be dated from the end of the 11th to early 12th centuries. The first fragment deals with the creation of mountains, rivers, and seas, including the different types of sea (color, consistency, viz. *Lebermeer*), whereas the second tells of rivers, spas, and wells in Italy, Spain, and Sardinia that have marvelous curative powers. The obvious gap between the two fragments must have had some transitional material, and there may well have been an introduction and an epilogue, but it is impossible to say how much is missing. Some personal travel experience containing information about Iceland is included in the first fragment, and mention is made in the second of a feud between two noblemen, but the text basically provides information about natural phenomena, starting with the creation, with a certain amount of geography thrown in. The source for much of the "natural science" may be found in Latin works, such as Isidor of Seville's "Etymologies." Other than the divine creation, there is little reference to theological matters.

Texts:
*Physiologus*:
    Maurer, Friedrich, ed. *Der altdeutsche Physiologus. Die Millstätter Reimfassung und die Wiener Prosa (nebst dem lateinischen Text und dem althochdeutschen Physiologus)*. Tübingen: Niemeyer, 1967 (= ATB, 67).
    *Maurer*, I, No. 4.

Wilhelm, Friedrich, ed. *Denkmäler deutscher Prosa des 11. und 12. Jahrhunderts.* Munich: Max Hueber, 1960 (= Germanistische Bücherei, 3). A: Text, pp. 4-28 (older [W223] and younger [W 2721] prose versions on opposite pages). B: Kommentar includes edition of Latin source, pp. 17-44.

> *Curschmann/Glier*, I, 192-197 (sel. with mod. Ger. trans.).
> *Haug/Vollmann*, 680-701 (sel. with mod. Ger. trans.).

*Merigarto*:
> *Ahd. Lb.*, XLI, 140-42.
> *Maurer*, I, No. 1.
> *Curschmann/Glier*, I, 198-203 (sel. with mod. Ger. trans.).
> *Haug/Vollmann*, 648-661 (with mod. Ger. trans.).

Translation:
Seel, Otto, trans. *Der Physiologus.* Übertragen und erläutert von O. S. Zürich, Stuttgart, 1960 (mod. Ger. trans.).

Translation and Facsimile:
Voorwinden, N. Th. J., ed. & trans. *Merigarto. Eine philologisch-historische Monographie.* Leiden, 1973.

## Natural Science—Bibliography

Eis, Gerhard. "Zum Merigarto." *PBB* 82 (1960) 70-76. Repr. in: G. E. *Kleine Schriften.* Amsterdam, 1979. Pp. 71-78.

Claims Passau as the likely location of the poet, see Voorwinden (below).

Henkel, Nikolaus. *Studium zum Physiologus im Mittelalter.* Tübingen: Niemeyer, 1976 (= Hermaea, N.F., 38).

Schmidtke, Dietrich. *Geistliche Tierinterpretation in der deutschsprachigen Literatur des Mittelalters.* Berlin: n.p., 1968.

Voorwinden, Norbert. *Merigarto. Eine philologisch-historische Monographie.* Leiden, 1973 (= Germanistisch-anglistische Reihe der Universität Leiden, 11).

A very complete discussion of previous research, the text itself, the dialect, poetic form, sources, and the provenance of the poem with interesting historical considerations.

## Salvation History

History beginning with Lucifer's rebellion, the creation and man's subsequent fall, the eventual incarnation, crucifixion, and resurrection, and the ultimate Day of Judgment was a very important and popular kind of historiography in the Middle Ages. It involved learning the essential facts of the Christian world view. The first two poems in this section are examples of such writing and are among the best-known poetic works of EMHG literature.

The *Ezzolied* (Song of Ezzo) exists in two manuscripts: the Vorau Sammelhandschrift (see above, p. 75), fol. 128$^{rb}$-129$^{rb}$ (V) and in cod. germ. 278, fol. 74$^v$ of the Bibliothèque Nationale et Universitaire Strasbourg (S). The original poem can be dated to the years 1057-65 on the basis of historical references to Bishop Gunther of Bamberg and to Ezzo himself, both of whom are named in V. The title, *Cantilena de miraculis Christi*, taken from the reference naming the *Scholasticus* Ezzo, is somewhat misleading. Both versions, the much shorter, fragmentary S (7 strophes), and the longer V, clearly deal with salvation history. Of course, V does include the miracles of Christ in the narration of that part, but the idea of "miracle" may be applied to all parts of salvation history. Many attempts to determine what was in the Ur-Ezzo have been made without consensus. Nor is there agreement on whether the poem was written in long lines with internal rhyme (Maurer) or in rhymed couplets (Schröder). If indeed V is a redaction and expansion of the original work, the expansion may be seen in the addition of material of a homiletic intent, the display of erudition by the redactor, and the inclusion of things that he thought were lacking but may not have been in Ezzo's original intent.

Of special interest is the prologue in V, in which it is stated that Bishop Gunther of Bamberg (1057-1065) commissioned the poem, Ezzo wrote it, and someone named Wille composed the tune, whereupon all who heard it hastened to become monks, or to live like monks, possibly in lay convents, or to go on a crusade—the meaning of those lines is uncertain, but Bishop Gunther did lead a crusade to the Holy Land in 1064/65 and died there shortly before the return trip. In the older S-version the audience is addressed as *"iu herron"* ("You gentlemen"), indicating to some that a group of noblemen was being addressed, thereby making *Ezzolied* for some the first vernacular poem addressed to a noble lay audience. On the other hand, *"iu herron"* could also refer to clerics, e.g. Canons Regular.

The *Ezzolied* is important in that it breaks the long silence in German poetry mentioned above. Its content may be divided roughly into three main sections: a. the creation, the fall of man, and OT history up to the time of Christ; b. the life of Christ, including his birth, youth, miracles and teaching, through his crucifixion and resurrection; c. a homiletic part dealing with prefigurations of redemption in the OT, the allegorical meaning of the crucifixion, concluding with praise of the Trinity and thanks for redemption. It is a lively poem, the authorial voice does not hesitate to speak in the first person, to use exclamations (often in Latin), to address God, and to rejoice in the anticipated homecoming in redemption from sin.

**Summa Theologiae** is the name given to another poem in the Vorau *Sammelhandschrift*, fol. 97$^{ra}$-98$^{va}$, (titled "De sancta Trinitate" in the manuscript by another hand) that has salvation history as its background. Written in the first decades of the 12th century, the text of 324 lines in rhymed couplets (Schröder) or some 160 long lines with internal rhyme (Maurer) is in strophic form, with 10 (or 5-6) lines per strophe. The poem is a concise poetic explication of the basic tenets of Christianity as revealed in salvation history and at the same time a sermon-like discussion of the proper form a Christian life should take to ensure return to the presence of God after Judgment Day. The poet, obviously a learned man, had a fine command of theological matters, but his presentation is not for the scholar, rather for the interested layman who has little or no knowledge of Latin but who needs information and guidance. Therefore the verses do not have the rhapsodic quality of the *Ezzolied*, but they do provide clear, vernacular expression of theological concepts. The language seems to show the influence of the

Latin background to a certain extent. The poem must have attained some degree of popularity, since two other fragmentary versions have survived.

About half the poem deals with the nature and properties of God, the fall of Lucifer, the creation of man as replacement for the fallen angels, the significance of the creation for man and man's place in creation, Adam's fall, and man's condition before salvation. In the second half the poet discusses the process of salvation culminating with Christ on the cross; the challenge of the cross to man; man's relationship to God, his fellow-man, creation, and the devil; the situation of the soul after salvation became possible; how man should live in the world with respect to God's commands; and the Last Judgment, concluding with hymnic praise to God.

In contrast to the concise *Summa Theologiae* the poem known as **Das Anegenge** (The Beginning) is rather extensive. It too is a salvation history, divided into two parts: the longer Old Testament part beginning with the creation and ending after the flood (the actual *Anegenge*), and the shorter New Testament part dealing with the life of Christ. However, each part is embellished with an allegorical introduction describing how the subsequent events came about, and much of the poem is of an exegetical nature, designed to explain the facts of salvation history to an untutored public. Some of the commentary refutes common misconceptions (e.g. Adam and Eve were *not* created at the same time) or attempts to answer questions that people might easily pose (e.g., How could Noah round up so many animals in such a short time? Answer: HE [= God] was his hunting companion and drove them all to the ark). It is a combination of biblical paraphrase, didactics, and homily. The poem contains 3,242 lines in rhymed couplets and is divided into sections of varying length. The language is Bavarian and the poem is usually dated to the last quarter of the 12th century. It may be found in the Vienna *Sammelhandschrift* 2696 of ca. 1300.

Another longer poem, **Die Rede vom Glauben** (Discourse on Faith) by an author who names himself in the epilogue as *"Der arme Hartmann"* ("Poor Hartmann") is not based directly on salvation history but rather on the Nicean Creed. It consisted originally of about 3,800 long lines, of which 400 were missing from the only extant manuscript, the Strasbourg-Molsheim *Sammelhandschrift* (CV,16b) that was destroyed by fire in 1870. However, the edition published by Massmann in 1837 is probably a true copy of the original. In the prologue, Hartmann addresses his discourse to laymen and includes himself in that category. The poem falls into three parts following the creed: God the Father, Jesus Christ, and the Holy Spirit and generally explains the individual functions of the Trinity. In the first (shortest) part God's attributes are described. In the second part Christ is presented as the only begotten son of the Father, the Wisdom of God in the Creation, the Word of God, the victor over Satan, who descended from heaven to become a human. The significance of salvation, Christ's resurrection, ascension, and the Last Judgment are also explained. The Holy Spirit in the third (longest) section provides inspiration and advice to mankind. This is illustrated in a series of legendary exempla, but the contemporary scene is also used as examples of what not to do. Courtly life with its worldly interests and appetites is repeatedly criticized and the ascetic life praised. An epilogue concludes the poem. The date of composition is probably before the middle of the 12th century.

Texts:
*Ezzolied*:
  *Ahd. Lb*, No. XLIII.
  *Henschel/Pretzel*, No. 1.
  *Waag/Schröder*, I, No. 1.
  *Maurer*, I, No. 1.
  *Curschmann/Glier*, I, 80-91 (with mod. Ger. trans.).
  *Haug/Vollmann*, 566-595 (with mod. Ger. trans.).
*Summa Theologiae*:
  *Henschel/Pretzel*, No. 2.
  *Waag/Schröder*, I, No. 8.

Facsimile:
  Vorau Sammelhandschrift (see above, p. 75).
*Das Anegenge*:
  Neuschäfer, Dietrich, ed. *Das Anegenge. Textkritische Studien. Diplomatischer Abdruck. Kritische Ausgabe. Anmerkungen zum Text*. Munich, 1966 (= Medium aevum, 8).
*Rede vom Glauben*:
  *Maurer*, II, No. 46.

## Salvation History—Bibliography

Freytag, Hartmut. "Ezzos Gesang. Text und Funktion." In: *Geistliche Denkformen in der Literatur des Mittelalters*. Ed. by Klaus Grubmüller, et al. Munich: Fink, 1984 (= Münstersche Mittelalter-Schriften, 51). Pp. 154-170.

Argues against the idea of an "Ur"-Ezzo, stresses unity of the Vorau version, seeks commonalities with the Strasbourg version, and examines the reasons for the composition of the poem.

_____. *Kommentar zur frühmhd. Summa Theologiae*. Munich: Fink, 1970 (= Medium Aevum, 19).

Detailed commentary on the poem with special attention to sources, previous editions, and interpretations. Modern German translation of the text and extensive bibliography.

Gentry, Francis G. "Arbeit in der mittelalterlichen Gesellschaft: Die Entwicklung einer mittelalterlichen Theorie der Arbeit vom 11. bis zum 14. Jhdt." In: *Arbeit als Thema in der deutschen Literatur vom Mittelalter bis zur Gegenwart*. Königstein/Ts.: Athenäum, 1979. Pp. 3-28.

Jacobs, Jef. "Der descensus ad inferos als Bericht und Exempel in frühmhd. religiöser Dichtung." *ABäG* 26 (1987): 17-34.

*Anegenge* discussion pp. 22-27.

Marchand, James W. "The Ship Allegory in the *Ezzolied* and in Old Icelandic." *Neophil.* 60 (1976): 238-250.

Interesting study of the allegory going beyond what the title would suggest.

Murdoch, Brian O. *The Fall of Man in the Early Middle High German Biblical Epic. The "Wiener Genesis," the "Vorauer Genesis," and the "Anegenge."* Göppingen: Kümmerle, 1972 (= GAG, 58)

Discussion of the texts and their contemporary theological backround.

_____. *The Recapitulated Fall. A Comparative Study in Medieval Literature.* Amsterdam: Rodopi, 1974 (= Amsterdamer Publikationen zur Sprache und Literatur, 11).

See also Rupp, 1971 (above) for *Das Anegenge, Summa Theologiae,* and Hartmann's *Rede vom Glauben.*

For literature on Armer Hartmann's *Rede vom Glauben,* see article by Kunrad Kunze in *VL²* 1 (1978): 450-454.

## The Proper Life

The works to be considered in this section generally fall under the generic term *Reimpredigt,* or "rhymed homily." As such they are admonitory verses to a lay public concerning what the proper Christian life should be. Of course, the background is salvation history (see C, above) because that involves man's ultimate destination, but the emphasis here is on the life in this world that is required to assure salvation. This does not necessarily mean that people were suddenly concerned about their souls; there is a long Latin literary tradition dealing with such matters. But this type of poetry may be related to the general interest in religious life among the laity and some of the evangelical zeal of churches in towns and cities, not the monasteries, that we have noted before.

The *Memento mori* is the most important of these sermonizing poems. The title itself expresses its message, and it begins with the lines: "Now think, men and women, where you are going to end up. You love this infirmity and think that you will always be here. However lovely you think it is, you shall have it only a short while. However much you would like to live for a long time, you will have to die." The poet warns against being caught up with the delights of the world, the folly of believing that one will always be here, and the danger of denying justice to the poor. In short, one should prepare for the next life during the short time of life on earth. It is impossible to know when death will come on the journey of life, but come it surely will. The poem closes with a rhetorical reprimand for the deception of the world and a prayer to God to take pity on the souls of men.

The *Memento mori* is to be found in the same manuscript as the Strasbourg-version of *Ezzolied* (see above, p. 81 f.), and the original was probably composed in the last quarter of the 11th century. The dialect is Alemannic. The poem is divided into 19 strophes, a total of 76 long lines (Maurer). In the last line, there is mention of a certain "Noker" as the author, but it has not been possible to identify him with any certainty.

Another poem that deals even more specifically with social matters in relation to salvation is entitled *Vom Rechte.* It is difficult to find a good, short expression in English for *Reht.* Certainly, it does mean "Justice," the "Right," or the "Law," but here it seems to stand for the broader concept of the divinely ordained, established order of things in the world. Naturally, that order would be "just" or "right," but the poet spares no words in explaining that that order is not always observed by man and that no one is indeed so noble, high, or mighty as *Das Recht*. Putting oneself above the "Law" will surely have dire consequences for the salvation of one's soul. The proper Christian life is characterized by loyalty, truthfulness, and reliability. Wealth and power lead to pride and exploitation of the poor. Masters and mistresses should be fair in their treatment of their servants and share the profits of their common work. Lies and slander are to be avoided. Greed is a shameful trait. The relations between men and women should also be subject to God's laws, and by all means one should consult one's priest for advice on how to lead a proper life. The descriptions of human behavior are taken very vividly from everyday country life and show a keen appreciation of human foibles. All in all, it is a fascinating, lively "Reimpredigt" and impresses with its style and seriousness of purpose.

*Vom Rechte* is found in the Millstatt *Sammelhandschrift* (see M, above, p. 75), fol. 135$^v$-141$^v$. The text is in poor condition and presents editorial problems. There are 549 lines in rhymed couplets in 30 stanzas of varying length (Schröder) or half that many long lines (Maurer). The dating is also difficult, 1150-1160? The language is Austrian (Carinthia).

**Die Wahrheit** (The Truth), similar to *Vom Rechte* in theme, but much shorter, would seem to have been written by a fiery evangelist. It is in the Vorau *Sammelhandschrift* (see V, above, p. 75), cod. 276, fol. 96$^{ra}$-96$^{rb}$ and comprises 182 lines in rhymed couplets. The author has provided the title himself in line 151: "This song is called 'The Truth'." The truth is that although we are away from home, heaven is our homeland, but it is uncertain that we shall get there. The poet wants to convert his listeners to turn away from a life that will surely lead to hell by describing the horrors of hell and the delights of heaven. He warns against the devil and urges loyalty to the Lord, to the church and the scriptures. He threatens and cajoles his audience, using rhetorical questions and exhortations. One can almost imagine him thumping his bible as he preaches! *Die Wahrheit* is usually dated from the middle to the second half of the 12th century.

Thematically close to the *Reimpredigt* but stylistically different is a longer allegorical poem entitled **Die Hochzeit** (The Wedding). Somewhat reminiscent of the "Song of Songs" as the wedding of the church to Christ, *Die Hochzeit* begins with the story of a powerful king who had sent his disobedient servants into an abyss, whence they continue to make trouble. The king decides to marry a beautiful maiden in order to have an heir and to assure the proper order of things. After the maiden gives her agreement to the king's messenger, preparations for a gorgeous wedding are started, and the maiden then comes to her bridegroom for the splendid festival. However, throughout the narration of the story the poet explains the allegorical interpretation of almost all the elements. It is not a consistent, single allegory, rather a seemingly random, disconnected discussion in almost free association of this aspect or that. Nevertheless, the significance of each event invariably has reference to true Christian living and the proper order of things, in sum a moral, perhaps even anagogical exegesis, quite in the manner of typical biblical exegesis in sermons, but here of the poet's own fictional story.

*Die Hochzeit* is a lengthy work, almost 1100 lines in stanzas of varying length. It is found right after *Vom Recht* in the Millstatt manuscript (see above), fol. 142$^r$-154$^v$. The text is likewise in poor condition. The poem is usually dated to 1160.

Two poems usually attributed to **Der sog. Heinrich von Melk** (The so-called Heinrich von Melk) are to be found in the youngest of the EMHG *Sammelhandschriften*, Vienna cod. 2696 (ca. 1300). The first poem is actually in two distinct but loosely connected parts: fol. 165$^r$-171$^r$: **Von dem gemäinem lebene**, (The Life of Society in General), and fol. 171$^r$-178$^v$: **Von des tôdes gehugede (Erinnerung an den Tod**, i.e., Memento mori). The second poem, fol. 303$^r$-312$^v$, is called: **Vom Priesterleben** (The Life of Priests). In v. 1032 f. of the first poem the poet gives his name as "Heinrich" and asks for God's mercy for himself and for a certain Abbot *Erchennenfride*. Since an Abbot Erchenfried is attested at the monastery of Melk from 1122 to 1163, and the language of the poems would be compatible with the dialect of that area, the poet has been named "Heinrich von Melk," although there is no historical record of anyone of that name. There is also considerable doubt whether the same author wrote both parts of the first poem or, indeed, the second poem at all. In addition to the question of authorship, the dating of the works is uncertain, with estimates running from ca. 1160 to the early 13th century. The poems are written in rhymed couplets with lines of a varying number of syllables.

Nevertheless, there are certain similarities in the poems: strong social criticism of all classes, especially of the clergy and the wealthy against a background of Christian ideals; the consequences of sinful life in the hereafter; and even the satirical nature of the poetry. The clergy is the target for the author's sharpest censure for such sins as simony, lascivious conduct, disregarding their vow of celibacy, and willingness to let the rich do as they please while castigating the poor. The powerful and wealthy laity is taken to task for attacking one another like wolves, for overweening pride and decadent life at court. The knights can only brag about their successes in love and in fighting. Even the poor are condemned for trying to dress like the nobility. In all of this and especially in the "Memento mori" part, there is the admonition to forswear such sinful behavior before it is too late. One can never know when death will strike, and death itself is portrayed in repulsive images.

The stridency of the remarks, especially about the clergy, by a man who was probably a member of some lay brotherhood, is striking. Of course much had been written before in church circles about the necessity of reform and of observing one's sacerdotal obligations, but that had been largely intramural and, of course, in Latin, hence not accessible to the laity. Here it is all out in the open for all to hear in their own tongue, and we should probably assume that with the increasing economic prosperity in the 12th century and the growth of the cities, there was a larger public that might be interested in reading, if they could, or hearing poetic works like these. It is no longer a question of what constitutes the established order of things and how to observe it, but of a sharp critique of the social order as it existed at that time.

Texts:
*Memento mori*:

*Ahd. Lb.*, No. XLII.

*Maurer* I, No. 5.

*Curschmann/Glier* I, 148-157 (with mod. Ger. trans.).

*Haug/Vollmann*, 662-671 (with mod. Ger. trans.).

*Vom Rechte*:

*Maurer* II, No. 29.

*Waag/Schröder* II, No. VIII.

*Haug/Vollmann*, 752-783 (with mod. Ger. trans.).

*Die Wahrheit*:

*Henschel/Pretzel*, No. 3.

*Maurer* I, No. 18.

*Waag/Schröder* II, No. XI.

*Die Hochzeit*:

*Maurer* II, No. 30.

*Waag/Schröder* II, No. IX.

*Haug/Vollmann*, 784-849 (with mod. Ger. trans.).

*Heinrich von Melk*:

Heinzel, Richard, ed. *Heinrich von Melk*. Berlin, 1867. Repr. 1983.

Kienast, Richard, ed. *Der sogenannte Heinrich von Melk. Nach R. Heinzels Ausgabe von 1867 neu hrsg*. Heidelberg, 1946.

*Maurer* III, Nos. 52 & 53.

*Curschmann/Glier* I, 154-175 (sel. with mod. Ger. trans.).

Translation:

Schützeichel, Rudolf, trans. *Das alemannische Memento mori. Das Gedicht und der geistig-historische Hintergrund*. Tübingen, 1962. Pp. 127-133. (mod. Ger. trans.).

## The Proper Life—Bibliography

Carne, Eva-Maria. "Der Aufbau der 'Wahrheit'." *MLN* 84 (1969): 448-451.

Dunstan, A. C. "Sources and Text of the MHG Poem 'Die Hochzeit'." *MLR* 20 (1925): 310-316; *MLR* 21 (1926): 178-186.

Freytag, Wiebke. "Das Priesterleben des sogenannten Heinrich von Melk. Redeformen, Rezeptionsmoden und Gattung." *DVjs* 52 (1978): 558-580.

Discussion of parallels to the "Offendiculum" of Honorius Augustudonensis in Strophe 1-10 of Heinrich's prologue and his retorical transformation of them.

Ganz, Peter. " 'Die Hochzeit': *fabula* und *significatio*." In: Johnson, L. P., H.-H. Steinhoff, R. A. Wisbey, eds. *Studien zur frühmhd. Literatur. Cambridger Colloquium 1971*. Berlin: Erich Schmidt, 1974. Pp. 58-73.

Sees not only the connection to allegorical religious literature and the sermon but also to contemporary secular heroic poetry to provide the *prodesse* and the *delectare* for the audience.

Gentry, Francis G. "Noker's *Memento mori* and the Desire for Peace." *ABäG* 16 (1981): 25-62.

The "Memento Mori" viewed as reflecting the political and social disintegration resulting from the investiture controversy.

Kaiser, Gert. "Das *Memento mori*. Ein Beitrag zum sozialgeschichtlichen Verständnis der Gleichheitsforderung im frühen Mittelalter." *Euph.* 68 (1974): 337-370.

Murdoch, Brian O. "Die sogenannte 'Wahrheit.' Analyse eines frühmhd. Gedichts." In: *Akten des V. Internationalen Germanisten-Kongresses Cambridge 1975, Vol. 2.* Bern: H. Lang, 1976. Pp. 404-413.

See also Rupp, 1971 (above) for *Memento Mori.*

Scholz-Williams, Gerhild. "Against Court and School. Heinrich von Melk and Hélinant of Froidmont as Critics of Twelfth-Century Society." *Neophil.* 62 (1978): 513-526. Follows the argument that Heinrich wrote only the *Erinnerung an den Tod* and sees in it criticism of courtly culture à la Hartmann's *Armer Heinrich.*

Schröbler, Ingeborg. "Das mhd. Gedicht vom 'Recht'." *PBB* 80 (1958): 219-252.

Speicher, Stephan. *"Vom Rechte." Ein Kommentar im Rahmen der zeitgenössischen Literaturtradition.* Göppingen: Kümmerle, 1986 (= GAG, 443).

Line-by-line commentary on the text, discussion of its relationship to contemporary sermon literature, with extensive bibliography.

## PERSONAL RELIGIOUS EXPERIENCE

If one thinks of "personal religious experience" in terms of more modern confessional writings, one is bound to be disappointed. Although there are several *Sündenklagen* (Laments of Sins) to be considered here, it is difficult to read these as personal confessions and laments. The individual element tends to be missing in favor of the typical or formulaic, although some do have a more personal tone. Poems of this type follow the older Latin tradition of the planctus, but as they were written in the vernacular, they were intended for the instruction and use of the laity.

The oldest is the **Millstätter Sündenklage** (Millstatt Lament of Sins) from the first third of the 12th century in the Millstatt *Sammelhandschrift* (see above p. 75). It is on the last few leaves of that manuscript, is in poor condition, and contains 864 lines in rhymed couplets, or 432 long lines in 70 strophes of varying length (Maurer). After a short hymn of praise to God the Creator and Almighty, the poem falls into three parts: first, an appeal to God for mercy followed by a discourse on God's judgment, the terrors of hell, and the delights of paradise; second, a confession and the lengthy lament of sins; finally, a prayer to God to hear his plea for forgiveness and protection. The sins confessed, although formulated as personal sins, cover almost the entire range of possible sins, both in the general part of the confession and in the specific part, in which the poet accuses the various parts of his body for having carried out his sinful deeds (e.g. his feet for being quicker to take him to a prostitute or on a raiding expedition than to church), this being a variation on the old argument between the body and the soul. He repeatedly refers to biblical figures who had been saved such as Daniel, the three youths in the fiery furnace, Lazarus, or those whose sins had been forgiven like the woman taken in adultery as models for God's mercy, and he pleads to be treated in a similar fashion.

The **Vorauer Sündenklage** (Vorau Lament of Sins) is similar in many respects but is addressed not only to God but, in considerable detail, to the Virgin Mary as the mediatrix between man and God. Because of this a more personal, human plea is presented in the initial part of the lament. The second part, the actual confession and request for forgiveness, gives a lengthy list of sins accompanied by abject self-accusation (e.g. "I am the worst man who ever took the name of being a Christian.") and is directed to God and Christ. The third part repeats the request for forgiveness, with reference to biblical figures who had been saved, as in the Millstatt lament, and the poem ends with a prayer for help in the struggle with Satan by means of an armor made up of abstract qualities, such as proper Faith, Patience, and Humility. The text of the poem as copied in the manuscript is far from perfect, so that it is difficult to tell how many lines the original must have had. The number varies in modern editions from 846-858 lines in rhymed couplets. The Vorau lament may be dated between 1250-1260. It is much more sophisticated, creative, and lively in its language and style than Millstatt.

Three poems to the Virgin Mary exemplify a type of religious poetry that is well known in Latin hymns and becomes increasingly popular in vernacular lyrics. It is based on the feeling that Mary as the mother of Jesus is someone who can intercede for mankind with Christ and provide help. We can discuss the three as a group: *Das Melker Marienlied* (Melk Song to Mary) from the first half of the 12th century, *Das Arnsteiner Mariengebet* (Arnstein Prayer to Mary) from the middle of the 12th century, and *Die Mariensequenz aus Muri* (Marian Sequence from Muri) from the end of the 12th century. In all three poems Mary is addressed by conventional signs and attributes associated with her, many of them taken from the Old Testament; flower on the rod of Jesse, blooming almond branch on Aaron's rod, closed gate, light from the burning bush of Moses, etc. But each poem or song has its own individuality. The *Melker Marienlied* (Cloister Melk, Ms. 383, $1^r$) is a simple hymn of praise to Mary in 14 stanzas of six lines each in rhymed couplets with the refrain "Sancta Maria" concluding each stanza. It stresses the prefigurations of Mary, her role as mother of Christ, and other allegorical figurations, including the Eve-Mary typology. There is no direct request for intercession. The *Arnsteiner Mariengebet* (State Archives Wiesbaden, Ms. C 8, fol. $129^v$-$135^v$) is sometimes called a *Lied* or a *Leich*, but it is definitely a prayer in substance although it incorporates praise of the Virgin using conventional Marian symbolism. The beginning and the ending of the prayer are damaged. All that remains are 327 lines in strophes of various length in rhymed couplets. The author identifies herself as a woman (". . . hear me, a sinful woman," v. 19), and she speaks as a devout woman not only for herself but for all women and all poor people, begging Mary for intercession with her son and for help in leading a proper life and at the time of death. The *Mariensequenz aus Muri* (Muri Ms. 69, fol. $33^v$-$36^r$, Codex Engelbergensis 1003, fol. 115, plus one fragment) follows the metrical pattern of the Latin sequence *Ave praeclara maris stella*. In fact, the first three lines are a translation of that and the poem was surely intended to be sung to that melody (one of the manuscripts has neumes). There are a total of 69 lines including the introduction (3 lines) and the conclusion (4 lines). The main body of the poem is divided into seven double sections of one to eight lines each (in Schröder/Waag) or one to six lines each (Maurer) in modern editions. The poem begins with praise of Mary, using the usual figurative attributes and covering her life from the Annunciation to the birth and nursing of Jesus. The main thrust of the prayer is for inspiration, help, and intercession predicated on Mary's special position as virgin mother of Christ.

Texts:
*Millstätter Sündenklage*:
   *Maurer*, II, No. 24.
*Vorauer Sündenklage*:
   *Henschel/Pretzel*, No. 9.
   *Maurer, III*, No. 50.
   *Waag/Schröder*, II, No. 12.
*Melker Marienlied*:
   *Maurer*, I, No. 13.
   *Waag/Schröder*, II, No. 15.
   *Haug/Vollmann*, 858 (with mod. Ger. trans.).
   *Wehrli*, No. 2. (with mod. Ger. trans.).
*Arnsteiner Mariengebet*:
   *Maurer*, I, No. 19
   *Waag/Schröder*, II, No. 10.
*Mariensequenz aus Muri*:
   *Maurer*, I, No. 20.
   *Waag/Schröder*, II, No. 17.
   *Wehrli*, No. 3 (with mod. Ger. trans.).

## Personal Religious Experience—Bibliography

Brinkmann, Hennig. "*Ave praeclara maris stella* in deutscher Wiedergabe. Zur Geschichte einer Rezeption." In: *Studien zur deutschen Literatur und Sprache des Mittelalters. Festschr. für Hugo Moser zum 65. Geburtstag*. Berlin: Erich Schmidt, 1974. Pp. 8-30.

Kolb, Herbert. "Das Melker Marienlied." In: Jungbluth, Günther, ed. *Interpretationen mhd. Lyrik*. Bad Homburg: Gehlen, 1969. Pp. 47-82.

A very close reading of the text stressing its relationship to the sermon and to contemporary allegorical interpretation.

Schäfer, Gerhard M. *Untersuchungen zur deutschsprachigen Marienlyrik im 12. und 13. Jahrhundert*. Göppingen: Kümmerle, 1971 (= GAG,48).

For "Melker Marienlied," pp. 19-24; "Arnsteiner Mariengebet," pp. 24-31; "Mariensequenz aus Muri," pp. 35-44. These poems, among others, are seen as early steps leading to the much later *Marienleich* of Frauenlob.

Schröder, Werner. *Vom "Rheinauer Paulus" zur "Millstätter Sündenklage". Aspekte der Poetisierung volkssprachiger kirchlicher Gebrauchstexte im 12. Jahrhundert*. Stuttgart: F. Steiner, 1986 (= Akad. d. Wiss. u. d. Lit. Mainz. Abh. d. Geistes- und Sozialwiss. Kl., 1986/3).

Also *Vorauer Sündenklage*, pp. 66-71.


## HISTORICAL POETRY

The four poems in this group deal with historical figures, but they are not historiography in the ordinary sense of the word. They are creative literary works based on notable people of the past and legendary figures. One should also keep in mind that there is a strong religious background to each of these works, frequently of a didactic nature.

The first two poems, the *Annolied* (Song of St. Anno) and *Kaiserchronik* (Chronicle of the Emperors), are in a way related. Both deal in part with salvation history, world history, and legendary figures. The *Annolied* begins with a short survey of salvation history, ending with Cologne and its saints in recounting the spread of Christianity. The second part is world history, tracing its traditional four empires, Babylonian, Persian, Greek, and Roman, the last of which is connected to its current extension, the German *translatio imperii*. The story of St. Anno, Archbishop of Cologne (1056-1076), forms the third part and qualifies as a legend because of the miracles that led to his canonization. The *Kaiserchronik*, on the other hand, has the course of world history as its central structure but uses references to salvation history and legendary figures to interpret it.

Anno was a very important and influential man of his day. He was named Archbishop of Cologne in 1056 by Henry III and in that capacity exerted the spiritual and temporal power of a prince of the church and empire. Upon the death of Henry III, Anno was involved in the regency of Queen Agnes, established for the minority of Henry's son. In fact, Anno organized the abduction of Henry IV from Kaiserswerth to Cologne in 1062, became regent himself until 1064 and tutor of young Henry until the latter attained his majority in 1065. In his bishopric, Anno fostered the growth of the city, furthered the activity of the church, and founded the reformed monastery of Siegburg. He was a strict ruler, forcefully putting down a rebellion of the Cologne merchants against his authority in 1074 that had a devastating effect on the city, but he eventually became reconciled with the citizenry. He was buried in the monastery in Siegburg upon his death and was canonized in 1183.

No manuscripts of the *Annolied* exist. It has survived in a partial printed edition of 1597 by Vulcanius and a complete one by Martin Opitz in 1639. It consists of a total of 878 verses organized in 49 stanzas of varying length and was probably written about 1077, possibly by a monk in the monastery of Siegburg. It has been speculated that the *Annolied* was written in support of Anno's controversial candidacy for sainthood. This remarkable poem contains a wealth of interesting material from a variety of sources which the author used with considerable originality for the historical parts. The source for the life of Anno itself is unknown although the author may have been acquainted with Lampert von Hersfeld's obituary for Anno in his *Annals* of 1078-79. It is unlikely that he knew the *Vita Annonis* of Abbot Reginhard of Siegburg (before 1088). In the 11th century somewhat similar Latin chronicles that work biography and city history into the mainstream of salvation and world history are to be found in the same geographical area, but the *Annolied* is unique in vernacular poetry and in its attempt to integrate biography into the two kinds of history.

The *Kaiserchronik* is, as we have said, structured primarily on world history. It is a huge work of over 17,000 lines with a rich manuscript tradition. There are three versions of it, the oldest (A) in the Vorau *Sammelhandschrift* (see above, p. 75), fol. 1$^{ra}$ - 73$^{vb}$. This version alone is found in three complete manuscripts and twelve fragments, while the two other longer versions (B and C), essentially continuations, are attested to in twelve complete manuscripts and ten fragments. In addition, prose redactions and translations of it into Latin occur in the tradition. The language of the *Kaiserchronik* is Bavarian, and it was probably written in Regensburg between 1126 and 1147, possibly by a single author, although there are indications that lead one to believe that several authors may have worked on it. No patron for this extensive work is mentioned, but it is likely that patronage came from the nobility rather than from the church. The sources for the material in the *Kaiserchronik* come from many Latin and vernacular sources. One early part on Caesar and the Germans is a re-working of some 225 lines of the *Annolied*.

The *Kaiserchronik* traces the history of the Roman empire from the founding of the city by Romulus and Remus to the time of Conrad III. High points are the establishment of the empire by Julius Caesar, who had help from the German peoples he had conquered and may have been born in Trier himself; the transformation of the heathen empire into a Christian one by Constantine; and the translation of the empire to Germany by Charlemagne. All emperors are judged by whether they were good or bad rulers in the Christian terms of a *rex justus et pacificus*. Evil is considered the work of the devil, whereas good is divinely inspired, and rulers come to evil or good ends accordingly. However, the *Kaiserchronik* is not only about emperors but also about popes and certain legendary figures whose stories fall supposedly during the reign of a particular ruler. Some of the best known legends are the ones about Sylvester, Faustinianus, and Crescentia. They function frequently as exempla in which virtue is rewarded after endless tribulations and vice punished and are intended to support the imperial ideology of the poem and to entertain a lay audience.

Two other "historical" poems may be considered together because they are the first German poems with French sources: the *Alexanderlied* (Song of Alexander) of Pfaffe ("priest" or "cleric") Lamprecht and the *Rolandslied* (Song of Roland) of Pfaffe Konrad. This is a significant development as German vernacular literature and even court life begin to turn increasingly towards French culture for their models during the second half of the 12th century.

The *Alexanderlied* comes from the French *romans d'antiquité*, whereas the *Rolandslied* takes its subject matter from another French literary genre, the *chansons de geste*. The *Alexanderlied* is found only in the Vorau *Sammelhandschrift* (see above, p. 75) between the Old Testament and New Testament materials on fol. 109$^{ra}$-115$^{va}$. It is a poem of 1533 lines in rhymed couplets. The author, Pfaffe Lamprecht, names himself in the poem, but his name is practically all that is known about him. He is the author of a fragmentary *Tobias* (see above, p. 77) and obviously was versed in Latin and French. His language is Mosel-Franconian. Lamprecht's *Alexanderlied* is sometimes called the *Vorauer Alexander* and is usually dated at around 1150.

Lamprecht tells the life of Alexander from his birth to his great victory over the Persian King Darius. His French source was the *Roman d'Alexandre* by Albéric de Pisançon, a fragment of only 105 lines of the beginning extant, based on the Latin Pseudo-Calisthenes account of the storied events of Alexander's life which was so popular in the Middle Ages. In his prologue Lamprecht stresses the theme of transitoriness and vainglory in his tale but not in an admonitory manner. His main interest is in the tremendous feats that Alexander performed during his lifetime and all the wonderfully outstanding events of his life. Alexander is admired as an exceptional ruler and model for princes. The defeat of Darius at the very end seems rather abrupt, leading to the question of whether Lamprecht's source only went that far or whether Lamprecht either finished it off quickly or left it unfinished. No patron for the poem is mentioned or known.

The *Strasbourg Alexander* from the Strasbourg-Molsheim *Sammelhandschrift* that was lost in the fire in 1870 is a more modern reworking of Lamprecht's work in terms of style, language, and rhyme. Dated ca. 1170, it continues the biography of Alexander from his victory over Darius until his death. Here Alexander's journeys to exotic lands in the East and his encounters with fantastic peoples and creatures form the main emphasis, but the motif of *vanitas* is still there in the episode where Alexander comes to the gates of Paradise and is given a small stone as token of submission. An old Jew interprets the stone for him: all the gold in the world can not outweigh it, but a little dirt and flowers can tip the scales radically against it. Alexander learns the vanity of human striving from this example and returns home to Greece where he rules for twelve more years. The *Strasbourg Alexander* is based on Latin sources rather than French. The author is unknown, but he surely had a religious education.

> Konrad's *Rolandslied* is the story of Charlemagne's campaign against the Saracens in Spain, in the course of which Marsilie, the Saracen leader, feigns surrender, only to attack the rearguard of the withdrawing Christian forces upon the advice of the traitorous Genelun, who had been sent to negotiate a peaceful submission. In the course of the fighting, the heroic fighter Roland is killed when he delays summoning aid by sounding his horn. However, Charlemagne takes drastic revenge by slaughtering the Saracens, including the forces of mighty King Paligan which have come to assist Marsilie. Genelun is executed after the heathens have been defeated. *Rolandslied* is a crusading epic, pitting the Christians against the heathens. Charlemagne is the loyal servant of God who fights for the just cause against the forces of evil. Roland dies the death of a martyr, as do all the other Christians. It is popular history, based on the defeat of the retreating Frankish rearguard by the Basques in 778: Good triumphs over Evil, the great Christian heroes defeat those treacherous heathen, and Justice overcomes Treason.

Konrad's version differs from his French source in many respects but most strikingly in the fact that he tones down the nationalism and emphasizes the religious aspect of the conflict. As a result, his poem is almost double the length of the original (9,094 lines in rhymed couplets). He names himself in an epilogue and tells that he had translated the French source first into Latin and then into German. He also mentions as patron Henry the Lion, whose English wife, Mathilde, had encouraged the translation. The poem can therefore be dated after 1168, the year of their marriage, probably around 1170. There are two complete manuscripts of the poem and four fragments, attesting to its popularity. The language is Bavarian, and the poem is presumed to have been written in Regensburg. Konrad's *Rolandslied* had a strong influence on later authors, above all on Wolfram von Eschenbach, in the composition of his *Willehalm* (see p. 194 ff.).

Texts:
*Annolied*:

Bulst, Walther, ed. *Das Annolied. Hrsg. von Martin Opitz MSCXXXIX. Diplomatischer Abdruck, besorgt von Walter Bulst.* Heidelberg, 1946 (= Editiones Heidelbergensis, 2).

Nellman, Eberhard, ed. & trans. *Das Annolied. Mittelhochdeutsch und Neuhochdeutsch.* Stuttgart: Reclam, 1979, [3]1986 (= UB, 1416). (Text and mod. Ger. trans.).

*Maurer*, II, No. 22.

*Curschmann/Glier*, No. 14 (Text and mod. Ger. trans.).

*Kaiserchronik*:

Schröder, Edward, ed. *Die Kaiserchronik eines Regensburger Geistlichen.* Berlin, 1895 (repr. 1964) (= MGH Chroniken, 1).

Bulst, Walther, ed. *Die Kaiserchronik. Ausgewählte Erzählungen. 1. Faustinianus. Nach dem Vorauer Text.* Heidelberg, 1946. *2. Crescentia. Nach dem Vorauer Text.* Heidelberg, 1946 (= Editiones Heidelbergensis, 5 & 6).

*Haug/Vollmann*, No. XII, 1-3 (Sel. with mod. Ger. trans.).

Translation:

Mayer, Joseph Maria, trans. *Der Kaiser und der Könige Buch oder die sogennante Kaiserchronik. Gedicht des 12. Jahrhunderts. In freier Prosa-Bearbeitung hrsg. und mit Anmerkungen versehen.* Munich, 1874 (mod. Ger. trans.).

See also Nellmann (above).

Texts:

*Alexanderlied*:

Kinzel, Karl, ed. *Lamprechts Alexanderlied nach den drei Texten mit den Fragmenten des Alberic von Besancon und den lateinischen Quellen hrsg. und erklärt von Karl Kinzel.* Halle, 1884.

Ruttmann, I., ed. *Das Alexanderlied des Pfaffen Lamprecht (Straßburger A). Text, Nacherzählung, Worterklärungen.* Darmstadt: Wiss. Buchges., 1974.

*Maurer*, II, No. 45 (*Vorauer Alexander*).

*Curschmann/Glier*, No. 20 (Sel. from *Straßburger Alexander* and mod. Ger. trans.).

*Rolandslied*:

Wesle, Carl, ed. *Das "Rolandslied" des Pfaffen Konrad.* Tübingen, [3]1985 by Peter Wapnewski (= ATB, 69).

Kartschoke, Dieter, ed. & trans. *Das Rolandslied. Mittelhochdeutscher Text und Übertragung.* Frankfurt/M., 1970 (= Fischer Taschenbuch, 6004). (Text and mod. Ger. trans.).

Richter, Horst, ed. *Pfaffe Konrad. Das Rolandslied. Text, Nacherzählung, Wort- und Begriffserklärungen, Wortliste.* Darmstadt: Wiss. Buchges., 1981.

*Curschmann/Glier*, No. 22 (Sel. and mod. Ger. trans.).

Translations:

*Alexanderlied*:

Thomas, J. W., trans. *The "Strassburg Alexander" and the Munich "Oswald."* Columbia, SC: Camden House, 1989 (= Studies in Ger. Lit., Ling., and Cult., 44). Engl. prose trans.

See also *Curschmann/Glier*, No. 20 (above).

*Rolandslied*:

Thomas, J. W., trans. *Priest Konrad's "Song of Roland."* Translated and with an Introduction by J. W. Thomas. Columbia, SC: Camden House, 1994 (= Studies in Ger. Lit., Ling., and Cult.). Engl. prose trans.

See also Kartschoke, Richter, and *Curschmann/Glier*, No. 22 (above).

Facsimile:

Werner, W., and H. Zirnbauer, eds. *Das Rolandslied des Pfaffen Konrad. Faksimile-Ausgabe des Codex Pal. Germ. 112.* 1970.

# Historical Poetry—Bibliography

*Annolied* and *Kaiserchronik*:

For bibliography on the *Annolied* see Eberhard Nellmann's text and translation (above). His afterword gives an excellent, short introduction to the work. See also his article in $VL^2$ 1 (1978): 366-371, and the *Kommentar* in *Haug/Vollmann*, pp. 1425-1449.

Liebertz-Grün, Ursula. "Zum *Annolied*. Atypische Struktur und singuläre politische Konzeption." *Euph.* 74 (1980): 223-256.

Comes close to being a *Forschungsbericht* of more recent *Annolied*-literature but also discusses the politics behind it.

Nellmann, Eberhard. *Die Reichsidee in deutschen Dichtungen der Salier-und frühen Stauferzeit. Annolied, Kaiserchronik, Rolandslied, Eraclius.* Berlin: Erich Schmidt, 1963 (= PSuQ, 16).

Treats the political ideas in the four poems before 1200.

Ohly, Friedrich. *Sage und Legende in der "Kaiserchronik." Untersuchungen über Quellen und Aufbau der Dichtung.* Münster, 1940. Repr. Darmstadt: Wiss. Buchges., 1968.

Monumental study of the sources of the poem resulting in the conclusion that the poet was highly original in his conception and based his poem more on legends and hagiography than on chronicles.

For additional bibliography on the *Kaiserchronik*, see Eberhard Nellmann, $VL^2$ 2 (1980): 19-23.

## *Alexanderlied*:

Fischer, Wolfgang. *Die Alexanderkonzeption des Pfaffen Lambrecht.* Munich: Eidos, 1964 (= Medium Aevum, 2).

Stein, Peter K. "Ein Weltherrscher als *vanitas*-Exempel in imperial-ideologisch orientierter Zeit?" In: R. Krohn, et al. *Stauferzeit.* 1979. Pp. 144-180.

Analysis of the poem as the result of changing political perspectives of the role of emperor in the *Straßburger Alexander* as opposed to the earlier Vorau version.

## *Rolandslied*:

Ashcroft, Jeffrey. "*Miles dei—gotes ritter:* Konrad's *Rolandslied* and the Evolution of the Concept of Christian Chivalry." *FMLS* 17 (1981): 146-66.

Kartschoke, Dieter. *Die Datierung des deutschen Rolandslieds.* Stuttgart: Metzler, 1965 (= Germanistische Abhandlungen, 9).

Argues for a final completion date of ca. 1172.

Murdoch, Brian. "The Treachery of Ganelon in Konrad's *Rolandslied.*" *Euph.* 67 (1973): 372-77.

Richter, Horst. *Kommentar zum Rolandskied des Pfaffen Konrad—Teil I.* Bern: H. Lang, 1972 (= Kanadische Studien zur deutschen Sprache und Literatur, 6).

Detailed commentary of the first 2760 lines, illuminating the function of the theological aspects peculiar to this German version of the story vis-à-vis the French *chanson.*

# Middle High German Literature under the Hohenstaufens 1170-1273

## HISTORICAL BACKGROUND

German literature of the High Middle Ages, the remarkable flowering described as classical MHG literature, the *mittelhochdeutsche Blütezeit*, is inextricable from the name of Hohenstaufen, the reigning house that gained dominance in Europe during the latter half of the twelfth century. It had first achieved significance in 1079, when Agnes, daughter of the Emperor Henry IV, had married Frederick of Staufen who was then created Duke of Swabia. It was his father, Frederick of Büren, who in about 1077 had built the castle now known as Hohenstaufen, not far from Stuttgart, one of the first of the many castles throughout Swabia which became the strongholds of the dynasty and important administrative centers.

On the death of Henry V in 1125 the Salian inheritance passed to the Hohenstaufens, who did not, however, as yet assume the imperial crown, even though Henry himself had designated his nephew, Frederick II of Swabia his successor. Breaking the tradition of hereditary succession to the German crown, the princes elected Lothar of Supplinburg, Duke of Saxony. The inevitable conflict with the Hohenstaufens lasted for the larger part of Lothar's reign, and the episode represented a significant assertion of the power of the princes.

When Lothar died in 1138, there was another setback to the hereditary principle, when Lothar's nominee, his son-in-law Henry the Proud, Duke of Bavaria and Saxony, was rejected in favor of the long-term anti-king, the Hohenstaufen Conrad III, formerly Duke of Franconia. Henry the Proud, whose only son was Henry, known as the Lion, died in suspicious circumstances in 1139.

Conrad III died in 1152, on his return from the Second Crusade. The son whom he had originally nominated to succeed him had died two years earlier, and his only other son was still a child. Recognizing the urgent need for a strong opposition to the Saxons under Henry the Lion, who had long attempted to lay claim also to Bavaria, Conrad had taken the step of naming as his successor not that second son of his, but his nephew, Frederick of Hohenstaufen, Duke of Swabia, a man of thirty at the time.

This was a popular nomination: Frederick, often called Frederick Barbarossa, was already known as a statesman and a warrior who had participated in the crusade. Most important, he stood in exactly the same relationship to the Welf and Hohenstaufen dynasties—his mother was the sister of Henry the Proud and his father brother to Emperor Conrad—and looked as though he might unite the divided Germany. It all seemed auspicious, and perhaps if he had devoted himself to the state of affairs in Germany instead of becoming embroiled in turbulent relations with Italy and bitter confrontations with successive popes, the course of the Hohenstaufen dynasty would have been very different, and, with it, the course of European history.

For the time being, however, the stability of the Hohenstaufen dynasty was assured, and, thus also, the power of the German Empire, the Holy Roman Empire as it was to be called in time to come. This was the environment which nurtured the literature which dominates medieval Germany, the *staufische Klassik*, which reached its peak in the very early years of the thirteenth century, coinciding with the peak of chivalry and the dominance of the knightly class. The poets of that age often, though not in all cases, came from that class, and their works were certainly intended for a knightly audience. The decline of that class and its increasing substitution by the middle classes coincide likewise with the decline of courtly literature, and this at a time when Hohenstaufen power was gradually but irrevocably waning.

The Hohenstaufens under Frederick I may have appeared invincible, but their position was often held on a thread, and the almost constant opposition of Church and State gave rise to a volatile situation. It is also important to bear in mind that events in the far reaches of the Empire had resonances in that part which concerns us for the study of medieval German literature.

Crucial was the position of Sicily, the future of which was significantly affected by the marriage in 1186 of Frederick's son Henry to Constance, daughter of King Roger of Sicily of the Hauteville dynasty. The basis of the union was blatantly political: to preserve the succession in the event of the death of the reigning king, William IV, who had no heir. Potentially, also, the marriage would mean the union of the enormously wealthy kingdom of Sicily with the Empire, and the consequent diminution of papal power.

Henry was to concern himself with Italy, while Frederick returned to Germany, under threat of excommunication by Pope Urban III for arranging the marriage without papal approval. As things turned out, this excommunication did not take effect, because matters of even greater significance intervened: the surrender of Jerusalem to Saladin, the death of Urban III and, in 1190, the death by drowning of Frederick himself as he led his forces into the Third Crusade. The fact that the Empire passed without challenge to his son Henry VI is testimony to the achievements of Frederick Barbarossa, but his son was a ruler of quite a different caliber, lacking the charisma of his father.

Henry and Constance were crowned in Rome in 1191, Henry having laid claim to Sicily, too, on the death of William of Sicily, in 1189, but the union of this kingdom with the Empire depended on the continuation of the Hohenstaufen dynasty, something which could be threatened by the princes if the occasion arose, and certainly by a powerful pope. Henry VI did try to establish the principle of the hereditary empire, but he failed, although he succeeded in having his young son elected as king in 1196, shortly before his own death in 1197, an event which plunged Germany into a state of anarchy during the ensuing fifteen years of conflict between the Hohenstaufens and the Welfs.

Ironically enough, these were years which saw the upsurge of courtly literature in Germany, and it was precisely in Thuringia, which was severely affected, that a rich literary center flourished at the court of Count Hermann I. This flowering is an unambiguous testimony to the power and wealth of the noble lords, and their new role as patrons of the arts, not to mention the less tangible but frequently observed coincidence of significant periods of artistic creativity with times of social unrest. The picture of courtly society, idealized in the concept of the court of King Arthur, may well have been an attempt to block out the negative features of reality, yet the most effective narrative poets of the day, astute observers as they were, did not provide an unreservedly positive view. It is possible to discern a certain criticism in Hartmann's *Iwein*, for example, or to see Gottfried's *Tristan* as an attack on society. In the outspoken comments of Walther von der Vogelweide, moreover, we gain a powerful insight into the prevailing malaise as well as some of the most specific references to political events.

The child Frederick was three years old when his father died, and his mother, the Empress Constance, died in 1198. Although there was plenty of support for him as the appointed heir, there was a need to avert a state of chaos developing in the period before he attained his majority. Therefore, his uncle, Philip of Swabia, agreed, after some initial reluctance, to be crowned, with the support of the majority of the great lords and bishops. Once more, however, the death of the pope precipitated a crisis: on the accession of Innocent III, who saw the potential threat of an Empire which was composed of Germany, central Italy and Sicily, there was a plausible rival candidate in the form of Otto of Brunswick, son of Frederick Barbarossa's old enemy Henry the Lion of Saxony. He, too, was crowned, and Germany was thrown into a civil war, with the Welfs supported by Richard the Lionheart and the pope on the one side, and the Hohenstaufen cause supported by Philip Augustus of France on the other.

This double election was thus not merely a German issue but much wider in its implications and capable of resolution only on a broader, European scale. The German Empire no longer held the dominant position it had held during the earlier Middle Ages, but was dependent on decisions taken and moves made elsewhere in Europe. Moreover, the situation did not by any means remain constant. Richard the Lionheart died in 1199, and the subsequent shift in loyalty of some of Otto's most significant supporters was followed by a period during which the pope also relented and transferred his favor to Philip. The murder of Philip himself in 1208, assassinated by a personal enemy, changed the whole course of events.

Otto was crowned emperor in 1209, and in 1211 he marched his armies into southern Italy, to the consternation of the pope, for whom a union of Sicily and the Empire under Otto was just as threatening as the same union under the Hohenstaufens. With no other choice open to him, the pope turned to Frederick, who had meanwhile attained his majority and been elected king in 1211 and crowned in Mainz in 1212.

In 1214, at the battle of Bouvines, Otto's army was defeated by the cavalry of Philip Augustus of France who, in an act of blatant symbolism, transferred the imperial banner, the golden eagle left battered on the battlefield, to Frederick. Frederick was crowned emperor at Aachen in 1215, and Innocent III declared himself in favor of him at the great Lateran council of that same year. Shortly after his coronation, Frederick made a public declaration of his intent, underlining it by having the body of Charlemagne displayed in its magnificent shrine in Aachen and then personally hammering the first nails into the sarcophagus. This was the successor to Charlemagne, who aimed at nothing short of world dominion and whose first step was to announce a crusade: a clash with Innocent III was inevitable.

Frederick II had spent his entire life in his mother's kingdom of Sicily, and he was a complete stranger to the country of his father, its customs, even its language. By the time of his election as emperor, however, he had powerful allies among the German princes, whose authority had increased during the years of conflict between Otto and Philip. With no hereditary succession established, the princes had enjoyed considerable independence, to the extent that the great families possessed power and sometimes popularity which rivalled that of the emperor. Since an election was necessary before the title of Emperor could pass from father to son, it meant that even the ploy of having the heir elected at a very early age was dependent on the goodwill and the support of the princes. Thus the monarchy in Germany was weakened at a time when the reverse was happening in England and France.

The intelligent and highly cultivated Frederick, who is numbered among the foremost literary patrons of the age, felt infinitely more at home in Sicily than in Germany. For the time being, however, expediency dictated that he remain in Germany, although as it turned out he spent only nine of the thirty-eight years of his reign there. He had promised Innocent III that he would transfer the kingdom of Sicily to his infant son Henry, but the death of the pope released him, in his own mind, from this undertaking, and he committed himself instead to the task of having Henry elected King of the Romans, thus establishing the succession and enabling himself to return to Sicily.

In 1220 Frederick achieved his ambition of being crowned emperor in Rome. He also renewed his crusading oath which had earlier been ignored by Innocent III. In 1218 Pope Honorius had been obliged to call on him to participate in a crusade which lacked united leadership, and by 1220 this need was all the more urgent. Following his coronation, however, Frederick was more concerned with his kingdom of Sicily and neglected his obligation to the disastrous crusade. He was permitted by Honorius to postpone his departure, promising in 1225 to set out in 1227. With this end in mind, he married Isabella of Jerusalem, his wife Constance, mother of Henry VI, having died in 1222. Isabella, sometimes called Yolande, was fourteen and the daughter of the King of Jerusalem, who held the title, however, from his deceased wife. It seemed desirable that a husband of Frederick's stature should present himself, to defend her inheritance, and to assume, as he did with alacrity, the title of King of Jerusalem.

Although he did commence the postponed crusade in August 1227, he almost immediately became very ill, stricken with the same affliction, which may have been typhoid or cholera, which claimed many of his men, including his close friend and deputy, Ludwig IV von Thüringen, son of Hermann I, who had been one of the great patrons of German literature until his death in 1217. Although there is no reason to suppose that Frederick's illness was other than genuine, it gave the new pope, Gregory IX, an excuse to excommunicate him on the grounds that he had broken his oath.

When he was fully recovered, he prepared to depart again in June 1228, against the expressed command of the pope. Frederick saw it as imperative to succeed in a crusade if he were to put pressure on the papacy and secure his rule in the Empire and in Sicily. As King of Jerusalem he was expected to destroy Islam, and this was his route to universal authority. By 1229 he had recovered the most important areas conquered by Saladin, and he had himself crowned in the Church of the Holy Sepulcher in Jerusalem, asserting that his authority came from God.

The return of Jerusalem was achieved by negotiation with al-Kamil, and this conquest by diplomacy was suspect to both Muslims and Christians. The pope, for his part, seized the opportunity of the absence of the impenitent and excommunicated crusader to engage in war against Sicily, left now undefended and, as he saw it, wrongfully held by Frederick.

His claim to the title of King of Jerusalem was contested when, soon after the birth of his son Conrad, his wife Isabella died. Amid accusations—unproven and actually against all sense in the circumstances—that he had been responsible for her death, it was maintained that the rightful heir to his mother's title was the child. Conrad IV did indeed bear the title King of Jerusalem in the future, though Frederick continued to lay claim to it for the time being. Having placed Germany in the decidedly unstable care of his son Henry, Frederick returned from the Holy Land to Italy. He did not return to Germany until 1235, when the rebellion of his son Henry forced him to take action.

Henry had been crowned king at Aachen in 1222 and placed by his father under the guardianship of Ludwig von Wittelsbach, Duke of Bavaria and Count Palatine of the Rhine. Some mystery surrounds the murder of Ludwig in 1231, and it may indeed have been a consequence of his undue influence on his ward, which seemed to have led to an alienation of the latter from his father and Frederick's suspicion that his son was too close to the pope for his liking. The action which Frederick took was extreme, but, in the opinion of some, justified by his desire to preserve his Empire. Henry was arrested and imprisoned in various places, until his suicide in 1242, committed, it is believed, because he feared that his father had worse in store for him, but Frederick apparently lamented his son's death deeply.

Assessments of the reign of Frederick II differ, depending on the perspective from which it is viewed. A fascinating and complex figure, he achieved much, but not for Germany, although we cannot overlook his impact as a patron of literature. His obsession with his mother's kingdom led to his virtual neglect of the larger part of his Empire. Yet for some spectators, the glory of the Hohenstaufen house attaches to him, despite the fact that he presided over its decline. He failed to exploit the great potential of the German nation, and he allowed internal strife, not least within his own family and among his own supporters, to dissipate the inherent energy of the vast regions under his crown.

The death of Frederick II in 1250 marked an important turning-point, signalling the end of the dominance of the German Empire and heralding an era when one can more accurately speak of its individual components. Of course this was not an abrupt change, and much of the 13th century is characterized by uncertainty and crisis.

It is probably true to say that the social changes of the period determined the literary environment and accounted for some of the literary developments. Crucially it was a courtly culture deriving from France but developing native German features which promoted the environment in which the remarkable literature of the "classical" MHG period flourished. The literary centers were the great courts of Europe, the imperial court itself but increasingly the smaller courts of powerful and discriminating princes, for whom the patronage of literature could reflect on their own prestige and ensure them lasting fame. Some of these patrons were surely motivated by altruism and even considerable aesthetic judgment in their nurturing of literature at courts which, with the focus on lavish feasts and celebrations, provided the ideal venue for the encouragement of artistic talent. Indeed, some of the patrons were also not undistinguished performers themselves, particularly in the field of the love lyric, and well-equipped to influence the manner and the standard of the presentations they were supporting. In some cases it was the noble ladies who exerted an influence, since the knights very often left the task of learning to read to their women-folk. Although there is a dearth of hard evidence of the patronage of ladies, the outstanding example of Queen Eleanor of Poitou cannot have been entirely isolated, and, as the Middle Ages progressed, other less well-known ladies are mentioned, often in passing it is true, as having had an impact on individual works in German. In the course of the 13th century, other patrons emerged: significant merchants and members of influential local families in a society which was moving increasingly into the towns.

During the period under consideration, Germany passed from being an essentially agrarian country to being a land peppered with towns, many of them little more than large villages, but some of them important centers of the growing commerce. From an essentially feudal society, with its sharp divisions between the nobility and the peasantry, there emerged a society in which new groupings formed and gained eminence. Although the larger part of the population was made up of poor people, craftsmen and merchants looked to their own ranks for leadership and power. The new classes gained in confidence with the increasing demand for their skills. Economic expansion, the growth of the towns and the greater mobility of the population were all factors which affected the literature of the thirteenth and fourteenth centuries. Among the factors which account for the growth of literacy is the need of merchants to communicate on a day-to-day basis. The increasing use of the vernacular to support the ever more complex demands of administration meant that a basic level of literacy became a possibility for a broader range of the population. Increasingly during the thirteenth century the education of the laity was a factor which accounted for a change of emphasis in the nature of literature. Literacy and with it literature were no longer the prerogative of the Church, and restrictions were lifted in many directions. Education brought with it a greater receptivity to new thoughts and ideas, and this at a time when the relatively circumscribed world of the earlier Middle Ages had been opened up by the Crusades. This meant an exposure to a wider, more exotic dimension and the intermingling on many levels of challenging new forces.

From the peak of courtly literature in Germany, around 1200, we can observe a gradual broadening of perspective which gains in momentum as the century progresses, though not without some efforts to maintain the status quo. The élitist literature of the *Blütezeit*, works aimed at the nobility and composed for the most part by its members or at least by those for whom chivalry was an important guiding ethos, gives way to a wider range in which accepted values can be challenged and even overthrown. Gradually the previously inconceivable begins to happen: works of literature start to concern themselves with the lower classes, are directed at much more mixed audiences, and the poets are no longer exclusively from the upper classes or at least composing under their patronage. Side by side with this widening of the horizons of literature is a broadening in its artistic range by the addition of new genres and the development of original and experimental forms.

### History (1170-1273)—Bibliography

Abulafia, David. *Frederick II. A Medieval Emperor*. London: Allen Lane (Penguin), 1988; Paperback: London, NY, etc.: Oxford UP, [2]1992.

The most recent major study of Frederick II, it really brings the subject to life. Excellent maps of pertinent areas.

Ehrismann, Otfrid, and Hans Heinrich Kaminsky. *Literatur und Geschichte im Mittelalter*. Kronberg/T: Athenäum. 1976.

A useful paperback which puts the literature of the "Stauferzeit" into its historical background.

Fleckenstein, Josef (Bernard S. Smith, trans.). *Early Medieval Germany*. Amsterdam, New York, Oxford: North-Holland, 1978 (= Europe in the Middle Ages. Selected Studies, 16).

Fuhrmann, Horst. *Deutsche Geschichte im hohen Mittelalter von der Mitte des 11. bis zum Ende des 12. Jahrhunderts*. Göttingen: Vandenhoeck & Ruprecht, 1978. Engl. trans. by Timothy Reuter. *Germany in the High Middle Ages, c. 1050-1200*. Cambridge: Cambridge UP, 1986.

Kantorowicz, Ernst. *Frederick the Second 1194-1250*. (Authorized English Version by E.O. Lorimer), London: Constable, 1931.

A stimulating account, quite controversial in some of its views.

Masson, Georgina. *Frederick II of Hohenstaufen. A Life*. London: Secker and Warburg, 1957.

A very readable account, with a tone and emphasis different from Abulafia and Kantorowicz, and worth reading as a complement to either or both.

Riley-Smith, Jonathan. *The First Crusade and the Idea of Crusading*. Philadelphia: Univ. of Pennsylvania Press, 1986. Paperback, 1991.

____. *The Crusades. A Short History*. London: Athlone, and New Haven: Yale UP, 1987.

____. *What Were the Crusades?* London: Macmillan, [2]1992.

This little book (97 pages) attempts to answer the question posed by the title and reveals its very complex nature. See also the two items above for more detail.

Runciman, Steven. *A History of the Crusades*. 3 vols. Cambridge: Cambridge UP, 1951-54.

Now somewhat dated but still much valued.

### A Note on the Language of the Period

During the latter decades of the 12th century, the German language came into its own as a written means of communication for a wide range of activities and, centrally for us, for literature. Although Latin continued to be used in many areas of a society which was to a large extent dominated by the Church, the growing society of knights and citizens turned increasingly to the vernacular. The growth of literacy led to the demand for secular literature, and the obvious medium was German. Although Latin remained the official language, German was often used alongside it. There is thus extant a large number of manuscripts dealing with everyday matters in Germany, and, by virtue of the fact that they were, broadly speaking, legal documents, they were very frequently dated. It is thus possible to form a reasonably sound impression of the state of the language and the distribution of dialects. The provenance of a particular document, however, may not be assumed with absolute certainty. The scribe, for example, may have used a form of German different from that implied by the place of origin as indicated on the seal.

The knowledge thus gained may be applied, albeit with considerable caution, to the literary works of the age. These are rarely dated, and information about author and origin must be pieced together from the available evidence. When working with texts, it is important to realize that in most cases the extant manuscripts are very much later than the original composition. Manuscripts representing the earliest written form of the work are rare and often fragmentary. When multiple copies exist, these often contain considerable variations, suggesting that copies were made from copies and display evidence of several hands at work within one manuscript. Obviously the quality of the scribes varied, and we know that some were scrupulous in copying while others may have taken it upon themselves to "correct," emend, add, or subtract on occasion. Very often the original language will have been contaminated with the language of the scribe, which may well be chronologically or geographically distant from it, or perhaps both. Since most of the literary texts of the Hohenstaufen period are handed down to us in manuscripts produced mainly in southern Germany, it is the language of Alemannia and East Franconia which prevails, whatever the origin of individual poets.

The apparent uniformity of language found in many edited texts today almost certainly did not exist but is rather the result of attempts by certain eminent literary scholars, headed by Karl Lachmann in the first half of the 19th century, to promote the idea of a standard language for the classical MHG period. Thus many of the great works of the period can be read in a pleasant and accessible form which is, however, a largely artificial language. For a more realistic impression of their original state, one has to go to the manuscripts themselves. Fortunately, these are now becoming increasingly available in facsimile editions, or in editions which are more faithful in recording the manuscript versions, however taxing these may be for the modern reader.

Nevertheless, it seems likely that there was a certain amount of standardization in the language used for the transmission of literary works. The courtly language which the poets employed was probably different from the regional dialect of their normal communication, but this is not really an argument for the existence of a single standard language. A much more obvious unifying factor was the sheer uniformity of subject matter. This means that there is a relatively circumscribed range of vocabulary and phraseology. Central ideas of chivalry and courtly lifestyle are expressed in words and phrases which inevitably recur, but this is less indicative of a standardized language than of the consistency of the content of the literary works. In addition, imitation and the concept of an exemplary mode of expression undoubtedly played an important part in the composition of literary works, whether lyric or narrative, courtly or heroic.

Naturally enough, it is the language of chivalry which dominates any study of the German language of the late 12th century and the 13th. Here the native German word often survived side by side with the adopted counterpart from French or Provençal (thus, for example, *rîter* and *chevalier, geselleschaft* and *massenîe, vroide* and *joie, sicherheit* and *fianze*). At the same time, the distinction between the ethos of the courtly romances and the heroic epics is frequently discernible in the preference in the latter (particularly the *Nibelungenlied* and *Kudrun*) for nouns and adjectives regarded as old-fashioned or even unseemly by their "courtly" contemporaries: thus, nouns like *helt, degen, recke* were largely covered by the courtly *rîter* in the works of Hartmann and Wolfram, while the *Nibelungenlied* and *Kudrun* express approval in terms like *balt, ellenhaft, snel*, adjectives rarely used in the courtly romance which favors the seemingly more elegant *edel, küene, wert*.

The literature of the latter decades of the 12th century and on into the 13th was increasingly influenced by French culture. French customs, manners, and dress spread from west to east into German-speaking areas during this time and interest in the more fashionable French literature grew rapidly. France became the treasury of good behavior and noble concepts, and it is therefore not surprising that French words and expressions were taken up in German, in many cases to be adopted, modified and to occupy a permanent place in the German language, even after the decline of chivalry made some of the vocabulary redundant. There are words which occur in modern German and raise no comment but whose existence in the language derives from this period, when they were taken into German from their French sources and accorded a permanent place in the language. In many cases their French origin is barely identifiable, save to the informed linguist. R. E. Keller (see LANGUAGE—BIBLIOGRAPHY; Chapt. 5, "The Hohenstaufen Flowering," 236-335), in his thorough survey of the "borrowed vocabulary" of this period, lists a great many words which relate to "chivalry and its life" (e.g., *Abenteuer, Admiral, Fasan, Plan, Thron, Turm*), to "warfare and equipment" (e.g., *Banner, Buhurt, Harnisch, Turnier*), "entertainment" (e.g., *Melodie, Pinsel, Posaune, Tanz*), "luxury goods" (e.g., *Alabaster, Ingwer, Rosine, Scharlach, Zinnober*).

Keller also demonstrates that it was not only French which influenced German at this time, although this had the strongest impact but that, leaving aside the language of courtly literature, German was enriched from other sources, too—Flemish and Dutch and Italian, and, with lasting implications for the modern German language, from Latin (*Advokat, Argument, Disziplin, Element, Metall, Provinz, Prozeß, Regiment, Student, Text, Universität*, to name but a few of the very common words which he cites as dating from this period).

For further detailed information on the language of the classical MHG period, see Maurer/Rupp ("Die höfische Blütezeit," 189-253), Schieb ("Mittelhochdeutsch," 347-385) and Penzl (*Mittelhochdeutsch*) in LANGUAGE—BIBLIOGRAPHY (p. 5 f.), in addition to Keller (above).

## Middle High German Language—Bibliography

Gärtner, Kurt, and Hans Hugo Steinhoff. *Minimalgrammatik zur Arbeit mit mittelhochdeutschen Texten*. Göppingen: Kümmerle, 1976 (= GAG, 183).
Summary overview of the differences between MHG and NHG.

Paul, Hermann/ Mitzka, Walter. *Mittelhochdeutsche Grammatik*. Tübingen: Niemeyer, [18]1960.
One of the comprehensive, standard MHG grammars.

Saran, Franz/ Nagel, Bert. *Das Übersetzen aus dem Mittelhochdeutschen*. Tübingen: Niemeyer, [3]1957.
Excellent advice for translators, sample translations from well-known MHG texts, metrics, and valuable glossary of important words of high-frequency, with etymologies.

Walshe, M. O'C. *Middle High German Reader, with grammar, notes and glossary*. Oxford: Oxford UP, 1974, and often reprinted.


## PRE-COURTLY EPICS

Not all EMHG literature had been concerned with religious matters. In the latter decades of the period (early to mid-12th century) several rather lengthy epics dealing with worldly affairs were composed by anonymous poets. These have frequently been referred to as *"Spielmannsepen"* (minstrel epics), although modern scholars are not particularly satisfied with the term, so that the term *"Spielmannsepen"* is usually preceded by *"sogenannte"* (so-called). It might be better to call them "pre-courtly epics," because they generally lack the elegant manners and setting of the courtly epic even though the action does take place at various courts. They are similar to courtly epics in that the hero is tested and proves his worth so that a happy ending results, but unlike courtly epics they are characterized by formula-like language (possibly a reflection of the oral poetry from which they seem to derive), an exaggerated manner of expression, great interest in rich clothing and armor, generosity in bestowing gifts, fantastic motifs, and burlesque comedy. Some may have been based on historical events and thus are related to later heroic epics like the Dietrich-epics (see p. 390 ff.). Five of the six epics included here all have the motif of a bridal quest (*Brautwerbung*), a common motif of the oral poetry of many countries. Two of the pre-courtly epics, *König Rother* and *Herzog Ernst*, probably result from the transformation of oral historical saga material into written epics, whereas the other three, *Oswald*, *Orendel*, and *Salman and Morolf*, deal with legendary material also from oral sources. *Graf Rudolf*, on the other hand, seems to have had an OF source, like the *Rolandslied* and the *Alexanderlied*, and it may well have been an oral version of a *chanson de geste*.

**König Rother** is an epic in rhymed couplets of about 5,200 lines. It exists in only one virtually complete manuscript (Heidelberg Cpg 390) from the end of the 12th century and in fragments of three other manuscripts that attest to its popularity well into the 14th century. The unknown author, surely an educated cleric, refers occasionally to the "books" as his source so that a written source may already have existed, although such references could be merely a device to substantiate the veracity of his tale. The language is a curious mixture of low and high German, but the poem seems to have been intended for a Bavarian audience, since names of two Bavarian noble families, the Tengelingen and the Dießen, occur. The name Rother may be a reflection of the Langobard king, Rothari (d. 652), yet his residence in the southern Italian city of Bari may suggest the influence of a more contemporary figure, the Norman king, Roger II of Sicily (d. 1154). The work is generally assumed to have been composed about 1160-70.

King Rother, acting on the advice of his nobles, who are concerned about the royal succession, decides to seek the hand of the beautiful daughter of King Constantine of Constantinople. This is no easy task because all previous suitors have lost their lives. Therefore, Rother is advised to send his trusted and devoted Count Lupold with eleven other counts as an embassy to King Constantine. Each count is to be accompanied by 12 knights magnificently equipped with costly armor, horses, clothing, and treasure. Upon arrival in Constantinople, they make an extremely favorable impression at court, especially on the queen, but when Lupold announces the purpose of their mission, Constantine refuses to promise them his daughter and has all the guests thrown into prison. He has the treasure seized that they had brought along on their ships, entrusting it to his chamberlain for safe keeping.

A year passes and Rother is distressed that his men have not returned. The mounting of a military campaign against Constantine is rejected since the men, if not already dead, would surely be killed when the army approached. An alternate plan is adopted: Rother is to go to Constantinople himself with a small group of his men disguised as Dietrich, a refugee who has been forced to leave Rother's lands. Among the vassals with him are King Asprian, a giant of fearsome appearance, and Witold, another threatening giant, who has to be kept in chains. Arriving in Constantinople, they frighten the inhabitants, but when Constantine hears Dietrich's story, he grants him asylum.

Dietrich demonstrates his generosity by lavish gifts to other refugees in the city and gains thereby an army of 5,000 men. Although intimidated by the giants, everyone is impressed by Dietrich, the queen in particular, who voices regret that Constantine had not given his daughter to Rother, arguing that he must really be the most powerful king, if he had indeed exiled a man of Dietrich's qualities. The princess's curiosity is piqued by what she hears about Dietrich, and she eventually arranges for him to come secretly to her chamber, where he reveals his true identity to her and she her favor for him. While not disclosing that Dietrich is Rother, they plan to get Rother's messengers released from prison, at least temporarily, as an act of Christian compassion. Dietrich pledges his life to Constantine that the prisoners will not leave the city. They leave their cells, get cleaned up and reclothed, and their quarters are refurbished. There is great rejoicing when Rother signals his identity by playing a certain melody on his harp, thus proving his true identity to the princess.

Suddenly news comes that the heathen King Ymelot from Cairo is approaching with the largest army ever assembled. "Dietrich" and his men, including the prisoners, offer to help Constantine. The two armies make camp near each other outside the city. At night, Rother and his men slip into the heathen camp and capture Ymelot, turning him over to Constantine as a prisoner. In the turmoil of the defeat of the heathen army, Rother returns quickly to Constantinople and spreads the word that Constantine has been killed. When the ladies ask for help, Rother has them brought to his ship, but he takes only the princess on board, disclosing his identity to the queen and telling her that the news of Constantine's defeat and death was merely a ruse to get the princess away. The queen is quite happy with this turn of events as Rother and the princess sail away, but Constantine is in a rage, lamenting the loss of his daughter. To make matters worse, Ymelot manages to escape also.

Upon his return to Bari, Rother finds that he needs to reassert control over his lands and travels to the north. In his absence, an unscrupulous minstrel sent by Constantine arrives in Bari. He uses a ruse to get the princess aboard his ship and sails back to Constantinople with her. When Rother returns he summons all his vassals and holds a council to determine what to do to get the princess back. They decide to take just 30,000 men to sail to the vicinity of Constantinople and to hide in the woods. Rother and a few others will enter the city disguised as pilgrims. There they learn that Ymelot had escaped and has now returned and captured Constantine. The princess is to be married to Ymelot's son that very evening. The "pilgrims" make their way into the banquet hall and hide under the table where the princess is seated. Rother slips her a silver ring with his name on it. This causes her to become so obviously elated that everyone is convinced that Rother must be somewhere in the hall.

Since all entrances are blocked, Rother and his men put their trust in God and arise from under the table. Given the choice of how he wishes to be executed, Rother chooses hanging in the forest (where his army is concealed!) but insists that all 30 heathen kings be present. All agree to go out there. Meanwhile the 5,000 men of the city, whom Dietrich/Rother had helped previously, arm themselves to go out to free him. When the gallows is being set up, those Christians attack and free Rother and his two companions. Then Rother blows his horn, and his army, including the giants Asprian and Witold, come rushing out of the woods to slaughter the heathens. Constantine and the city are spared for the sake of God, and the king brings his daughter and all the ladies out to meet Rother. The Queen, after accusing Constantine of the sin of arrogance, gives the princess back to Rother.

Rother, his wife, and his men return to Bari, where Rother's wife gives birth to a son, Pippin, who is later to become the father of Charlemagne. Rother rewards all his vassals with fiefs and lands, to which they all retire. Twenty-two years later, Pippin is knighted in Aachen, and Rother and his wife, following the advice of an old vassal, renounce the world and enter a monastery to prepare for the after-life.

We have recounted the events of the story in some detail in order to show many of the features of this type of epic: the council with the noble vassals, the bridal quest and re-quest, the great attention to feats of arms, the disguises, the clever ruses, the danger-ous situations, the stereotypical figures (e.g., Constantine), the fierce giants, and the noble and generous ruler. It is all high adventure, with occasional flashes of humor, that surely must have entertained a medieval audience. However, there is also a subtext that should not be overlooked: Rother is the very model of the ideal Christian ruler, and Constantine just the opposite. Rother seeks and accepts advice—Constantine is so arro-gant that he does not listen to anyone; his wife sees things more rationally than he does! Rother is exceedingly generous, altruistic—Constantine a bit reluctant to open his purse, except when circumstances force him to do so. Rother is fair-minded and merciful (though not necessarily to the heathens!)—Constantine is selfish, despotic, willing to deal with the heathens, and not always trustworthy. The remaining epics of this kind can be treated somewhat more summarily.

Text:
Frings, Theodor, and Joachim Kuhnt, eds. *König Rother.* 1922, repr. Halle, 1954,1961, and 1968 (= Altdt. Texte für den akademischen Unterricht, 2).
de Vries, Jan, ed. *König Rother.* Heidelberg, 1922 (= Germanische Bibliothek, 2. Abt. Bd. 13).
Pornbacher, Hans and Irmtraud, eds. *Spielmannsepen I.* Darmstadt: Wiss. Buchges., 1984. Pp. 1-222. Includes MHG text and close mod. Ger. re-telling.
*Curschmann/Glier*, I, No. 23 (Sel. with mod. Germ. trans.).

Translations:
Lichtenstein, Robert, trans. *König Rother. English.* New York: AMS Press, 1969. xv, 118 p. Repr. from the edition of 1966, Chapel Hill (= Univ. of North Carolina Studies in the Germanic Langs. & Lits., 36). (Engl. verse trans.).
Kramer, Günter, trans. *König Rother. Geschichte einer Brautwerbung aus alter Zeit.* Berlin, 1961. (Mod. Germ. trans.).
See also Pornbacher, H. and I. (above).

***Herzog Ernst*** lacks the bridal quest motif of *König Rother*, but there is much more adventure in the strange lands of the East to entertain an audience. In addition, the poem has a frame-story of political intrigue and warfare centering around the relationship of the Emperor and Duke Ernst of Bavaria that may reflect the problems of the empire during the 12th century.

Orphaned early in life, Ernst is raised by his mother, Duchess Adelheid of Bavaria, who eventually accepts an offer of marriage by the widower Emperor Otto. After the wedding Ernst comes to Otto's court and is initially treated as if he were Otto's own son. However, his privileged position is jeopardized by Heinrich, the jealous Count Palatine of the Rhine and nephew of Otto, who slanders Ernst by telling Otto that Ernst is conspiring with other princes to kill Otto and seize the throne. Although this is totally untrue, Otto believes it and sends Heinrich to Bavaria to pillage the countryside. Baffled and anxious, Ernst assembles his nobles and goes to Otto to declare his innocence and to beg him to relent, but Otto is adamant and insists that the nobles support him. Later, during an assembly of the court in Speyer, Ernst, his good friend Wetzel, and another man are able to get into the emperor's quarters and find him consulting with Heinrich. Ernst kills Heinrich, but Otto just barely escapes, declares Ernst an outlaw, and marches with the imperial army into Bavaria against Ernst. After resisting his attacks for over five years and almost at the end of his resources, Ernst gives up, deciding to go to the Holy Land with a few faithful men to fight the Saracens.

On the way to Constantinople, Ernst assembles quite an army of men. They then sail off in ships for the Holy Land. However, a storm destroys twelve of the ships, and Ernst in his ship is buffeted by the storm for three months before finally reaching land. At this point a series of encounters with strange creatures in different lands begins. (This comprises almost two-thirds of the entire poem and would be too long to describe in detail here. A summary accounting must suffice). In the land of Grippia they encounter strange creatures with heads and long necks like cranes; sailing from there, they are drawn inexorably to the magnetic mountain where they are shipwrecked; the surviving eight men are carried off by griffins as food for their young, but they manage to escape from the nest, travel out through an underground river, and find a wonderful jewel that later is to become the famous "orphan" in the German imperial crown; they come next to Arimaspi, a land of one-eyed people, whom they help fight against their enemies, a race of people with huge flat feet; then they fight long-eared people, help pygmies against the cranes, and defeat a race of giants. After six years in Arimaspi, Ernst and his company, including now representatives of the various people they had done battle with, leave and eventually return home via Babylon and Jerusalem. Ernst travels secretly from Bari to Rome and then on to Bamberg, where in the meanwhile Otto had realized that he had treated Ernst unjustly. Dressed as a pilgrim, Ernst begs Otto for forgiveness, finally receives it, and is reinstalled in his land as Duke of Bavaria.

There are two complete manuscripts of *Herzog Ernst*, one of which (Nürnberg 2285) bears the date 1441, the other (Vienna 3028) is also from the 15th century. This version, probably from the early 13th century, is called *Herzog Ernst B* to differentiate it from an earlier "A" version, of which we have three fragments. A comparison of the overlapping parts of "A" and "B" reveals that "B" has kept the same sequence of events while improving the rhyme and expanding some of the descriptions and dialogues to make it more "courtly," so that "B" may be considered a reasonable facsimile of the text of "A." There are ca. 6,000 lines in rhymed couplets. The language of "B" is Middle Franconian, whereas "A" is Rhine Franconian. A Latin letter in a Tegernsee manuscript compiled in 1186 requesting the loan of "the German book of Herzog Ernst," provides evidence that the earlier "A" version probably existed by ca. 1160. Some scholars believe that there may even have been an earlier Latin version of the tale. There are numerous later versions of *Herzog Ernst* both in German and Latin dating into the 15th and early 16th centuries to attest to its lasting popularity.

The sources for *Herzog Ernst* are of two sorts: people and events in German history for the frame-story and oriental fairy tale motifs, Greek and Roman ethnography, and Hellenistic travels. Whether the poet was acquainted with these through oral tradition or written Latin sources is uncertain. The names Otto and Adelheid are reminiscent of Otto the Great, whose second wife was Adelheid of Italy and whose son, Liudolf of Swabia rebelled against him in 953-55. However there are also similarities closer chronologically to the time of composition in the revolt of Duke Ernst of Swabia against his stepfather, Conrad II, in 1026-30, or the struggle of Henry the Proud of Bavaria against Conrad III and the feuding between the Welf and Staufen families in the 12th century. The political subtext this time seems to be the problematic relationship between the dukes of the realm and the emperor, where a rather tentative balance is ultimately achieved and the authority of the emperor maintained.

Texts:
Bartsch, Karl, ed. *Herzog Ernst*. Vienna, 1869. Repr. Hildesheim: Georg Olms, 1969.
See Pornbacher, Hans and Irmtraud (above), pp. 223-461.
See also Sowinski (below).

Translations:
Thomas, J. Wesley, and Carolyn Dussère, trans. *The Legend of Duke Ernst*. trans., with an introduction by J. W. T. and C. D. Lincoln: Univ. of Nebraska Press, 1979 (Engl. prose trans.).

Sowinski, Bernhard, trans. *Herzog Ernst. Ein mittelalterliches Abenteuerbuch.* In der mhd. Fassung B nach der Ausgabe von Karl Bartsch mit den Bruchstücken der Fassung A. trans., with notes and an afterword by B. S. Stuttgart: Reclam, 1970 (= UB, 8352-57). (MHG. text and mod. Germ. prose trans.).
See also Pornbacher, H. and I. (above).

The material for **Oswald** is the legendary life of St. Oswald, the historical King of Northumbria in the 7th century, described by Bede in the 8th century. It is difficult to discern precisely how the story traveled from England to Germany to become a pre-courtly epic, although St. Oswald was venerated in southern Germany in the 12th and 13th centuries. Still, we are not even sure that German versions existed in the EMHG period. Extant texts are in various manuscripts and printed versions from the 15th and 16th centuries and may be traced at most to the 14th century. Yet most scholars feel that a 12th century version probably did exist because of the bridal quest and other similarities to *König Rother*. It may be that *Oswald* lost favor with the courtly audiences of the 13th century, only to become popular again at a later time.

There are several different versions of *Oswald* in verse and in prose, but two main versions stand out: the so-called "Munich Oswald" (four mss. represented by Munich Cgm 719) with just over 3,500 lines in rhymed couplets in Bavarian dialect and the "Vienna Oswald" (three mss. represented by Vienna 3007) with 1465 verses in Silesian dialect. Of the two, Munich presents more entertaining adventure material, whereas the Vienna version stresses the edifying, Christian legendary side of the story. Obviously, the "Munich Oswald" has more of the characteristics of the pre-courtly "Spielmannsepen" that we are dealing with here.

Like Rother, Oswald seeks a suitable (equal in rank) bride and is advised by a pilgrim that he can find one overseas, a heathen princess named Pamige, whose father, Aran, kills all suitors. The pilgrim also advises Oswald to send a remarkable raven, suddenly divinely endowed with the power of speech, as his emissary. The raven flies to the east, enduring all sorts of trials on the way, and eventually wins the assent of the princess, who had secretly wanted to convert to Christianity all along. After a hazardous return trip the raven reports to Oswald, who sets out the next spring with a huge army to gain the princess. After journeying for over a year the army arrives near Aran's castle and makes camp. Oswald wants to send the raven to Pamige, only to discover that he had forgotten to bring the raven along. In response to Oswald's prayer for help, God sends an angel to England to fetch the raven, who miraculously reaches Oswald in four day's time. The princess, in conversation with the raven, advises Oswald to come to the castle with a smaller group of his men disguised as goldsmiths and to set up a tent before the walls and display their skill at making gold ornaments. As if miraculously, in response to Oswald's prayer, twelve of his men turn out to be master goldsmiths and the plan can be put into action.

King Aran is tricked into leaving the castle with his men to go hunting for the golden stag that the goldsmiths had fashioned. The princess then, with a little deception and some divine assistance, escapes from the castle, joins Oswald in his tent, and they immediately flee by ship. King Aran pursues them by sea with a great army and catches up with Oswald on a shore, where a great battle takes place, in the course of which all heathens are killed save Aran himself. Aran agrees to convert to Christianity if God will bring his men back to life and if water can be produced from the sheer face of a cliff. Both things happen;

Oswald baptizes all the heathens and returns to England with the princess. Before their marriage Christ appears in the guise of a pilgrim and begs Oswald for one thing after another, finally including his kingdom and Pamige, his bride-to-be. Each time Oswald is ready to honor his request, but Christ reveals himself, returns everything to Oswald, stipulating that Oswald and Pamige live in a chaste marriage. They do this for two years, after which they die and go directly to heaven. Oswald becomes one of the Fourteen Auxiliary Saints (Helpers in Need).

*Oswald* is, as can be seen, a strange mixture of adventure and pious legend. The mixture never quite succeeds. Oswald does practically nothing on his own. Whenever he needs help, divine assistance is at hand and more or less automatically gets him out of every tight situation. The most interesting character in the epic is the raven, who is given real human qualities. He is a Christian, likes to eat and drink, is easily offended and needs to be mollified; he plays chess and displays a very courtly manner while providing a certain amount of comedy for the story.

Text:
Curschmann, Michael, ed. *Der Münchner "Oswald."* Tübingen, 1974 (= ATB, 76).
Schröder, Walter J., ed. *Spielmannsepen II: "Sankt Oswald," "Orendel," "Salman und Morolf." Texte. Nacherzählungen, Anmerkungen und Worterklärungen.* Darmstadt: Wiss. Buchges., 1976. Pp. 1-130 (Text of Baesecke's edition of 1907, with close mod. Ger. retelling).

Translation:
Thomas, J. Wesley, trans. *The "Strassburg Alexander" and the "Munich Oswald."* Columbia, SC: Camden House, 1989. Pp. 83-118 (= Studies in German Literature, Linguistics, and Culture, 44).
See also Schröder, W. J. (above).

The story of **Orendel**, who acquires and wears the Seamless Garment of Christ, is even more a mixture of themes and motifs than *Oswald*: the bridal quest, crusading against the Saracens and the freeing of Jerusalem, the adventures of the late Hellenistic Appollonius of Tyre, the fairy tale of the youngest son who leaves home and wins the queen and her land, legendary material about the "Gray Garment of Christ" and its connection with the city of Trier, not to mention Christian miracles and saints' lives.

In very rough outline, Orendel, the third son of King Ougle of Trier, sets out with a huge army to win Bride, the Queen of Jerusalem, as his bride. After a series of terrible calamities, he arrives alone with God's aid at the home of a fisherman, who takes him on as a helper. Orendel obtains the "Gray Garment" which was found in the belly of a whale that he had caught and heads for Jerusalem wearing the garment. There he acquires armor, participates in a tournament, in which he defeats many knights. With God's help he also overcomes several giants and their armies and wins the hand of Bride as a result. However, an angel informs him that his marriage to Bride is not to be consummated for nine years.

There follows a series of battles with heathens in which Bride takes an active part in the fighting in defense of Jerusalem and elsewhere. An angel summons Orendel to return to Trier, which is under siege by the heathens. After successfully lifting the siege, Orendel leaves his "Gray Garment" hidden in a stone sarcophagus there and returns to Jerusalem. The city and the Holy Sepulcher are occupied by the heathens and must be freed in a number of struggles in which Bride again participates in important ways until the liberation is accomplished. At that point, an angel appears and tells Orendel and Bride that they must never consummate their marriage; they have only six months and two days to live. They immediately retire to a monastery and at the end of the allotted time they ascend to heaven.

*Orendel*, a poem of almost 4,000 lines in rhymed couplets, existed in only one manuscript from 1477 in Strasbourg. This was lost in the fire in 1870, but a copy from 1818 exists in Berlin (Ms. Germ. 817a). There are also two printed editions, both from 1512 in Augsburg, one in verse and one in prose, by two different printers using different sources. The time of composition is generally thought to be in the latter half of the 12th century and tied to the history of Trier, for it was in the 12th century that the church in Trier made its claim to possess the "Seamless Garment of Christ," culminating in the placing of the garment in the main altar of the cathedral in 1196. The printed versions of 1512 may have been in connection with the exhibition of the garment at Emperor Maximilian's request in that very year. The last public exhibition was in the summer of 1959. Nothing is known about the author who was probably a cleric, possibly from the vicinity of Trier. Stylistically, *Orendel* is characterized by its paratactic organization of episodes and the repetition of poetic formulas, perhaps hinting at an oral source. The figure of Queen Bride as an active participant in the fighting in close alliance with Orendel is unusual for a pre-courtly epic.

Texts:
Steinger, Hans, ed. *Orendel*. Halle: Niemeyer, 1935 (= ATB,36).
See also Schröder, W.J. (above), pp. 131-266. Steinger's text with following mod. Germ.
re-telling.

Translation:
Simrock, Karl, trans. 1845.
See Schröder, W.J. (above).

*Salman und Morolf* is another bridal quest story but this time with a twist:

Salman's wife is spirited away and must be regained. Of course, Salman (i.e., the Old Testament King Solomon, here the Christian King of Jerusalem) first wins his wife, Salme, against the wishes of her father, the heathen King Cyprian, and has her baptized. Another heathen king, Fore (= Pharaoh), wants Salme as his wife and comes to Jerusalem with an army to claim her. Salman defeats the army and takes Fore prisoner, but Fore with the aid of a magic ring makes Salme fall in love with him. She helps him escape and goes with him to heathen territory. Solomon's brother Morolf is sent as a pilgrim to Wendelsee in heathendom to find Salme, does locate her, is taken captive twice but finally succeeds in getting away to return to Jerusalem. Salman and Morolf then go to Wendelsee to get Salme back, and here the sequence of events is almost identical with those in King Rother's second trip to Constantinople, to regain his wife after she had been re-abducted by her father's minstrel (see above). Fore's sister returns to Jerusalem with them.

Salman and Salme remain in Jerusalem for seven years, during which time Salme bears Salman a son. However, at the end of seven years, Salme is abducted again, this time by the disguised King Princian of Akers (= Akkon), who makes her fall in love with him by dropping a magic ring into a goblet of wine and having her drink from it. They flee, and once again Morolf is dispatched to find Salme. He does so after a number of adventures and disguises and returns to Jerusalem with the news that she is in Akers. This time Salman does not go himself but sends Morolf with an army to get Salme back. He does this by freeing her from a prison on a cliff in the sea with the help of a mermaid and six dwarfs. Princian and his brother are killed in the ensuing fight, Morolf brings Salme back to Salman, and then kills the unfaithful woman while having her let blood. Salman mourns her death and has her buried in the cathedral. He then marries Fore's sister and lives with her for thirty more years.

There are several elements in this lively tale: Oriental saga material about the fabled King Solomon from Talmud and Kabbala sources, the apocryphal Testament of Solomon, and Muslim stories about him; the widespread tale of the Unfaithful Wife; and the late "Spruchgedicht von Salomon und Markolf" (14th century), in which Salomon's proverbial wisdom is lampooned in a "disputation" with Markolf, who has a witty, coarse, sometimes obscene counter for every profound pronouncement by Salomon. This part of *Salomon und Markolf* probably goes back to the biblical "Liber sapientiae," also known as the "Wisdom of Solomon" in the Apocrypha. It is followed in the poem by a series of comic tales (*Schwankerzählungen*), the last of which resembles a part of our *Spielmannsepos* and may share a common source with it. Stories about Solomon are also to be found among later Russian folk songs and tales, but the connection to the German versions is not clear.

At the center of *Salman und Morolf* is the enchanting beauty of Salme. She is irresistible to almost every man except Morolf, and the problem is how to keep Salme from the clutches of others who have succumbed to her beauty even at a distance. In this respect the relationship between man and wife is quite different from that in *Orendel* where Bride and Orendel are very devoted to one another. However, we never get the feeling that Salme is anything more than a fascinating trophy. In contrast to Bride she actually does very little on her own. The real main persona is, of course, the colorful and resourceful Morolf who dominates the action scene by scene and creates the dramatic and comic effects of the poem. He appears to have a rather acute insight into human nature, clearly recognizes that Salman is under Salme's spell, and eventually decides to put an end to it by killing her. Salman's subsequent marriage to Fore's sister provides a solution to the fateful love aroused by Salme in others.

Instead of rhymed couplets the anonymous poet uses a strophic form that is now generally known as the "Morolf"-strophe. It has the rhyme scheme: a, a, b, x, b, with x being a so-called "orphan" or unrhymed line. There are generally four stresses, with each line ending on a stressed syllable. As with the other *Spielmannsepen*, we have only late sources, four manuscripts from the late 15th century, one of which was lost in the Strasbourg fire of 1870, a fragment lost in Dresden in 1945, and two printed versions from the 15th and 16th centuries. One of the manuscripts is bound together with the *Spruchgedicht* "Salmon und Markolf." All the manuscripts seem to have been illustrated. The original is usually dated to the late 12th century because of the overlapping with *König Rother* which seems to have been borrowed from *Salman und Morolf* and the reference to Akkon as a Christian city, captured by the crusaders in 1191.

Texts:

Vogt, Friedrich, ed. *Die deutschen Dichtungen von Salomon und Markolf.* Halle, 1880 (repr. 1976).

Karnein, Alfred, ed. *Salman und Morolf.* Tübingen: Niemeyer, 1979. (ATB, 85).

See also Schröder, W. J. (above), pp. 267-429. Vogt's text, followed by mod. Germ. prose retelling.

Translation:

See Schröder, W. J. (above), pp. 399-429.

*Graf Rudolf* exists only in fourteen fragments from one manuscript totalling some 1,400 lines so that it is difficult to put together a coherent story from them (the leaves alpha-delta are in the Stadtbibliothek Braunschweig, sig. 5; and leaves A-K are in Göttingen, sig. Cod. Ms. philol. 187,4). Six parts of the tale have survived, but we can only speculate on what has been lost.

In the normal arrangement of the fragments there is, first, the pope's call for a crusade, which Graf Rudolf of Arras heeds, and his arrival in Jerusalem. The second part shows Rudolf fighting against the Saracens at Askalon in the service of the Christian King of Jerusalem. Third, the Christian king's ambition to have his court equal or surpass that of the Emperor in Rome and Rudolf's part in teaching it courtly attitudes and practices. Fourth, Rudolf fighting against the Christians in the service of the heathen King Halap and Rudolf's love for Halap's daughter. Fifth, in Constantinople, Halap's daughter is baptized under the name of Irmingart. Rudolf is apparently a prisoner somewhere else, but he escapes from prison and returns to Constantinople. Six, the beginning of his return journey home with Irmingart, interrupted by an attack by robbers.

There are several remarkable aspects to *Graf Rudolf*. It has a realism about it that other *Spielmannsepen* lack, perhaps reflecting actual conditions in the Holy Land at that time. The description of the fighting and Rudolf's escape from prison and his survival are realistically portrayed. Furthermore, courtly mores and practices, including the love story, play an important role, so that it seems to be a kind of transitional work between pre-courtly and early courtly literature, if one can make so fine a distinction. Certain events in it show a positive attitude towards the Saracens and appear to foreshadow Wolfram von Eschenbach's *Willehalm* (see below, p. 194 ff.): the Saracens are noble knights—the heathen King Halap, in fact, is more noble than the Christian King Gilot; women dressed as soldiers defending a castle; and the lament over the early death of a young nephew. In addition, Rudolf's fighting on the heathen side is more than just a means to a successful bridal quest.

The poem should be dated between 1170 and 1185, probably before the fall of Jerusalem in 1187. We know nothing about the author. The dialect seems to be a kind of northern Middle German, but whether it is Hessian or Thuringian is uncertain. Some attempts to identify the source as an OF *chanson de geste* have been made, but they are not convincing. There are few, if any, references to a source at all, although the poet does give his narrative persona some profile by occasionally commenting on the action. His language uses a number of formulaic expressions but in general is not stylistically very different from the epics discussed above. The poem lacks a beginning and an ending, where one might expect possibly to find something about a patron or a reason for writing it. On the whole, it is an intriguing work, tantalizing to the scholar.

Text:
Ganz, Peter F., ed. *Graf Rudolf*. Berlin: Erich Schmidt, 1964 (= PS&Q, 19).

Translation:
None available.

## Pre-Courtly Epics—Bibliography

Blamires, David. *Herzog Ernst and the Otherworld Voyage. A Comparative Study*. Manchester: Manchester UP, 1979.

A good English introduction to the poem and its place in world literature and the folklore of fantastic voyages.

Bräuer, R. *Literatursoziologie und epische Struktur der deutschen "Spielmanns"- und Heldendichtung*. Berlin: Akademie-Verlag, 1970.

Curschmann, Michael. *Der Münchener Oswald und die deutsche spielmännische Epik*. Munich: Beck, 1964 (= MTU, 6).

Extremely valuable, often cited as a basic study of the genre.

_____. *Spielmannsepik. Wege und Ergebnisse der Forschung von 1907-1965. Mit Ergänzungen und Nachträgen bis 1967*. Stuttgart: Metzler, 1968.

Excellent review of research for the period covered.

Gellinek, Christian. *König Rother. Studie zur literarischen Deutung*. Bern: Francke, 1968.

Haug, Walter. "Das Komische und das Heilige. Zur Komik in der religiösen Literatur des Mittelalters." In: Schröder, Werner, ed. *Wolfram Studien*, VII. Berlin: Erich Schmidt, 1982. Pp. 8-31.

Discussion of the general topic, then specifically on the Munich *Oswald*.

Meves, Ulrich. *Studien zu König Rother, Herzog Ernst und Grauer Rock (Orendel)*. Frankfurt/M.: P. Lang, 1976.

Schröder, Walter Johannes. *Spielmannsepik*. Stuttgart: Metzler, 1962, [2]1967 (= Sammlung Metzler, D, 19).

A handy volume with concise information on the topic and fairly detailed plot summaries. Bibliography but now dated.

_____, ed. *Spielmannsepik*. Darmstadt: Wiss. Buchges., 1977 (= WdF, 385).

A collection of significant articles on the topic, reprinted from various journals, etc.

Urbanek, Ferdinand. *Kaiser, Grafen und Mäzene im "König Rother."* Berlin: Erich Schmidt, 1976 (= PSuQ, 71).

Waremann, Piet. *Spielmannsdichtung. Versuch einer Begriffsbestimmung*. Amsterdam: J. van Campen, 1951.

See also the introduction to Peter Ganz's edition of *Graf Rudolf* (above) and his article in *VL*[2] 3 (1981): 212-216 for further information and bibliography.

# EARLY COURTLY ROMANCES

There are basically three types of Old French narrative literature that were adopted and adapted in Germany: the *chansons de geste*, dealing with Charlemagne and his paladins; the *romans d'antiquité*, which produced vernacular versions of many of the Greek and Roman tales; and the *romans courtoises*, whose subject matter stems from Celtic sources and includes the stories of King Arthur and his knights. We have already mentioned an early German version of the first type, Konrad's **Rolandslied** (see p. 94), and Lamprecht's **Alexander** (see p. 93 f.) is an example of the second. However, they are not courtly epics, and we have included them in the category of EMHG historical literature. Nor are the *Spielmannsepen* that we have called pre-courtly epics truly "courtly," although we could discern some courtly characteristics in several. Despite the fact that they usually involve bridal quests, notably missing from all of them is the figure of the courtly lady and the motif of courtly love, celebrated in the love lyrics of the Occitan and French troubadors/trouvères and the German minnesingers (see section on Minnesang, pp. 224 ff.).

Courtly literature is literature that is centered on courtly life, produced for a courtly audience, and composed to reflect the tastes and idealized values of the thin upper stratum of medieval society that composed the court, the nobility. Elegant manners and appearance were most important. Proper bearing and breeding were indispensable, and honor, reputation, and fame were qualities to strive for with courage and knightly skill. Largesse was a mandatory virtue, and anyone who was interested in material gain for its own sake was surely of low status, not courtly. Above all, the pursuit of courtly love, that paradoxical sublimation of emotions, appears to have fascinated noblemen and ladies alike, whether practiced as described in literature or not.

The court was not only the focus of the courtly narrative, it also provided the poets with the economic support that made it all possible. We know relatively little about most of the poets themselves, but it is generally assumed that they were laymen, probably with a clerical education, in the service of a feudal lord and commissioned to write. The tastes of the lord undoubtedly determined the choice of subject matter for the narrative, yet the personality of the poet is undeniably apparent in most instances.

This new type of literature developed very rapidly in the span of one generation in Germany alongside some of the more traditional poetry. Stylistic changes occurred that made the "earlier" literature appear dated and clumsy. The strophic form of heroic poetry disappeared in favor of the rhymed couplets of French courtly narrative, and the tendency towards more regular metrical patterns, especially in the number of unaccented syllables between the four main stressed syllables in each line, increased. The new narrative literature was meant to be read, either privately or aloud before an audience, whereas the older literature in stanzas was undoubtedly sung. Poets seem to have tried to avoid rhymes that would not be pure in other dialects, although assonance still persisted. In addition there were lexical changes brought about by the adoption of fashionable words and expressions from the French into German. The language of German chivalry, for instance, was dominated by the French terms of courtly life.

## Early Courtly Romances—Bibliography

Ruh, Kurt. *Höfische Epik des deutschen Mittelalters. Teil 1. Von den Anfängen bis zu Hartmann von Aue.* Berlin: Erich Schmidt, [2]1977 (= GLG, 7).

A comprehensive monograph on the genre. The first part covers what we have called "precourtly" and "early courtly" epics of the 12th century, including the "courtly" Arthurian romances of Hartmann von Aue.

Two epic poems mark the beginning of German courtly literature: The ***Tristrant*** of Eilhart von Oberge and the ***Eneide*** of Heinrich von Veldeke. Eilhart's work is based on the so-called *"estoire,"* a postulated OF *roman courtoise*, and Heinrich's is a German re-working of the OF ***Romans d'Eneas***, a *roman d'antiquité*.

Eilhart von Oberge's ***Tristrant*** (note spelling!) is probably the oldest complete version of the tragic love story of Tristan and Isolde of which we have any definite knowledge. It may have had the same source as the OF fragmentary versions by Beroul and Thomas, but it is quite different from them and may be closer to the original *"estoire."* Gottfried von Straßburg's fragmentary version, which people usually think of when Tristan and Isolde are mentioned, definitely has Thomas's version as its source (see p. 157 f.). Eilhart's version is usually dated to about 1170, but there is a considerable difference of opinion among scholars about that, with some arguing for a later date. The main problem is whether Eilhart's work precedes Heinrich von Veldeke's *Eneide* or follows it.

Attempts have been made to identify Eilhart with a certain Eilhardus de Oberge, a vassal of Henry the Lion, whose name is mentioned in eight legal documents from 1189-1207. A town named Oberge still exists today near Braunschweig, and this would fit well with the idea that Eilhart's original poem was written in Low German. However, a dating that late would seem to conflict with the style of the poem and certain other features that speak for an earlier date and a Middle German dialect. Furthermore, the area of the lower Rhine where French courtly literary influence was felt earliest would be more likely. The poet is therefore considered to have been of the generation before the recorded Eilhardus, probably a member of the same family who had traveled to that lower Rhine area. There is also a possible connection to the court of Countess Agnes of Loon (Looz), the patroness of Heinrich von Veldeke. Her daughter married the first Wittelsbach, Otto von Scheyern, and that might account for the existence of the early Regensburg *Tristrant*-fragments.

The poet is named in the three complete manuscripts that do exist as, variously, "von Hobergin her Eylhart" (D), "vom Baubenberg Segehart" (H), and "von Oberengen Enthartte" (B), and in the late prose version (P, printed 1484 or 1498) he is called "Filhart von oberet." The three manuscripts are late paper manuscripts: Dresden (D) dated 1433, East Middle German; Heidelberg (H) between 1460-75, Swabian; and Berlin (B) dated 1461, Swabian, which contains Gottfried's unfinished *Tristan* supplemented by the conclusion of Eilhart's *Tristrant*. It is difficult to say whether these manuscripts represent Eilhart's original work or whether they reflect the results of a courtly revision of the 13th century as has been suggested. There are also three groups of early fragments: Magdeburg (M), parchment, end of 12th century, Upper German with Low German elements;

Regensburg (Rd, Rm, Rr), parchment, end of the 12th century, Upper German; and Stargard (St), parchment, end of the 12th-beginning of the 13th century, Middle German. In addition there is a Czechoslovakian *Tristram* (C), a translation based on various sections of Eilhart, Gottfried, and Heinrich von Freiberg, in two manuscripts: Strahov, 1449, and Stockholm, 1483. Finally, there are two prints of the prose romance *Histori von Tristrant und Ysalden* (P) of 1484 and 1483 and 14 other prints up to 1664, thus attesting to the continuing popularity of the work.

In the prologue the narrator admonishes his listeners to behave and not disturb the telling of the story because it is a useful one, tells the truth about Tristrant and Isalde, and is a story of both joy and grief.

The story itself begins with the circumstances surrounding Tristrant's birth and early life: he is the son of Blankeflur, the sister of King Marke of Cornwall, who has eloped with Rivalin of Lohenois. Blankeflur gets sick and dies at sea, her son is cut from her womb and survives. As he grows up Tristrant is instructed in all courtly manners and practices by Kurneval, a squire. These include knightly combat and other physical skills, courtly behavior, and the ability to play the harp and other instruments.

As a youth, Tristrant, wishing to see foreign lands, travels to Cornwall with Kurneval and a retinue, which is pledged not to reveal his identity, and offers to serve King Marke. Impressed by Tristrant's excellent manners, Marke takes him on, and Tinas, the lord high steward, becomes Tristrant's protector and mentor.

When Morolt of Ireland arrives, demanding tribute from Marke, Tristrant asks to be knighted, reveals his noble lineage, and persuades the reluctant King Marke to allow him to fight Morolt in single combat, when no other nobleman is willing to accept Morolt's challenge.

The duel takes place on an off-shore island. Tristrant wounds Morolt mortally with a blow through the helmet, leaving a sword splinter embedded in the wound, but Tristrant is wounded himself by Morolt's poisoned spear. Morolt is taken home by his men but dies before Isalde can cure him, though she does remove the splinter from his skull and saves it. No doctor can heal Tristrant's festering wound so that he finally asks to be put in a boat alone with his harp to die at sea rather than to annoy people with the stench. Driven by a storm, Tristrant is washed up on the shore of Ireland, where he pretends to be a minstrel, attacked by robbers at sea. Princess Isalde is finally able to heal the poisoned wound, and Tristrant eventually returns to Cornwall.

Marke wants to make Tristrant his heir, but his closest relatives urge him to take a wife. Marke finally agrees to marry, but only the woman whose strand of golden hair had been dropped in the hall by a swallow. The relatives are unhappy, but Tristrant offers to find the woman, to prove that he was not seeking to be Marke's heir himself. With a group of 100 men, he sets sail, trying to avoid Ireland (anyone from Cornwall found there is to be killed immediately!), but unfortunately they are swept there by a gale.

Once again Tristrant resorts to a ruse, assuming the name of Tantris and claiming that he and his men are merchants hoping to sell their wares in Ireland. Hearing about a dragon that has been plaguing the land and fearing that he may be discovered, Tristrant decides to die attempting to kill the dragon rather than wait and be killed. The next day he comes upon the dragon, kills it, and cuts the tongue out, but is badly burned in the process. He goes to a spring to cool off, puts the tongue under his armor, and lies down in the spring in pain. The lord high steward finds the dead dragon and, believing the person who had killed the dragon to be dead, decides to claim that he had slain it and also to claim the reward that the king had offered: the hand of Princess Isalde in marriage.

Isalde cannot believe that the steward had actually killed the dragon, rides out with two trusted servants, Brangene and Perenis, finds the unconscious Tristrant, and brings him back. She bathes him herself and revives him, but while cleaning his sword as he is lying in the bath, she notices the notch in it, and remembers the splinter from Morolt's skull. It fits the notch exactly! Although Isalde wants to kill Tristrant out of revenge, Brangene points out that, if she does so, she will have to marry the cowardly steward. Rather than do that, she gets her father to pardon the man who had killed the dragon. Tristrant, having compared Isalde's hair with the one found by Marke, realizes that Isalde is the woman he is seeking, and after forcing the steward to back down, asks for Isalde's hand for Marke. The king agrees and lets Isalde go.

To assure success in the marriage between Isalde and Marke, Brangene is given a love potion for the two to drink at their wedding. The potion has the effect that those who drink it will always love one another, but for four years they will have to be together daily or suffer sickness; if they do not speak to one another for a week, they will die. On the voyage back to Cornwall, Tristrant and Isalde put into a harbor to rest. They drink the potion by mistake and become sick. Brangene knows what has happened when she finds the potion missing and tells Kurneval, who arranges for Tristrant to go to Isalde. Tristrant does so, and they become lovers, thereby curing their illness.

Once Tristrant and Isalde are back in Cornwall, the problem arises as to how to keep Marke from finding out that Isalde is no longer a virgin. On the wedding night, Tristrant arranges that there be no lights in the room, and Brangene is substituted for Isalde in Marke's bed. Tristrant and Isalde then sleep together, in the same room with Marke and Brangene, and the substitution is never discovered.

There follows a series of escapades in which the lovers manage to meet secretly and avoid discovery, but Marke's vassals are suspicious and denounce Tristrant. Marke does not want to believe them, and they continue their plotting to trap Tristrant and Isalde. Eventually Tristrant is caught almost in the act when a wound in his leg opens while he is in bed with Isalde, leaving an unmistakable trace of blood. Both Tristrant and Isalde are sentenced to death, but on the way to his execution Tristrant manages to escape by leaping from the window of a chapel which he had been allowed to enter for prayer and by landing safely in the water far below.

Isalde is given to the lepers to suffer the most shameful death, but Tristrant rescues her, and they flee together to the forest. There they build a hut and live by hunting game and fishing. It is a hard life, and they suffer greatly despite their love. Tristrant always sleeps with his drawn sword between them, and that custom serves them to good advantage when Marke's hunter discovers the lovers asleep. He runs to tell Marke, who comes alone, sees the sword, replaces it with his own, and lays his glove on Isalde without awakening either of them. However, they realize that Marke has been there, fear that he will return to kill them, and flee deeper into the woods. Four years after having drunk the potion, when its power has begun to wane, Tristrant goes to the hermit Ugrin, who advises him to give Isalde back to Marke. Marke agrees to take Isalde back, but Tristrant must leave the country. Tristrant does so, leaving his dog to Isalde.

After some time at King Arthur's court as one of his knights and a return to Marke's court on a hunting expedition with Arthur and his men, in the course of which he is unsuccessful in being together with Isalde, Tristrant travels to another land where he makes the acquaintance of Kehenis, whose sister, Isalde White Hands, Tristrant eventually marries, although he knows that she is not the equal of Isalde. The marriage is not consummated for a year, and Isalde White Hands complains about it to her brother, who confronts Tristrant. To show Kehenis that Isalde is superior to his sister, Tristrant and Kehenis go to Marke's court, arrange for a secret meeting with Isalde, and Kehenis is forced to admit that Tristrant is right in his assessment. This is the first of a series of trips that Tristan makes in various disguises to see Isalde.

The remainder of the poem deals with the various adventures of Tristrant and Kehenis, who assist each other in many ways. In the course of the last of these, Kehenis is killed and Tristrant severely wounded by a poisoned lance. Knowing that only Isalde can heal him, Tristrant sends a message to Cornwall, asking Isalde to come. However, she arrives too late. Tristrant has already died, having been told that she was not coming, whereupon Isalde lies down beside the dead Tristrant and dies herself. In an afterword by Eilhart, we learn that Marke was finally told about the potion and regretted greatly that he did not know in time to have treated them better. He has a rosebush planted over Isalde's grave and a grapevine over Tristrant's. The two vines grew together inseparably.

Several features of Eilhart's poem mark it as an early courtly epic. The overwhelming love of Tristrant and Isalde caused by the potion is a courtly form of the well-known irresistible Ovidian variety. It produces a genuine physical love-sickness in the two and is seen as an excuse for their adulterous behavior. Their love is a given, existing in its own right. The description of their reactions to this overpowering love, especially Isalde's, is something new in German literature (unless Heinrich von Veldeke's *Eneide* precedes it!). They examine their feelings, wondering in interior monologues what is happening to them after they have drunk the potion. Isolde's long discourse on her situation (ca. 200 lines) is especially noteworthy. In fact, Eilhart portrays their inner thoughts more than once as they ponder their options in various situations.

Another given is the courtly setting. Both Tristrant and Isalde are ideal creatures of the court, attractive, accomplished, born to courtly life. Marke's vassals, the barons, are quite properly intent on trying to maintain the king's honor, but in doing so become the enemies of the lovers. It is an actualization of the situation depicted in Minnesang: the feudal lord's wife has become his vassal's lady, and the courtiers have become the *huote*, those people at court who watch over every move the lovers make. In Eilhart's work both the lovers and feudal society are paradoxically justified in their positions, although Eilhart does not refer to this overtly. In a way, the one cannot exist without the other. Tristrant and Isalde discover this when they live together in the forest for four years. Despite their love, they are ultimately unable to remain away from the court and must return, even if it means separation.

Above all, it is a tale of knightly adventure like most courtly romances, not only a love story. Eilhart says in his prologue that "no one ever heard a better tale of worldly intent, of manhood, and of love." It is packed with action, risk-taking, combat, and intrigue. Tristrant lives every bit as much by his wits as by his sword. He seems to recognize that fate and luck play a large role in life, and he does not hesitate to take his chances.

Eilhart's style is quite straightforward. He has a tendency towards parataxis, stringing uncomplicated sentences together. In dialogue he frequently uses stichomythia, which enlivens his verse with its short alternating utterances and replies. He employs a narrative persona, who occasionally comments on the action or addresses his fictional audience with his opinions or questions. He uses assonance in rhyme but less as he goes along, judging from the old fragments. All in all, it is a well-structured, entertaining work that undoubtedly deserves the popularity it enjoyed.

Texts:
Lichtenstein, Franz, ed. *Eilhart von Oberge*. Strasbourg: Trübner, 1877 (= QuF, 19).
Bußmann, Hadumod, ed. *Eilhart von Oberge. Tristrant. Synoptischer Druck der ergänzten Fragmente mit der gesamten Parallelüberlieferung.* Tübingen: Niemeyer, 1969 (= ATB, 70).
Buschinger, Danielle, ed. & trans. *Eilhart von Oberg. Tristrant. Edition diplomatique des manuscrits et traduction en français moderne avec introduction, notes et index.* Göppingen: Kümmerle, 1976 (= GAG 202). Mss. H, D, and B.

Translations:
Thomas, J. Wesley, trans. *Eilhart von Oberge's Tristrant*. Lincoln & London: Univ. of Nebraska Press, 1978 (Engl. prose with lengthy introduction).
Buschinger, Danielle and Wolfgang Spiewok, transls. *Eilhart von Oberg. Tristrant und Isalde.* Göppingen: Kümmerle, 1986 (= GAG 436). (Mod. Ger. prose).
See also Buschinger, Danielle—text edition with modern French trans. (above).

Heinrich von Veldeke's **Eneide** is a landmark work in German courtly literature. Even contemporaries and immediate successors felt that courtly literature began with Heinrich. Gottfried von Straßburg in the famous review of poets in his *Tristan* credits Heinrich, saying: *er impfete daz erste ris / in tiutscher zungen* (4738 f.—he grafted the first shoot on [the tree of] the German language), and Wolfram von Eschenbach, among others, acknowledges Heinrich as his *meister*. Heinrich wrote not only the *Eneide* but also a life of the legendary St. Servatius and numerous lyric poems as well.

Heinrich was born near Hasselt in the Belgian province of Limburg in the area of the lower Rhine. At least a von Veldeke family is documented in the service of the Counts of Loon and of the monastery of St. Trond. His **Servatius** was written under the patronage of Agnes von Loon (documented until 1175) or her daughter of the same name, who married the Bavarian Duke Otto of Wittelsbach about 1169. Hessel, Dean of the Servatiusstift in Maastricht (documented 1171-76), also supported his work. Heinrich probably began work on the *Eneide* about 1170. According to the epilogue to the *Eneide*, he had finished almost four-fifths of that work by about 1175, when he gave the manuscript to Countess Margarete of Cleve to read. At her wedding to Landgrave Ludwig III of Thuringia, it was taken, much to the chagrin of Margarete, from a lady who was entrusted with it, by a Count Heinrich, presumably the brother of the Landgrave, and removed to Thuringia. Nine years later Heinrich was invited to Thuringia to finish his *Eneide* for the Count Palatine, later Landgrave, Hermann, who was a literary patron and at whose court a number of noted poets were supported. Hermann was particularly interested in the *romans d'antiquité* and commissioned the writing of German versions of several poems of that genre as well as of other genres. One further historical event is important for the chronology of Heinrich's life: Friedrich Barbarossa's famous court festival at Mainz in 1184, at which two of his sons received their swords. Heinrich mentions having been in attendance there when he describes the wedding celebration of Eneas and Lavinia in his *Eneide* as the greatest festival ever save Barbarossa's (13222-13252). Heinrich died presumably around 1200.

Heinrich's *Servatius*, a poem of some 6,000 lines, based on a Latin vita, is considered to be an earlier work. It falls into two distinct parts with roughly the same epilogue at the end of each. The first part describes the life of St. Servatius, the 4th century bishop who was born in Armenia but was called by God to Tongeren. He moved later to Maastricht, where he was captured by the Huns. Although he managed to convert Attila to Christianity, at least for a time, the city was eventually ravaged and Servatius died. Immediately, miracles were reported at his gravesite, and these comprise the material for the second part of the poem. Only fragments from ca. 1200 of the original work are extant, but there is a revision of the complete poem in a manuscript of the 15th century. The language of the fragments is in Veldeke's native Limburg dialect, and that supports the position that the poem was originally written in that dialect.

The original language of the *Eneide* is much more problematical. There are seven more or less complete manuscripts (B= Berlin, early 13th cent.; H= Heidelberg, 14th cent.; M= Munich, 13/14th cent.; E= Eibach, 14th cent.; h= Heidelberg, 15th cent.; G= Gotha, 15th cent.; w= Vienna, 1474) and seven fragments, a very rich manuscript tradition, which attests to the popularity and importance of the work. Three of the manuscripts are illustrated, one of them (B) is exceptionally beautiful.

Although we know that Heinrich began work on his *Eneide* in his native Limburg, *all* the manuscripts are in High German or even Upper German, rather than the Low German that one might expect. Two alternative explanations are possible: Heinrich wrote at first in Low German, but the poem was then revised in Thuringia by someone else, and when Heinrich arrived nine years later, he finished it off in High German or continued writing it in Low German and had the ending revised. Some support for this view may be found in the epilogue to the poem, where it is stated that in Thuringia the story was written differently from what it would have been if it had stayed in Heinrich's possession (13460-63). Then the epilogue goes on to talk about how Heinrich came to Thuringia to finish the poem. The other possibility is that Heinrich, well aware that some rhymes in his native Limburg dialect would not be rhymes in High German, avoided such rhymes for the purpose of making it possible to translate his work into High German, or he made use of what has been called the "Middle High German Poetic Language" and composed the poem himself in High German.

The question of the language of composition is really impossible to answer with certainty. Even the High German manuscripts have some Low German characteristics, and scholars are still divided in their opinion. However, this has made it very difficult to produce a reliable text of the poem. The first editor, Ettmüller, gave up trying to establish a text of the original and chose the best oldest manuscript, B (= Berlin), for his edition (1852). Then Behagel, who consulted all available manuscripts, produced an edition (1882) that was substantively more accurate by using more reliable younger manuscripts

(G and h) as his main sources than Ettmüller did, but he translated the text into what he considered to be Veldeke's native Limburg dialect. Frings and Schieb came next in 1964. They used the *Servatius*-fragments as the basis for their more precise analysis of Heinrich's language, but they published a diplomatic text of G in parallel with their own reconstruction of the Old Limburg dialect. However, the basis for choosing a particular variant from *all* the manuscripts for their new text was its closeness to or distance from what they had determined to be "Altlimburgisch." Their edition aroused great controversy upon its appearance, and it has generally not been accepted by other scholars. The most recent edition by Kartschoke (1986) is a compromise. He reproduces the Ettmüller text, but has notes at the end to call attention to other possible variants. One most annoying result of this situation is the lack of uniformity in quotations and references in scholarly works.

Heinrich's main source was the OF *Roman d'Eneas* (ca. 1160), but he also used Virgil's *Aeneid* on occasion. Nevertheless, the story-line in both *Eneide* and the OF *roman* is quite similar, as opposed to Virgil's poem. Both begin with a brief account of the siege and fall of Troy, followed by the escape of Aeneas from the city and his adventures up to the arrival at Carthage, whereas Virgil begins *in mediis rebus* with the stormy passage at sea and the arrival in Carthage. Then he has Aeneas recount the earlier events of the fall of Troy to Dido. The OF and the German versions stick to a strict chronological sequence even if it means being repetitious. The love affair with Dido and her death after Eneas leaves continue the course of events, followed by Eneas's trip to the underworld and the conversation with his father who tells him that the founder of Rome will come from his offspring.

Upon Eneas's arrival in Italy, King Latinus is prepared to give him his daughter Lavinia in marriage, but Lavinia has already been promised to Turnus, who becomes the chief opponent, along with Lavinia's mother, of Eneas. The Trojans quickly construct a fortress and several battles ensue with Prince Pallas fighting on Eneas's side and Queen Camilla, the Amazon, fighting on Turnus's. Both are killed in the fighting and are given splendid funerals. Against her mother's advice, Lavinia falls in love with Eneas and he with her. The fighting finally comes to an end despite an armistice that is violated, with a duel between Turnus and Eneas, in which Eneas slays Turnus. Lavinia's mother dies in a fit of anger, and the splendid wedding festival begins. At the end of the work Heinrich connects Eneas's progeny with the founding of Rome and an enumeration of its rulers up to the time of Augustus and the birth of Christ.

The role of the gods with the exception of Venus is diminished, as one might expect in Christian versions. The medieval poets emphasize or elaborate on many things important to courtly life: descriptions of clothing, furnishings, banquets, funerals, combat, and horses. Love in its Ovidian formulation is manifested more prominently in monologues and dialogues than it is in Virgil's poem. There is also considerable expansion of the ending of the poem. Virgil's Lavinia plays a much smaller role, and his poem ends rather abruptly with the death of Turnus, giving approximately the same amount of space to the Italian part as to the preceding section, whereas in the medieval versions the love between Eneas and Lavinia is developed much more fully. That and the enhanced role of Camilla greatly expand the latter half of the poem from the more equally balanced structure found in Virgil, even leading some scholars to suggest a tripartite structure for the medieval versions. The OF *Roman d'Eneas* has 10,156 lines as opposed to the *Eneide* with 13,527, much of the excess of which is due to the greater detail in the description of battles and courtly ceremonies.

Heinrich von Veldeke was famous for his treatment of the theme of love. Wolfram von Eschenbach praises his skill in describing how love begins but then criticizes Heinrich for not having told us how to keep it (*Parz.* 292,20). We have seen that Ovidian love is typical for early courtly literature in Eilhart's *Tristrant*, and it is obvious that there are many parallels between the love monologues of Isalde in Eilhart's work and those of Dido and Lavinia in the *Eneide*. This has led to a lot of scholarly discussion as to which poet was the first and which the imitator. It is also a consideration in the respective dating of each poem. The most recent research holds Eilhart as the originator and Heinrich as the imitator and expander, thereby placing Eilhart's work at an earlier date, and we concur with that position.

As we have indicated, there are actually two love monologues in the *Eneide*, the first being Dido's, which begins as a dialogue between Dido and her sister Anna after Eneas has left her and continues monologically a few lines later (2295-2319, 2355-2422), ending with Dido's suicide. It is basically a lament about her condition but includes a description of the physical and mental effects her love for Eneas has had on her. The second monologue is Lavinia's and comes as a consequence of her mother's teachings about love when she urges Lavinia to love Turnus and reject Eneas. In the course of the dialogue with her mother, Lavinia asks a series of naive questions about love, and her mother attempts to answer them (9735-9990). Lavinia remains unconvinced that she wants to love Turnus or even anyone at all after hearing about love's symptoms, and her mother flies into a rage at the thought that Lavinia might want to love Eneas. Shortly thereafter, Lavinia sees Eneas riding with some of his men before the walls. She suddenly notices how handsome he is, when Venus shoots an arrow into her heart, and she begins to understand what her mother had been trying to tell her about love. Her famous monologue is actually in four parts (10061-10388, 10400-10435, 10476-10496, 10725-1084) in each of which she comments on the very things her mother had told her about love.

Although the women's monologues have received most of the attention, we should not forget that there are monologues on love by both Tristrant in Eilhart's poem and Eneas in Veldeke's. After Lavinia has an arrow with her letter to Eneas affixed to it shot down from the fortress to land at his feet and Amor shoots Eneas with his golden arrow, Eneas too must suffer the pangs of love-sickness. His symptoms are described, and he reacts angrily to them initially, then launches into a lengthy monologue on love (11043-11338) during the course of the night when he is unable to sleep.

Veldeke's emphasis on courtly aspects of his narrative must have been of considerable interest to his contemporaries. Much has been written about his views on the various rulers, his emphasis on moderation as a necessary quality of the ideal courtly figure, his casting of the heroes of antiquity as knights, the lengthy descriptions of fighting, the sumptuousness and splendor of courtly ceremonies, and above all his depiction of the power of love that can end tragically or happily, as fate would have it. The modern reader may not find such features quite so fascinating. Indeed, they do tend to get wearisome and repetitious. Obviously tastes change, yet one cannot deny the regard Heinrich's successors had for his skill.

Veldeke's lyric poetry is also highly esteemed. We do not know just when his poems were written. Some suggest early in his career, before *Servatius*, others between the parts of that poem, or during the nine years when his *Eneide* was lost to him. For more information on his lyric, see the section on lyric poetry (see p. 245 ff.).

The other OF *roman d'antiquité* that was translated into German at the court of Hermann von Thüringen is the *Liet von Troye* (1190-1210) by Herbort von Fritzlar from the *Estoire de Troie* (ca. 1160-65) by Benoit de Sainte-Maure. We should also mention the German version (from the Latin) of Ovid's "Metamorphoses" by Albrecht von Halberstadt (ca. 1190 or ca. 1210), which may also have been commissioned by Hermann von Thüringen. Strangely enough the OF *Roman de Thèbes* (after 1150) was apparently never translated into German.

Texts:
Ettmüller, Ludwig, ed. *Heinrich von Veldeke*. Leipzig, 1852 (= Dichtungen des deutschen Mittelalters, 8).

Behaghel, Otto, ed. *Heinrichs von Veldeke Eneide*. Heilbronn, 1882, repr. 1970.

Schieb, Gabriele and Theodor Frings, eds. *Henric van Veldeken. Eneide*. Berlin, 1964 (= DTM, 58).

Kartschoke, Dieter, ed. and trans. *Heinrich von Veldeke. Eneasroman*. Stuttgart: Reclam, 1986 (= UB, 8303). (MHG text with mod. Ger. prose trans., introduction and notes).

Salverda de Grave, Jacques, ed. *Eneas. Roman du XIIe siècle*. 2 vols. Paris, 1925-29, repr. 1964, 1968. (= Les Classiques Français Du Moyen Age, 44 & 62).

Schöler-Beinhauer, Monica, ed. and trans. *Le Roman d'Eneas*. Munich, 1972 (= Klassische Texte des romanischen Mittelalters in zweisprachigen Ausgaben, 9). (OF text with mod. Ger. prose trans., intruduction).

Frings, Theodor and Gabriele Schieb, eds. *Sente Servus - Sanctus Servatius*. Halle/Saale, 1956. (= Die epischen Werke des Henric van Veldeken, 1).

Translations:
*Curschmann/Glier*, Vol. 1, pp. 416-441 (Sel., lines 9735-9990 and 13093-13252).
Kartschoke, Dieter (see above).
Schöler-Beinhauer, Monica (see above).

## Courtly Love, *Tristrant*, and *Eneide*—Bibliography

**Courtly Love:**

Boase, Roger. *The Origin and Meaning of Courtly Love. A Critical Study of European Scholarship*. Manchester (Eng.): Manchester UP; Totowa, NJ: Rowman & Littlefield, 1977.

Bumke, Joachim. *Die romanisch-deutschen Literaturbeziehungen im Mittelalter. Ein Überblick*. Heidelberg: Winter, 1967.

Ferrante, Joan M., et al. (eds). *In Pursuit of Perfection. Courtly Love in Medieval Literature*. Port Washington, NY: Kennikat Press, 1975.

Liebertz-Grün, Ursula. *Zur Soziologie des "Amour courtois."* Heidelberg: Winter, 1977 (= Beihefte zum *Euphorion*, 10).

Newman, F. X., ed. *The Meaning of Courtly Love*. Albany, NY: State Univ. of NY Press, 1968.

Schnell, Rüdiger, *Causa amoris. Liebeskonzeption und Liebesdarstellung in der mittelalterlichen Literatur*. Bern: Francke, 1985 (= Bibliotheca Germanica).

**Eilhart's *Tristrant*:**

Buschinger, Danielle. "La Structure du *Tristrant* d'Eilhart von Oberg." *Études Germaniques* 27 (1972): 1-26.

____. *Le "Tristrant" d'Eilhart von Oberg*. Diss. Université de Paris IV. Université de Lille III: Service de reproduction des theses, 1974. 2 vols. 1071p.
Exhaustive study of *all* aspects of the poem.

Bußmann, Hadumod. "Der Liebesmonolog im frühhöfischen Epos. Versuch einer Typbestimmung am Beispiel von Eilharts Isalde-Monolog." In: Glier, Ingeborg. *Werk-Typ-Situation: Studien zu poetologischen Bedingungen in der älteren deutschen Literatur*. Stuttgart: Metzler, 1969. Pp. 45-63.

**Heinrich von Veldeke's *Eneide*:**

Dittrich, Marie-Luise. *Die "Eneide" Heinrichs von Veldeke. I. Teil: Quellenkritischer Vergleich mit dem Roman d'Eneas und Virgils Aeneis*. Wiesbaden: Steiner, 1966.
*The* basic study of the relationship of Veldeke to his sources.

Groos, Arthur. " 'Amor and His Brother Cupid': The 'Two Loves' in Heinrich von Veldeke's *Eneit*." *Traditio* 32 (1976): 239-255.

Klein, Thomas. "Heinrich von Veldeke und die mitteldeutschen Literatursprachen. Untersuchungen zum Veldeke-Problem." In: Klein, Thomas, and Cola Minis. *Zwei Studien zu Veldeke und zum Straßburger Alexander*. Amsterdam: Rodopi, 1985 (= Amsterdamer Publ. z. Spr. u. Lit., 61).

Peters, Ursula. *Fürstenhof und höfische Dichtung. Der Hof Hermanns als literarisches Zentrum*. Konstanz: Universitätsverlag Konstanz, 1981 (= Konstanzer Universitätsreden, 113).

Sacker, Hugh. "Heinrich von Veldeke's Conception of the *Eneid*." *GLL* 10 (1956/57): 210-218.

Sinnema, John R. *Heinrich von Veldeke*. New York: Twayne, 1972 (= TWAS, 223).
Comprehensive treatment of Heinrich von Veldeke's life and works.

## THE "CLASSICS"—COURTLY LITERATURE

We have already defined courtly literature implicitly by explaining why pre-courtly and early courtly literature are *not*, strictly speaking, "courtly" (see p. 117). Therefore we shall not expand further on that topic but rather turn now to a type of literature that is almost synonymous with courtly literature. In fact, it is usually considered to epitomize the genre. We are speaking here of Arthurian romance, which developed in France principally in the works of Chrétien de Troyes and very rapidly became the most popular form of narrative in that country, virtually replacing the *chansons de geste*, in the latter half of the 12th century. Arthurian romance spread very quickly to Germany and other

European lands and indeed has provided material for literary and creative works of all kinds even to the present day.

## King Arthur and the "Matter of Britain"

The *matière de bretagne*—and here we are speaking of both Great Britain and Brittany on the French coast of the Channel—stems from the Welsh and Cornish areas of Britain and undoubtedly crossed the Channel to Brittany or, possibly, through the mediation of the Norman French after the conquest, spread throughout France, and then on to the rest of Western Europe. The precise origins and routes of transmission have been the subject of much scholarly discussion over the years, but it seems likely that ancient Welsh tales about mythic heroes are the ultimate source of the material, and, if that is true, we would be dealing with the realm of folklore.

However, it is very possible that an historical Arthur did exist at one time, but whether he was a king and whether he ever had a Round Table or actually performed all the feats attributed to him is quite another matter. The name Arthur is probably Roman in origin and could date to the period of the Roman occupation of Britain. Arthur is mentioned first by Nennius, a priest of South Wales, in his *Historia Britonum* of about 800. There he is called "dux bellorum," a kind of field marshal, fighting alongside the kings of the Britons against the invading Saxons and defeating them in twelve battles, the last of which took place at a certain Mount Badon. Arthur is described as a valiant warrior, of great physical strength, a devout Christian fighting against the pagan Saxons. An earlier historian, the Welsh St. Gildas, writing about 540, writes of the battle as a crucial one, that stopped the Saxons' westward advance and brought peace for 44 years. Gildas does not mention Arthur by name, but it seems likely that Arthur was the leader of the Britons in that battle. The "Bellum Badonis" is also mentioned in the *Annales Cambrae* (Welsh Annals) from the second half of the 10th century. There Arthur is credited with having carried the Cross on his shoulders (or shield) for three days and nights and earned the victory. In another battle, at Camlann, Arthur is said to have been killed along with a certain Medraut, possibly a reference to Arthur's treasonous nephew Modred of later versions.

These and numerous other references to Arthur would indicate that a popular tradition of Arthur already existed at the time Geoffrey of Monmouth wrote his monumental *Historia Regum Britanniae* (1130/36) and made Arthur known as a king of heroic proportions. Although Geoffrey lived and died in England, he may well have been born in Brittany, where an Arthur-tradition, stemming from Cornwall, is thought to have existed. Geoffrey could have gone to England in the years following the Norman conquest. At any rate, his *Historia* seems intended to raise the status of the Anglo-Norman royal house by providing it with a glorious ancestor who descended from the Trojan-Roman line and who could rival Charlemagne in the scope of his conquests. Indeed, according to Geoffrey, Arthur, the son of Uther Pendragon, was crowned at the age of 15, fought against the Saxons in the lands around the North Sea, and established his court at Caerleon, where he held festivals and tournaments at Pentecost. He was supposed to have conquered Gaul by defeating a giant in single combat and the Roman army under Emperor

Lucius and was on his way to take Rome when he was forced to return to Britain because of the treachery of his nephew Modred, who had seized Queen Guenhuvara and the throne. Upon his return, Arthur killed Modred in battle in Cornwall but was mortally wounded himself and taken to the island of Avalon, the place from which his mighty sword had come. Geoffrey's *Historia*, if not historically accurate, was at least very popular—there are over 200 extant manuscripts—and it was quickly rendered into the vernacular languages.

The most important "translation" for our purpose here is the *Roman de Brut* by the Anglo-Norman poet Wace of ca. 1155, although there are also Anglo-Saxon versions. It greatly expands Geoffrey's version (nearly 15,000 rhymed couplets in Norman French, as opposed to Geoffrey's 600 Latin lines), stressing as it does the courtly aspects and introducing the idea of the Round Table as a feature of Arthur's court. The figure of Arthur changes also from that of a conquering imperial ruler to that of a courtly feudal lord. Wace omits or tones down the cruelty and savagery attributed to Arthur by Geoffrey and is clearly more interested in presenting the details of life at court, the festivities, the costumes, the knightly combat; all things that would be of interest to the courtly audience of his day and that were admittedly calculated to please a patron such as Henry II of England and his new queen, Eleanor of Aquitaine, to whom Wace presented a copy of his work. It is also interesting to note that Wace refers to tales circulating about Arthur, so that we can assume that not all his additions to Geoffrey's *Historia*, including the Round Table, were of his own invention but rather come from an oral Arthurian tradition. Eighteen manuscripts and six fragments of Wace's *Roman* exist today.

### Chrétien de Troyes

Although Wace's *Roman de Brut* does indeed have a lot to tell about Arthur, we should not forget that it is essentially a re-working of Geoffrey's *Historia* and starts all the way back with Aeneas's grandson, Brutus, as the progenitor of the kings of England, Arthur being just one of the kings, albeit an outstanding one. Chrétien, on the other hand, does not claim to be writing history per se but rather telling "true" stories about Arthur and his knights, referring occasionally to books or tales that may or may not be trustworthy, i.e. he is either being faithful to a reliable source, or he criticizes other stories that are told orally for not being true; his is the correct version.

Chrétien tells us something about his own life in prologues to two of his works. Two certain dates have been established: 1164 and 1190, so that his works may be dated to the latter half of the 12th century. Whether Chrétien was born in Troyes is not known, but he surely did live there, and his language shows indications of the dialect of the Champagne. He undoubtedly had a clerical education, though he was probably not a cleric himself. Chrétien's Arthurian romances are *Erec, Cligès, Lancelot* or *Le Chevalier de la Charrette, Le Chevalier au Lion* or *Yvain*, and *Perceval* or *Li Contes del Graal*. In these, Arthur and his court form the background from which the titular hero departs and to which he returns after successfully completing a series of perilous, frequently fantastic adventures that usually bring him a wife, a kingdom, and fame. In most of the tales the hero achieves apparent success rather quickly, only to be found at fault, whereupon he undertakes to correct his fault and ultimately restores his honor, this time on a more certain basis.

Arthur himself is a rather passive figure, but he represents the highest ideals of chivalrous conduct. Needless to say, the brilliance of his court is described in detail, the Round Table plays a central role in the assembling of his knights—only the best are admitted to that elite group—and lovely courtly ladies are present for all festivities, which take place, most often at Pentecost. Courtly love, not the overpowering Ovidian variety found, for example, in Veldeke's *Eneit*, but rather the kind in which the knight strives to earn the love of his lady through worthy deeds, is the norm, and it usually involves a splendid wedding festival. Ladies are the ones to be pleased, and the knights are subservient to them. The Arthurian world is clearly an intriguing imaginary world with little, if any, connection to reality, although it seems to take itself seriously. Above all, it is entertaining and exciting.

However, Chrétien, despite his apparent pleasure in telling a good story, shows a serious side in his tales. They deal very often with the real problems of courtly society: conflicts of duties, keeping one's word, failure to live up to the obligations of a ruler, proper knightly behavior, and good deeds in social situations (e.g., helping people in distress). In a way, Chrétien seems to be trying to create role models for the new courtly society for which he was writing by demonstrating how members of that society should act. Or, looked at in another way, he was giving literary form to the aspirations of courtly society by idealizing it. In either case, he struck a responsive chord in his contemporaries not only in France but almost immediately in Germany and other European countries as the numerous translations and imitations of his works attest.

## Arthurian Literature—Bibliography

**General:**

Brogsitter, Karl Otto. *Artusepik*. Stuttgart: Metzler, 1965 (= Sammlung Metzler, 38).
Informative, concise treatment. Almost half devoted to Arthurian literature in German.

Köhler, Erich. *Ideal und Wirklichkeit in der höfischen Epic*. Tübingen: Niemeyer, 1956.
A seminal study based on a sociological approach to courtly literature.

Lacy, Norris, ed. *The New Arthurian Encyclopedia*. New York & London: Garland Publishing, 1991.
Revised and expanded edition of *The Arthurian Encyclopedia* (1986). Excellent reference work on all aspects of the subject.

____, and Geoffrey Ashe. *The Arthurian Handbook*. New York & London: Garland Publishing, 1988 (= Garland Reference Library of the Humanities, 765).
A critical survey, intended for a broad audience, covering origins, early and modern periods, the arts. Includes a chronological table, extensive (114 pp.!) Arthurian glossary, and good bibliography. Very useful.

Loomis, Roger Sherman, ed. *Arthurian Literature in the Middle Ages. A Collaborative History*. Oxford: Oxford UP, 1959.
A monumental series of essays by eminent scholars. A bit dated now, but still very useful.

____. *The Development of Arthurian Romance*. New York: Harper and Rowe, 1964. Repr. of original edition, London: Hutchinson & Co., 1963.

Very readable, concise treatment, expounding Loomis's theory of Welsh origins of Arthurian literature.

Ruh, Kurt. *Höfische Epik des deutschen Mittelalters*. Vol. 1: *Von den Anfängen bis zu Hartmann von Aue*. Berlin: Erich Schmidt, 1967. [2]1977 (= Grundlagen der Germanistik, 7). Vol. 2: *"Reinhart Fuchs", "Lanzelet", Wolfram von Eschenbach, Gottfried von Straßburg*. Berlin: Erich Schmidt, 1980 (= GLG, 25).

A very comprehensive study of the courtly epic. Especially valuable sections on the major authors and their works. Can be used as reference or read straight through.

Schultz, James A. *The Shape of the Round Table. Structures of Middle High German Arthurian Romance*. Toronto: University of Toronto Press, 1983.

A structural examination of MHG Arthurian romances, demonstrating quite convincingly that the bipartite model of the canonical romances (*Erec, Iwein, Parzival*) is not prescriptive for the genre as a whole. Brief summaries of less familiar epics in an appendix.

**Chrétien de Troyes:**

Texts and Translations:

Bryant, Nigel, trans. *Perceval. The Story of the Grail*. Cambridge: D. S. Brewer, 1982. Repr. 1986. Prose trans. of Chrétien's *Perceval* complete; the first and second continuations, Gerbert de Montreuil's continuation, and the third continuation (Manesier's continuation) partially translated, but with summaries of other parts.

Carroll, Carleton W., ed. and trans. *Chrétien de Troyes, Erec et Enide*. New York: Garland Publishing, 1987 (= GLML, A,25). OF text and prose transl.

Cline, Ruth Harwood, trans. *Yvain or The Knight of the Lion*. Athens: Univ. of Georgia Press, 1984. Verse trans.

____. *Perceval or The Story of the Grail*. Athens: Univ. of Georgia Press, 1983. Verse trans.

Kibler, William W., ed. and trans. *Lancelot, or The Knight of the Cart*. New York: Garland Publishing, 1981 (= GLML, A,1). OF text and prose trans.

____. *The Knight with the Lion, or Yvain*. New York: Garland Publishing, 1985 (= GLML, A,48). OF text and prose trans.

____. *Arthurian Romances*. Harmondsworth: Penguin, 1991 (= Penguin Classics). Engl. trans. of *all* of Chrétien's romances in one vol.

Nolting-Hauff, Ilse, ed. and trans. *Iwein*. Munich, 1962, [3]1983 (= Klassische Texte des roman. Mittelalters, 2). OF text and mod. Ger. prose trans., with introduction.

Owen, D. D. R., trans. *Chrétien de Troyes, Arthurian Romances*. London & Melbourne: Dent, 1987 (= Everyman's Classics). Prose transl. of *Erec and Enide, Cligés, Lancelot, Yvain, Perceval*.

Pickens, Rupert T., ed. and William W. Kibler, trans. *Li Contes del Graal*. New York: Garland Publishing, 1990 (= GLML, A,62). OF text and prose trans.

Secondary Literature:

Frappier, Jean. *Chrétien de Troyes: l'homme et l'oeuvre*. Paris: Hatier, 1957. English trans.: *Chrétien de Troyes: The Man and His Work*. Trans. by Raymond J. Cormier. Athens: Ohio UP, 1982.
Comprehensive study of Chrétien, somewhat dated, but still important.

Jones, Martin H., and Roy Wisbey, eds. *Chrétien de Troyes and the German Middle Ages*. Cambridge/London: D. H. Brewer, 1993 (= Publs. of the Institute of Germanic Studies, 53).
Papers from a 1988 conference at the Institute. 9 of the 19 papers are on Hartmann's adaptations of Chrétien's *Erec et Enide* and *Yvain*.

Kellermann, Wilhelm. *Aufbaustil und Weltbild Chrestiens von Troyes im Percevalroman*. Halle/Saale: Niemeyer, 1936 (= Beihefte zur Zeitschrift für romanische Philologie, 88). Repr. Darmstadt: Wiss. Buchges., 1967.
A landmark study of Chrétien and his works with emphasis on his *Perceval*.

Lacy, Norris, J., Douglas Kelly, and Keith Busby, eds. *The Legacy of Chrétien de Troyes*. Amsterdam: Rodopi, 1987-88. 2 Vols.

## Hartmann von Aue

Hartmann von Aue deserves credit for having introduced the Arthurian romance to German audiences through his translations of Chrétien's *Erec* and *Yvain*, but he was also known as a lyric poet; as author of a poetic lament about love, usually referred to as *Diu Klage* or *Das Büchlein* and as the author of two other non-Arthurian tales: *Gregorius* and *Der arme Heinrich*. He was admired by Gottfried von Straßburg (see p. 167) who praises him in the famous excursus on contemporary poets in his *Tristan*, saying:

> Hartman der Ouwære,
> ahî, wie der diu mære
> beid' ûzen unde innen
> mit worten und mit sinnen
> durchvärwet und durchzieret!
> wie er mit rede figieret
> der âventiure meine!
> wie lûter und wie reine
> sîn kristallîniu wortelîn
> beidiu sint und iemer müezen sîn!
> si koment den man mit siten an,
> si tuont sich nâhe zuo dem man
> und liebent rehtem muote.
> swer guote rede ze guote
> und ouch ze rehte kan verstân,
> der muoz dem Ouwære lân
> sîn schapel unde sîn lôrzwî.
> (4619-35)

*(Ah, how Hartmann of Aue dyes and adorns his tales through and through with words and sense, both outside and within! How clear and transparent his crystal words both*

*are and ever must remain! Gently they approach and fawn on a man, and captivate right minds. Those who esteem fine language with due sympathy and judgment will allow the man of Aue his garland and his laurels*—Trans. A. T. Hatto)

And Gottfried is not the only poet to praise Hartmann: Rudolf von Ems (see p. 340) mentions him in his *Alexander* and in his *Wilhelm von Orlens*, and Heinrich von dem Türlin (see p. 358 ff.) eulogizes Hartmann in *Diu Crône*. Wolfram von Eschenbach (see p. 174 ff.), on the other hand, challenges Hartmann to have "his" (Hartmann's) King Arthur and Queen Ginover treat young Parzival properly when he arrives at their castle, otherwise Wolfram will drag Hartmann's Lady Enite and her mother Karsnafite (in *Erec*) through the mill and lower their reputations by defending his friend with jibes at them (*Parz.* 143,21-144,40). In two other places (*Parz.* 253,10-14; 436,4-22) he criticizes Lunete for having advised Laudine in Hartmann's *Iwein* to marry Iwein, the knight who had just killed her husband.

Wolfram's references to Hartmann and his characters from *Erec* and *Iwein*, interesting as they may be in terms of the reception of Hartmann's works, are important for the dating of Hartmann's life and works since they provide the only sure clue that we have. Wolfram must have been composing his *Parzival* some time after the year 1203 since he refers to the siege of Erfurt of that date (379,18) so that Hartmann's works—it is generally assumed that *Iwein* was his last work—must already have been finished before the time when Wolfram was working on his *Parzival*, probably a few years after 1203. Attempts have also been made to use either the dates of the Barbarossa crusade of 1189-90 or that of Henry VI in 1197-98 on the basis of several of Hartmann's lyric poems that supposedly suggest that Hartmann had participated in a crusade after the death of his liege lord, but this is merely conjecture.

We are left therefore with the commonly accepted dating of his birth as ca. 1160-65 and of his death in or after 1210. His narrative works were probably written in the following order: *Erec, Gregorius. Der arme Heinrich, Iwein*, beginning around 1185 and with his last work about 1200 or shortly thereafter. *Diu Klage* is thought to be an early work, and his lyric poetry may have been early also, but the poems (see p. 257 ff.) could have been written at any time. We are also left in the dark about the precise circumstances of Hartmann's life despite the fact that he identifies himself in each of his narrative works. In *Der arme Heinrich*, for example, he begins by saying: *Ein ritter sô gelêret was/ daz er an den buochen las/ swaz er daran geschriben vant:/ der was Hartman genant,/ dienstman was er zOuwe.* (1-5. There was a knight so learned that he read books, whatever he found written in them: his name was Hartmann, a ministeralis at Ouwe). From this and from other references in his works we may conclude that he must have had a clerical education that included a thorough grounding in Latin and knowledge of classical authors, exceptional for a knight of that period, but who his liege lord was at Ouwe or even which particular village or town he meant is uncertain. The suffix -au survives to this day in place names in Swabia and Switzerland. His language is Alemannic, and he may have had ties to the Zähringen family in Swabia, but he names no patron in any of his works. He surely had a good command of French, since there are only a few instances in his versions of Chrétien's works where he apparently misunderstood his source. That may support the idea that he was a ministerialis of the Zähringens, who were related by marriage to French noble families and owned lands in Burgundy. The mother of Berthold IV (1152-86) was Clementia of Namur, and his son, Berthold V (1186-1218), was married twice to daughters of French counts: Ida of Boulogne and Clementia of Auxonne. Berthold V is named by Rudolf von Ems as a literary patron, but there is no record that the family ever possessed any Chrétien manuscripts. Consequently, there is unfortunately not enough hard evidence to support this or any of the theories that have been advanced about Hartmann's patron or liege lord.

### General Hartmann—Bibliography

Boggs, Roy A. *Hartmann von Aue. Lemmatisierte Konkordanz zum Gesamtwerk.* 2 vols. Nendeln: KTO Press, 1979.

Combined listing for major works, one listing for lyric poetry; index of names; rhyme index.

Clark, Susan L. *Hartmann von Aue. Landscapes of the Mind.* Houston, TX: Rice Univ. Press, 1989.

A close reading of Hartmann's major works with emphasis on the interior world of the mind and the exterior world of landscape.

Cormeau, Christoph, and Wilhelm Störmer. *Hartmann von Aue. Epoche—Werk—Wirkung.* Munich: Beck, 1985 (= Beck'sche Elementarbücher).

Probably the best, recent comprehensive introduction to Hartmann and especially to the social-historical background of his life and works. Includes a chronological table and a section on Hartmann-reception through the ages.

Hasty, Will. *Adventures in Interpretation. The Works of Hartmann von Aue and Their Critical Reception.* Columbia, SC: Camden House, 1995.

This is a relatively brief, critical examination of research on all aspects of Hartmann's life and works. Extensive bibliography. Very good as a recent, detailed introduction to the subject.

Jackson, W. H. *Chivalry in Twelfth-Century Germany: The Works of Hartmann von Aue.* Cambridge: D. H. Brewer, 1994.

Argues strongly for the idea of development in the protagonists in Hartmann's works as characteristic of the social dynamism in German chivalry of the period.

Kuhn, Hugo, and Christoph Cormeau, eds. *Hartmann von Aue.* Darmstadt: Wiss. Buchges., 1973 (= WdF, 359).

A collection of important articles on most of Hartmann's works, reprinted from various journals from 1951-1970 with two earlier exceptions. A fine sample of research for the twenty-year period.

McFarland, Timothy, and Silvia Ranawake, eds. *Hartmann von Aue. Changing Perspectives: London Hartmann Symposium.* Göppingen: Kümmerle, 1988 (= GAG, 486).

Papers from a 1985 symposium at the Institute of Germanic Studies, London, on the works of Hartmann. Excellent collection presenting more recent scholarly views.

Neubuhr, Elfride. *Bibliographie zu Hartmann von Aue.* Berlin: Erich Schmidt, 1977 (= Bibliographien zur deutschen Literatur des Mittelalters, 6).

Excellent bibliography but unfortunately, like many of the bibliographies in this series, never updated.

Sparnaay, Hendricus. *Hartmann von Aue. Studien zu einer Biographie.* 2 vols. Halle, 1933-38. Repr. Darmstadt, 1975, with foreword by Christoph Cormeau.
An exhaustive study of every scrap of evidence on Hartmann's life and works. Still valuable for its source material but obviously otherwise dated.

Wapnewski, Peter. *Hartmann von Aue.* Stuttgart: Metzler, 1962, [7]1979 (= Sammlung Metzler, 38).
Brief, very informative, well-balanced introduction to Hartmann. Later editions have updated bibliography, but the text itself is unchanged.

See also M. Jones and R. Wisbey, *London Chrétien Symposium* (above).

## Hartmann's Arthurian Romances: *Erec* and *Iwein*

*Erec*, the first Arthurian romance in German, is probably a "translation" of Chrétien's work of the same name. Medieval "translations" should not be confused with our modern conception of the term, for they can include paraphrase, commentary, expansion, abbreviation, criticism, and re-shaping of the original as well as, at times, virtually literal translation. About the only constants between the source and the translation are the individual events and, usually, their sequence.

Strangely enough, Hartmann's *Erec* exists in only one, almost complete manuscript, and it is a very late one: the *Ambraser Heldenbuch*, compiled by Hans Ried at the request of Kaiser Maximilian I about 1510. The beginning is defective in that two pages have been lost, so that the opening part in Chrétien about Arthur and the hunt for the white stag is lacking. There are also three manuscript fragments in Wolfenbüttel from the 13th and 14th centuries. However, questions have been raised as to whether Chrétien's *Erec* was Hartmann's sole source, as stated in one of the fragments, but missing from the text in the Ambraser Heldenbuch, or whether he knew other versions of the tale. These would include Welsh versions, the Mabinogi *Gereint*; or the source of the ON *Erexsaga*; or an oral version differing somewhat from Chrétien's; or Chrétien's source in another (lost) version that had already been translated into German. All of these suggestions try to account for the fact that Hartmann's version differs from Chrétien's to a considerable extent, yet the arguments are not compelling. Most differences can be explained as Hartmann's desire to make aspects of French culture understandable to a German audience or as emphasizing points that he must have thought were important for his audience at this early stage of their acquaintance with the courtly romance. Hartmann's *Erec* is certainly an expansion of Chrétien's (almost 10,200 lines, with the beginning lost vs. just under 7,000 lines for Chrétien), and the question of Hartmann's source, if indeed other than Chrétien, is still unresolved and possibly unresolvable.

*Erec* is the story of a young knight who attains fame, wife, and crown too rapidly, then jeopardizes his position through lack of maturity, but in a series of adventures that test him severely he gradually gains the understanding and experience that make him an exemplary knight and ruler of his kingdom.

Erec's sudden rise to renown begins with an episode that shames him: he is whipped across the face by the insolent dwarf of the knight Iders fil Niut and is helpless to defend himself or exact retribution since he is completely unarmed. To make the shame even greater, the lashing is witnessed by Queen Ginover and her ladies, whom he had been accompanying on a social outing. Thus deeply embarrassed and humiliated, Erec leaves the ladies and rides off in pursuit of Iders, seeking revenge for the insult.

His chase of Iders takes him to Tulmein, where a contest is to be held the next day to see whether any knight can defeat Iders and claim the prize of a sparrow hawk for his lady, who would thereby be acclaimed the most beautiful. Iders had previously won the prize twice for his lady. The contest is the occasion for a festival at the castle of Duke Imain with many people in attendance, but Erec shuns the court, finally finding lodging in town at the home of the impoverished Count Koralus, who lives there in humble quarters with his wife and daughter. Koralus and Erec's father had been squires and then knighted together, but Koralus had lost all his wealth and property through no fault of his own. Nevertheless, he is still able to provide Erec with armor, although old-fashioned and out of condition from disuse, for the combat with Iders on the next day. Needless to say, Koralus's daughter, Enite, is very beautiful, and Erec offers to marry her if he can defeat Iders.

This he does after a lengthy and arduous fight. Iders is forced to yield; his dwarf is punished, and they, along with Iders's lady, are sent to King Arthur's court at Karadigan where Iders is to surrender to Ginover, to bring her the happy news of Erec's great victory, and to say that Erec will be there the next day. At Arthur's court, the king has returned from the hunt for the white stag (missing from the beginning of Hartmann's *Erec*), in the course of which Arthur himself had captured the stag and thereby earned the right to kiss the most beautiful lady at the court. Ginover persuades him to delay until Erec returns, having heard from Iders of Enite's beauty. Back at Tulmein, everyone celebrates Erec's great victory and Enite's beauty, signified by the sparrow hawk. At Erec's insistence, Duke Imain agrees to hold the celebration at Count Koralus's house and to provide the food and drink for the occasion.

On the following day, Erec and Enite take leave of Enite's parents and set out on horseback for Karadigan, exchanging loving glances all the way. Arrived at the court, Enite is welcomed by Ginover and whisked away to be bathed and dressed in suitable fashion. When she then appears before the assembled court, all the knights declare that she is the most beautiful lady ever seen, and Arthur claims his reward with a kiss. Eventually, the impatiently awaited wedding is held amidst illustrious guests from far and wide, and a magnificent festival follows the ceremony itself. Three weeks later a great tournament (Erec's first!) is held, and, of course, Erec distinguishes himself and is declared to be the best knight in the tournament. It is then time for Erec to return to his father's kingdom with his bride, his apprenticeship at Arthur's court now having been completed in exemplary fashion.

At Karnant in Destregales, the land of Erec's father, King Lac, the newlyweds are welcomed warmly, and old King Lac abdicates his throne in favor of his son, thereby making Erec and Enite king and queen. However, Erec begins to spend more time in bed with Enite than he does acting like the bold knight that he is, and soon people become dissatisfied with their lazy king, who has neglected his knightly duties and brought his court into disrepute. They blame and curse Enite for the sorry state of the court. This disturbs Enite greatly, and, thinking her husband asleep, she laments her sorrow aloud, thus awakening him. He compels her to tell him the reason for her lament, and after hearing her out, prepares to ride out alone with her, ostensibly for pleasure, but concealing his armor and his real intent of redeeming his lost honor. Enite is to ride ahead of him dressed splendidly and is forbidden to say a single word, regardless of what she might see or hear.

With this, a double series of adventures begins, in the course of which Erec survives a number of dangerous encounters mainly because Enite disregards his order to remain silent and warns him in time:

The first series begins with Erec's defeat of three, then five robbers in the forest, as a result of which Enite is forced to take care of the eight captured horses. Following those two episodes comes one in which a count treacherously offers hospitality to Erec and Enite with the intent of killing Erec in order to win Enite, with whom he has fallen in love. Here again Erec, having been warned by Enite, escapes and defeats the pursuing count and his men. The next episode is an encounter with the dwarflike King Guivreiz le petiz, whom Erec finally forces to surrender even after having been wounded in the difficult duel they fight. Guivreiz becomes Erec's vassal and friend, but the next day Erec and Enite continue on to Arthur's court, or rather camp, for Arthur and his knights are out in the forest on a hunt. Erec apparently does not deem himself worthy of the honors shown to him by Arthur and his knights because he insists on riding off alone with Enite the next day after having received a magic bandage to heal his wound.

The second series of adventures starts when Erec and Enite encounter the wife of a knight named Cadoc. She begs Erec to free her husband who has been captured and is being terribly mishandled by two giants. Erec agrees to help, tries by peaceful means to get the giants to release Cadoc, and when they refuse, Erec attacks the giants, killing both of them. Cadoc is rescued and told to go to Queen Ginover in Britain. The next episode begins when Erec returns to where he had told Enite to wait. Exhausted by his struggle with the giants and with his wounds re-opened in that fight, Erec falls unconscious from his horse, pale from loss of blood. Enite believes him to be dead and commences a lengthy lament, in which she blames herself for Erec's death, wishes to die, rails at God for her ill-fortune, and is about to commit suicide when another count, this time named Oringles, comes up and stops her. He is smitten by her beauty, and he and his men take Enite to Limors, his castle, carrying the unconscious Erec on a litter. At the castle preparations are made for an immediate wedding, but Enite adamantly refuses. When Oringles strikes her, she cries out, thereby rousing Erec from the bier on which he had been lying in state. Quickly seizing a sword, Erec slays Oringles, and he and Enite escape in the ensuing panic among the guests.

After a touching reconciliation in which Erec acknowledges Enite's steadfast loyalty and apologizes for the hardships she had suffered, they unwittingly encounter Guivreiz and his men on the road through the forest at night. The two knights meet in combat because in the darkness each is unaware of the identity of his opponent. This time it is Guivreiz who is victorious, unhorsing the weakened Erec, but Guivreiz, alerted by Enite's cry, soon discovers that he has been fighting with his friend and takes Erec and Enite to Penefrec, one of his castles, where they stay two weeks so that Erec can recover fully from his wounds.

With Erec and Enite reconciled and Erec restored to health, it would seem that the second series of adventures had ended and it would be time for Erec to return to Arthur's court, having reestablished his honor. But one final adventure awaits him: Joie de la curt, the most dangerous of all. This involves a duel with Mabonagrin, a knight who has been living in a magic garden of delights with his wife, having pledged to remain there alone with her until someone defeats him in single combat. Eighty knights have already lost their lives in the attempt, their heads having been placed on stakes at the entrance to the garden and their ladies kept in the nearby castle of Brandigan. Erec eventually succeeds in defeating Mabonagrin and returning him and his wife, who turns out to be a cousin of Enite's, to courtly society and the ensuing "joie de la curt."

The eighty ladies then accompany Erec to Arthur's court where they are welcomed as lovely additions to that illustrious company. Erec and Enite, of course, receive great acclaim and his honor is fully restored. Word comes that Erec's father has died, and Erec and Enite then return home to Karnant to re-assume the throne amidst great jubilation. Erec becomes an exemplary ruler, attentive to Enite's wishes, to be sure, but now in a proper way.

It has been necessary to describe the action in *Erec* in some detail because *Erec* is not only the first truly courtly epic in German, but it also became the prototypical Arthurian romance in the view of Hugo Kuhn, whose 1948 study (see below) established the characteristics of *the* courtly romance for many scholars, even though not very many romances actually follow the pattern closely. In addition, *Erec* has so many motifs that are found in other courtly epics that a simple brief summary did not seem appropriate for our purposes.

As we have noted earlier, the differences between Chrétien's version and Hartmann's are considerable. We can say in general that Hartmann has expanded the descriptions of courtly life and ceremony, there is less direct dialogue but more authorial intrusions and commentary on the action in a frequently moralizing, didactic tone. Indeed, the work as a whole may be read as a treatise on learning the proper, socially responsible attitude of a ruler. Hartmann shows a strong idealistic tendency as, for example, when he stresses the value of the inner nobility of Enite and her father despite outward poverty. They are poor also in Chrétien, but their human qualities are not stressed as they are in Hartmann.

Several specific differences should be mentioned: Hartmann greatly expands the ending of Chrétien's version by introducing the 80 widows. Erec shows compassion for and sympathy with the ladies and with his victory over Mabonagrin is able to restore them to Arthur's courtly circle, thereby demonstrating an appropriate altruism. Furthermore, Hartmann's *Erec* does not stop with the triumphant return to Arthur's court. Erec and Enite return to Karnant, thus emphasizing their roles as ideal rulers. There is a significant difference in the reconciliation between Erec and Enite at the end of the episode at Limors. In Chrétien, Erec forgives Enite for her words and for her offense, which forced him to leave Karnant. He has apparently been testing her and is now sure that she loves him perfectly and he pledges his service to her. In Hartmann, on the other hand, it is Erec who asks Enite's forgiveness for his inappropriate behavior and for having tested her so severely.

There are several questions that have occupied scholars aside from the question of Hartmann's source mentioned above: How can the structure of *Erec* be viewed? Is there development in Erec? Enite? Can religious analogies be applied to Erec? What is Erec's basic problem: pride? sloth? society? recklessness? Can one speak of "transgression" in the case of Enite? Why does Erec leave Karnant in the first place? Is *Erec* a treatise on marriage? These and many more questions are treated in Will Hasty's useful overview of research on *Erec* (see above; pp. 36-51), a convenient starting point for access to the immense amount of scholarship on problems of interpretation.

Texts:
Cramer, Thomas, ed. and trans. *Hartmann von Aue. Erec. Mittelhochdeutscher Text und Übertragung.* Frankfurt/M.: Fischer, 1972 (= Fischer Taschenbuch, 6017). MHG text, with mod. Ger. trans., notes, and introduction.
Leitzmann, Albert, ed. *Erec.* Tübingen: Niemeyer, [6]1985, ed. by Christoph Cormeau and Kurt Gärtner (= ATB 39). The standard text.
Schwarz, Ernst, ed. and trans. *Erec. Iwein. Text, Nacherzählung, Worterklärungen.* Darmstadt: Wiss. Buchges., 1964.

Translations:
Cramer, Thomas (see above).
Keller, Thomas, trans. *Erec. By Hartmann von Aue.* New York: Garland Publ., 1987. (= GLML, 12) Eng. prose trans. with extensive introduction.
Mohr, Wolfgang, trans. *Hartmann von Aue. Erec.* Göppingen: Kümmerle, 1980 (= GAG, 291). Mod. Ger. prose trans.
Resler, Michael, trans. *Erec by Hartmann von Aue.* Philadelphia: Univ. of Pennsylvania Press, 1987. Engl. prose trans., with extensive intro. and notes.
Schwarz, Ernst (see above).
Thomas, J. Wesley, trans. *Erec by Hartmann von Aue.* Lincoln: Univ. of Nebraska Press, 1982. Engl. prose trans. with introduction.

Facsimile:
Unterkirchner, Franz, ed. *Ambraser Heldenbuch. Vollständige Faksimile-Ausgabe.* Graz: Akad. Druck- u. Verlagsanstalt, 1973. (= Codices selecti, 42).

### *Erec*—Bibliography

Fisher, Rodney. "Erecs Schuld und Enites Unschuld bei Hartmann von Aue." *Euph.* 69 (1975): 160-96.

Erec seems to blame Enite for his own failure in their marriage until he eventually overcomes this fault and recognizes its cause towards the end of the story.

Jacobson, Evelyn M. "The Unity of *wort* and *sin*: Language as a Theme and Structural Element in Hartmann's *Erec*." *Seminar* 27 (1991): 121-35.

Kuhn, Hugo. "*Erec*." In: *Festschr. f. P. Kluckhohn u. H. Schneider.* Tübingen: Niemeyer, 1948. Pp. 122-47. Repr. in: H. Kuhn. *Dichtung und Welt im Mittelalter.* Stuttgart: Metzler, 1959. [2]1969. Pp. 133-50. Also in: Kuhn/Cormeau, 1973, above, 17-48).

An important article on the structure of *Erec* and the Arthurian romance in general (but see also James Schultz in ARTHURIAN LITERATURE—BIBLIOGRAPHY, above).

McConeghey, Patrick. "Women's Speech and Silence in Hartmann von Aue's *Erec*." *PMLA* 102 (1987): 771-83.

Okken, Lambertus. *Kommentar zur Artusepik Hartmanns von Aue.* Amsterdam/Atlanta GA: Rodopi, 1993. 564 p. (= Amsterdamer Publikationen zur Sprache und Literatur, 103).

This is a very thorough and detailed commentary to Hartmann's *Erec* and *Iwein*, providing an immense amount of background information. Two appendices by Dietrich Haage deal with medical matters and the ouroboros motif (the description of the stirrups on Enite's saddle) respectively. Extensive bibliography.

Quast, Bruno. "*Getriuwiu wandelunge*: Ehe und Minne in Hartmanns *Erec*." *ZfdA* 122 (1993): 162-80.

Ranawake, Silvia. "Erec's *verligen* and the Sin of Sloth." In: *London Hartmann Symposium*, 1988 (see above). Pp. 93-115.

Sees Erec's failure at Karnant not as result of *minne* but rather as analogous to the sin of *acedia*, a very human, social failure. His journey of penance is one of rehabilitation, resulting in elevation to the status of true *miles christianus* in the service of *caritas*.

See, Geoffrey. "An Examination of the Hero in Hartmann's *Erec*." *Seminar* 27 (1991): 39-54.

Sterba, Wendy. "The Question of Enite's Transgression: Female Voice and Male Gaze as Determining Factors in Hartmann's *Erec*." In: *Women as Protagonists in the German Middle Ages: An Anthology of Feminist Approaches to MHG literature*. Ed. by Albrecht Classen. Göppingen: Kümmerle, 1991. Pp. 57-68.

*Iwein*. In many ways the situation of Hartmann's *Iwein* is quite the opposite of that of his *Erec*. Here again, to be sure, the source is a work of Chrétien, his *Chevalier au Lion* or *Yvain*, but this time Hartmann stays much closer to his source than he did in his *Erec* (*Yvain*—6,879; *Iwein*—8,166 lines). Also, there are 32 *Iwein* manuscripts extant, 15 complete ones and 17 fragments as opposed to only one complete and two fragmentary *Erec* manuscripts (see above). However, despite the rich tradition it has been impossible to determine a stemma. Usually, either A (Giessen), B (Heidelberg), or both have served as the basis for scholarly editions since they are the oldest (13th century), although they differ from each other. In addition, there has been quite a bit more scholarship done on *Erec*, where there seem to be more problems, than on *Iwein*, though *Iwein* is not without problems, too. And finally, the major crisis for the respective protagonists is the opposite one: Erec suffers from inactivity (*verligen*), whereas Iwein gets into trouble because he is carried away by too much knightly action and misses the date for his promised return to his wife.

Iwein, a young knight at King Arthur's court, seizes his opportunity for fame and fortune when he hears the report of his kinsman Kalogrenant's (mis-)adventure at the magical fountain ten years previously. Hoping to get to the fountain before Arthur can, he slips away from the court secretly and repeats the stages of Kalogrenant's adventure. At the delightfully situated fountain where nature is unblemished, he pours water from it onto the stone, thereby immediately causing a violent storm to erupt. When the storm subsides, he sees the lord of the forest riding up to confront him. A brutal duel ensues in which Iwein manages eventually to wound his opponent severely by slicing through his helmet with his sword. Realizing that he is about to die, the knight quits the fight, and his horse carries him swiftly back to his castle with Iwein in hot pursuit, obsessed with the desire to capture or kill the knight to prove his victory in the duel and so avoid mockery, particularly from the scornful Sir Kei.

At the castle gate, Iwein leans forward over his horse's neck to deliver a finishing blow to his opponent, and at that very moment the portcullis slams down, narrowly missing Iwein's back, and impaling his horse just behind the saddle, killing it. The knight is carried through a second gateway, tripping a second portcullis, and trapping Iwein in the room-like space between the two portcullises. Lunete, a lovely maiden, enters the space from a side door, recognizes Iwein as the one knight who a long time ago at Arthur's court had greeted her politely when no one else there had done so, and gives him a magic ring that will make him invisible as long as he holds it in his hand. When she leaves, the people of the castle enter, flailing about with their swords, searching unsuccessfully for the invisible Iwein, in order to avenge the death of their lord. While Iwein looks on, the body of the slain lord of the castle is carried past, followed by his grief-stricken wife, Laudine. Iwein is immediately overwhelmed with love for her and sorely regrets having caused her sorrow.

Lunete then hatches a clever plan to persuade Laudine to marry the knight who had killed her husband, Ascalon, by arguing that the fountain and Laudine's lands now have no protector after the death of Ascalon, that King Arthur is due to arrive in under a fortnight, and that Iwein is surely a better knight than Ascalon was—he had, after all, defeated Ascalon. Lunete's calculated maneuvering eventually succeeds, and Iwein and Laudine are married. King Arthur and his knights arrive as expected, pour water from the fountain on the stone, and when the ensuing storm abates, Sir Kei is granted the first duel with the defender (Iwein). Kei suffers a humiliating defeat; Iwein comes forward to greet Arthur and all repair to the castle for a huge celebration. When Arthur is about to leave, Gawain takes Iwein aside, warns him that he might fall into the error of Erec by staying home too much with Laudine, and persuades him to come along with him to continue winning honors in tournaments. Laudine reluctantly grants Iwein leave of one year's duration with the strict admonition that he *must* return before that time expires. She gives him a ring in token of their commitment to one another.

After more than a year has passed, Iwein suddenly realizes that he has stayed away too long and that it is now too late. Lunete appears before Arthur's court, publicly charges Iwein with unfaithfulness, and demands the return of Laudine's ring. The blow to his honor, the humiliation, the loss of his self-respect, and the undeniable fact of his own guilt have a devastating effect on Iwein, driving him to madness. He flees to the forest and lives there like a wild man, completely naked, for some time until the maid of the Countess of Narison finds him sleeping and heals him of his madness with a magical salve. Recovered, Iwein helps the Countess by defeating and capturing Count Aliers, who had been ravaging her land and besieging her castle. However, Iwein refuses all favors and takes his leave.

From this point on, Iwein undergoes the following series of adventures:

> He saves a lion engaged in a struggle with a dragon by killing the dragon. In appreciation the lion then becomes his companion, Iwein is ever after known as the "Knight with the Lion."

> Iwein returns to the magic fountain and finds Lunete imprisoned in the chapel. She is to be burned at the stake the next noon for having given treasonous advice to Laudine. Realizing that his failure is the reason for her plight, Iwein promises to be her champion when he returns the next day.

> At a nearby castle that night he learns that the land has been ravaged by the giant, Harpin, two of the lord's sons have been hanged, and two more will be the next morn-

ing unless the lord turns his daughter over to the giant. Because the lord's wife is Gawain's sister, Iwein agrees to fight the giant and kills him in the morning with the aid of the lion.

He then returns to the magic fountain in the nick of time to save Lunete in a trial by combat, killing her accuser, the steward, and defeating his two brothers, again with the help of the lion. He deliberately conceals his identity from Laudine when she thanks him and leaves immediately, though both he and the lion are wounded.

After two weeks at a nearby castle, Iwein and his lion travel on. They are overtaken by a maiden, who asks for Iwein's help as champion for the younger daughter of the Count of the Black Thorn, to represent her in a trial by combat with the champion of her older sister before King Arthur on a given date. Iwein agrees to help, but before that they come to a castle where 300 ladies are held captive by two giants and forced to make elegant clothing in a type of medieval sweatshop. Iwein, again aided by the lion, is able to kill the giants and return the ladies to their noble station in life.

At Arthur's court, Gawain is preparing to fight incognito when Iwein and the younger daughter arrive just in time. The evil older sister has secured Gawain's service to support her attempt to disinherit her younger sister after their father's death. Iwein, of course, appears as the "Knight with the Lion." Thus the two good friends begin their fight without recognizing each other. The duel lasts all day until at nightfall they stop, each one wounded but without advantage over the other. When they then mutually disclose their identities, the combat is declared over, Gawein admits to having supported the wrong side, and King Arthur enforces an equal settlement of the estate between the two sisters.

Iwein has restored his honor but is still afflicted by love for Laudine. He slips away from court again with the lion and goes to the magic fountain once more in the hope of forcing a reconciliation. When he pours the water on the stone this time, the most terrible storm of all time arises. Laudine feels the need for a protector more than ever and asks Lunete for advice. Lunete suggests the "Knight with the Lion," but only on the condition that Laudine swear an oath to help him "regain his lady's favor." This she does, Lunete goes out, finds Iwein, and brings him to the castle where he and Laudine are finally reconciled, even though it had taken some clever deception on Lunete's part.

Although we have mentioned the various ways in which *Iwein* differs from *Erec*, there are a surprising number of marked similarities in structure and motifs. Both heroes attain early success, honor, and marriage, then have to repair their shattered reputations. Although it may not be too clear in the case of Erec, both redeem themselves by a change in the basis for their chivalry. Iwein, in particular, changes from a self-centered hero to a knight whose deeds are performed in the service of others. Structurally, the court of King Arthur is the starting point of the adventures. During the course of each story, there is an intermediate return to Arthur's court (in *Erec* at the hunt in the forest, and in *Iwein* Arthur comes to the fountain) and a final ending at his court where both heroes regain their honor (in *Iwein* not quite final; the reconciliation with Laudine is yet to come). Furthermore, there is the duel with the unrecognized friend (Guivreiz and Gawain) which is the last step, save one, in the process of rehabilitation. Both Erec and Iwein have the problem of establishing a lasting love and marriage relationship with their respective wives and of learning to assume their proper roles as rulers.

Although Chrétien's *Yvain* was surely Hartmann's immediate source, scholars have found earlier traces of the Iwein-figure in the historical Owen, son of Uriens, in Welsh sources of the 7th and 9th centuries and in Geoffrey of Monmouth's *Historia Regum Britanniae* (see above, p. 128). It seems that heroic figures developed from the historical ones, resulting euhemeristically in tales like the story "Owen and Luned" in the Welsh *Mabinogion*. How these then were transmitted to Chrétien is still uncertain, but there seems to be a fairy tale background to *Yvain* in the figure of Laudine, in the magical fountain, in the sudden storm caused by the pouring of the water, and in the figure of the protector. Other fairy tale elements would be the magic salve that heals Iwein of his madness, the magic ring that makes the bearer invisible, the dwarfs and giants, and the thankful lion, although that is a very old classical motif. All of these have their narrative function in Chrétien's and Hartmann's romances.

We have said earlier that there may be fewer problems involved in interpreting *Iwein* than in *Erec*, yet in many ways *Iwein* is more difficult to deal with. Among the points discussed in the secondary literature is the question of Hartmann's attitude toward Arthur and his court, indeed toward chivalry in general. Some scholars have detected traces of irony, whereas others see Hartmann's work as an *adaption courtoise* of Chrétien. Another question is the interpretation of Ascalon, with some maintaining that it was a sinful, uncourtly, unnecessary act by Iwein that is responsible for his downfall. They point to Hartmann's description of the pursuit and killing as done *âne zuht* (without restraint or regard for the rules of chivalry, l. 1056). Others view it less judgmentally and sympathize with Hartmann's exculpatory explanation. In addition, there is the question of why Laudine gives Iwein leave to be absent for a year, especially because she has been convinced of the need for a protector of the fountain as a compelling reason for marrying Iwein in the first place. Who, indeed, will defend the fountain while he is gone? As in *Erec*, the problem of the hero's development is also present here, perhaps more obviously so, in that we see all his deeds after his madness as in the service of others. For some this is a melding of the chivalric with the religious. Finally, the degree that Hartmann was responding to the social situation of his day has also been the subject of discussion, especially as it might have pertained to the rise, ambition, and self-reflection of the ministeriales.

Hartmann's *Iwein* must have been a very popular work, judging from the number of extant manuscripts. There are other later versions of the story, but they depend largely on Chrétien's work: the Old Norse *Ivens Saga* (ca. 1230), the Swedish *Ivan, The Knight of the Lion* (ca. 1303), and the Middle English *Ywain and Gawain* (ca. 1350). The Welsh "Owein and Luned" from the *Mabinogion* (earliest MS ca. 1225) probably shares a common Anglo-Norman source with Chrétien. Hartmann's work was well known, referred to, and even borrowed from by other German authors of courtly epics. Ulrich Füeterer's *Yban* (ca. 1480) in his *Buch der Abenteuer* is based on Hartmann's version.

We are very fortunate to have some illustrations of Hartmann's *Iwein* in the form of a fresco cycle at Castle Rodeneck near Brixen in the Tyrol. Identified in 1972 and cleaned, the frescoes date from the early 13th century and depict eleven scenes from Iwein's first adventures. The Hessenhof in Schmalkalden (Thuringia) also has illustrations on its walls, seven picture strips, with 26-27 scenes from Iwein's adventures. These date likewise from the first half of the 13th century. Although they may have originally been planned to depict the entire story, they concentrate on the early parts up to the episode with the lion, and there was not much room left for the rest. Some are missing, others in poor condition. In a different medium, from the first half of the 14th century, are two scenes of the Malterer Embroidery, which show Iwein wounding Ascalon and, accompanied by Lunete, meeting Laudine for the first time. The embroideries are in the Augustiner Museum in Freiburg i. Br.

Texts:
Bech, Fedor, ed. *Hartmann von Aue. Dritter Theil., Iwein, oder der Ritter mit dem Löwen.* Wiesbaden, 1869. [4]1902. Repr. 1934 (= Dt. Klassiker des MAs, 3).

Benecke, Georg F., and Karl Lachmann, eds. *Iwein, der riter mit dem lewen getihtet von dem hern Hartman, dienstman ze Ouwe.* Berlin: 1827. 7th edition with title: *Iwein. Eine Erzählung von Hartmann von Aue.* Completely re-edited by Ludwig Wolff. 2 Vols. Berlin, 1968. (Vol. 1: Text; Vol. 2: Critical apparatus and notes). This is the standard edition. Vol. 1 also available separately as paperback.

Cramer, Thomas, ed. and trans. *Hartmann von Aue. Iwein. Urtext und Übersetzung.* Berlin & New York: De Gruyter, 1968. [3]1981. Text of 7th edition of Beneke, Lachmann, and Wolff, with facing mod. Ger. prose trans. and copious notes, with bibliography.

Henrici, Emil, ed. *Hartmann von Aue: Der Ritter mit dem Löwen.* Halle (Saale): Waisenhaus, 1891/93. Part 1: Text; Part 2: Notes (= Germanistische Handbibliothek, 8).

McConeghy, Patrick M., ed. and trans. *Hartmann von Aue. Iwein.* New York & London: Garland Publ., 1984 (= GLML, A19). Modified version of Wolff's 1968 text, with facing Engl. prose trans., informative introduction, bibliography, and notes to the text.

Steinger, Hans, ed. *Iwein.* In *Erec/Iwein.* Eds. Hans Naumann and Hans Steinger. Leipzig: Reclam, 1933 (= Dt. Lit. in Entwicklungsreihen, Höfische Epik, 3).

Translations:
Cramer, Thomas (See above).
McConeghy, Patrick M. (See above).
Thomas, J. Wesley, trans. *Iwein.* Lincoln: Univ. of Nebraska Press, 1979. Very readable Engl. prose trans., with lengthy intro.

Facsimiles:
Heinrichs, H. Matthias, ed. *Hartmann von Aue. Iwein. Handschrift B.* Köln, Graz: Böhlau, 1964. (= Dt. Texte in Handschriften, 2). Photocopy of Ms. B (Giessen) in original size, brief introduction.

Okken, Lambertus, ed. *Hartmann von Aue. Iwein. Ausgewählte Abbildungen und Materialien zur handschriftlichen Überlieferung.* Göppingen: Kümmerle, 1974 (= Litterae, 24).

See also F. Unterkirchner's facsimile of the entire Ambraser Heldenbuch listed above in section on *Erec.*

## *Iwein*—Bibliography

Batts, Michael. "Hartmann's *humanitas*: A New Look at *Iwein.*" In: *Germanic Studies in Honor of E. H. Sehrt.* Coral Gables, FL: Univ. of Miami Press, 1968. Pp. 37-51.

Beneke, Georg Friedrich. *Wörterbuch zu Hartmanns Iwein.* Göttingen: Dietrich, [2]1874. Repr. Wiesbaden: Sändig, 1965.

Buschinger, Danielle. "Hartmann von Aue, adaptateur du 'Chevalier au lion' de Chrétien de Troyes." In: *Littérature et société au moyen age*. (Actes du colloque des 5 et 6 mai 1978). Ed. by D. Buschinger. Paris, 1978. Pp. 371-91.

Close comparison of Hartmann's version with Chrétien's, special attention to differences in detail.

Clifton-Everest, J. M. "Christian Allegory in Hartmann's *Iwein*." *GR* 48 (1973): 247-59.

Cramer, Thomas. "*Sælde* und *êre* in Hartmanns *Iwein*." *Euph.* 60 (1966): 30-47. Also in: Kuhn-Cormeau, 1973. Pp. 426-49 (above).

Interpretation based on the guilt of Iwein for his killing of Ascalon (*âne zuht*).

Curschmann, Michael. "*Der aventiure bilde nemen*: The Intellectual and Social Environment of the Iwein Murals at Rodenegg Castle." In: M. Jones and R. Wisbey, eds. *London Chrétien Symposium* (see above). Pp. 219-27.

Hasty, Will. "The Natural Order of Things in Hartmann's *Iwein*: The Adventure of Paradox." In: W. H. *Adventure as Social Performance. A Study of the German Court Epic.* Tübingen: Niemeyer, 1990. Pp. 17-37.

The paradoxical role of *aventiure* as a means of gaining honor in courtly society in the case of Iwein.

Hatto, Arthur T. " 'Der Aventiure Meine' in Hartmann's *Iwein*." In: *Medieval German Studies Presented to Frederick Norman*. London, 1965. Pp. 94-103.

Applies Gottfried's term to the "hidden" meaning in Iwein's awakening in Hartmann and Chrétien.

Kaiser, Gert. " 'Iwein' oder 'Laudine'." *ZfdPh* 99 (1980): 20-28.

Critical response to Mertens's Laudine monograph (below).

McFarland, Timothy. "Narrative Structure and the Renewal of the Hero's Identity in *Iwein*." In: *London Hartmann Symposium, 1985* (See above). Pp. 129-57.

Addresses the problem of "development" in Iwein by examining his two monologues and his two dialogues with Laudine in the second cycle and demonstrating the changes in orientation that have taken place in the course of these structural elements.

Mertens, Volker. *Laudine: Soziale Problematik im "Iwein" Hartmanns von Aue*. Berlin: Erich Schmidt, 1978 (= Beihefte zu *ZfdPh*, 3).

The problems of women rulers and Hartmann's sympathetic portrayal of Laudine, but see Kaiser (above).

Okken, Lambertus (See *Kommentar zu den Artusepen Hs. v. A.* above).

Ranawake, Silvia. "Zu Form und Funktion der Ironie in Hartmanns *Iwein*." In: *Wolfram-Studien VII*. Ed. by Werner Schröder. Berlin: Erich Schmidt, 1982. Pp. 75-116.

Examines Hartmann's use of irony based on a close comparison with Chrétien's version.

Robertshaw, Alan. "Ambiguity and Morality in *Iwein*." In: *London Hartmann Symposium, 1985* (See above). Pp. 117-28.

Describes the ambiguity of the author's attitude towards Iwein's action in the first part of the work, then his obvious approval following Iwein's recovery from his madness and increasingly ethical motivation.

Sacker, Hugh. "An Interpretation of Hartmann's *Iwein*." *GR* 36 (1961): 5-26.

Salmon, Paul. " 'Ane zuht.' Hartmann's von Aue Criticism of Iwein." *MLR* 69 (1974): 556-61.

Challenges the significance of the expression regarding Iwein's guilt.

Zutt, Herta. *König Artus, Iwein, der Löwe: Die Bedeutung des gesprochenen Worts in Hartmanns Iwein.* Tübingen: Niemeyer, 1979.

## Hartmann's *Gregorius* and *Armer Heinrich*

With those two works by Hartmann we leave Arthurian romance and turn to Christian legend. *Gregorius* is quite clearly a legend, almost a saint's life or exemplum, with a moral, but the genre of *Armer Heinrich* is not so easily determined. To be sure, it does recount the miraculous cure of a leper, and in that respect would seem to fall into the category of Christian legend, but some would see it rather as a medieval novella with a fairy-tale ending. In any case, both seem to have been popular works in their day and are still among the most frequently read texts by modern students of MHG. Both have been re-interpreted by 20th-century authors: *Gregorius* by Thomas Mann in his short novel *Der Erwählte* (1951) and *Armer Heinrich* by Gerhart Hauptmann in his drama *Der arme Heinrich* (1902).

*Gregorius* exists in six complete manuscripts and five fragments, ranging from the 13th to 16th centuries. It has not been possible to establish a definite stemma, but two of the oldest manuscripts, A (Rome, Bibliotheca Vaticana, Cod. Regin. Lat. 1345) and B (Strasbourg, former Johanniter-Library, Cod. A 100) usually are used as the basis for modern editions, despite the fact that neither one records the prologue. That is found in only two of the manuscripts, J (Berlin, Staatsbibliothek Stiftung Preußischer Kulturbesitz, Ms. germ qu. 979) and K (Konstanz, Stadtarchiv, Hs. A I 1). The text, including prologue and short epilogue, contains 6,004 lines. There is a Latin translation by Arnold of Lübeck of 1210-13 and numerous German prose versions beginning in the 14th century. Hartmann's source was a version of the OF *La Vie du Pape Saint Grégoire*, which is preserved in six manuscripts from the 13th to 15th centuries, and the legend itself may go back to the middle of the 11th century, but the idea of a "Pope Gregory" has no historical basis. None of the existing manuscripts appears to have been Hartmann's source. Nevertheless, additions and expansions by Hartmann can be identified with some certainty. He seems also to inject his own comments on the action and to have a good overview of all the events of the story in mind, emphasizing as he does the total structure of the tale.

> *Gregorius* is a medieval Oedipus story with a double incest, in that Gregorius himself is the product of an incestuous brother-sister relationship. The young noble twin siblings of Aquitania are orphaned at the death of their father and, beginning with an entirely proper mutual affection, they are lured by the devil into an excessive devotion to one another that eventually leads to the sister's pregnancy. The brother undertakes a pilgrimage to Jerusalem to do penance and dies of love-sickness en route. The sister gives birth to Gregorius secretly, then has Gregorius put into a small cask, laid in a boat, along with some money and an ivory tablet on which is inscribed the circumstances of his birth and a plea that he

be baptized, schooled, and requested to pray for his sinful parents. Thereupon the boat is pushed away from shore, and Gregorius is entrusted to the waves and God's mercy.

The boat with the child is found by two fishermen, who turn the child over to the abbot of a near by monastery. They are paid for their silence and under a pretext Gregorius is raised in the family of one of the fishermen, yet under the watchful eye of the abbot. As he grows up Gregorius becomes a gifted pupil in the monastery school and seems destined for a monastic career, but he eventually learns that he is not the fisherman's son when his "mother" gives vent to years of pent-up resentment, which he overhears "by chance" following an incident during which, quite uncharacteristically, he has struck his "brother." Gregorius wants to leave and become a knight, but the abbot tries to persuade him otherwise in a lengthy argument. Finally, however, the abbot does agree to have Gregorius outfitted for knighthood, but he makes one last attempt to dissuade him: he gives Gregorius the tablet that tells of his noble lineage and his sinful birth, believing that this will lead him to embrace the monastic life in order to atone for the sins of his parents, but Gregorius is happy to learn that he is of noble family, and he wants only to find his land and his parents. He sets sail, leaving his ultimate destination in God's hand.

After surviving a storm, Gregorius arrives at a fortified city that is being besieged by a suitor of the lady of the land in an attempt to compel her to marry him. She is actually Gregorius's mother, who had not married, having preferred to lead an ascetic life. However, when Gregorius defeats the suitor, thereby freeing the land, and after her vassals strongly urge her, the lady agrees to marry Gregorius, being strongly attracted to him and ignoring any niggling doubts she may have when she recognizes the material of the clothes he is wearing as being that which she placed in the boat with her child "or very like it." He proves to be an able ruler, until his wife/mother happens to get hold of his ivory tablet and realizes that she is married to her own son. When Gregorius too learns their true relationship, he tells his mother that she should continue to rule her land and do penance through good works for her sins. He then leaves immediately to find a place where he can do severe penance himself in the wilderness.

A mean fisherman, suspicious of Gregorius's intent, shackles him to a rocky island in the middle of the lake and throws the key into the water. Seventeen years later, papal legates arrive at the fisherman's house. They had come as the result of identical dreams indicating that that was where they would find the next pope. The fisherman finds the key in a fish he had caught to serve as a meal to the legates, he rows them out to the rock, and they find Gregorius still alive but most reluctant to leave his rock. He is eventually convinced that God has forgiven him his sin, goes with the legates to Rome, and is crowned Pope. At length his mother arrives on a pilgrimage to Rome, receives absolution from Gregorius, and stays in Rome until her death.

*Gregorius* begins with a rather lengthy prologue of 176 lines, in which the author accuses himself of having composed works for worldly rewards. He points out that it is misguided to postpone penance for sins, thinking that there will be time to do that later in life, since that attitude does not allow for the eventuality of an unexpectedly quick death. Therefore, he wants to lighten the burden of his sins by telling the truth in the firm belief that no man's sin is too great not to be pardoned if he has genuine contrition. He will tell a story of a man who sinned terribly, to serve as an example for all sinful people who despair of God's grace. They do not have the proper faith to do penance after confession and believe that they will be forgiven. They will travel on the easy road to perdition. They should rather choose the difficult road of blessedness that leads to a sweet end. Then, using a somewhat adapted version of the biblical simile of the Good Samaritan, he describes the traveller attacked by robbers and left half-dead. But God provided the wounded man with two pieces of clothing: Fear (that he should die) and Hope (that he would not be damned). In addition, spiritual loyalty and remorse for his sins poured the oil of Grace and the wine of Christian faith into his wounds and healed him. Grace also lifted him up on its shoulders and carried him to where he could be cured, just as Christ, the Good Shepherd, took the sinner home. The man survived his wounds, i.e. sins, because he did not succumb to the sin of *desperatio* (*zwîvel*), doubt that man can be forgiven. That is the greatest sin of all, the one that can not be forgiven. Hartmann then names himself as the author of the "strange tale" of such a man, whom he calls "the Good Sinner," saying that he is aware of the shocking nature of the story he has to tell.

The comments on sin and salvation through contrition and penance in the prologue underline the main theme of *Gregorius*, but scholars are divided on the question of Gregorius's culpability. Generally speaking, one can differentiate between subjective (willful, intentional) and objective (unintended, unknowing) sinfulness. The incest of Gregorius's parents is considered subjective, although Hartmann does have the Devil seduce the twins, and the sister does not cry out in protest because it would destroy their honor. The brother then does the proper thing: undertaking a pilgrimage to Jerusalem, and the sister renounces marriage, preferring to lead a celibate life of contrition and penance. The state of Gregorius, the product of the incest, is not so certain. He was no willing participant in the incest, and whether his baptism cleared him of original sin or whether he inherited the sins of his parents is not clear, although the thinking of the day was firmly that he did not. We only know that God did not let him perish on the water and brought him safely to the fishermen and the abbot.

If Gregorius is not a sinner by virtue of his birth, then perhaps he becomes sinful through his actions in the course of the story. Is his desire to leave the monastery and become a knight a sin? Should he have stayed there and atoned for the sins of his parents? Is the role of a knight essentially sinful? Is his mother's decision to marry him, motivated as it was by her need for a protector or possibly even an heir, another sin? Is she wrong in failing to pursue her recognition of the material? Is she perhaps blinded by erotic attraction to a handsome young man? Can either of them be blamed for the second incest? These are questions that scholars have addressed in a variety of ways. We are left after the revelation of the second incest with Gregorius's advice to his mother not to despair of God's grace but to live a life of penance through good works. As for Gregorius himself, he has again discovered that he is not the person that he had thought himself to be. He wishes only to flee the world, to remove himself as far as possible from all human contact, to devote himself to penance. This may be, as some have suggested, a reflection of the eremitical movement of the day and not connected directly to any particular instance of sinfulness. The tendency of more recent criticism seems to be skeptical of theological influences and to be willing to look at *Gregorius* more in terms of the final outcome of the story. For a more detailed review of research, see Hasty (above), pp. 52-67.

Texts:

Neumann, Friedrich, ed. *Hartmann von Aue. Gregorius der gute Sünder.* Wiesbaden: Brockhaus, 1958. 5th edition by Christoph Cormeau, 1981 (= Deutsche Klassiker des Mittelalters, NF 2). Introduction, MHG text, notes, and commentary.

Paul, Hermann, ed. *Hartmann von Aue. Gregorius.* Halle: Niemeyer, 1882. 13th edition by Burghart Wachinger. Tübingen: Niemeyer, 1984 (= ATB, 2). The standard edition.

Schwarz, Ernst, ed. *Gregorius. Der arme Heinrich. Text, Nacherzählung, Worterklärungen.* Darmstadt: Wiss. Buchges., 1967. MHG text, mod. Ger. retelling, bibliography.

Sol, Hendrik B., ed. *La Vie de Pape Grégoire. Huit versions francaises médiévales de la légende du bon pêcheur.* Amsterdam, 1977. First edition of all versions of Hartmann's OF source.

Translations:

Buehne, Sheema Zeben, trans. *Gregorius, the Good Sinner.* New York: F. Ungar, 1966. Bilingual edition, introduction by Helen Adolf.

Kippenberg, B., ed. and trans. *Hartmann von Aue. Gregorius der gute Sünder.* Stuttgart: Reclam, 1963, etc. (= UB, 1787). MHG text of F. Neumann, mod. Ger. trans., afterword by H. Kuhn.

Zeydel, Edwin H., trans. *Gregorius: A Medieval Oedipus Legend.* Chapel Hill: Univ. of North Carolina Press, 1955. Repr. New York: AMS Press, 1966 (= UNC Studies in the Germanic Langs. and Lits., 14). Introduction, Engl. verse trans., and notes.

Facsimile:

Heinze, Norbert, ed. *Hartmann von Aue, Gregorius. Die Überlieferung des Prologs, die Vaticana-Handschrift A und eine Auswahl der übrigen Textzeugen.* Göppingen: Kümmerle, 1974. (= Litterae, 28). Photocopies of A with selection of parallel texts.

For bibliography on *Gregorius* see *GREGORIUS* AND *ARMER HEINRICH*—BIBLIOGRAPHY (p. 153 f.).

*Der arme Heinrich* is a shorter epic poem of 1,520 lines, like Hartmann's other narrative works, in rhymed couplets. It has been difficult to determine precisely the form of Hartmann's original tale because there are only three complete manuscripts of it extant, along with three short fragments, and there are considerable differences in the tradition. Hermann Paul, the editor of the original ATB edition (1882) used A (Strasbourg, Stadtbibliothek, destroyed in the fire of 1870, but preserved in a reliable copy of 1784), dated to 1330-50, as his *Leithandschrift*. The B version is found in B$^a$ (Heidelberg, Universitätsbibliothek, cpg. 341), dated 1320-30, and B$^b$ (Genf-Cologny, Fondation Martin Bodmer, Cod. Bodmer 72, previously Kalocza, Ms. 1) of 1320-30. Of the three fragments, C (St. Florian) and E (Munich) are earlier, first half and second half of the 13th century with only 61 and 117 verses, respectively. D (Indersdorf) is second half of the 14th century. Subsequent editors, Albert Leitzmann and Ludwig Wolff, were not so strict in following A, preferring to use philological methods to produce what has become a generally accepted text. The most recent editor, Gesa Bonath (1984), tends to side with Wolff's text but has provided variants at the foot of each page so that the manuscript tradition can be viewed easily. Despite what seems to be a meager manuscript tradition, there is reason to believe that *Der arme Heinrich* was quite popular. There are numerous references to it in a variety of texts of the 13th and beginning 14th centuries.

We have mentioned the problem of determining the genre of *Armer Heinrich* and the fact that scholars have had divergent views on the subject. It would seem at first glance

to be a simple Christian tale of an attempted cure for leprosy using the blood of an innocent maiden that is rendered unnecessary by divine intervention, but then one would
expect that the former leper would have ended up as a saint or at least have entered a
monastery. The latter is, in fact, the way the B version does end, rather than in the marriage with the maiden in A, but that seems to have been a change by someone who
wanted to give the tale a more pious twist. The connection to the fairy tale lies in the
happy ending where the poor maiden marries the prince, and the notion of a novella as
genre lies in the sudden drastic change in Heinrich's life and its astonishing consequences, plus other formal aspects. Still, there is no way to avoid the didactic thrust that
Hartmann gives to the work, and that could place it squarely into the genre of a religious
exemplum, but it is surely not a conventional one if one considers the extensive role of
the maiden and her motivation.

The events of the story are quickly recounted:

In the prologue, Hartmann first identifies himself as the author with the famous lines:
*Ein ritter sô gelêret was/ daz er an den buochen las/ swaz er dar an geschriben fand:/ der
was Hartman genant,/ dienstman was er zOuwe.* (There was a knight so learned that he
read whatever he found in books: his name was Hartmann, a ministerialis in Ouwe). Then
he describes his purposes in looking around for a story: to entertain people, to praise the
honor of God, and to gain the favor of people. He has found a tale that he will interpret for
people who will reward him, hoping that anyone who hears or reads his story will pray for
his salvation.

Heinrich, a noble lord in Ouwe in Swabia, is described as a man of many excellent
qualities that had gained him high renown in the world as an exemplary courtly knight and
ruler. Suddenly, for no apparent reason, his splendid life, like Job's, comes crashing down.
He is afflicted with leprosy. Hartmann does not disclose why Heinrich should have been
singled out, but sickness, particularly leprosy, was generally considered to be punishment
from God for sins. Heinrich's first impulse is to find the best doctors, to see if there might
possibly be a cure for his illness. He travels first to Montpelier then to Salerno, both important centers of medicine in the Middle Ages, where he is given little hope that he can be
cured. But he does learn that a possible, but unlikely cure exists: the blood from the heart
of a virgin, given of her own free will, and, of course, thereby costing her her life.

Accepting the impossibility of such an event, Heinrich returns home, gives up his lands
and possessions, and retires to one of his remote farms far from the world of the court, to
await his inevitable death. The farmer and his wife have an eight-year old daughter, among
their other children, who takes a particular liking to Heinrich, being around him and serv-
ing him all the time. He returns her attention with trinkets and other gifts, admiring her
"sweet spirit" (*süezer geist*) and calling her affectionately his "wife" (*gemahel*). After
three years the farmer finally asks Heinrich whether there is not a cure for his leprosy by
the doctors in Salerno. Heinrich goes into a lengthy discourse on his illness and its reason,
apparently putting into words for the first time his recognition of his own responsibility for
his state: he had forgotten that God was responsible for his successful life. He accuses
himself of being a "world-fool" (*werlttor*), of having pride or *superbia* (*hochmuot*), for
which he is being punished by God, but he does mention the cure that he had been told by
the doctor in Salerno—all this within earshot of the daughter.

The focus of the action now turns away from Heinrich, and a major part of the story—structurally the center of it—is devoted to the maiden and her attempts to persuade her parents to let her sacrifice herself for him. She does this in a series of emotional arguments with her parents on successive nights. Her reasoning is this: if Heinrich dies, the family will have a new feudal lord who will surely not treat them as well as Heinrich has; when she grows up she will have to marry, something she knows will be unpleasant; if she can heal Heinrich, she will be certain of going straight to heaven. The parents are astonished at the wisdom she expresses, are finally convinced that the Holy Spirit is speaking through their daughter and reluctantly accede to her wishes. Heinrich at first refuses: what would people say, if he accepted and the cure did not work after all? Then he is surprised when the parents give their consent. At length, he and the maiden set out for Salerno.

There the doctor at first tries to talk the maiden out of her plan and is at pains to emphasize that the cure will not take place if she is in any way under pressure but then takes her to his operating room. Heinrich waits outside. The girl rips off her clothing and leaps to the operating table where she is fastened securely, and the doctor begins to sharpen his knife. Hearing this from outside, Heinrich peers through a crack in the door and sees the maiden in all her beauty lying there. He looks at her, then at himself, and has a complete change of heart (*metanoia*), his values are completely reversed, and he is willing to submit to God's will. He rushes in and stops the operation. At this the girl is absolutely furious. She curses Heinrich for his cowardice, but Heinrich accepts her fury calmly, and they prepare to travel home. At that point God (*cordis speculator*) looks into the hearts of both of them and relieves them of their suffering by healing Heinrich so that by the time they return home Heinrich looked as he had twenty years earlier.

His return is celebrated joyfully by all his people; he takes charge of his lands once again and, like Job, is wealthier and enjoys greater honors than before his illness. His vassals urge him to marry to ensure the succession in his realm, but they cannot agree on a wife for Heinrich, until he points out that he owes everything to the maiden and that he wants to marry her. All agree, although the maiden is not even asked, and Heinrich and the maiden are married. They have a sweet long life on earth and, we are assured, attain eternal life in heaven.

We do not know what Hartmann's source may have been. Since he mentions his search of books for a story in the prologue and uses the verb *diuten* (to interpret) when he speaks of telling ther story, it has been assumed that he probably had a Latin source. There are Latin exempla, *Heinricus pauper* and *Albertus pauper*, of the 14th and 15th centuries, but these themselves seem to have been influenced by Hartmann's tale. References to leprosy go back to biblical sources, and cures for it using human blood were known in antiquity. In the Middle Ages, the numerous legends of St. Sylvester who cures the Emperor Constantine of leprosy through baptism after Constantine had refused to try a bath in the blood of children is similar to *Armer Heinrich*, and the Amicus and Amelius legend, which has numerous versions in several languages, tells of the friend sacrificing his children to save his friend from leprosy, only to find that the children have been miraculously brought back to life. See also Konrad von Würzburg, *Engelhard* (p. 350 f.).

The name Heinrich and the fact that he is "von Ouwe" have raised some speculation that the story may have come from the history of the family of Hartmann's liege lord or possibly even Hartmann's own family. The unusual marriage of a nobleman to a farmer's daughter, even though the farmer was a freeman, may account for the fact that Hartmann's family had been reduced to the state of ministeriales, or Hartmann may have wanted to honor his own lord by telling the story. Unfortunately, there is no record of such a family, let alone a family with such a history, and thus the origins remain problematic.

Much attention has been paid to addressing the question of Heinrich's "sin." Since leprosy was considered punishment for sin, one should assume that that is the case for Heinrich, but Hartmann's narrator, if one reads closely, does not identify a specific reason for the leprosy. He merely describes Heinrich's fall from grace. Of course, Heinrich himself, is quite convinced that he is being punished for *superbia*, for having forgotten God, for thinking that he had acquired his position in life through his own merit. Perhaps that is what Hartmann had in mind after all. Certainly, it is significant that Heinrich's *metanoia* takes place when he suddenly begins to think more of the girl than he does of himself, submits to God's will, and stops the operation. Some scholars see *Armer Heinrich* as criticism of courtly society with the blame for Heinrich's sickness resting on that society. Others view Heinrich as someone whose sin lies in refusing to accept God's will rather than in the society itself. At any rate, Heinrich's suffering must be considered at least as the result of a faulty set of priorities. When he finds the right orientation, the cure can begin.

Hartmann notes that God has been testing Heinrich, as He did Job, but also the maiden. She seems to be such a faithful, compassionate girl, and her offer to sacrifice herself for Heinrich so truly Christian that we are left to wonder why she should have been tested, too. Some scholars maintain that she, like Heinrich, is too extreme: he in his worldliness, she in her otherworldliness. There is also the question of her motivation: is she really doing this for Heinrich, or is her main interest in her own salvation? Would she have done it for any other leper? However one decides to answer such questions, the figure of the maiden is quite remarkable in the work. She takes up a major portion of the narrative with her arguments, when Hartmann presents her inner feelings in considerable detail. This is quite unusual for a female figure in MHG literature, and some see her manipulation of her parents as not entirely positive. In general, *Armer Heinrich* is more a narrative examining the thoughts of the characters than their actions.

The role of the physical beauty of the girl and the eroticism of the scene in Salerno has been treated by many scholars, with some seeing it as a reflection of her spiritual beauty, while others go so far as to see an erotic bond between Heinrich and the young girl right from the start. There can be no doubt that the beauty of the maiden is the catalyst for Heinrich's *metanoia*, however one wishes to interpret it. Finally, we should not overlook the happy ending—at least it seems to be happy—in the marriage. This, too, has been problematical for many scholars, as we have already indicated.

Texts:
de Boor, Helmut, ed. *Hartmann von Aue. Der arme Heinrich. Mhd. Text und Übertragung.* Hamburg-Frankfurt a. M., 1963. [15] 1981. MHG text with mod. Ger. prose trans.
Gierach, Erich, ed. *Der arme Heinrich von Hartmann von Aue. Überlieferung und Herstellung.* Heidelberg, 1913. [2] 1925. Critical text and text of A and B in parallel.
Maurer, Friedrich, ed. *Hartmann von Aue, Der arme Heinrich nebst einer Auswahl aus der*

*"Klage", dem "Gregorius" und den "Liedern."* Berlin, 1958, [2]1968 (= Slg. Göschen, 18).

Mettke, Heinz, ed. *Hartmann von Aue. Der arme Heinrich.* Leipzig, 1974. Critical text and diplomatic edition of all manuscripts save Bb.

Paul, Hermann, ed. *Hartmann von Aue. Der arme Heinrich.* Halle: Niemeyer, 1882. Tübingen: Niemeyer, [15]1984, by Gesa Bonath. [16]1996, by Kurt Gärtner (= ATB, 3). The standard edition.

Translations:

Bell, Clair Hayden , trans. *Peasant Life in Old German Epics: "Meier Helmbrecht" and "Der arme Heinrich."* New York: Octagon Books, 1965. Engl. prose trans.

See de Boor (above).

Okken. Lambertus , trans. *Hartmann von Aue. Der arme Heinrich. Ein mittelhochdeutsches Märchen.* Amsterdam/Atlanta, GA: Rodopi, 1989. Mod. Ger. prose trans.

Pretzel, Ulrich , trans. *"Hartmann von Aue*, Der arme Heinrich." In: U. Pretzel. *Deutsche Erzählungen des Mittelalters.* Pp. 1-23. Mod. Ger. prose trans.

Rautenberg, U. (ed.), and S. Grosse, trans. *Hartmann von Aue. Der arme Heinrich.* Stuttgart: Reclam, 1961, etc. (= UB, 456). Mod. Ger. prose trans.

Facsimiles:

Müller, Ulrich, ed. *Hartmann von Aue, Der arme Heinrich. Abbildungen und Materialien zur gesamten handschriftlichen Überlieferung.* Göppingen: Kümmerle, 1971 (= Litterae, 3). Photocopies of manuscripts.

Sommer, Cornelius, ed. *Hartmann von Aue, Der arme Heinrich. Fassung der Handschrift Bb. In Abbildung aus der Kaloczaer Kodex.* Göppingen: Kümmerle, 1973 (= Litterae, 30). Photocopy of manuscript Bb.

## *Gregorius* and *Armer Heinrich*—Bibliography

Christoph, Siegfried. "Guilt, Shame, Atonement and Hartmann's Gregorius." *Euph.* 76 (1982): 207-21.

The dilemma of shame/honor and guilt/atonement as a basis for interpretation.

Cormeau, Christoph. *Hartmanns von Aue "Armer Heinrich" und "Gregorius." Studien zur Interpretation mit dem Blick auf die Theologie zur Zeit Hartmanns.* Munich, 1966. (= MTU, 15).

Examines concepts of early scholastic terminology (e.g., *ignorantia*) and attempts to find instances of them in the two works. An important study in its day and still very much worth reading.

Jones, Martin H. "Changing Perspectives on the Maiden in *Der arme Heinrich.*" In: *London Hartmann Symposium* (see above). Pp. 211-231.

Review of various interpretations of the maiden and her motivation for her sacrifice. Takes the maiden's words at face value and relates them to ideals of chastity of the time.

See also Kuhn/Cormeau, *Hartmann von Aue* (above): 8 articles on *Gregorius*, 5 on *Armer Heinrich.*

Kühnel, Jürgen. "Ödipus und Gregorius." In: *Psychologie in der Mediävistik* (Papers from a symposium at Steinheim an der Murr, 1984). Ed. J. Kühnel. Göppingen: Kümmerle, 1985 (= GAG, 431) Pp. 141-70.

Margetts, John. "Observations on the Representation of Female Attractiveness in the Works of Hartmann von Aue with Special Reference to *Der arme Heinrich.*" In: *London Hartmann Symposium* (see above). Pp. 199-210.

Interprets the scene in Salerno as having a strongly sexual/erotic aura (sadism, masochism, bondage). Considers also scenes in *Erec* and *Iwein* where female beauty arouses a sexual response.

Mertens, Volker. *Gregorius Eremita. Eine Lebensform des Adels bei Hartmann von Aue in ihrer Problematik und ihrer Wandlung in der Rezeption.* Munich: Artemis, 1978 (= MTU, 67).

Interpretation of *Gregorius* on the basis of the social situation of the day with special attention to patrons and possible audience.

Schwarz, Werner. "Free Will in Hartmann's *Gregorius.*" In: *Beiträge zur mittelalterlichen Literatur.* Ed. P. Ganz. Amsterdam: Rodopi, 1984. Pp. 25-44.

Seiffert, Leslie. "The Maiden's Heart. Legend and Fairy-tale in Hartmann's 'Der arme Heinrich'." *DVjs.* 37 (1936): 384-405.

Still valuable study of genre aspects of the work.

Tobin, Frank J. *"Gregorius" and "Armer Heinrich." Hartmann's Dualistic and Gradualistic Views of Reality.* Bern: Herbert Lang, 1973 (= Stanford German Studies, 3).

Wailes, Stephen L. "Hartmann von Aue's Stories of Incest." *JEGP* 91 (1992): 65-78.

Theme of incest in *Gregorius* as subtext in Freudian interpretation of *Der arme Heinrich.*

Wynn, Marianne. "Heroine without a Name: The Unnamed Girl in Hartmann's Story." In: *German Narrative Literature of the Twelfth and Thirteenth Centuries* (Roy Wisbey Festschr.). Ed. by Volker Honemann, et al. Tübingen: Niemeyer, 1994. Pp. 245-59.

The controversial theme of the forced marriage of the maiden who had wanted martyrdom, examined in relation to women's roles in Hartmann's day. The fact that she has no voice in the marriage must have produced a mixed reception.

## Hartmann's *Diu Klage*

*Diu Klage—Das Büchlein* is a didactic poem in the form of a debate between the Body and the Heart on the subject of courtly love. As such it could possibly have been treated along with Hartmann's love lyrics, which we have included in the general section on *Minnesang* (see p. 224 ff.), but related as it may be in theme, it is quite different in form, style, and apparent purpose. There has been little unanimity among editors and scholars on the title of the work. Some prefer *Die/Diu Klage*, others *Das (erste) Büchlein*, still others *Das Klagebüchlein* or *Klage-Büchlein*. To complicate matters further, the sole manuscript containing the work, the *Ambraser Heldenbuch* (Vienna Nationalbibliothek, Cod. Ser. Nov. 2663), has Hartmann's work at $22^{va}$—$26^{va}$ and another "Büchlein" immediately following Hartmann's work at $26^{vb}$—$28^{rb}$. This so-called *Zweites Büchlein* was once thought to belong to Hartmann's oeuvre, but subsequent scholarship has demonstrated that it does not. Two of the modern editions of Hartmann's *Klage* also have the text of *Das zweite Büchlein.*

The superscript by the scribe, Hans Ried, in the manuscript reads: *Ein schone Disputatz. Von der Liebe. Soeiner gegen einer schonen frawen gehabt. und getan hat* (a fine disputation on Love such as was had and pursued for a lovely lady). "Disputation" in the sense of Latin *disputatio*, a formal debate, here on the topic of Love, places the work in the long rhetorical tradition of antiquity and, since the debate is between Body and Heart, close to other dualistic debates, namely, the one between Body and Soul, as in the *Visio Fulberti*. The topic of Love suggests acquaintance with Chrétien's no longer extant *Ars Amatoria*, Ovid's *Remedia Amoris*, the *De arte honeste amandi* of Andreas Capellanus, and with the term *klage* (lament, complaint), the Romance *salut d'amour*. The *klage* in the sense of "complaint" has legal implications, and one does indeed find legal terminology in the "Büchlein." It may also be akin to allegorical MHG "Minnereden," a genre that could have been developing at approximately the time Hartmann was writing but flourished much later in the 14th and 15th centuries (see p. 423 f.).

Most important, however, is the didactic nature of the poem, but Ovidian instruction in love is not the point, nor is love an end in itself, but rather a means to make a young man find his place in society by teaching him the important virtues and social skills to please his chosen lady and thereby enable him to be pleasing to "God and the World." All this is presented as a kind of fictive inner biography of the poet himself, identified as Hartmann in v. 29, as the result of the chosen lady's refusal to listen to him.

The actual disputation then begins when the Body charges the Heart with leading it astray and laments the suffering it must endure. The Heart rejects the accusation and begins to explain what must be done to win the lady's favor: persistent effort and a proper frame of mind. Otherwise love is not worth much. The struggle itself is the important thing, and the body must sacrifice its desire for ease and comfort. A rapid-fire of one-line exchanges (stychomythia) between the two leads to an agreement to work together when the Body is willing to follow the Heart's instruction.

The Heart has three main pieces of advice for the Body: a. Love is incompatible with ease (*gemach*), cf. *Erec*, which may have been written just after or during the composition of the *Büchlein*; b. The lover is required to have the chief Christian and aristocratic virtues: *milte* (generosity), *zuht* (proper bearing), *diemuot* (humility), *triuwe* (loyalty), *stæte* (constancy), *kiuscheit* (chasteness), *shame* (modesty), and *manheit* (manly bravery); c. If these virtues can be combined, the young man will have *sælde* (bliss, blessedness, good fortune, charisma—hard to define), vv.1301-26, and God and the World will love him (v. 1346). An extended allegory is used in which the required virtues are described and employed: a magic potion, brought by the Heart from France and concocted of herbs (the virtues listed above) with God as the herbalist is to be mixed and drunk to produce the state of *sælde*. Then with constancy and propriety the reward will be gained.

The poem is written in rhymed couplets for the dispute (the first 1644 lines), then breaks into stanzas of varying lengths for the final plea to the lady by the Body (from v.1645 to the end at v.1914). The stanzas are rhymed a,b,a,b,..., but with different alternating ("crossed") rhymes within each stanza. There is a definite structure in the work, most recently described as being based on combinations of the numbers 4 and 8. Dialogue between Body and Heart is dominant structurally with no dialogue in the prologue and the monologic plea to the lady in the stanzas at the end. The fact that Hartmann seems so concerned with the structure and less adept at other aspects of poetic writing has made most scholars consider the *Klage* to be an early work. In many ways it is virtually unique in German literature of the period and, although perhaps not great poetry, is interesting in that it advocates a way for a knight to earn acceptance by the secular world *and* by God: a *ritterliches Tugendsystem* (system of knightly virtues), a concept that at one time played an important role in scholarly discourse on MHG literature (see BIBLIOGRAPHY, below).

Texts:
Keller, Thomas L., ed. and trans. *Hartmann von Aue. Klagebüchlein.* Göppingen: Kümmerle, 1986 (= GAG, 450). MHG text with Engl. prose trans. on opposing pages, lengthy intro.

Schirokauer, Arno/Petrus W. Tax, ed. *Hartmann von Aue. Das Büchlein.* Nach den Vorarbeiten von A. Schirokauer zu Ende geführt und hrsg. von P. Tax. Berlin: Erich Schmidt, 1979 (= PSuQ, 75). Text with extensive intro., notes, and wordlist.

Wolff, Ludwig, ed. *Das Klagebüchlein Hartmanns von Aue und das zweite Büchlein.* Munich: Fink, 1972 (= Altdeutsche Texte in kritischen Ausgaben, 4). Edited text with variants of ms. and other editions.

Zutt, Herta, ed. *Hartmann von Aue. Die Klage. Das (zweite) Büchlein.* Berlin: de Gruyter, 1968. Diplomatic text of the ms. and edited text with variants from other editions on opposite pages.

Translation:
See Keller (above).

Facsimile:
See F. Unterkirchner's facsimile of the entire Ambraser Heldenbuch listed above in the section on *Erec.*

## *Diu Klage*—Bibliography

Eifler, Günter, ed. *Ritterliches Tugendsystem.* Darmstadt: Wiss. Buchges., 1970 (= WdF, 56).

Collection of reprinted studies on the topic beginning with Ehrismann's seminal study (1919) and ending with two from 1964, thereby covering the major contributions to the discourse.

Gewehr, Wolf. "Hartmanns Klage-Büchlein als Gattungsproblem." *ZfdPh* 91 (1972): 1-16.

Mertens, Volker, *"Factus est per clericum miles cytherius*: Überlegungen zu Entstehungs-und Wirkungsbedingungen von Hartmanns *Klage-Büchlein.*" In: *London Hartmann Symposium* (see above). Pp. 1-20.

Seiffert, Leslie. "On the Language of Sovereignty, Deference and Solidarity: The Surrender of the Accusing Lover in Hartmann's *Klage.*" In: *London Hartmann Symposium* (see above). Pp. 21-52.

Wisniewski, Roswitha. "Hartmanns Klagebüchlein." *Euph.* 57 (1963): 341-69.

Discussion of the terminology and the literary background of the argument between "Heart" and "Body."

Zutt, Herta. "Die formale Struktur von Hartmanns 'Klage'." *ZfdPh* 87 (1968): 359-72.

The structure of the poem as the result of numerical composition.

## Gottfried von Straßburg: *Tristan*

Although he is extraordinarily reticent about revealing his identity and other factual details of his life, Gottfried is in many ways very much a presence in the poem. It may be that he would have divulged at least his name at the end of his work. As it is, others have supplied that name, together with his place of origin: Rudolf von Ems (*Wilhelm von Orlens* 2185-6; *Alexander* 20621) and Konrad von Würzburg (*Herzmære* 9; *Die goldene Schmiede* 97), and Gottfried's continuators, Ulrich von Türheim (see p. 372 ff.) and Heinrich von Freiberg (see p. 374 f.). The initial G of the opening acrostic may be Gottfried's own clue to his identity, but it may also be the initial letter of *Grâve* (Count) and thus supply a clue to the unanswered question of the identity of his patron, whose name, as the following acrostic suggests, was Dietrich.

The social standing of Gottfried must likewise be adduced, because there is again no documentary evidence to guide us. Those who refer to him in the Middle Ages use the designation *meister*, but this is in itself ambiguous, since it could be used for one who was of the citizen class (i.e., not a knight), but also to denote academic status, the degree of *magister*. Both may well be applicable to Gottfried, who is never given the title *her* and whose indifference to chivalry verges at times on disdain and would seem to preclude any likelihood that he was himself of the knightly class, still less a practicing knight. In contrast, his learning is manifest and it has been suggested that he could have gained his scholarly distinction at the University of Paris. In this respect, as in so many others, Gottfried stands apart from the other significant names of the *Blütezeit*, for whom chivalry was a way of life, if not in practice, then certainly by inclination. His learning, too, goes beyond that of Hartmann von Aue, whose work reflects the formal education of the cathedral or monastery school, but perhaps not very much more, and it is of quite different kind from Wolfram's, which appears to have been pieced together from a wide range of experience but is definitely not rooted in anything very conventional.

Gottfried's *Tristan* shows a close acquaintance with literature, both contemporary and classical, a knowledge of music, art, and architecture, of law and theology. His command of the German language is of the finest, with a predilection for word-play and allegory unmatched by his contemporaries. The notion that his education might have destined him for the Church but that this clearly did not accord with his philosophical make-up is entirely acceptable. The designation *clericus* has been suggested for him, but the further suggestion that he may have held office, perhaps as a diplomat, perhaps in the local or episcopal secretariat, must remain an unsubstantiated, though attractive, speculation. Despite his indifference to knighthood and all that goes with it, he is obviously well versed in the manners and accessories of the court, and he can use its wiles to his own ends in this poem, which, on one level, may be seen as a critique of the society that forms the background to his idealized love.

### The Source:

Gottfried is adamant that he is committed to one source alone, that by Thomas von Britanje, who is believed to have composed in England, possibly at the court of Henry II, in the literary French of the Angevin courts, though with traces of Anglo-Norman.

Beyond such generally accepted supposition, however, little is known of him, and the dating of his work is contentious, with some critics placing it before 1160, and others favoring a date closer to 1180/1190. His *Tristran* (note spelling!) is largely lost, with only fragments surviving, yet it can be reconstructed fairly confidently by reference to the works which are believed to derive from it, the most significant of which is the Norwegian *Tristramssaga*. The reconstruction of Thomas's poem is first and foremost the achievement of Joseph Bédier, who, in the very early years of the twentieth century, produced two volumes devoted to *Tristran*. The surviving fragments of Thomas's work, a little over 3100 lines in all and largely relating to the end of the story, are believed to constitute about one-sixth of the original.

The situation with regard to Thomas's version has changed, and with it some of the established preconceptions about Gottfried's poem, since the discovery very recently of the so-called "Carlisle fragment" containing 154 lines which correspond approximately to lines 11958-12678 of Gottfried. These cover the conversation prior to the drinking of the potion, the drinking of it, and the response of the lovers to the onset of their passion and continue through to the arrival in Cornwall. Not least of the discoveries resulting from this exciting find is that the play on the word *lameir* in Gottfried is already present in the source. The fragment was published for the first time in a recent issue of *Romania* (see *TRISTAN*—BIBLIOGRAPHY) and will clearly have repercussions for *Tristan*-scholarship.

Apart from this recent development, it is one of the most remarkable literary chances that the greater part of what survives of the work of Thomas can conveniently be appended to Gottfried's great fragment, to give a fair impression of how Gottfried presumably intended to complete his work, since we have his explicit declaration of allegiance to Thomas in his Prologue. A. T. Hatto has made effective use of this chance by juxtaposing his translation of Gottfried's *Tristan* with his translation of the surviving fragments of Thomas. In doing so he not only allows his readers to read the story of Tristan and Isolde to the end which Gottfried probably intended, but he also demonstrates the sharp differences in emphasis and style between the two, though with the caution that we should perhaps not judge the quality of Thomas, for whom Gottfried clearly had considerable admiration, from the extant fragments of his work (Hatto, trans., p. 362).

The Manuscripts:

The transmission of the poem is fairly uniform in the eleven "complete" manuscripts. Of these M (Cod. germ 51 of the Bavarian State Library in Munich) and H (Cod. pal. germ. 360 of the University Library in Heidelberg) date from the thirteenth century, and both contain the continuation of Ulrich von Türheim (see p. 372 ff.). B (Cologne), F (Florence), N (Berlin) and W (Vienna) date from the fourteenth century: B and F contain Ulrich's work, and F the continuation by Heinrich von Freiberg (see p. 374 ff.). The remaining five are all a century later. There are in addition some fifteen fragments, for the most part from the earlier period. A detailed description of the manuscripts can be found in the edition by Marold (see below).

Considerable controversy surrounds the question of whether Gottfried composed anything other than *Tristan*. The manuscripts ascribe to him one very conventional love song (*Diu zît ist wünneclich*)—dismissed as not authentic by some scholars, though now included somewhat tentatively in the latest edition of **Minnesangs Frühling**—some didactic strophes and a hymn of praise to the Virgin. The great Heidelberg manuscript contains two songs which are there attributed to Ulrich von Lichtenstein but one of which Rudolf von Ems appears to be attributing to Gottfried (*der wîse meister Gotfrid*, **Alexander** 20621 ff.), leading some critics to conclude that both are in fact the work of Gottfried von Straßburg, but others would argue against this. For a discussion of the arguments, see G. Weber, Sammlung Metzler, 15, pp. 7-10.

## The Poem:

When Gottfried came to compose his *Tristan* at the height of the *Blütezeit* (ca. 1210), the story of the lovers bound by a magic potion was already familiar to the German public through the version by Eilhart von Oberge (see p. 118 ff.). The legend was one of the most popular, if not *the* most popular, love stories of the Middle Ages, with versions throughout Europe. The essence of the story remains the same, but the details are different, and, as Gottfried himself maintains, many have told the tale, but few have told it properly, that is, in accordance with his view of a mutual passion between two people unto death. In Gottfried's essentially courtly version, the material receives its ultimate expression, in a work, which, unfinished though it may be, dominates the development of the Tristan story and attains an undisputed position as one of the literary pinnacles of the German Middle Ages. For most people it is the *Tristan par excellence*, though admittedly for some not least because it supplied the basis for Wagner's masterpiece.

Central to the story of Tristan and Isolde is the drinking of the potion, and, although some would doubt that Gottfried, with his sharp intellect and sometimes devastating regard for the truth, could really have believed in a magic potion, he could certainly not decline to make it the cause of their love. It occupies a central position, quite literally, at the core of his poem, and Gottfried's description of this scene is one of the high points of the poem, with some of the finest poetry in MHG and full of dramatic tension. An issue which has taxed scholars is whether the potion is indeed the cause of love between them or whether Gottfried uses it to exonerate Tristan and Isolde as they embark on a relationship which, on the face of it, must have been shocking to the medieval audience. Some have insisted that love already exists between the pair, demonstrated in their closeness as they play and sing together; in Isolde's refusal to kill Tristan as he sits in his bath and she stands over him with the sword in her hand, knowing now that this was the sword which killed her uncle Morold; and even, perversely, in the hatred which she declares for him when he visits her on the boat just before they drink the potion.

However, the love potion is represented as the immediate cause of their love, and in this respect Gottfried shows the power of love of which he is fully aware, an overwhelming force which turns everything upside down, just as even the dregs of the potion, when hurled into the sea, churn up an elemental force. Love comes in many guises in *Tristan*— as the ambusher of hearts (11711), the reconciler (11721), the physician (12164), to name but a few—but it cannot be ignored. If Gottfried hardly ever mentions the potion again, this is not because it did not exist. Rather it assumes the status of a symbol, of a tremendous mutual passion of whose effects and consequences he is in no doubt. In the story of Rivalin and Blanscheflur he has, after all, already shown himself fully aware of the impact of love and more than capable of demonstrating it. Within the story of Tristan and Isolde, he is adamant about certain aspects of the potion, which distinguish his account from that of his predecessors. Marke does *not* drink the potion, of that he is sure, for this fatal attraction between two people cannot include a third person. Thus he explicitly dismisses those versions which maintain that the drink which Marke and Isolde consume on the wedding night was the same drink, reminding us that Brangaene had thrown it overboard (12655 f.). Another feature of earlier versions and most crucially of Eilhart's, that the effect of the love potion could diminish with time, is similarly repugnant to Gottfried, and, if his Tristan was to follow that of Thomas and marry the second Isolde, then this could only have been a marriage without love, for Gottfried's ideal of love endures unto death, indeed *is* death.

Most of the actual events of Gottfried's *Tristan* are present already in the earlier versions, but his work is remarkable for the emphasis which he places on some of these, often in accordance with his greater concern for abstractions, and for some of his outstandingly important additions.

Gottfried's poem begins with forty-four lines in quatrains, an opening which speaks of the nature of art and the criticism of art and whose main purpose may well be as a vehicle for the acrostic: G(= Gottfried? or Grâve?), DIETRICH, T(presumably Tristan, matched by the I which begins line 45).

Very much more important is the actual Prologue, in which Gottfried states his purpose in the most emphatic terms, dedicating his work to the "noble hearts" (*edeliu herzen*, first mentioned at v. 47) who alone will comprehend this story of a love which he elevates here and throughout his poem above the everyday emotion of those who belong to the ordinary world and for whom love is undiluted joy. "May God permit them to live in joy!" he declares (54), while he and those who share his understanding of the proper nature of love will go a different way, enduring suffering and sorrow as the natural concomitants of this higher emotion. The Prologue, in which Gottfried resumes the rhyming couplets of the courtly romance which are the principal metrical form of the poem, is inseparable from the work as a whole. It is the first and one of the greatest passages in the work, and it demonstrates the special nature of Gottfried's language and thought, and the inextricability of the two. He presents the essential duality of love in language which plays with antitheses, speaking of

> ir süeze sur, ir liebez leit,
> > ir herzeliep, ir senede not,
> ir liebez leben, ir leiden tot,
> > ir lieben tot, ir leidez leben.
> (Ranke ed., 60-63)

(Its sweet bitterness, its dear sorrow, its heart's joy, its yearning pain, its dear life, its sorrowful death, its dear death, its sorrowful life.)

Gottfried is *the* master of language among the poets of the German courtly period, and his virtuosity shows itself very early on in his *Tristan*, as he plays with words and concepts in a sometimes quite daring way. Thus he tells us, for example, of his tale:

> daz entsorget sorgehaften muot,
> daz ist ze herzesorgen guot.
> (79-80)

(It takes care away from the care-laden spirit. It is good for the cares of the heart.)

It is good for a man to be occupied, for sorrow increases when there is no distraction from it:

> swa so der müezege man
> mit senedem schaden si überladen,
> da mere muoze seneden schaden.
> bi senedem leide müezekeit,
> da wahset iemer senede leit.
> durch daz ist guot, swer herzeclage
> und senede not ze herzen trage,
> daz er mit allem ruoche
> dem libe unmuoze suoche:
> da mite so müezeget der muot
> und ist dem muote ein michel guot.
> (82-92)

(Whenever a man at leisure is overburdened with the anguish of love, leisure increases the anguish of love. Leisure side by side with the pain of love increases the pain of love. Thus it is all to the good that someone who in his heart is bearing the heart's lamentation and love's tribulation should earnestly seek distraction for himself. That way his spirit will find release and it will be a great boon for his spirit.)

Gottfried's obvious pleasure in language and his manipulation of it to his own ends is evident and leads, for example, to his invention of a word like *bemæren* (125: to supply someone with a story, i.e., a *mære*). However, this is not just language for its own sake. Gottfried is intent at all times to tell his story of exemplary lovers, and he exploits his language to do this. Thus, at what one could describe as the first peak of the prologue, he arrives at three explicit lines, which again make effective use of chiasmus. He is about to tell of a lover and a loveress:

> ein senedær unde ein senedærin,
> ein man ein wip, ein wip ein man,
> Tristan Isolt, Isolt Tristan.
> (128-130)

(A lover and a loveress; a man, a woman; a woman, a man; Tristan, Isolt; Isolt, Tristan)

It is sometimes held that Gottfried, who shows himself decidedly irreverent towards orthodox Christianity, has created a religion of love in this poem, and already in his prologue he uses the language and imagery of Christianity to do so. As the prologue reaches its conclusion, he sums up his commitment to his theme of love and the telling of his story in two powerful quatrains which refer to love as bread:

> Deist aller edelen herzen brot.
> hie mite so lebet ir beider tot.
> wir lesen ir leben, wir lesen ir tot
> und ist uns daz süeze alse brot.

> Ir leben, ir tot sint unser brot.
> sus lebet ir leben, sus lebet ir tot.
> sus lebent si noch und sint doch tot
> und ist ir tot der lebenden brot.
> (233-240)

(That is bread to all noble hearts, and thus the death of both of them lives on. We read of their life, we read of their death, and that is to us as sweet as bread.
Their life, their death *are* our bread. Thus lives their life, thus lives their death. Thus they live still and yet are dead, and their death is bread to the living.)

The Eucharistic echoes are evident, as they will be again in the Love Grotto, where the lovers have no need of food, sustained as they are by love (16819-16820), and the echoes are further stressed by the interrelationship of love and death which will run through the poem. The potion itself which will bind them in eternal love is, in the words of Brangaene, "death to both of them" (11706): the vial which contained it and even the journey which has brought them to this point are *veic* (death-laden, 11693, 11698). Yet, in accordance with his nature as a "noble heart," Tristan, when he learns what has happened to them, gladly embraces the death which their love must inevitably mean to them:

> "ez wære tot oder leben:
> ez hat mir sanfte vergeben.
> ine weiz, wie jener werden sol:
> dirre tot der tuot mir wol.
> solte diu wunnecliche Isot
> iemer alsus sin min tot,
> so wolte ich gerne werben
> umb ein eweclichez sterben."
> (12495-12502)

("Whether it be life or death, it has poisoned me gently. I do not know how that other death will be, but this death is good for me. If the blissful Isolde is always to be my death like this, then I shall gladly woo eternal dying.")

Although the audience has been alerted to the nature of the story and, after the early naming of the two central characters, must be awaiting the crucial event, known to everyone, of the drinking of a magic potion, that event does not occur until far into the poem. Nevertheless, its shadow hangs over the first half of the work, and a chain of episodes leads inevitably to the climax on the boat between Ireland and Cornwall. The first of these episodes, which is devoted to the bitter-sweet love story of Tristan's parents, serves several functions: as a miniature love story in its own right, but, more significantly, establishing the nature of love and its effects and founding the story of Tristan himself very firmly in that of his parents.

The parental history was a popular feature of medieval romances, but, no less than Wolfram in his *Parzival*, Gottfried uses it in a way which transcends the traditional. The comparison with the story of Gahmuret is an obvious one, for Riwalin, too, is an intrepid knight errant, and his story is an important prelude to that of his son. However, Gottfried is not really interested in Riwalin's chivalry, although the fact that he is a knight of some reputation and considerable personal attractiveness is significant in securing for him a place at Marke's court and inevitably in the heart of Marke's sister. His conflict with Morgan, and the truce which enables him to go away for a year in the hope that he may benefit from the example of Marke, his subsequent intervention on behalf of Marke in the course of a war and his apparently fatal wounding, and his actual death in action against his own old enemy Morgan: all these events are passed over quickly by Gottfried, for they are no more than supporting events which surround the main action, which is the dawning of love between Riwalin and Blanscheflur, the consummation of this love and the conception of Tristan, and the tragic deaths of the two lovers.

Riwalin and Blanscheflur have no need of a love potion, but Gottfried describes the overwhelming impact of their passion in terms which anticipate those he will later use to tell of the effects of the potion upon Tristan and Isolde. What dominates, here too, is the awareness of a bewildering force which changes the lives of both young people and places them outside the society to which they belong. In the rapid train of events, there is no time for their love to mature nor for them to reveal it to Marke and the court he represents. Tristan is conceived in an act of deception, though innocent enough one might say, when Blanscheflur goes in disguise to see her lover for one last time, believing that he is dying. Desperate to conceal the truth from the outside world, they elope to Riwalin's country, deceiving Marke, who will be deceived repeatedly by their son and his beloved in time to come.

Already in this vignette, Gottfried is raising issues which will dominate in the major love story that follows. The juxtaposition of joy and sorrow, so adamantly defined as the nature of true love in the Prologue, is present in this brief and tragic love, and even more important is the specific juxtaposition of love and death, in the central scene of the conception of Tristan, as Blanscheflur, in giving her love to the "dying" man, restores him to life, yet receives from him a new life which will mean her own death (1308 ff.). The reciprocity in true love underlined in the Prologue is emphasized here too, in lines which echo that earlier statement of the theme of the poem:

> sus was er si und si was er,
> er was ir und si was sin;
> da Blanscheflur, da Riwalin,
> da Riwalin, da Blanscheflur,
> da beide, da leal amur.
> (1358-1362)

(Thus was he she and she was he, he was hers and she was his; there Blanscheflur, there Riwalin, there Riwalin, there Blanscheflur, there both of them, there true love.)

This is true love, but it contains the seeds of death, not only for these two lovers, but for the child which Blanscheflur is now carrying and whose birth will coincide with her death.

Tristan is thus born of a doomed love, but he also inherits, along with the chivalry of his father, the capacity for deception and subterfuge of his mother. Indeed, his very birth is enshrouded in deception, when it is announced that he is the child of Floraete, and his name is deliberately chosen to convey the sadness which is his fate. In other respects, however, the next generation is by no means a replica of the preceding one. Tristan has all the shrewdness and foresightedness which seemed to be lacking in his somewhat shallow father, of whom Gottfried has explained that, like most young people, he is *selten vorbesihtic* (seldom/never careful or cautious, 302). Tristan is the exception to this rule, seemingly constantly a step ahead of everyone else and extraordinarily circumspect: thus, for example, he is quick to invent a story when he meets the pilgrims on his arrival in Cornwall (2695, ff.) and, despite his agony, he has the perspicacity to disguise the terrible wound which he receives in the combat with Morold (7131 ff.). In this respect, Isolde is a match for him, so that together they can muster the kind of defense which they will need to protect their love from a threatening society. Nor is the cunning which they practice viewed in a negative light by Gottfried, who sees it, of course, as the necessary means to counteract the opposition of a court which is hostile to their love and capable of sinking to any depths in order to trap them and outwit them.

From the moment they drink the potion, Tristan and Isolde are placed in opposition to the society to which, hitherto in the poem, they have been shown to belong. Gottfried tells us that the world has been turned upside down (*verkeret*, 11889), but this is the world which, until now, he has been at pains to show as the norm. King Marke is an exemplary ruler of a harmonious court where high standards prevail, and Riwalin is not mistaken in expecting to find abundant honor there. The picture which Gottfried gives, both initially when Riwalin comes to Tintagel and later, when Tristan arrives there and is received with warmth and hospitality, is a thoroughly positive one, but this can only be the case while there is no threat to it. Any intervention from outside, like the challenge from Morold or, more lastingly, the alien force of the passion produced by the love potion, reveals the weaknesses in the structure. This must, of course, be so, for Gottfried has declared the pre-eminence of the love of Tristan and Isolde in the Prologue, and all other standards must prove invalid in comparison with it.

The suffering which he has declared to be the essential concomitant of joy in love has no place in the pleasure-loving court of King Marke, and his own love for his wife, intense in its own way, is a paltry emotion which can be disparaged and ridiculed. This is evident from the humiliating events of the wedding-night, when Marke is not even aware of the substitution of Brangaene in the bridal bed. What right to consideration has a man who cannot distinguish his bride from her confidante, in his obsession, which is emphasized more and more, with the physical side of love? The degradation of Marke continues: from his contemptible association with the dregs of the court, the dwarf Melot and the steward Marjodoc, to his preparedness to use frankly unregal tricks in order to ensnare the lovers, and his pathetic reversal as he peers in at them through the little windows high up in the Love Grotto and is overwhelmed with desire for his beautiful wife. Any sympathy which might attach to him as he gazes down at them in the orchard, with no sword between them this time, is dispelled by his feeble decision to leave them while he goes off to find witnesses. On one level, of course, Marke appears to gain what he wants, for, although he knows that Isolde does not love him, she is queen where he is king (11733), and this humiliating compromise is probably enough for a man who has been so diminished in stature.

The world of Marke is that ordinary world of which Gottfried speaks in his Prologue and which he rejects as the proper environment for love in the idealized form which is his principal concern. For the first 11,000 lines or so, this is the world in which Tristan and Isolde operate. It is in this society that Tristan gains supremacy as a traditional hero with a range of superlative talents and achievements. In this respect, one could argue that Gottfried is fulfilling the expectations in his audience of a courtly romance akin to the Arthurian romances, though the only sign of Arthur in *Tristan* comes when Gottfried compares the ideal existence in the Love Grotto to the court of Arthur which it surpasses (16859-16865). However, Tristan rises above the traditional, displaying a more complex array of skills which include music and literature, a close knowledge of hunting and all that goes with it, the mastery of foreign languages and prowess at chess. Siegfried-like, he may slay a dragon, yet he has already gained the admiration of the court of Ireland by his command of *moraliteit* (8004), that all-embracing concept of exquisite behavior which he is able to impart to the young Princess Isolde. It is hardly surprising that this exemplary young stranger should gradually encounter opposition and jealousy from the inhabitants of the court of Marke, which begins to show itself vulnerable and insecure when challenged.

Gottfried is gradually preparing the way for the revelation of Marke's court and Marke himself as negative forces, but he is also demonstrating the originality of his whole poem, which stands very much on its own in its age and defies precise generic definition. It is above all the episode of the *Minnegrotte* which distinguishes Gottfried's *Tristan* from other versions of the Tristan-story as well as from the more conventional courtly romance. This episode is rightly seen as the peak of the poem and has evoked most debate among scholars, eliciting a wide range of interpretations of the work.

In this episode (16621 ff.), Gottfried makes his most important addition to the material of his source. In Thomas, the lovers are banished from the court and find a secluded place in the forest where they can spend time together. Gottfried, on the other hand, develops the whole idea of a cave devoted from time immemorial to the pursuit of love. Tristan deliberately chooses this place which he came upon long before while out hunting, and he undertakes the two-day journey from the court with Isolde and Curvenal. It is in a rugged mountain region, and the path to it is fraught with hazards, just as the pathway of true love is perilous for those martyrs who pursue it (17085). The cave itself is a *cluse* (16806), the word used by Wolfram to describe the hermitage of Trevrizent, or the place of retreat and worship which Sigune has had built when Parzival meets her on the third occasion. Inside, however, this cave in the rocks opens up into something closer to a great church, or a temple perhaps, and this Gottfried describes in great detail, concentrating first of all on the physical appearance of it, its architectural features (16703 ff.), before, some two hundred lines later, interpreting these features in terms of the significance of the place. Thus the roundness of the cave signifies the simplicity of love, the absence of cunning or deceit (16931 ff.), its breadth the endless power of love (16837), its height love's aspiration which knows no bounds (16939 ff.). The vaulting of the cave is gathered in by the keystone, the crown of virtues set with precious stones and the focus of admiration for those who behold it (16944 ff.). The smooth white wall betokens the purity of love (16963), the firm green of the marble floor its constancy (16969 ff.). At the center of the cave is a bed—for sensuality is by no means absent in Gottfried's ideal love, of that there should be no doubt—but it is made of crystal, as befits the nature of love (16977 ff.).

Gottfried expends considerable time on the door of the cave, bronze, with a latch and a lever, and two bars, "each one a seal of love" (17016), the one of cedar, denoting the wisdom and understanding inherent in proper love, the other of ivory, pure and chaste (17026). Thus deceit and treachery are excluded from the cave, which needs no lock or key to guard it against these things which have no part in love. Tristan and Isolde come there and gain access because they are noble hearts who have a right to enter, but of course Marke, even if he tried to enter by the door, which instinctively he does not do (17491 f.), could not gain entry. Indeed, when he does come there, he resorts to clambering up in order to peer in at the lovers through the little windows placed high up in the cave and interpreted now by Gottfried as standing for kindness, humility, and good breeding (*güete, diemüete, zuht*, 17063). With the ambiguity which causes so many problems in the interpretation of the poem, Gottfried assures us that what shines in through those windows is honor (*ere*, 17068).

Honor, on one level, suffuses this place where, for an indefinite period, the lovers dedicate themselves to the pursuit of this high ideal of love, unimpeded by the constraints of society. Yet it is precisely the honor which, on another level, they have sacrificed which prevents this *wunschleben* (16846) from being absolute perfection and which, presumably, leads them to accept Marke's invitation to return to the court. In fact, Gottfried says as much, when he explains that they were happy "more for the sake of God and their honor than for any other reason" (17696 ff.). Even before Marke urges them to refrain from the tender looks and intimate talk which betray the love which he has just told his councillors he no longer believes to exist between them, Gottfried has said that the lovers will never again be able to indulge in their love so freely or so joyfully (17702 ff.). The idyll in the Love Grotto is over, and it is only partially balanced by the desperate assignation in the orchard which spells the end of their time together at the court and makes Tristan's departure essential. Gottfried describes the lavish preparations which Isolde makes for a bed draped in the finest materials, and the place she selects is sheltered from the sun, yet this rendezvous is contrived in the only place now available to them, in the middle of Marke's own court, where no one, least of all the brooding Brangaene, can prevent his entering and discovering them (18139 ff.). The picture which greets him is as stylized as the earlier one in the Love Grotto, but this time the message is explicit, for there is no sword between them to confuse him and tell him what he would like to believe. Only a waverer (*zwivelære*) like Marke would hesitate to act upon the evidence of his own eyes, but then Gottfried has already condemned Marke for his blindness (see below).

The protracted scene of parting marks the end of the love story as Gottfried tells it, but presumably he intended to tell of the deaths of both lovers, in accordance with his declared allegiance to Thomas. The usually accepted explanation of the fact that his poem breaks off in mid-action, in mid-thought one might say, as Tristan contemplates his position, drawn as he is to the second Isolde and feeling himself forgotten by the first, who has apparently not cared enough for him to send messengers to look for him, despite his own undying love for her, is that Gottfried died before he could complete his work. Earlier suggestions that he underwent some kind of moral reversal which made him antagonistic to his own material were never given much credence, though there is something to be said for the view that he had, after all, told his story to the end, through the Prologue and at the time of the drinking of the potion. *How* the lovers were to die may not have been that important to him. It has also been well observed that he has explored the material of Thomas which tells of death and lamentation in his account of the grief of Blanscheflur, three times over in fact, and that he therefore perhaps never intended to use it again. Nevertheless, it is relevant that his continuators clearly saw his work as in need of completion, and both Ulrich von Türheim and Heinrich von Freiberg lament that he died before he could finish it.

Whatever the explanation, *Tristan* remains a fragment, and a certain amount of the difficulty in interpreting it stems from that fact. Yet one might justifiably think that precisely with Gottfried we were given abundant guidance on matters of interpretation, for, fragment though it may be, *Tristan* is consistently interspersed with lengthy passages without parallel in the source or anything remotely comparable in other versions of the events. These are the *excursi*, or digressions as they are sometimes called, a term which is misleading because close examination reveals that they are actually closely related to the narrative and intended to play a part in it, whether directing it in some way, or suggesting how the audience should be viewing events.

The so-called "literary excursus" (*Literaturstelle, Dichterschau*, 4588-45907) which Gottfried inserts at the point of Tristan's investiture has received a great deal of scholarly attention. It is important as a critique of his predecessors and his near-contemporaries, telling us something about his own literary standards, and it is often seen as first and foremost a vehicle for an onslaught on Wolfram von Eschenbach, almost certainly the "friend of the hare" who goes leaping about the field and whom Gottfried disparages for the complexity and waywardness of his narrative. In contrast, he admires the "crystalline words" of Hartmann von Aue, to whom he accords the laurel wreath of narrative poetry. How Gottfried arrives at this passage is interesting, too, for, though he would seem to be eager to seize the opportunity for such a discourse, his actual pretext is a different one, for he professes inadequacy in the face of the task of describing Tristan's elevation to the knighthood, and even when he returns to that stage of his narrative, he quickly turns aside again and leads eventually into his allegorical account of the four *richeite* (4975:

A.T. Hatto translates this elusive concept with "splendours") which contribute to the equipping of Tristan for the ceremony.

In his *excursi*, especially those dealing with aspects of love, Gottfried guides his audience at crucial stages of the progress of the narrative and often when a contrary standpoint might seem to present itself. What concerns him above all in these passages is the place of apparently negative emotions in love (like anger and jealousy, 13031 ff.; doubt and suspicion, 13776 ff.) and the negative environment which acts against the flourishing of love. In this connection he condemns the practice of surveillance (*huote*), particularly in one of his longest discussions of love and its place in a hostile society, represented by Marke. It is Marke's own fault if he allows himself to be deceived, blinded as he is by lust (17738 ff.). In this passage Gottfried makes his most forthright statements about the relationship between the sexes and their respective roles in society, condemning the view of woman as an inferior being and asserting her right to dispose of her love and her body as she chooses. Yet this is far from an advocacy of promiscuity, for what he is extolling is moderation and a proper regard by a woman for her womanhood (18051).

Despite its highly abstract tone, this passage is inextricable from the events of the poem, for Isolde is at this very point about to summon Tristan to the orchard, frustrated as she is by the constraints placed upon her by Marke and desperate for the physical fulfillment without which their love cannot survive. Gottfried's way of guiding his listeners as he tells the story of the lovers is remarkable. Throughout the poem, from the Prologue on and perhaps particularly in the Love Grotto, where they are pursuing an age-old custom in their dedication to love, treading in the paths of the giants of old (16695-6), the lovers are not only named individuals, Tristan and Isolde, but also a man and a woman, the representatives of ideal lovers everywhere and at all times. This duality is reflected in the style, the lengthy passages of something akin to sermonizing within pure narrative. It also shows itself in the use which Gottfried makes, particularly in the early stages of the work, of the quatrains which interrupt the flow of the couplets and often sum up a situation in more general terms, or highlight the essence of what he has just related or is about to relate. Thus, for example, he laments the death of Blanscheflur, following so soon upon the death of Riwalin:

> Owe der ougenweide,
> da man nach leidem leide
> mit leiderem leide
> siht leider ougenweide!
> (1751-1754)

(Alas for the sorrowful sight when after grievous grief one sees a sight more sorrowful with even greater grief.)

Or, speaking of Tristan's determination to avenge the death of Riwalin at the hand of Morgan, he remarks:

> Ir aller jehe lit dar an,
> haz der lige ie dem jungen man

                    mit groezerem ernest an
                    dan einem stündigen man
                    (5099-5102)

(Everyone is in agreement that a young man is more likely to be afflicted with anger than a mature man.)

Some of these quatrains have an almost proverbial tone to them, but others are exceedingly artistic purveyors of a central truth which is essential to the poem. Thus he says of love:

                    Si dunket schoener sit dan e.
                    da von so turet minnen e.
                    diuhte minne sit als e,
                    so zegienge schiere minnen e.
                    (11871-17875)

(It later seems more beautiful than it did before and because of this the law of loving grows more precious. If later love seemed as it did before, then soon the law of loving would perish.)

Tristan and Isolde have just drunk the love potion and are beginning to experience its effects, and Gottfried inserts this quatrain and plays with the two distinct meanings of the word *e* (the noun "law" and the adverb "previously") to assert a basic premise: that love must grow and change if it is to survive. The ideal of love which he has propounded in the Prologue is here given a new and extended task: not only must it embrace suffering and sorrow along with joy, but it must be prepared to evolve and resist any temptation to remain static. Perhaps herein lies the answer to the teasing question of why the lovers leave the Grotto and return to a court which will oppose them and force changes upon them. Society manages to divide them physically, but, in that conclusion so frustratingly denied to us, death would surely have guaranteed the survival of their love.

## Principal Trends in *Tristan*-Scholarship

The earliest commentators on the poem, among them the great scholar Karl Lachmann and the poet Eichendorff, were outraged by what they saw as its immorality, even when they admitted that the language and style of the poem were admirable. "So much beauty wasted on the hideous," was Eichendorff's devastating assessment. The excellent account by Rosemary Picozzi provides objective information on the fluctuations of *Tristan*-scholarship from its early condemnation, through those who saw the origins of the story in remote mythologies (Picozzi, p. 87 ff.) and what Picozzi calls the "biographical studies" of the mid-nineteenth century (pp. 92-97) which sought to interpret the poem with somewhat spurious assumptions about Gottfried's own life, to the examination of the relationship between Gottfried and his declared source which followed the conclusive identification of some fragments by a certain Thomas (pp. 98-105). Particularly through the work of Bédier, the originality of Gottfried and his special qualities began to be acknowledged.

With this redressing of the extreme reactions of earlier critics has come, throughout the present century, a flood of deeply committed and very varied interpretations of the poem. Again, Rosemary Picozzi provides a thorough and balanced account of the range of these interpretations, and she has isolated the principal studies which should be taken into account in considering the history of *Tristan*-scholarship (pp. 108-154). Inevitably, though, her work stops at the late 1960s, and it can probably best be complemented by the latest revision in the Sammlung Metzler series and by the volume edited by Adrian Stephens and Roy Wisbey.

Of the older scholars, the names associated above all with *Tristan* are Ranke, Schwietering, and Weber, whose works are classics of their kind. Central to their studies of the whole poem is the preoccupation with the nature of the love extolled by Gottfried, its relationship to conventional religion and to medieval mysticism, and the extent to which it accords with courtly values. More recently, attention turned to other specific aspects of the poem, its content and meaning, but also to its language and form. Significant studies of symbolism are those by Petrus Tax and Ingrid Hahn, whose methods and conclusions are very different, but who both cast important new light on the understanding of this problematic work. Rosemary Combridge, a British scholar writing in German, opened up a whole new area of consideration with her examination of law in *Tristan*, a subject which proves to be extraordinarily fruitful to an understanding of specific situations within the poem. To approximately the same period belong the various articles by Rainer Gruenter, now conveniently gathered in one volume, which concentrated most significantly on the character of King Marke and, in the long article entitled "Das *wünnecliche tal*," on the *locus amoenus* and the whole subject of Gottfried's descriptions of the natural setting. The complete studies by W.T.H. Jackson and, more recently, by Hugo Bekker offer substantial food for thought, even when some of the findings may appear to be taken to extremes. The extensive work of William C. McDonald has appeared in two wide-ranging volumes which place Gottfried's poem in its broad context and demonstrate many of its intrinsic qualities most effectively. In the present generation of younger scholars, Mark Chinca has devoted a whole volume to the study of the poetics of *Tristan*, while the work of Kathleen Meyer has also indicated some important new directions in the examination of Gottfried's language and of the function of allegory in establishing the genre of the poem.

This brief indication of the range of *Tristan*-scholarship, like our bibliography below, must necessarily be selective, but it should serve to indicate both the vitality of that scholarship and the fertility of the poem itself. *Tristan* appears to be no more amenable to definitive interpretation than it was in the early stages of its research, and that, no doubt, is to be expected with a work which, like the love of which it relates, must grow and change even as we look at it.

Texts:
There are three major editions of the poem, none of them *the* definitive edition but all in their way very reliable, particularly in the recent re-workings of them:
Bechstein, Reinhold, ed. *Gottfried's von Strassburg Tristan*. Wiesbaden, 1869-70 (= Deutsche Classiker des Mittelalters 7-8). Edited, with notes and commentary by Peter Ganz. Wiesbaden: Brockhaus, 1978. 2 vols. (= Deutsche Klassiker des Mittelalters, NF 4).

Marold, Karl, ed. *Tristan.* Leipzig, 1906 (= Teutonia 6). 3rd reprint reissued by Werner Schröder, incorporating the additions and emendations by Friedrich Ranke and revised by E. J. Schmidt, with Schröder's own preface. Berlin: De Gruyter, 1969. Repr., 1977.

Ranke, Friedrich, ed. *Tristan und Isold.* 1930. 14th repr., Dublin/Zürich: Weidmann 1969. Corresponds to the (partial) re-edition (1958) by Ranke's pupil E. Studer, whose heralded complete new edition did not materialize, in part pre-empted by the new edition of Marold.

Weber, Gottfried, ed. *Gottfried von Straßburg. Tristan.* Darmstadt: Wiss. Buchges., 1967. Ranke's text, with mod. Ger. retelling by Werner Hoffmann.

Translations:

Hatto, Arthur T., trans. *Tristan, with the "Tristran" of Thomas.* Trans. with an introduction by A.T.Hatto. Harmondsworth: Penguin, 1960, and many times reprinted (= Penguin Classics, L98).

Krohn, Rüdiger, trans. *Tristan.* Stuttgart: Reclam, 1981 (= UB 4471-73). Ranke text with Mod. Ger. prose trans., commentary, and afterword by Rüdiger Krohn.

Kühn, Dieter, trans. *Tristan und Isolde von Gottfried von Straßburg. Tristan: eine Fortsetzung/ Ulrich von Türheim.* With the collaboration of Lambertus Okken, Frankfurt/M.: Insel, 1991. Mod. Ger. trans.

See also Weber, Gottfried (above).

Schach, Paul, trans. *The Saga of Tristram and Isönd.* Lincoln: Univ. of Nebraska Press, 1973. Engl. trans. of ON version, with introduction.

## *Tristan*—Bibliography

Batts, Michael S. *Gottfried von Straßburg.* New York: Twayne 1971. (= TWAS, 167).

A reliable basic introduction in English, but, of course, now rather out of date on questions of current scholarship.

Bekker, Hugo. *Gottfried von Straßburg's "Tristan": Journey through the Realm of Eros.* Columbia, SC: Camden House, 1987 (= Studies in German Literature, Linguistics, and Culture, 29).

One of the more recent studies of the whole poem and one of the few in English, but the approach is a very specific one and sometimes the arguments are rather strained.

Benskin, M., T. Hunt, and I. Short. "Un nouveau fragment du *Tristan* de Thomas," *Romania* 113 (1992-95): 290-319.

(See under "Sources," above.)

Buschinger, Danielle, and Wolfgang Spiewok, eds. *Tristan und Isolde im europäischen Mittelalter.* Ausgewählte Texte in Übersetzung und Nacherzählung. Stuttgart: Reclam, 1991 (= UB, 8702)

Although not strictly secondary literature, this is a useful little volume which presents substantial portions of the principal *Tristan* texts of European literature, translated into German, with a commentary and an introduction. Helpful for those seeking to put the German versions into context.

Chinca, Mark. *History, Fiction, Verisimilitude: Studies in the Poetics of Gottfried's Tristan.* London: MRHA & Inst. of Germanic Studies, 1993 (= MHRA Texts & Dissertations, 18; Bithell Series of Dissertations, 18).

Outstanding, in-depth study of Gottfried's poetics.

Combridge, Rosemary N. *Das Recht im "Tristan" Gottfrieds von Straßburg.* Berlin: Erich Schmidt, 1964 (= PSuQ, 15).

Unfortunately not available in English, this is a major contribution. The examination of central episodes in the light of the legal implications is very fruitful.

Ferrante, Joan M. *The Conflict of Love and Honor. The Medieval Tristan Legend in France, Germany and Italy*. The Hague/Paris: Mouton 1973.

A wide-ranging study of the Tristan story, which places Gottfried's version usefully in its context and contains a great deal of detailed material, both on *Tristan* in particular and in comparison with other versions.

Gruenter, Rainer. *Tristan-Studien, hrsg. v. Wolfgang Adam*. Heidelberg: Winter, 1993.

A collection of significant writings on *Tristan*, published in the 1950s and 1960s by an eminent scholar. All are, of course, in German. A central preoccupation is the description of landscape, particularly in the longest article, "Das *wünnecliche tal*," pp. 65-141.

Hahn, Ingrid. *Raum und Landschaft in Gottfrieds "Tristan."* Munich: Eidos, 1963 (= Medium Aevum, 3).

Jackson, W. T. H. *The Anatomy of Love: The "Tristan" of Gottfried von Straßburg*. New York: Columbia UP, 1971.

An excellent account of the whole poem. Provides a balanced examination of the central theme of the work, though written from a standpoint of unambiguous admiration for the poem.

____. "The Stylistic use of Word-Pairs and Word-Repetitions in Gottfried's 'Tristan'." *Euph.* 59 (1965): 229-251.

A fruitful examination of a central feature of Gottfried's language.

____. "The Literary Views of Gottfried von Strassburg." *PMLA* 85 (1970): 992-1001.

A study of the literary excursus which leads to some much broader analysis of the whole poem.

Jaeger, C. Stephen. *Medieval Humanism in Gottfried von Straßburg's "Tristan and Isolde"*. Heidelberg: Winter, 1977.

____. "The Testing of Brangaene: Cunning and Innocence in Gottfried's *Tristan*." *JEGP* 70 (1971): 189-206.

____. "The Crown of Virtues in the Cave of Lovers: Allegory of Gottfried's *Tristan*." *Euph.* 67 (1973): 95-116.

This and the two preceding works by Jaeger give reliable guidance in English on central concerns of *Tristan*-scholarship. Also clear and informative is his article in the *Arthurian Encyclopaedia* (New York: Garland, 1986, pp. 249-256); *New Arthurian Encyclopedia* (New York: Garland, 1991, pp. 206-211).

Johnson, L. Peter. "Gottfried von Straßburg: *Tristan*." In: *Mittelhochdeutsche Romane und Heldenepen*, Stuttgart: Reclam, 1993 (= UB, 8914: Interpretationen) Pp. 234-255.

Included here, even though it is in German, as one of the most recent essays on the poem, and easily available in the Reclam volume.

____. "Gottfried von Straßburg 'Tristan'." In: *Medieval Literature. Part Two: The European Inheritance*. Harmondsworth: Penguin, 1983. Pp. 207-221.

A lively article, in the first volume of the *New Pelican Guide to English Literature*, ed. by Boris Ford.

McDonald, William C. *The Tristan Story in German Literature of the Late Middle Ages and Early Renaissance.* Lewiston: Edwin Mellen, 1990.

_____. *Arthur and Tristan. On the Intersection of Legends in German Medieval Literature.* Lewiston: Edwin Mellen, 1991.

Meyer, Kathleen J. "The Ambiguity of Honor in Gottfried's *Tristan*: lines 17694-17699." *Neophil.* 70 (1986): 406-415.

On the basis of the examination of these six lines, Kathleen Meyer makes some perceptive observations about the levels of honor in the work; also stimulates thought about the complexity of Gottfried's language more generally.

_____. "Allegory and Generic Ambiguity in Gottfried's *Tristan.*" In: *Genres in Medieval German Literature*, ed. by Hubert Heinen and Ingeborg Henderson. Göppingen: Kümmerle, 1986 (= GAG, 439). Pp. 47-58.

A useful examination of the relationship between *Tristan* and the contemporary romance and the role of allegory in fulfilling the expectations of the audience and of creating a distinctive genre.

Okken, Lambertus. *Kommentar zum Tristan-Roman Gottfrieds von Straßburg.* Amsterdam: Rodopi, 1984-88. 3 vols.: I, 1984; II, 1985; III, 1988 (= Amsterdamer Publikationen zur Sprache und Literatur, 57, 58, 81).

Exhaustively thorough commentary on the text (Ranke's) with attribution of all sources of information on words and expressions and other aspects of the work. Three appendices: music (M. van Schaik); clothing and armor; and medicine (H. M. Zijlstra-Zweens), in Vol. 2; addenda in Vol. 3, and appendix on medicine by B. D. Haage. Outstanding bibliography.

Peiffer, Lore. *Zur Funktion der Exkurse im "Tristan" Gottfrieds von Straßburg.* Göppingen: Kümmerle, 1971 (= GAG, 31).

Although individual excursi have been discussed, this is the only work which sets out to consider their total contribution to the poem.

Picozzi, Rosemary. *A History of Tristan Scholarship.* Bern: Herbert Lang, 1971 (= Canadian Studies in German Language and Literature, 5).

Another very useful work in English, which provides a clear account of earlier scholarship and, in particular, a survey of 20th-century interpretations of the poem. Comprehensive bibliography.

Ranke, Friedrich. *Die Allegorie der Minnegrotte in Gottfrieds "Tristan".* Berlin, 1925 (= Schriften der Königsberger Gelehrten Gesellschaft, geisteswiss. Kl., 2). Repr. 1973 in Weber, WdF, 320 (below).

Schröder, Werner. *Über Gottfried von Straßburg* (Kleinere Schriften Band V. 1973-93). Stuttgart: S. Hirzel, 1994.

Contains some wide-ranging contributions to *Tristan*-scholarship, published over two decades by Werner Schröder.

Schwietering, Julius. *Der "Tristan" Gottfrieds und die Bernhardische Mystik.* Berlin, 1943 (= Abh. d. Preuß. Akad. d. Wiss., 1943. Phil.-hist. Kl., 5). Also in: J. S., *Mystik und höfische Dichtung in Hochmittelalter.* Tübingen, 1960, [2]1962. Pp. 1-35, and J. S. *Philologische Schriften.* Munich, 1969. Pp. 338-61.

_____. "Gottfried's *Tristan*," *GR* 29 (1954): 5-17.

Stephens, Adrian, and Roy Wisbey, eds. *Gottfried von Straßburg and the Medieval Tristan Legend.* Cambridge: Brewer and the Institute of Germanic Studies, 1990 (= Arthurian Studies, 23; Publs. of the Inst. of Germanic Stud., 44).

18 papers from an Anglo- North American conference held at the Institute in London in 1986.

Steinhoff, Hans-Hugo, comp. *Bibliographie zu Gottfried von Straßburg.* Berlin: Erich Schmidt 1971 (= Biblio. z. Dt. Lit. d. Mas., 5). II. Berichtszeitraum 1970-1983. Berlin: Erich Schmidt, 1986 (= Biblio. z. dt. Lit. d. Mas., 9).

The best, most complete bibliography available; has been kept up to date until 1983.

Tax, Petrus. *Wort, Sinnbild, Zahl im Tristanroman. Studien zum Denken und Werten Gottfrieds von Straßburg.* Berlin: Schmidt 1961. [2]1971 (= PSQ, 8).

Important, among other things, for its allegorical-symbolic interpretation and the role of ambiguity in *Tristan.*

Weber, Gottfried. *Gottfrieds von Straßburg "Tristan" und die Krise des hochmittelalterlichen Weltbildes um 1200.* Stuttgart: Metzler, 1952. 2 vols.

_____, and Werner Hoffmann. *Gottfried von Straßburg.* Stuttgart: Metzler, 1962. [5]1981 (= Sammlung Metzler, 15).

Concise, convenient compendium of information about Gottfried, his *Tristan*, and scholarly research in that area.

Willson, H. Bernard. "Vicissitudes in Gottfried's *Tristan*." *MLR* 52 (1957): 203-213.

_____ "Gottfried's *Tristan*: The Coherence of Prologue and Narrative." *MLR* 59 (1964): 595-607.

This and the article above it are now rather out of date in some respects, but they remain readable and sensitive interpretations.

Wolf, Alois, ed. *Gottfried von Straßburg.* Darmstadt: Wiss. Buchges., 1973 (= WdF, 320).

This volume assembles and reprints 23 significant articles from 1925-69, thereby affording an overview of research.

_____. *Gottfried von Straßburg und die Mythe von Tristan und Isolde.* Darmstadt: Wiss. Buchges., 1989.

Discusses Gottfried's *Tristan* against the background of other versions reflecting the "myth" of Tristan and Isolde.

## Wolfram von Eschenbach

Few would dispute the position of Wolfram von Eschenbach as the most significant single figure of medieval German literature. He may not scale the lyric heights of Gottfried von Straßburg (see p. 157 ff.), nor justifiably lay claim to the crystalline words of Hartmann von Aue (see p. 132). He does not take issue with the social and political problems of his day with the pungency of Walther von der Vogelweide, nor does he demonstrate quite the same versatility in poetic form as Heinrich von Morungen. Yet he transcends all of them in the range of his material and the power of his language. Though he is deeply rooted in his age and inseparable in so many respects from the climate of the High Middle Ages and although his work abounds in local color, Wolfram von Eschenbach justifiably ranks as a substantial figure in world literature. The wider dissemination of his works, particularly through translations into English, has furthered his reputation.

Wolfram von Eschenbach names himself in his two great epics, *Parzival* (114,12) and *Willehalm* (4,19), and he seems to be supplying a mass of autobiographical details throughout his works, e.g., that he had a wife (*Parz.* 216,28), a sister (*Parz.* 686,29), a daughter whose dolls are not as beautiful as the heathen knights (*Wh.* 33,24). In fact, however, it is not easy to ascertain how much of this is factual information and how much it should be attributed to his pose as narrator. When he remarks that he and his brother are as one (*Parz.* 740,29) or that he would not disdain the man whom his daughter chose as her husband (*Wh.* 11,23-24), this has the ring of a poetic generalization rather than a piece of personal information. Nor does the fact that he elevates the state of marriage necessarily tell us, as some have assumed, that he himself enjoyed a happy married life. We must thus distinguish between what we know for sure about his life and what we should treat with some circumspection.

He was probably born in about 1170, and his death will have occurred some time after 1220. He may have acquired a reputation as a Minnesänger prior to the composition of *Parzival*, where he speaks of himself as being "something of a Minnesänger" (114,13), but it is impossible to date his extant songs with any certainty, or do more than suggest the order in which they may have been composed. It seems likely that some early attempts at love songs may have been lost or even destroyed by the poet himself, including possibly one at least in which he said something which was taken amiss by the ladies (*Parz.* 114,23). That *Parzival* predates *Willehalm* is not in dispute (cf. *Wh.* 4, 20-24), and, despite some early views that *Titurel* was an early work, the consensus is now that it, like *Willehalm*, belongs to the period towards the end of Wolfram's life and may, like it, have been left a fragment because he died in the process of composition. Another view is that he deliberately left them unfinished for some reason (see below).

Wolfram's place of origin is now generally believed to be the little town of Ober-Eschenbach not far from Nuremberg. Despite the existence of rivals, this town has been known officially since 1917 as Wolframs-Eschenbach. There is documentary evidence that a von Eschenbach family has been associated with this town since the late 13th century, and it was here that a grave purporting to be Wolfram's was seen in 1608. This memorial, which is nowhere to be seen today, appears to have been erected by the von Eschenbach family who perpetuated the connection with the great poet by bestowing his name on successive generations throughout the later Middle Ages. That they appear to have had a family emblem quite different from the one attributed to Wolfram in the Manesse anuscript is only one of the problems which somewhat cloud the issue. Wolfram betrays considerable acquaintance with Franconia in references in both *Parzival* and *Willehalm*, yet his only precise reference to his place of origin is in *Parzival*, when he speaks of *wir Beier* (121,7), although at that time Franconia was not actually a part of

Bavaria. However, since the reference is to the foolishness of the Bavarians, and since he may well have been performing to an audience of Bavarians, the likelihood is that he is wishing to add to the mocking remark by associating himself with them. This would be very much his style. It might be expected that Wolfram's language would supply some conclusive evidence about his origin, but, in the absence of more research on the matter, we are left at best with the conclusion that his language is Franconian with Bavarian features.

When it comes to the question of Wolfram's social standing, doubt has been cast on his own central statement *schildes ambet ist mîn art* (My inherited nature is the service of the shield: *Parz.* 115,11), a view perpetuated by the famous depiction of him as a knight in the Manesse manuscript. He may have been a ministerialis, an unfree knight in the service of a lord, but modern scholars have come to doubt whether this was the case, despite his reference earlier in *Parzival* to his knightly word of honor (15,12). Certainly, whether he was an active knight or not, he is in sympathy with the ideals of chivalry and shows again and again in his works that he understands the demands of the calling, appreciates its strengths and its weaknesses, and, on a more practical level, is familiar with the details of the life of the fighting man. He may perhaps have been a fairly humble man, whose own aspirations and elevation to the nobility by later generations have encouraged a different impression. Indeed, the prevailing impression which he himself offers in his work is of a poor man, in whose house even the mice had a poor deal (*Parz.* 184,29-185,2). The likelihood is that he had no house to call his own, and that he was dependent for his material well-being on a patron and his own poetic art. That he was a layman, despite his profound faith and his preoccupation with religious matters, is accepted and in particular supported by the praise of near-contemporaries. Wirnt von Gravenberg (see p. 314 ff.), though first and foremost a pupil of Hartmann von Aue's, nevertheless praised the "wise man of Eschenbach", of whom he spoke the famous words: *leien munt nie baz gesprach* (Never did the mouth of a layman speak better).

On the matter of his education, Wolfram's own pronouncements have been examined, brought into question, and occasionally dismissed. The famous lines in *Parzival* have sometimes been regarded as Wolfram's teasing exaggeration, rebutting the proud boasting of his contemporaries, particularly Hartmann von Aue, but probably also Gottfried von Straßburg:

> ine kan decheinen buochstap.
> dâ nement genuoge ir urhap:
> disiu âventiure
> vert âne der buoche stiure.
> (115,27-30)

(I do not know a single letter of the alphabet. Many people take that as their starting-point. This story moves along without books to steer it.)

Of course, it is not impossible that Wolfram had no formal education: as a poor man he would hardly have had the means to acquire one in an age when only a very small minority was granted the privilege of schooling. Those who subscribe to this view point to the evidence that his knowledge had been gained by listening and that he never once claims to have *read* his source. There is no evidence of a knowledge of Latin, which would have been expected of one who had had a formal education, and his knowledge of French, though apparently quite extensive, could well have been acquired aurally, hence the signs of mishearing of sounds and the instances where he appears to have misunderstood his sources. His broad knowledge in a wide range of spheres—medicine, precious stones, distant places, literature, and legend—could have been gleaned by an intelligent, alert mind and retained in an extraordinarily acute memory. He may have travelled quite widely in his lord's service, and he almost certainly conversed with a wide range of people. It is just possible that he had no need of books. However, the other school of thought dismisses such a likelihood and attributes Wolfram's assessment of his literacy to his playful disparagement of learning. He does not want to be thought of as a learned man; what guides him is something which is entirely natural to him, which, in an allied passage in *Willehalm*, he calls *sin*:

swaz an den buochen stêt geschriben,
des bin ich künstelôs beliben.
niht anders ich gelêret bin:
wan hân ich kunst, die gît mir sin.
    (2,19-22)

(I have remained ignorant of those things which are written in books, and I am tutored in one respect alone: if I have any skill, this comes from my own mind.)

This mind was evidently one of enormous scope and flexibility judging from the range of Wolfram's work. His rejection of the formality of language and thought which seems implicit in his declaration of his lack of learning means that he is free to give rein to his fertile imagination and the originality of his expression. If he gives the impression that he is ignorant in matters of detail, of foreign languages and geography for example, it is probably as much an aspect of his deliberate pose as it is a reflection of the actual situation. In this, as in other respects, one must admit to a high degree of uncertainty or perhaps of deliberately contrived ambivalence.

The first critical edition of the complete works of Wolfram von Eschenbach appeared in 1833, the product of the eminent and immensely industrious philologist Karl Lachmann. This single volume, which contains—in this order—the *Lieder, Parzival, Titurel* and *Willehalm* was re-edited by several scholars (Moriz Haupt in 1854 and again in 1872; Karl Müllenhoff in 1879; Karl Weinhold in 1891) before the 1926 edition by Eduard Hartl which has remained the authoritative edition, frequently reprinted. The only other complete edition is that by Albert Leitzmann (1902-1906), which is essentially based on the Lachmann readings but often provides more helpful punctuation. Editions of the individual works are treated in the relevant sections below.

Lachmann made the important decision to divide *Parzival* and *Willehalm* into sections ("Books") which correspond to the divisions marked in the great St. Gall manuscript (D) by large illuminated letters. This principle results in a division of *Parzival* into sixteen Books and *Willehalm*, as it stands, into nine. Whether such sections indicate how much was performed at one sitting is impossible to say, but it is an attractive idea. The elusive answer to this question would supply some useful information about performance and also about the structure of the poems. Within the Books, the edition divides the whole text into thirty-line sections (*Dreißiger*), which accords with the division of the major manuscripts from Book V of *Parzival* on, and throughout *Willehalm*, where smaller illuminated capitals mark the beginning of each section. Books I, II, and III of *Parzival* and Book I of *Willehalm* do not end on completed *Dreißiger*. The assumption is that Wolfram, or perhaps his scribe, had not established the principle from the beginning of the works, or, in the case of *Willehalm*, that the last but one couplet was omitted for some reason, since the existing concluding couplet of the first Book has a thoroughly final ring to it. At any rate, quotations from *Parzival* and *Willehalm* are always given with the number of the *Dreißiger* first, followed by the line number within the thirty-line section, as seen in the quotations above.

The large number of manuscripts of both *Parzival* and *Willehalm* (more than eighty of *Parzival*, of which sixteen are complete, and twelve complete manuscripts of *Willehalm* with numerous fragments) leads us to assume that both were very popular works in the Middle Ages. *Titurel* survives in only three manuscripts, of which only one (G) contains the 164 strophes which appear to represent the totality of Wolfram's fragments, but this need not necessarily be taken as a sign that the work was less popular. On the contrary, it seems likely that even in this state the work was well received, provoking the continuation which was supplied in full measure by Albrecht, who managed to gain popularity for it precisely because he succeeded in persuading his audience that he was in fact Wolfram von Eschenbach (see p. 381 ff.). The Songs are not handed down in a single manuscript devoted to Wolfram's lyric. Although seven of the extant songs are contained in the great lyric collections A, B, and C (see 225 ff.), two songs which rank as the most striking survive only in manuscript G of *Parzival*, where, along with the text of *Titurel*, they constitute an important, though incomplete, collection of Wolfram's work.

Judging from the number of manuscripts of his works, Wolfram was popular in the Middle Ages, though one of the most important contemporary references to him is far from complimentary. This is the attack on him as the "friend of the hare" (*des hâsen geselle*) and the "teller of wild tales" (*der mære wildenære*) by Gottfried von Straßburg in the literary excursus in *Tristan* (4636-88). There is little doubt that he is referring to Wolfram in his blatant criticism of a fellow poet whom he apparently disliked for his complex and obscure style. We may even suspect that Gottfried saw Wolfram as a rival and perhaps, in his heart of hearts, as a superior artist. Gottfried could also have been expressing an opinion held among some of Wolfram's listeners, who may have been perplexed by the complicated style and the many twists and turns of a narrative which they nevertheless admired and enjoyed.

### Wolfram von Eschenbach—General Bibliography

Bumke, Joachim. *Wolfram von Eschenbach*. Stuttgart: Metzler, [6]1991 (= Sammlung Metzler, 36).

A most authoritative and thorough introduction to Wolfram and his individual works, offering clear guidance through the mass of existing scholarly research. Earlier editions are also very good, but this latest one has been completely revised and the bibliography brought up to date. The best work of its kind and a "must" for any study of Wolfram.

_____. *Die Wolfram von Eschenbach-Forschung seit 1945. Bericht und Bibliographie.* Munich: Wilhelm Fink, 1970.

Excellent, complete bibliography of Wolfram scholarship for the period 1945-70 with thorough, even-handed discussion of all important studies. In greater depth than the item above for the period covered.

Dalby, David. *"Der mære wildenære." Euph.* 55 (1961): 77-84.

A study of the term *der mære wildenære* (*Trist.* 4664), coming to the conclusion that it means *gemieteter märenfänger* (hired trapper/snarer of tales), hardly a compliment, if indeed aimed at Wolfram.

Decke-Cornill, Renate. comp. "Wolfram-Bibliographie. 1984-86. In: *Wolfram-Studien,* X. Berlin: Erich Schmidt, 1988. Pp. 207-33.

A continuing bibliography in the *Wolfram-Studien,* an organ of the Wolfram von Eschenbach Gesellschaft, since 1984. The *Studien,* appearing irregularly, were started by Werner Schröder in 1970 and have been continued since Vol. 11 (1989) by J. Heinzle, L. P. Johnson, and G. Vollmann-Profe. Aside from the bibliography, an excellent source for recent articles on Wolfram and his age.

Ganz, Peter. "Lachmann as an Editor of MHG Texts." In: *Probleme mittelalterlicher Überlieferung und Textkritik. Oxforder Colloquium, 1966.* Ed. by W. Schröder and P. Ganz. Berlin: Erich Schmidt, 1968. Pp. 12-30.

Fascinating review of Lachmann's life and his principles of editing texts.

Gärtner, Kurt, and Joachim Heinzle, eds. *Studien zu Wolfram von Eschenbach. Festschrift für Werner Schröder zum 75. Geburtstag.* Tübingen: Niemeyer, 1989.

Contains 37 articles mainly in German on a variety of aspects of Wolfram's life and works. Especially interesting as a panorama of contemporary Wolfram research by scholars in Germany, France, England, and the U.S.A.

Green, Dennis, and L. Peter Johnson. *Approaches to Wolfram von Eschenbach. Five Essays.* Bern: Peter Lang, 1978 (= Mikrokosmus. Beitr. z. Litwiss. u. Bedeutungsforschung, 5).

Essays are mainly on *Parzival,* how Wolfram composed, and one on Wolfram's lyric poems by two well-known scholars. Very much worth reading.

Heffner, Roe-Merrill S., comp. *Collected Indexes to the Works of Wolfram von Eschenbach.* Madison, WI: Univ. of Wisconsin Press, 1961.

Extremely useful index for locating key words and phrases and for establishing Wolfram's usage of particular terms.

Nellmann, Eberhard. *Wolframs Erzähltechnik. Untersuchungen zur Funktion des Erzählers.* Wiesbaden: Steiner, 1973.

An interesting study of authorial intrusions in Wolfram's narrative works, the creation of a narrative persona, and his relationship to his audience.

Norman, Frederick. "The Enmity of Wolfram and Gottfried." *GLL* 15 (1961/62): 53-67.

Discussion of the problem of dating medieval works on the basis of references to other poets, ending with analysis of Wolfram-Gottfried "feud."

Poag, James F. *Wolfram von Eschenbach.* New York: Twayne, 1972 (= TWAS, 233).

A useful first introduction to Wolfram in English for the general reader.

Pretzel, Ulrich, and Wolfgang Bachofer, comps. *Bibliographie zu Wolfram von Eschenbach.* ²1968. Berlin: Erich Schmidt, 1968 (= Biblio. z. dt. Lit. d. Mas, 2).

Complete Wolfram bibliography approximately to date of publication. Items are listed chronologically in various categories. Excellent index. Unfortunately not continued and brought up to date.

Ruh, Kurt. *Höfische Epik des deutschen Mittelalters II: "Reinhart Fuchs," "Lanzelet," Wolfram von Eschenbach, Gottfried von Straßburg.* Berlin: Erich Schmidt, 1980 (= GLG, 25).

A comprehensive view of Wolfram and his work in the context of a study of German courtly literature.

Rupp, Heinz, ed. *Wolfram von Eschenbach.* Darmstadt: Wiss. Buchges., 1966 (= WdF, 57).

A collection of 22 important articles on Wolfram and his works dating from 1946 to 1961, conveniently reprinted in one volume.

Schreiber, Albert. *Neue Bausteine zu einer Lebensgeschichte Wolframs von Eschenbach.* Frankfurt/M.: Diesterweg, 1922. Reprint 1975 (= Deutsche Forschungen, 7).

An early attempt to assemble all possible information on Wolfram's life; at times rather bold and imaginative conclusions, but the data are still there.

### Parzival

The relative datings of Wolfram's *Parzival* and Gottfried's *Tristan* depend on the assumption that the Prologue to *Parzival* was added at a later date than the composition of the early Parzival story, with the remainder of the Parzival Books and the whole of the Gawan action later still. Wolfram's *Parzival* and Gottfried's *Tristan* thus belong to the first decade of the 13th century and were probably directed at the same or a very similar audience. Indeed, it ranks as one of the most fascinating features of medieval German literature that two great narrative works with diametrically opposing attitudes to such central social issues as love and marriage appeared almost simultaneously.

Although, like Gottfried, Wolfram took a familiar story as the core of his first narrative poem, *Parzival* is an altogether more complex work than the unfinished French poem of Chrétien de Troyes, *Perceval* or *Li conte du Graal* (ca. 1180-90), which was his immediate source. If one discounts Wolfram's references to Kyot who is now by common consent agreed to be a fiction designed to tease his audience with his (Kyot's) fantastic history of the Grail, then the likelihood is that some of the most significant material in *Parzival* was invented by Wolfram himself. Substantial portions of the poem, notably the story of Parzival's father Gahmuret and the extension of it to tell of his other son Feirefiz, have no counterpart in Chrétien. Wolfram has expanded and deepened his French source in numerous significant ways (Chrétien: ca. 8,900 lines, vs. ca. 15,000 in the corresponding parts in Wolfram, out of a total of 24,810 lines). The traditional story of the search for the Grail attains a profound spiritual meaning, and although, for want of a better term, *Parzival* can be called an Arthurian romance, it far transcends the normal expectations of the genre. The considerable portion of the work which is devoted to Gawan is no subsidiary plot centered on a secondary hero but an integral part of the work.

A first reading of *Parzival* is likely to provoke comment on the multitude of characters and the complexity of plot, with its episodes often interweaving in a bewildering way. A useful initial approach is thus to attempt to unravel this apparent confusion and reveal the structural divisions.

The sixteen Books are allocated to the narrative in the following broad way:

I. Wolfram introduces his work with a brief but very dense Prologue, which contains some of the most complicated language and imagery in the poem (1,1-4,26). His story will tell, he predicts, of great loyalty, the nature of womanly woman, and of man's manly courage (4,9-13). The true hero of the tale, a bold man but one who only slowly achieves wisdom, is as yet unborn (4,24).

He turns first to the story of the knight Gahmuret, the second son of Gandin, who dies in combat. Declining his elder brother's offer of a share in his inheritance, Gahmuret seizes the opportunity to ride off in search of adventure, which he finds in abundance. In particular, he serves the *bâruc*, the Caliph of Baghdad, with whom he forms a close friendship. After much travelling he comes to the land of Belakane, a beautiful heathen queen whom he saves from a threatening situation and marries. Although he loves her deeply, he grows restless after a time and leaves her secretly, on the pretext that the difference in faiths has come between them. She is left to give birth to their child alone, and when he is born, a strange boy spotted black and white, she calls him Feirefiz Anschevin.

II. In spite of himself, Gahmuret finds himself deeply in love with the widowed Queen Herzeloyde, and he agrees to marry her, but only on condition that he be free to practice his chivalry at regular intervals, so that he does not abandon her as he did his first wife. However, it is an urgent call from his friend the *bâruc* which finally separates them. He dies in a distant heathen land and is buried there. This time it is Herzeloyde who must give birth in grief, and the child is Parzival.

III. Desperate to ensure that her son be spared the fate of his father, Herzeloyde withdraws into the wasteland of Soltane, far from the court and all that goes with knighthood. Her child grows up surrounded by her love but deceived of his kingly way of life (118,2). His inherited nature is too strong for her, however, and she cannot stop him departing in search of chivalry once he learns of its existence from some passing knights. She gives him some very disconnected and incomplete advice which he will remember at intervals in the future, sometimes with negative consequences.

This Book contains some of Parzival's most significant early encounters: with Jeschute (129,27 ff.), with his cousin Sigune who is grieving over her dead lover, Schionatulander (138,9 ff.), the Red Knight Ither whom he slays (145,7 ff.), and the old knight Gurnemanz with whom he stays for two weeks and who teaches him some important lessons but also gives him the fateful piece of advice that he should not keep asking questions (162,20 ff.). Although he is attracted to Gurnemanz's young daughter Liaze, he knows that he is not yet ready to settle down and that in any case he must win his lady when the time comes, and he rides away.

IV. He fights on behalf of the lovely young woman Condwiramurs and marries her. They rule together over her kingdom and all is well for a whole year, but then he is prompted to leave her, to go and see how his mother is faring but also because he knows that, as a knight, he must maintain his chivalry.

V. He comes to a strange castle where an elaborate ceremony takes place, amidst much luxury and obvious wealth, but accompanied by a prevailing mood of sorrow. He sees a procession of lovely maidens, culminating in a beautiful woman who, as he knows, has given him her cloak to wear and who is carrying a precious stone (the Grail) on a piece of green material. His kindly host, a man who is clearly suffering, gives him a sword. Mindful of the advice of Gurnemanz that he should not ask too many questions, he remains silent. After a night troubled by dreadful dreams, he wakes up determined to help these people, since it is clear that they are in some kind of trouble, but the castle is empty and he rides away, with some words of abuse from a page at the gate echoing in his ears (248,26-30).

He meets his cousin Sigune for the second time and she upbraids him for failing at the castle and sends him away without holding out any hope that he could ever make amends at the Grail Castle (255,24-29).

He meets Jeschute again and is able to repair the wrong he had done her much earlier by assuring her husband, whom he has defeated in a fierce duel, that she has not been unfaithful to him.

VI. His magnificent defeat of Orilus, the husband of Jeschute, means that his reputation has reached King Arthur, who now sends out to invite him to join the Round Table. It is in fact Gawan who persuades him to accompany him to the Court, when he discovers him in a trance as he contemplates some drops of blood in the snow which remind him of the beauty of his wife (282,1 ff.). However, after a warm welcome, Parzival's fortunes are plunged into the depths when Cundrie arrives on a mule to accuse him of having failed to express compassion at the Grail and to assure the whole company that they are disgraced by his very presence among them (311,30 ff.). Hardly has she left when a knight comes in to accuse Gawan of having committed a terrible act of discourtesy by slaying a man in the act of greeting him. Both men must leave the Court in order to attempt to right their reputations.

VII. This Book is devoted to the exploits of Gawan, who finds himself fighting at Bearosche as the knight of the young girl Obilot. He leaves at the end of the Book, after having resolved an awkward situation for his "lady's" sister and father by his feats of arms.

VIII. Gawan becomes embroiled in a decidedly unchivalrous adventure, when he is (wrongly) accused of seducing the desirable and very forward Antikonie. Central to the escapade is his undignified defense of the pair of them, when he hurls chessmen at the pursuing crowd and has to resort to using a chessboard as a shield. Again, he rides away, this time only just managing to retain a measure of reputation.

IX. At the heart of the poem is this lengthy Book, devoted exclusively to Parzival, who has been wandering around in search of the Grail without really knowing how to find it and attempting to enhance his chivalric reputation by means of fighting. The Book again contains a series of crucial meetings for Parzival. The first is his third meeting with Sigune (435,6-442,25), who is now gentler towards him but still convinced that he has no expectation of coming to the Grail a second time. She commends him to God, and, more practically, directs him in the tracks of Cundrie who visits her regularly with food brought from the Grail Castle. Although the tracks fade out, he does have a further important experience, this time meeting a group of pilgrims, including two beautiful young women, on Good Friday (446,6-451,23). They are attracted to this desolate young knight and feel great sympathy for him. They invite him to join them, but, conscious that he has rejected the God to whom they are devoted, he reluctantly declines their invitation. As he rides away, he is deeply moved by this encounter, however, and decides that he should give God another chance. He lets his horse take its own path and comes to the cell of the hermit Trevrizent (452,13-15).

In the two weeks he spends with Trevrizent he learns many things that are of the utmost importance to him: of the relationship between them, the love of God, the nature of the Grail and the fact that they both belong to this select family (Trevrizent is his uncle). The information comes only gradually, and it culminates in Parzival's ability to confess his sin of having killed Ither, a relative, and of being the one who rode away from the Castle without having asked a question. Trevrizent is compassionate to him and, before Parzival leaves, he takes his sins from him but urges him to continue his life of chivalry, understanding as he now does that he must do so in the service of God.

X. Wolfram turns again to Gawan, who now meets the lovely Orgeluse and commits himself to her service, despite the warnings he receives from her and from others. He undergoes a series of adventures of fairly traditional "Arthurian" nature and endures much mockery from her. At the end of the Book he comes within sight of Schastel Marveile.

XI. Seeking to discover the secret of this wondrous castle, Gawan learns that four hundred ladies are imprisoned there by the evil magician Clinschor. He is successful in the dangerous adventure of the Bed of Wonders and thus frees the women, among whom are his grandmother, his mother, and his sister.

XII. Having proved himself to this extent, Gawan now applies himself to the demands of Orgeluse, who requires that any would-be suitors should fetch a garland from a tree in a garden guarded by the powerful Gramoflanz, the slayer of her beloved Cidegast. Since his death she has sent numerous knights to their deaths at the hand of Gramoflanz, but Gawan manages to pluck the garland successfully (603,30). When Gramoflanz appears and admits that this man has indeed gained the trophy, he reveals also that he has sworn never to fight with any man singly, save the son of King Lot, against whom he has a deep grievance because, as he tells him, King Lot killed his father in the act of greeting him. When Gawan identifies himself as that son of King Lot, Gramoflanz arranges to engage in combat with him at an appointed time, and in the presence of King Arthur himself, since he can see that, following the exploits at Schastel Marveile, he is not at present in a fit state to fight. Gawan returns triumphant to Orgeluse who at last concedes that he has won her love.

XIII. The already intricate situation is further complicated by the fact that, as we now learn, Gramoflanz is conducting a secret love affair with Itonje, the sister of Gawan. He is thus torn between his love for her and his obligation to fight her beloved. A message is sent to King Arthur, asking him to appear at the appointed time to witness this combat.

XIV. Parzival is brought back into the narrative when he engages in combat with Gawan, neither recognizing the other. Only sheer chance prevents the inconceivable outcome that Parzival might slay his friend and kinsman, and the two of them go back to Arthur's encampment, where Parzival is received with great joy. This represents the peak and the conclusion of the Gawan adventures, but Parzival, aware that he is out of place amidst the ensuing celebrations, slips away.

XV. He encounters a magnificently attired heathen knight and launches into combat with him. In the course of the fierce fighting, Wolfram reveals that each is the son of Gahmuret, for the man is none other than Feirefiz Anschevin. Once more fate seems to intervene, when, at the climax of a tremendous battle between two well-matched opponents, Parzival's sword breaks (744,11). Recognition ensues, and Parzival returns to Arthur's Court, this time with his half-brother. At the height of the welcome that follows, Cundrie arrives, with the announcement that Parzival has been named on the Grail and may now go with a companion to Munsalvæsche. He selects Feirefiz to accompany him, and they ride away.

XVI. When they come to the Grail Castle, Parzival falls on his knees before the suffering Anfortas, his uncle, and prays to the Trinity, then, rising to his feet, he addresses the Question to him. (795,29). Anfortas is immediately restored to health and great beauty. The announcement on the Grail stone has named Condwiramurs too, and she is on her way to join him. He rides to meet her, calling in on the way at the cell of Trevrizent, who is astounded to learn that, after all, he has succeeded (798,1 ff.). He meets Condwiramurs and sees his twin sons for the first time (800,20-21). Together they journey to the Grail, and Parzival remembers that they are passing close to the place where he last saw Sigune. She is now dead and he places her in the coffin with her lover (804,30-805,2). When they all return to Munsalvæsche, the Grail procession again escorts the Grail before them, and it now becomes apparent that Feirefiz, as a heathen, cannot see it. In his desire for the maiden who carries the Grail, he gladly accepts baptism and immediately sees the Stone (818,20-23). He returns with his bride to the East, where together they spread the message of Christianity: their son is the fabled Prester John. Of the two sons of Parzival, Wolfram tells how Kardeiz inherited his worldly kingdoms (803,21), while the story of Loherangrin, who serves the Grail, becomes entwined with that of the Swan Knight, whose marriage comes to a tragic end when his wife demands to know where he comes from. Wolfram concludes his poem by declaring that he has brought Parzival to the place for which Fortune intended him.

At the heart of Wolfram's *Parzival* is the theme of the search for the Grail, and in this central aspect of his work Wolfram immediately shows himself to be highly original. The Grail itself is not, as it is traditionally and certainly in Chrétien, a chalice or a bowl, but a unique and precious stone, endowed with a number of magic qualities. These, however, are not all evident when the Grail first appears in the poem, carried out in the great ceremony which Parzival witnesses in Book V, but—a characteristic feature of Wolfram's narrative technique—they are gradually revealed and explained. One particular aspect of the Grail company is its political role. Children are called to the Grail society, grow up there and become knights and ladies. Whenever a queen is needed, a lady is sent out openly to become the wife of the ruler (e.g., Herzeloyde in her first marriage), or when a king is required, the men are sent out incognito to become lords of the land (e.g., Lohengrin), a function of the Grail as a divine message center or placement bureau.

Wolfram's Grail embraces a strange mixture of properties. Purely physical attributes, like its capacity to summon up food and drink in abundance and in response to desire, and to allow itself to be carried only by a selected person, despite its otherwise tremendous weight, exist alongside other qualities which make it an unambiguously spiritual object with a special provenance and imposing a unique destiny on its intended king. The progress of Parzival towards the Grail is thus, on one level, the progress of a knight towards his goal comparable with the search for *âventiure* of Hartmann's Erec or Iwein, or Wolfram's own Gawan. On another level, it represents a deeper and very much more complicated movement towards his individual fulfillment. Parzival has a predestined role in a selected family, and the idea of a chosen dynasty is one which Wolfram introduces and develops crucially. A significant dimension of the poem is thus the complex structure which he builds up on the family of Titurel, to whom the Grail was entrusted by the neutral angels after Lucifer's rebellion against God. The current king, Titurel's grandson Anfortas, has transgressed the dictates of the Grail by seeking love outside its ordinance and must suffer terribly in consequence. Parzival is the next in line, but his accession depends on his fulfilling certain individual requirements.

Although Parzival's future may appear preordained, failure is not only possible but, as it ultimately turns out, inevitable. His first visit to Munsalvæsche, the Grail Castle, ends in disaster, when he neglects to ask the question which he does not even know exists but which turns out to be a simple expression of compassion for a suffering fellow human being. In the context of the whole poem, it is evident that Parzival's omission must be expected in one who is as yet so inexperienced and, in particular, so wrong-headed in his relationship with God. His ability to articulate what appears to be a very simple and obvious question will come only after much suffering and indeed after a period of alienation from God has led to a proper and deeper understanding of His nature. A fruitful relationship with other people can only arise on the basis of a properly adjusted relationship with God.

At the center of Wolfram's *Parzival*, Book IX contains the essence of the spiritual thought of the poem. He learns from his uncle, the hermit Trevrizent, that God is the true Lover (466,1). He comes to realize how mistaken he has been in believing that his relationship with God could be on a tit-for-tat basis and in blaming God for, as he believes, failing to reward his service and causing him to suffer so terribly. Parzival, as future Grail King, must clearly have a solid faith, but Wolfram does not advocate that he should serve God, as Trevrizent does, in isolation from the world, and the end of Book IX finds Parzival leaving the hermitage to pursue his life of chivalry in a heightened form, knowing as he now does that knighthood must be harnessed to man's other responsibilities and that chivalric glory for its own sake (*prîs*) is a superficial pursuit.

Wolfram's purpose is not, however, to denigrate chivalry. On the contrary, he understands both its strengths and its weaknesses and seems to see it as an ultimately positive pursuit. In expanding the role of Gawan in his poem and making this hero into a significant counterpart figure, he gives his poem an important additional dimension. Wolfram's own assertion that he turns to Gawan and his adventures because he recognizes that it may become tedious for his audience if he concentrates exclusively on the one man

(338,7 ff.) is plausible enough, and one important function of the substantial Gawan part of the poem, apart from conveying the impression of the passing of time, is doubtless to provide a counter-balance to the somber account of Parzival's progress.

It might be going too far to speak of "comic relief," but the more light-hearted tone of the Gawan action does cut across the dominant seriousness of Parzival's story. Gawan is Parzival's friend and kinsman, and he is an exemplary knight of Arthur's Round Table. He also represents a norm which Parzival himself attains and transcends. From the time the two are juxtaposed in Book VI, the essential difference of temperament between them is made clear, for all the parallelism of their situations. Both are required to act to restore their damaged reputations after the accusations of *untriuwe* (faithlessness) which have been leveled at them in public at Arthur's Court. Gawan's way ahead is clearly defined: he must appear at a certain place and an appointed time if he is to rebut the accusation that he killed King Kingrisin in the act of greeting him. Parzival's future is far less clear, and his only hope is to come to Munsalvæsche again and to express the compassion which, out of a false sense of correctness (*zuht*), he suppressed on the earlier occasion. However, he has no knowledge of the whereabouts of the Grail Castle, and those who profess to be informed on the matter—Sigune, Cundrie, and Trevrizent—are convinced that there is no possibility of a second chance. In any case, his distance from Munsalvæsche is less a question of geography than of personal fitness.

That the paths of Parzival and Gawan are parallel but on different levels, in accordance with the differences between them in temperament and in destiny, is emphasized by Wolfram's references to Parzival in the adventures which primarily concern Gawan. That Parzival is the true hero of the poem (*des mæres hêrre*, 338,7), its "true stem" (678,30), as Wolfram puts it, is never forgotten, even though he devotes Books VII, VIII, XI, XII, XIII and a large part of XIV exclusively to Gawan. Passing mention of Parzival occurs repeatedly; often he is engaged in the same exploit as Gawan; sometimes he is on the opposite side; sometimes other characters report that they have seen him in their travels. When they come together in the magnificent combat in Book XIV, this is quite obviously the goal of Gawan's chivalrous tests. Yet, equally obviously, it is only a stage for Parzival himself and when the end of Book XIV shows Gawan firmly where he belongs, in the Arthurian setting, Parzival assumes center stage again as the work moves to its conclusion.

Not least among Wolfram's achievements in *Parzival*, then, is a work whose central plot is a twofold one. Parzival and Gawan both pursue their personal goals, and each is accorded the highest place within his own context. For each the fulfillment of that personal destiny is linked with the love of a woman. Condwiramurs is inextricable from the Grail as the inspiration and the goal of Parzival, while for Gawan his ultimate success in terms of Arthurian chivalry wins him the hand of Orgeluse. It is Wolfram's masterly stroke to have linked the two realms precisely through the figure of Orgeluse, the woman who is almost as beautiful as Condwiramurs but not quite (508,22-23) and who has only ever known rejection from Parzival himself, who compared her unfavorably with the Queen of Pelrapeire, his beloved wife (618,19-619,14). It was, we learn, Orgeluse who caused Anfortas to transgress when he pursued her love even though she was not designated for him by the Grail law.

That Wolfram chose to employ a character from his source like this says much for the way in which he uses Chrétien's unfinished tale. The spiteful, worldly woman who is Gauvain's partner in the French version is deeply integrated into Wolfram's narrative, and in the process she acquires a depth and a history not even hinted at by Chrétien. It would be facile—and run the risk of sounding condescending—to emphasize that Wolfram has created a work of larger proportions than Chrétien was attempting, especially since we do not know for certain how Chrétien would have concluded his work. However, we can probably assume that Wolfram is following the rough outline of what Chrétien might have intended, at least insofar as Perceval's eventual return to the Grail Castle is concerned. Even if that is indeed the case, his *Parzival* is in many ways still a definite reconception of the basic material.

To substantiate this idea one need only compare those episodes which are already present at least in embryo in Chrétien's *Perceval* without regard to the ending. The encounter with the woman in the tent, the killing of the Red Knight, the drops of blood in the snow, the meeting with the group of pilgrims, are just some examples of such episodes that Wolfram has taken up in his work, and comparison between the two works reveals how he has expanded and deepened them, integrating them into the broader structure of his poem and often giving them a new significance. Nowhere is the development of a single character more fruitful than in the case of the *germaine cousine* who becomes Wolfram's Sigune figure. She occurs four times in all, reappearing at crucial points in Parzival's progress and attaining a name and a history all her own which may well have inspired Wolfram's own *Titurel* fragments (see below).

The central narrative of Wolfram's *Parzival* is a complicated and subtle structure, but it is also set in a framework which is all Wolfram's own and which adds a further important dimension to the whole work. The story of Gahmuret and his two wives is a colorful story of knight errantry and tragic love. It also supplies the parental history, not just for the central hero but, in accordance with the complexity of Wolfram's poem, for his half-brother, the black and white Feirefiz, whose dramatic return into the action in Book XV constitutes the high point in Parzival's chivalrous career and leads directly, through the shattering of the sword of Ither on the helmet of Feirefiz, to God's forgiveness and the resultant success of Parzival at the Grail. This is in itself an important function of the Gahmuret story, but the poignant love story of Gahmuret and Belakane finds its appropriate conclusion in the marriage of Feirefiz and the Grail Bearer. The baptism which Belakane would have accepted, had she only known that this was what Gahmuret wished of her (57,6-8), is achieved by her son. However, Wolfram does not leave it at that, and in the broad and far-reaching reconception of his material, the message of Christianity travels to the East with Feirefiz and his bride.

The second marriage of Gahmuret produces Parzival himself, of course, and this story, too, assumes much greater significance through Wolfram's emphasis on *art*, that which is inherent in a human being and predisposes his nature and ultimately his whole existence. Parzival's dilemma is to a large extent caused by his parentage and the need that he has to reconcile the urge for chivalry which he inherits from his father with the task laid upon him as the son of Herzeloyde and thus as a member of the Grail Family. When Parzival fails to ask Anfortas about his suffering, he is neglecting his duty as a member of that family, though he does not understand this, until his maternal uncle Trevrizent explains it to him and attributes also to him the sins of having caused the death of his mother and having killed his kinsman Ither, the Red Knight. These burdens Parzival must carry until, with God's Grace and against all expectations, he receives a second chance. When he slightly reformulates the question he puts to Anfortas, he acknowledges that he is addressing his blood relative. Trevrizent had told him that the man who came to the Grail should have asked: *"hêrre, wie stet iwer nôt?"* ("My lord, what is the nature of your suffering?" 484,27), but he adds his significant personal touch when he eventually comes before Anfortas and asks: *"Oeheim, waz wirret dier?"* ("Uncle, what ails you?" 795,29). Wolfram himself underlines Parzival's own awareness of the importance of the clan when he sums up his story at its close. He has told, he says, "how Herzeloyde's child strove for the Grail and won it, as it was ordained that he should do" (827,6-7). There is still more, however, in this assessment, for inherited destiny combines with personal courage and effort in Parzival's achievement, and the ingredients cannot be separated.

We have remarked already about the extraordinary number of *Parzival* manuscripts that are extant: at latest count 86, of which 16 are complete, the rest fragmentary. There is one early printed text of 1477. The manuscripts fall generally into two groups designated by the two main manuscripts: D (St. Gallen, Stiftsbibliothek, 857, from the second quarter or third of the 13th century, Alemannic) and G (Munich, Bavarian State Library, Cg. 19, dated same as D, Alsatian/Alemannic, with 12 illustrations, 3 on a side). Both are parchment manuscripts. Most manuscripts fall into the G-group, and the question of priority has not been settled, nor has the precise filiation, especially of the G-group. Lachmann used D as his *Leithandschrift*.

Texts:
Lachmann, Karl, ed. *Wolfram von Eschenbach*, Berlin, 1833. [6]1926 by Eduard Hartl. Repr. Berlin: de Gruyter, 1965. Contains all Wolfram's works. *Parzival* pp. 13-388. *Parzival* available also as *Studienausgabe* (paperback) with text only.
Bartsch, Karl, ed. *Wolfram's von Eschenbach Parzival und Titurel.* Leipzig, 1870-71. [4]1927-32 by Marta Marti (= Dt. Classiker d. Mas, 9-11). Handy footnotes with aids to trans.
Leitzmann, Albrecht, ed. *Wolfram von Eschenbach.* Vol. 1, *Parz.* Book I-VI 1902. [7]1961 by Wilhelm Deinert; Vol. 2, *Parz.* Book VII-XI 1903. [6]1963 by Blanka Horacek; Vol. 3 *Parz.* Book XII-XVI 1903. [5]1965 by Wilhelm Deinert; Vol. 4 *Willehalm* Buch I-V 1905. [5]1963; Vol. 5 *Willehalm, Titurel*, Songs 1906. [5]1963 (= ATB, 12-16) Editions until 1950 Halle (Saale): Niemeyer, then Halle and Tübingen.
Martin, Ernst, ed. *Wolframs von Eschenbach Parzival und Titurel.* Halle (Saale), 1900 and 1903. Part I: Text. Part II: Commentary (= Germanistische Handbibliothek, 9 1.2). Martin's text has never been quite fully accepted, but his line-by-line commentary is still very valuable.
Nellmann, Eberhard, ed. and Dieter Kühn, trans. *Wolfram von Eschenbach: Parzival.* Frankfurt/M.: Deutscher Klassiker, 1994. 2 vols. (= Bibliothek deutscher Klassiker, 7/8). MHG text with facing mod. Ger. trans. by D. Kühn (revision of his 1986 trans., below). Valuable commentary by Nellmann.

Spiewok, Wolfgang, ed. and trans. *Wolfram von Eschenbach: Parzival*. 2 vols. Stuttgart: Reclam, 1981, repr. 1994 (= UB 3681/2). Lachmann text with mod. Ger. trans.

Weber, Gottfried, ed. *Wolfram von Eschenbach: Parzival*. Darmstadt: Wiss. Buchges., ³1977. Lachmann text, with mod. Ger. re-telling by Werner Hoffmann.

Translations:
See Nellmann, Spiewok, and Weber (above).

Hatto, Arthur T., trans. *Wolfram von Eschenbach. Parzival*. Harmondsworth: Penguin, 1980 (= Penguin Classics). A brilliant translation into Engl. prose, with two substantial introductions and a helpful list of names.

Kühn, Dieter (see Nellmann, above). Also, _____ , trans. *Der Parzival des Wolfram von Eschenbach*. Frankfurt/M.: Insel, 1986. I. Teil: Leben, Werk und Zeit des W.v.E.; II. Teil: Parzival. Earlier version of the mod. Ger. trans. in Nellmann.

Mustard, Helen, and Charles Passage, trans. *Wolfram von Eschenbach. Parzival*. New York: Random House, 1961 (= Vintage Books, V-188). Engl. prose trans., not as accurate as Hatto's, but with good intro., index of names, and helpful genealogical table.

Mohr, Wolfgang, trans. *Wolfram von Eschenbach: Parzival*. Göppingen: Kümmerle, 1977 (= GAG, 200). Mod. Ger. verse trans.

Stapel, Wilhelm, trans. *Parzival. Übersetzung*. Hamburg, 1937. Reprinted Munich: Albert Langen, 1950 et seq. Mod. Ger. prose trans.

## *Parzival*—Bibliography

So much has been written on Wolfram, and his *Parzival*, in particular, that it is impossible to give an adequate sample of it in a short list of a few representative works. The reader is referred to the WOLFRAM VON ESCHENBACH—GENERAL BIBLIOGRAPHY and the pertinent parts of the works listed there for *Parzival*-studies, e.g., Bumke (Metzler, pp. 47-206; bibliog. alone, pp. 173-206!), or the other bibliographical works there as a start. However, the reader may wish to look at some of the following works, most of which are in English.

Blamires, David. *Characterization and Individuality in Wolfram's "Parzival."* Cambridge: Cambridge UP, 1966.

A helpful, though somewhat lengthy and repetitious study of Wolfram's methods of depicting his characters.

Fourquet, Jean. *Wolfram d'Eschenbach et le "Conte del Graal." Les divergences de la tradition du "Conte del Graal" de Chrétien et leur importance pour l'explication du "Parzival."* Paris, 1938 (= Publ de la Faculté de l'Université de Strasbourg, 87; Thèse Strasbourg, 1938). Paris: Presses universitaires de France, ²1966 (= Publ. de la Faculté des Lettres et Sciences humaines de Paris-Sorbonne, Études et Méthodes, 17).

A landmark study of Wolfram's relationship to the Chrétien manuscript tradition showing that he used at least two *Perceval* ms. traditions for different parts of *Parzival* and revised his work several times.

Green, Dennis H. *The Art of Recognition in Wolfram's "Parzival."* Cambridge: Cambridge UP, 1982.

A very thorough, fruitful examination of Wolfram's narrative technique: how he tells the story by "revealing while concealing."

Kratz, Henry. *Wolfram von Eschenbach's 'Parzival.' An Attempt at a Total Evaluation.* Bern: Francke, 1973.

A very long, rather sober view of the poem that reads the poem against the grain of contemporary criticism.

Mergell, Bodo. *Wolfram von Eschenbach und seine französischen Quellen: II. Teil: Wolfram's Parzival.* Münster i. W.: Aschendorffsche Verlagsbuchhandlung, 1943 (= Forschungen z. dt. Sprache u. Dichtung, 11).

A detailed comparison of Chrétien's *Perceval* and Wolfram's *Parzival*. Valuable for the wealth of material, though the conclusions drawn must be treated with some caution.

Sacker, Hugh. *An Introduction to Wolfram's 'Parzival'.* Cambridge: Cambridge UP, 1961.

A useful basic introduction for the English reader, though now somewhat outdated. A conscientious attempt to elucidate the complex happenings of the work and to suggest some fairly straightforward interpretations.

Schröder, Werner, comp. *Die Namen im "Parzival" und im "Titurel" Wolframs von Eschenbach.* Berlin: de Gruyter, 1982.

A valuable index of the proper names, noting all occurrences, variant spellings, possible sources, and family relationships, if any. See also the name index for *Willehalm* in his *Willehalm* edition.

Wapnewski, Peter. *Wolframs "Parzival." Studien zur Religiosität und Form.* Heidelberg: Winter, 1955 (= Germanische Bibliothek. Reihe 3).

A very even-handed study of the problem of Parzival's guilt and the religious background of the work.

Weigand, Hermann J. *Wolfram's "Parzival." Five Essays with an Introduction.* Ed. by Ursula Hoffmann. Ithaca & London: Cornell UP, 1969.

A collection of articles from 1938-1956 by a distinguished scholar that illuminate Wolfram's originality and his artistry.

Wynn, Marianne. *Wolfram's Parzival. On the Genesis of its Poetry.* Frankfurt/M.: Peter Lang, 1984 (= Mikrokosmos, 9).

A stimulating study of the creative process in Wolfram's work with many valuable insights into the poem itself.

### Titurel

Most critics today would accept the view that this puzzling work, which exists as two fragments and has been very sparsely handed down to posterity, is Wolfram's last work, or that it was composed in a pause in his work on *Willehalm*. Thematically, however, it cannot be separated from *Parzival*, and for that reason we place it here. The title comes from the name of the old Grail King in the first line of the poem and is somewhat misleading. Titurel does have a lengthy monologue to open the poem, but young Schionatulander and Sigune soon seize center stage, suggesting to some scholars that it should really be re-titled "Schionatulander and Sigune."

As far as we can judge, it is almost entirely the product of Wolfram's imagination. Certainly no literary source has been uncovered for it, and we should probably look no further than Wolfram's own intriguing comment, placed in the mouth of Sigune when she tells Parzival of Schionatulander that "a hound's leash brought him his agonizing death" (141,16). Although she goes on to explain that Schionatulander died in the service of herself and Parzival, and to lament the love which she withheld from him in life and now commits to him in death, the connection between a hound's leash and a knight in armor remains unexplained, tantalizingly left hanging in the air. One can but speculate whether Wolfram found himself called upon to provide an explanation, or whether, more calculatingly, he had deliberately offered this foretaste of a tale which he was proposing one day to tell.

As it stands, *Titurel* does not supply the explanation, either, though, brief as it is, it goes a long way towards hinting at the background to the tragic story of Sigune and Schionatulander which runs like a thread through Parzival's own story. More than that, it hints at a work of considerable dimensions which might, in Wolfram's hands, have tackled some of the issues which preoccupied him elsewhere: the joy of young love, its sweetness and its pain, the demands of formally declared *minne*, and the hazards of the life of chivalry. By returning to the theme of the Grail family, he raises again the issues of inheritance, not just of obligation and of material goods but of abstracts like the capacity to love and to suffer. Indeed, we see the suffering of the family of Titurel from another perspective and recognize that Sigune's tragic love is a part of a broader legacy which she carries as a member of that family, and no one is better qualified to explain this to her than Herzeloyde, of whose tragic love we are well informed in *Parzival*. Moreover, her inherited fate is matched by that of her lover Schionatulander, who is none other than the grandson of Gurnemanz, to whom Wolfram had given such moving words about the toll exacted by chivalry (*ir zagel ist jâmerstricke haft*: its tail is fraught with sorrow, *Parz.* 177,26). Indeed, in enumerating the losses he had sustained, Gurnemanz had mentioned the death of his son Gurzgrie, husband of Mahaute and, as *Titurel* reveals, the father of Schionatulander. By linking the works in this way and increasing the complexity of the relationships, Wolfram underlines one of his central themes, that of *art*, the inherited nature which cannot be suppressed. Indeed, he seizes this theme from the very beginning of the first *Titurel* fragment, which shows the old king Titurel abdicating and handing down to his heirs the custody of the Grail which, as Trevrizent had explained to Parzival, was a sacred trust in the hands of his family. At the same time, Titurel spells out his awareness of the capacity of this family to love with constancy, for this is a part of their inheritance (4,4).

Titurel speaks positively of the future and seems to hold out the hope that his young heirs will thrive, but he himself must succumb to age and infirmity. The whole thrust of the first fragment is towards the recognition of the transience of human life and the fragility of happiness. Wolfram achieves this by his references to those whom his listeners already know from *Parzival*, the five children of Frimutel, and above all Sigune and Schionatulander who, from the moment of their appearance in the fragment, are overshadowed by the memory of Sigune cradling her beloved in *Parzival*, praying by his coffin in her cell and, eventually, united with him in that coffin. Much of the material overlaps with what we know from the earlier work—the love of Gahmuret and

Herzeloyde, and the departure of Gahmuret on his last journey—but the emphasis is different here, for at the forefront is the next generation of lovers, who address one another in the language of courtly love and whose love is unclouded, for them, by any premonition of future disaster. Such premonition exists, however, expressed by Herzeloyde herself and certainly in the mind of the listener, for Sigune and Schionatulander are pursuing a pattern which has been established in their respective families and whose end is, in any case, known to us.

The first fragment ends with Sigune's ecstatic declaration that she is now free to love Schionatulander before the eyes of the world, having revealed her feelings to her aunt, Herzeloyde. Before that, Schionatulander had received the blessing of his friend and older kinsman, Gahmuret, for a love which promises to be a happy and fulfilled one. What lies between this and the opening of the second fragment is unknown, and the second fragment plunges us deep into a new and fateful episode in the forest. Schionatulander catches hold of a hound which has escaped from a hunting party, and Sigune begins to read the story which is inscribed on its leash. In the process she inadvertently lets it go and the dog escapes into the woods. It now becomes imperative to her that she should read the story to its conclusion, and the whole future of the love of the pair of them depends on Schionatulander's ability to capture the dog again and bring it to her. He gladly accepts her challenge which brings him the prospect of such rich reward, and the fragment ends on a mood of joyful optimism, with only the memory of *Parzival* to darken it. How this lovers' pact led to the poignant scene which greets Parzival's eyes in Book III of *Parzival* remains untold.

Much speculation surrounds this strange and haunting work. The suggestion that Wolfram may have intended to compose an unfinished work is too 'modern' an idea, and in any case it chimes badly with the evidence that the medieval audience clearly required a completion and even believed that this was supplied by the blatantly ill-fitting work of Albrecht (see p. 381 ff.). Equally unlikely is the suggestion that Wolfram found himself unable to sustain the intricate poetic form which he had apparently invented for this unique work. Despite the emphasis on the exuberance of youth, there is a maturity about the poem which suggests that it is a work of relative old age, and the most likely explanation is that Wolfram died before he could complete it. The most important piece of internal evidence on chronology comes in strophe 82a which is now usually believed to be genuine and which refers to the death of Hermann von Thüringen: this would lead to a dating of *Titurel* after 1217.

There is something to be said for the view that the first fragment is one completed section of a work which was to be composed of a series of comparable sections, in a sense self-contained and related less with one another than with the central theme of love. This would have been a unique concept, but then few can doubt that *Titurel* is something of an experiment. Whatever its structural flaws, it attains a high degree of success in the evocation of mood, the bitter-sweetness which results from the juxtaposition of youth and age, joy and sorrow, love and death. This is the mood which prevails from the somber opening passages, with the abdication of the frail old man who places all his hopes in the future, to the vitality of love declared and accepted and the eager departure of the young knight Schionatulander as he hurtles towards the death which we know awaits him.

For a work which stands very much alone in its generation, Wolfram departed from the metrical form of the courtly romance. In place of the rhyming couplets used by Hartmann and Gottfried, and indeed by Wolfram himself for his other two narrative works, *Titurel* has an intricate strophic form which resembles in some of its features the metrical form of early German love songs and in some ways suggests a debt to the *Nibelungenlied*. Yet, when all is said and done, we have in *Titurel* a unique metrical pattern, not consistently maintained, it is true, but basically the four line strophe looks like this:

1. 8 stresses with caesura after the 4th stress (4+4)
2. 10 stresses with caesura after the 4th stress (4+6)
3. 6 stresses with no caesura (6)
4. 10 stresses with caesura after the 4th stress (4+6)

The first and second long lines rhyme, as do the third and fourth lines. The placing of the caesura has been the subject of considerable disagreement among scholars, some of whom refuse to accept that there is anything systematic about its occurrence.

The strophe is altogether surprisingly flexible and capable of expressing on the one hand the somber tone of the poem and on the other its youthful exuberance. At times it moves slowly and elegantly; at others it sweeps along with a vitality which accords with its optimistic evocation of young love and boundless energy. As in the *Nibelungenlied*, the long line can often express a balance or a contrast, while frequent enjambement conveys the idea of a constant forward movement, a thrusting towards the inevitable, perhaps.

The mood of the poem moves between the tragic and the joyful, and Wolfram's command of different poetic modes—lyric, dramatic and epic—contributes to the special quality of the fragment. That Wolfram was master of all these moods is evident from his other narrative works, as indeed also from his lyric as we shall see, and a central concern of his throughout his oeuvre is the power of love and its impact on the human beings whom he presents with such subtlety and understanding.

Texts:
See the standard edition by Lachmann, pp. 389-420; also, Bartsch-Marti edition, vol. 3; Leitzmann edition, vol. 5; and the one by Martin, Part I (above).
Gibbs, Marion E., and Sidney M. Johnson, eds. *Wolfram von Eschenbach. "Titurel" and the "Songs."* New York: Garland, 1988 (= GLML, A,57). MHG text and Engl. trans., intro., and notes.
Heinzle, Joachim. *Stellenkommentar zu Wolframs "Titurel."* Tübingen: Niemeyer, 1972 (= Hermaea. Germanistische Forschungen, NF, 30). Both a detailed commentary and an edition.
Mohr, Wolfgang, ed. *Wolfram von Eschenbach. Titurel. Lieder.* Göppingen: Kümmerle, 1978. (= GAG, 250). MHG text and revision of old Simrock Ger. verse trans.
Schröder, Walter J., ed., and Gisela Hollandt, trans. *Wolfram von Eschenbach. Willehalm. Titurel. Text, Nacherzählung, Anmerkungen und Worterklärungen.* Darmstadt: Wiss. Buchges., 1971. Lachmann's text and mod. Germ prose trans. and notes.

Translations

Passage, Charles E., trans. *Titurel. Wolfram von Eschenbach. Translation and Studies*. New York: Ungar, 1984. First complete Engl. trans., with substantial discussion. See also Gibbs/Johnson, Mohr, and Schröder/Hollandt (above).

Facsimile:

Heinzle, Joachim, ed. *Wolfram von Eschenbach. "Titurel." Abbildung sämtlicher Handschriften mit einem Anhang zur Überlieferung des Textes im "Jüngeren Titurel."* Göppingen: Kümmerle, 1973 (= Litterae, 26).

## *Titurel*—Bibliography

Again, the reader is directed to the comprehensive treatments of Wolfram's oeuvre in the WOLFRAM VON ESCHENBACH—GENERAL BIBLIOGRAPHY, e.g., Bumke (Metzler, pp. 275-292).

Haug, Walter. "Erzählen vom Tod her. Sprachkrise, gebrochene Handlung und zerfallende Welt in Wolframs Titurel." In: *Wolfram Studien VI*. Ed. Werner Schröder. Berlin: Erich Schmidt, 1980. Pp. 8-24.

An interesting approach which seems to justify the fragmentary nature of the work for inner reasons.

See Heinzle (above). This most important work on *Titurel* takes into account all previous work and examines the text or text possibilities in detail.

See Mohr (above). His afterword (pp. 101-61) is an excellent introduction to *Titurel* with special attention to the structure and composition.

See Passage (above). The major part of this work is an elaborate attempt to identify possible sources. Valuable and informative discussion of *Jüngerer Titurel*.

Richey, Margaret F. "The *Titurel* of Wolfram von Eschenbach: Structure and Character." *MLR* 56 (1961): 180-193.

A very useful introduction in English, which questions whether Wolfram really intended more.

See Schröder, Index of proper names in *Parz.* and *Tit.* (above).

Wolff, Ludwig. "Wolframs Schionatulander und Sigune." In: *Studien zur deutschen Philologie des Mittelalters. Friedrich Panzer zum 80. Geburtstag*. Ed. Richard Kienast. Heidelberg: Winter, 1950. Pp. 116-30. Repr. in Rupp (WdF, 57, pp. 549-69) and L. W., *Kleinere Schriften zur altdeutschen Philologie*. Ed. Werner Schröder. Berlin: de Gruyter, 1967. Pp. 246-61.

A long article providing a comprehensive interpretation of *Titurel*, including the question of Sigune's guilt.

### *Willehalm*

If *Parzival* can be dated with reasonable certainty to the first decade of the 13th century, the date of composition of Wolfram's other great epic is more problematic, and, as already discussed, we cannot know for certain whether *Willehalm* or *Titurel* is the last work. In both cases the date of 1217, the death of Hermann von Thüringen, is important, for it is usually assumed that the patron who explicitly provided the story of Guillaume (3,8-11) is dead when Wolfram mentions him for the last time (417,22-26) and that it may in fact have been his death which led to the premature "conclusion" of the poem. The date of 1212 as the earliest possible date for the beginning of composition suggests itself on two counts: the new siege weapon, the *trabucium (drîboc)*, which is used at the siege of Oransche (111,9; 222,17) was not introduced until 1212; Wolfram refers mockingly to the coronation of Otto IV, an event which occurred in 1212 and could probably not have been mentioned in such terms until after Otto's death in 1218. It is probably reasonable to place the work somewhere towards the end of the second decade of the 13th century, although some scholars would place it a little later.

The generic category of *Willehalm* is another problem. Already his *Parzival* had stretched the concept of the courtly romance, but that remains essentially what it is. *Willehalm* retains the metrical form of the courtly romance, the rhymed couplet, but the poem is a unique fusion of the courtly and the heroic, with elements of the saintly legend attaching to it. Like *Titurel*—indeed one might venture to say like *Parzival*, too— *Willehalm* is a unique work which defies categorization. Kurt Ruh suggested that it was a *genus novum*, an *Opus mixtum* (1980, p. 190), while an attractive suggestion is the term "tragic romance" (*tragischer Roman*: Werner Schröder, 1979). Another important area of debate is the question of how one should view the figure of Willehalm himself, whether this is the story of a man's progression towards sanctity, whether one can justly speak of a "development" at all in his case, or whether in designating him a saint Wolfram is assuming a knowledge in his audience of the story of Willehalm beyond the events of his poem. To Giburc, too, Wolfram attributes the unofficial designation *heilic vrouwe* (403,1), prompting the assumption that he is thinking of her as a martyr, a woman who must suffer for her faith and for her love. The existence of such controversy and speculation prepares the new reader for a work which has its own special challenges.

Whereas for his *Parzival* Wolfram had turned to the *matière de Bretagne*, to a favorite story of the Middle Ages, the search for the Grail, and specifically to the version of Chrétien de Troyes, the material for *Willehalm* has its roots in the historical figure of Count William of Toulouse, a cousin of the Emperor Charlemagne, who served both Charlemagne himself and his son, the future Emperor Louis the Pious. History tells of his military exploits and, in particular, of his leading role in the siege and subsequent conquest of Barcelona in 801. Contributing if anything even more to his renown is the account of his religious devotion and the fact that, towards the end of his life, he became a monk and entered the monastery which he himself had endowed in 804, the monastery known today as Saint-Guilhem-du-Désert in the valley of Gellone. The most important quasi-biographical account is contained in the early 12th century *Vita sancti Wilhelmi*, which makes it clear that William was remembered as a saint but also as a knight with all the makings of a significant heroic figure. Doubtless this, and the stories which will have circulated, contributed to the cycle which emerged in the later 12th century and to which was connected the *chanson de geste* which Wolfram must have known. We cannot know for sure which version Wolfram will have used as his source, and the existing manuscripts can only provide an approximate guide to the material which was available to him, but it is usually accepted that his source was a version of the *Aliscans*, which, in its turn, was probably based on the *Chançun de Willame*. The *Aliscans* is usually dated, with some caution, between 1180 and 1190 and exists in thirteen manuscripts which, as is common with *chansons de geste*, vary markedly. Even the oldest of them, the Arsenal manuscript now in Paris, can convey only an approximate impression of what Wolfram will have had handed on to him. The current consensus is that manuscript M, the St. Mark's manuscript in Venice, is the closest to what Wolfram will have used, but this is a 14th century manuscript, and it contains a great many errors and omissions.

*Chansons de geste* are composed in *tirades* or *laisses*, stanzas of a varying number of ten-syllabic (five stresses), assonating lines. Each *laisse* is a more or less self-contained unit, frequently connected to the preceding and subsequent stanza by a line or so that recapitulates the content of the *laisse* and is then paraphrased at the beginning of the next stanza. In some manuscripts (e.g. the Arsenal ms.) each *laisse* ends with a non-assonating line (*vers orphelin*). Wolfram, as we have said, uses the familiar rhymed couplets (four stresses) of the courtly romance. Since the extant manuscripts of *Aliscans* vary so widely in the total number of lines, as may be typical of heroic poetry, especially that based on oral tradition, it is impossible to say for sure how long Wolfram's source may have been. Modern printed editions of *Aliscans* contain some 8,500 lines. *Willehalm*, even in its unfinished form, runs to 14,000.

Wolfram tells us that his patron, Hermann von Thüringen, made known to him a story which was circulating among foreigners at that time (5,7). The precise choice of subject, then, was someone else's, yet Wolfram appears to have found in this material an appropriate vehicle for his thought, even though, at a late stage of his fragment, he may appear to protest that he is ill at ease with this account of what he describes as "slaughter" (*mort* 401, 30) and challenges another to take it over from him (402, 28-30). Equally, though, such passages may be interpreted as Wolfram characteristically reveling in his narrative in the full knowledge that no one could do it greater justice. Those who see in them signs of a Wolfram who is losing heart after the death of his patron probably fail to remember how often he teases his audience elsewhere, and perhaps they also overlook the fact that, immediately after them, Wolfram embarks on his Book IX, with its moving opening prayer to Giburc. This hardly looks like a dispirited or a failing poet.

A comparison between *Aliscans* and *Willehalm* shows that Wolfram has related essentially the same events as far as his work goes. Whether he would have completed his poem in the same way as his source is a matter of conjecture and cannot be divorced from the discussion of the "ending" and of Wolfram's overall perspective, which is markedly different from that of the French version. As we have noted, *Willehalm*, even as it stands, is almost twice as long as the *Aliscans*, and, although at times it is very close to the source, it is certainly a reworking rather than anything like a translation. One striking example of difference is the depiction of the heathen knights. In *Aliscans* they are denigrated to semi-human devils, the slaughter of whom by the Christians can only be considered a good deed. For Wolfram, however, though many of the heathens have an exotic appearance, they are the equals of the Christians in chivalric qualities. Like the Christians, they are noble knights, fighting for the love of their ladies. Unfortunately, they are misguided in their religion: that is the only real difference. Increasingly as he proceeds, Wolfram shows considerable independence in his conception of his material, to the extent that one wonders, indeed, if he could have remained faithful to it to the end.

After a beautiful opening prayer to the Trinity, followed by Wolfram's brief introduction of himself and his purpose, the narrative proper of *Willehalm* begins in the middle of the action.

Previous history: Willehalm, pursuing the Saracens in battle, gets too far ahead of his forces and is captured by the heathens. In captivity he gets to know Arabel, the queen of his captor Tybalt. They fall in love, she desires to convert to Christianity, helps Willehalm escape and returns to Oransche with him where she is baptized with the name of Giburc. Naturally, her husband wishes to force her to return. He elicits the help of her father, Terramer, the most powerful Saracen ruler, and together they raise an immense expeditionary force.

At the beginning of the poem, they have come ashore and are fighting with Willehalm and his men not far from Oransche. Outstanding in the battle is Vivianz, Willehalm's young nephew, but he finally dies of his wounds when the overwhelming might of the heathen forces determines the outcome. Willehalm loses all his men but manages to get back to Oransche, having killed the noble Saracen king, Arofel, and using Arofel's armor to disguise himself while eluding the heathens. He is the sole survivor, apart from some prisoners whom he is able to free.

The next day, by mutual agreement, Willehalm leaves Giburc in the hope of raising a new army with help from Louis, son of Charlemagne and King of France, to fight the heathens. He receives a very cold welcome at court in Laon, as a result of which he threatens to kill the Queen, his sister, and finally forces agreement to his plan with the help of Princess Alyze, his niece, and other members of his family who pledge their support.

While at Laon, Willehalm sees a young giant, Rennewart, who had been acquired by the king from merchants, who had kidnapped him in heathendom. Because he will not convert to Christianity, he is kept as a kitchen boy, suffering untold humiliation, until Willehalm asks for his services. (Rennewart had been a playmate of Alyze and the two are secretly in love). Rennewart is delighted to serve Willehalm and asks only for a huge iron-clad club as his weapon.

The army then sets out for Oransche, with Rennewart repeatedly forgetting his club in his eagerness to participate with all the rest. Meanwhile, at Oransche, Giburc and her ladies have been defending the castle successfully against the Saracen siege. From the walls she engages in conversations with her father about religious matters, but he continues alternately to beg her to return or to threaten her with death. After a while the heathens retire to their ships to get away from the foul air of the siege. They burn their camps.

At this moment Willehalm and his allies arrive in Oransche, thinking that the smoke is from the burning castle, only to be greatly relieved to see that they have free access to Oransche. The assembling of forces continues. Rennewart, late as usual, forces the reluctant French troops, who were leaving, to return to Oransche, with the promise that he will lead them in the upcoming battle. Just before the next day Giburc and Rennewart meet and seem almost to realize that they are actually brother and sister, when Giburc gives him splendid armor. Before the battle begins, a series of speeches is made to boost morale, but Giburc, although urging revenge for the fallen heroes of the first battle, pleads for mercy, if possible, for the heathen. They are, after all, also God's creatures.

The battle is then joined, the Christians fight bravely, and this time are successful, due in no small part to Rennewart's efforts. But in the rout of the heathen forces, Rennewart is missing. Willehalm is greatly grieved at his loss. He makes arrangements for the proper burial of the slain heathen kings and then leaves the battlefield. Here the poem ends, or breaks off, as the case may be. There is no resolution of the Rennewart story.

Placed centrally between the two battles is Wolfram's evocation of the love of Willehalm and Giburc, conveyed in the contrasting moods of their tender love scenes and the militant defense of the fortress by Giburc. The poem is altogether remarkable for the sharp contrasts which it achieves and which reflect Wolfram's central message of love and war. Any initial impression that fighting dominates proves to be unfounded, for the admittedly magnificent descriptions of the two battles are supported by action of other kinds and by a great deal of speech. Nevertheless, there seems to be a definite intensification of the struggle from the first battle to the second. What had started out largely as a family matter, the battle to return Giburc to Tybalt, changes noticeably in the second to not only a conflict between Christianity and Islam but also to a contest between the Holy Roman Empire and the mighty powers of the Orient for control of the West.

If Willehalm is essentially the man of action, the commander of the Christian forces, Giburc is the focus of debate. To her Wolfram gives the responsibility of propounding the Christian message, as she defends her faith in a series of conversations with her father (215,10-221,26) and in her address to the assembled Christian forces before the second battle, when she maintains her allegiance to her adopted faith yet urges the Christian knights to demonstrate compassion in the event of victory (306,1-311,6).

Where *Parzival* had shown the emergence of one man into the light, the "conclusion" of *Willehalm* is less unambiguously hopeful. Parzival has to discover faith in God. One man's struggle for a proper understanding of the nature of God has been replaced in *Willehalm* by an unshakeable belief in the omnipotence of God, and specifically of God the Creator, Who has brought into being Christians and heathens alike. Compared with the complexity of the plot of *Parzival*, there is in *Willehalm* a marked simplicity, even though, beneath the account of love and war, lies the perennial and unsolved problem of the conflict of faiths and the suffering of the human race. To be sure, Willehalm is victorious in military terms in the second battle, and Terramer is put to flight, yet there is no suggestion that this is a lasting resolution to the religious and political conflict. How Wolfram would have concluded his work is a central area of scholarly speculation, but it seems unlikely that he could have countenanced the somewhat facile ending of his source, for his work has addressed deeper issues in a more complex way.

Central to any consideration of the relationship between *Willehalm* and the source, and the problem of the "ending," is the figure of Rennewart. The circumstances of his life at the French court and his love for the Princess Alyze are uncovered by Wolfram in characteristic manner, gradually and with hints of future revelations and a happy outcome, until we come to know that he is, in fact, the brother of Giburc, a prince himself. The scene of mutual recognition which is present in the completed source is postponed in *Willehalm* and has no place in Wolfram's fragment. What assumes a greater significance is his role as the right-hand man of Willehalm, fighting as a non-Christian against his own Saracen relatives, his leadership of a contingent of men who had attempted to desert, and his disappearance from the poem before its "end."

For most critics the fact that Rennewart's fate remains untold is the firmest indication that Wolfram cannot have meant the work to be completed as it stands, and certainly the medieval audience would have felt disappointed at this failure to tell to its end the story of one who had become a very significant figure in the poem, and possibly a favorite character, providing a certain amount of comic relief but nonetheless essentially a serious dimension of the whole work. The need was more than satisfied in some ways by the lengthy continuation by Ulrich von Türheim (see p. 377 ff.), who certainly provided the conclusion to the story of Rennewart and went on to tell, as does the source, of how Willehalm entered the monastery and died there. However, nobody would wish to assert that this continuation is aesthetically in tune with Wolfram's great poem. As with the successful masquerade practiced by Albrecht (see p. 381 ff.), it tells us much about the emphasis which the medieval audience laid on the story for the story's sake that in the majority of the manuscripts Wolfram's incomparably superior poem is placed between the *Willehalm* (or *Arabel*, as it has been called) of Ulrich von dem Türlin and the *Rennewart* of Ulrich von Türheim (see p. 377 ff.).

Of all medieval German works only Wolfram's *Parzival* exists today in more manuscripts than his *Willehalm*, attesting surely to the popularity of both poems. Altogether there are 88, with 12 complete ones and 76 fragments. Only one complete manuscript dates to the 13th century: the St. Gall manuscript Stiftsbibliothek 857, called K by Lachmann, G by Schröder. It is a *Sammelhandschrift*, containing, among other works, *Parzival* D and *Nibelungenlied* B, as well as *Willehalm*. Ms. G/K is the *Leithandschrift*, followed less closely by Lachmann than by Schröder in their editions.

Texts (by publication date):
See Lachmann, Karl, (above, Pp. 422-640) and Leitzmann, Albert, (above, Vols. IV and V).
Kartschoke, Dieter, ed. and trans. *Wolfram von Eschenbach. Willehalm.* Berlin: de Gruyter, 1968. Text of Lachmann's 6th edition, with side-by-side mod. Ger. trans. and extensive notes on the text.
Schröder, Werner, ed. *Wolfram von Eschenbach. Willehalm.* Berlin: de Gruyter, 1978. A monumental piece of editing, based on all mss., with extensive introduction on the text and index of foreign words and proper names.
Kartschoke, Dieter, ed. *Wolfram von Eschenbach. Willehalm.* Berlin: de Gruyter, 1989 (paperback). Text of Schröder's edition, with revised mod. Ger. trans., but no notes.
Heinzle, Joachim, ed. and trans. *Wolfram von Eschenbach. Willehalm,* Frankfurt/M.: Deutscher Klassiker, 1991 (= Bibliothek des MAs, 9). Normalized text of Ms. G, with abbreviations resolved; mod. Ger. trans. on opposing pages; a detailed *Stellenkommentar,* not only on text, but also on trans.; 16 color illus., 12 black/white, of the miniatures in the Wolfenbüttel codex Wo. with an essay by Dorothea and Peter Diemer; a list of variants; an index of names.
_____. *Wolfram von Eschenbach. Willehalm.* Tübingen: Niemeyer, 1994 (= ATB, 108). Same text as edition above, but with variants at foot of each page, no trans., no illus., paperback.

Translations:
See Kartschoke, 1968 and 1989 (above).
Schröder, Walter J., and Gisela Hollandt, eds. *Wolfram von Eschenbach. Willehalm. Titurel.*

*Text. Nacherzählung. Anmerkungen und Worterklärungen.* Darmstadt: Wiss. Buchges., 1971. Lachmann text with notes and mod. Ger. retelling.

Unger, Otto, trans. *Wolfram von Eschenbach. Willehalm.* Göppingen: Kümmerle, 1973. Mod. Ger. verse trans.

Passage, Charles E., trans. *The Middle High German Poem of Willehalm by Wolfram of Eschenbach.* New York: Ungar, 1977. Engl. prose trans. with list of 404 proper names and their sources.

Gibbs, Marion E., and Sidney M. Johnson, trans. *Wolfram von Eschenbach. Willehalm,* Harmondsworth: Penguin, 1984 (= Penguin Classics). Engl. prose trans. with intro., second intro., notes, and index of names.

See Heinzle, 1991 (above).

Facsimiles:

*Wolfram von Eschenbach, Willehalm mit der Vorgeschichte des Ulrich von Türlin und der Fortsetzung des Ulrich von Türheim. Vollständige Faksimile-Ausgabe im Originalformat des Codex Vindobonensis 2670 der Österreichen National Bibliothek.* Kommentar von Hedwig Heger. Graz: Akademische Druck- und Verlagsanstalt (= Codices selecti, 46).

Montag, Ulrich, ed. *Wolfram von Eschenbach. Willehalm. Die Bruchstücke der Großen Bilderhandschrift. München, Cgm 193,III.* Stuttgart: Müller u. Schindler, 1985.

## *Willehalm*—Bibliography

For a long time research on *Willehalm* remained in the shadow of *Parzival.* It was a commonplace for studies of *Willehalm* to begin with a comment on how much like a "stepchild" it had been treated. That all changed around 1960 when interest developed under the influence of scholars like Joachim Bumke and Werner Schröder. That interest has continued to the present day, so that it is impossible to present an adequate sample. Again we should like to refer the reader to the comprehensive studies listed in the WOLFRAM VON ESCHENBACH—GENERAL BIBLIOGRAPHY, e.g., Bumke (Metzler, pp. 207-274) and list only a few significant items here.

Bumke, Joachim. *Wolframs "Willehalm." Studien zur Epenstruktur und zum Heiligkeitsbegriff der ausgehenden Blütezeit.* Heidelberg: Winter, 1959 (= Germanische Bibliothek. 3. Reihe).

Although this book has been to a large extent overtaken by the research of the past decades, it remains a very important interpretation and point of departure for other scholars.

Decke-Cornill, Renate. *Stellenkommentar zum III. Buch des "Willehalm" Wolframs von Eschenbach.* Marburg: Elwert, 1985 (= Marburger Studien zur Germanistik, 7).

One of three line-by-line commentaries on different Books on *Willehalm.* Cf. Happ and E-J Schmidt (below).

Greenfield, John. *Vivianz: An Analysis of the Martyr Figure in Wolfram von Eschenbach's "Willehalm" and in His Old French Source Material.* Erlangen: Palm & Enke, 1991 (= Erlanger Studien, 95).

A thorough study of the Vivianz-figure in *Willehalm* and *Aliscans.* Cf. also Lofmark's *Rennewart* (below).

Happ, Erich. *Kommentar zum zweiten Buch von Wolframs "Willehalm."* Diss. Munich, 1966.

Cf. Decke-Cornill (above) and E.-J. Schmidt (below).

Kiening, Christian. *Reflexion—Narration. Wege zum "Willehalm" Wolframs von Eschenbach.* Tübingen: Niemeyer, 1991 (= Hermaea, NF, 63).

Examines the interaction of narrative and non-narrative (i.e., "reflective") portions of the poem. First chapter highly theoretical and complex, but the bulk of the study makes a significant contribution to Wolfram scholarship.

_____. "Wolfram von Eschenbach: *Willehalm.*" In: *Mittlehochdeutsche Romane und Heldenepen.* Ed. by Horst Brunner. Stuttgart: Reclam, 1993 (= UB, Interpretationen, 8914). Pp. 212-32.

A very useful, brief, but thorough general interpretation.

Lofmark, Carl. *Rennewart in Wolfram's "Willehalm". A Study of Wolfram von Eschenbach and His Sources.* Cambridge: Cambridge UP, 1972 (= Anglica Germanica, Series 2).

This elegantly written and very lucid study of the sources for the Rennewart episodes goes beyond the boundaries implied in the title and has remained a central work on *Willehalm.*

_____. "Das Problem des Unglaubens in Wolframs *Willehalm.*" In: Gärtner/ Heinzle (eds.), (1989). Pp. 399-414.

Excellent summary of the problem. Conclusion: the realization that conflict between Christian and heathens will persist. It will not be resolved through force or logic, only through Christian charity.

Mergell, Bodo. *Wolfram von Eschenbach und seine französischen Quellen. I. Teil: Wolframs Willehalm.* Münster: Aschendorffsche Verlagsbuchhandlung, 1936 (= Forschungen zur dt. Sprache u. Dichtung, 6).

Detailed comparison of Wolfram's *Willehalm* and *Aliscans.* Contains much valuable material, but some of the conclusions are questionable in the light of later scholarship.

See also Rupp, WdF, 57, pp. 388-548, for five important earlier articles on *Willehalm.*

Schmidt, Ernst-Joachim. *Stellenkommentar zum IX. Buch des "Willehalm" Wolframs von Eschenbach.* Bayreuth, 1979 (= Bayreuther Beiträge zur Sprachwissenschaft, 3). See also: Heinzle, Joachim, "Beiträge zur Erklärung des Neunten Buches von Wolframs *Willehalm.* Aus Anlaß des Kommentars von Ernst-Joachim Schmidt." *PBB* 103 (1981): 425-436. Addenda and corrections. Cf. Decke-Cornill and Happ (above).

Schmidt, Ronald Michael. *Die Handschriftenillustrationen des "Willehalm" Wolframs von Eschenbach. Dokumentation einer illustrierten Handschriftengruppe.* Wiesbaden: Reichert, 1985. Vol. I: Text.; Vol. II: Illus.

Art historical study of the illustrated *Willehalm*-mss. and their iconography, with black-white illus. in Vol. II.

Schröder, Werner. *Der tragische Roman von Willehalm und Gyburg: Zur Gattungsbestimmung des Spätwerks Wolframs von Eschenbach.* Wiesbaden: Steiner, 1979 (= Akad. d. Wiss. u. d. Lit., Mainz; Abh. der Geistes- u. Sozialwiss. Kl., 1979, 5).

Very sensible discussion of the genre of *Willehalm*, leading to the designation "tragic romance."

Wiesmann-Wiedemann, Friederike. *Le roman du "Willehalm" de Wolfram d'Eschenbach et l'épopée d' "Aliscans."* *Étude de la transformation de l'épopée en roman.* Göppingen: Kümmerle, 1976 (= GAG, 190).
Comparison of the two works from the point of view of structure, meaning, and the position of the author.

## The Songs

Although Wolfram's renown rests on his narrative poems, his contribution to the medieval German lyric is an important one and his originality is very much in evidence here, too. It should probably not surprise us, given the importance he attaches to human relationships and the central role of love in his works, that the conventions of the Minnesang give way in his greatest love songs to powerful evocations of passion.

There is good reason to suppose that Wolfram may have composed songs of the more traditional Minnesang type which, possibly because they were not well received or perhaps because he himself was not at ease with the basic ideas, did not find their way into the manuscripts. As already indicated, he speaks of himself in *Parzival* as "something of a Minnesänger" (114,13), but whether one takes this as a self-deprecatory remark or the opposite depends on how seriously one should regard Wolfram's apparent self-revelations. Carl von Kraus expressed the ambiguity of the remark well when he described it as "bescheiden ausgedrückt und dabei stolz gedacht" (expressed modestly while at the same time proud in thought). It would seem to suggest, in either case, a dating for the songs of about 1200, but, as far as the extant songs are concerned, it is virtually impossible to be sure about their chronology.

Only seven songs are now generally regarded as authentic, with two others no longer accepted as being by Wolfram. One of these (*Maneger klaget die schoenen zît*) had already been dismissed by Lachmann, while the other (*Guot wîp, ich bite dich minne*) has been the subject of much debate and is now no longer generally included among Wolfram's songs.

Of the remaining seven, five are dawn songs, while the other two display elements of the Minnesang, handled by Wolfram with characteristic originality. The song which begins *Ein wîp mac wol erlouben mir* (A woman can well allow me . . .) strikes one, on the face of it, as extraordinarily uninspired for Wolfram, but a closer look suggests that it is perhaps not meant to be taken seriously at all, that it is a parody of the Minnesang, and may indeed be echoing a song by Walther von der Vogelweide which begins in very similar fashion (111,22) and is itself a parody of another song, by Reinmar von Hagenau (X). Wolfram here gathers together a collection of typical phrases and clichés from the love lyric, compounding the effect of his mockery by speaking, not of the sweet nightingale which accompanies the wooing described by his contemporaries but of three birds with very different connotations: the falcon, which swoops on its prey, the owl which can see in the dark, and the stork which treads so lightly that it does no damage to the crops. When he concludes the song by comparing himself with this harmless bird, he not only introduces a quite new element into the courtly lyric but seems to be asserting his innocence vis-à-vis the ladies, a stance which may be linked with his apparent references in

*Parzival* to some (lost?) criticism which he has uttered of one lady in particular (114,5-6; 114,19-20; 337,5).

The other song which does not belong among Wolfram's dawn songs begins with the powerful evocation of the sights and sounds of springtime: *Ursprinc bluomen, loup ûzdringen* (Springing up of flowers, bursting forth of leaves), but its early promise is not fulfilled, as after the brilliance of the first two strophes, when the poet speaks of his singing all year through and compares it with the birds who confine their songs to May-time, Wolfram drifts into a much more conventional mode. Thus the last three strophes use the language of the Minnesang to describe the relationship of service and reward which is its core and with which, one cannot but suspect, Wolfram was not much in sympathy. This song, too, may be a parody, or it may simply be Wolfram's contribution to a genre which was fashionable but not to his liking.

It is in the dawn song that Wolfram shows himself master of the lyric. Although he cannot be said to have invented the dawn song, or even to have introduced it into German literature, he is unrivalled in his command of this subgenre which depends so much on the intensity of the situation which it treats. It eschews the artificiality of the conventions of the Minnesang and replaces them with a relationship which rings very true and prompts a myriad of emotions.

A number of suggestions have been put forward about the order of Wolfram's songs, and, as far as the dawn songs are concerned, the order in which one reads them to some extent affects the interpretation: however, the reverse is also the case. One cannot speak of a developing relationship in the four powerful songs which describe the illicit lovers lying together as day breaks and the pain of their parting, yet they contain differing ingredients and each makes a distinctive impact. Only the fifth of the group, which may not necessarily be the last and is in fact the fourth in Lachmann's edition, *Der helden minne ir klage* (The lament of secret love . . .), presents a different view, with its elevation of married love as the supreme state which permits the lovers to await the dawn together, untroubled by fear of discovery. It can thus be seen as a kind of antithesis of the dawn song. Those who seek an autobiographical element have even suggested that this was a euphoric Wolfram composing shortly after his own marriage. However, a more recent interpretation of this puzzling song is that it is not to be taken seriously at all, but that it is a parody which uses the language and motifs of the dawn song in order to proffer an ironic advocacy of married love.

The four songs which are quite unambiguously dawn songs demonstrate Wolfram's sense of the dramatic, the more powerful because it is conveyed through the medium of the lyric. At the heart of all four lies, of course, the loving couple, pursuing their illicit love with tremendous passion tinged increasingly with despair and fear, knowing as they do that the coming of day threatens their relationship, their honor and their very lives. Beyond the intimacy of their embraces is the outside world, society itself, which means that, as day dawns, they must part.

There are two other examples in German of a type of love poem which had become established in Provence as early as the second half of the 12th century, but the dawn songs by Dietmar von Aist and Heinrich von Morungen (see p. 242 ff. and p. 255 ff.), exquisite as they are in their separate ways, cannot compare with the impact of Wolfram's highly charged presentation of illicit love threatened by convention. Moreover, they lack the third character, the watchman, who is already present in some of the French examples but becomes a powerful, active figure in Wolfram, entering into the drama, sometimes as an onlooker, sometimes an intermediary and even urging the lovers to remember what they owe to him as the one who made their meeting possible. In the song *Von der zinnen wil ich gên* . . . (Lachmann's No. 5: I will go down from the battlements . . .) the watchman occupies center stage as he debates with himself about whether he should interrupt the love-making with his announcement of the day: his dilemma is as great as theirs. The conversations between the lovers, too, express their different but equally distressing pressures, for these are two real people caught up in a hopeless human situation. It has also been well observed that Day itself is a character in its own right, though not a human one, particularly in the great song where Day claws its way through the sky (No.2: *Sîne klâwen durch die wolken sint geslagen*).

To express the diversity of human emotions which imbue his dawn songs, Wolfram uses also a diversity of metrical form, and indeed the form and the language of these songs supports the originality of their substance and gives them their special quality.

Wherever they should be placed chronologically—and this is a matter on which there can really be no certainty—Wolfram's songs, and above all his dawn songs, represent a complement to his narrative. In them he conveys in lyric form the tenderness which he describes, for example, in Parzival's reunion at dawn with his wife Condwiramurs after so many years of separation (800,20 ff.) or the yearning of Sigune for Schionatulander in *Titurel* (117-121). The tension which he evokes as day comes ever nearer shows the same mastery of atmosphere which pervades *Willehalm*: as Willehalm rides towards Oransche at night at the end of Book IV and sees the redness of the sky which tells him that his fortress is on fire, for example, or the bleakness of the battlefield as he assesses his losses among the corpses after the second battle (451,1 ff.). Although Wolfram's output in the realm of the pure lyric appears to have been relatively small, it is nevertheless a significant part of his whole oeuvre.

Texts:
See Lachmann edition, pp. 3-10; Leitzmann edition, Vol. 5., pp. 185-94.
Moser, Hugo, and Helmut Tervooren, eds. *Des Minnesangs Frühling*. Stuttgart: S. Hirzel, [36]1977. Vol. 1, pp. 436-51. With explanatory notes: Vol. II, pp. 116-19.
von Kraus, Carl, ed. *Deutsche Liederdichter des 13. Jhdts.* [2]1978. Vol. I, pp. 596-604. With extensive commentary: Vol. II, pp. 646-707.
Wapnewski, Peter, ed. *Die Lyrik Wolframs von Eschenbach. Edition. Kommentar. Interpretation*. Munich: Beck, 1972. MHG text, mod. Ger. prose trans., commentary, and interpretations. See also, Wolfgang Mohr, *"Titurel", Lieder* (above), pp. 76-99: MHG text and mod. Ger. verse trans.
See also Gibbs/Johnson, *"Titurel" and the "Songs"* (above), pp. 70-110: MHG text, Engl. prose trans., notes, and comments.

Translations:
See Wapnewski, Mohr, and Gibbs/Johnson (above).

Facsimiles:

See illustrations in Wapnewski (above) and other facsimile editions of the main mss. of Minnesang in MINNESANG—BIBLIOGRAPHY (p. 235 ff.). Some (partial) illustrations also in Gibbs/Johnson (above).

## Songs—Bibliography

See the sections on Wolfram's Songs (Lieder) in the works listed in the WOLFRAM VON ESCHENBACH—GENERAL BIBLIOGRAPHY, e.g., Bumke (Metzler, pp. 39-46).

Hatto, Arthur T., ed. *Eos. An enquiry into the Theme of Lovers' Meetings and Partings at Dawn in Poetry.* London: Mouton, 1965.

An enormous volume which gives a comprehensive account of the dawn song, with numerous examples and translations. See in particular the chapter on medieval German dawn songs by A. T. Hatto (pp. 428-472) and on Old Provençal and Old French by B. Woledge (pp. 340-389).

Sayce, Olive. "Die Syntax der Lieder Wolframs." In: Gärtner/Heinzle (1989). Pp. 535-48.

Skillful, illuminating syntactical analysis by a most knowledgeable scholar of medieval lyric poetry.

See especially Wapnewski (above).

An extremely valuable contribution to research on Wolfram's songs. It may adopt some idiosyncratic editorial policies and viewpoints but is nonetheless very important. Truly a "complete" edition, with clear reproductions of the mss., diplomatic *and* edited versions of the texts, discussion of editorial decisions, and interpretations.

Wynn, Marianne. "Wolfram's Dawnsongs." In: Gärtner/Heinzle (1989). Pp. 549-58.

Taking the refreshing position that medieval lyric poetry must have had some basis in social reality, this is a fascinating examination of possible real backgrounds of the participants in the dawn songs.

# "HEROIC" POETRY

## *Nibelungenlied*, the *Klage* (and *Kudrun*)

At about the same time as Hartmann von Aue was composing his *Iwein*, a work which can reasonably be seen as the classic Arthurian romance in German, and Wolfram was probably beginning his *Parzival*, a poem of very different character by an unknown author appeared to contribute another vital perspective to this extraordinary literary era. The impact of the *Nibelungenlied* owes much to its timing at the very beginning of the 13th century, presenting as it does material that is essentially heroic in a manner that made it compatible with courtly culture. The poem's success, both then and now, is due to the fascinating fusion of these essentially opposed qualities, as well as to its many intrinsic strengths. It would be misleading to speak of a harmonizing of opposites, for this is a work which challenges by its sheer ruggedness, its many contradictions, and the questions which it poses and sometimes fails to answer. Perhaps it is precisely these facets which have ensured that the *Nibelungenlied* is arguably the most popular of the great works of the German Middle Ages, and that it has provoked, and continues to provoke, a stream of scholarly literature.

From the time of its rediscovery by Johann Jacob Bodmer, in the middle of the 18th century, the *Nibelungenlied* has been an important focus of interest, and the poem has prompted a succession of retellings. Clearly this work with its roots so far back in the Germanic past, is uniquely amenable to reinterpretation in terms of the circumstances and history of successive generations and even centuries. This is because at its core are emotions and passions which are tragically close to the surface in human beings and motivate their behavior no matter what the precise context. The French scholar Ernest Tonnelat characterized it aptly as "un poème humain." Love and hate, jealousy and the thirst for power, are all recognizable forces in human conduct, and they all play a role in a poem which combines personal histories with the account of the fortunes of whole dynasties and even of nations.

The *Nibelungenlied* poet is attentive to detail, yet he paints with a broad brush in his evocation of large areas in time and place. The scope of the poem earns it the designation "epic," while the adjective "heroic" identifies its substance and its ethos, despite the courtly veneer which may well have been its only assurance of survival in the climate of the early thirteenth century.

### The Manuscripts

That the poem was well received in its own time is suggested by the abundance of manuscripts, 10 complete, 35 in all. Some of these can be dated as late as the 16th century, but the three most important—A, B, and C—are close to the date of composition, in the 13th century. However, probably none of them is what might be termed *the* "original" manuscript. The suggestion is that the work was circulating in various forms, some of them via oral transmission and that none of these existing oldest manuscripts should be regarded as the true prototype.

Manuscript A, from Hohenems in the Vorarlberg and now in the Staatsbibliothek in Munich (Cod. germ. 34) was favored by Karl Lachmann, who believed it to be the oldest of the three. Manuscript B is now generally thought to be earlier, possibly as early as the first half of the 13th century. This fine manuscript contains also Wolfram's *Parzival* and *Willehalm* and can be seen in the Stiftsbibliothek in St. Gallen, Switzerland (Ms. 857). It provided the basis for the edition by Karl Bartsch, originally published in 1866 and many times reprinted. The third manuscript (C), the Donaueschingen manuscript (Fürstl. Fürstenbergische Hofbibliothek, Ms. 63), probably dates from about the same period, and this too has been the object of significant scholarly editions by Friedrich Zarncke (1856) and Adolf Holtzmann (1857), and, much more recently by Heinz Engels (1968), Werner Schröder (1969), and Ursula Henning (1977).

Texts:
Among the many editions, the following are the most important and/or most readily available:
Bartsch, Karl, ed. *Das Nibelungenlied*. Wiesbaden: Brockhaus, [13]1956, ed. by Helmut de Boor; [22]1988, ed. by Roswitha Wisniewski (= Deutsche Klassiker des Mittelalters). Usually

considered the "standard" edition, based on Ms. B.

Batts, Michael S., ed. *Das Nibelungenlied. Paralleldruck der Handschriften A, B und C, nebst Lesarten der übrigen Handschriften.* Tübingen: Niemeyer 1971. With 99 text reproductions. A very important work which draws together the textual material in parallel in one volume.

Brackert, Helmut, ed. and trans. *Das Nibelungenlied.* Frankfurt/M.: Fischer, 1971. 2 vols. (= Bücher des Wissens, 6038-39). MHG text, mod. Germ. trans., notes, and afterwords.

Hennig, Ursula, ed. *Das Nibelungenlied nach der Handschrift C.* Tübingen: Niemeyer, 1977 (= ATB 83).

Hoffmann, Werner, ed. and trans. *Das Nibelungenlied. Kudrun. Text. Nacherzählung. Worterklärungen.* Darmstadt: Wiss. Buchges., 1972. MHG text with mod. Ger. re-telling.

Lachmann, Karl, ed. *Der Nibelunge Not mit der Klage. In der ältesten Gestalt mit den Abweichungen der gemeinen Lesart.* Berlin, 1826. [6]1960, ed. by Ulrich Pretzel. (Based on Ms. A).

Translations:

Hatto, Arthur T., trans. *The Nibelungenlied.* Harmondsworth: Penguin, [2]1969. Engl. prose trans., valuable introduction and appendices.

Kramer, Günter, trans. *Das Nibelungenlied. Mit 33 Zeichnungen von Ernst Barlach.* Berlin: Verlag der Nation, 1982. Mod. Ger. prose trans., with afterword and 2 short essays (1 on the Barlach sketches).

Mowatt, D. G., trans. *The Nibelungenlied.* London: Dent, New York: Dutton, 1965 (= Everyman's Library). Engl. prose trans.

Ryder, Frank G., trans. *The Song of the Nibelungs.* Detroit: Wayne State UP, 1962. Engl. verse trans.

See also Brackert and Hoffmann (above).

Facsimile:

Duft, Johannes, ed. *Das Nibelungenlied und Die Klage.* Ms. B (Cod. Sangall. 857). Cologne/Graz: Böhlau, 1962 (= Deutsche Texte in Handschriften, 1).

Hornung, Hans, ed. *Das Nibelungenlied in spätmittelalterlichen Illustrationen. Die 37 Bildseiten des Hundeshagenschen Kodex, Ms. Germ. Fol. 855 (Berlin).* Bozen (Tyrol): Verlagsanstalt Athesia, 1968. Color facs. of ms. leaves with illus. and text.

## The History of *Nibelungenlied* Research

As indicated already, the *Nibelungenlied* has enjoyed a special position as a focus of scholarly interest in medieval German literature, and, for some reason, the past fifteen years or so have seen a spate of critical works to add to the abundance of existing literature on the poem. Indeed, the work seems capable of tolerating more comment than almost any of its contemporaries and of provoking fresh responses from anyone who approaches it. This means, of course, that the task of presenting the secondary literature is particularly difficult, but, as is so often the case, the volume in the Sammlung Metzler series is an excellent starting point. The original volume by Gottfried Weber has now been completely reworked and expanded by one of the foremost authorities on the heroic epic, Werner Hoffmann, whose latest edition (1992) takes account of the more recent interpretations and offers a lucid account of the essential scholarly standpoints on such controversial issues as the origins of the poem and its composition in the *Blütezeit* (see *NIBELUNGENLIED/KLAGE*—BIBLIOGRAPHY, below).

The serious study of the *Nibelungenlied* must inevitably also embrace the study of its impact when it was rediscovered in the 18th century as well as of the way it has consistently resurfaced in the history of German literature since then. The study of the reception of the poem has become an important focus of research, thoroughly documented in the works by Otfrid Ehrismann listed below. Matters such as these cannot be divorced from questions of the fluctuations in the interpretation of the poem itself, or, to put it quite simply, the question of what, if anything, the poet had in mind beyond the telling of a rattling good tale.

Werner Hoffmann highlights the principal trends in research on the poem in his first chapter (Metzler, 1992). This succinct survey provides a chronological account of the history of *Nibelungenlied* scholarship, from its rediscovery by Bodmer, through the fundamental work of Lachmann and Heusler, which was concerned largely with matters of genesis, to the more interpretative writings of older Germanists—Friedrich Panzer (1870-1956), Dietrich Kralik (1884-1959), Ernest Tonnelat (1877-1948), Bodo Mergell (1912-1954), Gottfried Weber (1897-1981), Friedrich Maurer (1898-1984)—and thence to some of the significant contributions of the more modern period, by Bert Nagel, Werner Schröder, and Werner Hoffmann himself. Other important names which stand out in the past twenty-five years or so are Theodore Andersson, Hugo Bekker, Michael Curschmann (*VL*$^2$ 6, 1987, 926-969), Otfrid Ehrismann, Joachim Heinzle, Heinz Ihlenburg, Winder McConnell, Jan-Dirk Müller, Heinz Rupp. The volume in the WdF Series contains, as usual, some central articles which reflect the chronological development of research in the field. The preponderance of the secondary literature is in German, but the reader dependent on English will find a stimulating "introduction to a second reading," which goes far beyond an introduction, in the translation by A.T. Hatto. The books in English by McConnell and Bekker listed in the bibliography offer wide-ranging and often astute guidance on central issues, while the most recent contribution in English, that by Neil Thomas, *Reading the "Nibelungenlied,"* is likely to prove a valuable accompaniment to any re-reading of the poem.

### The Dating of the Poem

The *Nibelungenlied* in the form in which we read it today is usually dated to 1200 or just a little after, a dating which owes much to the presumed relationship between the poem and Wolfram's *Parzival* and must also depend on the date assigned to the latter. A thorough assessment of the arguments is contained in Hoffmann (Metzler, 1992, pp. 104-112). The most persuasive "evidence" comes in Wolfram's reference to the "advice" of Rumolt (*Parz*, 420,25-30), who, in the *Nibelungenlied*, had urged the Burgundians not to go to the land of Etzel. Such a mention would only carry weight with an audience which had the incident in the earlier work fairly fresh in its mind.

### The Author

We have even less evidence to guide us on the identity of the author of the poem, although the likelihood is that he was a cleric. This means: not a priest—which he almost certainly was not, given the nature of the material—but a clerk, an educated man who had gone through a formal education and was employed, probably at court, in some kind of official capacity. Attempts to identify him precisely have failed, and his anonymity is an essential part of his role as narrator of this quasi-historical story. He intrudes very little on his account of events, rarely passing judgment or expressing an opinion or offering any guidance as to how the audience should be responding. That he was familiar with courtly customs and some of the external features of chivalry need not suggest more about him and his provenance than that he wished to accommodate the taste of the age in which he lived. Early attempts to adduce that he was himself a knight have not received much support, and there is nothing substantial to uphold the view that he may have been writing for a knightly patron. Even the favored opinion that he was active in Passau is not entirely proven, although there is every reason to connect him with the general area of the Danube.

## The Genesis of the *Nibelungenlied*

The question of the source or sources of the *Nibelungenlied* is a very complex one, and it is beset by the existence of fashions in scholarship which have prevailed over the generations. Not until relatively recently was the poem considered as a literary entity meriting interpretation as such. Earlier scholarship was intent on seeing it as a compilation of not entirely compatible elements, and even then opinions differed about the nature of the ingredients and the way in which they had come to be mixed. Doubtless the most fruitful approach is one which combines these two distinct approaches and sees that an understanding of how the poem came into being can support and enhance our appreciation of it as a work of literature.

Not disputed is the existence within the *Nibelungenlied* of two quite separate strands of legend: the story of Brünhild and the death of the mighty Siegfried at the hand of his Burgundian relatives, and the fall of the Burgundian dynasty. The two are linked in the poem by the figure of Kriemhild, the wife first of Siegfried and then of the emperor Etzel, and the second "part" is made dependent upon the first when she uses her second marriage to gain revenge for the murder of her first husband. The question remains as to when these two separate strands became linked.

Although the opening of the poem, in two of the principal manuscripts, speaks of the "old tales" (*alte mæren*) which tell of the marvelous deeds of heroes of old and seems to presume a knowledge of these in the audience, these tales cannot be conclusively adduced. The preponderance of earlier *Nibelungenlied* scholarship concerned itself, to the point of obsession, with the attempt to establish the likely sources, but it must be admitted that even today little absolute certainty prevails, though there are matters on which there is a high degree of consensus.

As early as 1816, Karl Lachmann put forward the view which for a long time commanded almost universal respect, that the poem was a compilation of independent lays, composed by individual poets. This *Liedertheorie* had its source in Lachmann's training as a classical scholar, a similar theory having been advanced about the identity of Homer, on the basis that the works ascribed to him could not be the work of one single poet. The idea that the *Nibelungenlied* was the product of a number of minds—and in his later development of his theory (1836) Lachmann demonstrated his belief in 20 separate *Lieder*, though not necessarily each by a different poet—was attractive to the Romantics who saw it as a great national epic, the product of a whole nation. Indeed, the designation *Volksepos*, though now eschewed, enjoyed popularity as encapsulating all that the poem seemed to represent. The pre-eminence of Lachmann meant that the basic idea was generally accepted, with variations, throughout the nineteenth century, until, in fact, a new theory, or series of theories, came to rival it, in the successive publications of the Swiss scholar, Andreas Heusler. His name dominated *Nibelungenlied* studies for the first half of the 20th century, following the publication of his first revolutionary work *Lied und Epos in germanischer Sagendichtung* in 1905. His view was of a work which had come into existence by a process of *Anschwellung* (swelling up): lays had achieved epic stature by a process of organic growth.

Heusler saw the *Nibelungenlied* in its final form as the merging of two branches which embraced five separate entities: two stages of the legend of Brünhild, in the 5th or 6th century, and towards the end of the 12th century, and three stages of the legend of the Burgundians, in the 5th or 6th century, the 8th century and in the 1160s. Most significant of all is his postulation of this last work, which he called the *ältere Not* (older [version of the] suffering or fall, i.e., of the Nibelungs), and which even the most skeptical of Heusler's successors believe to have existed, a lengthy epic by a poet from the Danube region. This considerable poem is believed to have formed the basis for the second part of the *Nibelungenlied*, and many of the problems and inconsistencies in that work are attributed by scholars to the existence of the older version, which, though not now extant in any tangible form, may well have provided significant portions of the *Thidrekssaga* too. This Norwegian work tells first and foremost of the exploits of Dietrich von Bern (Theodoric of Verona), but it contains also Nibelung material of more archaic nature than the *Nibelungenlied* itself. Its narrator, composing in the middle of the 13th century, speaks of having obtained his material from North German merchants, thus appearing to corroborate the opinion that an older version of the poem was circulating, if not the *ältere Not* itself, then one of similar age and kind.

It was Heusler's view—an oversimplified view perhaps but essentially a cogent one—that five considerable poets had contributed to the material which the sixth and greatest, the "Last Poet," molded into the work that emerged at the beginning of the 13th century. His task had been to link the two strands, giving approximately equal weight to each, and ensuring continuity by the use of the same strophic form throughout. In the process of creating this single entity, he had added material and refined both the plot itself and his telling of it in accordance with the ethos and taste of his own age. Even Heusler conceded that the relationship between the two basic strands had long been assumed, if not formally articulated, and that the task of relating the death of Siegfried to the fall of the Burgundians was less a conceptual than an artistic matter. It is almost inconceivable that the author of the *ältere Not* had not provided some background in the form of an account, however cursory, of the death of Siegfried and the circumstances which led to it.

Succeeding decades have revealed the oversimplifications in Heusler's theories, of which he himself was aware, and they have shown that the poem contains a multitude of other ingredients which can be identified elsewhere in European literature. Later scholars have drawn attention also to other elements which contributed to the evolution of the poem and which were present in the literary and historical environment of the early 13th century. The poem has been shown to be much less isolated than once appeared, and its intrinsic qualities are appreciated alongside its position within the Middle High German *Blütezeit* (see in particular, the work of Friedrich Panzer for an early argument along these lines). That is not to say that Heusler's basic views have been discredited, though there have been attempts to disregard them: they have rather been modified and expanded in the light of more recent findings. Above all, modern scholarship has shifted its emphasis, so that, although the genesis of the *Nibelungenlied* remains an entirely valid concern, it is seen as one element among many in the consideration of a poem which appears to be infinitely complex. See Heusler, Hoffmann (1992 and 1987), Andersson in *NIBELUNGENLIED/KLAGE*—BIBLIOGRAPHY (below), and Hatto (above, Appendix 4).

## The Form

One of the many features which sets the *Nibelungenlied* apart from its contemporaries is its form. It is composed in strophes containing four long lines, broken by a caesura. Each half-line contains four beats and the lines rhyme in pairs. The songs of Der von Kürenberg (see p. 239 ff.) have a similar, if not identical, meter, an observation which had led to the suggestion, not generally upheld, that this poet of love who showed a strong sense of the dramatic in his songs was in fact the author of the epic. It is much more likely that both were inspired by an established metrical pattern of Germanic origin, familiar in Austria in the latter half of the 12th century and thus accessible to both poets. Earlier debates about whether Der von Kürenberg was its inventor and whether the postulated *ältere Not* was already in this form have proved ultimately inconclusive. Likewise difficult to decide with any certainty is whether the poem was meant to be recited or actually sung, though the latter possibility is far from excluded. Probably both modes of performance occurred.

What is evident is that the meter will have aided the progress of the narrative very effectively, with the long lines accommodating the enjambement which conveys the passages of description (e.g. 281-283, the description of Siegfried's first sight of Kriemhild) and the more staccato movement achieved by the division into half-lines lending itself to terse comment and the impression of decisive action (e.g., 2219-2220, the death of Rüedeger at the hand of Gernot). Examples abound, sometimes closely following one another, so that the texture of the narrative is remarkably varied, given that, on the face of it, the rhythm remains the same. The capability of the meter to express contrasting moods will surely have guaranteed a lively rendition, while the very fact that the poet cannot always sustain the rhythm with absolute precision excludes any likelihood of monotony.

In this poem the juxtaposition of joy and sorrow and the rapid fluctuations in human existence are emphasized, and the poet uses his long line, balanced either side of the caesura, to express such contrasts most effectively. Thus we find lines like:

er was ir noch vil vremde,    dem si wart sider undertân (46,4)

(He to whom she was later to become devoted was still quite unknown to her.)

and

durch sîn eines sterben    starp vil maneger muoter kint (19,4)

(Because of his single death many a mother's child died.)

The last example, coming as it does at the end of the first *âventiure*, is also the first example of a recurrent feature of the poem: the prediction of disaster to come—a dominant element throughout the narrative—in the final line of an *âventiure*, seemingly pointing to the continuity of the action and no doubt inviting the audience to return for more. A large proportion of *âventiuren* end in this way, until the last ones, when the catastrophe predicted is being played out before us (see 138,4; 324,4; 876,4; 1100,4; 1505,4; 1649,4; 1757,4; 1848,4; 1920,4; 2080,4).

The division of the *Nibelungenlied* into 39 sections, known as *âventiuren* stems from the oldest manuscripts, which differ in this respect markedly from the manuscripts of the courtly romances of the same period, where new sections are indicated at most by large illuminated initial letters. The sections in the *Nibelungenlied* vary considerably in length, giving little guide to the amount offered at each performance, and are traditionally preceded by a brief heading which supplies the central content (e.g., *wie Sîfrit erslagen wart, wie die Burgonden zuo den Hiunen kômen*), again an innovative feature stemming from the earliest manuscripts.

## The Poem Itself

The substance of the *Nibelungenlied* is remarkably single stranded, a quality which is underlined by the frequent references to ultimate disaster. From the beginning, the poet is moving inexorably towards his conclusion, undistracted by the multitude of events along the way, all of which are ultimately seen to play their part in the achievement of that conclusion.

The basic story can be quickly told: the lovely princess Kriemhild, sister to the three kings of Burgundy, marries the handsome and fabulously strong Siegfried, in a marriage ceremony alongside another couple, Kriemhild's eldest brother, Gunther, and Brünhild, whose enormous physical strength stems, like Siegfried's, from a supernatural source. Indeed, Brünhild has consented to marry Gunther only because she has been deceived into believing that he has defeated her in a trial of strength, whereas in reality the victor was Siegfried, disguised in his magic cloak. Similarly disguised, he contrives to subdue her on Gunther's behalf on the wedding night. The double deception leads eventually to the death of Siegfried, at the hand of Hagen, one of Gunther's vassals and a dominant force at the Burgundian court.

Kriemhild's grief and desire for revenge lead her to bide her time until, in marriage to the mighty King Etzel of Hungary, she sees her opportunity. She invites her brothers and their companions, explicitly Hagen, to a reunion in Etzel's palace and there instigates hostilities which culminate in mass slaughter, the deaths of all her brothers, the death of Hagen at her hand, and her own death at the hand of the trusty warrior Hildebrand.

Such a synopsis, accurate enough in itself, fails to convey the quality of the *Nibelungenlied*. It omits mention of the scope of the poem, which traverses vast reaches of time and place and encompasses a range of human emotions, all pitched at their very height. The characters have a larger-than-life quality which is strangely combined with their capacity to appear, on one level at least, quite real. The work is full of action, and this action is both physical—movement and constant happenings—and more inward, with the characters acting and reacting as events overtake them. The latter aspect contributes, too, to an essential feature of the poem, and one of its central areas of debate, for it may be argued that the characters in the poem have little or no control over their destiny, that they are the victims of a force quite outside them. Equally valid, however, is the view that they are themselves the authors of what befalls them and that the whole work contains some kind of message about human behavior.

Certainly it is impossible to remain neutral in one's response to the *Nibelungenlied*, and the variety of critical writings on it demonstrates the power which it exercises and has exercised over many generations. All we can hope to do is indicate some of the central areas of discussion, concentrating on those works and standpoints which have achieved a measure of "classic" status, and indicating the direction of most recent research on the work. The poem falls naturally into two roughly equal parts on either side of the nineteenth *âventiure*, which, telling as it does of "how the treasure was brought to Worms," constitutes a kind of hinge between the two. The Nibelungen treasure was originally won by Siegfried in one of his early exploits when he slew the two kings of Nibelungenland, Schilbung and Nibelung, and appropriated the *hort*, but he then gave it to his wife as part of her dowry, so that it is intimately related with him and their marriage and thus represents to her, apart from its colossal material value, a link with the happiness which has already been taken from her by his murder. Both aspects of the *hort* mean that its subsequent loss to her provides Kriemhild with a second powerful reason for revenge and a double grievance against Hagen which will culminate in her cold-blooded killing of him at the end of the poem.

There is altogether in the *Nibelungenlied* an overriding sense of the consequential. One is constantly aware that if a particular event had not occurred, or a particular action not been taken, then the whole course of the poem would have been different. One can say, for example, that if Siegfried had not pronounced himself the vassal of Gunther when they came to Isenstein. . . , if he had not been so foolish as to take the ring and the girdle from Brünhild on the wedding night and give them to his wife. . . , if Hagen had not happened to arrive on the scene in front of the cathedral and find Brünhild in tears. . . , then everything would have been different and presumably better. Equally, though, we are aware that everything happens as it must happen, in accordance with the poet's assertion in the first *âventiure* (17,3) and reiterated in the last (2378,4) that all joy turns to sorrow in the end. There is no restraining the course of events. It is anticipated in general terms early in the poem and becomes increasingly more clearly defined as it proceeds. Exactly how Kriemhild's beloved, the falcon of her early dream (13), will perish in the claws of two eagles, cannot be known in that first *âventiure*, but that it will happen cannot be in doubt after its closing two strophes, which contain, in miniature, the whole story:

18,4 sît wart si mit êren     eins vil küenen recken wîp.

19 Der was der selbe valke,     den si in ir troume sach,
   den ir beschiet ir muoter.     wi sêre si daz rach
   an ir næhsten mâgen,     die in sluogen sint!
   durch sîn eines sterben     starp vil maneger muoter kint.

(Later she became the noble wife of a very bold warrior. He was that same falcon whom she had seen in her dream which her mother had explained to her. How terribly did she take revenge for that upon her closest kinsmen who killed him later! Because of the death of this one man, many a mother's son died.)

The audience knows what is going to happen, but the characters in the poem, even if they did know, would apparently be powerless to avert it. Even the seemingly omnipotent Hagen has to accept that he can do nothing to prevent the inexorable course of events, though he may put it to the test when he hurls the chaplain overboard in a vain attempt to prove that the water-sprites (*mêrwîp*) were wrong when they predicted that only this man, of the whole company, would return alive (1576-1580). The poet's audience, conditioned from the start to the hopelessness of the situation, cannot be surprised by the corroboration of the truth when the chaplain scrambles ashore, but even it can hardly fail to be moved by the resigned gesture of Hagen as he smashes the boat to pieces, knowing that it will not be needed again (1583).

Surprise, then, cannot be a feature of this poem, in which the poet has laid his cards so firmly on the table from its very start, and yet it does contain considerable tension, as it moves towards the long-awaited revelation of how his predictions will be fulfilled. This is, indeed, a masterly narrative. It enthralls from beginning to end, and probably what engages the modern reader is, at heart, little different from that which seems to have appealed to the 13th century listeners, a fascinating story in its exploration of human emotions, revealing the depths in human relationships in a way that is simple and direct and even, at times, verging on the crude.

One of the outstanding qualities of the *Nibelungenlied* is its dramatic brilliance, achieved by the evocation of vivid scenes—like Siegfried's arrival in Worms (71 ff.), the contests between Brünhild and Gunther/Siegfried in *âventiure* 7, Siegfried's show of bravado during the hunt immediately before his death, to name just a few of the many— and by confrontation, like the great quarrel between the queens in *âventiure* 14, Kriemhild's reception of the Burgundians and especially of Hagen when they come to Gran (1737 ff.), or, a confrontation of a different kind, the moving exchange between Hagen and Rüedeger, when Hagen requests Rüedeger's shield (2194 ff.). There is surely little in stage-drama to match the moment when Hagen is brought fettered in front of Kriemhild and defiantly refuses to reveal the whereabouts of the treasure (2371), nor the swiftness of the dénouement which follows.

One speaks readily about the *Nibelungenlied* in terms normally reserved for conventional drama, referring also to the vividness of the setting, for example, of the great cathedral in Worms or the forest clearing with the spring and the linden tree where Siegfried meets his death. One recalls the brilliantly observed moments of human reactions: the coy reluctance of the young daughter of Rüedeger to kiss the fearsome Hagen (1665-1666), or, in the same *âventiure*, her mother's sadness when she has no choice but to give

Hagen the one gift he requests, the shield which belonged to her dead kinsman Nuodung (1699). A single gesture speaks volumes when, observing that Kriemhild has made a point of kissing her brother Giselher, Hagen tightens the straps of his helmet, knowing as he does that this is no friendly reunion (1737,4) and that he must not drop his guard.

The poet manages to convey such pregnant moments with little obvious skill in using language. If anything, he succeeds because he says so little, focusing on the impact of the visual impression contained in a situation which he has conveyed with quite unusual skill. This is due in part to our constant awareness, which he never allows to slip, of what is going on, and partly it is due to the fact that people in the *Nibelungenlied* behave with extraordinary consistency. Brünhild tells Hagen *diu mære* (864,2), but, because we know both so well, we know that what she tells him and what he hears may not necessarily be the same thing, and that it may in neither case correspond to the events which we have just witnessed. In the scene between Hagen and Rüedeger, there is no point in protesting that Hagen could have picked up any number of shields from the ground around him, because we know that the exchange is saying something specific and enormously important, ensuring that the noble Rüedeger, drawn into the conflict against his friends because he has no choice, can transcend that conflict and die in it without prejudicing his immortal soul.

Considering just a handful of examples of this kind reveals the extraordinary subtlety of this poet, of whom A. T. Hatto can say: "It is marvelous that the Nibelung poet can say so much so well with so wretched an epic diction" (*Traditions*, p. 191). To be sure, there is much in the language of the *Nibelungenlied* that is repetitive and formulaic, ordinary to the point of being trite. It is, after all, the language of heroic literature, with which the courtly touches sit somewhat uncomfortably. The poet rarely indulges in imagery, and the moments which might warrant the designation lyrical—Siegfried's first sight of Kriemhild (281-283), for example, or the burgeoning love between the young couple (293-295)—are extremely rare. Nevertheless, there are moments of tenderness elsewhere, and sometimes the impact is particularly powerful when they come unexpectedly: the despair of the mourning Kriemhild as she demands that the magnificent coffin be opened up and she lifts the handsome head of her husband with her white hands for one last kiss (1068-1069). Even at such moments, however, the stark reality of the poem is very much present, for the tears which she sheds are blood, and her agony is precariously balanced between grief and lust for revenge. Different, of course, but very effective in its juxtaposition of stark realism and tenderness is the gesture of Hagen in restoring Eckewart's sword to him (1634): there is no disguising that they are on a doomed journey, but there is still room for gratitude and compassion.

Despite the brilliant moments of the poem, some critics have focussed on its imperfections, those points that do not quite add up, or where the poet seems to have slipped up, or where we may be dealing with something left over from an earlier stage of the development of the story. In this area of what one might call inconsistencies are some question marks which hang over some of the major characters. How, for example, does the virtuous princess Kriemhild of the early *âventiuren* become the she-devil (*vâlandinne* 1748,4; 2371,4) of the second part? Is this, as some would maintain, a psychologically sound development, given the suffering which she must endure, or is it a totally unrealistic and unacceptable change? Are the signs of her later wayward strength already discernible in her apparently flippant rejection of her mother's interpretation of her dream (14-18)? To what extent is it possible to think of the whole poem as "the tragedy of Kriemhild"? Is she victim or instigator? The latter question could equally be posed with regard to Hagen, who provokes diametrically opposed assessments. Some critics see him as a loyal vassal, intent on the best interests of his royal masters, while for others he is motivated by self-interest, consumed with greed and the lust for power and enraged by the usurpation of his role by the outsider Siegfried. The poet himself seems to be ambivalent in his depiction of Hagen, who is capable of extremes of ruthlessness— for example, when he kills Siegfried in cold blood and then places his corpse outside Kriemhild's door, and , much later, when he strikes off the head of the young son of Kriemhild and Etzel—and sensitivity, as in the scene already mentioned when he restores Eckewart's sword, or, more centrally, in the encounter with Rüedeger.

It is hard to see Gunther, too, as a consistent character: a king of immense reputation and power, yet a weakling when it comes to action; a man quite unable to win for himself the bride on whom his heart is set; a husband who responds to his wife's whims and needs constant advice from those about him. Yet precisely this man behaves with unambiguous courage in the final stages of the poem, seeming to restore his reputation of kingly supremacy in the fighting and not meriting the ignominious fate which his sister inflicts on him, when she has him beheaded and herself brandishes the head before Hagen (2369).

In the character of Siegfried himself, the contrasting textures of the poem are most striking, for this is a hero in the old style, with a history of dragon-slaying and mighty conquests in strange lands where he gained not only the great treasure but the horny skin which renders him almost immortal and the cloak of invisibility (*tarnkappe*, 97,3) which enables him to perform deeds beyond the capability of ordinary men. Yet this superman is vain and petulant, a prey to very human weaknesses which, in the long run, will cause his undoing. When the poet tells us, in the enigmatic way he has, that he *does not know* if Siegfried removed Brünhild's ring and girdle *out of arrogance* (680,2), he is almost certainly telling us that that was precisely the reason. Siegfried has all the arrogance of one who sees himself as beyond the reach of ordinary mortals, and when he commits the further act of stupidity of giving these highly significant objects to his wife, he unwittingly seals his fate. One can argue about whether he is an innocent victim of the treachery of others or a conspirator in his own destruction, but the fact remains that he is clearly no match for the cerebral agility of Hagen.

If Hagen meets his match in Kriemild, then Brünhild is the true counterpart of Siegfried, coming as they both do from the shadowy world of legend which is one of the major ingredients of the first part of the poem. In the second part, the poet is dealing with events and figures which derive, however hazily, from the real world of historical fact. This is the world of the migrations which brought Rüedeger as an exile to the court of Etzel, who may bear little resemblance to the traditional conception of Attila the Hun but contributes to the higher degree of reality which pervades the poem towards its conclusion, when together with the other semi-legendary, semi-historical figures, Dietrich and Hildebrand, he survives to contemplate the carnage.

The end of the *Nibelungenlied* is slaughter and lamentation on a grand scale commensurate with the epic which precedes it. Nothing remains to tell, and the poet takes refuge in his assertion that he cannot say what happened afterwards (*waz sider dâ geschach*, 2379,1). This is the fall of the Nibelungs (*der Nibelunge nôt*, 2379,4). Manuscript C, however, contains the alternative description which has given the name commonly accepted today to the poem: *der Nibelunge liet*.

With his closing statements the poet has set his seal on the action and would appear to be ruling out all possibility of a continuity. Not for him the extensive glimpses into the future which Wolfram gives in his *Parzival* (see p. 184), or the assurances of the happy-ever-after in this world and the next which characterize all Hartmann's narrative works. This is hardly surprising, for the poet has been adamant that all joy turns to sorrow, and he has never intimated that a reversal was possible.

### The *Klage*

This attitude makes it most unlikely that another work, the **Klage**, which is appended to the *Nibelungenlied* in all the main manuscripts was by the same author. Most critics believe that the *Klage* was composed about 1220. Its sermonizing tone and much of its language suggest that its author was a man of the church intent on conveying an essentially Christian message in an attempt to redress the unmitigated gloom and the total absence of hope of the *Nibelungenlied*. The form of the poem is quite distinct from its predecessor, 4360 lines in rhyming couplets, and its whole mood is completely different. In its attempt to supply a sequel to the *Nibelungenlied*, it strikes a tone which combines the elegiac with the moralizing. In no way does it match the *Nibelungenlied* in narrative skill, but it is interesting for what it tells us about medieval expectations, the demand for a story to be told to its absolute end, regardless of aesthetic considerations. In this respect it can be compared with the continuations of Wolfram's *Willehalm* and his *Titurel* (see p. 377 ff.), which, judging from their very existence, were clearly acceptable to an audience more concerned with the account of events than with questions of artistic coherence.

After an opening which recapitulates the major events of the *Nibelungenlied*, particularly in its closing stages, the *Klage* tells of how the dead were lamented by Etzel and his surviving companions. In contrast to the judgments which seemed to be implied as the *Nibelungenlied* came to its terrible end, Kriemhild is defended for her loyalty to Siegfried which means that she can be exonerated from blame, while Hagen is heaped with unambiguous abhorrence. In an attempt to attribute responsibility for the devastation, Etzel blames himself for having brought down the wrath of God by—a strange feature already present in manuscript C of the *Nibelungenlied*—renouncing his assumed Christian faith and returning to heathendom, while the poet puts into the mouth of the Bishop of Passau, informed of the terrible train of events, the opinion that pride has brought about the fall of the Burgundians. The Bishop instructs his clerk, one Conrad, to write down in Latin the events related to him by Swemmel, the messenger known to us from the *Nibelungenlied* who is here given the task of conveying the news of the disaster.

Ends which did not strike one as particularly loose in the overwhelming cataclysm of the *Nibelungenlied* are tied. Rüedeger's widow Gotelind is informed of what has happened, as is Ute, the mother of Kriemhild, and both women are said to die of grief, adding to the toll. The prevailing sense that nothing remains is lightened in the *Klage* by the description of the investiture of the young son of Gunther and Brünhild, who will wear the crown in succession to his father and on whom, presumably, rests the responsibility for restoring a semblance of order and even of hope. Brünhild herself is thus afforded a new status, after the events of the *Nibelungenlied* had seemed to cast her into oblivion. Dietrich, now married to Herrat, the niece of Queen Helche, promises to provide Giselher's young widow—who, in the *Klage*, is given the name Dietlinde—with a new husband to help her in the burdensome task which now falls to her of managing her father's estates.

This somewhat facile attempt to redress the unmitigated gloom of the great poem which preceded it may not be greatly admired from an artistic standpoint, but it perhaps merits rather more attention for its intrinsic qualities than it has received. It is repetitious and at times ponderous, but there are moments of human insight and compassion such as had no place in the *Nibelungenlied*. The language, though owing much to its predecessor, contains echoes of the courtly romances which it resembles also in its form, and also, from time to time, one discerns attempts at imagery which recall, not the *Nibelungenlied* at all, but the colorful idiom of, say, Wolfram von Eschenbach.

The *Klage* was certainly never meant to be read, or heard, in isolation from the *Nibelungenlied*, but it should not be dismissed too lightly, for it is a work which is capable of casting new light on established perspectives both for its contemporaries and for the modern reader.

Text:
There are many editions of the work, usually appended to editions of the *Nibelungenlied*. The MHG text is probably most accessible in the following edition:
Bartsch, Karl, ed. *Diu Klage. Mit den Lesarten sämtlicher Handschriften.* Leipzig, 1875. Repr. Darmstadt: Wis. Buchges., 1964.

Translation:
McConnell, Winder, trans. *The Lament of the Nibelungen (Diu Chlage).* Columbia, SC: Camden House, 1994 (= Studies in German Lit., Ling., and Cult.). Engl. prose trans. of the *Klage*, adjacent to a transcription of Ms. B of the poem. Intro. augmented by pertinent enlightening footnotes throughout.

Facsimile:
See facs. of *Nibelungenlied* ed. by Duft (above).

### Kudrun

The *Klage* may well be seen as the first manifestation of the reception of the *Nibelungenlied*, and it also provides an important link with another work which followed quite a bit later and which otherwise might stand in even more puzzling isolation. This is *Kudrun*, which has for the most part remained in the shadow of the *Nibelungenlied* and certainly must be considered in relationship to it, but deserves also independent treatment. For that reason we have decided to treat it separately, in its chronological position, and together with the post classical heroic literature represented by the Dietrich epics (see p. 390 ff.).

## The Impact of the *Nibelungenlied* after the Middle Ages

Although the *Nibelungenlied* itself, and with it the *Klage*, was clearly a popular work in the decades and the century or so which followed its composition, and although its influence is felt in the later heroic works of the German Middle Ages, there is no extant evidence of the works which must surely have come into existence in imitation of it. The explanation would seen to lie in the overwhelming impact of the *Nibelungenlied*, which meant that all other efforts paled into insignificance and were never allowed to endure. This is strange enough, but even stranger is the fact that the *Nibelungenlied* itself appears to have fallen into oblivion in the course of the 16th century, when the only evidence that it ever existed is in the admittedly very popular "Lied vom Hürnen Seyfried." This poem circulated in printed versions and achieved dramatic form at the hand of Hans Sachs in 1557. The material seems then to have survived in quasi-historical re-tellings in prose, the oldest extant edition dating, however, from as late as 1726. By that time the material and the form were in any case so transformed that its origins in the *Nibelungenlied* are barely recognizable.

Thus, when Manuscript C came to light in 1755 in the library at Hohenems, its significance was not appreciated, even when it was published in part in 1757 by J. J. Bodmer and then in its entirety in 1782 by Christoph Heinrich Myller. The explanation for this indifference, even among the educated—or perhaps especially in such circles—lies in the pre-eminence of Classical taste at that period. It was not until the Romantics evoked a new interest in the concept of the national and in particular of the German that the material of the *Nibelungenlied*, with its roots deep in the Germanic past, began to inspire a new enthusiasm.

It is probably true to say that, since that time, it is this poem of all the works of the *Blütezeit* that has maintained its position in the forefront of the minds of the German-speaking public. It was frequently edited and printed during the nineteenth century, apparently a text much favored in the home and at school. Its essentially dramatic qualities were much appreciated, above all by Friedrich Hebbel in 1855-1860 and Richard Wagner in 1853, who, in their very different ways, seized the material both for the impact of its message and for its amenability to large-scale performance. Thus, in the middle of the 19th century, the *Nibelungenlied* was given new and ambitious transformations by two considerable, though highly contentious, artists. At the same time, lesser names saw the potential in the stories of individual characters of the poem, and since that time, the *Nibelungenlied* has consistently provided the inspiration for novels and short stories, plays and films. Although some critics understandably draw a veil over the way in which the material was used for nationalistic purposes in the Weimar Republic, and later under the National Socialist regime, this is a phase which has its place in the vast history of the reception of the *Nibelungenlied*. The most comprehensive account of this period is given by Francis G. Gentry, but fairly balanced information is also available in the works of Otfrid Ehrismann, Werner Hoffmann, and in the little introductory volume by Joachim Heinzle (see below).

## *Nibelungenlied/Klage*—Bibliography

The suggestions under this heading can be no more than guidance for those wishing to extend their knowledge of the *Nibelungenlied* and its sequel, and of the mass of literature surrounding them. We follow our usual practice of recommending some of the central secondary works, but also in particular highlighting fairly recent works in English. Most of these contain substantial bibliographies, which will direct readers in specific areas.

Andersson, Theodore M. *A Preface to the Nibelungenlied*. Stanford, CA: Stanford UP, 1987.

Of interest to anyone seeking a thorough insight into this complex material.

Bäuml, Franz H., and Eva-Maria Fallone, comps. *A Concordance to the Nibelungenlied*. Leeds: Maney & Son, Ltd., 1976.

Concordance based on the Bartsch-de Boor text.

Bekker, Hugo. *The Nibelungenlied. A Literary Analysis*. Toronto: Univ. of Toronto Press, 1971.

Detailed examination of the main aspects of technique and structure of the poem based on close reading of the text.

Bostock, J. Knight. "The Message of the *Nibelungenlied*." *MLR* 55 (1960): 200-212. Also in German in Rupp, WdF, 54, pp. 84-109, with title: "Der Sinn des Nibelungenlieds." See also K. C. King (below).

An attempt to establish the meaning of the poem in its demonstration of the effects of pride. Well worth reading.

Dürrenmatt, Nelly. *Das Nibelungenlied im Kreis der höfischen Dichtung*. Lungern: Buchdruckerei Burch & Cie., 1945.

An important book in its time and still often cited, it relates the poem to its literary context.

Ehrismann, Otfrid. *Das Nibelungenlied in Deutschland. Studien zur Rezeption des Nibelungenlieds von der Mitte des 18. Jahrhunderts bis zum ersten Weltkrieg*. Munich: Fink, 1975 (= Münchner Germanistische Beitr., 14).

See comments to next item.

_____. *Nibelungenlied 1755-1920: Regesten und Kommentare zu Forschung und Rezeption*. Gießen: Schmitz, 1986 (= Beitr. zur deutschen Philologie, 62).

This and the book above, with their detailed documentation, are invaluable reference works for anyone interested in the lasting impact of the *Nibelungenlied* beyond the Middle Ages. Some inevitable overlap, and of course no coverage of the past decade.

_____. *Nibelungenlied. Epoche-Werk-Wirkung*. Munich: Beck 1987 (= Arbeitsbücher zur Literaturgeschichte).

Conforms to the general pattern of the series and provides a comprehensive account of the central issues of the poem, including its reception from the 18th century to the present. Interesting section devoted to the use of the poem as a school text, not least as an instrument of fascism.

Gentry, Francis G. "Die Rezeption des Nibelungenliedes in der Weimarer Republik." In: *Das Weiterleben des Mittelalters in der deutschen Literatur*. Ed. by J. F. Poag and G. Scholz-Williams. Königstein/Ts: Athenäum, 1983. Pp. 142-156.

Gillespie, George T. *"Die Klage* as a Commentary on *Das Nibelungenlied."* In: *Probleme mittelhochdeutscher Erzählformen: Marburger Colloquium 1969.* Ed. by Peter F. Ganz and Werner Schröder. Berlin: Erich Schmidt, 1972 (= Publ. of the Inst. of Germanic Studies, Univ. of London, 13). Pp. 153-177.

Detailed study of the relationship of *Klage* to *Nibelungenlied,* seeing it as Christian exegesis of the personages and the events.

Hatto, Arthur T. "Medieval German." In: *Traditions of Heroic and Epic Poetry, Volume I,* Ed. by A. T. Hatto. London: MHRA, 1980. Pp. 165-195.

An interesting article, placing the work in the broad context of medieval German literature, and, beyond that, of world literature.

Haymes, Edward R. *The Nibelungenlied. History and Interpretation.* Urbana & Chicago: Univ. of Illinois Press, 1986 (= Illinois Medieval Monographs, 2).

An attempt "to view the *Nibelungenlied* within its specific historical and literary horizons to a greater extent than has been attempted in the past."

Heinzle, Joachim. *Das Nibelungenlied. Eine Einführung.* Munich: Artemis, 1987. Frankfurt/M.: Fischer Taschenbuch Verlag, [2]1994 (= Literaturwiss. Fischer, 11843).

Useful short, but comprehensive introduction to *Nibelungenlied.* Very informative narrative bibliography on the various areas of interest.

_____, and Anneliese Waldschmidt, eds. *Die Nibelungen. Ein deutscher Wahn, ein deutscher Alptraum. Studien und Dokumente zur Rezeption des Nibelungenstoffs im 19. und 20. Jahrhundert.* Frankfurt/M.: Suhrkamp, 1991.

Valuable essays by various scholars on the reception of Nibelungen-materials, with numerous interesting illustrations.

Heusler, Andreas. *Nibelungensage und Nibelungenlied. Die Stoffgeschichte des deutschen Heldenepos.* Dortmund: Ruhfus, [6]1965.

Originally published in 1920, Heusler's work remains an enthralling piece of scholarship and essential to anyone seriously concerned with the evolution of the poem and research on that evolution.

Hoffmann, Werner. *Das Nibelungenlied. Interpretation von Werner Hoffmann.* Munich: Oldenbourg, 1969. [2]1974 (= Interpretationen zum Deutschunterricht).

See comments to next item.

_____. *Das Nibelungenlied.* Frankfurt/M.: Diesterweg, 1987 (= Grundlagen und Gedanken zum Verständnis erzählender Literatur.)

These two small but densely written books (above) are useful within their own terms, although they do not set out to offer much that is new.

_____. *Das Nibelungenlied.* Stuttgart: Metzler, [6]1992 (= Sammlung Metzler, 7.)

An authoritative handbook for anyone wishing to study the poem in scholarly depth.

Huber, Werner. *Auf der Suche nach den Nibelungen. Städte und Stätten, die der Dichter des Nibelungenliedes beschrieb.* Gütersloh: Presentverlag Heinz Peter, 1981.

Not particularly of scholarly value, but beautiful color illustrations of contemporary places associated with the Nibelungs, with text in German, English, and French.

King, K. C. "The Message of the *Nibelungenlied*—a Reply." *MLR* 57 (1962): 541-50. See also in German: Rupp, WdF, 54, pp. 218-36, with title: "Der Sinn des Nibelungenlieds—eine Entgegnung."

Written in response to the article by Bostock (see above). Both articles can also be found in the volume *Selected Essays on Medieval German Literature by K. C. King*. Ed. by J. L. Flood and A. T. Hatto. London: Inst. of Germanic Studies, 1975. Pp. 126-145 and 146-161.

Maurer, Friedrich. *Leid. Studien zur Bedeutungs- und Problemgeschichte, besonders in den großen Epen der staufischen Zeit*. Bern: Francke 1951. [4]1969 (= Bibliotheca Germanica, 1)

In his classic book on suffering and sorrow as manifested in the works of the German Middle Ages, Maurer devotes a substantial section to the *Nibelungenlied* (pp. 13-38).

McConnell, Winder. *The Nibelungenlied*. Boston: Twayne, 1984 (= TWAS, 712).

Good, informative general introduction to the poem.

_____. "The Problem of Continuity in *Diu Klage*." *Neophil.* 70 (1986): 248-55.

A short but interesting article examining the relationship between the two works and making a case for the importance of the *Klage*, despite its artistic inferiority to the *Nibelungenlied*.

Mergell, Bodo. "Nibelungenlied und höfischer Roman." *Euph.* 45 (1950): 305-36.

An important article in its day, reprinted in Rupp, WdF, 54, Pp. 3-39.

Mowatt, D. G., and Hugh Sacker. *The Nibelungenlied. An Interpretative Commentary*. Toronto: Univ. of Toronto Press, 1967.

General introduction, emphasizing literary value, plus detailed running commentary on the text with at times novel readings.

Müller, Jan-Dirk. "Das Nibelungenlied." In: Horst Brunner, ed. *Mittelhochdeutsche Romane und Heldenepen*. Stuttgart: Reclam, 1993. Pp. 146-72 (= UB, Interpretationen, 8914).

A readable and lucid appraisal of the poem on the basis of a consideration of central issues and principal characters and episodes.

Nagel, Bert. *Das Nibelungenlied. Stoff-Form-Ethos*. Frankfurt/M.: Hirschgraben Verlag, 1965. [2]1970.

Useful interpretive study based on its basic materials, structure, and ideology.

Panzer, Friedrich. *Studien zum Nibelungenlied*. Frankfurt/M.: Diesterweg, 1945.

Examines the Romance, Roman, and historical elements in the *Nibelungenlied*, along with its pre-history, the poet and his provenance.

_____. *Das Nibelungenlied. Entstehung und Gestalt*. Stuttgart: Kohlhammer, 1955.

A distinguished scholar's attempt at a total interpretation as culmination of his scholarly preoccupation with the poem over many years.

Rupp, Heinz, ed. *Nibelungenlied und Kudrun*. Darmstadt: Wiss. Buchges., 1976 (= WdF, 54).

Collection of significant articles (16) on the 'Nibelungenlied' from 1950-65 and on 'Kudrun' (7) from 1956-70.

Schröder, Werner. *Nibelungenlied-Studien*. Stuttgart: Metzler, 1968.

This is a collection of essays, some of them already published elsewhere, covering some central topics, such as the idea that the work is first and foremost the tragedy of Kriemhild, the concept of the epic in the poem and the question of the Nibelungen treasure.

Thomas, Neil. *Reading the "Nibelungenlied."* Durham: Univ. of Durham, 1995 (= Durham Modern Language Series, GM 5).

A refreshing little volume which probes more deeply into more of the issues of the poem than the title might suggest. Places the poem in its broad cultural and literary context, and includes certain aspects of the modern German cultural condition. Good bibliography for recent items.

Tonnelat, Ernest. *La chanson des Nibelungen. Étude sur la composition et la formation du poème épique.* Paris: Société D'Édition: Les belles lettres, 1926 (= Publications de la Faculté des Lettres de l'Université de Strasbourg, fascicule 30).

A comprehensive study of the *Nibelungenlied* by a distinguished French scholar. Some views out of date, but study is worth reading. Stresses the unity of composition and the literary-historical elements.

_____. *La Légende des Nibelungen en Allemagne au XIX siècle.* Paris: Publications de la Faculté des Lettres de l'Université de Strasbourg, fascicule 119, 1952.

Wailes, Stephen L. "The *Nibelungenlied* as Heroic Epic." In: *Heroic Epic and Saga. An Introduction to the World's Great Folk Epics.* Ed. by Felix J. Oinas. Bloomington: Indiana UP, 1978. Pp. 120-43.

A stimulating analysis of the poem, which departs from the consideration of levels of the heroic in it.

Weber, Gottfried. *Das Nibelungenlied. Problem und Idee.* Stuttgart: Metzler, 1963.

One of the first studies of the work as a whole, a classic interpretation, which contains chapters devoted to the central characters, to chivalry and to questions of the place of Christianity in the poem. Fundamental to *Nibelungenlied* research and frequently cited.

Wunderlich, Werner, and Ulrich Müller, eds., with assistance of D. Scholz. *"Waz sider da geschach": American-German Studies on the Nibelungenlied. Text and Reception. With bibliography 1980-1990/91.* Göppingen: Kümmerle, 1992 (= GAG, 564).

Selection of papers from the Kalamazoo International Congresses 1990 and 1991 gives some idea of recent discourses. 10-year bibliography cites 686 items!

# The Medieval German Lyric

The flourishing of the lyric in the Middle Ages in Germany is amply demonstrated by the substantial collections in the manuscripts, most of which contain love poetry alongside poetry of more obviously didactic nature. As far as the love lyric is concerned, the manuscripts provide us with impressive evidence of a tradition that continued over a lengthy period and maintained a certain consistency, while affording the opportunity for individual poets to emerge with often striking originality and for a multitude of diverse trends to exist within the tradition.

## THE MINNESANG

When one thinks of the lyric of the German Middle Ages, one is thinking first and foremost of the Minnesang, the love lyric based essentially on a fictitious relationship between a knight and his high-born lady. Yet within what would seem at first sight to be a rather unpromising, static pose, there lies a variety of expression, and individual poets come into their own with a remarkable diversity of form and content. We are dealing, moreover, with a European, indeed a worldwide phenomenon, the German manifestation of which shows both liberal borrowings and substantial individuality.

We shall begin with the earliest examples of the love lyric in German, in the middle of the 12th century, and continue through the "courtly period," which produced some of the finest examples, coinciding with the great narrative works of MHG, but also a mass of minor poets. Then we shall trace both the decline of the tradition and the way in which it broadened out into a questioning, sometimes innovative, and strikingly fresh mode. Later we shall look at other kinds of lyric poetry, more precisely didactic poetry, which actually belongs chronologically with our consideration of the narrative literature of the later 13th and the entire 14th centuries.

Our interest will lie in the principal trends of Minnesang, in the specific qualities of its most important individual exponents, and in the multiplicity of questions which confront scholars in this field. Because of the large scope of this section, bibliographic information will be included wherever appropriate rather than altogether at the end of a larger section. The following will, it is hoped, balance the demands of a chronological and a thematic approach.

### The Origins of the Minnesang

Poems based on the idea of love and service are common throughout medieval Europe, and what became known as the Minnesang probably has its most important ultimate source in classical models which were brought into northern Europe by wandering scholars and, like much of the narrative, were adopted and subsequently adapted from Old French and Old Provençal lyrics. The theory that there were Arabic origins, fostered in the courts of southern France and Andalusia, is an attractive one, but it is difficult to prove, not least because of the barriers of language. The link between the love lyric and poems, either in Latin or in the vernacular, in praise of the Virgin Mary, is likewise a tenuous one at an early stage, although the Marian lyric of the 13th and 14th centuries is an important, but separate, development (see p. 422). The earliest love poems in German suggest a native tradition, but this too is elusive and is unlikely to have constituted the basis for what was to become a highly sophisticated art, essentially based on the court.

At the height of the influence of medieval French literature on German, in the decades which span the turn of the 12th and 13th centuries, the impact of the lyrics of the troubadours and the trouvères was crucial at the German courts, which were undoubtedly highly receptive to this fashionable mode. It is reasonable to assume considerable direct contact between the French poets and their German counterparts, who, imitating at first, soon came to establish their distinctive tradition.

## Minnesang Origins—Bibliography

Brinkmann, Hennig. *Entstehungsgeschichte des Minnesangs.* Halle: Niemeyer, 1926 (= *DVjs* Buchreihe, 8). Repr. Darmstadt, 1971.

A landmark comprehensive study that is still valuable today.

Dronke, Peter. *Medieval Latin and the Rise of the European Love Lyric.* Oxford: Clarendon, 1966. 2 vols, I: Problems and interpretations, II: Medieval Latin love poetry: texts.

____. *The Medieval Lyric.* London: Hutchinson, 1968. [3]1996.

Provides an introduction to the medieval lyric, both secular and sacred, for the period 800-1300 in Romance and Germanic languages using specific outstanding examples.

Waddell, Helen. *The Wandering Scholars.* London, 1927. London: Constable, [7]1934 (revised & enlarged). Reprinted often; reissued 1954 in paperback by Pelican Books.

A classic work on the rise of the Latin lyric in the 12th and 13th centuries. Eminently readable, with its many insights into the background of Minnesang.

Wechssler, Eduard. *Das Kulturproblem des Minnesangs. Studien zur Vorgeschichte der Renaissance. I. Minnesang und Christentum.* Halle, 1909. Repr. Osnabrück, 1966.

An interesting early work which is sometimes disparaged for its method. Gives a fascinating impression of the array of comparable lyrics at this period.

## The Manuscripts

The manuscripts containing these poems were produced some time after the original composition and may not always give a clear idea of the quantity of a poet's output. Probably a certain amount has been lost; some songs may never have been recorded.

The earliest extant manuscript containing some of the poems under consideration is the **Codex Buranus**, MS M (Bayerische StB. Munich, clm. 4660 and 4660a), dating from the early 13th century and including some poems in German, along with a preponderance of Latin poems, also known as *Carmina Burana*. The manuscript was originally in the library of the monastery of Benediktbeuern in Upper Bavaria and contains some indication of the music attaching to the poems.

The **Small Heidelberg Manuscript**, MS A (UB Heidelberg, cod. pal. germ 357), is the earliest of the three major Minnesang manuscripts, but, unlike the other two, it is not illustrated. Most of it is believed to be the work of a single, 13th-century scribe, probably an Alsatian, with a few later additions, probably from the 14th century. We can reasonably assume that this text, despite some apparent errors, is as close as we can come to the original text, and the manuscript contains material not recorded elsewhere.

MS B is usually called the **Weingarten Manuscript** (Württembergische LB Stuttgart, cod. HB XIII.1) because it arrived at the monastery of Weingarten in the 17th century, probably from its origins in Constance. It is now in the Landesbibliothek in Stuttgart. Most of the work is by one scribe, with sections added by four others. The 25 named poets who make up the main part of this manuscript are headed by Emperor Heinrich VI, with others following in order of social standing. There are some illustrations and some empty pages, presumably intended for later additions, and both point to a patron of substance, since parchment was an expensive commodity. It is likely that it was instigated by Heinrich von Klingenberg, Bishop of Constance from 1293 to 1306. He was a significant political figure, head of the royal chancellery under Rudolf I of Habsburg. Linked with the Manesse family, he was known to be interested in poetry.

The manuscript of the Minnesang with which we are most familiar, from the frequent reproductions of its beautiful illustrations, is the **Large Heidelberg Manuscript**, MS C (UB Heidelberg, cod. pal. germ. 848), traditionally known as the **Manesse Manuscript** because it is believed to have been prompted by the Manesse family in Zürich. The many fine illustrations, some of which are very detailed, are liberally adorned with gold and silver. The current state of the manuscript—with pages cut out, sections stuck or sewn in, spaces and additions—all suggests that it was compiled in the course of quite a long period of time. The original section contains 110 poets, with others added at a later date. The evidence indicates that it was begun in about 1300 and continued up to about 1340. Included is a high proportion of Swiss poets, many from the Zürich region. One of these is Johannes Hadloub, known as Hadlaub, who supplies the important reference to the Manesse family as collectors of poetry.

Although manuscripts A, B, and C are the most significant compilations of the Minnesang, there are a large number of others, some of them fragments. MS J, the **Jenaer Liederhandschrift** (UB Jena, Ms. El. f. 101), held at the University of Jena since its foundation in 1558, is the earliest manuscript with a large number of melodies. Although its provenance is uncertain, its language and the origin of many of the poets represented points, interestingly, to North Germany. MS R (StB Preußischer Kulturbesitz, Berlin, Ms. germ. fol. 1062), from Riedegg in Austria, is the most important record of the poems of Neidhart. Predating all these is the so-called *Carmina Burana* already mentioned.

The largest manuscripts, and in particular the great Heidelberg one, are well worth looking at for a variety of reasons. They show the very large number of songs recorded and close examination reveals the complexity of the editorial task and the problems involved. In addition, they are intrinsically very beautiful and even the excellent facsimiles convey an authentic impression of the extravagant decoration and suggest the dedication which prompted such lavish expense and the skill of execution.

Facsimile editions:

MS M: *Carmina Burana. Facsimile-Ausgabe der Benediktbeurer Liederhs. und der Fragmenta Burana (Clm. 4660 u. 4660a) der Bayer. StB München.* Ed. by Bernhard Bischoff. Vol. 1: Facsimile, Vol. 2: Introduction. Munich: Prestel Verlag/ Brooklyn, NY: Institute of Medieval Music, 1967.

MS A: *Die Kleine Heidelberger Liederhs. Cod. Pal. Germ. 357 der UB Heidelberg.* Vol. 1: Facsimile, Vol. 2: Introduction by Walter Blank. 1972. Also: *Die kleine Heidelberger Liederhs. in Nachbildung mit Geleitwort und Verzeichnis der Dichter und der Strophenanfänge.* Ed. by Carl von Kraus. Stuttgart: Omnitypie Ges. Nachf. L. Zechnall, 1932.

MS B: *Die Weingartner Liederhs. (Landesbibliothek Stuttgart, HB XIII I.* Vol. 1: Facsimile, Vol. 2: Essays by W. Irtenkauf, K. H. Halbach, R. Kroos, O. Ehrismann (transcription). Stuttgart: Müller & Schindler, 1969.

MS C: *Codex Manesse. Die große Heidelberger Liederhs. Facsimile-Ausgabe des Cod. Pal. Germ. 848 der UB Heidelberg.* 1975 ff. Commentary by Walter Koschorreck and Wilfried Werner, 1981.

See also the very informative catalogue of the exhibition in 1988: Mittler, Elmar and Wilfried Werner. *Codex Manesse. Katalog zur Ausstellung vom 12. Juni bis 2. Oktober 1988.* UB Heidelberg, 1988.

See also: Walther, Ingo F. with coll. of Gisela Siebert, ed. *Codex Manesse. Die Miniaturen der Großen Heidelberger Liederhs.* Frankfurt/M.: Insel, 1988. Color reproductions (reduced size) of all the miniatures.

For complete information on the Ms. and its history, see: Jammers, Ewald. *Das königliche Liederbuch des deutschen Minnesangs. Eine Einführung in die sogennante Manessische Handschrift.* Heidelberg: Schneider, 1965.

MS J: Tervooren, Helmut, and Ulrich Müller, eds. *Die Jenaer Liederhs. In Abbildung.* Göppingen: Kümmerle, 1972 (= Litterae, 10).

A full account of the smaller manuscripts is contained in: Schweikle, Günther. *Minnesang.* Stuttgart: Metzler, 1989 (= Sammlung Metzler, 244). A very useful comprehensive introduction to the whole subject of Minnesang.

## Music

Given the ample evidence that a significant feature of the poems with which we are concerned is that they were, in fact, songs, and that the art of the Minnesang was not least a vocal art, it is strange and frustrating that the manuscripts provide so little idea of the music. Although the *Carmina Burana* manuscript contains some indications of the musical renderings, they are unhelpful in that they give no hint about pitch or tempo. The substantial collection of melodies in J belongs with a group of very minor poets whose songs can mostly be categorized as didactic. Other evidence of the melodies attaching to, for example, Neidhart's songs, is so late as to raise doubts about the extent to which they correspond to the original rendering. We are thus left with an exasperating void in our knowledge of how the most famous songs will have sounded and the need to supply this seemingly important dimension from the evidence available, in the form mentioned above or from the music which is sometimes attached in the Romance manuscripts.

One is left to toy with the thought that perhaps this dimension was not in fact so important, that the virtuosity evident in the language, the metrical structures, the playing with words and images, and so on, were actually of paramount importance, whereas the music was deemed to be no more than an accompaniment which could, in any case, be subject to considerable adaptation by individual performers. There is little or no evidence to substantiate the popular view of the medieval poet accompanying himself on a musical instrument, though some instruments undoubtedly constituted a separate form of courtly entertainment. All the more important is the verbal artistry which must dominate any study of the Minnesang.

## Music—Bibliography

McMahon, James V. *Music of Early Minnesang*. Columbia, SC: Camden House, 1990 (= Studies in German Lit., Ling., & Cult., 41). Written for the literary scholar, not the musicologist.

Taylor, Ronald J. "The Musical Knowledge of the Middle High German Poet." *MLR* 49 (1954): 331-338.

____. *Die Melodien der weltlichen Lieder des Mittelalters*. Stuttgart: Metzler, 1964. I: Darstellungsband, II: Melodienband (= Sammlung Metzler, 34 & 35).

____. *The Art of the Minnesinger. Songs of the Thirteenth Century Transcribed and Edited with Textual and Musical Commentaries*. 2 Vols. Cardiff: Univ. of Wales Press, 1968. 2 vols. This and the two other items above are significant contributions by a scholar who has a particular expertise in this aspect of the discipline.

## Minnesang—Editions

1a. Lachmann, Karl, and Moriz Haupt, eds. *Des Minnesangs Frühling*, 1857. Subsequent revisions by Friedrich Vogt and numerous editions. [30]1950 ed. by Carl von Kraus, with subsequent reprintings: Stuttgart: Hirzel, [35]1970. (Text only, no notes).

1b. Moser, Hugo, and Helmut Tervooren, eds. *Des Minnesangs Frühling. Unter Benutzung der Ausgaben von Karl Lachmann und Moriz Haupt, Friedrich Vogt und Carl von Kraus*. Stuttgart: Hirzel, [36]1977. Bd. I: Texte, Bd. II: Editionsprinzipien, Melodien, Handschriften, Erläuterungen.

The early editions contained the "Namenlose Lieder" and twenty named poets, ending with Hartmann von Aue. In this edition, some of the poems attributed to Spervogel in all preceding editions appear under the name of Herger. Two additional poems which appear in the manuscripts under the name of Gottfried von Straßburg are included as are the songs of Wolfram von Eschenbach.

A computer data file edition of *Minnesangs Frühling* based on Moser-Tervooren, [38]1988 has been compiled by Jean L. C. Putmans and is available from Kümmerle Verlag, Göppingen (1993) on 3.5" disk. Introduction, texts, and word-lists.

**Note**: Traditionally the poems were identified according to their page and line number in the original edition, but a major change effected by Moser and Tervooren has simplified this rather unwieldy system: poets are now numbered, from I to XXIV, with their individual poems similarly given Roman numerals and strophes Arabic numerals. Lines are numbered in groups of 5. To facilitate identification, the original numbering is given in the right-hand margin. The new system is gradually becoming established, but of course most of the critical literature before the past fifteen years or so uses the older notation. Some of the recent scholarship supplies both references: thus XIX (Heinrich von Morungen) XIII.1,5 = 133,17. The second volume contains sections on editorial principles, melodies, and manuscripts, and notes on the individual poets and individual poems.

1c. ____, eds. *Kommentare zu "Des Minnesangs Frühling."* Bd. III/1: Carl von Kraus, *Des Minnesangs Frühling. Untersuchungen.* Leipzig, 1939. Durch Register erschlossen und um einen Literaturschlüssel ergänzt. Stuttgart: Hirzel, 1981.

Reprint of von Kraus's valuable "Untersuchungen" to accompany the new edition.

1d. ____, eds. *Kommentare zu "Des Minnesangs Frühling."* Bd. III/2: *Des Minnesangs Frühling. Anmerkungen.* Nach Karl Lachmann, Moriz Haupt und Friedrich Vogt. Neu bearbeitet von Carl von Kraus. Zürich, [30]1950. Durch Register erschlossen und um einen Literaturschlüssel ergänzt. Stuttgart: Hirzel, 1981.

Reprint of the notes to the poems from von Kraus's last edition (1a), including the notes of earlier editors.

2. von Kraus, Carl, ed. *Deutsche Liederdichter des 13. Jahrhunderts.* Tübingen: Niemeyer, 1952. 2 vols., I: Text, II: Kommentar.

Composed with the explicit intention of editing all those poets of the 13th century who had *not* recently been accorded scholarly editions, it thus represents a major complement to *Minnesangs Frühling,* and, containing as it does 69 poets (including Gottfried von Straßburg and Wolfram von Eschenbach and a group of unidentified poets), it shows the abundance of lyric poets in the century, many of whom have not achieved any degree of eminence but were nevertheless amply recorded in the manuscripts. Poems are identified in a manner broadly the same as that in the new edition of *Minnesangs Frühling.* The companion volume, *Kommentar,* was completed by Hugo Kuhn following the death of Carl von Kraus (Tübingen: Niemeyer, 1958).

These two major works (1a-d and 2) provide the basis for any serious study of the German lyric from about 1150 to the end of the 13th century. In the discussions below it is understood that texts of the poems will be found in these two major sources unless otherwise indicated by reference to selected editions, editions of individual poets, and anthologies. However, mention should perhaps be made at this point of two very useful editions:

3. Sayce, Olive, ed. *Poets of the Minnesang.* Oxford: Clarendon, 1967. With introduction, notes, and glossary.

A one-volume "introduction to the essentials of the subject." A very comprehensive work, containing a selection from the anonymous poems of the mid-12th century and from 26 named poets, spanning the period up to about the end of the 13th century. Exceptionally clearly set out, with footnotes which aid the interpretation of individual poems supported by fuller analyses and metrical summaries at the back of the volume. Introduction and glossary are likewise clear and to the point, informative without overwhelming with detail. Select bibliography directs the reader to some of the major issues of a general and a specific nature. Altogether the most useful and

manageable book on the subject available in English. Texts have been newly established from the manuscripts, and textual variants are clearly indicated.
4. Brackert, Helmut, ed. & trans. *Minnesang: Mittelhochdeutsche Texte und Übertragungen.* Frankfurt/M: Fischer Taschenbuch Verlag, 1983.
A very useful paperback volume containing a good representative selection of texts in MHG with adjacent translations into modern German. Also, an informative afterword with notes on individual poets and songs and on technical matters such as meter.

## Meter

We know that the songs of the Minnesänger were sung, even though our knowledge of the melodies is very scant. However, it is evident that meter was a vital component, and a knowledge of MHG metrical practices is essential for any study of Minnesang.

The classic work on meter is in three volumes of formidable detail: Heusler, Andreas. *Deutsche Versgeschichte. Mit Einschluß des altenglischen und altnordischen Stabreimverses.* Berlin: de Gruyter, 1929 ff. Repr. [2]1956. 3 vols. I: Grundbegriffe. Der germanische Vers, II: Der altdeutsche Vers, III: Fnhd. u. Nhd. Vers (= Grundriß der germanischen Philologie, 8). More manageable summaries will be found in Walshe (71-85) and Sayce (1967 xx-xxiii) and, in German, in Schweikle (1989 154-164). See also: Paul, Otto, and Ingeborg Glier. *Deutsche Metrik.* Munich: Hueber, [9]1961 (MHG metrics pp. 37-99).

Essentially the principle is one of stress, and the normal metrical unit ("foot") which corresponds to the normal speech pattern is a stressed syllable (*Hebung*), indicated /, followed by an unstressed syllable (*Senkung*), indicated x. The first foot is often preceded by an unstressed syllable, which is called the anacrusis (*Auftakt*), sometimes indicated A. Thus the first line of the song by Wolfram von Eschenbach (MF III) would be scanned as follows:

x(A)  /  x  /  x  /  x  /
Ein wîp mac wol erlouben mir

Here we have an anacrusis followed by four feet.

Although this pattern is the norm, there are variations. An individual foot may contain one stressed and two unstressed syllables (a dactyl), and sometimes this pattern is sustained over more than one foot and even throughout a poem:

/  x  x  /  x  x  /  x  x  /  x
Leitlîche blicke unde grôzlîche riuwe
/  x  x  /  x  x  /  x  x  /
hânt mir daz herze und den lîp nâch verlorn.

This opening of a song by Heinrich von Morungen (XIII) is given its stately movement by Morungen's fondness for dactyls. Note that elision takes place between words when a word ending with a vowel is followed by a word that has an initial vowel (*herze und = herz' und*).

Equally, a foot may contain no unstressed syllable at all, as is the case with the second foot of the opening of this famous early song:

```
/  x   /   /  x   /
Du bist mîn, ich bin dîn
```

What gives a line its distinctive quality and ultimately establishes the rhythm of a poem is the cadence, the ending of the line. The traditional designation follows that of Heusler and, in its simplest terms, is as follows:

1. Masculine (*männlich voll* = mv) describes two situations:

a) where the final beat falls on a stressed syllable, not followed by an unstressed syllable:

```
x  /  x  /  x  /  x  /
Ich wil von ir niht ledic sîn (Reinmar der Alte IX,3,1)
```

b) where the final beat falls on a *short* stressed syllable followed by an *unstressed* syllable. In this respect it is very important to note the distinction in classical MHG between short and long vowels (thus *sagen* but *vrâgen*; *tote* = godson but *tôte* = corpse). Note that in the following example *klagen* (with *short* stem vowel) is treated as if it were a word of only *one* syllable:

```
x  /  x  /  x  /  x  / , x  x   /
Sît ich den sumer truoc riuwe unde klagen (Hartmann von Aue I,1)
```

2. Feminine (*weiblich voll* = wv). The final beat falls on a long stressed syllable, followed by an unstressed syllable. A long stressed syllable is one which contains a long vowel or a diphthong, or a short vowel followed by a double consonant. Thus, for example:

```
x /  x  /  x  /  x  /  x  /  x
Owê, war umbe volg ich tumben wâne (Heinrich von Morungen XVII,1,1)
```

and

```
/  x   / x  x  / x  x  /  x
Ursprinc bluomen, loup ûz dringen (Wolfram von Eschenbach VI,1,1)
```

3. Feminine double stress (*klingend* = k): in this case the last beat falls on a final syllable immediately after a stressed long syllable:

```
/  /  x  /  x  /  x  /  /
Grôz angest hân ich des gewunnen (Morungen XXXII,3,1)
```

4. Metrically incomplete (*stumpf* = s): here the final foot is missing, and a rest is postulated. Thus, in the following, long line, which should contain eight beats, the second half line ends in a rest:

```
x   / x  /   x  / x /  /   x / x  /  (/)
Mich dunket niht sô guotes noch sô lobesam (Anonymous X,1)
```

This cadence is used with great effect by Walther in his refrain *tandaradei* in "Under der linden an der heide", where the suggestion that something is missing evokes a multitude of innuendoes.

Not surprisingly, the development of metrical form in the lyric is one of increasing complexity. The early songs are mostly in the long eight-beat line, sometimes broken by a caesura, which characterizes early Germanic poetry and confirms the idea of a native tradition. There are also examples of an even simpler, four-beat line. Sometimes the two are mixed, as in this strophe by Der von Kürenberg(I,1):

> 'Vil lieben vriunt <*verkiesen*>, daz ist schedelîch;
> swer sînen vriunt behaltet, daz ist lobelîch.
> > die site wil ich minnen.
> > > bite in, daz er mir holt sî, als er hie bevor was,
> > > und man in, waz wir redeten, dô ich in ze jungest sach.'

('It is not good to abandon a beloved friend, but if a man keeps his friend then this will earn him praise, and I will welcome such behavior. Ask him to be kind to me as he used to be, and remind him of what we said to one another when last we met.')

This strophe demonstrates several other features of the form of that period: the rhyming in couplets, the acceptance of assonance, and the short, unrhymed line, often described as the "orphan" (*Waise*).

As time went by and the impact of the Romance lyric came to be felt in matters of theme and language, so too did the form become more complex, and most notably, the tripartite division became frequent. In this arrangement, there are two identical groups of lines, the *Stollen*, which together form the *Aufgesang*, followed by a third section which is different in form (the *Abgesang*). If one were to think of this with its musical accompaniment, then the first and second portions would have the same melody, the third a distinct one. Sometimes there was a corresponding change in emphasis in the content. An example would be the following first strophe of a song by Friedrich von Hausen (XII,1):

> Ich lobe got der sîner güete,
> > daz er mir ie verlêch die sinne,
> daz ich si nam in mîn gemüete;
> > wan si ist wol wert, daz man si minne.
> Noch bezzer ist, daz man ir hüete,
> > danne iegelîcher sînen willen
> > > spræche, daz si ungerne hôrte,
> > > und mir die vröide gar zerstôrte.

(I praise God who in His loving kindness ever prompted me to take her into my heart, for she is truly worthy of love. It is better that she should be protected than that anyone should declare his unwelcome intentions and as a result completely destroy my happiness.)

The first four lines, rhyming ab,ab, constitute the *Aufgesang*, the remaining four the *Abgesang*. While the *Aufgesang* praises the virtue of the lady, the *Abgesang* breaks new ground with its treatment of the related but essentially new theme of *hüete*, surveillance. The *Aufgesang* and the *Abgesang* are linked here by meter and by the fact that the ab rhyme continues into the *Abgesang*, followed by the cc (hôrte: zerstôrte) of the last two lines.

The following strophe by Heinrich von Morungen (I,1) shows another more intricate manipulation of the threefold structure:

> Si ist ze allen êren ein wîp wol erkant,
>  schoener gebærde, mit zühten gemeit,
>   sô daz ir lop in dem rîche umbe gêt.
> als der mân wol verre über lant
>  liuhtet des nahtes wol lieht unde breit,
>   sô daz sîn schîn al die welt umbevêt,
>    Als ist mit güete umbevangen diu schône.
>  des man ir jêt,
>   si ist aller wîbe ein krône.

(She is a woman famous for her great honor, beautiful in gesture and with joyful good-breeding, so that praise of her circulates in the Empire. Just as the moon radiates across the land at night, bright and huge, so that its light embraces the whole world, so too is the lovely lady encircled with virtue. Because of this people say of her that she is the crown of all ladies.)

The strophic form would be expressed:

> 4mv a
> 4mv b
> 4mv c
> repeated
>
> 4wv d
> 3mv c
> 3wv d

The short penultimate line which links back to the rhyme of the *Aufgesang* is deliberately startling in its effect, and the repetition of the rhyme binds the strophe more closely together. Sometimes the effect of binding parts of the poem together is achieved by the echoing of a particular rhyme between one strophe and another, or even all the strophes of the poem: such echoes are called *Responsionen*.

Altogether the development in the art of the Minnesang was towards greater complexity and a virtuosity in the manipulation of metrical form which matched the increasing diversity of theme and language. Almost certainly there will have been times when the handling of the metrical pattern became, if not exactly an end in itself, nevertheless a vital component of the poet's expertise. Consider, for example, the deliberate playfulness in this strophe by Heinrich von Morungen, the movement of which continues throughout the song (VIII):

Sach ieman die vrouwen,
die man mac schouwen
in dem venster stân?
diu vil wolgetâne
diu tuot mich âne
sorgen, die ich hân.
Si liuhtet sam der sunne tuot
gegen dem liehten morgen.
ê was si verborgen.
dô muost ich sorgen.
die wil ich nu lân.

(Has anyone seen the lady who is standing at the window? The beautiful one takes away all my sorrows. She shines like the sun on a bright morning. Previously it(= she) was hidden away and I could only grieve, but now I will leave my grief behind.)

Mastery of form is one of the principal poetic features of Morungen, and Walther von der Vogelweide displays great dexterity in his adaptation of meter to suit his widely ranging themes. In the songs of Wolfram von Eschenbach, too, the relatively small number of songs is marked by an extraordinary command of highly individualized metrical patterns.

## Types within the Genre

Certain distinct types of song are recognized within the overall concept of the Minnesang, although there are times when these may overlap. The woman's lament (*Frauenklage*) is quite frequent at the earlier stage, with some of the anonymous poets, Der von Kürenberg, and Dietmar von Aist excelling in songs which present the situation from the point of view of the woman, while Meinloh von Sevelingen and Kaiser Heinrich, at their rather later date, were also capable of displaying this allegiance to the older tradition alongside the more modern viewpoint. The latter placed the lady at some distance from the emotion, as the recipient of devotion from her knight but rarely herself displaying an active involvement in it. Yet even as ardent an adherent of the convention as Reinmar von Hagenau could bring himself to offer the woman's standpoint in the famous song in which she pours out her feelings to the messenger, only to retract them at the end (XXVIII).

Actual dialogue is rare until Wolfram von Eschenbach and Neidhart, but it is a component of some of the dawn songs (*tageliet*), a common type in European love poetry of the period. It probably entered medieval German poetry with the charming song 'Slâfest du vriedel ziere?' ('Are you asleep, my lovely love?') which is attributed to Dietmar von Aist (XIII). The lovers are sleeping in the open air and are awakened by the birds' song, only to realize that they must part. As time went on, the emotion and dramatic potential of this situation was exploited, notably by Heinrich von Morungen and Wolfram von Eschenbach. The dawn songs of Wolfram represent the peak of this form of love lyric in German, combining as they do the lyrical and the epic qualities inherent in the very concept of a perfect mutual love threatened from outside and alien to the society in which it is conducted (see p. 202 ff.). On the face of it, it seems a very long way from Dietmar's delicate portrayal of the parting of two lovers in the early morning to Wolfram's majestic song "Sîne klâwen durch die wolken sint geslagen" (MF II; see p. 204), yet they are part of a continuum, which in turn belongs to this tradition in world literature.

A common type of song, particularly in the earlier poets, is the *Wechsel*, in which, as the word suggests, there is an exchange between the man and the woman, not as a direct conversation, for very often the pair are far apart, but in a series of strophes which relate, to a greater or lesser extent, to one another. They are commenting on the same situation, displaying their respective viewpoints, and sometimes the language and thought of the one is taken up by the other. Moreover, the strophes are bound together by the same metrical pattern. Many examples of the *Wechsel* will be found, among them Friedrich von Hausen IX, Albrecht von Johansdorf VIII, Heinrich von Morungen X, XXVIII, and XXX, which is also a dawn song and a lament.

A variation on this is the address of each to a messenger, in itself a development of the messenger song (*botenliet*). There are two distinct types of messenger song, the one in which the messenger himself speaks (cf. Dietmar von Aist, XI; Walther von der Vogelweide L.112,35; Reinmar von Hagenau XXVII, which is a conversation between the lady and the messenger) and that in which one or other of the couple, or sometimes each in turn, addresses the messenger, who does not himself speak (cf. Der von Kürenberg,I; Dietmar von Aist,II).

The crusading song is a development of the love lyric, often having its source in the conflict between the service of the lady and the service of God. The earliest examples in German stem from Friedrich von Hausen, V, VI, VII, but it is a significant aspect of the work of a number of other poets: Hartmann von Aue, VI, XVII; Albrecht von Johansdorf, II, IIIa, V, XIII; Reinmar von Hagenau, XXX, XXXI. In a poet like Walther von der Vogelweide, the theme of the crusade and the exhortation to participate in it lead to songs which are no longer within the category of the Minnesang but belong to his broader contribution in the field of political and philosophical poetry.

## Minnesang—Bibliography

Among the great deal of literature available, the following should be especially useful:

Bergner, Heinz, ed. *Lyrik des Mittelalters. Probleme und Interpretationen*. Stuttgart: Reclam, 1983. 2 vols. (= UB, 7896, 7897).

Vol. 1 contains Middle Latin (Paul Klopsch), Old Provencal (Dietmar Rieger), Old French (Friedrich Wolfzettel); Vol. 2 has MHG (Ulrich Müller), Middle English (Heinz Bergner) lyric poems, with mod. Germ. trans. and interpretations. Highly recommended as source for comprehensive sample of Minnesang.

Edwards, Cyril, Ernst Hellgart, and Norbert Ott, eds. *Lied im Deutschen Mittelalter. Überlieferung, Typen, Gebrauch*. (Papers of the Chiemsee-Colloquium, 1991). Tübingen: Niemeyer, 1996.

Papers on a wide variety of lyric types and other aspects of MHG (and later) lyric poetry. Affords a good overview of contemporary research.

Fromm, Hans, ed. *Der deutsche Minnesang.* Darmstadt: Wiss. Buchges., 1961. [5]1972 (= WdF, 15).

Reprint of 10 significant articles on Minnesang from 1914 to 1956.

____, ed. *Der deutsche Minnesang, II. Band.* Darmstadt: Wiss. Buchges., 1985 (= WdF, 608).

Reprint of 15 additional important articles by leading scholars from 1960 to 1981.

Goldin, Frederick, ed. and trans. *German and Italian Lyrics of the Middle Ages.* Garden City, NY: Anchor Press/Doubleday, 1973. Part I: German Lyrics. Part II: Italian Lyrics. (= Anchor Books, AO-71).

Sel. of poems by various poets with short intros., texts with facing English prose trans. German lyrics: pp. 1-201.

Jungbluth, Günther, ed. *Interpretationen mittelhochdeutscher Lyrik.* Bad Homburg, Berlin, Zürich: Gehlen 1969.

A collection of original essays by acknowledged experts in this field.

Müller, Ulrich, ed. *Minne ist ein swaerez spil. Neue Untersuchungen zum Minnesang und zur Geschichte der Liebe im Mittelalter.* Göppingen: Kümmerle, 1986 (= GAG, 440).

Nine essays by individual specialists. Listed here because it is a fairly recent book and readily available, it is definitely for the more informed reader.

____. In: Heinz Bergner (1983, II, 7-227).

Excellent selection of poems, discussion of background, translations, and interpretations.

Räkel, Hans-Herbert S. *Der deutsche Minnesang. Eine Einführung mit Texten und Materialien.* Munich: Beck, 1986 (= Beck'sche Elementarbücher).

For someone who is trying to deal with individual poems, possibly without a great deal of additional guidance. Quite a number of well-selected examples are presented with translations and analyses. Serves the purposes of both the relative beginner and the more informed reader.

Richey, M.F. *Essays on Mediaeval German Poetry.* Oxford: Blackwell; New York: Barnes & Noble, [2]1969.

Originally published in 1943, this volume is a basic introduction to some of the most important examples of the Minnesang. The assessments seem sometimes rather old-fashioned, but they are still quite perceptive introductions to a first reading of the poems, some of which are given in translation.

Sayce, Olive. *The Medieval German Lyric 1150-130. The Development of Its Themes and Forms in their European Context.* Oxford: Clarendon, 1982.

This is a most authoritative study and very much to be recommended. Extremely clearly set out and very readable, a substantial complement, much wider in its range and purpose, to the other volume by Olive Sayce listed above.

Schweikle, Günther. *Minnesang.* Stuttgart: Metzler, 1989. [2]1995 (= Sammlung Metzler, 244).

One of the completely revised volumes in the series, it constitutes a clear and scholarly handbook on the subject, with numerous bibliographical items.

_____, ed. *Minnesang in neuer Sicht.* Stuttgart: Metzler, 1994.

This contains 16 articles on a wide range of issues, some of them fairly general, others relating to specific poems.

Tervooren, Helmut, comp. *Bibliographie zum Minnesang und zu den Dichtern aus "Des Minnesangs Frühling."* Berlin: Erich Schmidt, 1969 (= Biblio. z. dt. Lit. d. Mas., 3).

Excellent bibliography, arranged by topics, as far as it goes (1968). Unfortunately not continued.

Thomas, J. Wesley. *Medieval German Lyric Verse in English Translation.* Chapel Hill: Univ. North Carolina Press, 1968 (= UNC Studies in Germanic Langs. & Lits., 60).

Contains brief introductions to groups of poets and individuals, followed by translations into English verse. A useful first introduction to the subject.

Wapnewski, Peter. *Waz ist Minne. Studien zur mittelhochdeutschen Lyrik.* Munich: Beck, 1975.

Another series of essays, all by Wapnewski, and some quite provocative. Particularly pertinent for Walther von der Vogelweide.

Wehrli, Max, ed. and trans. *Deutsche Lyrik des Mittelalters.* Zürich: Manesse, 1955. [2]1962. 36 miniatures from the Manesse Ms.

Sel. from MHG texts, with Mod. Ger. trans. A very pleasant volume, perhaps more decorative than scholarly in its intention though it contains some pertinent comments.


## Spruchdichtung

Moving away from the realm of the love lyric, we need to consider also this important component of medieval German lyric. The term *Spruch* is used in modern German to denote a type of poetry usually of a didactic nature. It is a word associated particularly with the work of Walther von der Vogelweide who, alongside his large contribution to the Minnesang, composed a great many strophes of different content, often quite weighty poems which were, however, almost certainly intended to be sung, hence the controversy which surrounds the appropriateness of the word *Spruch* which seems to suggest recitation rather than singing. Often the basis of a *Spruch* was a proverbial phrase or an aphorism, although this could often be contained, usually at the beginning of a poem or as its pithy conclusion, in a series of connected strophes.

Examples of the *Spruch* are found in the work of Herger and Spervogel, in the early period, while later Reinmar von Zweter, Heinrich von Meißen (otherwise known as Frauenlob), and Der Marner were among the most significant poets active in this field in the post-Walther period. The manuscripts do not make a distinction between the Minnesang and this gnomic poetry, including songs of both kinds indiscriminately for the most part, although sometimes there appears to be an attempt at sectionalizing. Sometimes it is difficult to impose a distinction, since an element of didacticism may be present in what is essentially a love song, for example, and some poets were equally at home in both kinds of composition.

## The *Leich*

This peculiarly Germanic type of poem deserves special mention. The word *Leich* is used to describe a sequence of unequal strophes and it is a genre which was developed during the 13th century in German. Originally the word *leich* referred to a song which was accompanied by an instrument, but at the back of the development is the French word *lai* which described a form well established in the Old French period and corresponded to the Old Provençal *descort*. The subject matter of both *lais* and *descorts* is largely secular, with love and loyalty dominating as themes, but the possibility of religious themes existed for the *lai*, as it came to do increasingly for the *leich*. In German, there were two distinct developments: the religious *leich* and the secular *leich*. The only poet of whom we can definitely say that he produced an example of both is Konrad von Würzburg (see p. 356). The term *leich* to denote a special kind of poetic composition occurs for the first time in Ulrich von Lichtenstein's *Frauendienst*, who provides what amounts to a definition before his own example (1373, 2 ff.). It is clear from what he says that the *leich* is distinct from a *liet*: it can be read, but it is intended to be accompanied by instruments, and in particular Ulrich mentions that many a fiddler was grateful to him for pitching the notes so high.

There are a number of other examples of what may be called the secular *leich* throughout the 13th century (Otto von Botenlouben, Der von Gliere, Konrad von Würzburg) , some of them coming into the category of *Tanzleich*, since the emphasis on the musical accompaniment led naturally to the association with dancing (Tannhäuser, Ulrich von Winterstetten).

Manuscript C attributes to Ulrich von Gutenberg a work which comes under the category of *leich* and is the only example of a secular *leich* in *Des Minnesangs Frühling*, which does, however, contain what may well be the first example of a *leich*, one which falls into the category of "religious *leich*" and is attributed to Heinrich von Rugge. This is recorded, however, only in a Latin manuscript containing various theological writings (manuscript N): it has thus been kept distinct from the other songs in the Minnesang tradition which are attributed to Heinrich von Rugge and recorded in the principal Minnesang manuscripts.

One of the principal examples of the religious *leich* is that by Walther von der Vogelweide. This is a complex prayer addressed to the persons of the Trinity, and to the Virgin Mary as mediator between God and sinful man ("Got, dîner trinitate, . . ."). It does not surprise us that Walther, who dominates German lyric poetry for a generation and makes an enduring impact on it, tried his hand at this distinctive form of the lyric, just as Konrad von Würzburg, one of the great masters of the narrative, was to do after him.

## THE EARLY LYRIC

The earliest songs extant in German probably go back to the middle of the 12th century, possibly even a little before 1150, and, despite some attributions in the manuscripts, they are usually described as "anonymous." They are characterized by a simplicity of thought and structure, often single strophes, and probably emerge from a native German tradition, untouched as yet by the Romance influences which were soon to put their stamp on the love poetry of medieval Germany. However, it is possible to point to Latin models at this very early stage.

The tiny poem "du bist mîn, ich bin dîn" (I.VIII) stands in many anthologies as one of the very earliest of German love poems. The text is contained in a love letter, written in Latin, and purporting to come from a young woman. This simple declaration of love and the presumption that it is returned is expressed in six lines whose metrical structure is more intricate than might at first sight seem the case. Similarly, much is contained in what appears to be a very simple little poem: the mutuality of this love which will last for ever and the image, recurrent in the folk song, of the lost key to the heart in which the beloved is secured.

It is notable that the lady is the speaker in this little poem, as in a number of these very early examples, and it is her love that is declared. This point is worth noting, because in the "traditional" Minnesang, the knight often dominates, and the lady is a shadowy figure, the object of his devotion but often herself quite passive. At this early stage, there is recognition of the suffering of the woman, as in the little lament "Grüenet der walt allenthalben" (I.VII), which is recorded in the *Carmina Burana* in juxtaposition to what appears to be a rather clumsy Latin translation. Here, too, the extraordinary economy of the strophe yields much, in the plaintive cry of the lady for her absent lover, who has ridden away from her and remained away so long, leaving her alone and unloved against the contrasting background of the forest in full growth.

The relationship between nature and love is a powerful ingredient in a number of these songs. In " 'Sô wol dir, sumerwunne!' " ('Hail to you, joys of summer!': VIII. V, where it is attributed to Dietmar von Aist), nature seems to be in tune with the lady's sense of loss, and in " 'Diu linde ist an dem ende nu jârlanc lieht unde blôz' " (I. XI), the opening line, with its description of the bereft linden tree, leads to a bitter recognition on the part of the lady of her lover's infidelity. In " 'Mich dunket niht sô guotes noch sô lobesam' " (I.X: 'It seems to me that nothing is so good nor so worthy of praise'), the more optimistic view of love is expressed by the lady in her description of the rose and the singing of the birds in the forest.

It is not easy to distinguish the tone of these early anonymous songs from others of about this period which can be attributed to named poets. The difference lies often in their form, as the single strophe gave way to a rather more complex metrical structure. To this slightly later stage of the early period of German lyric poetry belongs a group of poets sometimes described as the "Danubians", who were probably active in about 1150-1170. The earliest of these with at least a partial identification is **Der von Kürenberg** (II), whose work is extant only in the large Heidelberg manuscript, with 15 strophes under his name. This name, however, may have been given to the poet by the compiler of the manuscript only on the evidence of the lines in which the lady tells how she heard a knight singing "in Kürenberges wîse" (II.2,3), a phrase which is usually taken to be a reference by the poet to his own characteristic melody. Where he came from and when he was composing are also a matter of speculation, although the assumption is that he was active in Bavaria or Austria in the second half of the 12th century.

Of these 15 strophes, 10 are *Frauenstrophen* and 5 *Männerstrophen*, and, although the single strophe poem was doubtless favored at this time, there is clear metrical evidence that some of these strophes should be seen as pairs, the one a response to the other, though not to be construed precisely as a reply. This type of poem, the *Wechsel*, was popular at this time, and it brought out both the sense of a mutual relationship and a certain dramatic quality, with the figures of the man and the woman, each speaking in his and her context and often in distinctive language, yet with the strophes linked by meter and sometimes by a particular word or phrase. Thus we have, for example, the vivid poem already mentioned, in which the lady describes herself on the battlements late at night and threatens to force a knight to submit to her unless he leaves her lands, while, in the second strophe, the knight hastily orders his horse and his armor, anxious to leave her land rather than submit to her will. In the other poem clearly falling into the category of *Wechsel*, the lady sends a message through a third party, bidding him to *remind* her knight of what they said to one another at their last meeting, while the response uses the same verb, asking her why she *reminds* him of the pain of separation (II.I).

The existence of these two fairly clear-cut examples of the *Wechsel* leads to a problem with what is probably the best known of the Kürenberger's poems, the falcon song which has prompted some lively if inconclusive debate among scholars (II.6-7):

'ich zôch mir einen valken    mêre danne ein jâr.
    dô ich in gezamete    als ich in wolte hân
        und ich im sîn gevidere    mit golde wol bewant,
        er huob sich ûf vil hôhe    und floug in anderiu lant.

Sît sach ich den valken    schône fliegen:
    er fuorte an sînem fuoze    sîdene riemen,
        und was im sîn gevidere    alrôt güldîn.
        got sende si zesamene    die geliep wellen gerne sîn.'

('I nurtured a falcon for more than a year. When I had made it as tame as I wanted it to be and had entwined its plumage with gold, it flew up and away into other lands. Since then I have seen the falcon flying and looking beautiful. On its foot it was wearing silken ribbons and its plumage was all red gold. May God bring together those who wish to love one another.')

Much hinges on whether the strophes constitute a *Wechsel*, with the man speaking first, or whether both strophes should be attributed to the lady.

These strophes have a vitality and freshness all their own, and there is every reason to think of them as relating to an existing native tradition, which had already given rise to the anonymous songs treated above. The lady is as much in evidence as the knight, and her love is expressed in urgent, often suppliant tones. Yet there is already a hint of imperiousness in her demeanor, as there will be increasingly and overwhelmingly as the Minnesang tradition develops. Moreover, there are other features which will become characteristic motifs of the genre, and which suggest, already at this early stage, the influence of Romance models. One of the most evident of these is the need for security, in a world peopled by spies threatening the well-being of the lovers (II.1,3; II.8,3). The awareness of this danger leads to the man's instruction to his lady that she should practice subterfuge and, just as the morning star hides itself, direct her attention towards another man so that no one will know the true state of affairs between the pair of them (II.11).

For an interpretation of this song and an assessment of some of the literature, see Wapnewski (1975, 23-46).

Probably just a little later than Der von Kürenberg is a poet who resembles him in a number of ways yet shows some significant developments. **Dietmar von Aist** (VIII), likewise from the Danube region, appears to have been more prolific and more varied in tone and technique, if the evidence of the manuscripts is to be trusted. However, it is precisely the discrepancies in the manuscript tradition which cause the problems in attribution, since the 30 strophes assigned to Dietmar in the three principal manuscripts are not consistently so assigned, and the diversity of the material attributed to him suggests that the poems cannot all be by him. Indeed, there are some poems which are attributed to Dietmar in one manuscript and to other, named, poets elsewhere. All this confusion suggests that, at the time of the compilation of the manuscripts, there were deemed to be sufficient likenesses among these poems as to justify their inclusion under the single name where no other obvious authorship presented itself, although the disparities may well have been evident even then. It is also, of course, possible to see Dietmar as a poet of some range, capable of bridging the early period and its later developments. A further complication is that the Dietmar von Aist recorded historically is of a date too early—his death is recorded in 1171—to justify the attribution of all these poems to him. Again we are left with an unanswerable question, but the usually accepted view is that the Dietmar von Aist who composed the bulk of the poems under his name is a later member of the same family and not himself historically attested.

Although, like Der von Kürenberg, he did apparently compose single strophe poems, there is a preponderance of poems of two and even three strophes. Again, there is an inclination towards the *Wechsel*, and, as in Kürenberg, the strophes are linked by metrical form and, sometimes quite loosely, by theme or situation. In II, the messenger is used to convey between two people the thoughts of love and grief at separation. There is also in the poems an awareness of the suffering implicit in love, and, not least, the need for the lovers to protect themselves from the spiteful onlookers.

As in the anonymous songs, nature is in tune with their love, and, in III, the optimistic tone reflects the end of winter and the coming of spring:

> Ahî nu kumet uns diu zît,    der kleinen vogellîne sanc.
> ez grüenet wol diu linde breit,    zergangen ist der winter lanc.
> nu siht man bluomen wol getân,    an der heide üebent sie ir schîn.
> des wirt vil manic herze frô,    des selben troestet sich daz mîn.

(Ah, now the time is coming for the singing of the little birds. The lovely broad linden tree is turning green; the long winter has passed. Now we can see the beautiful flowers, showing themselves on the heath. Many a heart rejoices at this and my own finds consolation.)

An idea which will become a characteristic feature in the later Minnesang is of the edifying power of love:

> du hâst getiuret mir den muot.
> swaz ich dîn bezzer worden sî,    ze heile müeze ez mir ergân.
> (III.2,2-3)

(You have raised me inwardly, and if I have become a better person because of you, then may this bring salvation to me.)

Perhaps the following poem (II,4-5) demonstrates most effectively the qualities of the *Wechsel*:

> Uf der linden obene    dâ sanc ein kleinez vogellîn.
> vor dem walde wart ez lût.    dô huop sich aber daz herze mîn
> an eine stat da'z ê dâ was.    ich sach die rôsebluomen stân,
> die manent mich der gedanke vil,    die ich hin zeiner frouwen hân.
>
> 'Ez dunket mich wol tûsent jâr,    daz ich an liebes arme lac.
> sunder âne mîne schulde    vremedet er mich menegen tac.
> sît ich bluomen niht ensach    noch enhôrte der vogel sanc,
> sît was mir mîn vröide kurz    und ouch der jâmer alzelanc.'

(High up in the linden tree a little bird was singing, making its noise at the edge of the forest. Then did my heart go back again to where it previously had been. I saw the roses blooming there, reminding me of the many thoughts which I have of a lady.
'It seems to me a thousand years at least since I was lying in the arms of my beloved. Now without any fault of mine he has been estranging me from him for many a day. Since then I have not seen the flowers nor heard the song of the birds; since then my joy has been short-lived, and my grief all too long.')

Here we have the same situation viewed from the perspective, first of the man, then of the woman. Both lament their separation in wistful, yearning terms. The birds' song and the flowers link the strophes, yet, whereas for the man they bring with them the memory of his lady, the woman fails to see or hear them, so great is her sorrow.

Two charming and important songs are attributed to Dietmar in manuscript C but regarded as not authentic Dietmar by a number of editors. These are the poignant woman's lament "Ez stuont ein frouwe alleine" (A lady was standing alone: IV), and the poem which begins " 'Slâfst du, friedel ziere?' " (Are you asleep my lovely love?: XIII) and is the earliest extant example of the dawn song in German. Editors who argue that these are not by Dietmar point to their archaic features and prefer to include them among the anonymous poems. However, since other editors continue to include them among Dietmar's songs and since they are too significant to be overlooked, they are included here, as examples of those poems which contribute to the range in the poems attributed to Dietmar, a range which, for some, is in itself too great to be acceptable.

IV describes the lady standing alone and gazing across the heath land, waiting for her lover to return. When she sees the falcon in flight, this prompts her lament, in which she points to the good fortune of the bird, which can fly wherever it chooses and select any tree in the forest. The implied envy of the freedom of the falcon is made more concrete when she transfers the verb choose (*kiesen*) to herself, for she has chosen a man, yet this has given rise to hostility from other lovely ladies. The poem ends with a cry of woe: 'Alas, why do they not leave me my love? I do not covet any of their sweethearts!' So much is implied in this subtle poem: the pain of separation and the strain of waiting, the restrictions imposed on the woman in this clandestine love affair, the social pressures and the spitefulness which have parted them. The poem is dominated by the single image of the soaring bird, free to pursue its own desires. The falcon, as we have already seen, and as we know from Kriemhild's famous dream, was a favorite symbol of love and of the beloved.

The same lingering sadness and the recognition of the pain of parting characterize the three-strophe dawn song:

'Slâfst du, friedel ziere?
man weckt uns leider schiere;
ein vogellîn sô wol getân
daz ist der linden an daz zwî gegân.'

"ich was vil sanfte entslâfen:
nu rüefstu, kint, Wâfen.
liep âne leit mac niht sîn.
swaz du gebiutest, daz leiste ich, vriundin mîn."

Diu frouwe begunde weinen:
'du rîtest hinnen und lâst mich eine.
wenne wilt du wider her zuo mir?
owê du vüerest mîne vröide sant dir!'

('Are you asleep, my lovely love? They will soon be waking us. A splendid little bird has hopped on to the branch of the linden tree.'
"I had fallen asleep very gently, but now,my child, you have given the call to arms. Joy without sorrow may not be. Whatever you command, my beloved, that I shall do."
The lady began to weep: 'You are riding away and leaving me alone. When will you come back to me? Alas, you take my joy away with you!')

More important than the arguments about the authenticity of this poem are its intrinsic qualities. The three slight strophes speak of love fulfilled yet threatened, and the two figures play an equal role against a background which is not so much described as implied: dawn, the bird's song, the linden tree, all ingredients of the dawn song, which enters German literature now apparently for the first time, to be raised two or three decades later by Wolfram von Eschenbach to an artistic peak (see p. 203 ff.). Yet already in this very early example in German, the poet, whether Dietmar von Aist or some other, unknown poet, manages to express the urgency of the situation and to convey the sense of threat which leads to the man's need to ride away, leaving the woman to lament alone.

In a fragile, lyric form, the dramatic potential is very much in evidence, as it so often is in these early poems.

The sense one has of Dietmar von Aist, as represented in the manuscripts, bridging the old and the incipient new is maintained in the work of the third poet in this group, **Meinloh von Sevelingen** (III), whose place of origin was almost certainly the town now known as Söflingen near Ulm on the Danube. While the single strophe which dominates is reminiscent of the older lyric, elements of a more reflective view of love emerge, as well as a much more developed sense of the relationship as one of service for reward. In this respect, Meinloh, composing in about 1180, anticipates the more cerebral, analytical mode of the "classical" Minnesänger. The influence of the Romance lyric is evident in poems which set out much more explicitly than ever before in German the conventions of courtly love. In place of the delicately impressionistic presentation of a mutual relationship which inflicts joy and sorrow on both parties is an unequal relationship in which the lady, superlatively beautiful and virtuous, dominates the man, who extols the edifying powers of love, addressing his admiration directly to his lady, or through a messenger. However, the lady is not yet the obdurate creature who comes to characterize so much of the later lyrics. She, too, is committed to this love and, stronger party that she is, she will defend it in spite of the opposition of rivals and spies. It looks, then, like a new view of the old relationship, but the tone is more one of confidence and even happiness. A certain defiance in face of hostility has replaced the yearning tone of the earlier lyrics.

Three further names belong within this early group: **Der Burggraf von Regensburg**, **Der Burggraf von Rietenburg**, and **Kaiser Heinrich**. Of these, the first two almost certainly belonged to the same family and were probably close contemporaries, though the poems of Der Burggraf von Regensburg have more in common with the older lyric, while those of Der Burggraf von Rietenburg look rather towards the future, with their reflections on the nature of love, and the concept of service (*dienst*), to be performed with constancy (*stæte*) and bring suffering (*swære*) as its reward. Indeed, *minne* is *ein sælic arbeit* (a blessed toil), he tells us, though the modern editors prefer *ein saelikeit* (a blessing), expressing in a simple antithesis the familiar duality of love (II,3).

A glance at the poems of the two burgraves shows the essential difference between them, with Regensburg favoring the Germanic long line familiar in Der von Kürenberg and Meinloh von Sevelingen and Rietenburg anticipating the short lines and tripartite form which characterize the later lyric with its marked Romance influence.

On the early lyric in general, see especially Räkel (1986, 21-39).

**Kaiser Heinrich** (IX) stands at the head of manuscripts B and C, where he has 3 poems attributed to him. The illustrations depict him with crown and scepter, and, despite some doubts which have been cast on his identity, there is general agreement that this is indeed the Emperor Heinrich VI, son of Friedrich Barbarossa. When he speaks of the lands over which he rules and the crown he wears and asserts that he would sacrifice them for the sake of his love, he is not playing with images but talking in real terms, though using recognizable poetic language. As in Rietenburg, there are "modern" elements in these three poems. They show the exposure to Romance models and the capacity to absorb their influence, alongside more archaic features. Two of the songs consist of two strophes each, one of them (I) indisputably a *Wechsel*, the other (II) probably also one. The third song (III) consists of four strophes in the more complex tripartite form and it comes much closer to the ideas of the conventional Minnesang, as the lover laments his separation from his lady yet hopes for fulfillment and reward.

In the poems of Kaiser Heinrich, Romance elements were already being assimilated into poems in the older mode, and, in the years and decades which followed, the influence of the Romance lyric becomes more apparent. The effect of the troubadours was on both form and substance, and, hardly surprisingly, this influence is observable in a group of poets who were geographically closer to France. Of these the best known is **Heinrich von Veldeke** (XI), whose reputation rests, however, more on his version of the *Roman d'Eneas* (see p. 122 ff.) than on his lyric output, substantial though this was, and Friedrich von Hausen, who stands for the beginnings of Minnesang in the Rhineland.

When Gottfried von Straßburg, in his literary excursus, praises Heinrich von Veldeke, he seems to be referring to his impact on both epic and lyric poetry in Germany. "Wie wol sanc er von minnen!" exclaims Gottfried (Ranke edition 4728), and the likelihood is that he is thinking of his contribution to the love lyric, as he almost certainly is when, some lines later, he refers to his words and melodies (4750). Gottfried's famous tribute to Heinrich von Veldeke for having grafted the first shoot in the German tongue (4738-4739) may refer to his lyric or his epic, or to both, but what is important is that Veldeke, who almost certainly composed in his native dialect, was nevertheless well known in High German regions and that Gottfried recognized his achievement in bringing French material into Germany.

Coming as he did from Veldeke near Spalbeke, in the medieval duchy of Lorraine, now Belgium, Heinrich von Veldeke was uniquely well placed to assimilate both French and German elements, and his lyric shows the unmistakable adoption of Romance conventions and attitudes. Veldeke composed his *Eneit* at the court of Hermann von Thüringen, and there, too, he was undoubtedly exposed to French influences in the art and culture which Hermann nurtured. Veldeke may well have been a prominent performer at the famous festival in Mainz in 1184, when the Emperor Barbarossa knighted his two sons and which Veldeke describes at first hand in relation to the wedding feast of Aeneas and Lavinia (see p. 124).

In typical Minnesänger fashion, love for Heinrich von Veldeke both demands service for reward and represents an edifying force. He is fully aware of the price exacted by love in terms of suffering and prolonged waiting, yet the emphasis is on the happiness to be gained rather than on the misery endured. There is a robust enjoyment of love explicit in his poetry, and sometimes this tips over into humor. Equally,though, he can write reflective, analytical poetry, with the analysis directed rather at the nature of love itself than at the effects on the lover. Thus he plays with the ideas, and the very word, of love in the following strophe (XII):

> Swer ze der minne ist sô vruot,
> daz er der minne dienen kan,
> und er durch minne pîne tuot,

*<wol im, derst ein sælic man!>*
Von minne kumet uns allez guot,
diu minne machet reinen muot,
waz solte ich sunder minne dan?

(Whoever is so wise in matters of love that he knows how to serve love and endures anguish on account of love *<good for him: he is a fortunate man!>*. From love all good things come to us. Love makes the mind pure. What then should I do without love?)

In accordance with the mood of happiness and enjoyment of love—a mood not generally observable in German love poetry until perhaps Heinrich von Morungen (see p. 252 ff.)—is the abundance of descriptions of nature. Nature had played a part in the earlier lyric, but Heinrich von Veldeke devotes quite lengthy descriptions to the natural setting, sometimes comparing it with the specific relationship or with the prevailing circumstances in the world at large. Thus, for example, the following poem (VII):

In den zîten, daz die rôsen
    erzeigent manic schoene blat,
sô vluochet man den vröidelôsen,
    die rüegaere sint an maniger stat
    Durch daz, wan sî der minne sint gehaz
und die minne gerne noesen.
got müez uns von den boesen loesen.

Man darf den boesen niht suochen (alt.: vluochen),
    in wirt dicke unsanfte wê,
wan si warten unde luochen,
    alse der springet in dem snê:
    Des sint sî vil deste mê gevê,
des darf doch niemen ruochen,
wan si suochen birn ûf den buochen.

(At the time when roses show many lovely petals, anyone who is unhappy is damned; there are critics all around who hate love and want to harm it. May God free us from those evil people.
You don't need to damn evil people. They are often terribly miserable anyway, for they lurk and spy [on lovers], like someone leaping [around blindly] in the snow [= a snow bank? a snowstorm?]. Consequently, they are all the more hostile, but don't bother about that because they are just looking for pears on a beech tree.)

A certain didacticism sometimes intrudes in Veldeke's poetry, as it does in this admittedly rather puzzling poem, and this tendency, often manifested in his single strophes, leads to a quality of *Spruchdichtung* in some of his poems, a significant new form at this stage, but one which was to develop in the more skillful hands of Walther von der Vogelweide (see p. 273 ff.).

Indeed, there is in Heinrich von Veldeke a mixture of tones which singles him out and possibly may account for his somewhat isolated position, for his work, for all its significance, did not provoke imitation. Other factors may, of course, also have played a part:

his originally isolated position geographically, and his language which, Gottfried's fulsome praise notwithstanding, may conceivably have constituted a barrier. This language is problematic to us, too. It is most likely that he wrote in his native dialect, but the manuscripts transmit this in a hybrid form which is largely High German but with Low German features. In 1947 Theodor Frings and Gabriele Schieb published a reconstruction of the poems in the Limburg dialect, and, despite the misgivings expressed about this enterprise and its success or otherwise, this is the form in which many editors present Veldeke's work. In the above quotations, we have chosen the normalized Middle High German of the manuscripts: in the 1977 edition of *Des Minnesangs Frühling*, the two versions are set side by side.

## THE "CLASSICAL" MINNESÄNGER

**Friedrich von Hausen (Hûsen) (X)** was a close contemporary of Veldeke's and was almost certainly also present at the great festival in Mainz in 1184. Indeed, the records show that he was in the entourage of Friedrich Barbarossa, and it was in his company, in the course of the Third Crusade, that he met his death, as the result of a fall from his horse in 1190. We thus know more about him than is often the case, and we have a picture of him as a courtly diplomat and as a crusader: the manuscripts depict him in this latter role.

His significance for the Minnesang is not only in his own right but as the instigator of a German tradition of courtly love lyric. Unlike Veldeke, he had his imitators and followers, but, like Veldeke, he was himself profoundly influenced by Romance predecessors, to the extent that at times precise models for his lyrics can be identified. The basic situation dominates: the man serves the lady with a devotion which is spoken of in terms of feudal allegiance. All hopes of happiness rest in the favor of the lady. She is a paragon of virtue, but in all likelihood he will not be rewarded despite his constancy (*stæte*) towards her. The lady is a shadowy figure, the passive recipient of this devotion but apparently unaware of his suffering if not positively indifferent to it. The tone of Hausen's poetry is controlled and measured: the conventions of secrecy and of never uttering criticism of his beloved are maintained in language and form which are themselves cool and controlled, with a tendency to analysis and an almost cerebral aloofness.

This controlled demeanor is well contained in the Provençal verse forms, with the tripartite division into *Stollen* and *Abgesang* lending itself to what is at times an intricate argument continuing over two or three strophes or sometimes even more. The following example, in which Hausen pursues the advantages and disadvantages of surveillance (*huote*), may serve to demonstrate much that is typical of him (XII):

> Ich lobe got der sîner güete,
> > daz er mir ie verlêch die sinne,
> daz ich sie nam in mîn gemüete;
> > wan si ist wol wert, daz man si minne.
> Noch bezzer ist, daz man ir hüete,
> > danne iegelîcher sînen willen

spræche, daz si ungerne hôrte,
und mir die vröide gar zerstôrte.

Doch bezzer ist, daz ich si mîde,
    danne si âne huote wære,
und ir deheiner mir ze nîde
    spræche, des ich vil gern enbære.
Ich hân si erkorn ûz allen wîben.
    lâze ich niht durch die merkære,
        vrömede ich si mit den ougen,
        si minnet iedoch mîn herze tougen.

Ein lîp was ie unbetwungen
    und doch gemuot von allen wîben.
alrêst hân ich rehte bevunden,
    waz man nâch liebem wîbe lîde.
Des muoz ich ze manigen stunden
    der besten vrowen eine mîden.
        des ist mîn herze dicke swære,
        als ez mit vröiden gerne wære.

Swie dicke ich lobe die huote,
    dêswâr ez wart doch nie mîn wille,
daz ich iemer in dem muote
    werde holt, die sô gar die sinne
Gewendet hânt, daz sî der guoten
    enpfrömden wellent staete minne.
        dêswâr, tuon ich in niht mêre,
        ich vereische doch gerne alle ir unêre.

(I praise God for His goodness in that He ever granted me the good sense to take her into my heart, for she is truly worthy to be loved. It is better that she should be guarded than that anyone should express his desire which she did not wish to hear and which would completely destroy my joy.

Yet it is better that I should avoid her than that she should be without surveillance and anyone speak to her out of spite for me, something which I could well do without. I have chosen her from among all women. Even if I do not neglect anything on account of the spies but keep my eyes away from her (for example), nevertheless my heart will love her secretly.

A man has always been unafflicted by all ladies, although he has not been unaware of them. Now for the first time I have really discovered what a man suffers on account of a beloved woman. Because of this I must often avoid one of the best ladies. Because of this my heart is often heavy when it would like to be joyful.

However often I may praise surveillance, in truth it was never my intention to be well inclined towards those who have so applied themselves to distancing the virtuous lady from steadfast love. Indeed, even if I never do anything else to them, I should nevertheless be glad to hear of their dishonor.)

Yet, before we give the impression of a poet so controlled as to be monotonously long-suffering, we should point to the occasional flashes of humor or self-mockery, as when he tells how he has sometimes been so deep in thoughts of love that he has wished people good morning in the evening (V,5-7) or when he reveals that his lady has told him that, though he may be called Aeneas, she is no Dido, ready to die of love for him (I,1-5). And, although he maintains his determination never to speak ill of his lady, he can at times turn his anger against Love itself, as he shows in the poem which begins with the lament "Wâfenâ, wie hat mich minne gelâzen!" (Alas, how has Love forsaken me!) and ends with his threat to poke out Love's crooked eye in revenge (XV).

Friedrich von Hausen's generally reserved, analytical style is well suited to a new theme which was already present in Romance poetry and which he introduces into the Minnesang. He was, after all, a crusader, and his commitment to the service of God is well expressed in poems which speak of the conflict between his duty to love and his religion. It is unclear, and indeed probably impossible to say with any certainty, in what order he composed his lyrics, but his decision to turn to the service of God, not as a rejection of worldly love but as a natural progression towards a higher goal, seems to be the logical continuation of the questions which he has already posed about love. In the poem already mentioned, he has gone to the heart of the matter with his question (XV, 3, 1-3):

> Waz mac daz sîn, daz diu welt heizet minne,
> und ez mir tuot sô wê ze aller stunde
> und ez mir nimet sô vil mîner sinne?

(What can that be that the world calls love and that causes me such pain at all times and so deprives me of my senses?)

It is God Himself who has encouraged him to love his lady (XII,1,1-3) and he has remained true to her despite her failure to grant him a reward (V,4). That, however, seems to be the crux: since no reward is forthcoming from her, he will turn his service—the same word—towards God:

> nu wil ich dienen dem, der lônen kan.

(Now I propose to serve Him who knows how to reward.)

Even so, the decision is not that clear-cut. God supersedes his lady as the foremost object of his devotion but that does not mean that he does not love her, to the extent that, in one famous and characteristically self-analytical poem, he represents his dilemma as a conflict between his heart and his body, the former wanting to remain behind with his lady while the latter wants to go off and fight the heathens (VI). There is not much color in the lyric of Friedrich von Hausen, in the way one can think of Veldeke's poems as colorful, or Morungen's as we shall see, yet this poem gains a vividness from our awareness that the poet was to perish as a crusader, in the service of God and, indirectly, of his lady.

See: Jackson, W. T. H. "Contrast Imagery in the Poems of Friedrich von Hausen."
*GR* 49 (1974): 7-16. Repr. in: W. T. H. Jackson. *The Challenge of the Medieval Text.*
New York: Columbia UP, 1985. Pp. 37-48.

It is possible to speak of a "school" of Friedrich von Hausen, poets who, in the last
decades of the 12th century, furthered this new German style of courtly love lyric. To this
group belong Ulrich von Gutenberg, Bligger von Steinach—remembered less for his
poetry than for Gottfried von Straßburg's enthusiastic praise of him in his literary excursus (4691 ff.)—Bernger von Horheim, Hartwig von Rute and Graf Rudolf von Fenis.
The two last named came from Bavaria and Switzerland, respectively, but the others
were geographically closer to Hausen and may have known him personally. Although
close examination reveals individual traits, the poets are linked by their conception of
love as *swære*, suffering to be endured with more or less equilibrium, and by their adherence to Romance models. Sometimes precise parallels can be drawn with troubadour
lyrics, but more often it is a case of a more general resemblance in thought and, of
course, in form.

Another poet of probably about the same period, at the turn of the 12th and 13th
centuries, is **Albrecht von Johansdorf** (XIV), whose quality is perhaps overshadowed
by the more obvious virtuosity and diversity of his contemporaries, yet whose very consistency demands attention here. His presentation of love has none of the playfulness one
finds elsewhere in the Minnesang but is characterized by an earnestness all its own. This
is not the cerebral, cool analysis of Friedrich von Hausen, but the unpretentious expression of an experience which has a certain ring of authenticity. The sense of an equality in
the relationship justifies the usually accepted division of the following strophes between
the lady and the man (VIII):

> 'Wie sich minne hebt, daz weiz ich wol:
>   wie si ende nimt, des weiz ich niht.
> ist daz ichs inne werden sol,
>   wie dem <*herzen*> herzeliep beschiht,
>     Sô bewar mich vor dem scheiden got,
>     daz wæn bitter ist.
>     disen kumber vürhte ich âne spot.
>
> Swâ zwei herzeliep gevriundent sich,
>   und ir beider minne ein triuwe wirt,
> die sol niemen scheiden, dunket mich,
>   al die wîle unz sî der tôt verbirt.
>     Waer diu rede mîn, ich tæte alsô:
>     verliure ich mînen vriunt,
>     seht, sô wurde ich niemer mêre vrô.
>
> Dâ gehoeret manic stunde zuo,
>   ê daz sich gesamne ir zweier muot.
> dâ daz ende unsanfte tuo,
>   ich wæne wol, daz sî niht guot.
>     Lange sî ez mir unbekant.

und werde ich iemen liep,
der sî sîner triuwe an mir gemant.'

Der ich diene und iemer dienen wil,
diu sol mîne rede vil wol verstân.
spræche ich mêre, des wurde alze vil.
ich wil ez allez an ir güete lân.
Ir gnâden der bedarf ich wol.
und wil si, ich bin vrô;
Und wil sî, sô ist mîn herze leides vol.

('I know full well how love begins, but I do not know how it ends. If I am to discover how love befalls a heart, then may God protect me from a parting which, I believe, is bitter. I truly fear that misery.

Whenever two hearts are bound in friendship and their love becomes one single loyalty, it seems to me that no one should separate them, as long as death spares them. If it were my business this is what I should do: if I were to lose my friend I should never be happy again.

It takes many hours for two people to join together. When the end is painful, then I really think that is not good. May it remain unknown to me for a long time and, if I ever become dear to anyone, let him be mindful of his loyalty towards me.'

She whom I serve and always will serve shall fully understand what I am saying. If I were to say anything more, that would be too much. I propose to leave it all to her goodness. I am in sore need of her mercy, and if she desires it, then I am happy. And if she desires it, then my heart is full of sorrow.)

Although Albrecht von Johansdorf's lyric shows some range of metrical pattern, there is, as indicated, a relative uniformity of tone, a seriousness which does not admit of the playfulness of some other Minnesänger. That does not mean, however, that he is not capable of manipulating familiar ideas in an original way, as in the poem where he engages in a debate with his lady. The repartee is quite lively, as he laments his wasted service of her in the following two strophes, the second and third of a long poem of seven strophes (XII):

"Mînen senden kumber
    klage ich, liebe vrouwe mîn."
'wê, waz sagent ir tumber?
    ir mugent iuwer klage wol lâzen sîn.'
        "Vrowe, ich enmac ir niht enbern."
        'sô wil ich in tûsent jâren niemer iuch gewern.'

"Neinâ, küneginne!
    daz mîn dienst sô iht sî verlorn!"
'ir sint âne sinne,
    daz ir bringent mich in selhen zorn.'
        "Vrowe, iuwer haz tuot mir den tôt."
        'wer hât iuch, vil lieber man, betwungen ûf die nôt?'

("My dear lady, I lament my yearning misery." 'Alas, you foolish man, what are you saying? You must abandon your lament.' "My lady, I cannot give it up." 'Then I will never grant you your wish in a thousand years.'
"Oh no! your majesty! let my service not go to waste!" 'You have lost your senses if you make me so angry.' "My lady, your hostility is killing me." 'My darling man, who has forced you into this trouble?')

His protestations that her beauty has caused him his anguish are lost on her, however, and although she finally holds out the prospect of reward to him, this is not in the way he had hoped (XII,7,3 ff.):

'iu sol wol gelingen,
     âne lôn sô sult ir niht bestân.'
          "Wie meinent ir daz, vrowe guot?"
          'daz ir dest werder sint unde dâ bî hôchgemuot.'

('You will be very successful: you will not remain without reward.' "What do you mean, virtuous lady?" 'That you shall be all the nobler, and happy too.')

Personal edification is hardly what he had looked for from this relationship.

The conventional frustrations of courtly love lead elsewhere to a surprising possibility that Johansdorf puts as a question: would it be proper and not inconstancy to offer allegiance simultaneously to two women, in secret, of course? (IV,2). The answer comes in a blunt rejoinder, which most editors and commentators interpret as coming from the woman, and not, as the manuscripts have it, from another man:

"wan solz den man erlouben unde den vrouwen niht."

(wan = man: "The men shall be allowed to do it, but not the ladies.")

The lady in Johansdorf's poems is not always the distant recipient of devotion but a genuine participant who is capable of surprising anger and indignation and of experiencing the joy of love and the pain of separation when, as in some of the songs, the man is about to depart on a crusade (II; XIII). The crusading songs show the service of God, not, as in Friedrich von Hausen, as an extension of the love of the lady, but as something which can exist side by side with it. Even when he asks Love to release him, it is in the expectation that the absence will be temporary (XIII, 2, 1-2):

Minne, lâ mich vri!
     du solt mich eine wîle sunder liebe lân.

(Love, let me free! You must leave me for a while without joy.)

The rather delicate charm of the songs of Johansdorf is in sharp contrast to the vividness of **Heinrich von Morungen** (XIX), with his color and powerful imagery, his sensuality, and his evocation of love as a force less to be questioned than to be confronted. At the heart of Morungen's songs is the devotion of the knight to his high-born lady in a relationship which has no expectations of fulfillment. Yet his grief and failure are presented in a way which suggests that they are positive experiences. Not for him the reflection of Friedrich von Hausen or the delight in self-pity of Reinmar von Hagenau. Heinrich von Morungen knows how to elevate his suffering by describing it in grand and imaginative terms, as in one of his most remarkable poems, which begins with a striking image (XXXII):

Mir ist geschehen als einem kindelîne,
    daz sîn schoenez bilde in einem glase gesach
unde greif dar nâch sîn selbes schîne
    sô vil, biz daz ez den spiegel gar zerbrach.
    Dô wart al sîn wunne ein leitlich ungemach.
alsô dâhte ich iemer vrô ze sîne,
dô ich gesach die lieben vrouwen mîne,
    von der mir bî liebe leides geschach.

Minne, diu der werelde ir vröude mêret,
    seht, diu brâhte in troumes wîs die vrouwen mîn,
dâ mîn lîp an slâfen was gekêret
    und ersach sich an der besten wunne sîn.
    Dô sach ich ir liehten tugende, ir werden schîn,
schoen unde ouch vür alle wîp gehêret,
niuwan daz ein lützel was versêret
    ir vil vröuden rîches <*rôtez*> mündelîn.

Grôz angest hân ich des gewunnen,
    daz verblîchen süle ir *mündelîn* sô rôt.
des hân ich nu niuwer klage begunnen,
    sît mîn herze sich ze sülher swære bôt,
    Daz ich durch mîn ouge schouwe sülhe nôt
sam ein kint, daz wîsheit unversunnen
sînen schaten ersach in einem brunnen
    und den minnen muoz uns an sînen tôt.

Hôher wîp von tugenden und von sinnen
    die enkan der himel niender ummevân
sô die guoten, die ich vor ungewinne
    vremden muoz und immer doch an ir bestân.
    Owê leider, jô wânde ichs ein ende hân
ir vil wunnenclîchen werden minne.
nû bin ich vil kûme an dem beginne.
    des ist hin mîn wunne und ouch mîn gerender wân.

(It happened to me as to a child who caught sight of his lovely image in a mirror and went to take hold of his own reflection with such force that he shattered the mirror. Henceforth all joy was grievous suffering for him. Thus did I too think I would always be happy when I saw my beloved lady, from whom suffering befell me along with joy. Love, who increases the joy of the world, look, she brought my lady to me in a dream, when I was enveloped in sleep and contemplating the peak of my delight. Then I saw her lovely virtues, her noble aspect, more beautiful and more splendid than all other women, save that her blissful little <*red*> mouth was a little damaged.

I was very distressed that her little mouth so red should grow pale, and because of this I have begun to lament again, since my heart exposed itself to such sorrow that I should see through my eyes such suffering, like a child who, untutored in wisdom, glimpsed his shadow in a fountain and had to love it until his death.

The heavens cannot encompass anywhere a woman more elevated in virtues and in sensibility than the noble lady whom I must keep away from in order to avoid harm and yet remain constant to forever. Alas, in truth I thought that I had reached the end with respect to her blissful, noble love, but now I am hardly at the beginning, and so my joy and my yearning hope are all gone.)

Familiar elements of the classical Minnesang are here: the absolute devotion to the lady and the knowledge that this love can come to nothing; the need for secrecy; the praise of the lady as a paragon of virtue and beauty. What is remarkable about the poem is the confident grasp of the hopeless situation and, even more, the power of the language and the imagery, couched in the sedate movement of Morungen's favored dactyls. Although there is evidence of a troubadour model for this song, there is nothing comparable in German, and altogether the very substantial corpus of Morungen—there are 35 songs attributed to him in the manuscripts—marks a new and brilliantly effective stage in the development of the German lyric.

In some ways it has a very "modern" ring to it, with the undisguised impression of personal experience and the emphasis on the visual and the tangible. Yet the relationship of which it tells is firmly medieval, and, through it all, one retains the awareness of a fiction: the Minnesang is emphatically supra-personal, but what Morungen achieves is the awareness of a powerful, almost demonic force, which touches its victims in a deeply emotional way which could be mistaken for something personal.

When Morungen sets out the dilemma of loving above one's social status, he achieves a poem of great power and conviction (XV). Here the traditional lament for unrequited service is transformed by the sense—whether autobiographical or not is irrelevant—of a personal experience. His assertion that he has selected a lady above the sun anticipates the grand image of the final strophe, by which time the lady and the sun have merged and her unlikely descent to his level is made parallel to the coming of evening which he anticipates as the only solace he can hope for. Similarly he contrives to convey the impression of optimism and hopelessness in the final line: wân is, after all, a foolish, ill-based hope, and a concept recurrent in the Minnesang. The speaker is an emperor without a crown, without a land, or so he tells us (XXVIII): the whole point of his love is that, true to the tradition, it must remain unrequited, but that is no impediment when it comes to deriving the maximum effect from his condition.

His persistence in the face of the unresponsiveness of his lady is expressed in varied and vivid terms: shouting into a deaf forest (VIa, 2,1-2), teaching a bird to speak (VIa,3,1-2), felling a tree without tools (VIa,38-9). In all these cases, he is expressing the hope that perhaps, just perhaps, he may yet succeed.

Although the essential position at the heart of Morungen's songs is a conventional one, there is nothing conventional in his handling of it. What distinguishes him is the variety of his corpus and what can be described as the sheer poetic skill of his execution.

Morungen is arguably the greatest poet of his age in terms of his command of form and his use of language and imagery, but he is exclusively the poet of love, whose achievement lies in his evocation of the extremes of passion implied in love and his imaginative, sometimes extravagant, evocation of its power. Even though in general he respects the convention which forbids him from openly criticizing his lady, he leaves us in no doubt that she provokes him to anger at times, and he even goes so far as to accuse her of being a murderess (XXXIV). Yet even this idea he turns around, for if she imagines that by killing him she will ensure that he never sees her again, she is mistaken: his soul will serve her soul in the next world.

Perhaps the nearest Morungen comes to the self-pity which characterizes many of his fellow Minnesänger is when he gives instructions that the inscription on his gravestone should tell how much he loved her and how indifferent she was to him (VIII). When he refers to the "sin" which she has committed against him (3,8), he transgresses the rules of the genre. Yet this accusation that she has driven him to his death is contained in a poem notable for its lightness of tone and its deliberately playful meter.

This necessarily short account can do no more than suggest the special quality of Heinrich von Morungen. What his large corpus shows is the variety attainable within what appears at first sight a restricted genre. Morungen was almost certainly a professional poet, who, as he puts it, "was born to sing" (XIII,1,7). If people doubt the sincerity of his love because he disguises his grief with his singing, then this is a misconception which he has to bear, for he has an obligation to entertain the people irrespective of his own sorrow (XIII,2). Although sorrow is abundantly present in Morungen's songs and elegantly conveyed, he is probably at his best when he is expressing the sheer exuberant joy of love, as in the ecstatic "In sô hôher swebender wunne . . ." (IV), when he describes his sensation of flying and when all nature seems to be in tune with his happiness. If a single word could characterize a poet, perhaps in the case of Morungen it is that word *wunne*, and such joy can exist side by side with an awareness of sorrow, as it does most effectively in Morungen's dawn song, which is also simultaneously a song in celebration of love and a lament, all contained in the form of a *Wechsel* (XXX):

> "Owê,—
> Sol aber mir iemer mê
>   geliuhten dur die naht
> noch wîzer danne ein snê
>   ir lîp vil wol geslaht?
>     Der trouc diu ougen mîn.
>     ich wânde, ez solde sîn
>     des liehten mânen schîn."
>   Dô tagte ez.

> 'Owê,—
> Sol aber er iemer mê
>   den morgen hie betagen?
> als uns diu naht engê,
>   daz wir niht durfen klagen:

"Owê, nu ist ez tac,"
als er mit klage pflac,
dô er jungest bî mir lac.'
Dô tagte ez."

"Owê,—
Si kuste âne zal
in dem slâfe mich.
dô vielen hin ze tal
ir trehene nider sich.
Iedoch getrôste ich sie,
daz sî ir weinen lie
und mich al umbevie.'
Dô tagte ez.

'Owê,—
Daz er sô dicke sich
bî mir ersehen hât!
als er endahte mich,
sô wolte er sunder wât
Mîn arme schouwen blôz.
ez was ein wunder grôz,
daz in des nie verdrôz.
Dô tagte ez.

("Alas, shall her exquisite body ever again shine through the night towards me, whiter than snow? It tricked my eyes. I thought it must be the light of the bright moon." Then day dawned.

'Alas, shall he ever again wait for day to dawn here? Then may night pass away from us without our having to lament "Alas, now it is day", as he said so plaintively, when he last lay by my side.' Then day dawned.

"Alas, she kissed me in my sleep times without number. Then did her tears fall. But I consoled her, telling her to leave her weeping and embrace me." Then day dawned.

'Alas, that he has so often gazed at me! When he uncovered me he was wanting to see my arms bare, without clothing. It was a miracle that he never grew tired of this.' Then day dawned.)

See in particular: Wapnewski (1975 65-73), on Morungen's dawn song.

Not for nothing has the colorful Morungen, though sparsely attested historically, found his way into legend, partly corroborated, which tells of pilgrimages and journeyings, possibly to India and Persia, and of his devotion to St. Thomas culminating in his death in the monastery of St. Thomas in Leipzig in 1222.

See: Tervooren, Helmut, ed. *Heinrich von Morungen. Lieder.* Stuttgart: Reclam, 1975 (= UB, 9797). Sel. MHG text with mod. Ger. trans., intro. and notes.

See also Menhardt, H. "Zur Lebensbeschreibung Heinrichs von Morungen." *ZfdA* 70 (1933): 209-34; Pretzel, Ulrich. "Drei Lieder Heinrichs von Morungen" (MF 127,1; 131,25; 136,1). In Jungbluth (1969, 110-120); Müller, Ulrich, in H. Bergner (1983, II, 100-105) for interpretation of "Owê,—soll aber mir iemer mê . . ."; and Jackson, W. T.

H. "Persona and Audience in Two Medieval Love Lyrics," *Mosaic* 8 (1975): 147-159. Repr. in: W. T. H. Jackson. *The Challenge of the Medieval Text.* New York: Columbia UP, 1985. Pp. 49-65. This article compares Morungen's "Owe, war umbe volge ich tumben wane" with "Lo tems vai e ven e vire" by Bernard de Ventadorn.

See also: Goldin, Frederick. *The Mirror of Narcissus in the Courtly Love Lyric.* Ithaca, NY: Cornell UP, 1961: esp. pp. 107-166 on Morungen.

Before passing to Reinmar von Hagenau who represents in many ways the antithesis of Heinrich von Morungen, we insert at this point another poet who, belonging to about the same period as these two, is very different from both of them. **Hartmann von Aue** (XXII) is well known as the author of narrative poems (see p. 132 ff.), and his contribution to what can strictly be described as the Minnesang is, perhaps not surprisingly, rather limited and relatively less effective. Bearing in mind the relationship between his narrative works and their French sources, it is also not surprising that his lyric shows an acquaintance with Romance models. It is likewise to be expected that, as a poet in the mainstream of literary composition at this prolific period, he tried his hand at the lyric. What we can gather about his personality and temperament from his narrative works does not suggest that he would be very much at home in a convention which verged at times on an elaborate game.

Among the eighteen songs attributed to him, very few reflect an adherence to the conventions of Minnesang. When he writes within the convention, as he is quite capable of doing, Hartmann is formally successful but thematically less convincing. Although he uses the familiar language and formulae, there is something rather hollow in his praise of love. He is at his most distinctive when he admits to his discomfort in the traditional role of the hapless lover and challenges the norm as he does in the poem described in German as the *Unmutslied* because of its tone of discontent (XV):

> Maniger grüezet mich alsô
> —der gruoz tuot mich ze mâze vrô—:
> "Hartmann, gên wir schouwen
> ritterlîche vrouwen."
>     mac er mich mit gemache lân
>     und île er zuo den vrowen gân!
>     bî vrowen triuwe ich niht vervân,
>     wan daz ich müede vor in stân.
>
> Ze vrowen habe ich einen sin:
> als sî mir sint, als bin ich in;
>     wand ich mac baz vertrîben
>     die zît mit armen wîben.
>         swar ich kum, dâ ist ir vil,
>         dâ vinde ich die, diu mich dâ wil;
>         diu ist ouch mînes herzen spil.
>         waz touc mir ein ze hôhez zil?
>
> In mîner tôrheit mir beschach,
> daz ich zuo zeiner vrouwen gesprach:

"vrowe, ich hân mîne sinne
gewant an iuwer minne."
    dô wart ich twerhes an gesehen.
    des wil ich, des sî iu bejehen,
    mir wîp in solher mâze spehen,
    diu mir des niht enlânt beschehen.

(Many a man greets me like this, and the greeting pleases me only a bit: "Hartmann, let's go and look at courtly ladies!" Let him leave me in peace and hurry off to the ladies himself! I am not sure how to behave with ladies except that I stand in front of them incapable of doing anything.

I have just one idea as far as ladies are concerned: as they are towards me, so am I to them, for I can better pass my time with ladies of low birth. Wherever I go there are many of these, and I shall find the one who desires me. This one will be my heart's desire too. What use is it to me to aim too high?

It happened to me once, fool that I am, that I said to a lady: "My lady, I have turned my thoughts to your love." Then I got a funny look, and because of this, let me tell you, I intend to look only at ladies who will not permit such a thing to happen to me.)

There is no mistaking the tone of self-mockery as he depicts himself as an outsider in the game of love, but this is not a man weighed down by his own inadequacy, and he places the responsibility firmly with the ladies, asserting, as Walther von der Vogelweide was to do after him, that he would rather spend his time with ladies of lower social status. The question "waz touc mir ein ze hôhez zil?" foreshadows Walther's famous "si sint mir ze hêr" (see p. 272). There is no evidence to suggest a precise influence here, in either direction, but perhaps there are signs of a more prevalent disaffection with the whole convention, which poets were challenging in their own ways.

Hartmann's contribution to the love lyric is his extension of the concept of love to include his commitment to his unidentified lord and his grief at his death. There is considerable controversy surrounding the authenticity of some of the poems attributed to Hartmann. The dating of his lyrics within his oeuvre is also problematic, and the relative chronology impossible to establish with any certainty. The profound poem "Diz waeren wunneclîche tage" (These could be happy days: XVI), the authenticity of which is now generally accepted, gains in depth if it is read as a lament for the death of a beloved husband, a widow's lament in the manner of Reinmar's (see p. 266), rather than the expression of grief at separation. It is also more poignant if one sees it as the expression of personal grief, placed in the mouth of the widow, yet still reflecting the poet's own sense of loss.

The song which has always constituted a crux for the chronology of Hartmann's works shows his movement away from the conventional singing of love towards the crusading song (XVII). The tone is again one of challenge to the Minnesingers, but this time there is a confidence as he replaces one love with another:

Ich var mit iuweren hulden, herren unde mâge.
    liut unde lant die müezen sælic sîn!
ez ist unnôt, daz ieman mîner verte vrâge,

ich sage wol vür wâr die reise <mîn>.
Mich vienc diu minne und lie mich varn ûf mîne sicherheit.
nu hât si mir enboten bî ir liebe, daz ich var.
ez ist unwendic, ich muoz endelîchen dar.
wie kûme ich bræche mîne triuwe und mînen eit!

Sich rüemet maniger, waz er dur die minne tæte.
wâ sint diu werc? die rede hoere ich wol.
doch sæhe ich gern, daz sî ir eteslîchen bæte,
daz er ir diente, als ich ir dienen sol.
Ez ist geminnet, der sich durch die minne ellenden muoz.
nu seht, wie sî mich ûz mîner zungen ziuhet über mer.
und lebte mîn her Salatîn und al sîn her
dien bræhten mich von Vranken niemer einen vuoz.

Ir minnesinger, iu muoz ofte misselingen,
daz iu den schaden tuot, daz ist der wân.
ich wil mich rüemen, ich mac wol von minnen singen,
sît mich diu minne hât und ich si hân.
Daz ich dâ wil, seht, daz wil alse gerne haben mich.
sô müest aber ir verliesen underwîlen wânes vil:
ir ringent umbe liep, daz iuwer niht enwil.
wan müget ir armen minnen solhe minne als ich?

(I journey forth with your blessing, my lords and my kinsmen. Good fortune to the land and the people! No one needs to ask about my journey, for I shall tell you where I am going. Love took me prisoner and released me in exchange for my word of honor, but now it has ordered me to go away. There is nothing for it: I must go without fail. How little would I break my oath and betray my loyalty!

Many men boast of what they do in the name of love. I hear the words but where are the deeds? However I should like to see that she commanded one or other of them to serve her as I am meant to serve her. That is really love when a man must go into exile for the sake of love. Just see how love forces me out of my native land across the sea! And if my lord Saladin were still alive and all his army, they would not get me a single step out of the land of the Franks. [Alternatively: And if my lord were still alive, Saladin and all his army would not get me. . . . ]

You Minnesingers, you must often go wrong. That which harms you is your vain hope. I will boast that I can sing of love, since love has me and I have it. That which I desire, look: that thing desires me too. You on the other hand must sometimes lose much foolish hope, for you strive for love which does not want anything to do with you. Why can you poor things not love such love as I do?)

This sounds like the Hartmann of *Gregorius*, with its serious tone and unmistakable religiosity, and of course the beginning of that work contains Hartmann's declaration that he is turning his back on the frivolous matters with which he has concerned himself. It is more than likely that he is thinking of his attempts at conventional love songs when he says that. Whether this poem represents Hartmann's last word on the subject is impossible to establish with absolute certainty, but it does have a ring of finality about it.

See: von Reusner, Ernest, ed. *Hartmann von Aue. Lieder.* Stuttgart: Reclam, 1985 (UB, 8082). Sel., with trans. into mod. Ger., introduction, and notes.

See also the section on Hartmann von Aue in Räkel (1986 108-118), which contains, along with some general information on chronology and biography, translations, and comments on the two songs quoted here.

The other poet usually thought of as constituting the peak of the Minnesang is **Reinmar von Hagenau** (XXI), whose special qualities could hardly be more distinct from those of Heinrich von Morungen. Together these two remarkable poets, composing at approximately the same time, at this vital conjunction of literary talents in medieval Germany, demonstrate the potential of the convention and contradict any impression that it was a monolithic development. Reinmar's exquisite verses present love as a spiritual experience whose effect is principally grief and resignation. Like Friedrich von Hausen, but with greater delicacy and subtlety, Reinmar reflects on the nature of love. Whereas Hausen could be said to analyze *minne*, Reinmar analyzes his thoughts and feelings about it. If the keynote of Morungen's poetry is *wunne*, joy in the rare fulfillment of love and even in the knowledge of its hopelessness, that of Reinmar is sorrow, which is expressed in a multiplicity of terms (*sorge, leit, kumber, swaere, trûren*). Yet, perversely, this sorrow is endowed with positive force, and not for nothing does Reinmar pride himself that no one bears his grief with such elegance (*sô schône*) as he does (XII,5,3-5).

The great Heidelberg manuscript distinguishes this Reinmar from other poets of the same name, particularly Reinmar von Zweter, who is abundantly represented in this manuscript, by adding the identification "der Alte." The commonly accepted addition of "von Hagenau" to the name Reinmar stems from what is usually taken to be a reference to him by Gottfried von Straßburg, when, in speaking of the lyric poets—"the nightingales"—he laments that the leader of them all, the one from Hagenau who bore their banner, has fallen silent (4778-4781). Gottfried does not mention the name Reinmar, so the assumption that he is referring to him is derived from the fact that Reinmar was indeed foremost among the lyric poets before Walther von der Vogelweide, to whom Gottfried accords the task of taking up the banner of the nightingales (4798-4801). There is a Hagenau in Alsace, and it is usually assumed that this is the place referred to by Gottfried, though other possibilities in Austria have been suggested. The commonly assumed connection between Reinmar and the court of Vienna is also based on somewhat slight evidence: the "widow's lament" (XVI) is a lament for a Liutpolt, usually taken to be Leopold V of Austria, who died in 1194 and who is assumed to have been Reinmar's patron. The commonly held view of Reinmar as court poet at Vienna where he met and initially influenced the younger Walther von der Vogelweide, though attractive and entirely feasible, is thus based on assumption and hard to substantiate. It is, however, the view on which much scholarship is based (cf. Bumke *Mäzene*, 168-171). There is much to suggest that Reinmar and Walther were active at the same court at the same time, and there is firm evidence that Walther's early career was based in Vienna (see p. 267). The idea of the court of Vienna as a focus of the Minnesang at its height is not seriously disputed. Assuming also that the *Tristan* reference is indeed to Reinmar leads to a date of probably shortly before 1210 for his death.

The manuscript tradition of Reinmar's poetry is very complex. He appears to have been a most prolific poet, although the manuscripts are not unanimous in their attributions to him: some poems are attributed elsewhere to other poets, and there is some confusing overlap with Hartmann von Aue and Walther von der Vogelweide. Given the fact that Walther did apparently make reference in his own work to that of Reinmar (see p. 269 ff.), and assuming that it is right to think of them as having been in contact, it is hardly surprising if there was some confusion in this instance about the authenticity of individual poems. A further complication arises from the fact that the manuscripts do not always coincide about the number of strophes in a particular poem or about the ordering of the strophes.

The very fact that Reinmar was undoubtedly a prominent poet who was likely to have been the focus of a school adds to the complexity of the manuscript tradition, since it is highly likely that not all of the immense corpus stemmed from Reinmar himself and, in particular, that the admixture of frankly weaker poems may be explained by the possibility that they were actually by his less gifted pupils. Much of the work of successive editors has thus been in establishing authenticity, with some, notably Carl von Kraus, emphatically excising a large number of poems from the corpus, and Maurer rehabilitating most of these on the grounds that they were probably early, less successful attempts. The conclusions of these two highly respected scholars represent two extreme procedures, and it is likely that a proper assessment lies somewhere in between. The most recent edition of *Minnesangs Frühling* has eight poems headed Pseudo-Reinmar, and sixty printed under his name, with indications of opinions on the matter of authenticity. It is entirely satisfactory for our purpose here to concentrate on the core of Reinmar's work, those poems whose authenticity has never been brought into question. Even these represent a very large contribution to the genre.

The tone which dominates in Reinmar, as already indicated, is one of rejection and resignation. He behaves with exemplary patience and unfaltering devotion to a lady whose dominant demeanor is indifference. Put like that, one could give the impression of a monotonous series of poems of unvarying character—something approaching a dirge perhaps—but this is not the case. Not only does the situation vary, but the poet's perception of that situation too.

It would be possible to select a great many poems to demonstrate the most prevalent features of Reinmar's lyric. The following five strophes do not constitute the most remarkable or the most famous of his poems, but they are chosen precisely for that reason: their typicality (VIII):

Sô vil sô ich gesanc nie man,
    der anders niht enhete wan den blôzen wân.
daz ich nû niht mêre enkan,
    des enwunder nieman: mir hât zwîvel, den ich hân,
      Allez,daz ich kunde, gar benomen.
      wanne sol mir iemer spilende vröide komen?
        noch sæhe ich gerne mich in hôhen muote als ê.
        mich enscheide ein wîp von dirre klage

und spreche ein wort, alse ich ir sage,
mirst anders iemer wê.

Ich alte ie von tage ze tage
und bin doch hiure nihtes wîser danne vert.
hete ein ander mîne klage,
deme riete ich sô, daz ez der rede wære wert,
Und gibe mir selben dekeinen rât.
ich weiz vil wol, waz mir den schaden gemachet hât:
daz ich niht verheln kunde, swaz mir war.
des hân ich ir geseit sô vil,
daz sî daz niemer hoeren wil.
nu swîge ich unde nîge dar.

Ich wânde ie, ez wær ir spot,
die ich von minnen grôzer swaere hôrte jehen.
des engilte ich sêre, semmir got,
sît ich die wârheit an mir selben hân ersehen.
Mir ist komen an daz herze mîn
ein wîp, sol ich der vol ein jâr unmære sîn,
und sol daz <. . . . . . . . .> alse lange stân,
daz si mîn niht nimet war,
sô muoz mîn vröide von ir gar
vil lîhte ân allen trôst zergân.

Sît mich mîn sprechen nû niht kan
gehelfen noch gescheiden von der swære mîn,
Sô wolde ich, daz ein ander man
die mîne rede hete zuo der sælde sîn;
und iedoch niht an die stat,
dar ich nu lange bitte und her mit triuwen bat.
dar engan ich nieman heiles, swenne ez mich vergât.
nu gedinge ich ir genâden *noch*.
waz sî mir âne schulde doch
lange tage gemachet hât!

Und wiste ich niht, daz sî mich mac
vor al der welte wol wert gemachen, obe si wil,
ich gediende ir niemer mêre tac.
jô hât si tugende, der ich volge unz an daz zil,
Niht langer wan diu wîle ich lebe.
noch bitte ich sî, daz sî mir liebez ende gebe.
waz hilfet daz? ich weiz wol, daz si ez niht entuot.
doch *tuo* si ez dur den willen mîn
und lâze mich ir tôre sîn
und neme mîne rede vür guot.

(Never did any man sing as much as I, possessing nothing but the simple hope. Let no one be surprised if now I can do it no longer, for my doubt has completely deprived me of everything that I was capable of doing. When can joy ever come dancing towards me? I should like to see myself again in high spirits, as I was before. Unless a lady separates me from this lament and says a word to me, as I do to her, I shall always be in pain.

I get older by the day and yet I am no wiser this year than I was last. If someone else had my reason for complaint, then I would advise him that it was worth talking about, yet I can give myself no advice. I know full well what has caused me such harm: that I did not know how to conceal what was ailing me. Because of this I told her so much that she does not wish to hear it. Now I keep silent and bow to her.

I used to think that those whom I heard talking about the great suffering of love were joking, but I have paid a high price for that, God knows, since I have seen the truth in myself. A lady has entered my heart and if I am to mean nothing to her for a year and more and if it. . . . is to last so long that she takes no notice of me, then the joy which I derive from her must very likely completely vanish and leave me with no hope.

Since what I say cannot help me nor separate me from my suffering, I would like another man to have my words for his good fortune. And yet not at that place where I have been beseeching now for such a long time and have been beseeching loyally. I do not want anyone to have good fortune there when it is lost to me. But I still hope for mercy from her. What long days she has made for me without my wanting them!

And if I did not know that, if she wants to, she can make me honorable in the eyes of the whole world, I would not serve her for a single day longer. Truly she is virtuous, whom I shall follow to the very end, no longer than as long as I live. Yet still I beg her to grant me a happy end. What use is that? I know very well that she will not do it. Yet let her do it for my sake and allow me to be her fool and accept what I say as good.)

Our text follows the order of manuscript A, and the very fact that the order is different in the three manuscripts containing all five strophes, while one, manuscript B, contains only strophes 2, 1, and 5, points to an important feature of Reinmar's style. He does not describe a developing relationship, nor does he, as Friedrich von Hausen does, move logically in his argument from one point to the next. Rather does he present a series of reflections, connected by a common theme of course, but not intended to suggest any progression. The thought is predictable here: all that remains to him is a very slight hope (*wân*); doubt or despair (*zwîvel*) has deprived him of all else; he yearns for joy (*vröide*) and the return to his previous buoyant spirits (*hôher muot*): the lady could if she so desired put an end to his lament (*klage*), but, if she does not, then his lot is lasting suffering (*mirst anders danne wê*). The second strophe, which is actually placed first in the other three manuscripts, laments that, though he grows older by the day, he is no wiser this year than last. He would know how to advise someone else, but he cannot help himself. He blames himself for having revealed his feelings to his lady so often that she no longer wishes to hear anything from him. He will keep quiet and submit. The tone of self-accusation and even self-mockery leads, in the order of manuscript A printed here, to the recognition that, before he himself experienced love, he did not take seriously what others said about it. Now he is receiving his just deserts and experiencing the indifference of a lady at first hand. He will lose all hope (*trôst*) if she continues to pay no heed to him. The fourth strophe shows him in a more selfless mood, wishing that his words may help another man, since they cannot do anything about his own suffering. He does not begrudge anyone else the well-being (*heil*) which eludes him. Yet still he hopes for the lady's favor (*genâde*), lamenting that she has made his days so long through no fault of his. The final strophe reaffirms his determination to stay loyal to her service, convinced as he is that his esteem in the eyes of the world rests in her, all-virtuous as she is. He will pursue his goal to the very end of his life. Yet still he pleads with her to put an end to his misery, though he knows that she will not do so. The final lines express both his awareness of his foolishness and his determination not to give up pressing his suit on his obdurate lady.

As already mentioned, this poem is not particularly remarkable and does not find its way into popular anthologies, but it is chosen here to demonstrate a norm against which the more distinctive poems can be measured. The restraint which he maintains here and determines to maintain is characteristic of his pose, while the lady exerts her influence not by what she does so much as by what she does not do, through the reflection of her in him. There are a number of poems which corroborate this impression, but that does not mean that there are not variations on the way it is expressed.

In the song which begins "Ein wîser man sol niht ze vil . . ." (XII), he betrays a certain exasperation and even irritation. People say that constancy (*staete*) is a virtue, indeed the prime virtue but what good has this done him? If the devotion (*triuwe*) which he bestows on her goes unrewarded, then no one must be surprised if from time to time he is angry. On the other hand, just as sorrow can follow on from joy, so perhaps can joy succeed sorrow, and anyone who wishes to be happy should be prepared to suffer too and to experience both states with proper moderation. There is nothing better in all the world than patience and a man who practices that will always arrive at his desired goal. So, too, he hopes to come through safely ("alsô dinge ich, daz mîn noch werde rât").

The next strophe is the one which contains Reinmar's firm declaration about his art: no matter how profound his suffering he will bear it with elegance and restraint. Even if his lady oppresses him day and night, he will react gently and accept her hostility as though it were love. Yet the last line betrays the truth behind the mask:

owê, wie rehte unsanfte daz mir doch tuot!

(Alas, how harshly that afflicts me!)

He is really suffering very much despite appearances. The final strophe again juxtaposes joy and sorrow in what seems to be a powerful statement of his experience of love:

ich weiz den wec nu lange wol,
    der von der liebe gât unz an daz leit.
der ander, der mich wîsen sol
    ûz leide in liep, der ist mir noch unbereit.
        Daz mir von gedanken ist alse unmâzen wê,
        des überhoere ich vil und tuon, als ich des niht verstê.

(I have long since known very well the way which leads from joy to sorrow: the other one which is supposed to direct me out of suffering and into joy, is still not ready for me. Because I am so overwhelmingly afflicted by suffering, I often fail to hear things and behave as though I do not understand.)

The next lines are surprisingly forceful for the restrained Reinmar: if love yields nothing but discomfort (*ungemach*), then let it be cursed. The final line, which is sometimes taken as a broader comment from Reinmar about his art, sums up his perception of love:

> die selben ich noch ie in bleicher varwe sach.

(I have always seen that thing in pale colors.)

Love, for Reinmar von Hagenau, has a sickly hue, and his poetry tends towards the pastel shades.

This is a very interesting and much discussed poem, which again contains much which is characteristically Reinmar. Much scholarly discussion centers on the ordering of the strophes, and indeed the question whether the six strophes constitute a single poem or should rather be divided into two poems of three strophes each. The order assumed above follows that of manuscript E, while manuscript A records only the first three strophes, with the second and third reversed. Such textual difficulties point to a feature already mentioned: that there is no obvious sequence of argument in Reinmar's work. Moreover, one does well to remind oneself that the Minnesang is not to be read as autobiography and that, in Reinmar von Hagenau perhaps more than anyone else, what we admire is the sheer art of his analysis of feelings which were possibly more thought than felt. (An interesting examination of this particular poem is that by Friedrich Neumann in our bibliography.)

If Gottfried's appraisal is to be relied upon and if we measure the reputation of Reinmar by the elegy by Walther von der Vogelweide (see p. 273), we can probably judge that Reinmar was highly regarded by his contemporaries and that, to a considerable extent, his poems may be viewed as quintessential Minnesang. Possibly the relatively restrained admiration of some distinguished early critics who point to the absence of passion and the lack of obvious musicality in Reinmar, speaks for the distance of the modern period from a convention which is so deeply rooted in the courtly ethos of the Middle Ages and of which Reinmar is an unsurpassed exponent.

Reinmar's mastery of the courtly conventions extends to his representation of the woman's standpoint, in songs which conform to the earlier traditions of the *Wechsel* and the *Frauenklage* and which reveal the woman as more than just a shadowy figure and the object of devotion. She, too, is capable of love, but she is also aware of the social pressures which could act against them. In one poem which stands out as more lively and even verging on restrained humor, the lady pours out her feelings to the messenger but in the end retracts what she has said and begs him not to pass on a word of it (XXVIII). This poem presents, in the mouth of the lady, the basic dilemma of the Minnesang with all its hazards, and it even sums up the paradox of courtly love in words which might be seen to anticipate Walther von der Vogelweide:

> Minne heizent ez die man
> unde mohte baz unminne sîn.
> wê ime, ders alrêst began.

(People call it love and yet it might better be called unlove. Woe to the man who ever embarked upon it!)

This does not sound like the lady who returns her lover's advances with rejection and indifference.

Reinmar's capacity to put himself into the position of the woman is demonstrated in one of the poems in which one senses real emotion, whether truly experienced or vicariously imagined. This is the widow's lament, which, as already mentioned, plays a part in establishing the small amount of factual information about Reinmar (XVI). For some critics, the poem goes no further than a commissioned funeral lament, but such a dismissive assessment overlooks the poignant sense of loss and the sense of isolation attributed to the woman mourning her lost lord. If the poem ends with a somewhat conventional commendation to God, one should not forget the wistful opening: people say that the summer has come and that she should behave as she used to do, but how can she, when the source of all her joy lies in his grave? The passion which some miss in Reinmar is there in her description of her reaction to his death. This may be anatomically implausible, but the effect is powerful:

> dô man mir seite, er wære tôt,
> dô wiel mir daz bluot
> von deme herzen ûf die sêle mîn.

(When they told me he was dead the blood welled up out of my heart and into my soul.)

With a corpus as large as Reinmar's and within the limitations of this introduction, we can only hope to convey his special quality and direct our readers towards the extensive oeuvre and the mass of critical literature. Within the Minnesang he represents a high point, yet he contributes only a part to a development which, even as he was composing, was beginning to be challenged, broadened, and even broken up.

See: Räkel (1986 143-170); Schweikle, G., *Reinmar: Lieder*. Stuttgart: Reclam, (UB, 2745); Schweikle, G. (1994, 182-215), "War Reinmar 'von Hagenau' Hofsänger zu Wien?"; F. Neumann: "Reinmars Lied: 'Ein wîser man sol niht ze vil' (MF 162,7)." In Jungbluth (1969, 153-168).

Already it is evident that the Minnesang is no monotonous recital of a single theme, far from it, and we have already seen how poets of distinction emerged to uphold the convention in highly individualized ways and even to challenge it. If Reinmar von Hagenau and Heinrich von Morungen represent, in very contrasting ways, Minnesang at its peak, three other poets, composing at about the same time, or just a little later, contributed in a way which shows simultaneously their dependence on the tradition and their very original quality. If we place Walther von der Vogelweide, Wolfram von Eschenbach, and Neidhart under three separate headings, this is because they all three take German lyric poetry into unprecedented directions. There is every reason to question the very term Minnesänger as applied to them, yet, as will emerge, they grow out of that tradition, if only because in many ways they contradict it.

In the case of Wolfram von Eschenbach, whose contribution to the lyric is a small but very significant one, we have treated his songs together with the rest of his work, rather than here, where they might also justifiably belong. Thus, for Wolfram's lyric, see pp. 202 ff.

It is not possible to establish **Walther von der Vogelweide's** place of origin, but he tells us that he learned his art—*singen unde sagen*—in Austria, and the single piece of documentary evidence is in the household accounts of Wolfger von Erla, Bishop of Passau, from which we learn that a large sum had been paid to Walther to enable him to purchase a fur coat. The date is November 1203, and Wolfger is known to have been travelling in Austria at that time. It is usually assumed that Walther was at the court of Vienna, that he met Reinmar von Hagenau there and subsequently left Vienna and Reinmar behind when he began a life of wandering, which one can trace in his poems from his appeals to some of the most significant literary patrons of his day for support. The existence of a feud between Reinmar and Walther is much debated, but there is a fair amount of evidence to suggest that the two went their separate ways when Walther began increasingly to attack some of the basic precepts of the Minnesang and to establish himself as a poet of very independent mind. What all this means is that Walther, more than any other German lyric poet of the period, is deeply rooted in the Middle Ages yet very much an innovator. However, even though in his own work he took the German lyric into totally new directions, he remains surprisingly isolated. There is no school of Walther von der Vogelweide and no real successors: he disrupted existing trends yet did not really provoke imitation, perhaps because his whole manner was so individual. His poetry stands very much on its own as a massive corpus of great diversity.

Walther's appeal to modern readers lies probably in the remarkable scope of his poetry. He is a master of a wide range of metrical forms, but the same may be said of Reinmar von Hagenau and Heinrich von Morungen. Walther speaks of love, but he also confronts issues of human concern, topical and universal. He appears never to lack an opinion, and he expresses himself with a forthrightness that is frequently provocative and sometimes shocking. Certain terms are commonly used to denote the types of Walther's poems, and these certainly have their uses, but there is considerable overlap among them. In particular, the love songs and the so-called *Sprüche* often have elements in common, which makes rigid separation ultimately undesirable, even if it is helpful in the handling of such a large mass of material. Within these two main areas, there is a wide range of other categories.

In the absence of documentary evidence, it is usual to think of Walther's lifetime as spanning about 1170 to about 1230, a relatively long period in those days and one which embraced some turbulent times, much of which he reflected in his work. By their very nature the political *Sprüche*, which often treat specific events, can be dated, so that in this area one can talk confidently of chronology. In the case of the love songs, the situation is far less clear, and attempts to point to development are based to a large extent on assumptions. It is, however, reasonable to think of a youthful Walther adopting the conventions of the Minnesang which surrounded him and only gradually coming to question some of their premises. The extent to which he was engaged in a feud with Reinmar, an idea which colored much earlier scholarship, can be overestimated, although there is clear evidence that some songs by both poets do contain responses to one another. Nor is it possible to trace with absolute certainty a progression in his attitude to the conventions of courtly love. Again, the earlier view that he went along with norms of *hôhe minne*, rejected them in his songs of equal love (his so-called *Mädchenlieder*) and then moved to a new and elevated form of courtly love which was a revised, transcending view of the earlier attitudes, is too simplistic.

Any development is unlikely to have been so clear-cut and, judging from Walther's political poems, we can probably assume that his allegiances, in this respect too, were often dictated by expedience. Walther was, after all, a professional poet, and, innovative as he was in many respects, he must have had to satisfy the expectations of his courtly audience, at least to some extent, by giving his listeners the more conventional love songs to which they were accustomed. It is reasonable to suppose that his performances will have contained elements of the new and consciously quite shocking, side by side with old favorites which the audience knew and called for. The manner and circumstances of performance are largely a matter for surmise, but it would seem unrealistic to think, as was once the popular idea, of a strict chronological progression, with Walther abandoning standpoints once and for all as he moved to a new phase.

Nevertheless, even if one is cautious about implying rigid chronological divisions, it is convenient to see Walther's love songs as falling into distinct kinds: thus he was as capable of extolling courtly love as his contemporaries, directing his praise at a noble and inaccessible lady, but his most significant innovation was the idea that love could exist between equals, or that the lady in question could be a young girl of low social rank. We have already seen that other Minnesänger sometimes questioned the phenomenon of love to which at other times they appeared quite subservient, and Walther, with the sharp critical tone which gives such a distinctive edge to his *Sprüche*, can be remarkably direct in his onslaught on a relationship which is sometimes anything but positive.

Even if we disregard those songs which have become attached probably erroneously to his name in the manuscripts, we are left with an oeuvre of vast proportions, of which only a slight impression can be given in this introduction. His popularity in his own age is suggested by the fact that the three main manuscripts, A, B and C, have a large amount under his name, and that a great many of the lesser manuscripts, particularly E, record his work. Some individual poems were obviously considered very significant in their own day and may exist in several of the manuscripts, although not always in quite the same form.

The following will suggest some possible approaches to Walther's large oeuvre in three main areas: love poetry, *Sprüche*, and late poems. These divisions may appear somewhat disparate, but they represent a tried and tested way of handling Walther's extensive and varied corpus.

Love songs:

A small group of songs is accepted as being by a youthful Walther very much under the influence of traditional Minnesang. One of these: "Dir hât enboten, frowe guot" (120,16), is recorded in *Minnesangs Frühling* under the name of Hartmann von Aue

(XII). Most scholars would now accept it as Walther's, but the varying attribution in the manuscripts between Hartmann and Walther only underlines Walther's early conformity to the conventions. Another song which is assigned with little hesitation to the period just before 1198 is the messenger song "Frowe, vernemt dur got von mir diz mære" (112,35). Lachmann described it as unworthy of Walther, a somewhat harsh criticism which can only be made in the knowledge of what Walther was to achieve as he developed his individual style. Even at this early stage, there is evidence of an exuberance which suggests less the influence of Reinmar or Hartmann than of Heinrich von Morungen. An example is the following first two strophes of five (109,1 ff.):

> Ganzer fröiden wart mir nie sô wol ze muote:
> mirst geboten, daz ich singen muoz.
> sælic sî diu mir daz wol verstê ze guote!
> mich mant singen ir vil werder gruoz.
> diu mîn iemer hât gewalt,
> diu mac mir wol trûren wenden
> unde senden fröide manicvalt.

> Gît daz got daz mir noch wol an ir gelinget,
> seht, sô wære ich iemer mêre frô,
> diu mir beide herze und lîp ze fröiden twinget.
> mich betwanc nie mê kein wîp alsô.
> ê was mir gar unbekant
> daz diu Minne twingen solde
> swie si wolde, unz ichz an ir bevant.

(I have never experienced such complete joy. I have been ordered to sing. Blessed be the woman who understands and gives me credit for it! Her very noble salutation prompts me to sing. She who ever has power over me may turn aside my sadness and send me abundant joy.
If God grants me success with her, who forces me body and soul towards joy, then, look, I should be happy for ever more. No woman has ever constrained me like this. I never knew at all that Love could force someone any way it wanted, until I discovered it in her.)

There is much in these two strophes, and in what follows, to suggest that Morungen was an early model, and the likeness is in the handling of the meter as well as in the substance, with the conception of the power of love, the emphasis on the physical beauty of the beloved and the awareness of the poetic vocation.

Apparently it did not take Walther long to break out of any mold which he had assumed, and the date of 1198 is usually seen as a crucial turning point, marking his departure from Vienna and the beginnings of a period of wandering which brought with it a much greater freedom in his treatment of the theme of love. Indeed, it is more than likely that the independent-minded Walther had already broken away from the influence of Reinmar, and that the questioning tone was already evident before he left Vienna.

There is evidence to support the popular idea of a feud between Reinmar and Walther: some poems clearly do represent a riposte from the one to the other. It is easy to exaggerate this relationship, but there is no denying that Walther is intending to reply when he explicitly adopts the melody of his rival in the poem headed "in dem dône Ich wirbe umb allez daz ein man" (111,22). No one, least of all the Viennese audience, will have failed to take in this retort to Reinmar's poem X. The relationship between the two songs, the image of chess and the reference to the stealing of a kiss, is blatant, but it may have led critics to assume a more sustained feud than actually existed.

The so-called "sumerlaten-lied" (the song of the summer twigs 72,31) is important not only as a component in what may have been a series of songs in which the two prominent poets of the court of Vienna reacted to one another. It also shows Walther's ability to employ the language and manner of the convention for his own ends. His devotion to his lady is expressed in terms reminiscent of Reinmar, yet increasingly the sincerity is brought into doubt, until a complete reversal is achieved in the last line of the fourth strophe, which mimics Reinmar's desperate cry "stirbet sî, sô bin ich tôt" (if she dies, then I am dead IX,3,8) with the defiant opposite statement: "stirb ab ich, sô ist si tôt" (but if I die, then she is dead). The real tone of this song, the challenge to conventional *minne* comes firmly in the humor of the final strophe:

> Sol ich in ir dienste werden alt,
> die wîle junget si niht vil,
> so ist mîn hâr vil lîhte alsô gestalt,
> dazs einen jungen danne wil.
> sô helfe iu got, hêr junger man,
> sô rechet mich und gêt ir alten hût mit sumerlaten an.

(If I am to grow old in her service, all the while she is not getting much younger, then perhaps my hair will be so gray that she will wish for a young man. Then, young sir, may God help you and may you take my revenge for me and apply the young twigs of summer to her old skin.)

This is not the resigned self-pity of Reinmar, for revenge is at hand. The somewhat risqué reversal of the norms of the Minnesang shows Walther well able to manipulate the convention and to play with its established features. Indeed, it would seem that he did this increasingly as he challenged the idea of love, the very word *minne*, and even posited a new relationship based on mutual affection and comparable social status.

We have already seen that, far from simply accepting the conventions of the Minnesang, some of its foremost proponents questioned it, and this is especially true of Walther. In what we shall come to recognize as his forthright manner in his political and social poems, he challenges the very essence of *minne* in songs like the following one which tussles with the dilemma of love in no uncertain terms (69,1):

> Saget mir ieman, waz ist minne?
> weiz ich des ein teil, sô wist ichs gerne mê.
> der sich baz denn ich versinne,
> der berihte mich durch waz si tuot sô wê.
> minne ist minne, tuot si wol:

tuot si wê, so enheizet si niht rehte minne.
sus enweiz ich niht wie si danne heizen sol.

Obe ich rehte râten künne
waz diu minne sî, sô sprechet denne jâ.
minne ist zweier herzen wünne:
teilent sie gelîche, sost diu minne dâ:
sol abe ungeteilet sîn,
sô enkans ein herze alleine niht enthalten
    owê woldest dû mir helfen, frowe mîn!

Frowe, ich trage ein teil ze swære:
wellest dû mir helfen, sô hilf an der zît.
sî abe ich dir gar unmære,
daz sprich endelîche: sô lâz ich den strît,
unde wirde ein ledic man.
dû solt aber einez rehte wizzen, frouwe,
    daz dich lützel ieman baz geloben kan.

Kan mîn frowe süeze siuren?
wænet si daz ich ir liep gebe umbe leit?
sol ich si dar umbe tiuren,
daz siz wider kêre an mîne unwerdekeit?
sô kund ich unrehte spehen.
wê waz sprich ich ôrenlôser ougen âne?
    den diu minne blendet, wie mac der gesehen?

(Can anyone tell me what love is? I know a bit about it, but I would like to know more. If anyone is better informed than I, let him tell me why it hurts so much. Love is love if it does good. If it causes pain, then it is not proper love. In that case I do not know what it should be called.

If I guess rightly what love is, then say 'yes.' Love is the joy of two hearts. If they share equally then that is love, but if it is not to be shared, then one heart cannot contain it on its own. Alas, if only you would help me, my lady!

Madam, I am carrying too heavy a load. If you intend to help me, then hurry up about it. But if I mean absolutely nothing to you, then say so once and for all, and I will give up the battle and become a free man. But one thing you should know for sure, my lady: that no one can praise you better than I do.

Does my lady know how to make sweetness sour? Does she think that I give her joy in exchange for sorrow? Am I supposed to praise her for turning it all to my disfavor? Then I would be seeing things wrongly. Oh no! why am I talking like this, blind and deaf as I am? How can a man see when he is blinded by love?)

Central to the relationship he advocates here is its mutuality, and its capacity to bestow happiness. Moreover, this is no lovelorn suitor who is prepared to wait, but a free man who wants an answer once and for all and who is not going to be trifled with. Yet the defiance does not last, and the last two lines represent what appears to be a retreat and an acceptance of the power of love.

Walther's originality and his capacity to argue his case with great power are illustrated in one of his most substantial songs. It contains, in five strophes, some of his most important pronouncements on love. The song (47,36) begins with the striking statement:

> Zwô fuoge hân ich doch, swie ungefüege ich sî.

(There are two respects in which I behave correctly, no matter how incorrect I may be.)

It moves from his assertion that, as a professional poet, he adapts his mood according to the mood of his audience to an attack on the decline of courtly values which will echo in some of his *Sprüche*. The fault, he maintains, lies with the habit of women of leveling out the menfolk, of failing to discriminate as once they did. If the women were to be more discerning this would redound to the credit of both sexes. At this point (strophe 4), the song reaches its most famous pronouncement, as Walther plays with the two words *wîp* and *frouwe* and arrives at the conclusion that the generic word "woman" is superior to "lady", which implies social status but not necessarily superior worth:

> Wîp muoz iemer sîn der wîbe hôhste name,
> und tiuret baz dan frowe, als ichz erkenne.

("Woman" must always be the highest name for women, and it praises better than "lady", as I see it.)

The final strophe moves to the question of reward for praise and to the declaration that henceforth he will direct his praise to women who know how to express their gratitude, and it culminates in the provocative question:

> waz hân ich von den überhêren?

(What do I gain from the uppity ones?)

This echo of his statement, almost certainly of an earlier date, "si sint mir ze hêr" (56,27) may have struck a chord with his listeners, shocking them, as he must have intended, into some self-examination. It is possible to be too grand, of too lofty status. It is not far from this somewhat revolutionary argument to Walther's apparent substitution of *ebene minne* for *hôhe minne*, and even to his ability to envisage a young girl of humble birth as the speaker in a song which extols the joy of explicitly physical love. The charming song "Under der linden an der heide" (39,11) is one of his best known, appreciated by many modern readers even without its complicated literary and social context. The natural setting, the coy refrain and the delicate humor, all contribute to a song which is unique and which shows a further dimension of Walther, very different from the more solid, deliberating songs which we have just considered. To be placed alongside this famous song is another which has provoked a great deal of scholarly interpretation, another so-called "Pastoral poem", "Nemt, frouwe, disen kranz" (My lady, take this garland. . . . 74,20), which describes the man searching all summer through for his lost love after he has given her a garland of flowers to adorn her at the dance. Despite the debate surrounding the sequence of the strophes and the meaning of this poem, it manifests an intrinsic delicacy and charm in its elusive evocation of love, contrasting sharply with the mannered adherence to the conventions which Walther displays at other times.

Walther constantly surprises with his originality and his capacity to go to the heart of the matter. This must have been the case in his own day, too, when he seems to make no attempt to soften his comments or to protect his audience or the object of his comments from his pungency. The impression of a man who did not readily guard his tongue supports the view of a wandering poet who was dependent on patronage but did not always go about seeking it in the most tactful way. More than any other German poet of his day, he reflects the age in which he lived, and the turbulence of the events of his lifetime finds appropriate expression in this independent commentator.

Side by side with his extensive contribution in the field of the love lyric, Walther is known as the single poet who developed the *Spruch* into a significant genre with a wide range of subject matter. The two principal manuscripts, with good reason, depict Walther sitting on a stone with his head supported in one hand while his elbow rests on one leg crossed over the other. This is the pose of the thinker, and it is the way Walther pictures himself in the poem which all the manuscripts place first of the famous trilogy, known as the *Reichston* (8,4; 8,28; 9,16). The trilogy can be dated quite precisely, for the second and third poems make clear reference to the political turmoil of the double election in 1198 and the excommunication of Philip in 1201 (see p. 99). The first poem is probably rather earlier, but it too relates to the upheaval which followed the death of Henry VI in 1197. Walther's position is clear: he advocates the crowning of Philip of Swabia and, in the third poem he upbraids the pope—though taking care to assume the guise of a hermit—for championing Otto von Braunschweig.

When he came to compose his lament for the death of Reinmar von Hagenau, he did so with a candor which is one of his most characteristic qualities: he admits that he does not lament Reinmar the man (*lützel*), but he does grieve for the art which has perished with him. The two strophes (82,24 ff. and 83,1 ff.) are a strange mixture of formal lament and personal comment. When he recalls Reinmar's special contribution he does so by quoting one of his fellow poet's most famous lines ("sô wol dir, wîp, wie reine ein nam": Reinmar XIV,3,1), and the fulsome praise he utters seems to take little account of the controversy which may have existed between the two poets precisely regarding the praise of women. His admiration appears unstinting, yet the second strophe begins with the cynical comment that he grieves for Reinmar more than Reinmar would have grieved for him had the positions been reversed. What appears to be a genuine sense of loss leads to the wish that Reinmar had waited a while so that he could have died with him. How seriously one takes this expression of grief and the accompanying world-weariness may depend on whether Walther ever really convinces anyone that he was capable of profound commitment, and whether, indeed, another poem in the same *tôn* (*Leopoldstôn*) in which he longs for acceptance in Vienna should be construed as an expression of hope that he may assume Reinmar's vacated place (84,1).

Many of Walther's *Sprüche* are pungent comments on prevailing situations, like the two *Sprüche* which constitute a blatant attack on the papacy and specifically on the practice of placing an offertory box (*stoc*) in churches, ostensibly to gather resources for the planned crusade. The poems, which can thus be dated 1213 or just after, show Walther at his most forthright, maligning the pope and the clergy in unrestrained language (34,4 ff. and 34,14 ff.). The short, single-strophic poem, with its pithy dispatch, often of a single thought, was well suited to Walther's incisive mind, and he employs it to great effect.

The poems broadly under the heading of *Spruch* can be categorized according to their form (*tôn*). Traditionally these forms are given designations which correspond to their mood (like the *Unmutston* for the two *Sprüche* just discussed which treat his displeasure at the edict about the *stoc*), or to the principal recipient or subject of the more significant examples. Thus the two distinct forms referred to as the *Philippston* embrace poems which, for example, relate to Philip's coronation in 1198 (18,29), tell of his great feast in Magdeburg in 1199 (19,5), urge him to greater generosity (19,17; 16,36). The *König-Friedrichs-Ton* is used for a number of poems which are addressed to Frederick II, including the famous expression of delight and gratitude that he has at last received a fief from the "noble, generous king" (28,31). This poem, probably from 1220, matches the one in which Walther appeals for a secure home (28,1). As already mentioned, the famous trilogy, made up of three longer strophes (25 lines including an "orphan" rhyme in the concluding couplet) is designated the *Reichston*, while the elegies on the death of Reinmar von Hagenau are in the *Leopoldston*, so-called after the link with Leopold VI of Austria (cf. 84,1).

Many of these *Sprüche* combine personal and public elements in a very striking way. Thus, for example, the poem where Walther imagines himself measuring Otto according to his generosity and finding him wanting, while King Frederick shoots up in comparison (26,33), tells us as much about Walther in his pursuit of patronage as about his subject, as does the one in which he reminds Philip of the famous generosity of Saladin (19,17). Walther's personality—his reckless pursuit of his own ends sometimes and his forthrightness—pervades many of these *Sprüche*. They also reflect the age in which he lived, often in some detail.

Deeply rooted though he is in the Middle Ages, Walther stands out among his contemporaries for his handling of themes which are timeless. He does this sometimes in poems which might be deemed to be quite trivial, were it not for their contribution to the broad spectrum of his work. Thus he may employ the palindrome to convey a serious message about the upbringing of children (87,1), and the earnest advocacy of discretion in all things is couched in his deliberate artistry of the mirror image in each strophe. The poem which begins "Dô der sumer komen waz/ und die bluomen dur daz gras/ wünneclîchen sprungen" (94,11) promises to be a conventional love song, as it gathers images of an idyllic natural setting, yet it turns into a travesty of an idyll, with the rude awakening from the dream by a wretched crow and his wish that he could hurl a stone at it. In the end, the point of the poem emerges as a no doubt topical comment on the interpretation of dreams. The hint of self-mockery in this poem is present in another which seems to be balanced between love song and broader comment. "In einem zwîvellîchen wân" (In a state of pondering uncertainty . . . 65,33) describes him deep in thoughts of love, contemplating leaving his lady's service, and resorting to measuring a blade of grass to establish whether she loves him or not. It is very much Walther's unique contribution to play with the conventions which he appears to be overthrowing.

Walther's Late Songs:

In his late songs Walther strides out most firmly and reveals himself as a poet of stature. These are, for the most part, profound poems, in which the weighty themes are matched by eloquent language and form. The dominant tone is lament, for the passage of time and the dissipation of life, yet this is alleviated by the awareness of that which is lasting. Walther shows himself in the poems which are by common assent attributed to his relative old age to be a religious man whose view of this world is fashioned by his concept of the next. Thus, in his dialogue with Lady World, "Frô Welt, ir sult dem wirte sagen" (100,24), he reveals both an awareness of the joys of life, of which he has drunk to the full, yet also of the need to pay for them when the time comes. The view of the world, beautiful from the front but actually corrupt (100,9-12) is in line with the familiar medieval conception, given tangible expression in the figure at the south entrance to Worms Cathedral, which had been newly consecrated in 1181. The poem succeeds in combining the personal and the universal, in the idea of the conversation between the poet and Lady World as the time approaches when he must settle his debts with the *wirt*, the devil who has lured him with the superficial blandishments of the temporal. Despite the repeated protestations of the World who tries to hold him there, the last word is one of resolution and peace:

> ich wil ze hereberge varn.

(I will go to my resting place.)

Indeed, a courageous optimism dominates Walther's late poems, with their recognition of the frailty of the world and those who live in it. Yet his ultimate faith prevails even in the face of almost apocalyptic gloom (13,5):

> Owê waz êren sich ellendet tiuschen landen!
> witze unde manheit, dar zuo silber und daz golt,
> swer diu beidiu hât, belîbet der mit schanden,
> wê wie den vergât des himelischen keisers solt!
> dem sint die engel noch die frowen holt.
> armman zuo der werlte und wider got,
> wie der fürhten mac ir beider spot!
>
> Owê ez kumt ein wint, daz wizzent sicherlîche,
> dâ von wir hoeren beide singen unde sagen:
> der sol mit grimme ervaren elliu künicrîche.
> daz hoere ich wallære unde pilgerîne klagen:
> boume, türne ligent vor im zerslagen:
> starken liuten wæt erz houbet abe.
> nû suln wir fliehen hin ze gotes grabe.
>
> Owê wir müezegen liute, wie sîn wir versezzen
> zwischen fröiden an die jâmerlîchen stat!

aller arebeite heten wir vergezzen,
dô uns der sumer sîn gesinde wesen bat.
der brâhte uns varnde bluomen unde blat:
dô trouc uns der kurze vogelsanc.
wol im der ie nâch stæten fröiden ranc!

Owê der wîse die wir mit den grillen sungen,
dô wir uns solten warnen gegen des winters zît!
daz wir vil tumben mit der âmeizen niht rungen,
diu nû vil werde bî ir arebeiten lît!
daz was ie der welte meiste strît,
tôren schulten ie der wîsen rât.
wan siht wol dort wer hie gelogen hât.

(Alas, how honor is departing from German lands! Wit and courage, and in addition
silver and gold, whoever has both these things, and remains behind in shame [i.e., does
not go on a Crusade], how such a man will forfeit the reward of the heavenly emperor.
Neither the angels nor the ladies are well disposed towards him, beggar as he is in the
eyes of the world and of God; how he must fear the contempt of both of them!
Alas, a wind is coming, know that for a fact. We hear it spoken of in song and verse. It
will make its way through all the kingdoms, as I hear pilgrims lament. Trees and tow-
ers will be laid low in its path. It will blow the heads from strong men. Now let us flee
to the Grave of God.
Alas, idle people that we are, how have we been sat down here in this wretched place
with joy on either side of us! We could have forgotten all our troubles when the summer bade us join its company and brought us passing flowers and leaves. Then the
brief singing of the birds deceived us. Lucky the man who ever strove for constant (=
heavenly?) joy!
Alas for that melody which we sang with the crickets, when we should have been
warning ourselves in preparation for the winter-time! That we fools did not toil alongside the ant who is now worthily resting with the products of her labors! That has
always been the greatest dispute in the world: fools have always criticized the counsel
of the wise. It can easily be seen in the next world who has lied in this.)

This poem is typical of Walther's late lyric, combining as it does topical allusions,
albeit imprecise ones, to the turbulent state of affairs in Germany, with broader comment
on the human condition and the prospects for the world in general. The repeated *owê* sets
the tone of lament, and the stately meter affirms the *gravitas* which characterizes this
stage of Walther's career. In this poem, as elsewhere in Walther's late poems, a single
hope is highlighted: the prospect of a crusade is held out as the one firm goal which could
link this world and the next.

Unlikely as it is that Walther himself took part in a crusade, he nevertheless saw it as
a desirable ambition and although the poem beginning "Vil süeze wære minne" (76,22)
is a genuine crusading song, more famous is the poem which is given the title "Palästina-
Lied" (14,38), in which Walther speaks as though he had arrived in the Holy Land. In
this magnificent poem, written from this perspective, he speaks of the Birth and Crucifixion of Christ, the Resurrection and the hope for the future represented in the Second

Coming. Clearly a significant poem in its own day, the "Palästina-Lied" is transmitted in a great many of the manuscripts, though the number of strophes fluctuates. There is a measure of agreement that the seven strophes in manuscript A constitute the poem proper, with additional strophes recorded elsewhere. Certainly there is something to be said, in this deeply religious poem, for regarding the very number seven as significant. For the modern critic, a further important factor is that the poem is recorded with the accompanying music in the Münster fragment (MS Z): its discovery, as late as 1910, constituted one of the most exciting contributions to research in this area, since it provided also at least some indication of how other songs may have sounded in performance.

The crusading theme combines with world-weariness in Walther's famous "Elegy," "Owê war sint verswunden. . . ?" (124,1). This great late poem, possibly Walther's last and dated about 1228, together with "Under der linden an der heide" (see above), often represents Walther to more general readers today. The contrast between them could hardly be greater, yet it serves to demonstrate the quite extraordinary range, the delicate, swiftly moving little love song, with its coy innuendoes, and the majestic lines which constitute Walther's last great lament. Yet the tone of lamentation, again marked by the recurrent *owê* which frames all three strophes, is not the tone which prevails, for it is replaced in the end by a cry of jubilation (*wol*) at the prospect of a crusade which represents redemption and reward. Once more the personal and the broad political combine, as Walther grieves for the passing of his own time, the loss of friends and youth, the churning-up of fields and the destruction of the forest, yet also deplores the state of affairs in the country, epitomized in the careless head-dress of the ladies and the rustic attire of the knights, and focusing on the letters of excommunication which had reached the Emperor Frederick II, because he had not fulfilled his crusading oath (124,26). Just as he had done all those years earlier in his *Reichston* trilogy, Walther links the world of men with the natural world when he describes the birds as being made miserable by the lamentation of human beings (124,30). Indeed, if we think of these two great works as being separated by three decades, this sharpens our awareness of Walther as a committed commentator and an outspoken critic of his age.

Yet no introduction to the poetry of Walther von der Vogelweide is complete without a necessarily brief reference to a poem which, in artistic terms, is arguably even greater. This is the deeply personal farewell to the world "Ir reinen wîp, ir werden man" (You pure women, you noble men: 66,21) which Peter Wapnewski rightly describes as one of the most significant creations of MHG lyric (*Gedichte*, p. 250). Walther takes leave of the world which has brought him joy and fulfillment for the forty years and more he has sung in it. The second strophe brings the poignant image of the aged poet walking with a staff, but his concern is no longer with the physical but with the eternal. And if the youthful Walther shines through in the gently humorous debate between body and soul, and the admonition that the love which the body has desired is "not fish through to the backbone," the message of the poem remains clear: the mature Walther is looking beyond this world, to the reunion of body and soul in the next.

Editions:

Brunner, Horst, et al., eds. *Walther von der Vogelweide: Die gesamte Überlieferung der Texte und Melodien. Abbildungen, Materialien, Melodietranskriptionen.* Göppingen: Kümmerle, 1977 (= Litterae, 7).

Kuhn, Hugo, ed. *Die Gedichte Walthers von der Vogelweide, hrsg. v. Karl Lachmann, aufgrund der 10. von Carl Kraus bearbeiteten Ausgabe neu hrsg. v. Hugo Kuhn.* Berlin: de Gruyter, [13]1965. All references above are to this standard edition of Walther.

Maurer, Friedrich, ed. *Die Lieder Walthers von der Vogelweide.* Vol. 1: Die religiösen und die politischen Lieder. Tübingen: Niemeyer, [4]1974 (= ATB, 43); Vol. 2: Die Liebeslieder. Tübingen: Niemeyer, [3]1969 (= ATB, 47). Another standard (paperback) edition.

Richey, Margaret F., ed. *Selected Poems of Walther von der Vogelweide.* Oxford: Blackwell, 1948, [2]1959, [3]1965 ed. by Hugh Sacker. The third edition has made some minor but positive changes to this useful little book, intended explicitly "for the average undergraduate."

Ranawake, Silvia, ed. *Walther von der Vogelweide. Gedichte.* On the basis of the edition of Hermann Paul (1882). Part I: Der Spruchdichter. Tübingen: Niemeyer, 1996 (= ATB, 1). It is claimed that Paul's edition ([4]1911) gets closer to the original than subsequent editions. Introduction, notes, and bibliography have been brought up to date. Extant melodies included. Part II: Der Minnesänger (= ATB, 110) will appear in due course.

Schaefer, Joerg, ed. and trans. *Walther von der Vogelweide: Werke.* Darmstadt: Wiss. Buchges., 1972. MHG text with adjacent mod. Ger. trans. and copious notes to the texts.

Wapnewski, Peter, ed. and trans. *Walther von der Vogelweide. Gedichte. Mittelhochdeutscher Text und Übertragung.* Frankfurt/M: Fischer, 1986 (= Bücher des Wissens, 6052). Representative selection with MHG text and adjacent mod. Ger. trans., valuable notes.

Translations:

See Wapnewski (1986) and Schaefer (1972) above.

Betts, Frank, trans. *Songs and Sayings of Walther von der Vogelweide.* New York: AMS Press, 1977.

*Curschmann/Glier*, I, 578-656; II, 10-32. Sel., MHG text, with adjacent mod. Ger. trans.

## Walther von der Vogelweide—Bibliography

Halbach, Kurt Herbert. *Walther von der Vogelweide. 4. durchgesehene und ergänzte Auflage, bearbeitet von Manfred Günter Scholz.* Stuttgart: Metzler, [4]1983 (= Sammlung Metzler, 40).

A very full handbook, containing a mass of detailed information. Excellent introduction to Walther.

Jones, George F. *Walther von der Vogelweide.* New York: Twayne, 1968 (= TWAS, 46).

A useful, if basic, volume in the series (in English).

von Kraus, Carl. *Walther von der Vogelweide. Untersuchungen.* Berlin: de Gruyter, 1935.

Somewhat dated now, but still an important scholarly contribution to the study of Walther.

McFarland, Timothy, and Silvia Ranawake, eds. *Walther von der Vogelweide. Twelve Studies.* Oxford: Meeuws, 1982 (= Oxford German Studies, 13).

A fine collection of articles, all in English, on a range of specific issues relating to Walther.

Müller, Jan-Dirk, and Franz Josef Worstbrock, eds. *Walther von der Vogelweide. Hamburger Kolloquim 1988 zum 65. Geburtstag von Karl Heinz Borck.* Stuttgart: Hirzel, 1989.

Thirteen wide-ranging articles, based on papers given in German at a fairly recent conference.

Rump, Hans-Uwe. *Walther von der Vogelweide in Selbstzeugnissen und Bilddokumenten.* Hamburg: Rowohlt, 1974 (= Rowohlts Monographien).

One in the series, particularly useful for its many illustrations and the way in which it relates Walther's work to the contemporary context. Useful bibliography, largely of works in German.

Sayce, Olive: See the two works listed above in MINNESANG—BIBLIOGRAPHY. Substantial sections devoted to Walther: (1967 85-114; 1982 183-210).

Schweikle, Günther. "Die Fehde zwischen Walther von der Vogelweide und Reinmar dem Alten. Ein Beispiel germanistischer Legendenbildung." In: *Minnesang in neuer Sicht* (see above), pp. 364-89.

An interesting article on the whole question of the existence, or otherwise, of a feud between the two poets.

Wapnewski, Peter. *Waz ist minne. Studien zur mhd. Lyrik.* (see above in MINNESANG-BIBLIOGRAPHY).

Contains three articles on specific poems by Walther, pp. 74-180.

Wilmanns, Wilhelm. *I: Leben und Dichten Walthers von der Vogelweide.* 1882. 2. vollständige Auflage besorgt von Victor Michels. Halle, 1916. *II: Lieder und Sprüche mit erklärenden Anmerkungen.* 4. Auflage besorgt von Victor Michels. Halle, 1924.

These two volumes constitute the standard early commentary on Walther, important as a classic piece of scholarship but to a large extent modified and subsumed in later work.

Even as Walther von der Vogelweide was composing, still more or less within the courtly conventions which he was questioning, **Neidhart** was beginning to produce an enormous corpus, obviously very popular in his day and widely recorded in the manuscripts. Many of the poems under the name of Neidhart are disputed but their very existence points to the impact of the poet himself and the flood of imitators which his really quite revolutionary work provoked.

Although Walther may be said to have opened the way, in his advocacy of mutual love and his refusal to accept that *hôhe minne* was the single ideal, Neidhart forged ahead in a direction which Walther could probably not condone, still less emulate. The view of Walther's song "Owê, hovelîchez singen" (Alas for courtly singing . . . 64,31 ff.) as a diatribe specifically against Neidhart and his school, though previously fairly generally accepted, is now regarded with more caution. However, there can be little doubt that Walther is railing against the unruliness and, to him, discordant sounds penetrating the court. These were to become fashionable and even to some extent respectable in the work of Neidhart. It is probably a trend that Walther is objecting to in this case, rather than a specific person, but research has demonstrated fairly conclusively a relationship between the songs of the two poets. This would not be surprising, since they were almost certainly active in the same general region of Bavaria and Austria at approximately the same time.

The manuscript tradition of Neidhart is complex. Although the three principal manuscripts A, B, and C do record some of his poems, the bulk of his large corpus as we can identify it is contained in an Austrian manuscript dating from the late 13th or early 14th century (manuscript R). Also of importance, because it contains a large number of melodies attached to the Neidhart songs, is the much later manuscript c, which in other respects is less reliable, with a great number of unauthentic poems, some clearly imitations and some additional strophes inserted into original Neidhart songs. Its existence is, however, important, showing as it does the continuing popularity of Neidhart as long as two centuries after his original compositions.

Neidhart is assumed to have lived from about the last decade of the 12th century to about 1240. The only literary references to him are not particularly helpful in dating. Wolfram mentions him in a somewhat obscure allusion in *Willehalm* (312,15-18), but this tells us no more than that Neidhart's reputation for consorting with rustic friends was well known in about 1215. Wernher der Gartenaere seems to be expressing his admiration for Neidhart in a reference in *Meier Helmbrecht* (see p. 403 ff.), the central character of which may well have been inspired by Neidhart and his imitators: he maintains that Neidhart, *if he were alive*, would tell the story better (217-220). More important in establishing a *terminus ad quem* are references within the songs to Duke Frederick II of Austria, who succeeded his father in 1230 (No. 23,XII; No. 24,IX; No. 35,VII), and to events of 1235 and 1236 (No. 36,VII). The crusading song (No. 11) may refer to Leopold of Austria's expedition in 1217-1218, or it could be the crusade of Emperor Frederick II in 1228-29. In neither case does it suggest that Neidhart himself took part in a crusade, although he writes, as does Walther in his famous *Palästina-Lied* (see p. 276 f.), from the perspective of the Holy Land.

The status of Neidhart is likewise unclear. Both Wolfram and Wernher give him the title *"her,"* but there is no documentary evidence for his name, both parts of which may in any case be a part of a fiction which he assumed: in the poems he assumes the role on the one hand of "the jealous man" and on the other of "the man from the vale of sorrow." Not until the 15th century did the two names come together, for a long time to be attributed to the poet himself rather than to any figment of his poetic imagination. That the second component (von Reuental) corresponds to an actual place name, though possible, is far from certain.

The illustration in the Manesse manuscript shows "her Nîthart" holding forth to a group of peasants, who appear to be gathered round him in a friendly fashion. This depiction expresses the central feature of the work of Neidhart, who brought the pastoral, the rustic, and even the crude into the realm of the court for the first time. His songs are often double edged, managing simultaneously to jibe at the conventions of courtly love and to criticize the behavior of the peasants. Neidhart was a highly gifted poet who succeeded—at a time when Minnesang proper had probably yielded all that it could in the hands of its greatest exponents—in breaking new ground and establishing a very distinctive mode of lyric which was to prove extremely popular and endure, it would seem, throughout the remainder of the Middle Ages. Though little more than a decade or so younger than Walther von der Vogelweide, Neidhart exploited the situation which Walther had already begun to observe, opening up the cracks in what had for a brief period seemed a solid social structure and admitting new and sometimes shocking elements.

Neidhart's corpus is traditionally divided into his "summer songs" and his "winter songs." The groups are distinct, though they have important features in common. There is evidence to suggest that the winter songs were more popular: they are more prolifically transmitted, and there are many more imitations of them. The manuscripts vary considerably in such matters as the ordering of the strophes and the numbers of strophes. It would appear that the songs were circulating very widely and that strophes were sometimes added, by no means always by Neidhart himself.

Common to both summer and winter songs is the description of nature, which usually opens the poem, sometimes at some length. In the winter poems, the description has an edge to it: usually the emphasis is on the passing of summer, in accordance with the generally more serious tone of the winter songs, in which the somber evocation of the winter season is frequently matched by the theme of unrequited love and service.

The tone of the summer songs is altogether more cheerful. Usually they contain a lively dialogue, between a young girl and her mother, or between two girls. The theme is the joy of summer and the accompanying aspirations to love. The object of desire is the knight of Reuental, who is infinitely preferable to the peasant suitors who present themselves. The following song (No. 14) is fairly typical:

Ine gesach die heide
nie baz gestalt,
in liehter ougenweide
den grüenen walt:
bî den beiden kiese wir den meien
ir mägde, ir sult iuch zweien
gein dirre liehten sumerzît in hôhem muote reien.

Lop von mangen zungen
der meie hât.
die bluomen sint entsprungen
an manger stat,
dâ man ê deheine kunde vinden,
geloubet stât die linde:
dâ hebt sich, als ich hân vernomen, ein tanz von höfschen kinden.

Die sint sorgen âne
und vröuden rîch.
ir mägede wolgetâne
und minneclîch,
zieret iuch, daz iu die Beier danken,
die Swâbe und die Vranken!
ir brîset iuwer hemde wîz mit sîden wol zen lanken!

'Gein wem solt ich mich zâfen?'
sô redete ein maget.
'diu tumben sint entslâfen;
ich bin verzaget.
vreude und êre ist al der werlde unmære.
die man sint wandelbære:
deheiner wirbet umbe ein wîp, der er getiuwert wære.'

    'Die rede soltû behalten,'
sprach ir gespil.
'mit vröuden sul wir alten:
der manne ist vil,
die noch gerne dienent guoten wîben.
lât solhe rede belîben!
ez wirbet einer umbe mich, der trûren kan vertrîben.'

    'Den soltû mir zeigen,
wier mir behage.
der gürtel sî dîn eigen,
den umbe ich trage!
sage mir sînen namen, der dich minne
sô tougenlîcher sinne!
mir ist getroumet hînt von dir, dîn muot der stê von hinne.'

    'Den si alle nennent
von Riuwental
und sînen sanc erkennent
wol über al,
derst mir holt. mit guote ich im des lône:
durch sînen willen schône
sô wil ich brîsen mînen lîp. wol dan, man liutet nône!'

(Never did I see the heathland more beautiful, nor the green forest so radiant to behold. The two things show us that it is May Time. You girls, you must pair up and dance merrily in this lovely summertime.

The May is praised by many tongues. The flowers have sprung up everywhere, where previously there were none to be found. The linden tree stands in leaf, and courtly maidens begin to dance, or so I have heard.

They are free from care and full of joy. You handsome, lovely maidens, adorn yourselves so that the Bavarians will thank you, and the Swabians, and the Franks. Tie up your white dresses with fine silk sashes round your hips.

'For whom should I adorn myself?' asked a girl. 'The foolish ones have fallen asleep, and I am dismayed. Joy and honor do not matter to anyone. Men are fickle. Not one of them woos a lady because of whom he would earn praise for himself.'

'You should not talk like that,' replied her friend. 'We shall grow old happily. There are many men who would still like to serve good women. Leave that talk! There is one wooing me who knows how to banish sadness.'

'Then show him to me and let's see if he pleases me. This belt which I am wearing shall be yours. Tell me the name of the man who loves you so secretly. I dreamt last

night that you were thinking of getting away from here.'
'The man whom they all call the Reuentaler and whose song they know far and wide
is well inclined towards me. I shall reward him well for it, for I intend to adorn myself.
Come on then; they are ringing the bell for nones.')

Typical here is the description of nature which leads into the exhortation to the young
girls to adorn themselves for the approaching dance. This, in turn, leads into the conversation between the two girls, the one lamenting the lack of a love affair, the other urging
her to hope, since there are plenty of eligible men around. The song ends with the naming of the knight of Reuental as the one who desires her and for whom she will adorn
herself. The song uses the language and the conventions of courtly love yet mocks gently
at them, for the speakers are peasant girls and the context is a country dance.

The more complicated, tripartite form of the example just quoted is less characteristic
of the summer songs. They tend rather towards simplicity, often in strophes of five or six
lines, and although there is considerable variation in the lengths of the lines, the number
of rhymes is limited, as in the following short song (No. 5):

> Der walt stuont aller grîse
> vor snê und ouch vor îse.
> derst in liehter varwe gar.
> hebt iuch dar,
> stolziu kint,
> reien, dâ diu bluomen sint!
>
> Uf manegem grüenen rîse
> hôrte ich süeze wîse
> singen kleiniu vogelîn.
> bluomen schîn
> ich dâ vant.
> heide hât ir lieht gewant.
>
> Ich bin holt dem meien:
> dar ine sach ich reien
> mîn liep in der linden schat.
> manic blat
> ir dâ wac
> für den sunnenheizen tac.

(The forest was all gray with snow and ice, but now it is all brightly colored. Come on
then, you cheerful girls, and dance in a ring among the flowers.
On many a fresh green branch I heard little birds singing their sweet songs. I found
lovely flowers there. The heath is wearing its lovely garment.
I love the May Time. Then did I see my beloved dancing in the shade of the linden tree.
Many a leaf protected her from the hot sun of the day.)

The simplicity of form here is typical of the summer songs, yet less typical is its
essentially descriptive tone. However, many of the songs do contain substantial passages
like this, sometimes presumably from the poet, sometimes presented as from another

participant, usually one of the young girls, and often adjacent to the more characteristic passages of dialogue. An example is the following, which also gives a good idea of the lively tone of the dialogue. In this case it takes the form of an uninhibited quarrel between the young girl and her mother (No. 21):

'Nu ist der küele winder gar zergangen,
diu naht ist kurz, der tac beginnet langen,
sich hebet ein wünneclîchiu zît,
diu al der werlde vreude gît;
baz sungen nie die vogele ê noch sît.

Komen ist uns ein liehtiu ougenweide:
man siht der rôsen wunder ûf der heide,
die bluomen dringent durch daz gras.
schône ein wise getouwet was,
dâ mir mîn geselle zeinem kranze las.

Der walt hât sîner grîse gar vergezzen,
der meie ist ûf ein grüenez zwî gesezzen:
er hât gewunnen loubes vil.
bint dir balde, trûtgespil!
dû weist wol, daz ich mit einem ritter wil.'

Daz gehôrte der mägde muoter tougen;
si sprach: 'behalte hinne vür dîn lougen!
dîn wankelmuot ist offenbâr.
wint ein hüetel um dîn hâr!
dû muost âne dîne wât, wilt an die schar.'

'Muoter mîn, wer gap iu daz ze lêhen,
daz ich iuch mîner wæte solde vlêhen,
dern gespunnet ir nie vadem?
lâzet ruowen solhen kradem!
wâ nu slüzzel? sliuz ûf balde mir daz gadem!'

Diu wât diu was in einem schrîne versperret:
daz wart bî einem staffel ûf gezerret.
diu alte ir leider nie gesach:
dô daz kint ir kisten brach,
dô gesweic ir zunge, daz si niht ensprach.

Dar ûz nam sî daz röckel alsô balde,
daz was gelegen in maneger kleinen valde.
ir gürtel was ein rieme smal.
in des hant von Riuwental
warf diu stolze maget ir gickelvêhen bal.

('Now the cold winter has quite gone. The night is short, the day is beginning to lengthen. A lovely time is just beginning which brings joy to all the world. Never before nor since did the birds ever sing more sweetly.

A lovely sight meets our eyes. We see masses of roses on the heathland. The flowers are forcing their way up through the grass. The beautiful meadow was covered in dew when my friend gathered flowers for a garland.

The forest has quite forgotten its gray hue. Daytime perches on a green branch which is full of leaves. Make haste and bind up your hair, my dear playmate. You know very well that I wish to be with a knight.'

The girl's mother overheard this, and she said:'Keep your denials to yourself in future. Your fickle disposition is clear to see. Wrap a scarf round your hair. You will have to go without your clothes if you want to join the throng.'

'Mother, who gave you the right to make me beg my dress from you, when you never spun a single thread of it? Stop this racket! Where's the key? Open up the cupboard for me.'

The dress was locked up in a chest, which she pried open with the leg of a household tool. The old woman never saw a more terrible sight. When the girl broke open her chest her tongue kept quiet and she said not a word.

Straightaway she (the girl) took out the little gown which had been folded up small. Her belt was a narrow band. The proud girl threw her colored ball into the hand of the man from Reuental.)

There is obvious comedy here, in the attempt of the mother to prevent her daughter from going out by locking her dress in a cupboard and refusing to give her the key, and the girl's violent reaction, as she forces it open and dashes off to meet her beau, the knight of Reuental. Yet there is more subtle humor too, in the juxtaposition of the opening lines, with their unambiguously courtly language, with this scene of domestic strife.

Moreover, as this song demonstrates, Neidhart is distinguished from his slightly earlier contemporaries by the range of his language. To speak of a whole different ambience, that of the peasant milieu, he requires a different vocabulary, and he uses this side by side with the more familiar, abstract language of love and the courtly ideals.

This great variety of language and in particular of vocabulary is even more in evidence in the winter songs, which are also liberally sprinkled with the names of the peasants. It is to their activities, singing and dancing and celebrating, which sometimes tips over into raucous arguing, that much of these songs is devoted. The natural description is there, usually at the beginning, but this is in stark contrast to the main interest of the songs and the main setting, which is the peasant house. Similarly, the tone of yearning for lost love, not dissimilar at all from that in the classical Minnesang, is transformed abruptly into an account of uninhibited rivalry among uncouth peasants who force their attention upon the lady and see to it that the courtly suitor, the poet himself, is excluded. The tone is one of satire, and the intended audience was the court, the members of which will have reveled in the exposure of the ways of peasants yet, at the same time, probably enjoyed seeing their own manners and ideals sharply parodied in the activities of the presumptuous lower classes. It is a complex perspective, then, which lies at the heart of Neidhart's winter songs. Moreover, Neidhart's artistic genius, which contains elements of the dramatic as well as of the lyric, reveals itself in a diversity of ways, through the wide range of form and language, and the evocation of a variety of situations.

The total reversal of the courtly norms which had so recently prevailed and which even Walther had not sought to overturn speaks of an age when values were shifting at a rapid pace. The assumption by the peasants of the clothing and manners of the knights reflects a period when society was in turmoil. It is the environment which could lead to the distortions of which *Meier Helmbrecht* tells (see p. 403 ff.), and, in literary terms, it cannot be divorced from the developments which were taking place in the narrative. Neidhart's achievement is to express this revolution in a way which is itself revolutionary, combining passages of pure lyricism with earthy accounts of basic human behavior. The songs contain a strong element of caricature, and their relationship with the events of the outside world is tenuous. Although Neidhart may be reflecting the spirit of his times, he does not, for the most part, reflect actual events in the way that Walther did. Yet his popularity suggests that he judged the mood of his listeners very accurately, and in this respect he may be seen as speaking very much for his age.

Editions:
Haupt, Moriz, ed. *Neidharts Lieder*. 2. Auflage. Neu bearbeitet von Edmund Wießner. Leipzig, 1923. Repr. Stuttgart: Hirzel, 1986. Ed. by U. Müller, I. Bennewitz, and F-V. Spechtler. 2 vols. With afterward by the eds. and important bibliography. Neidhart's huge corpus is contained in this so-called *Große Ausgabe* which has yet to be replaced, though revision is long overdue.
Wießner, Edmund, and Hanns Fischer, eds. *Die Lieder Neidharts*. Tübingen: Niemeyer, [4]1984. Rev. by P. Sappler, with a music appendix by H. Lomnitzer. (= ATB, 44). All quotations and references are from this readily available paperback edition.

Selections with Translations:
Brackert, Helmut (*Minnesang* 170-180)
*Curschmann/Glier*, II, 674-696. Sel., MHG text, with adjacent mod. Ger. trans.
Lomnitzer, Helmut, ed. and trans. *Neidhart von Reuental: Lieder*. Stuttgart: Reclam, 1984 (= UB, 6927). Sel. with MHG text, plus mod. Ger. trans., intro., notes, plus section on the melodies with examples.
Wehrli, Max (*Deutsche Lyrik* 339-355).

### Neidhart—Bibliography

Brunner, Horst, ed. *Neidhart*. Darmstadt: Wiss. Buchges., 1986 (= WdF, 556). Comprehensive collection of 16 reprinted articles dating from 1908-1981.
See also: Olive Sayce (1982 217-233). The section on Neidhart is substantial and, as usual, full of sound information.

## POST-CLASSICAL LYRIC

Although the most famous names associated with the medieval German lyric belong to the peak of the Hohenstaufen period, the declining years of the dynasty and later saw a mass of productivity in this area, not by any means of high literary quality but significant for the overall development of the genre. Lyric poetry continued to thrive alongside the narrative, taking its inspiration from established trends, yet going off also into quite new directions. The manuscripts record a very large number of poets active throughout the 13th century and into the 14th, some of them continuing the Minnesang tradition and others developing the didactic lyric: some were active in both areas. It is very difficult to date most of these poets, and the manuscript transmission is possibly not a very reliable guide to the amount of work actually produced at the time. The majority of the poets are known only from the Manesse manuscript, and it is not surprising that Swiss poets constitute a high proportion. We thus have to accept that our knowledge of the prevailing situation is probably distorted, with a preponderance of lyrics dating from the period closer to the compilation of the manuscript as well as emanating from a closer geographical location. Thus if the later 13th century appears to be more prolific than the earlier decades, this should not be taken to suggest that the tradition lapsed after the classical period and was revived only later.

The huge collection in *Deutsche Liederdichter des 13. Jahrhunderts* by Carl von Kraus is a good guide to this very complex subject. Contained here are sixty-nine poets, including Wolfram von Eschenbach, but many of them are frankly unremarkable. It is also important to remember that Carl von Kraus deliberately excluded poets whose work had, at that time (1951), already been published either in collections such as *Des Minnesangs Frühling* and *Die Schweizer Minnesänger* (ed. Karl Bartsch, 1886. Repr. 1964) or in individual editions, as was the case with Walther von der Vogelweide, Neidhart, der Marner, Tannhäuser and Konrad von Würzburg. Inevitably, the omission of these important names gives a distorted impression.

The most accessible source of information in English is the book by Olive Sayce (1982), which provides a mass of useful information and highlights some of the principal trends in both the love lyric and the didactic lyric. She has also provided English translations of the quotations she uses for reference and analysis, and this is particularly helpful in an area where most of the works are available only in their original form.

The following sections present a selection of some of the principal poets of this period, indicating groupings and distinctive features. It would be misleading to devote time to many of the individual poets who are of relatively limited literary quality, even though, as part of the whole, they may be relevant.

The Hohenstaufen court continued to be a literary center under Henry VII, son of Frederick II, and a group of Swabian poets can be identified, their activity extending from before he was appointed to the stewardship of Germany in 1220 to beyond his deposition in 1235. Three names emerge as significant in what can hardly be termed a Swabian school, belonging as they do to different generations. What **Burkhard von Hohenfels, Gottfried von Neifen** and **Ulrich von Winterstetten** have most notably in common is the preoccupation with form and their technical virtuosity. That said, however, all three make quite individual contributions to the development of the lyric during the 13th century. Our references are taken from von Kraus, *Deutsche Liederdichter des 13. Jahrhunderts*.

In the eighteen songs recorded under his name, **Burkhard von Hohenfels**, the earliest of the three (c. 1220), reveals considerable variety and also some innovations. Although clearly influenced by his predecessors in the field of classical Minnesang and more immediately by Neidhart too, Burkhard demonstrates his individuality in amalgamating these elements and adding features all his own. His lyric is rich in imagery, some of it reminiscent of Wolfram von Eschenbach but differently used and altogether more ornate. Characteristic of him is the habit of heaping image upon image in a way which anticipates the "baroque" manner of later decades. The following strophe, the opening of XI is fairly typical:

> Dô der luft mit sunnen viure
> wart getempert und gemischet,
> dar gab wazzer sîne stiure,
> dâ wart erde ir lîp erfrischet.
> dur ein tougenlîchez smiegen
> wart si fröiden frühte swanger.
> daz tet luft, in wil niht triegen:
> schouwent selbe ûz ûf den anger.
> > fröide und frîheit
> > ist der werlte für geleit.

(When the air was mingled and tempered with the fire of the sun, the water gave its dowry and the earth was refreshed. With secret embraces it became pregnant with the fruits of joy. This was what the air did, and I am not deceiving you. Look for yourself out on to the meadow. Joy and freedom are spread out before the world.)

The poem, with its refrain characteristic of Burkhard, continues in similar vein, evoking the joy of love which is the keynote of much of his lyric. It culminates in a strophe of unrestrained ecstasy, in which the joy in loving is matched by the joy in nature:

> Sûsâ wie diu werde glestet!
> sist ein wunneberndez bilde,
> sô si sich mit bluomen gestet:
> swer si siht, demst trûren wilde.
> des giht manges herze und ougen.
> ein ding mich ze fröiden lücket:
> sist mir in mîn herze tougen
> stahelherteclich gedrücket.
> > fröide unde frîheit
> > ist der werlte für geleit.

(Whish! how the noble one (= the world) is glistening! It is a sight which brings forth joy when it adorns itself with flowers. Anyone who looks at it will be a stranger to sadness. Many a man's heart and eyes declare that this is so. One thing lures me to joy. It is stamped secretly firm as steel into my heart. Joy and freedom are spread out before the world.)

It cannot be denied, however, that the conscious artistry in Burkhard often means that he lacks the spontaneity and lightness of touch of his predecessors. There is something ponderous and overly conscious, for example, in IX, in which he sustains one of his favorite images, of the hunt, throughout five strophes. Burkhard is breaking new ground in this obsession with imagery, and his emphasis on rhyme patterns, though reminiscent of Heinrich von Morungen, suggests a trend in German poetry very much later than the mid-13th century. XIV, for example, could be dated somewhere in the 17th century, but for its obvious linguistic features:

Nîden    lîden    muoz diu reine
dur ir minneclîchen lîp.
schelten    gelten    kan si kleine,
sît ir weder man noch wîp
arge wârheit mac gesprechen.
sist sælden sundertriutel.
in der würzegarten kan si brechen
ir rôsen, ir bluomen, ir tugentfrühtig kriutel.

(The pure one must suffer envy on account of her lovely body. She knows little how to repay abuse since neither man nor woman can speak base truth of her. She is the precious darling of Fortune, and she can pluck her roses and her flowers and her virtuous little plants from the herb garden [of love].)

This is only the first strophe of a poem which continues in the same somewhat heavy-handed way. It contains also a very interesting feature of Burkhard von Hohenfels: his talent for inventing words (*sundertriutel, tugentfrühtig, wehselgedenken, wünschelgedenken*). Altogether one on his own in this period, then, Burkhard von Hohenfels is interesting as much as a phenomenon as for any intrinsic poetic qualities.

Possibly twenty years or so after Burkhard, another Swabian took this self-conscious artistry a little further. **Gottfried von Neifen** is attested at the Hohenstaufen court in the period of Henry VII's reign, and the range of the work recorded under his name, not all of which is authentic, speaks for the somewhat varied taste of the court, which could accept the frankly crude along with the more traditional courtly lyric. Like Burkhard, he enjoys playing with words and rhymes, but there are times when he pushes this playfulness into extremes, so that his work, highly influential at the time, has been criticized by modern scholars for its vacuousness. This is perhaps too harsh a verdict on a poet who employs certain techniques, notably rhyme and frequent repetition, with considerable skill. Moreover, even if his dominant theme is the traditional one of unrequited love and the lamentation for it, he is highly original in his use of a wide variety of metrical form, with considerable variation in length of line and a predilection for internal rhyming. Almost certainly the most important influence as far as form is concerned is the Old Provençal lyric. Although Carl von Kraus rejects as not authentic a large number of the songs under his name, Gottfried von Neifen nevertheless appears to have been a fairly prolific poet. This is not profound poetry, but what it lacks in thought it to some extent compensates for in sheer verbal artistry, though probably no one would maintain that this is artistry on any but a superficial level. One could select any number of his songs to illustrate his essential qualities, but perhaps the following first strophe of XIV will suffice to make the point:

Schouwet ûf den anger:
winter wert niht langer;
kleine vogel twanger.

diu heide ist worden swanger:
si birt uns rôsen rôt.
man hoert vogel singen,
man siht bluomen springen,
dur daz gras ûf dringen;
ir swære wil sich ringen
als in diu zît gebôt.
alsus enpfâhen wir den süezen meien!
wol ûf, ir hübschen leien!
wir suln die fröide heien,
vil froelîch tanzen reien.
ahî, solt ich mich zweien
mit ir diu mir mac wenden sende nôt.

(Look upon the meadow! The winter does not last any longer. It has brought forth little birds. The heath has become pregnant and gives birth to red roses for us. One can hear the birds singing and see the flowers springing up, pushing their way through the grass. Their sadness is vanishing as the season bids it do. Thus do we greet sweet May Time. Up now, courtly laity! We must encourage joy and dance merrily in a ring. Ah, if only I might pair up with the one who can banish my yearning sorrow!)

The object of his devotion, the queen of his heart who inflames him with love, is extolled throughout his poems for her physical beauty, epitomized above all in her red lips. Her sweet red mouth is praised, adored, and apostrophized again and again in verse which stands out for its undisguised eroticism and its blatant use of words for the sake of words. We can conclude with three strophes from the middle of XXVIII:

Wâ wart ie mündelîn sô rôt?
wâ wart ie baz gestalter lîp?
wâ wurden ie sô froelich stêndiu ougen,
diu mich hânt brâht in grôze nôt?
genâde, minneclîchez wîp:
ach hæte ich iuwer süeze minne tougen!
nu wizzet daz ich gerne bî iu wære.
genâde, rôsevarwer munt:
wan machest dû mich niht gesunt?
sprich zeiner stunt 'ich wil dir büezen swære.'

Nu lache daz ich frô bestê,
nu lache daz mir werde wol;
vil rôter munt, nu lache lacheclîche;
nu lache daz mîn leit zergê:
sô wirde ich sender fröiden vol.
nu lache daz mir ungemüete entwîche;
nu lache daz min sendiu sorge swinde;
nu lache mich ein wênic an,
sît ich dir niht entwenken kan,
ich sender man, unz ich dich lieplîch vinde.

Einmüetic dast ein lieplîch wort;
einmüetic dast der Minne gir;
einmüetic sendiu herzen fröide lêret;
einmüetic dast der liebe ein hort,
swie doch diu minneclîche mir
mit wîbes güete selten fröide mêret;
einmüetic mange süeze fröide machet;
einmüetic fröit ze manger stunt;
einmüetic dast ein lieplîch funt,
swâ rôter munt gein liebe lieplîch lachet.

(When did a little mouth ever become so red? When was there ever a more lovely body? Where were there ever such happy eyes which have brought me into such distress? Mercy, lovely lady: if only I had your sweet love in secret! But be assured that I should like to be with you. Mercy, rose-red mouth: why do you not make me well again? Just once say: 'I will make amends for your suffering.'
Now smile that I am happy; now smile that I am well again. Bright red mouth: smile smilingly. Now smile that my suffering is vanishing. Then I shall be filled with yearning joy. Now smile that my distress is vanishing. Now smile that my yearning sorrow disappears. Now smile just a little at me, since I cannot escape you, yearning man that I am, until I find you loving.
"United" is a loving word. "United" is the desire of love. 'United' brings loving joy to hearts. "United" is the treasury of love, however rarely my lovely one has ever increased my joy with womanly goodness. "United" makes many a sweet joy. "United" often delights. "United" is a precious discovery whenever a red mouth smiles lovingly in love.)

Although one may briefly glimpse the influence of Heinrich von Morungen in these strophes, the dominant impression is quite different and shows how far Gottfried von Neifen, in the middle of the 13th century, had come from the traditions of the classical Minnesang.

The constraints of the classical period in the love lyric had evidently been swept aside in favor of a preoccupation with form and blatant demonstrations of technical virtuosity in the work of a fellow Swabian of about the same period as Gottfried von Neifen. If anything, **Ulrich von Winterstetten** goes even further in his playful handling of words and rhymes, and, like Gottfried von Neifen but to an even greater extent, he employs the refrain as a characteristic feature of his songs. A member of a prominent family of ministeriales, Ulrich von Winterstetten was almost certainly the grandson of the patron of Rudolf von Ems (see p. 339) and Ulrich von Türheim (see p. 372), and his own contribution to the development of the love lyric is a not inconsiderable one.

Like Gottfried von Neifen, Ulrich von Winterstetten is a prolific poet, with a substantial corpus recorded under his name but, in his case, hardly any speculation about authenticity. Like his fellow Swabians, he is clearly working under the influence of his illustrious predecessors, and it is particularly Wolfram von Eschenbach who suggests himself as the model for one of Ulrich's more significant types of poetry: the dawn song. That is not to say that his contribution in this area reaches the heights of Wolfram, but it is interesting that he ventured into this relatively contained form of love lyric, while at the same time displaying the impact of Neidhart, in his use of village dialogue, and closely resembling the poet who in many respects can be seen as Neidhart's successor, Tannhäuser (see below). Thus, as is the case with Burkhard von Hohenfels and Gottfried von Neifen, Ulrich von Winterstetten takes up a variety of new directions, in forms and techniques, while, like them, not advancing the thought behind the Minnesang to any extent. It is interesting that at a time when the narrative was breaking new ground in terms of subject matter and thought, the love lyric had moved away hardly at all from the admittedly revolutionary modes of Walther and, more important still in this respect, of Neidhart, but was demonstrating its ability to evolve in many different ways as far as form and technique were concerned.

In Ulrich von Winterstetten, the thought is fairly conventional, with the familiar complaints about love, praise of the lady, and pleas to her and sometimes to Love itself dominating. It is as though this conventional material is little more than the means for Winterstetten to demonstrate his extraordinary skill in manipulating words and phrases. Thus the sentiment behind the following strophe could belong to sixty years earlier, the language in which it is couched not at all:

> Ich wil allen liuten    betiuten    mîns herzen klage
> und wie grôzen kumber    ich tumber    nu trage,
> wie mich sorge twinget    und singet    doch mir der lîp:
> seht daz muoz ich lîden    durch mîden    ein wîp.
> des muoz ich dem jâmerschricke    leider undertænic sîn.
> ich lig in ir minne stricke,    daz ist an mir worden schîn.
> sî kan senden smerzen    ûz herzen    vertrîben wol.
> rôse ob allen wîben    man si nennen sol.

(I wish to explain to everyone my heart's lament and tell them what great misery I am bearing now, foolish man that I am, how sorrow afflicts me yet how I go on singing. Look, I have to endure this through estrangement from a lady. Because of this I must submit to the horror of misery, alas. I am languishing in the bonds of her love, that is evident in me. She knows well how to drive yearning pain out of my heart. She should be called the rose of all women.)

This is the first strophe of XXI, a song which shares with the majority of Winterstetten's the characteristic of a refrain. The somewhat aggressive rhyming pattern here is another of his most striking features, taken to even greater extremes than in Gottfried von Neifen, and sometimes appearing to constitute the *raison d'être* of the poem. This is true both of his *Lieder* (songs with a regular strophic pattern) and of his *Leiche*, of which there are five under his name in the manuscript. The opening of the third *Leich*, for example, conveys the impression of an exercise in rhyming:

> Nemt war    wie gar    was der meie vollenbrâht,
> Des wât    zergât    die der sumer hât erdâht.
> Der sneit    sîn kleit    beide ûf berge und in dem tal,
> Dâ sanc    erklanc    der vil lieben nahtegal,

Aller sorgen frî   ûf grüenem zwî
ir muot    was guot,    ze sange snel.

(Observe how perfect is the May time, whose clothing, which summer has invented, vanishes. It [= summer] tailored its [= May's] dress both in the hill and in the valley. Then did the lovely nightingale sing and resound. Free from all sorrow on the green branch its spirit was good, bold in song. . . .)

And so the poem goes on, for 126 lines, impressing by the sheer daring and virtuosity, if not by the thought which verges on the banal. However, it is in poems like these, and there are many of them, that the German lyric shows its capacity to develop along unprecedented lines during the 13th century.

Geographically apart from the three Swabians, is the poet known as **Tannhäuser**, from the region of Nuremberg, active also in the latter half of the 13th century. He bears close resemblances to Winterstetten, in his predilection for the *Leich*, and, like Winterstetten, probably showing the influence of Neidhart in his evocation of the dance.

Tannhäuser is a somewhat mysterious figure who found his way into popular legend, and thence into Wagner's opera, but one of the puzzling features for the scholar is the relatively small output from one who appears to have been a professional poet. Manuscript C contains six *leiche* and ten poems consisting of thirty-seven strophes. One of these tells, in the first person, of the trials of a journey by sea (13,57), and the assumption that this may refer to the crusading expedition led by Frederick II in 1228-1229 (see p. 100 f.) has meant that a dating has been assumed for Tannhäuser which is in all probability too early. The striking depiction in the Manesse manuscript, of a knight in the habit of the Teutonic Order, doubtless also derives from this poem, which may not be autobiographical at all. The mystery is compounded by the existence in manuscript J of a penitential poem, which is almost certainly not by him though his name attaches to it and which is the source of the legend which told of his damnation by the Pope on account of his sinful service of the goddess Venus.

The existing poems provide evidence of a gifted poet, whose learning and capacity for irony are manifested in a mockery which is both directed at himself and at the courtly love lyric which he delights in parodying. His extant oeuvre, relatively slight though it is, gives the impression of a considerable breadth. In mood he ranges between the flippant and almost bucolic, and the deeply earnest contemplation of contemporary events, of which his poems give more impression than is usually the case. His connections with the declining dynasty of the Hohenstaufens is evidenced in a late *leich*, in which he laments the passing of an age and with it the loss of courtly values, but, like Walther von der Vogelweide before him, he is capable also of expressing personal grief, at the death of his lord, Duke Frederick II in 1246 and the deprivation which came to him personally as a result. Yet even in this deeply-felt poem, he manages a wry humor, as he rhymes his name *Tannhusære* with *swære* (grief) and *klagebære* (lamentable).

Editions:
Lomnitzer, Helmut, and Müller, Ulrich, eds. *Tannhäuser: Die lyrischen Gedichte der Hss. C und J. Abbildungen und Materialien zur gesamten Überlieferung der Texte und ihrer*

*Wirkungsgeschichte und zu den Melodien.* Göppingen: Kümmerle, 1973 (= Litterae, 13).

Siebert, Johannes, ed. *Der Dichter Tannhäuser. Leben—Gedichte—Sage.* Halle: Niemeyer, 1934.

Thomas, J. Wesley, ed. *Tannhäuser: Poet and Legend. With Texts and Translations of his Works.* Chapel Hill: Univ.of North Carolina Press, 1974 (= Univ. of North Carolina Studies in Germanic Langs. & Lits., 77). MHG texts with Engl. trans. and very useful introduction.

Translations:
*Curschmann/Glier*, II, 696-710.
See Thomas (1974) above.

As already mentioned, poets from what is now known as Switzerland constitute a very high proportion of those recorded in the Manesse manuscript, but these are, for the most part, not outstanding exponents of lyric poetry. To a large extent they are little more than imitators, notably of Walther von der Vogelweide. Like him, many composed both love songs in the Minnesang tradition and didactic verse which falls under the heading *Spruchdichtung*.

The important collection by Karl Bartsch, *Die Schweizer Minnesänger*, first published in 1886 and reprinted as recently as 1964, is now undergoing a complete revision by Max Schiendorfer. The references below are to the 1964 reprint. The volume contains 32 poets who can be fairly confidently located in Switzerland, and these range chronologically from **Graf Rudolf von Fenis**, otherwise known as **Rudolf von Neuenburg**, who belongs to the earlier period, along with Friedrich von Hausen and Heinrich von Veldeke, to the cleric **Rost, Kilchherre ze Sarnen**, whose death is recorded in 1329. Among these names few stand out as remarkable within the Minnesang tradition. Interesting is the diversity of social origins represented, aristocrats and clerics, patricians and itinerant poets. Some of these poets have a large body of work attributed to them (**Ulrich von Singenberg, Konrad Schenk von Landeck, Johannes Hadloub**), while others are represented by no more than a handful of songs. Some of the poems are fairly conventional, in the manner of the "classical" Minnesänger, occasionally (Ulrich von Singenberg) with a hint of parody, although some poets try their hand at a broader range (Hadloub) and even introduce new elements (Steinmar). Konrad von Würzburg who stands out as a figure of significance and originality in medieval German literature in the later 13th century, is sometimes included among the Swiss poets, but is better viewed independently (see p. 356 ff.).

The volume by Bartsch provides, along with the texts, an introduction to each of the poets included, and this still constitutes the best survey of this whole group of poets. The poet **Steinmar** is probably altogether the most original of the Swiss poets. His so-called *Schlemmerlied* (1), an innovative eulogy of the autumn season as the time to enjoy gastronomic pleasures, demonstrates a novel approach. The picture of Steinmar in the Heidelberg Manuscript shows a carousing group sitting beneath the falling leaves, awaiting the platter which is being brought to them. Along with traditional songs in praise of courtly love (2) and dawn songs (5), his oeuvre includes songs which are clearly to be seen as parodies of the convention (7, 11, 14) and even more down-to-earth songs in the rustic manner of Neidhart. In 8, a parody of a dawn song, the place of the watchman is taken by the herdsman, who wakens the humble lovers with the cry "Let the cows out!"

In 11, he appears to be using features of the Minnesang, in his lament for the passing of the summer and the loss of love, but this is a song of "niedere Minne" as opposed to "hohe Minne," and what he is really lamenting, as the refrain tells, is that his sweetheart will not let him come to her on her straw-bedding. At other times he employs the language and thought of the Minnesang proper in a more conventional way (2), though sometimes this is no more than a veneer that conceals a more original approach, as in 4, where the refrain tells how he is even further from receiving the sweet reward this year than he was the last. In this song, which almost lulls one into thinking that it is a serious song in praise of courtly love, the element of parody breaks through, when he tells how his heart jerks to and fro "like a pig in a sack."

Little is known about Steinmar, but it is likely that he belongs in roughly the same period as another of the more important names among the Swiss poets, **Johannes Hadloub**, whose presence in Zürich in 1302 is attested by the record of the purchase of a house. Like Steinmar, Hadloub composed a wide range of songs, and he is considerably more prolific than Steinmar, with 54 songs under his name, including three *leiche*. On the whole he is a less gifted poet, and his work is strongly derivative, borrowing liberally from classical Minnesang, Walther, Neidhart, and probably even from Steinmar himself. His most original contribution, however, is in those songs in which he offers little comic anecdotes, humorous accounts of usually catastrophic love exploits. This aspect of his work is reflected in his unique depiction in the Manesse manuscript. It contains two separate scenes, the one above the other, and they picture the two separate exploits related in poems 1 and 2. The first poem tells of how, disguised as a pilgrim he approached his lady as she went to early mass, hoping to deliver a letter to her in secret. The lady's demeanor in the illustration speaks for her rejection of him which in the poem he so laments, proclaiming that his heart is broken. The picture above this shows again the hapless lover, lying in front of her "als ein tôt man" (like a dead man) as the poem describes him (2,18), while her little lap-dog appears to be biting his hand, undoubtedly a reference to the bite which, according to the poem, he received from her when he held her hand so tightly (2,29 ff.). The whole of the first song is an amalgam of conventional ideas—he has loved her since childhood, her voice is sweet, her cheeks rose-red, and so on—and comic self-mockery.

Hadloub betrays a certain amount about himself and his way of life in his songs, unlike most of his predecessors and contemporaries, and he does this with a vitality and humor which survives his sometimes rather labored manner. Moreover, unlike Steinmar who favored simpler metrical forms, Hadloub is quite skilled in his manipulation of more complex structures, and in particular in his use of internal rhymes.

Texts and Translations:
Bartsch, Karl, ed. *Die Schweizer Minnesänger*. Frauenfeld, 1886. Repr. 1964. Newly rev. and ed. by Max Schiendorfer. Tübingen: Niemeyer, 1990. Vol. I: Texts.
Schiendorfer, Max, ed. and trans. *Die Gedichte des Zürcher Minnesängers Johannes Hadlaub*. Zürich: Artemis, 1986. MHG texts with adjacent mod. Ger. trans.
Thomas, J. Wesley, ed. and trans. *Medieval German Lyric Verse*. Chapel Hill, NC: Univ. of North Carolina Press, 1968 (= UNC Studies in Germanic Langs. & Lits., 60). MHG texts, with Engl. trans. and some brief introductory remarks on Hesse von Reinach, Kraft von

Toggenburg, Rudolf von Neuenberg, and Steinmar.
Max Wehrli (*Dt. Lyrik*, 1954 379 ff.) includes a translation of part of Steinmar's "Schlemmerlied."
See also: Olive Sayce (1982) 298-345; Steinmar 334-339; Hadloub 339-345.


## THE DIDACTIC LYRIC (SPRUCHDICHTUNG)

The term *Spruchdichtung* (poetry that makes a statement, a pronouncement, an observation, or a saying) is a convenient term to describe the wealth of poems dealing with religious and biblical themes, laments for the decline of personal and universal standards, panegyrics and eulogies, and accounts of contemporary affairs which were composed during the periods in the love lyric we have just discussed. It may not be strictly accurate, however, since most of these poems were intended to be sung, rather than spoken (*Spruch* = "saying," "aphorism"), but it does distinguish those works of a generally didactic nature from the Minnesang proper, although sometimes the two may overlap in specific cases. Indeed, the manuscripts sometimes hardly distinguish between the two kinds of poetry, although it is true that manuscript C has a preponderance of love songs, while manuscript J contains a large proportion of didactic material, much of it, not surprisingly given the assumed provenance of the compilation, from North Germany.

The earliest evidence for the didactic lyric in German takes us back to the last twenty years or so of the 12th century and to a corpus of material under the name **Spervogel**, which in the latest edition of *Minnesangs Frühling* is divided between **Spervogel** and **Herger**, the latter name being assigned to the more archaic poet whom older scholarship sometimes called "Spervogel I," or "der ältere Spervogel," or "Spervogel Anonymous," in recognition of the disparity of the work under this one name. Manuscript A had already acknowledged that there were probably two poets at work here when it divided the entries between "Spervogel" and "Der junge Spervogel." Even in this manuscript, however, the work which is clearly by the older poet is spread over both entries. The complicated situation is not made any clearer by the fact that Herger and Spervogel are unlikely to have been the real names of the poets, arising as both do from references as it were to third persons which have been assumed to refer to the poet himself in each case (MF VI,1,3; VII,II,2).

The six poems assigned to Herger are not so much intact poems in any usual sense, but rather groups of strophes linked sometimes by a common theme or sometimes by the repetition of significant words, or sometimes by both. Thus poem I begins with an address to his sons and an expression of regret that he has not the means to bequeath worldly goods to them, unlike Wernhart von Steinsberc, whom he praises for his generosity. This reference to one who may well have been his patron is linked with a reference to Rüedeger, renowned for his hospitality and openhandedness at Bechelaren (see *Nibelungenlied*, p. 205 ff.). III has as its linking thread two groups of animal fables, the first three strophes being unconnected anecdotes about a wolf, the second two strophes linked by the statement "zwêne hunde strîten umbe ein bein" ("two dogs were fighting over a bone"). IV and VI have religious themes: in IV the strophes are linked by the words "heaven" and "hell," and the themes of seeking the one and avoiding the other;

in VI, the three strophes are less obviously linked, as they deal in turn with the Crucifixion, the Resurrection, and God's almighty power over all creation. In V, he begins by telling how he cannot manage to shake the fruit from the trees of the orchard which he has entered; he proceeds to tell how a neighbor urged the separation of the good and the bad fruit, lest the latter contaminate the former; the third strophe appears to go off in a new direction, as it condemns the man who abandons his virtuous wife in favor of another, comparing him with a swine who leaves his pure stream and seeks out a dirty puddle; the fourth urges a man to temper his quest for honor with the concern for the well-being of his soul; the fifth, which may well have had a distinctly acquisitive purpose, tells of a farmer who, not seeing his grain come up one year, does not plant it again the next.

The tone of the later Spervogel is somewhat less personal, though the themes are generally similar: the advocacy of moderation and good sense, friendship and service, sound moral behavior, and the pursuit of a solid reputation. The latest edition of *Minnesangs Frühling* presents two groups: the first eighteen strophes according to manuscripts A and C, the second thirteen according to J, with a certain amount of overlap, thematically and sometimes verbally. Unlike the strophes under the name of Herger, these tend to be more self-contained, and their tone is sententious rather than narrative, often having a proverbial tinge. Just one example will serve to convey the flavor of these strophes (1,12):

> Wan sol den mantel kêren, als daz weter gât.
> ein vrömder man der habe sîn dinc, als ez danne stât.
> sîns leides sî er niht ze dol,
> sîn liep er schône haben sol.
> ez ist hiute mîn, morne dîn: sô teilet man die huoben.
> vil dicke er selbe drinne lît, der dem andern grebt die gruoben.

(One should adjust one's coat according to the weather. A strange [virtuous?] man should take things as they are. He should not be too miserable about his troubles and enjoy his happiness. Today it's mine, tomorrow yours: that's how they parcel out the land. How often does a man find himself in the grave which he has dug for someone else!)

These are quite entertaining strophes, and particularly when sung, as was obviously the intention, they no doubt passed away some pleasant hours. However, they can hardly rank as significant poetry, nor yet as profound thought, and German poetry had to wait for Walther von der Vogelweide (see p. 273 ff.) to give a special quality to the *Spruch*, elevating it as a genre beyond the pithy statement of home-spun philosophy which is largely contained in the work of Herger and Spervogel.

Among the didactic poets after Walther, one of the principal names is that of **Reinmar von Zweter**. Originally, or so he tells us, from the Rhineland, he was an itinerant poet who spent his early life in Austria. His career can probably be dated approximately 1225-1259, and his work is extensively recorded in a wide range of manuscripts, suggesting that he was extremely popular, though, to modern tastes, his work is somewhat pedestrian. His *Sprüche* treat the themes established by Walther, and in the principal manuscript which contains his work, the early 14th century manuscript D, they are grouped according to content: religious *Sprüche*, mostly in praise of the Virgin; *Sprüche* devoted to the theme of courtly love; *Sprüche* in which he writes of courtly and in particular of knightly virtues; political poems, in which he first supported Frederick II in his conflict with the Pope, but subsequently turned against him; poems about courtly life and the nobility. Above all he praises honor (*êre*) by which he understands not just the honor accorded to a person by his fellow men but an intrinsic inner worth. In advocating honor and personifying Honor as a noble young woman, greatly to be desired, he harnesses the themes and language of the Minnesang in a new way. This he does in a form known as the *Fraun-Ehren-Ton*. It is not a particularly successful poetic medium but he employs it in a way that must have been admired, since Reinmar von Zweter was included among the twelve great "masters" by the *Meistersänger* (see p. 302).

Other important didactic poets of the period are **Der Marner** and **Bruder Wernher** in the earlier part of the 13th century and, in the later part, **Der Meißner**, **Rumelant**, **Friedrich von Sunnenberg** and **Der Kanzler**. Also to be included in this group is **Heinrich von Meißen**, otherwise known as **Frauenlob**, who will be treated separately. The most important theme is religion which is central to all of these, with poems in praise of the Virgin very common, along with prayers and confessions, poems in praise of Creation, and others to record specific events in the Bible and to mark significant Christian occasions.

The earnest tone which characterizes most of these poems stems from the belief in the poet's role as counselor, as possessing a special gift from God, which enables him, indeed obliges him, to offer advice and warnings to his fellow men. Most of these poets were itinerants, dependent on the generosity of their patrons, and the theme of generosity is a recurrent one, with protestations of poverty coupled with pleas for help and praise of hospitality and kindness. There are laments for individual patrons and princes, and laments for the decay of virtue and good breeding, such as we have already found in Walther von der Vogelweide. Quite separate from the lyric which is clearly an extension of the Minnesang, is the much more impersonal, didactic lyric which praises love for its edifying powers as is the case in the following lines by Reinmar von Zweter (31,1 ff.):

> Die Minne lêrt die vrouwen schône grüezen,
> Diu Minne lêret manegen Spruch vil süezen,
> Diu Minne lêret groze milte,
> Diu Minne lêret groze tugent,
> Diu Minne lêret, daz diu jugent
> kan ritterlîch gebâren under schilte.

(Love teaches how to greet the ladies elegantly, Love teaches many charming poems, Love teaches great generosity, Love teaches great virtue, Love teaches young people to acquit themselves in courtly fashion beneath the shield.)

The central intention of these poems, to teach, is achieved by a variety of devices such as fables and proverbs. The immediately preceding example from Reinmar von

Zweter makes use of repetition, to hammer the point home, and repetition, parallels, lists and direct questions are all used by the poets within this general group.

Editions:

Müller, Ulrich, ed. *Politische Lyrik des deutschen Mittelalters: Texte*. 2 vols. Göppingen: Kümmerle, 1972. Vol. I (= GAG, 68) and 1974. Vol. II (= GAG, 84). An important and readily available edition of these poems, with commentary.

Roethe, Gustav, ed. *Die Gedichte Reinmars von Zweter*. Leipzig, 1887. Repr. Amsterdam: Rodopi, 1967.

Schönbach, Anton, ed. *Die Sprüche des Bruder Wernher*. Sitzungsber. d. kaiser. Akad. d. Wiss., Wien, Phil.-hist. Kl. 148,7 (1904); 150,1 (1905).

Strauch, Philipp, ed. *Der Marner*. Strasbourg, 1876. Reissued "mit einem Nachwort, einem Register and einem Literaturverzeichnis von Helmut Brackert", Berlin, 1965.

Translations:

See Wehrli (*Deutsche Lyrik*, 1954): Bruder Wernher (432 f.), Reinmar von Zweter (443-445), Der Marner (450-453). Sel., MHG text with mod. Ger. trans.

See Thomas (*Med. Ger. Verse*, 1968, 179 ff.): four songs by Reinmar von Zweter with intro. comments. Engl. trans.

## Spruchdichtung—Bibliography

Moser, Hugo, ed. *Mittelhochdeutsche Spruchdichtung*. Darmstadt: Wiss. Buchges., 1972 (= WdF, 154).

Reprint of 21 articles from mid 19th cent.-1970.

Sowinski, Bernhard. *Lehrhafte Dichtung des Mittelalters*. Stuttgart: Metzler, 1971 (= Sammlung Metzler, 103).

## LATER DEVELOPMENTS IN THE LYRIC

**Frauenlob** is the pseudonym of **Heinrich von Meißen**, an important figure who evokes some extreme reactions in literary critics. Dismissed by some for his mannered eccentricity, he is viewed by others as the very culmination of the kind of traditions we have been considering and the instigator of a totally new phase in medieval German literature. Probably much research remains to be undertaken on one who, in the fifty years or so surrounding the turn of the 13th and 14th centuries, produced an enormous amount of material, much of it in highly ornate, exaggerated style. There is no firm evidence for the legend that he founded the first school of *Meistersänger* in Mainz, but, like Reinmar von Zweter, he was named by the *Meistersänger* as one of their twelve masters. We do know that he died in Mainz in 1318, where he was buried amidst great ceremony in the vicinity of the cathedral, according to documentary evidence.

Although he produced a great many *Sprüche*, his fame rests largely on his three *Leiche*, among them the poem to the Virgin Mary which may have given rise to his pseudonym. In the illustration in the Manesse manuscript, the coat of arms of Frauenlob contains a depiction of the Virgin wearing a crown, a reference to the *Marienleich* which opens the entry under his name in that manuscript. His other attempts at this form are the sometimes disputed *Minneleich* and the *Kreuzleich*. Characteristic of them is what Max Wehrli has described as the "calculated linguistic orgy" and the "self-indulgent acrobatics of words and forms which threaten any identifiable content" (*Geschichte* 1980 453). Frauenlob delights beyond any of his predecessors in intricate word-play, exotic vocabulary and bold neologisms, but it might be said that he is doing no more than setting the seal on existing trends. His work looks forward rather than back, however, and he is rightly seen as the instigator of the fashions in style and ostentatious displays of learning which were to gain currency in the *Meistergesang*.

Texts:
Stackmann, Karl, and Karl Bertau, eds. *Frauenlob (Heinrich von Meißen). Leiche, Sangsprüche, Lieder.* Göttingen: Vandenhoeck & Ruprecht, 1981. 2 vols.

Translations:
See Thomas (*Med. Ger. Verse*, 1968 216-221) for English transls., and Wehrli (*Dt. Lyrik*, 1954 467-473.) for mod. Ger. transls.

## Frauenlob—Bibliography

Kuhn, Hugo. *Minnesangs Wende*. Tübingen: Niemeyer, 1952. [2]1967 (= Hernaea, NF, 1). Important scholarly work relating to this post-classical period, particularly to the lyric. Not easy to read. Contains useful, if rather complex, material.

Sayce, Olive: has a full and informative chapter on the didactic lyric (1982, 408-441). Particularly useful in this otherwise rather inaccessible field are her many quotations, together with translations into English.

Schröder, Werner, ed. *Wolfram-Studien X: Cambridger "Frauenlob"-Kolloquium 1986.* Berlin: Erich Schmidt, 1988. Fifteen papers on "Frauenlob" given at the meeting of the Wolfram von Eschenbach-Gesellschaft in Cambridge, UK, September 1986. Reactions to the Stackmann/Bertau new edition (see above).

In order to complete the picture of the medieval German lyric one must go forward almost a century, to the remarkable and vivid figure of **Oswald von Wolkenstein**, who in some ways continues the development firmly established in the High Middle Ages and in others stands on his own, as an innovator of considerable talent who looks forward to the broadening horizons of the Renaissance.

Indeed, this colorful adventurer/poet, who was born in 1377 and about whose life we know a great deal from his own testimony, goes way beyond 1400, but it would be remiss to exclude so dynamic and significant a figure from this survey of the development of the lyric. He is a very talented artist, both as poet and musician, and as a personality he represents the ruthless thrust of an age which was breaking away from the conventions and anticipating the spirit and indeed the brutality of the decades to come.

The impression of Oswald as a larger-than-life adventurer whose exploits as he ranged round the world are recorded in his poems owes much to the work of Beda Weber who first edited the songs in 1847 and then published a highly romanticized biography in 1850. It was not until 1930 that some of the historical inaccuracies were corrected and the picture somewhat redressed in another biography, this time by a descendant of Oswald, Arthur von Wolkenstein-Rodenegg, who unearthed some significant material from the family archives and opened the way for research which had a firmer basis in historical fact and in the proper analysis of his songs.

That does not mean, however, that biographical details are not highly relevant to a study of Oswald, and we do know more about him than about most Middle High German poets. His parents both belonged to the Villanders family, an eminent and wealthy dynasty in the South Tyrol, and his grandfather had acquired the castle of Wolkenstein in the Dolomites from which Oswald's father assumed the family name. The exact year of his birth is disputed, but 1377 is usually accepted as most likely. He died on 2 August 1445 in Merano.

The three manuscripts, A (in Vienna), B (Innsbruck), and c (Innsbruck) contain a very large corpus of songs, most of them with the accompanying melodies. There is a very high degree of correspondence among these manuscripts, and it is generally held that A and B were produced at the behest and to a large extent under the control of Oswald himself, and that c was a copy of B. The splendidly produced manuscript B contains the famous portrait of Oswald, with his puffy face, his mass of thick wavy hair and his missing right eye. This striking depiction of him, which may conceivably be the work of Antonio Pisanello, distinguishes Oswald von Wolkenstein sharply from the earlier Middle High German poets, whom we can identify only from the stylized representations of the manuscript illustrations. Whether he was born with one eye missing or whether he lost it in the course of his often violent life, we cannot know, but the latter possibility seems the more likely. His quasi-autobiographical writings tell of how he ran away from home at a very early age, travelled widely in Europe and in the East, landed himself often in conflicts and at least twice in prison. For substantial periods of his life he was in the service of the Emperor Sigismund.

Coming as he did from a wealthy family and not, like so many of his fellow poets of earlier decades, dependent on his work to earn him a living, Oswald had a high degree of independence, both in the freedom which he clearly indulged to go his own way in life and in the process to become embroiled in some of the significant events of his day, and in his artistic independence which enabled him, uninhibited by the need to satisfy a patron or a public, to range over themes and forms as the mood took him and thus to produce an oeuvre which combines the familiar with the highly innovative. When he tells of his numerous love affairs, it is not with the mannered restraint of the Minnesang, but with an exuberant sensuality and eroticism which verges on the coarse. He tells also of his travels, his involvement in politics and feuding, his proficiency in foreign languages and his musical accomplishment. His musical legacy does indeed testify to the influence of non-European elements, as well as to the impact of models far beyond his immediate homeland.

Texts:
Heimrath, Johannes, and Michael Korth, eds. and trans. *Oswald von Wolkenstein: Frölich geschray so well wir machen. Melodien und Texte.* Munich: Heimeran, 1975. Sel. of melodies and texts, trans. into mod. Germ., with helpful commentaries by Ulrich Müller and Lambertus Okken. An informative and entertaining book, liberally adorned with illustrations.
Klein, K. K., ed. *Die Lieder Oswalds von Wolkenstein.* 3. neubearbeitete und erweiterte

Auflage von H. Moser, N. R. Wolf und N. Wolf. Tübingen: Niemeyer, 1987 (= ATB, 55).

Wachinger, Burghart, ed. and trans. *Oswald von Wolkenstein. Eine Auswahl aus seinen Liedern. Mittelhochdeutsch und Neuhochdeutsch.* Stuttgart: Reclam, [2]1967 (= UB 2839/2940). A convenient selection, with mod. Ger. trans. and a commentary.

Translations:
See Wachinger (1967) and Heimrath (1975) above.
*Curschmann/Glier* III, 155-175. Sel., MHG texts with mod. Ger. trans.

## Oswald von Wolkenstein—Bibliography

Baasch, Karen, and Helmut Nürnberger. *Oswald von Wolkenstein mit Selbstzeugnissen und Bilddokumenten.* Rowohlt: Hamburg, 1986 (= Rowohlts Monographien).
Contains a great deal of information, some of it rather loosely related to Oswald, and many illustrations.

Jones, George F. *Oswald von Wolkenstein.* New York: Twayne, 1973 (= TWAS 236).
Good basic introduction to Oswald von Wolkenstein in English.

Müller, Ulrich, ed. *Oswald von Wolkenstein.* Darmstadt: Wiss. Buchge., 1980 (= WdF, 526).
A collection of essays and articles, dating from 1959 and covering a wide range of issues. A useful bibliography is appended.

——. *"Dichtung" und "Wahrheit" in den Liedern Oswalds von Wolkenstein: Die autobiographischen Lieder von den Reisen.* Göppingen: Kümmerle, 1968 (= GAG, 1)
The first major study of Oswald to interpret Oswald's songs as literature rather than as autobiography, this book is stimulating and illuminating, though when it appeared it seemed rather provocative.

Robertshaw, Alan. *Oswald von Wolkenstein: The Myth and the Man.* Göppingen: Kümmerle, 1977 (= GAG 178).
A useful, clearly set out investigation of Oswald's life and work, with some analyses of individual songs. Appended are some interesting contemporary documents in facsimile with transcripts.

Röll, Walter. *Oswald von Wolkenstein.* Darmstadt: Wiss. Buchge., 1981 (= Erträge der Forschung, 160).
A very convenient little volume, which covers the central issues and major scholarship.

The golden age of medieval German lyric poetry was long past when Oswald von Wolkenstein was composing his dynamic and highly individual songs, but its memory was revived and to some extent maintained through the activities of the **Meistersinger,** who in the 14th century and through several centuries to come attempted to emulate the Minnesingers at least in the outward observation of their forms and to impose strict rules on poetry and song. Although the early "schools" recognized twelve great masters and perpetuated their melodies, it later became compulsory for anyone aspiring to become a master to invent his own *ton*. The early meetings took place in churches, and the subject was meant to be suitably edifying and harnessed to the service of God. Thus the phenomenon had more in common with the *Spruch* than with the love lyric which it imitated in formal terms. Closely associated with the development of the Meistersang is the name of Hans Folz, who in the late 15th century distinguished the older tradition from the new and paved the way for increasingly secular subject matter.

## Meistersinger—Bibliography

Nagel, Bert, ed. *Der deutsche Meistersang*. Darmstadt: Wiss. Buchges., 1967 (= WdF, 148).

A collection of significant articles on the subject reprinted here. Unfortunately, none very recent.

\_\_\_\_. *Der deutsche Meistersang: poetische Technik, musikalische Form und Sprachgestaltung*. Heidelberg: Kerle, 1967.

\_\_\_\_. *Meistersang*. Stuttgart: Metzler, 1962 (= Sammlung Metzler, 12).

A concise comprehensive overview of "Meistersang," at least as of 1962.

Schanze, Frieder. "Meisterliederhandschriften." *VL*$^2$ 6 (1987): 342-356.

# Post-"Classical" Literature

## HISTORICAL BACKGROUND 1273-1400

From the peak of the dominance of the Hohenstaufens who give their name to the great period of medieval German literature which is the core of this book, we witness a steady decline, reflected early on in the laments of Walther von der Vogelweide and coloring much of the literature of the post-courtly period.

The entrenched hostility towards the Hohenstaufens from the papacy culminated at the Council of Lyons in 1245, when the Pope announced the deposition of Frederick II and summoned the electors to name a new king of the Romans. Although Frederick himself did not die until 1250 and was then succeeded by his son Conrad IV until his death in 1254, we are approaching, or in the eyes of some, already in, that period known as the Interregnum, the long period during which there was no crowned emperor and which ended in 1273 with the coronation of Rudolf von Habsburg. In the meantime, several candidates were elected to the title of King of Germany, although none was regarded as a full sovereign nor numbered among the emperors.

The first of these was William of Holland, elected as anti-king in 1247 with the support of the pope and reigning until his death in 1256, when two rival kings were elected, Richard of Cornwall and Alfonso of Castile. The position of neither was very solid: Richard was crowned legally enough but failed to gain the support of all the princes; Alfonso never entered the kingdom and was never crowned. Gradually the princes who had originally supported Alfonso acknowledged Richard, but he never obtained recognition from the pope, wary still of a revival of Hohenstaufen power in the form of one who was brother-in-law to Frederick II, who had married Richard's sister Isabella. The impact of Richard on German history was slight, his title little more than nominal, and he spent the greater part of his reign in England. His death in 1272 marks a turning-point and the appearance of the family which was to dominate Europe in centuries to come.

Rudolf von Habsburg emerged almost from nowhere to defeat the only other candidate for the imperial crown, King Ottokar of Bohemia, and he succeeded during the eighteen years of his reign in gaining a high degree of respect in a country which had long been on the brink, and sometimes over the brink, of anarchy. He also managed to remain on reasonably good terms with successive popes, a feat in itself in medieval Europe and one which had been notably lacking among the achievements of his predecessors.

What he did not manage to do was establish an hereditary principle of succession, and, since he had never been crowned King of the Romans himself, his attempt to have his own son Albert accepted as his heir failed. Although Albert was an obvious successor, he was far from popular with the electors, and once more a virtually unknown candidate emerged, Count Adolf of Nassau. He was clearly a compromise choice, the electors having declined to choose either of the others, Albert of Habsburg or Wenzel of Bohemia, knowing as they did that either choice would precipitate a war between Austria and Bohemia.

The young and rather colorless Adolf made little impression on the Empire and was deposed in 1298, only to die shortly afterwards in an ill-conceived battle of his own instigation, and, it is said, at the hand of the man who was to succeed him, Albert of Habsburg, who again presented himself as a candidate for the crown so desired for him by his late father and himself. His unanimous election and his coronation in Aachen remained unrecognized by the Pope, who despised him on personal grounds and also feared even the remotest link with the hated Hohenstaufens.

Albert reigned for ten years and had a salutary effect on the morale of Germany, but he made no claim to the imperial crown and, unlike his much more significant predecessors, he did not even pretend to be interested in Italy. He concerned himself rather with subjugating Hungary and Bohemia and with attempting to annex the Swiss cantons for his own family.

Albert was assassinated in 1308 by his nephew, who had a personal grudge against him, and he was succeeded by a man who possessed both admirable qualities of character and political acumen, Henry of Luxemburg who became Henry VII. His fruitful and compassionate rule was cut short by his murder in 1313, when, it is said, he was poisoned by a priest with Communion wine in the course of a war in Italy which he had joined in alliance with Pope Clement V.

Two candidates now emerged: Ludwig of Bavaria and Frederick of Austria, son of Albert of Habsburg. Following an election characterized by intrigue, both were proclaimed and both crowned on the same day, Ludwig in the right place, Aachen, but by the wrong person, the Archbishop of Mainz, and Frederick by the Archbishop of Cologne, the right person, but in Bonn, the wrong place.

The situation was further complicated by the fact that the papacy was vacant, following the death of Clement V and before the election of John XXII, a Frenchman. There was therefore no arbiter, always assuming that anyone had been prepared to put the matter to arbitration. Instead, a lengthy civil war ensued which ended only eight years later when Ludwig defeated Frederick and took him prisoner, alienating John XXII who had offered to intercede in the dispute. From now on the pope and Ludwig were engaged in irreconcilable conflict, and the pope demanded that Ludwig no longer call himself King of the Romans, a title which he had assumed without papal authority.

The hostility culminated in extreme events: a fifth excommunication for Ludwig, followed by his coronation at St. Peter's in Rome and his deposition of John XXII and appointment of an Italian of his choice as successor, Peter of Corvara, himself a bitter opponent of John XXII. Ludwig's rival, Frederick of Austria, died in 1330 and, in a changed and changing situation, Ludwig attempted to reconcile himself with the Pope, but in vain. In 1334, John XXII died and was succeeded by Clement V, who could not for political reasons lift his predecessor's sentence of excommunication, since it would have alienated the French.

With the beginning in 1337 of the war between England and France which was to last for a hundred years, Ludwig's position looked more promising. He and Edward III became allies, and Pope Benedict XI was persuaded by the French king Philip to encourage Ludwig to withdraw his support of England by holding out the prospect of release from excommunication. With the death of Benedict XI and the accession of Clement VI in 1342, the excommunication remained firm, however, and Ludwig further alienated the Pope by annulling the marriage of the heiress Margaret Maultasch of the Tyrol with the son of John of Bohemia and marrying her to his son, Ludwig of Brandenburg.

In 1346 Ludwig was deposed by the Pope, although Germany did not accept this deposition. The electors were persuaded to meet and nominated Charles of Moravia of the house of Luxemburg, the eldest son of John of Bohemia. He was crowned in Bonn in 1346, a year before the sudden death of Ludwig, still unabsolved.

Like his immediate predecessors, Ludwig had accumulated substantial inheritances: the house of Wittelsbach now possessed Brandenburg, Tyrol, Bavaria, and the Palatinate, although the ancient German rule of partition required that after each accretion the domain be divided among the sons of the house. This tended towards a dilution of personal power and a fragmentation of the power of the dynasties.

The reign of Charles IV commenced in inauspicious circumstances. The feeling in Germany against the deposition of Ludwig was strong, and so, therefore, was the antipathy for the pope; and his election had been achieved under duress and far from unanimously. Three of his rivals were easily disposed of, or ruled themselves out: Edward III of England, Frederick of Meissen and Ludwig of Brandenburg. A fourth, Günther of Schwartzburg persisted in his claims and was largely accepted as king, but Charles himself is believed to have disposed of him, by arranging for him to be poisoned. Thus by 1349, Charles faced no competition and applied himself to affairs in Germany before eventually being crowned in Rome by the representative of the pope in 1355.

Probably the most notable achievement, in political terms, of Charles IV was his issue of the Golden Bull in 1356, a document which, as one of its most significant effects, formalized electoral procedures evolved over the previous decades. In thirty articles, it set out what could be described as the first written German constitution. Its principal objective was to create some kind of order at royal elections, requiring that the election should be by majority decision, interpreted as unanimity, by the seven named electors: the king of Bohemia, the archbishops of Mainz, Cologne, and Trier, the count palatine of the Rhine, the duke of Saxony, and the margrave of Brandenburg. The archbishop of Mainz was to summon the electors to Frankfurt within three months of the death of the emperor, and specific rules were established for the conduct of the elections, from a limit on the size of the retinue of each elector to the order of casting ballots and counting the vote. The electors thus achieved an exalted position, but they also assumed strictly defined duties, and provision was made for annual meetings of the electors in an imperial city within four weeks after Easter, at which occasions they were to report on the districts within their purview. The Golden Bull also concerned itself with a variety of practical matters of administration and law, e.g., the circumstances in which feuding might be considered legal. The rights of the burgher, too, were clearly established with the prohibition of migration into the towns and the removal of legal status from country dwellers who moved into the towns. In this way, the Golden Bull attempted to define the privileges of members of society at all levels.

The reign of Charles IV was particularly important for the growth of literature and of the language. The center of gravity of the Empire was shifting towards the East. Ties with Poland and Hungary were added to his ties with France and the Rhineland. His court was in Prague, where, in 1348, he founded the university which at that time was the only one in central Europe. Prague became a city of great beauty and culture, and the chancellery there cultivated a language of particular elegance, which has an important place in the development of the German language (see Waterman 112 ff.). With the support of Charles and the skill of his chancellor, Johann von Neumarkt, Prague became a center of linguistic and literary significance to match its political importance. It gave due recognition to the great writers of the Italian Renaissance, Dante, Petrarch, and Boccaccio, who all wrote in Latin as well as Italian and provided appropriate models for the development of the vernacular on the basis of Latin styles.

The final chapter of the Golden Bull concentrates on the importance of language, acknowledging that the individuality of the different nations within the Empire depends on differences in customs, way of life, and language. The electors and their successors should be acquainted with languages other than German, specifically in that they should be taught Latin, Italian, and Czech from the age of seven. This linguistic range was symptomatic of the conception of the Empire as supranational. To the traditional shape of a "Frankish" Empire with Frankfurt, Aachen and Nuremberg as its centers was added the new dimension of Bohemia, which was to remain an important element in imperial history under the Luxemburg family and later under the Habsburgs. The reign of Charles IV was generally a period of relative peace. He concerned himself with administrative acts within Germany and maintained his distance from the affairs of Italy and potential clashes with the papacy. His success in increasing the territory under the authority of Bohemia and passing it on to his son is undeniable.

Charles's son Wenzel, who had already been elected and crowned at Aachen in 1376, having been recognized by Pope Urban V as King of the Romans, succeeded his father upon his father's death in 1378. His reign, in contrast to that of his father, was characterized by disruption and conflict, largely the product of his own unstable personality. That he was not deposed until 1400 was probably due to the equally chaotic state of the papacy at the time of the Great Schism, and, until the intervention of Boniface IX, his misdeeds were allowed to go unchecked, though certainly not unnoticed. The act of deposition pronounced by the Archbishop of Mainz as Arch-chancellor of Germany lists an array of crimes which range from the foolish to the brutal and which speak of a man who was in no way fit for the elevated office he had inherited without challenge over twenty years earlier.

In the course of the 13th and 14th centuries an important dimension of society grew up in the form of the patrician class. Its members were families engaged in commerce and particularly in long-distance trade, so that from their base in the large towns like Cologne, Lübeck, Magdeburg, Nuremberg and Regensburg, their influence, which could be political as well as mercantile, radiated throughout Europe. Such families attained high social standing, very often assuming surnames which were based on place rather than, as previously, on trade, and so implied territory; patricians were accorded the title "Dominus" or "Herr" and enjoyed a privileged lifestyle, living in substantial town-houses and exercising authority within urban society in matters relating to justice and policy. They thus assumed considerable power in a country which lacked a strong centralizing monarchy and in which success in long-distance trading bestowed its own status. Many of these families lasted for decades, even centuries, in the same town and became intimately associated with it. Inevitably, this hierarchical grouping provoked opposition from the lower orders and there are many records of rebellions by the lesser townsfolk, some of them quite violent but others having no more forceful intention than to ensure more participation in public decisions and policy making. There are important examples, however, of the overthrow of the patricians by well-organized lower groups, and the establishment of a more equitable rule within the towns. (On this whole issue, see Du Boulay, 141-159.)

The 14th and 15th centuries also saw the grouping of towns known as the Hanseatic League. This development had begun considerably earlier in other countries, notably in England, where merchants had joined together for more or less social purposes in groups which nevertheless had religious, political, and economic implications. The Baltic alliances of the 13th century led to the joining in 1347 of the Hansas of Lübeck and Hamburg into the more formal union which was to lead, in turn, to the widespread linking of towns and cities—and not only coastal towns—throughout northern Germany. The ruling class of the Hanseatic League was the merchants, although its members obviously included also the guilds of craftsmen which were assuming increasing importance both socially and economically. The gradual rise of the Hanseatic League was matched by its slow decline in the course of the 15th century, although the leading cities, above all Hamburg, Lübeck, and Bremen, retained their independence for many centuries and, of course, still retain their dominant positions along with their historical significance. (See J. Leuschner 144-147).

In the later 13th and the 14th centuries, despite the movement away from the countryside and into the towns, the populations of the great towns and cities of Germany, insofar as figures are available, were very small, compared with those of comparable cities elsewhere in Europe. Simultaneous with the desertion of villages throughout the land were the ravages of the plague which afflicted the urban population in particular, even before the onslaught known as the Black Death in the middle of the 14th century. Yet this same period was a time of growth in many directions, geographically towards the East and culturally in many respects, with the building of some of the great cathedrals (Cologne begun in 1248, Strasbourg c.1275, Naumburg c.1250-60) and work continuing on some of the earlier ones like Worms and Mainz, and the foundation of new universities (after Prague in 1348, Vienna in 1365, Heidelberg in 1386, Cologne 1388).

In such a period of contrast and change, it is not surprising that the writing of the later Middle Ages in Germany represents a strangely diffuse, in some respects discordant, array of types and individual examples. More and more the German language was used for practical purposes, yet that language was still a collection of dialects, with the written language reflecting the diversity of regional forms. However, there was an effort to establish a kind of standard language in the chancelleries, and it is reflected in the many legal documents issued at the imperial and local level. Yet it was to be many decades, centuries even, before Germany attained a genuine standard literary language, even such as may have existed for a brief period, within a very limited scope, during the *Blütezeit* in the early years of the 13th century.

### History (1273-1400)—Bibliography

Dollinger, Philippe. *The German Hansa*. Trans. from the French and ed. by D. S. Ault and S. H. Steinberg. London: Macmillan, 1970.

Probably the best complete account of the subject.

Du Boulay, F. R. H. *Germany in the Later Middle Ages*. London: Athlone, 1983.

A very full account of the most important aspects of Germany in the 13th, 14th, and 15th centuries. It takes up approximately from where Bäuml (see Resources, p. 14) and Haverkamp (see Resources, p. 13) leave off and probably offers the most useful background to our subject. Best read in conjunction with J.Leuschner (below).

Leuschner, Joachim. *Germany in the Late Middle Ages*. Amsterdam: North-Holland Publishing Company, 1980.

This is a translation by Sabine MacCormack in the series *Europe in the Middle Ages, Selected Studies* (Vol.17). Covering much of the same material as Du Boulay, it offers a different perspective and is written in a refreshingly readable style.

Pevsner, Nikolaus. *An Outline of European Architecture*. Harmondsworth: Penguin [6]1960 (Jubilee Edition).

This brilliant encyclopedic work provides much information on an area that we have not been able to cover.

Thomson, S. H. "Learning at the Court of Charles IV." *Speculum* 25 (1950): 1-20.

On the language of the period, see the works already listed by Waterman (Late Middle High German, pp. 97 ff.; Early New High German, pp. 102 ff.) and Wells (Chancery Style, pp. 125-6; Commercial German, including the Hanseatic League, pp. 127 ff.).


### TYPES OF POST-"CLASSICAL" NARRATIVE LITERATURE

The three great exponents of the courtly narrative, together with the anonymous poet who drew together the disparate threads which constitute the *Nibelungenlied*, gave to medieval Germany what can justifiably be called a "classical" literature, and it is no exaggeration to say that large portions of the literary composition of the later 13th century would be inconceivable without this foundation. By about 1220 the corpus was "complete," and those who now took up the task of composing narrative literature did so with a weighty burden of responsibility upon them either to continue a tradition so magnificently established or, in some cases, to take a new direction. Certainly the variety of narrative literature in German after 1220 and indeed for the remainder of the 13th century is one of its most remarkable features. If it never attains the artistic eminence of the works of Hartmann, Gottfried, and Wolfram, it nevertheless deserves the attention which it has increasingly commanded in recent scholarship for its diversity, sheer bulk and, in individual instances, the independence of approach which raises a poet or a particular work above the charge of mere imitation.

That said, however, it is clear that the poets of this post-classical period were writing in the shadow of the previous generation. Many of them took their illustrious predecessors as their models in matters of style as well as content, aware that they were unlikely to live up to them and often indulging in blatant expressions of humility. For others, the established traditions represented a challenge to be questioned or even overthrown, and some poems of the later period can be described as anti-works, addressing familiar material in a new and sometimes provocative way. We have seen that this new generation was composing against a background of social change, and some of these shifting values found their way into the works themselves. That is in no way to suggest, of course, that there was anything static or acquiescent in the works of the great masters of narrative: on the contrary, we have already seen that it is possible and even necessary to read these works as questioning and even criticizing a status quo which was constantly being brought into question by the historical events of the age.

Although the courtly narrative remained a favorite form for a long time, other literary forms emerged, with the historical or quasi-historical poem obviously finding favor with the audiences, while the shorter narrative in all kinds of guises entered German literature for the first time and attained, as in later centuries too, a very special artistic prominence. It is no easy task to present this mass of narrative composition in an orderly way. There are in this period some authors who merit consideration in relation to their whole, often quite diverse, oeuvre, but in other instances, it is a single work, sometimes by an otherwise unknown author and even sometimes anonymous, which demands attention. There must be a certain amount of cross-reference, then, but this in itself may serve to convey the right impression of a period of seventy years or so which produced some rather remarkable literature of uneven quality but rich in its variety and conflicting qualities. For a full picture of the age, readers are referred to the excellent literary surveys already discussed.

The Arthurian romance, which entered German literature with Hartmann von Aue's *Erec*, remains as a significant element in narrative literature until, with the anonymous *Lohengrin* somewhere in the 1280s, it undergoes a transformation, marking the end of the genre. In the intervening decades, and in the hands of artists of greater and lesser skill, the Arthurian material in German is used in a variety of ways and for differing purposes, but the exploits of Arthur's knights remained a fairly constant focus of attention.

For some of the post-classical poets, the task of completing and supplementing the works of their more highly gifted predecessors was a pressing one, and these "continuations" are in a category all their own, telling us a great deal about the taste of the next generation but also not to be disregarded for their intrinsic qualities.

The fascination with the heroic material furnished by the Germanic past found its continued expression, after the *Nibelungenlied*, in *Kudrun*, and in the tales which belong to the Dietrich epics.

As the 13th century progressed, narrative literature assumed a tone which in some respects could be described as more realistic. Historical accounts provided the source for many of the works of the period as well as contemporary situations which could be exploited for their political or social interest. Side by side with these, the humdrum events of everyday life afforded the material for much of the literature which took the form of short stories, exempla and entertaining cautionary tales, much of it beginning to approach drama in its presentation of action and character.

## NON-"CLASSICAL" WORKS OF THE LATE 12TH–EARLY 13TH CENTURIES

Perhaps an alternative designation for this first group of works should be "non-canonical," for want of a better term. Chronologically, as best we can date them, some are even contemporaneous with the "classical" works of Hartmann, Gottfried, and Wolfram but have never been considered quite their equal, yet they are individually extremely interesting for the scholar and many have received considerable attention as a result. We treat them here before turning to the works of the later 13th and 14th centuries.

### Ulrich von Liechtenstein: *Frauendienst*

It is difficult to decide just where Ulrich's *Frauendienst* belongs in any systematic scheme of MHG literature. His work has been described as the first autobiography in German, although the term should not be taken too literally. What he has written is a kind of narrative framework in the first person, the account of a series of adventures in the service of love, but it is interspersed with 58 poems thematically linked more or less to the work as a whole. With elements of autobiography, narrative and lyric poetry in his *Frauendienst*, he thus occupies an important place in our consideration of the divergent paths which were being pursued in the narrative of the 13th century. Perhaps his place here between the preceding section on lyric and just before other narratives of the early 13th centuries is quite appropriate for his unique poem.

For once we have a firm date for the death of this poet, 26 January 1275, and the dates which he himself supplies in the course of his work suggest that he was born in the first decade of the 13th century. This, for the Middle Ages, long life-span covers some significant and turbulent times in European history, and decades which saw some radical developments in German literature.

The *Frauendienst* almost certainly owes its existence to the fact that Ulrich von Liechtenstein was a Minnesänger, and this very individual work, a strange amalgam of content and with a diversity of tones, was probably conceived as a vehicle for the songs which it contains and which populate the work more densely as it proceeds. The fact that the songs appear in the great Heidelberg manuscript suggests that they may have been circulating independently of the rest of the work. They show Ulrich as a Minnesänger not of the highest rank, but conversant with the themes and manner of the genre and quite skilled in poetic technique. He was also clearly familiar with the narrative works of his age, as is evident in the story that he tells around these songs, although the actual concept is quite original. In addition to the songs, the narrative contains a number of letters, most of them in verse, and three little books (*büechel*), also in verse and likewise purporting to have passed between the poet and his lady. The form of these interpolations is varied, and different in turn from the predominant strophic form of the surrounding narrative, the 1850 strophes of eight lines each (14,800 lines), rhyming in couplets. The work is framed by a prologue and an epilogue, essentially didactic in tone and extolling the virtues of love and its service. The penultimate line supplies the name of the work, *vrowen dienst*.

If we are to believe what Ulrich tells us, then the scope of the narrative extends over more than thirty years, from before his investiture as a knight to the completion of the work thirty three years later (1845,1-4). Since he supplies a firm occasion for his investiture—the marriage of the daughter of Leopold of Austria with Albrecht of Saxony in Vienna in 1222 (39 ff.)—we can date the completion of the work to 1255 and thus see it as spanning a lengthy period of important developments in Middle High German narrative and lyric poetry. The *Frauendienst* did not apparently gain much popularity in its day—apart from the record of the songs separately in the Manesse manuscript, there is only one manuscript (Munich Cgm. 44) and two fragments of the work, all dating from the late 13th century—but it does not require much stretching of the imagination to place the work at the beginning of a long line of development which led to the epistolary novels of the modern period, although one would certainly hesitate to accord much responsibility for this development to Ulrich von Liechtenstein. Equally, we can see it in relationship to the prevailing trend in France and Italy towards semi-autobiographical works incorporating love songs which was to find its ultimate expression, some fifty or sixty years later, in Dante's *Vita nuova*.

In German medieval literature, the work stands on its own and thus contributes to the urge towards original composition which we have already noted so often in considering the narrative of the period. It also adds to our understanding of the way in which the Minnesang was transmitted: the notion of the songs as having been performed in public or at a small gathering is not contradicted here, but we also learn that they could be *written down* and *sent* in order to be *read* by or to the recipient. The preponderance of songs described as "dancing songs" (*tanzwîsen*) supplies a firm link with Neidhart (see p. 279 ff.), although the dominant theme of the songs and indeed of the whole of the narrative, of devoted service to the chosen lady even in the face of indifference or rejection, keeps Ulrich von Liechtenstein firmly within the development of the Minnesang from its earlier, more traditional manifestations.

Ehrismann (II. Teil, Schlußband, 263) describes the work, perhaps rather recklessly, as "ein Liebesroman," while conceding that Ulrich's true element is the lyric. Structurally, the work can be seen as falling into two unequal halves, with the first telling of his exploits in prolonged service of the lady who rejects him, before he turns his attention to another, less turbulent, relationship. A further balancing feature are the masquerades which constitute an important focus: his journeyings in the guise of Lady Venus in the first half and the campaigns which he undertakes as King Arthur in the second. The assumption of these roles gives some idea of the nature of this work, with its fantastic, burlesque elements and the tendency to self-mockery. He demonstrates his devotion to his lady in actions which exceed the norm of subservience of his predecessors, having his hare-lip operated on because she is repelled by his appearance and cutting off his own finger and sending it to her to show that, contrary to what she may think, he has suffered for her sake.

The lengthy accounts of tournaments no doubt owe much to his predecessors in the narrative field. Certainly one senses the influence of Wolfram von Eschenbach in the descriptions of combatants, and in the long lists of names, but behind the fiction one senses also the historical background in which Ulrich played a prominent and well-attested part. There is no point in attempting to associate the events of which he tells with actual historical occasions, but the vitality of the poem is increased by the awareness of the wide range of contexts in which the name of Ulrich von Liechtenstein occurs in contemporary records. He was an important figure in the historical landscape of his age, performing some of the primary functions in society, as steward, marshall, judge. As a literary figure he ranks perhaps as a phenomenon rather than as an artist of rank.

Although he is primarily remembered as the author of the *Frauendienst*, his other work, the **Frauenbuch** (c. 1257), preserved only in the *Ambraser Heldenbuch*, is similarly outspoken and somewhat isolated in its kind, a pungent debate between a lady and a knight, each blaming the sex of the other for the decline in courtly values. As in comparable works, a third party, in this case the poet himself, has the last word. The work is much smaller in scope and lacks the diversity so remarkable in the *Frauendienst*, but this lament for the passing of courtly virtues in a world bereft of love and a proper attitude towards the ladies, and the ultimate affirmation nevertheless of the role of woman, can be seen as a reflection of the age and one which, like the *Frauendienst* with its powerful first-person expression of opinion, continues a trend begun a number of decades earlier by Walther von der Vogelweide.

Texts:
Bechstein, Reinhold, ed. *Ulrichs von Lichtenstein Frauendienst*. Leipzig, 1888. 2 vols.
Spechtler, Franz Viktor, ed. *Ulrich von Liechtenstein. Frauendienst*. Göppingen:Kümmerle, 1987 (= GAG, 485).
____, ed. *Ulrich von Liechtenstein. Frauenbuch*. Göppingen: Kümmerle, 1989 (= GAG, 520).

Translation:
Thomas, J. Wesley, trans. *Ulrich von Liechtenstein's "Service of Ladies." Translated in Condensed Form into English Verse, with an Introduction to the Poet and the Work*. Chapel Hill: Univ. of North Carolina Press, 1969. 228 p. (= UNC Studies in the Germanic Langs. & Lits., 63). This partial trans. gives a very incomplete impression of the poems contained in the work. The fairly lengthy intro. may prove helpful.

Facsimile:
Peters, Ursula, ed. *Ulrich von Lichtenstein, Frauendienst ("Jugendgeschichte")in Abbildungen aus dem Münchener Cod. germ. 44 und der Großen Heidelberger Liederhandschrift*, Göppingen: Kümmerle, 1973 (= Litterae 17). Black and white.

### Frauendienst—Bibliography

Grubmüller, Klaus. "Minne und Geschichtserfahrung. Zum Frauendienst Ulrichs von Liechtenstein." In: *Geschichtsbewußtsein in der deutschen Literatur des Mittelalters.* Ed. by Christoph Gerhardt, et al. Tübingen, 1985. Pp. 37-51.

Heinen, Hubert. "Ulrich von Lichtenstein: Homo (il)litteratus or Poet Performer?" *JEGPh* 83 (1984): 159-172.

McFarland, Timothy. "Ulrich von Lichtenstein and the Autobiographical Narrative Form." In: *Probleme mittelhochdeutscher Erzählformen. Marburger Colloquium 1969.* Ed. by Peter F. Ganz and Werner Schröder. Berlin: Erich Schmidt 1972. Pp. 178-196.

Peters, Ursula. *Frauendienst. Untersuchungen zu Ulrich von Lichtenstein und zum Wirklichkeitsgehalt der Minnedichtung.* Göppingen: Kümmerle, 1971 (= GAG, 46).

## Wirnt von Gravenberg: *Wigalois*

Although it cannot rank with the great works of Hartmann, Gottfried, and Wolfram, it is probably true to say that, were it not for their dominance, *Wigalois* might be accorded a position in the first league of medieval German literature. Yet, having said that, one must also add that, were it not for the existence of the narrative works of Hartmann and of Wolfram's *Parzival*, there would probably be no *Wigalois* anyway. The fate of Wirnt von Gravenberg is like that of so many of the less-skilled poets of his generation and the generation which followed: he falls short when measured by the standards of his models, and is sometimes too little appreciated for qualities all his own. However, there have been consistent attempts to redress this almost inevitable prejudice by scholarly studies of *Wigalois* both in its own right and in relation to its literary context, and the work emerges as an entertaining tale, which makes use of familiar motifs and many of the features of the traditional Arthurian romance, yet succeeds in breaking new ground in some important respects.

Judging by the number of manuscripts (13 complete and 28 fragments), *Wigalois* was a popular poem at the time and went on to enjoy considerable approval in the later Middle Ages. There is a prose version of 1472, and between 1493 and 1664 nine printed versions appeared. The appeal of the story itself is reflected in the fact that versions of it also exist in Danish, Icelandic, Swedish, and Yiddish. Wirnt von Gravenberg himself became a literary figure, the central character in Konrad von Würzburg's *Der Welt Lohn* (see p. 345 f.).

Whatever claim on posterity he may thus have achieved, little is known about Wirnt. It is assumed that he originally came from modern Gräfenberg, near Erlangen, and was thus a fairly near neighbor of Wolfram von Eschenbach. He is referred to as *hêr* Wirnt by his contemporaries, and there are records of a noble family of Gravenberg. It is generally accepted that he was a knight who may well have earned his living as a poet/singer at a court. This may have been Dießen in Bavaria, the court of the counts of Andechs, or Meran, in Tirol, or perhaps Würzburg.

When it comes to the dating of *Wigalois*, there is similar uncertainty, though most scholars are inclined to date it about 1210. We assume with some confidence that Wirnt will have known *Iwein* as well as *Erec*, and certainly the first part of *Parzival*. This would lead us to a date after 1205, which coincides with the only firm historical reference: Wirnt mentions the death of a noble prince of Meran (8061-8064). This refers very likely to the death of Berthold IV of Andechs-Meran in 1204 and not to that of his son Otto who died in 1234. Those who favor the later date point to the tone of regret for the decline of courtly values and decent human behavior which surfaces repeatedly in *Wigalois*, but it can reasonably be maintained that similar nostalgia for the standards of a bygone age can be, and is, expressed by any generation and does not necessarily support a later dating at all. Rather is it in line with the cautionary tone which characterizes Wirnt's poem. Heinrich von dem Türlin in about 1220 and Rudolf von Ems in about 1235 seem to be referring to Wirnt as though he were dead and therefore the earlier dating has more to recommend it.

Wirnt tells us that he was told this story by a squire (11686 ff.) and most scholars accept this, but it has also been suggested that perhaps the squire is a figment of his imagination, a kind of Kyot (see p. 180) known only to Wirnt and enabling him to tell his story his own way while hiding behind a source. This sounds a little far-fetched, but not impossible. Yet, if we assume that the squire did exist, we are still left with a number of questions: In what circumstances did Wirnt hear the story? How much did he hear? What did he add to it? Did the squire himself have a written French source? Did he have to translate it for his listener? These questions are actually unanswerable, but it is usually now assumed that there was a French source, which may now be lost or may exist as the tale *Le Bel Inconnu* by Renaut de Beaujeu, a work which can be dated between 1190 and 1200 and to which *Wigalois* bears some close resemblances, particularly in the first part. Little is known about the French poet, except that he knew Chrétien's *Erec*, and, even if Wirnt did have access, via the squire, to this specific story, the German poet has almost certainly added a great deal all his own, based on his knowledge of Hartmann and Wolfram, and of other French tales circulating at the time.

Like his admired Hartmann von Aue, Wirnt wanted to teach and to entertain, and his prologue, which bears close resemblance to Hartmann's *Der arme Heinrich* and *Iwein*, makes this clear. The didactic tone of the poem persists throughout, combining sometimes rather strangely with the lively, almost racy, narrative style. Wirnt tells a good story very well, but he pauses frequently to caution his listeners, to draw attention to a point he wishes to make, and, very often, to express the wish that things were different today, and that people behaved better. He condemns greed and selfishness, basing his social criticism on the assumption that people have neglected the law of God. He does not hesitate to express his somewhat homespun philosophy in language which often has a proverbial ring to it ("a stag is never hunted down by sleeping dogs," 2884 ff.). This is no master of rhetoric, nor does he set out to be. He seems to wish to convey to his listeners his own unsophisticated moral standpoint in language which impresses by its simplicity rather than its elegance. He gives the impression of a sincere man with no great claims to fame as a poet, who has set himself a task in telling his story and fulfils it to the best of his ability and with some degree of success. One recalls not least the humor of the poem. Sometimes this takes the form of ironic comments at his own expense, more than just the formulaic expressions of modesty. There are little comic touches within the narrative which, while demonstrating his involvement with it, show, too, that he has a certain distance from it. This allows him to view with a wry smile, for example, the strange beast with fiery breath which plays about with him like a little dog.

On first sight it might appear that we are dealing with a fairly traditional Arthurian romance, in which a knight is exposed to a series of adventures of escalating difficulty and comes eventually to his goal. Yet even assuming an unvarying pattern to such romances, closer inspection shows this work to be different. Wigalois is no Erec or Parzival: he does not progress through error. His progress is rather seen to be preordained, and he moves from one stage to the next without distraction or any false step. He is, after all, the Knight of Fortune's Wheel, the elected one who bears the golden wheel as his emblem and for whom success is inevitable. From the moment that he sits on the stone at Caridoel, he unknowingly proclaims his special nature, which is immediately recognized by those for whom this is a unique and wondrous event. He proceeds through life protected by Fortune, whether this be expressed by the magic belt or, in tune with the religious symbolism which is apparent throughout the poem, by prayer. He cannot go wrong, whereas the tests that Erec, Iwein, and Parzival undergo lead to error and even catastrophe, and only thence, eventually, to rehabilitation and success. The trials of Wigalois are demonstrations of his special nature, and he meets them, no matter what their hazards, with equanimity.

Thus, though one can discern a duality in the structure of this poem, it is of a different nature from that which is stressed in Hartmann's courtly romances, and in *Parzival*, even though the pattern may seem to be the same (see Heinzle, 1973). The first series of adventures demonstrates the suitability of the hero to undertake his destined task, while the second series leads towards that final task, which has been heralded from the beginning, although its precise nature has been kept secret. Some critics see this work as merely a series of adventures, some of them rather wild and exaggerated, with little relationship between them. But the structure of the poem is actually carefully contrived, using the familiar techniques of parallels and groups of adventures of escalating ferocity, and emerges very clearly (see Thomas, Introduction, and Heinzle, 1973). At its most simple, this structure can be seen as a division into five parts, framed by a prologue and an epilogue.

Leaving aside for the moment the first part of the narrative proper which is devoted to the story of Wigalois, son of none other than Gawein, we can see the core of the narrative in the second, third and fourth "parts." These constitute a related series of adventures which begin when Wigalois commits himself to helping the mistress of Nereja, who has come to Arthur's Court in search of a superlative champion. The ensuing series of adventures—familiar exploits such as slaying knights and defeating giants—proves that he is capable of undertaking a most dangerous task, not least to Nereja, who, having hoped to secure the aid of Gawein himself, is decidedly irritated and skeptical when she is forced to settle for such a young knight.

From this point on Wigalois's inspiration and goal become the lovely Larîe, daughter of King Lar, who, it transpires, was killed by a heathen knight called Roaz. This is the task to which Wigalois has committed himself and which he can undertake only after a further series of adventures brings him into a very different realm of supernatural forces. A strange beast leads him to a castle where it assumes human form and reveals itself as the spirit of the murdered King Lar, whose castle burns down each night but is restored every day. King Lar tells him that he must rid the country of a dragon in order to prove himself fit for the task of avenging his death on Roaz and so winning the hand of Larîe. He accomplishes this seemingly impossible task and embarks on a further series of encounters, with a wild woman, a powerful dwarf, and a fire-hurling centaur. Eventually he enters the great hall of the castle of Glois, where he kills the heathen Roaz.

By now he has proved himself a fitting husband for Larîe and a splendid wedding takes place in what is now his rightful kingdom of Korntin, attended, among others, by Erec, Iwein and Gawein. This would seem to be the end of the poem, but Wirnt has other ideas. Instead of the predictable return to Arthur's Court and a swift reference to a happy-ever-after future, a further event brings the work to a much more original and, in some respects, more serious conclusion. News reaches the wedding guests of the death of a vassal, killed while journeying to the festivities. To avenge this, Wigalois places his father, Gawein, in charge of a military campaign. What ensues is no extravagant account of chivalrous activity but a serious and thought-provoking confirmation of the suitability of Wigalois to rule. Under his rule, we learn, the land which had been devastated is restored to prosperity, and he reigns as a wise and gentle king, combining political stability with the culture which his chivalry allows him to foster. We hear, too, of his son who also performed great deeds but whose story must, says Wirnt, be left to another who has the skill to tell it properly, because it requires a special talent. He will gladly guide such a man towards the story, since he knows where to find it, while he, for his part, has something else (not disclosed to us!) in mind. With a quick prayer, he ends his poem.

This, then, is no "ordinary" Arthurian romance. The final episode may be seen as a *Bestätigungsabenteuer* ("confirmation adventure"), but of a different kind from, for example, the Joie de la curt episode in Hartmann's *Erec* (see p. 135 ff.). The action does not return to Arthur's court; in fact Arthur significantly is not present at the wedding celebrations, and those illustrious knights of Arthur—Erec, Iwein, and Gawein—have a very different role to perform in righting the terrible wrong that has been done in the murder of a vassal. It is as though the poem is spreading out, to embrace some new thoughts, and perhaps even to reject the pre-eminence of the Arthurian court and the model of the Arthurian romance. For all Wirnt's allegiance to Hartmann and Wolfram, he, like them, is capable of going his own way, at least in thought and substance.

The figure of Gawein, too, is not the traditional one. This is not the "bachelor *par excellence*" as Paul Salmon calls him (Lit.Hist. p. 72), but a married man with a son. The charming episode which opens the poem, with Gawein being led into another realm, where he falls in love with the beautiful Florie, marries her, and leaves her to bear his son, is more than just a pre-history of the central hero. Gawein does not return, not because he becomes embroiled in chivalry and forgets her, but because he lacks the means, having left behind the magic belt which allowed him to come there in the first place. When, years later, he learns of her death, he vows to remain unmarried forever. This whole conception of one of the favorite figures of the chivalrous romance reverses our view of him and, like the whole poem, challenges our preconceptions.

Material similar to that contained in *Wigalois* was used later for poems in English (*Libeaus Desconnus* of the mid-14th century) and Italian (*Carduino* of about 1375) and the fifteenth century French prose version *Le Chevalier du Papegau,* which contains many of the *Wigalois* adventures. Certainly the impact of this story in the Middle Ages was significant, and Wirnt von Gravenberg's poem remains one of the most entertaining works of MHG, despite some disparaging criticism.

Perhaps, as a narrator, Wirnt von Gravenberg was not quite up to the demands of his material and his conception of it. The work is full of exotic adventures, extravagant details, and fantastic features. There is a sense of magic pervading it, which, in the hands of a greater practitioner, might have become truly memorable. The Christian symbolism is there but sometimes too labored to be effective. It is a strange mixture of brilliance and a certain pedestrianism, largely of style and expression, which means that it never quite fulfils its promise. Yet leaving aside the question of influence and models which makes the hypothesis a ridiculous one, we are aware that, had Hartmann and Gottfried and Wolfram and the author of the *Nibelungenlied* not existed, *Wigalois* would probably be greatly admired as a product of its age.

Text:
Kapteyn, J. M. N., ed. *Wigalois, der Ritter mit dem Rade. Von Wirnt von Gravenberc.* Bonn: Klopp, 1926. Though there are earlier editions, this is the one most readily available and usable.

Translation:
Thomas, J. Wesley, trans. *Wigalois. The Knight of Fortune's Wheel, by Wirnt von Grafenberg.* Lincoln: Univ. of Nebraska Press, 1977. English trans. with useful introduction, notes, and bibliography (together 99 pp.!).

### *Wigalois*—Bibliography

Cormeau, Christoph. *Wigalois und Diu Crône: Zwei Kapitel zur Gattungsgeschichte des nachklassischen Aventiureromans.* Munich: Beck, 1976.

Heinzle, Joachim. "Über den Aufbau des Wigalois." *Euph.* 67 (1973): 261-271.

Mitgau, Wolfgang. "Nachahmung und Selbständigkeit Wirnts von Gravenberg in seinem *Wigalois*." *ZfdPh* 82 (1963): 321-337.

Neumann, Friedrich. "Wann verfaßte Wirnt den *Wigalois*?" *ZfdA* 93 (1964) 31-62.

Saran, Franz. "Über Wirnt von Grafenberg und den *Wigalois*." *PBB* 21 (1896): 253-420. This and the following article by Saran, dated though they are, represent an important early stage in research on *Wigalois* and are often crucial to an understanding of subsequent criticism.

____. "Zum *Wigalois*" *PBB* 22 (1897): 151-157.

Schreiber, Albert. "Über Wirnt von Gräfenberg und den *Wigalois*." *ZfdPh* 58 (1933): 209-231.

Thomas, Neil. *A German View of Camelot. Wirnt von Grafenberg's "Wigalois" and Arthurian Tradition.* Bern: Lang, 1987.

____. *The Medieval German Arthuriad. Some Contemporary Revaluations of the Canon.* Bern: Lang, 1989 (= Euro. Univ. Studies. Series 1. German Lang. & Lit., 1153).

Pp. 105-138 are of particular concern here.

See also J. Wesley Thomas's introduction, notes and bibliography, in his translation (above).

## Wigamur

Wigamur appears to be a name modeled on that of the more famous Wigalois by the unknown author who composed this poem of a little over 6000 lines some time in the middle of the 13th century, or it may be that the name was borrowed from some other context, similarly unknown. There may have been a French source, although none has been identified, and the identifiable influences are not so much the works of Hartmann and Wolfram, as the lesser Arthurian romances, notably Ulrich von Zatzikhoven's *Lanzelet* and Wirnt's *Wigalois*.

The incomplete state of the only manuscript makes it difficult to assess the poem, which tells the story of the Knight with the Eagle, but it is clearly made up of familiar motifs. Like Lanzelet, Wigamur is abducted by a sea creature and brought up away from courtly influence and training. Then, like the ill-prepared young Parzival going off into the world, he comes almost by chance to hear about chivalry and gradually grows into a knight himself. As Iwein rescues a lion which becomes his inseparable companion, so does Wigamur rescue an eagle and is henceforth always associated with it. The adventures which ensue are the familiar ones of intervening in battles and taking sides in legal conflicts. Although he fights on behalf of ladies, he is unconcerned to gain the hand of any of them until the culminating adventure, which finds him unwittingly preparing to engage in combat with his own father, recognizing him in the nick of time and marrying the daughter of the king who had been his father's opponent and whose side he had taken. In this last adventure it is not hard to discern echoes of heroic antecedents as well as the familiar elements of the courtly romance.

There is not a great deal of originality in the substance of this work, probably composed somewhere around the middle of the century, and the narrator, probably an East Franconian, cannot lay claim to much in the way of poetic skill. *Wigamur* is another piece in the jigsaw puzzle of post-courtly narrative and a rather undistinguished piece in itself, although the article by David Blamires listed below succeeded in demonstrating that the poem was worthy of more serious attention than it had so far received. The suggestion by Stephen Wailes (*Arthurian Encyclopedia*, 628-629) that the flawed state of the manuscript reflects scribal indifference is plausible. The lack of a critical edition, to which he also refers, has meanwhile been rectified by Danielle Buschinger.

Text:
Buschinger, Danielle, ed. *Wigamur*. Göppingen: Kümmerle, 1987 (= GAG, 320).

### Wigamur—Bibliography

Blamires, David. "The Sources and Literary Structure of *Wigamur*." In: *Studies in Medieval Literature and Languages in Memory of Frederick Whitehead*. Ed. by W.

Rothwell, W.R.J. Barron, David Blamires, and Lewis Thorpe. Manchester: Manchester UP 1973; New York: Barnes & Noble, 1973. Pp. 27-46.

Gives some guidance in assessing the work with a detailed summary of the plot.

Ebenbauer, Alfred. "Wigamur und die Familie." In: *Artusrittertum im späten Mittelalter*. Ed. by Friedrich Wolfzettel. Gießen: W. Schmitz, 1984. Pp. 28-46.

## Konrad Fleck: *Flore und Blanscheflur*

The young lovers Flore and Blanscheflur, the heathen king's son and the daughter of a Christian captive, may not be so well known as Tristan and Isolde, yet their story was a popular one in the Middle Ages and told in many languages, but, unlike the story of Tristan and Isolde, not finding its way into the modern period.

Perhaps the reason for the relative obscurity of this rather charming love story is that it lacked the tragic grandeur of the story of the passion which had its source in the supernatural and whose only outcome could be death. Although the depth of the love of Flore and Blanscheflur is undoubted and leads them to heroic deeds, to the defiance of society, and, if need be, to the acceptance of death, the ultimate sacrifice is not required of them and the resolution is a harmonious and happy one.

As far as medieval German literature is concerned, the relative lack of impact of the story may also be due to the modest stature of its principal German narrator, the Alemannic poet Konrad Fleck, who conceals his identity, as he explains in his closing lines, lest anyone should think that he is boasting. As on other occasions (see p. 340), we have Rudolf von Ems to thank for the little that we know about the author of *Flore und Blanscheflur*, his name and his status as a knight (*Willehalm von Orlens*, 2221-4; *Alexander*, 3239-3242). The *Alexander* reference also mentions his having composed a version of the *Cligès* story, but we have no trace of this. Rudolf, not the severest of critics perhaps, speaks warmly of Fleck's story of the bitter-sweet love of Flore and Blanscheflur: this, after all, is the essence of the tale, though some might find in it a deeper preoccupation with religious differences. The inclusion of the poem in the list in *Willehalm von Orlens* provides our only clue to the likely date of around 1220.

There is ample evidence within Konrad Fleck's poem that he was writing under the influence of Hartmann von Aue and of Gottfried's *Tristan*, with some blatant imitation of the language of the former. His debt to Gottfried is less easy to assess, but it seems reasonable to suppose that he will have seen the great Alemannic poet of love as something of a model, even if his modesty, and even perhaps his morality, prevented a more tangible attempt to emulate him.

*Flore und Blanscheflur* is, after all, a very moral tale, in which love and virtue are closely linked. Flore remains steadfast to his commitment to his childhood sweetheart and when he is led to believe that she has died in his absence, his one thought is to follow her. She, for her part, remains true to him and the pressure which she endures from the *amiral* represents a kind of martyrdom. The strength of their love is manifested to all present when, condemned to die on the pyre, each declines to accept the magic ring which would represent life but only for one of them. Even the *amiral* is moved by this display of pure devotion and therein lies their salvation.

The story is told with a quite engaging simplicity, and its inherently sentimental qualities cannot be denied. The pair are born on the same day and smile at one another from
their respective cradles. Their love grows from their early childhood, but this love is
doomed, less because of the difference in religion than because of the social gulf between
them. They are parted by the devious king, Flore's father, who sends his son away on a
brief journey and in the meantime sells Blanscheflur to some merchants who take her to
Babylon. There she becomes the prospective bride of the *amiral*, a ruler, who is notorious
for his sexual appetite and his ruthless treatment of his discarded wives. Another trick
awaits Flore on his return: he is shown an elaborate tomb, supposedly that of his beloved,
but his mother, who is a more compassionate person than her husband, had actually persuaded him to spare Blanscheflur and send her away instead of putting her to death. She
intervenes again, this time to prevent the threatened suicide of her grief-stricken son, who
now learns the truth and resolves to find Blanscheflur. His journeyings bring him to Babylon where he manages to gain access to her prison and to enjoy an interlude of love-making with her until they are discovered and condemned to death by the *amiral*.

These are already the ingredients of an exciting and quite original story, although we
cannot know how much was contained in the French source of an unidentified Ruopreht
von Orlent (142-146), and the embellishments which Konrad gives to it maintain the
interest of the narrative: the description of the ornate tomb and Flore's desperate grief as
he beholds it (2099 ff.); the way he wheedles his way into the confidence of the guard by
engaging him in games of chess (5049 ff.); the bold plan when he secrets himself in a
basket of flowers to gain access to the tower where his beloved is imprisoned (5511 ff.);
the tender reunion of the young lovers (5849 ff.).

There are some memorable episodes in this poem, and it is only the comparison with
the narrative giants of the German Middle Ages which would lead one to the view that
this material would have been better served by a more skilled practitioner. The story
itself has its limitations, but if, as T. R. Jackson demonstrates, the theme of religion is as
worthy of consideration in the poem as the theme of love, one might have to admit that
it would have received more profound treatment in the hands of a Wolfram von
Eschenbach. Flore is a heathen, Blanscheflur is a Christian. This difference does not
prevent love growing between them, as it is destined to do from the very day of their
birth, nor is it a reason for the disapproval of the king, who is more concerned to arrange
a marriage which will be socially and politically advantageous. The behavior of King
Fenix, like that of the *amiral*, is ruthless and definitely reprehensible, yet there is no
suggestion that they behave as they do because they are heathens, and they are capable
of gentleness on occasions, notably where their personal aspirations are not under threat.
Flore's mother, a heathen like her husband, is an influence for good, and the *amiral* has
people at his court who are susceptible to goodness when they see it, as they do in the
pure love of Flore and Blanscheflur.

The virtue of Flore is there for all to see: he possesses the traditional qualities of the
knight, perseverance and loyalty, purity of mind and body, and generosity of spirit. The
fact that he is a heathen is not really important, but it is appropriate that he should eventually be baptized, possessed as he is of the *wâriu minne* which makes him steadfast to
Blanscheflur and to God, and which distinguishes him so sharply from the *amiral*, who

is motivated by *valsche minne*. The point is clearly made, but without emphasis, for this is not a poem in which didacticism intrudes: such explicit teaching as it contains is confined to the prologue and the epilogue. That does not mean, however, that the poem should be dismissed as a rather bland little tale of young love, and Jackson's article is helpful in showing that it warrants closer attention than it has so far received. Whether one should go so far as to accord it the status implied in the juxtaposition with the *Nibelungenlied* in the study by Hans-Adolf Klein is less clear. What is apparent is the unfortunate absence of a modern edition of the poem, and the fact that it is still—or rather, perhaps, as yet—inaccessible to an English readership.

Texts:
Sommer, Emil, ed. *Flore und Blanscheflur*. Quedlinburg, Leipzig: G. Basse, 1846.

Golther, Wolfgang, ed. *Tristan und Isolde und Flore und Blanscheflur*. Berlin & Stuttgart: Spemann, 1873 (= Deutsche National-Literatur, 3. Abt., 4. Bd, 2. Teil). Text, pp. 249-270; introduction, pp. 235-246.

Translation:
Pannier, Karl, trans. *Flore und Blanscheflur. Eine Märchendichtung von Konrad Fleck. Nach dem Mittelhochdeutschen übersetzt*. Leipzig: Reclam, 1915 (= UB, 5781-5783).

### *Flore und Blanscheflur*—Bibliography

See article by Peter Ganz in *VL*[2] 2 (1980) 744-747. A particularly useful introduction.

Jackson, T. R. "Religion and Love in *Flore und Blanscheflur*." *Oxford German Studies* 4 (1969): 12-25.

This is likely to be the most accessible study of the poem.

Klein, Hans-Adolf. *Erzählabsicht im Heldenepos und im höfischen Epos. Studien zum Ethos im "Nibelungenlied" und in Konrad Flecks "Flore und Blanscheflur,"* Göppingen: Kümmerle, 1978 (= GAG 226).

One of the very few complete studies published, this book examines the poem from a particular standpoint, as the title suggests, but it contains some interesting material of a more general nature in relation to the work.

## *Moriz von Craûn*

This relatively short work (1784 lines) by an unidentified poet commands a great deal of interest, although we have good reason to assume that it was not successful in its own day. There is only one manuscript, in the *Ambraser Heldenbuch*, and this is full of obscure and often obviously corrupt passages. There are no contemporary references to the poem. Thus our only knowledge of its existence dates from about 300 years after its composition, whenever precisely that may have been, which is in itself a matter of intense speculation.

It is rare for there to be such a wide divergence of opinion about the date of composition, especially when the arguments for the respective datings all seem extraordinarily plausible. Some critics would place its composition as early as 1180, about the time of Hartmann von Aue's *Erec*, while others maintain that it is inconceivable that it predates the other works of Hartmann, and, more importantly, of Wolfram and Gottfried, although such references as critics may find are oblique, and the only predecessor named by the poet is Heinrich von Veldeke (1160). It is more significant that it responds to the attitudes of the classical Minnesang, than that it seems to reflect some of the elements of the early love lyric, in the emotional involvement of the lady, for example, or the evocation of the background. While most would probably reject the extreme date of 1230, there is probably by now a consensus for a date in the region of 1220.

The identity of the poet remains unknown. An early suggestion (by Richard M. Meyer in 1895) that the work was part of a longer poem called the *Umbehanc* ("curtain," "tapestry") and that this is what Gottfried von Straßburg is talking about in his praise of Bligger von Steinach (*Tristan*, 4709 ff.) was not generally given credence, although a much more recent article by Heinz Thomas has revived the idea rather tentatively. Probably we have to accept the fact that the identity of the poet cannot be established, though it is possible to build up a picture of the kind of person he may have been.

It is generally agreed that he hailed from somewhere in the Rhineland on the basis of his language, insofar as the state of the manuscript allows this to be established, his knowledge of customs and places on either side of the Rhine, and his familiarity with chivalry as it was practiced across the border. His knowledge of the activities and attitudes of chivalry and, in particular, the detailed knowledge he conveys of the tournament, suggest that he may well have been a knight himself or at least in close touch with those who were actively engaged in the chivalric life. An attractive suggestion put forward by Ruth Harvey in her very full and extraordinarily readable study of the work is that he may have been given the story by a French knight when they met at a tournament and brought it home to translate it himself or have it translated. Certainly, the vividness of the description of the tournament points to a poet who was himself familiar with the procedures and, perhaps more importantly, the feel of such knightly engagement, and if we accept a poet with his home in the Rhineland, then there is no problem in accepting that from time to time he crossed the border to participate in tournaments in France.

This suggestion has the added attraction of providing an answer to the question of the source of the poem, though, tantalizingly, that source is lost. Most would agree, however, that there was probably a French source and not, as has been suggested, a Latin one. How much the German poet added to that source is a matter of conjecture, but it is reasonable to assume that he gave to the poem as we have it much of its marked individuality and in particular that highly characteristic sense of purpose which provokes so much lively debate among its critics.

Those who write about *Moriz von Craûn* point to its isolated position in medieval German literature, wherever as individuals they may situate it chronologically. Although one may find points of comparison and contrast in both lyric and narrative works of the period, it stands very much on its own in terms both of substance and genre. The term *Novelle* comes to mind albeit anachronistically, and indeed there is much about the poem which, despite its indisputably and crucially medieval origins, strikes one as surprisingly modern.

The poem begins with a substantial prologue (1-262), telling of the progress of chivalry from its birthplace in Greece, to Rome, and thence to France from where it spread to other lands, lingering wherever it found a welcome and passing on as soon as signs of decadence appeared. Such decadence manifested itself, in the view of the author, as a reluctance on the part of knights to overlook the price demanded by chivalry, and the growth of sexual abnormality. Of this latter, the prime example is Nero, on whose behavior and reputation the poet lingers long enough to mislead the scribe responsible for the superscription of the manuscript into thinking that this is the content of the poem which follows.

In fact, of course, the main character is the knight Maurîcius, who is extolled as a prime example of that chivalry so faithfully served in his native France. He is seen as entirely worthy of the reward of the Countess of Bêamunt whom he serves unceasingly.

At this point, with the two central characters named, the poet interrupts his narrative for a lengthy discourse on love (289-416), and the fact that he does so points to his conception of the serious purpose of his narrative. This may not be, stylistically, the best part of the work, with its loose syntax and its somewhat incoherent thought, but for him it is certainly an essential passage, which makes it clear that his work is a serious examination of the ethics of courtly love and a demonstration of the impossibilty of reconciling theory and practice.

Maurîcius plucks up courage to go to his beloved and ask for her favor. After teasing him with a show of reluctance which may or may not be founded in reality, she gives her formal consent, sealed with a ring, but not before exacting his agreement to her condition that he must bring a tournament to her castle. She maintains, somewhat incredibly one might think, that she has never witnessed a tournament.

Maurîcius sets out to fulfill this condition in an extreme manner. He has a magnificently contrived ship on wheels constructed which is drawn across the land and set up before her castle. No expense is spared in the lavish appointments of this extraordinary contraption, and a large portion of the poem is concerned with the description of the ship and the tournament which ensues, but not before a significant event occurs. The Count, the lady's husband, accidentally kills a knight in the throng which accompanies the excitement leading up to the fighting proper. By rights this tragic circumstance should bring an end to the tournament even before it starts, but Maurîcius is not to be deprived of this opportunity to demonstrate his chivalry, and he dismisses any objections to continuing. The Count retires in grief and shame, fearful for his soul, but Maurîcius distinguishes himself in the ensuing action which is described with great gusto and considerable exaggeration. His brilliance on the field is matched by the ostentatious displays of generosity in which he indulges afterwards, bestowing rich gifts on all who present themselves to receive of his bounty, as he breaks up the costly ship and dispenses its fabric and trappings with openhanded exuberance. After all, he can now be sure, or so he thinks, of receiving the favor of his lady.

When he receives a summons from her, he breaks off what he is doing—actually he is just starting to remove his leg-armor—and goes eagerly to a private chamber, richly decorated and dominated by a spectacularly appointed bed. The Countess keeps him waiting, ostensibly because she cannot yet leave her husband who is still in such torment about the deed he has perpetrated and needs her comfort. Maurîcius, weary from his excessive exertions and not a little irritated at being kept waiting, allows himself to be persuaded by the lady-in-waiting who has acted as messenger to fall asleep in her lap, with the assurance that she will wake him in good time when her mistress approaches. In fact, however, the

Countess takes them both by surprise and, refusing to allow the lady-in-waiting to wake him, declares that she no longer feels herself bound to one who has shown such disdain for their agreement as to let himself fall asleep. Despite the pleading of the lady-in-waiting, she goes away, determined that the bond between them be severed and regretting that she permitted it in the first place. She returns to the bed of her husband.

Maurîcius wakes up to this devastating news and sends the maid to plead with her, but in vain. Regardless of the propriety of what he is doing and of the fact that he is still in his battle-stained armor, he goes to their bedroom, where the clanking of his loosened chausse startles the Count who is lying there in his anguish, convinced that this apparition must be the devil come in pursuit of him. The Countess, who has managed, it seems, to fall asleep in the meantime, wakes up and recognizes her spurned suitor but prefers not to intervene when Maurîcius seizes his chance to exploit the situation and declares that he is, in fact, the ghost of the knight whom the Count slew. At this the Count leaps out of bed and strikes his shin-bone, rendering himself unconscious for the remainder of the night. Maurîcius takes his place in the marital bed, where the Countess, apparently not wishing to anger him further, offers herself to him. Having taken from her what he had wanted—and "what use is it", asks the poet, "to tell you what they were doing? You know just as well without my telling you what people do"—he gets up, removes the ring from his finger, returns it to her, and cancels the pact between them, telling her to go back to her husband and going off himself into a life of, if anything, greater renown than ever before.

The lady is left to lament her foolishness and, aided by her lady-in-waiting who, though sorry for her, recognizes the truth of the situation, comes to accept the fact that she has been punished for the wrong she has done. To her belongs the "epilogue," in which she laments her folly in not accepting the good advice of the maid and urges all lovers to beware lest they fall into guilt similar to that from which she must suffer for the rest of her life. It remains only for the poet to lament the inadequacy of his own skill and the poverty of the German language in telling such a story, and to express the wish that he might have done it better.

The poet's modesty at the end of his work belongs with the many formulaic expressions of inadequacy to be found in medieval literature, but it is true that we are not dealing here with a particularly talented literary artist. He cannot be ranked with the great names of the Middle Ages in Germany, yet this isolated little poem has an attraction and a fascination all its own. Even a synopsis has to be relatively lengthy in order to give an impression of the wealth of detail and the careful structure. This is unlike so many of the lesser works of the period that are often characterized by repetition, imbalance, and irrelevance and frequently are a chain of only loosely connected episodes.

At the heart of this work, in the manner of the *Novelle*, is a single event, the culmination of what has gone before and the impetus to what follows. When Maurîcius falls asleep while waiting for his beloved, nothing can ever be the same again. Exactly what happens, of course, depends on the poet's conception of his purpose, for this is a poem which, for all its undoubted value as an entertaining anecdote, has a distinctly didactic tone to it, as both the prologue and the lady's closing speech make clear. Yet, one asks oneself, what are we meant to conclude? Maurîcius is lauded as a prime example of knighthood, while the Countess is blamed, and accepts the blame, for not behaving according to the rules. He appears to get off scot-free, going from strength to strength in his acquisition of fame, while she is condemned to a future of shame and misery. What of her rights in the matter, one asks, and perhaps wonders that this work has not, as yet, been subjected to feminist analysis.

Although some critics have seen the poem as a parody of courtly manners, such a view is contradicted by the dominant seriousness of its tone. Yet there are moments of real comedy, often derived from the poet's observation of human behavior and sometimes, it is true, verging on the burlesque quality which anticipates the later *Schwankdichtung*. If one uses the term "Novelle" to convey the structure of the poem, one can also point to its dramatic qualities, as well as to the moments of something much closer to the lyric, notably the description of the lady contemplating her sad fate early one morning, as she stands at the window and the nightingale sings particularly sweetly in the background.

The characters of the work are no puppets but creatures of flesh and blood with very real opinions and responses, and it has been well said that none of them escapes quite unscathed, not even Maurîcius himself, who condemns himself, one might hold, to a life of action but precious little else. As for the Countess and her husband, one can but speculate about their future and perhaps see the Count as the innocent victim of a code which no longer seems entirely positive. We are not called upon to ask why it is he who is seen as the feeble bystander, when all he has done is unwittingly kill another knight and then do the honorable thing in withdrawing from the tournament, while Maurîcius himself does not earn opprobrium for what must have been a grave misdemeanor, if not actually a sin, in insisting that the tournament should go ahead after the initial calamity. No ambiguity surrounds the figure of the maid, who manages to maintain her integrity, despite the dilemmas in which she is placed and who belongs in the tradition of the faithful, sorely-tried woman servant, reminding us above all of Hartmann's Lunete but with echoes, perhaps also, of Brangæne.

One could go on indefinitely enumerating the issues which this apparently modest little work raises. It has been described as a problem poem, and that designation applies on many levels. Beneath the anonymity of its author, we sense a man of considerable originality, questioning the values of his age and presenting us with some of the concerns which may have occupied the ordinary knight. Strange though it may seem to describe as "realistic" a work which has as its centerpiece a great horse-drawn ship on wheels, there is a quality of realism about this poem, in which the poetic haze of Arthurian literature is strikingly absent. Often the realism lies in the insights into the behavior of the characters: Maurîcius not stopping to secure, still less to remove, his leg-armor in his eagerness to meet his lady, or the hapless husband knocking himself senseless as he leaps out of bed in terror. In the last resort, too, one might wish to describe as thoroughly realistic the way in which Maurîcius, having got what he thought he wanted, finds that he no longer wants it, or perhaps that he is prepared to forego it to make his point, or the way in which the lady hankers for what she has lost through her petulant refusal of it earlier.

Above all, we cannot help feeling that we are dealing here with "real" people, in a way we do not usually encounter them in the literature of the period. The poet was doubtless attempting to satisfy the tastes of his public when he told of a great ship trundling across the land laden with rich accoutrements or of a richly adorned bed, but he may have shocked them by his challenge of the conventions. He may have been saying things which made them uncomfortable in an age which disliked confusion and contradiction. Perhaps indeed, he may have ventured too far when he composed this story based on real people, the family of Beaumont, neighbors of his in Craon, although there is no evidence for the veracity of this particular anecdote. Certainly the poem was saved from oblivion only by the strange chances which surround the production and survival of the *Ambraser Heldenbuch*, and the fact that it commands such interest today speaks both for its intrinsic fascination and for the modern perception of the Middle Ages, which in so many respects it appears to contradict.

Texts:
Classen, Albrecht, ed. and trans. *Moriz von Craûn*. Stuttgart: Reclam, 1992 (= UB, 8796). MHG text, based on the standard edition, with mod. Ger. trans., some detailed notes, a brief afterword, and a very full bibliography.

Pretzel, Ulrich, ed. *Moriz von Craûn*. Unter Mitwirkung von Karl Stackmann und Wolfgang Bachofer im Verein mit Erich Henschel und Richard Keinast. Tübingen: Niemeyer, 1956, [4]1973 (= ATB, 45). The standard edition of the text.

Van D'Elden, Stephanie Cain, ed. and trans. *Moriz von Craûn*. New York: Garland, 1990 (= GLML, A69). Text is a diplomatic edition of that in the *Ambraser Heldenbuch* with introduction, English prose translation, and notes to the text.

Translations:
See Classen and Van D'Elden (above).
Pretzel, Ulrich, trans. "Moriz von Craûn." In: U. P., *Deutsche Erzählungen des Mittelalters*. Munich: C. H. Beck, 1971. Pp. 24-54. Mod. Ger. trans.

### *Moriz von Craun*—Bibliography

Borck, Karl Heinz. "Zur Deutung und Vorgeschichte des *Moriz von Craûn*." *DVjs*. 34 (1961): 494-520.

A readable, fairly general discussion of the poem.

Gentry, Francis G. "A Tale from a City: *Moriz von Craûn*." In: *Semper idem et novus. Festschrift for Frank Banta*. Ed. by F. G. Gentry. Göppingen: Kümmerle, 1988 (= GAG, 481). Pp. 193-207.

Argues for a French fabliau as source and sees *Moriz* as appealing to a bourgeois audience rather than a courtly one.

Harvey, Ruth. *Moriz von Craûn and the Chivalric World*. Oxford: Clarendon, 1961.

Although not claiming to be an exhaustive discussion of *Moriz von Craûn*, it is a very full study of the poem which goes beyond the apparent limitations of its title. Full of absorbing details, particularly of the historical and social background, it can well be used as a stimulating aid to the reading of the poem.

Kokott, Hartmut. " 'Mit großem schaden an eere' (v.1718). Zur Minne-Lehre des *Moriz von Craûn*." *ZfdPh* 107 (1988): 362-385.

Based on an examination of the characters of the knight and the maid, this article sees the poem as a warning against *minne*. It is a provocative approach, well argued.

Thomas, Heinz. "Zur Datierung, zum Verfasser und zur Interpretation des *Moriz von Craûn.*" *ZfdPh* 103 (1984): 321-365.

Not the easiest article to read, but it addresses some central problems and takes into account earlier research.

## Ulrich von Zatzikhoven: *Lanzelet*

This is the only work attributable to Ulrich von Zatzikhoven even though, right at the end of it, he seems to be suggesting that he could produce more if his patron, whoever that may have been, desired it. No one very much regrets that he was not more prolific, and assessments of this work are for the most part very harsh. Like Wirnt von Gravenberg (see above, p. 314 ff.), he suffers from comparison with his close contemporaries, Hartmann and Wolfram, although, in his case, there is really even less suggestion that he is trying to emulate them.

Ulrich is telling a story, and he does this rather better than most of his critics appear to think. Perhaps one of the truest and kindest assessments of his achievement is that by Frederick Norman, which comes at the end of his Afterword to the 1965 reprint of Hahn's edition of 1845. Indeed, this Afterword is altogether a balanced analysis of Ulrich's achievement and of his significance, certainly not exaggerating the former but giving due weight to the latter. Norman concludes: "Ein großer Meister ist der Dichter nicht. Trotzdem: er ist ein guter Erzähler, unbekümmert und problemlos. Einen *sin* hat seine *aventiure* nicht. Wir tun gut daran, keinen *sin* bei ihm zu suchen und ihn unbekümmert zu lesen" (The poet is not a great master. Nevertheless: he is a good storyteller, untroubled and unproblematical. His story does not have a special meaning. We shall do well not to seek a special meaning in him and to read him untroubled, p. 292).

This is probably quite a good starting point for a reading of *Lanzelet*, bearing in mind that the audience was looking to be entertained and only secondarily to be instructed. Those who disparage Ulrich's poem perhaps overlook its entertainment value in their vain search for the deeper meaning which we have come to expect through decades of research into medieval literature. Quite simply, Ulrich is telling the story of the knight Lanzelet who is abducted by a fairy in early childhood and brought up in a magical "otherworld" on an island inhabited only by women and then makes his way through a series of adventures to the Court of King Arthur and the accession to his own rightful kingship. His progress is similarly *unbekümmert* (untroubled), despite the horrors which he has to face, and neither he nor Ulrich himself pauses to ask awkward questions about the nature of his progress or the morality of his behavior. For all the influence of Hartmann von Aue and of Wolfram's *Parzival* which many critics discern, Ulrich's poem is devoid of depth or complexity, but within its own terms, it is actually quite successful.

Most important, however, is what *Lanzelet* contributes, by its very existence, to our understanding of the development of Arthurian romance and its route through Europe. No less an authority than R. S. Loomis devoted considerable time and effort to the poem, perhaps most significantly for our purposes, in his introduction and notes to the translation by Kenneth J. T. Webster. Although the introduction, like the translation itself, may now sound so dated, the material which it contains has not been superseded. Ulrich's *Lanzelet* gathers together many motifs from many and diverse sources which were to be taken up in later versions of the Lancelot story and in other Arthurian literature.

Rarely do we have such a clear account of how a MHG poet came upon his story as that which Ulrich supplies himself towards the end of his poem (9322 ff.). It was contained, he tells us in a *welschez buoch* (book in a Romance language—here probably French) which was in the possession of one Hûc von Morville who was one of the hostages given as part of the ransom for Richard Coeur de Lion to the Emperor Henry VI and Duke Leopold of Austria. This, we know, was in 1194, but we do not know how the book came into the hands, presumably temporarily, of Ulrich. He goes on to tell how he was prevailed upon to recount this French story of Lanzelet in German for no other reason than to gain higher esteem among good people. We can only guess at the fate of the book itself, for this source is lost, leaving Ulrich's version as our only evidence of a rich tradition at this period. Although Chrétien de Troyes had told the story of Lancelot in his *Chevalier de la Charette*, there is every reason to believe that this was not the source of Ulrich's source. Ulrich assures us on several occasions that he is telling the story as he received it, and it is inconceivable that he would have omitted the love of the hero for Queen Guinevere when he came to the latter part of his story, the abduction by Valerin, and the rescue by Lanzelet. This central feature of the Lancelot material is absent in Ulrich's version, and it is out of the question that he would have suppressed it for reasons, as has been hinted, of delicacy.

If one can speak of a single central feature in Ulrich's *Lanzelet*, it is probably that of the magic cloak which fits only the truly virtuous woman. The account of how the cloak is tried on by one lady after another, changing its shape and size according to the nature of each one, until it is seen to fit Iblis perfectly, is one of the most vivid episodes in the poem (5835 ff.) and almost certainly prompted the fragment attributed to Heinrich von dem Türlin (see p. 360 f.). The significance of the test is clear: Iblis is the most virtuous woman, just as Lanzelet, who alone succeeds in defeating one hundred knights in combat, is the supreme knight.

An Ulrich von Zatzikhoven is mentioned in a document of 1214 as the parish priest of Lommis, in Thurgau, and, although this cannot be proved, it is likely that this was the same man, although another candidate has been proposed. Not knowing what became of the *welschez buoch* we cannot be sure when he made his version of the story. Some critics place it soon after 1194, detecting traces of Hartmann's *Erec* and his *Gregorius* but not of *Iwein*, others point to echoes of *Parzival*, of which he may have known the early books, or perhaps a very early version. If, as some maintain, he was composing under the influence of the complete *Parzival*, then the earliest date shifts to about 1210, and this is probably the latest acceptable dating.

Ulrich's language lacks polish, and the structure of the poem is unsophisticated. However, there *is* a structure to it, with the adventures following one another in ascending degree of difficulty and the hero returning full circle to the mother from whom he was abducted and the kingdom which is rightly his. He marries four times, deserting his first wife, being deserted by his second, marrying his beloved Iblis, to whom he will ultimately return after an interlude during which he is bound to a third woman whom he tricks into letting him go. The poem ends with a long look into the future, with Lanzelet and Iblis living happily into old age and dying on the same day. Their four children will inherit their kingdoms, happily also four in number. The family ties and the stability lost to the young Lanzelet because of the dishonorable behavior of his father are assured for the future. Running through the first part of the poem is the motif of identity, for he can discover his name only when he has performed the most hazardous of his early adventures. This hero who spends his childhood on an island surrounded by mist is encircled by fairy tale motifs and moves between the "real" world and the world of magic.

Yet Ulrich does not attempt to evoke all this in poetic language; there is something strangely matter-of-fact about his account, but it must be emphasized again that he tells his story very well. It says something for his narrative powers that E. G. Littmann saw fit to devote a whole thesis to the study of his technique of creating suspense. The poem probably appealed to its audience for the sheer gusto of its telling, even if it disappoints modern critics because it appears to lack an earnestly defined purpose. Ulrich does not indulge in lengthy asides or discourses of his own, and the most he allows himself is the very occasional, throwaway remark, which reminds the audience of his existence, as a narrator with a task set before him, or the most commonplace expression of a simple philosophy, notably that things only happen when they are destined to.

It is unfair, however, to sum up the achievement of Ulrich von Zatzikhoven as *provozierende Trivialität* (provocative triviality), as René Perennec does in one of the most recent interpretations of the poem (p. 144), though Perennec, who has contributed substantially to the more recent scholarly attempts to detect a structure and a deeper meaning in the poem, is not alone in his overall dismissiveness. Bert Nagel speaks of "eine bedenkenlose Kompilation rohstofflicher Art" (unhesitating compilation of an unrefined kind—*Deutsche Dichtung um 1200*, p. 679); Hugo Kuhn sees the poem as an example of what he calls "niedere Artusepik" (minor Arthurian epic—*Annalen der deutschen Literatur*, p. 135), while, more recently, Barbara Thoran sums up the way most critics have viewed *Lanzelet* as "fast als Ärgernis in der mittelalterlichen deutschen Literatur" (almost a source of irritation in medieval German literature, p. 52). There have been a number of attempts to impose some depth on the poem, and indeed Barbara Thoran's own article is one of the most convincing. All too often these suffer, however, from the assumption that a work of this period, composed in the shadow of Hartmann and Wolfram, must have a meaning. Kurt Ruh goes a long way towards reversing the reputation of *Lanzelet* when he describes it as "zumindest der Intention nach ein neues Modell des Artusromans" (a new model of the Arthurian romance, at least in its intention—1975, p. 55). Yet, of course, the limitation here implied is important: no matter what the intention—and some would hesitate to rank it this high—Ulrich probably did not have the means to fulfill it.

Perhaps, in the long run, it is best to recall the closing words of R. S. Loomis in his Introduction to Webster's translation: "For no Arthurian romance, except perhaps *Tristan*, can the history of the whole and its parts be so fully reconstructed as for Ulrich's

*Lanzelet*. And its itinerary has taken us from Ireland through Wales, Brittany, Wales again, and Cumberland, to the imperial court at Mainz and the home of the priest of Thurgau" (19). If one views this indisputably rather modest work from this perspective one probably accords it its proper status. Its intrinsic qualities, though they remain a matter of some dispute, are less significant.

Text:
Hahn, Karl August, ed. *Ulrich von Zatzikhoven: "Lanzelet."* Frankfurt/M: Brönner, 1845. Repr. Berlin, 1965 (with a useful afterword by F. Norman) and again 1995.

Translation:
Webster, Kenneth G. T., trans. *Ulrich von Zatzikhoven: Lanzelet.* Revised and provided with additional notes and an introduction by Roger Sherman Loomis. New York: Columbia UP, 1951. (English trans. with much information on the source material, detailed notes on the text).

### *Lanzelet*—Bibliography

Combridge, Rosemary. "Lanzelet and the Queens." In: *Essays in German and Dutch Literature*. Ed. by W. Robson-Scott. London: Univ. of London, Institute of Germanic Studies, 1973. Pp. 42-64.

Jackson, W. T. H. "Ulrich von Zatzikhoven's *Lanzelet* and the Theme of Resistance to Royal Power." *GLL* 28 (1975): 285-297.

Littmann, E. G. "Techniques of Creating Suspense in Ulrich von Zatzikhoven's *Lanzelet*." Diss. Michigan, 1975.

Perennec, René. "Ulrich von Zazikhoven: *Lanzelet*." In: *Mittelhochdeutsche Romane und Heldenepen*. Ed by. Horst Brunner. Stuttgart: Reclam, 1993 (= UB, Interpretationen, 8914). Pp. 129-145.

A recent analysis of the work but very unsympathetic.

Ruh, Kurt. *Höfische Epik des deutschen Mittelalters*. Vol. 2. Berlin: Erich Schmidt, 1980. Pp. 35-49.

———. "Der *Lanzelet* Ulrichs von Zatzikhofen. Modell oder Kompilation?" In: *Deutsche Literatur des späten Mittelalters* (Hamburger Colloquium 1973). Ed. by Wolfgang Harms and L. Peter Johnson. Berlin: Eric Schmidt, 1975. Pp. 47-55.

Thoran, Barbara. "Zur Struktur des *Lanzelet* Ulrichs von Zatzikhoven." *ZfdPh* 103 (1984): 52-77.

A full and interesting analysis, though whether it is entirely convincing is a matter of opinion.

### The *Prosa-Lancelot*

This work is strangely isolated. Presumed to date from the first half of the 13th century and related by its substance firmly to the Arthurian literature of the classical Middle Ages in Germany, its appearance in prose at this very early period probably accounts for the fact that it does not seem to have achieved any real popularity in its time. The German audience was almost certainly not ready for this bombardment with a lengthy work in a quite alien medium, and there is reason to believe that the French version of which the

German work is largely a translation may itself have been intended for a select reading public rather than for the more familiar performance at court.

Interesting though the work is as a phenomenon—a piece of courtly narrative in prose but one which remained without imitation—it has been eclipsed by some of the other poems of the post-classical era, notably perhaps by the *Jüngerer Titurel* (see p. 381 ff.), which is likewise an isolated monument that expounds a totally new ethos. The impending demise of the Hohenstaufen dynasty and the years of the Interregnum (see p. 304 ff.) were beginning to cast their shadow, and the idealism of the Arthurian romances was being replaced by a didactic, questioning tone and a greater respect for realism. The death of Arthur at the hand of Mordred, the treacherous nephew who himself dies in this combat, means the death of the world of chivalry which he represented, and this is replaced by a new spiritual order whose focus is Lancelot's son Galaad. He assumes the role of hero of the quest for the Grail, in place of Perceval, in the French cycle which unites the story of Lancelot and his love for Queen Guinevere with that of the search for the Grail.

The anonymous Vulgate Cycle (c.1215-1235) marked the transition of Arthurian romance from verse to prose and contained five narratives which could be read in approximate sequence and covered the story of the Holy Grail and its quest, the death of Arthur, the story of Merlin and that of Lancelot. The translator, or possibly translators, of this material into German, concentrated on the three last portions of a work in French which was obviously popular in its time and exists in over one hundred manuscripts. Whether the German version is based directly on a French original, or—perhaps more likely—on a lost version in Middle Dutch, remains uncertain. It is similarly open to speculation whether the partial translation into German which survives was in fact all that was attempted. The existence of two fragments dating from the mid-13th century points to a date of about 1250 for the German Prose Lancelot, although the most significant evidence is in the complete manuscript version of the 15th century. Clearly, then, the work survived for some long period, although its literary impact was minimal.

Edition:
Kluge, Reinhold, ed. *Lancelot*. Berlin: Akademie-Verlag, 1948, 1963, 1974 (= DTM 42, 47, 63).
This edition is based on the Heidelberg manuscript (P), which contains the only complete version of the work and is dated ca. 1430.

### *Prosa-Lancelot*—Bibliography

Ruberg, Uwe. "Prosa-Lancelot." *VL*[2] 5 (1985) 530-546.

A substantial introduction to the work.

Speckenbach, Klaus. "Prosa-Lancelot." In: Brunner, Horst, ed. *Mittelhochdeutsche Romane und Heldenepen*. Stuttgart: Reclam, 1993 (= UB. Interpretationen, 8914). Pp. 326-352.

This contribution contains detailed synopses, accompanied by analysis of content and narrative technique.

*Wolfram-Studien* 9 (1986) is devoted to the work, based on the contributions at the Schweinfurter Lancelot-Kolloquium in 1984.

Kennedy, Elspeth. *Lancelot and the Grail. A Study of the Prose Lancelot*. Oxford: Clarendon, 1986.
There is a dearth of material in English. This volume is concerned primarily with the French original, but is illuminating in many areas.

## RUDOLF VON EMS AND KONRAD VON WÜRZBURG

These two names in particular dominate the post-classical literary scene in Germany and together span a large proportion of the later 13th century. Although, as we shall see, they are very different from one another, they are often spoken of in one breath, representing, with the sheer range of their prolific output, the capacity of medieval German literature to survive and to take some powerful new directions in the decades which followed the decline of the courtly influence.

The word "epigones" is often used to describe these two poets and their contemporaries and in the most literal sense it cannot be questioned: they were indeed born later than Hartmann, Gottfried, Wolfram, the anonymous poet of the *Nibelungenlied*, and Walther von der Vogelweide. However, the negative connotations of the concept may surely be challenged. We shall see that some of those who followed in the tracks of the outstanding "classical" poets clearly saw it as their task to emulate them, to continue where they had left off in some cases and in others to attempt to surpass them. Nevertheless, Rudolf von Ems and Konrad von Würzburg, in different ways, took medieval German literature forward both thematically and stylistically, yet their achievements are probably unthinkable without the inspiration of their predecessors, and it would be extravagant to claim for either of them the towering stature of their models.

### Rudolf von Ems

**Rudolf von Ems** is the most significant of the post-classical poets of the first half of the 13th century. The range of his work is interesting, as is his independence of those predecessors whom he explicitly so admires and whose influence is apparent at many points throughout his oeuvre. If one describes his works broadly as courtly narratives, this must be with due recognition that the term as applied here is stretched to embrace material not treated earlier and that, perhaps most remarkably, there is no sign of Arthurian material. This means that Rudolf von Ems can in no way be regarded as a mere imitator in an age which was to a large extent fettered by its allegiance to its immediate past. However, it must be admitted that he lacked the artistic skill to realize the potential of this freedom. He stands alone, but he is no isolated peak.

The range of his work may well be attributable to the range of his patrons rather than to any real breadth of interest on his own part, and his references to these patrons enable us to form a clearer picture than is possible in other cases of the progress of his career and, more important, the circumstances which gave rise to a particular work at a particular time, and its intended audience. His creative life seems to have begun somewhere around 1220, possibly with a work which predates *Der guote Gêrhart* but which has not survived, and to have ended with his probably sudden death in 1254, an event which may well account for the fragmentary state of two works conceived on a very large scale, his *Alexander* and his *Weltchronik*. The picture of his extant works is completed by *Barlaam und Josephat* and *Willehalm von Orlens*, two works of very distinct character which contribute to an oeuvre of considerable diversity of content yet possessing a discernible coherence in style and tone.

Characteristic of all his works is a deep seriousness which sometimes tips over into melancholy, a gloomy awareness of an age of decline and perhaps of personal inadequacy to the task in hand which goes beyond the formulaic expression of humility. He feels himself very much the pupil of the great masters of MHG narrative and in trying to emulate them, he shows his relative weakness. He seems most obviously to be attempting to model himself on Gottfried von Straßburg in matters of style, yet in terms of thought and approach the gulf between them is immense. In this respect, he is more akin to the sober Hartmann von Aue. There are times, particularly in *Willehalm von Orlens*, when the echo of Wolfram von Eschenbach is the clearest one. It is perhaps fair to say that Rudolf is at his best when he is not trying to imitate anyone, but simply telling a good story, as he is quite capable of doing, in a straightforward and interesting way.

There is a generally held opinion that *Der guote Gêrhart* is his most successful work, though some may regard this as surprising, considering that it is almost certainly an early work, if not actually his first. It has the clear structure of a *Rahmenerzählung* (framestory), 6920 lines long, with a Prologue balanced by an Epilogue, enclosing a story within a story. It has a clear sense of purpose, and its didacticism, though less ponderous than in Rudolf's later works, is evident. Expressed quite simply, the message of the poem is that a man should practice humility in all his worldly doings and make them subject to the will of God. The Emperor Otto errs when he boasts of his virtue and is made to realize that he can learn from a merchant. This is one of the most remarkable features of the poem in an age which was so conscious of social status, but it reflects the changing spirit of that age and contributes to the freshness of the work. The Emperor comes to recognize how mistaken he was when, not content with the praise of this world, he demanded that God reward him for what he regarded as his incomparable virtue by anticipating the rewards which awaited him in the next. Having extracted Gerhart's story from him, he not only admits that this man is indeed superior to him in virtue but, in having that story recorded for posterity, he ensures that many other people should also learn the lesson which he has learned. The tale restores the reputation of the Emperor, but it is essentially the story of Gerhart the merchant of Cologne.

Contained within his story is another with a familiar motif, and this is a type of story which will echo in Rudolf's *Willehalm von Orlens*, of a pair of lovers who are parted by whatever circumstances and then find one another again.

> The main part of the work is Gerhart's own account of how he came across a lovely young princess in captivity, together with a group of young knights and ransomed them with his worldly goods, bringing the young woman home with him and after a year arranging for her to marry his own son. In the middle of the celebrations her former bridegroom, the heir to the throne of England, Wilhelm, believed to have perished at sea, appeared. Gerhart insisted that he was her rightful husband and took the pair back to England. There

Gerhart himself was offered the crown but declined it and handed the kingdom over to Wilhelm. He himself returned to Cologne, a merchant still but one whose great virtue is apparent, esteemed by the world and valued by God.

Within the layers of the poem, the story is fairly simply told, with few digressions. The Prologue, with its play on the word *guot*, is almost certainly modelled on Gottfried von Straßburg's *Tristan*, but the thought of the poem, with the juxtaposition of this world and the next, and the possibility of reconciling their claims, seems to owe something to both Hartmann von Aue and Wolfram von Eschenbach.

Those who like to assign genres to literary works have some problems with this poem which in many respects stands alone and is quite self-contained, to the extent that Ludwig Kahn can describe it as "remarkable and almost revolutionary" (p. 211). He speaks of the innovation, "unheard of and astonishing," that Otto is "converted" by the example of a merchant, and it is indeed true that this is the first time in medieval German literature that a member of the rising middle class plays such an important, indeed central, part in a work. One might think of Wimar in Wolfram's *Willehalm* (130,17 ff.), who, alone at the French Court, offers hospitality to Willehalm on his arrival, thereby demonstrating that virtue is not the prerogative of the knight and that any individual may serve as an example of true courtesy.

There is good reason to assign *Der guote Gêrhart* to a type of literature called *Patrizierdichtung* (poetry about patricians), although Xenja von Ertzdorff argues for its inclusion under her extended definition of the courtly romance. The two views of the poem do not, however, exclude one another but merely serve to demonstrate its unique quality. Gerhart possesses the most praiseworthy human characteristics, charity and compassion, the dedication to the service of both his fellow men and of God, and—ironically, when one considers that his history is placed in his own mouth—humility. There is no suggestion that the work is a challenge to the nobility by the merchant class; it would probably be taking it too far to interpret it in that quasi-political way. The far-fetched idea that Gerhart be offered the English crown is dismissed when he himself declines it and returns to his native Cologne to live out his life as an esteemed citizen but with no suggestion that he has transcended his social status. This would seem to be a reiteration of the feudal order rather than any attempt to erode it, still less to overthrow it. True nobility is a quality of mind and heart: the merchant possesses it by nature, the Emperor can learn to cultivate it. The investiture of young Gerhart by the Bishop challenges our credulity, but it, too, serves to advance the message of the poem and provide a glimpse of a future in which divisions could be based on different criteria.

Rudolf von Ems clearly understood and appreciated the values of knighthood. He describes the ceremony of investiture in considerable detail, as he will do later in *Willehalm von Orlens*, where its inclusion is more obviously relevant to the narrative. In that work he describes himself as a *knappe*, a status differing hardly at all from that of *ritter*, save in the formal undertaking of the investiture (*Bumke Ritterbegriff*, p. 102). Xenja von Ertzdorff suggests that his failure to take this further ceremonial step may have been due to a lack of material means in one who appears to have been a professional poet of knightly birth (p. 52), like Hartmann von Aue, a *dienest man* (ministerialis, *Willehalm von Orlens*, 15629).

A ministerialis, then, but Rudolf's addition at that point *ze Muntfort* is not helpful in identifying his place of origin. It is the more specific reference to him by the continuator of his *Weltchronik* as "Rudolf von Ense" (33496) which suggests Hohenems near Chur in the Vorarlberg. Rudolf himself names Rudolf von Steinach as the instigator of *Der guote Gêrhart* (6836-7), and the information supplies a further important and acceptable piece of the puzzle. Rudolf von Steinach is known as a ministerialis in the service of the Bishop of Konstanz, and he is described by Joachim Bumke as the first patron of this class in medieval German literary history (*Mäzene*, p. 275). Elsewhere, indeed, Bumke casts doubt on whether Rudolf von Steinach can be described as the "patron" of Rudolf von Ems in the generally accepted sense (*Bumke Kultur*, p. 674-5). It is certainly not impossible that he had the means to commission such a work, but the equality of status between patron and poet makes this an unusual situation at this period, though perhaps it is not necessary to draw too many conclusions from the apparent familiarity of Rudolf's references to his namesake (6827, and see *Bumke Kultur*, p. 674).

Probably more important, though just as difficult to establish with any certainty, is how precisely the knowledge of the story itself came to the attention of either of the Rudolfs. There is no extant literary source, but it is possible that the original story was written to honor a valued family of merchants in Cologne. Rudolf explains at the end of his work that "a man" had found the story in Austria and conveyed its contents to Rudolf von Steinach, who asked the poet to write a version in German. According to Rudolf's poem, the Emperor Otto himself had instructed that the story be written down by the monks and made known for the edification of Christian people (6801-6814). The relationship between these two explanations remains unclear, but the idea of a person of high social standing learning from one of lower status is a theme known in classical literature. Perhaps more significant and closer to the medieval German context, there was a Yiddish story in circulation of a Rabbi, who, asking who would be his companion in paradise, was directed to a butcher who told of events in his virtuous life which bear very close resemblance to those in Gerhart's account.

If *Der guote Gêrhart* was intended for an audience at a relatively small court, the work usually assumed to have followed it, **Barlaam und Josaphat**, was aimed first and foremost at the monks in the monastery at Kappel near Zürich, whose abbot had commissioned it after placing the Latin translation by John of Damascus at the disposal of Rudolf von Ems. However, it was also meant to appeal to a broader, secular audience. The monks no doubt appreciated the serious tone of the poem, but the preponderance of sheer didacticism (*lêre*), of lengthy passages of biblical teaching, was surely aimed at a less-informed audience. The poem shares with *Der guote Gêrhart* this combination of an overt message transmitted within an effectively told story. Most critics, however, would probably point to the prolixity of this second work that verges at times on the tedious. That may be the modern evaluation of the poem, for the relative assessment of these first two works appears to have been different in the Middle Ages if one compares the 15 manuscripts and 31 fragments of *Barlaam und Josaphat* with the mere two extant manuscripts of *Der guote Gêrhart*.

The actual story of *Barlaam und Josaphat* is an interesting one, a kind of re-telling of the Buddha legend in a Christian context. A favorite legend of the Middle Ages, there were many versions of it in many languages, some of them fairly accurate translations from the Latin versions which continued the original Greek tradition.

The early part of the poem deals with the conversion by Barlaam of the young prince Josaphat, but the true theme is his conversion in turn of the great heathen race into which he was born and the fulfillment of the prophecy which was uttered at his birth. It is written in the stars that Josaphat should achieve what looks to be the impossible, bringing not only his own stubborn father to an understanding of Christianity but the whole land over which he rules with power and compassion, propagating his faith not just through his teaching but also through his example as a successful ruler.

This is not a work which advocates *contemptus mundi*. Josaphat is a worldly ruler who has a task to fulfill within the world, and only when he has completed it can he hand over his rule to his successor and withdraw to the spiritual life of the recluse. This last phase of his life on earth is seen to be the crowning achievement of a life well led, and it leads in turn to his rightful rewards in the next world. As in *Der guote Gêrhart*, material wealth and status are not despised but harnessed to a proper purpose in the service of God. When Josaphat, in the fullness of time, hands over his kingship to Barachias, this does not represent a rejection of secular authority and power. He has occupied the throne in an exemplary fashion, and the throne has its own validity, as the symbol of order and dignity within a God-fearing society.

Nor is the path which Josaphat follows an easy one. He must practice humility and resist temptation. His commitment to a celibate life is temporarily shaken when the Princess of Syria makes her conversion dependent upon his love for her. Once in the wilderness, he has to endure great trials to demonstrate his love of God. As in Hartmann's *Gregorius*, the only sin which cannot be redeemed is despair.

Hartmann von Aue's influence is often evident in this poem, though more often in the thought than in its execution. Josaphat's father, King Avenier, for example, is a perfect king, but, like Armer Heinrich, he is concerned only with the glory of this world, and therein lies his error. Josaphat achieves the ideal reconciliation of the claims of this world and the next. If one also senses the influence of Wolfram von Eschenbach in this message of eternal reward achieved by the passage through this world rather than away from it, this is also no coincidence, and Rudolf's admiration for Wolfram is explicit in the close resemblance between the opening passage of *Barlaam und Josaphat* and the Prologue to Wolfram's *Willehalm*.

Such relative heights of language and expression achieved by blatant imitation are rare in this poem, however, and for the most part we have here, as in *Der guote Gêrhart*, rather pedestrian narrative, interpolated in this case by lengthy passages which retell biblical stories and hammer home the Christian doctrine that Josaphat must learn from his teacher Barlaam. The sincerity of both works is apparent, however, and there can be little doubt that Rudolf was successful in achieving his purpose of combining good story-telling with a serious and significant message.

We can see that there are points in common between *Der guote Gêrhart* and *Barlaam und Josaphat*, although some critics would contrast the worldly character of the *Patrizierdichtung* with the dominantly religious nature of the second poem. Friedrich Sengle, for example, describes *Barlaam und Josaphat* as "reine Geistlichendichtung, Legende im vorhöfischen kirchlichen Sinn" (pure clerical poetry, a legend in the pre-courtly ecclesiastical sense, p. 81). The term "legend" probably describes both works as well as any, and the differences between them, as well as their similarities, may be attributed to their composition in a time of change, by a poet who, though many would rank him in the second class, tries his hand at a variety of types of literature and makes a fair attempt at all of them.

In **Willehalm von Orlens**, the work thought to be his third completed work and composed between 1235 and 1243, Rudolf comes closest to the chivalrous romance, and this in itself might account for the extraordinary popularity of the poem in its own time and throughout the Middle Ages, with resonances beyond that time. One could also point quite simply to the appeal of the love story which is at the heart of the poem, and of the two young people, Wilhelm and Amelie, whose exemplary devotion to one another through many trials ensured their place along with Tristan and Isolde on the frescoes in the summer house at the castle of Runkelstein near Bolzano. It is entirely appropriate, too, that their reputation, very much alive around 1400, should have merited their inclusion among the courtly lovers depicted here, given that Rudolf took as his model Gottfried von Straßburg and followed him, albeit at some distance, in this account of perfect love against the background of a sometimes unhelpful society. The echoes of Gottfried are evident in the language and style of the poem, in the playing with words and the frequent use of the acrostic.

Rudolf does not, of course, come close to his great master, but he is no mere imitator, and here, as in his other works, he makes his own unique contribution to an established tradition. The story tells of the trials and tribulations of the young lovers who are separated by intrigue, meet up again only to be parted, endure a lengthy absence from one another, and are reunited only when their devotion is acknowledged and when they have proved themselves in their separate ways. Linked to that, however, is another theme, of political power and kingly rule, of the machinations of state and the need for stable and benign governance. Moreover, the love of the two young people, expressed in various discourses on *minne* and in the form of letters passing between them, culminates in marriage. This is not, as in Gottfried's poem, a love which battles against society and has no place in it, but a partnership which can be integrated into a conventional and productive order.

> Wilhelm is the son of a count who dies in combat and a mother who dies of grief on learning of her husband's death. He is educated by his father's slayer, Jofrit of Brabant, who shows himself to be a conscientious man intent on making what amends he can to the boy orphaned because of him. He sends Wilhelm to the English court, where he falls in love with the Princess Amelie. Their secret betrothal is threatened by her father's decision

to marry her to the King of Spain, while Wilhelm himself is busy proving his knightly worth by great deeds back in his own land. His plot to rescue her from this forced marriage is discovered, and he is banished from England, condemned to a life without speaking until Amelie permits him to utter. Fate intervenes in the person of the sister of the English king, an abbess who is moved when she learns of their love and contrives their reunion. The poem ends with their marriage, the reconciliation with the King of England, and Wilhelm's accession to the rule of Brabant, following the abdication of his foster-father. After the death of his father-in-law, he becomes King of England as well, succeeded by his son, also called Wilhelm, while his other son, Jofrit, is destined, by Rudolf's contortion of history, to become the first King of Jerusalem, Gottfried von Bouillon.

Many of the ingredients are familiar. The tragic parental story is reminiscent of both *Tristan* and *Parzival*, while the account of the future accessions, with the sense they provide of a stable next generation, also perhaps points to the influence of Wolfram. Rudolf had himself used the idea of lovers separated and reunited in *Der guote Gêrhart*, but it is a familiar literary theme, used centrally in *Flore und Blanscheflur* (see p. 320 ff.). The motif of someone condemned to silence and only released by the beloved savors of the fairy tale.

Large portions of the poem, which describe scenes of fighting and show considerable insight into the strategy of battle, suggest that Rudolf may well have been influenced by Wolfram's *Willehalm*, and though he is clearly trying to emulate Gottfried in matters of style, there are times when the language, particularly the imagery of battle, has distinct echoes of *Willehalm* in this respect, too.

The didactic tone which was often rather intrusive in the two earlier works is less evident here, yet Rudolf is obviously making some important points about love and statesmanship and the desirability of chivalry's being harnessed to worthwhile causes. His description of the investiture of the young Wilhelm, the instructions regarding proper courtly behavior and much of the background material, all echo substance from the courtly romance of the classical period. The idea of the knight's being inspired by love and his progress through vicissitudes to success and a high position in society are themes which link Rudolf von Ems with his admired predecessors. Thus, in some respects, this work has a much more obvious place in a chain of development than Rudolf's two previous works, and it may have had a ready appeal in its own time precisely for that reason. Moreover, it has been convincingly argued, and it is not difficult to accept the fact, that the poem has significant political overtones.

Rudolf names as his patron for this work Konrad von Winterstetten (15662-15666), one of the most important ministeriales attached to the Hohenstaufen court, whose function as advisor to the young King Conrad IV may be seen to be reflected in the advice given to Wilhelm in this poem and in particular his training in kingship. In making the son of Wilhelm and Amelie into the historical figure of Gottfried von Bouillon, King of Jerusalem, Rudolf forges a link with Conrad, who, as the son of Isabella of Jerusalem, bore that same title. The work thus has a particular relevance to the Hohenstaufen dynasty and to the court at which it was to be performed. Although Rudolf refers to a French source made known to Konrad von Winterstetten by a fellow ministerialis,

Johannes von Ravensburg (15601 ff.), this work is lost to us, so we can only surmise how much of the overtly political content may have been Rudolf's addition, but it is quite evident that, for all his limitations, he had a fair degree of originality when it came to handling his material and molding it for its particular destination.

Rudolf's *Alexander*, a lengthy fragment dealing with the familiar material of the life of Alexander the Great, serves to demonstrate courtly qualities and to instruct in leadership. Like *Willehalm von Orlens*, it is seen as relevant to the prevailing situation, with the idealized Alexander as a model to the young Conrad. It is thus an unambiguous tribute to the Hohenstaufen rule and a vote of confidence in the continuity of that dynasty. Considering the quite elaborate information which Rudolf gives about his patrons and the genesis of his other works, it is surprising that no patron is named for *Alexander*. It has been held that there was plenty of opportunity for him to insert such information in the fragment as it stands (Junk, p. 752-3), but one could also argue that he might have withheld it for a substantial epilogue, which he did not reach. Of the three manuscripts, the two longer fragments break off at about the same point (Ms. B at 21623 and M at 21640), leading to the opinion that Rudolf ceased composing here. It is also generally believed that the work was written in two stages, the first up to 5015 before *Willehalm von Orlens*, and the remainder after it. Rudolf himself speaks in terms of "books," of which we have six, and, judging by the acrostics which head the books and, after the first which forms his own name, spell out the name ALEXA. . . , we conclude that he intended to write ten in all.

One can only guess why he failed to complete the work, but one notes that he had interrupted it once already, apparently to turn his mind to a more pressing task. He appears to have been someone who, naturally adaptable if not exactly versatile, was able to respond to expediency, and perhaps, after well over 21,000 lines, he felt he had made his point and that a new challenge awaited him in the form of the *Weltchronik*. We have seen that his other works tend to prolixity, and *Alexander* is no different in this respect, but one might have expected him to draw the work to some kind of conclusion. Perhaps the material itself, despite any topical insinuations he might give to it, was not that interesting to his audience, and the excessive didacticism and the intrusion of Rudolf's learning into his narrative make it very heavy-going today and may not have been very appealing to a 13th-century public.

One aspect of *Alexander* does, however, ensure its enduring interest to literary scholars, and it is one which it shares with *Willehalm von Orlens*. Both contain lengthy insertions on literature (*Willehalm von Orlens*, 2170-2300; *Alexander*, 3171-3298). Though doubtless inspired by the literary excursus in Gottfried's *Tristan*, the tone is less polemical and the purpose probably to inform rather than to evaluate, still less to attack. The passages have proved to be invaluable in dating medieval German poems, assigning authors and even uncovering the existence of otherwise unknown works.

Although, by stretching the term considerably, one may describe *Alexander* as a courtly romance, the tendency to pure history is indisputable, and this direction is maintained in Rudolf's last and enormously ambitious work, the *Weltchronik*, an undertaking which, one might suggest, was by its very nature doomed to remain incomplete. In this case Rudolf is clear about the inspiration of his work: it was commissioned by Conrad IV and intended, he tells us, to be "ein eweclih memorial" (an eternal memorial, 21697). We may find a double irony in the fact that Rudolf himself died during the writing of the great work, and that by then (1254) Conrad's days were numbered as were those of the Hohenstaufen dynasty itself.

Clearly, however, the *Weltchronik*, which Rudolf had brought "only" to the story of Solomon, was very popular in the Middle Ages. There are over 80 manuscripts of it, some of them incomplete, and its impact ensured that not only was there an almost immediate attempt to continue it by one who was blatantly less gifted than Rudolf himself but that the very idea of a chronicle of the world was established and thrived as a tradition throughout the later Middle Ages.

No one would claim that Rudolf von Ems is a poet of high rank. What he is, is a significant and very interesting figure in the literary landscape of the German Middle Ages. His roots are firmly in the early 13th century, with the frequent echoes of the predecessors whom he so admired and tried in some respects to emulate. It is, however, less productive to emphasize his shortcomings—his pedestrian style, his wordiness, his clumsy repetition—than to see him as someone who, in concept perhaps rather than in actual execution, took German literature a good many steps further forward. The range of his subject matter is interesting, and it does not really matter if one perceives that his choice was dictated by other people. Although one must concede that there is not a comparable variety in his style, he nevertheless does much to release Middle High German literature from some of its traditions and contribute to what Dennis Green has called the "explosion of new genres in the vernacular which characterizes the 13th century" (1986, 180, note 117).

Texts:
Asher, John A., ed. *Der guote Gêrhart*. Tübingen: Niemeyer, [2]1971 (= ATB, 56).
Ehrismann, Gustav, ed. *Weltchronik*. Berlin: Weidmann, 1915.
Junk, Victor, ed. *Willehalm von Orlens*. Berlin: Weidmann, 1905.
____, ed. *Alexander*. 2 vols. Leipzig: Hiersemann, 1928 and 1929.
Pfeiffer, Franz, ed. *Barlaam und Josaphat*. Leipzig: Göschen, 1843.

### Rudolf von Ems—Bibliography

Brackert, Helmut. *Rudolf von Ems. Dichtung und Geschichte*. Heidelberg, 1968.
One of the most authoritative books on the poet.
Von Ertzdorff, Xenja. *Rudolf von Ems. Untersuchungen zum höfischen Roman im 13. Jahrhundert*. Munich: Fink, 1967.
Another full study, which departs from the question of genre as implied in the title but contains much useful material of a more general nature.
Green, Dennis. "On the Primary Reception of the Works of Rudolf von Ems." *ZfdA* 115 (1986): 151-180.
Kahn, Ludwig. "Rudolf von Ems: *Der gute Gerhard*. Truth and Fiction in Medieval Epics." *GR* 14 (1939): 208-214.
Schnell, Rüdiger. *Rudolf von Ems. Studien zur inneren Einheit seines Gesamtwerkes*. Bern: Francke, 1969.

A full-scale analysis of the oeuvre, well worth reading for those who wish to study Rudolf von Ems in some detail, possibly in conjunction with the books by Helmut Brackert and Xenja von Ertzdorff.

Schröder, Edward. "Rudolf von Ems und sein Literaturkreis." *ZfdA* 67 (1930): 209-251.

A full account of the literary context of Rudolf von Ems.

Sengle, Friedrich. "Die Patrizierdichtung *Der gute Gerhard.*" *DVjs* 24 (1950): 53-82.

An interesting assessment of this particular work but with more general references to the other poems too.

Walliczek, Wolfgang. "Rudolf von Ems: *Der guote Gêrhart.*" In: *Mittelhochdeutsche Romane und Heldenepen.* Ed by. Horst Brunner. Stuttgart: Reclam, 1993 (= UB: Interpretationen, 8914) Pp. 255-270.

One of the most recent essays on Rudolf, readily available.

Wisbey, Roy A. *Das Alexanderbild Rudolfs von Ems.* Berlin: Erich Schmidt, 1966.

A detailed analysis of Rudolf's *Alexander.*

____. "Zum Barlaam und Josaphat Rudolfs von Ems." *ZfdA* 86 (1956): 293-301.

## Konrad von Würzburg

The name of **Konrad von Würzburg** is often linked with that of Rudolf von Ems, although they are almost a generation apart. The link lies in the view of both of them as successors to the dominant poets of the classical Middle High German period, but as in the case of Rudolf von Ems, neither can be dismissed as a mere imitator, and close study of Konrad von Würzburg reveals more differences than similarities between them. There is no suggestion that the later Konrad was in any way dependent on Rudolf: rather do both have their roots in the work of Hartmann, Gottfried and Wolfram, all of whom they clearly admired and emulated to a greater or lesser extent, while retaining the capacity to break new ground.

There is no mention of Konrad von Würzburg in the literary passage in Rudolf's *Willehalm von Orlens* (ca. 1240) and no firm evidence on which to base a date of birth, but his death is recorded in 1287. It is now generally agreed that he was born in Würzburg, firmly attested that he died in Basel, and there is evidence of a middle period spent in Strasbourg, or possibly as an itinerant with strong links with Strasbourg. He betrays his class with the words "wær ich edel" (if I were a nobleman) in one of his *Sprüche*, and he is usually described as a professional poet, dependent on his patrons, many of whom he names. Though not himself of the nobility, he composed for such an audience, and his works betray, to a greater extent than those of Rudolf von Ems, a nostalgia for a past dominated by courtly ideals. His preoccupation with matters of chivalry and its trappings, such as tournaments and heraldry, suggests a man who, while not actively associated with this area of life, admired it and lamented its demise. Moreover his actual knowledge of such matters is evident as is his knowledge of law and theology and classical and contemporary literature. He seems to have learned Latin early in his life and to have acquired a knowledge of French at a later stage, though for his earlier works he had been dependent on translations. The assumption is that he was educated in a religious institution, but his early schooling did not lead to a career as a cleric.

One of the most interesting and impressive aspects of the work of Konrad von Würzburg is his command of a wide range of types of literature, and in this respect he differs from Rudolf von Ems and from his illustrious predecessors. Although he did compose long romances, his most original, and possibly his most successful contribution is in the field of short narratives, those that are usually classified as "legends" or the sometimes quite pithy short stories best categorized with the German term *mære*. There are also works which defy generic attribution and stand very much on their own, though often providing a model for the future, and there is quite a large corpus of lyric poetry.

Given the range of subject matter and form, it is difficult to speak of characteristic features of his work, although his preoccupation with form and mastery of technique are important starting points for any study of Konrad von Würzburg. He seems to have seen poetic composition not, as Rudolf von Ems did, as something which could be learned but as a gift to be used with reverence. His *Klage der Kunst* (see below, p. 354 f.) reflects his own attitude to art as something worthy of special esteem.

The chronology of Konrad's works has been the subject of some controversy, with quite extreme opinions expressed. Much of the information about chronology is based on Konrad's own references to his patrons or, in some cases, those who were in some way linked with the works, although not patrons in the strict sense of the term. The following non-chronological account adopts an approach which is broadly generic, while indicating those respects in which some poems defy categorization. Matters of chronology are treated along the way as appropriate.

### The Shorter Works: *Das Turnier von Nantes, Der Schwanritter, Der Welt Lohn, Das Herzmære, Heinrich von Kempten*

This little work, *Das Turnier von Nantes*, is contained in only one manuscript, the so-called Leone-manuscript, the *Hausbuch* of Michael de Leone, who died in 1355. This very fine manuscript contains a collection of songs of, among others, Walther von der Vogelweide and Reinmar von Hagenau as well as Konrad von Würzburg, the *Klage der Kunst* and *Die goldene Schmiede*, and the *Turnier von Nantes*, a work of 1156 lines which stands alone in the oeuvre of Konrad. Unusually, Konrad does not name himself in this work, but there is now virtual unanimity that it is in fact correctly attributed to him: certain similarities can be noted with *Der Schwanritter* and *Der Trojanerkrieg*. It is an account of a single event for which no historical basis has been conclusively established, and, for some, an early example of *"Wappendichtung"* (heraldic poetry). Others maintain, however, that the extensive descriptions of armor and heraldic symbols are incidental and that this admittedly recurrent preoccupation of Konrad's is not the central concern of the work.

He intends rather to extol the courage and largess of the central figure, King Richart of England, who heads the German forces at the tournament in Nantes and defeats the knights led by the French king. It has been pointed out that Nantes is one of the traditional seats of King Arthur and that Konrad could just be nodding towards a literary context which otherwise plays no part in his works. To the Middle Ages, the generosity of Richard Lion Heart was legendary, and this poem opens with the account of how a certain King Richart von Engellant, renowned for his open-handedness, is prevailed upon by his nobles to give up his custom of giving to all and sundry for one year but circumvents this embargo by hurling gold and silver vessels out of the windows. After his victory in the tournament, he dispenses all his gains, and the poem ends with a eulogy of him.

The model of Richard Lion Heart is an obvious one, but there is convincing evidence that the poem was intended, perhaps also, to honor another Richard, earl of Cornwall, brother of Henry III of England. In May 1257, Richard was crowned in Aachen by the bishop of Cologne. He appeared to fulfill certain requirements for the holder of the German crown and in particular to have the advantage of not threatening the power of the princes, but his nomination was by no means unanimously accepted. Konrad's poem may be seen as an attempt to rally support for him, and the date of 1257/58 is thus a convincing one for a work which had already been shown to be early on stylistic and thematic grounds (see de Boor, 1967).

Because of its singular nature and the issues it raises of chronology, *Das Turnier von Nantes* is usually considered, as here, separately from several other shorter works which were probably composed at about the same time. These can more easily be grouped together and even categorized as short stories or *mæren*. The word novella also comes to mind, though it may be seen as an anachronism at this very early stage. Moreover, the following consideration of the works concerned—*Der Schwanritter, Der Welt Lohn, Herzmœre, Heinrich von Kempten*—will show how distinctive they all are and that the one feature they have in common is their relative brevity, which emerges as one of Konrad's narrative strengths.

**Der Schwanritter** may well have been composed at about the same time as *Das Turnier von Nantes*, possibly even a little earlier. It is contained in only one manuscript, and that is badly damaged, resulting in the loss of parts of the text and in particular of the beginning, which may have contained a mention of a patron. The end of the narrative speaks of the descent of the houses of Brabant, Geldern, Kleve and Rieneck from Gottfried of Bouillon and the association of the counts of Rieneck with the emblem of the swan heightens speculation about their sponsorship of the poem, though the arguments are no more conclusive than for the other names which are linked with Konrad's other works.

The poem treats a favorite legend of the Middle Ages, that of the mysterious Swan Knight, bound by secrecy and doomed to disappear if anyone tries to discover his name or his origin. In German literature we know of him from the end of Wolfram's *Parzival*, which looks into a future when Parzival's son Loherangrin will be forced to leave his wife when she demands to know his secret. The oldest literary form of the legend is the French *Chanson du Chevalier au Cygne* of about 1200, a cycle of stories relating to the life of Gottfried of Bouillon. The story was later to find its way into the longer romance, *Lohengrin* (see p. 385 ff.).

In Konrad's version Gottfried of Bouillon is not the grandson of the Swan Knight but his wife's dead father. The unnamed knight in the boat drawn by a swan appears just at the right time to defend the rights of two ladies in a legal battle over their inheritance. Having won the victory, he marries the daughter and in a passage lost to us in this damaged manuscript lives with her and their children until the day comes when she goes against the specific condition and causes him to leave, drawn away again by the swan. His wife is left to bring up their children, from whom the counts of Geldern and Kleve will be descended.

The poem is set in the time of Charlemagne and so has a touch of historical reality about it, although the central interest and problems of interpretation concern the symbolism. Stylistically the poem is more complex and more polished than some of Konrad's other short works, possibly reflecting the influence of his French source in the style as well as in the theme, but the essential beauty and mystery are marred, perhaps, by overlengthy descriptions of clothes, particularly of armor, and of combat. Another of Konrad's interests shows itself here in his long account of the legal process, and, again, some would say that this spoils the narrative.

More obviously "German" in theme and tone, despite its probable inspiration in a Latin sermon, *Der Welt Lohn*, a little work, is contained in seven manuscripts and two fragments and had considerable impact on the later Middle Ages. The concept of Lady World, beautiful on the outside and from the front, but hideous and corrupt when she turns her back, was known to German audiences from the personification by Walther von der Vogelweide (100,24), and for some reason Konrad makes another familiar poet, Wirnt von Gravenberg (see p. 314 ff.), the other central figure.

The poem makes a powerful impression in its 274 lines. Wirnt von Gravenberg is introduced immediately as the epitome of the courtly knight, who has devoted his life to worldly matters, earning esteem for his fighting and his service of ladies, in both of which activities he has been indefatigable. One evening he is deeply engrossed in a book of stories of *minne*, which he greatly enjoys, but he is interrupted by a visit from a spectacularly beautiful lady, perfection herself (84-85). She is wearing a crown and no one could pay the price of her clothes, even assuming they were available for purchase. The effect on the poet is tremendous: his color drains away and he is overcome with confusion. When he asks who she is, she tells him that she is the one whom he has served so faithfully all his life. Her emphasis is on the service which he has given her, and the reward which he can expect from her. Still he is puzzled, for he is not aware of having served her nor of ever having seen her before, and he asks her name. At last the revelation comes: "I am called the World, which you have desired for so long" (212-213), and she proceeds to show him the reward which awaits him. Turning her back on him, she reveals the ghastly truth, the creatures which eat away at her and transform her superficial beauty into foul-smelling ugliness. Her lovely face is distorted and pale as ash (236-238).

To the accompaniment of the narrator's curses, Lady World disappears, and the knight without further ado leaves his wife and children and sets out, with the Cross on his garments, to cross the seas and fight against the heathens. This is his way of making amends and in this Christian service he dies and so ensures the salvation of his soul.

The poem ends with an exhortation to all people to take note of this lesson and to know that the service of the world will demand a terrible price: "I, Konrad von Würzburg, give this advice to all of you: that you leave the world to go its own way, if you wish to preserve your souls."

The central picture of the poem is a powerful one, and some have seen that as its principal purpose, but the decision of the knight to leave everything and take up the Cross suggests that the work should more properly be seen as a piece of propaganda, an incitement to join the Crusade. It may therefore be dated about 1266. (The 7th Crusade ended in 1270, and, though instigated by King Louis of France, it was very much in the mind of the German public).

Why Konrad should have chosen to make Wirnt von Gravenberg his central figure is puzzling. He may simply have wished to refer to a known person with a literary background, and he seems to be wishing to discredit courtly literature, since Wirnt's obvious enjoyment in his reading is ultimately seen in a negative light. Most plausible perhaps is the suggestion that Wirnt von Gravenberg's own contention in the prologue to his *Wigalois* that he had composed the work "for the love of the world" (142), together with his closing lament on the transience of joy (11676 ff.) suggested both the commitment to worldly things and a subsequent retraction.

***Das Herzmære*** is another powerful little work, belonging similarly to the earlier period of Konrad's creative life (around 1260). Konrad tells in his prologue that he is about to tell a *schoene mære* about pure love (23). How pleasant this story is, is a matter of opinion, since the core of the account of the devotion between a man and a woman is the fact that the woman unwittingly eats the heart of her lover. Their devotion is manifested in his death when they are forced to separate by her jealous husband, and her self-inflicted death by starvation when she realizes what she has done. Konrad's reference to Gottfried von Straßburg who held, in his own Prologue, that the way to the understanding of perfect love lay in hearing the stories of other lovers (9-21), suggests his purpose: to raise his pair of lovers as models of devotion. As in *Tristan*, the commitment to love is placed on a higher plane than the demands of conventional morality. The husband is the villain of the piece, separating the lovers in the first place, intercepting the messenger who comes with the dead lover's heart for the lady, and tricking her into eating it by persuading her that it is a special delicacy to tempt her appetite. If he then receives his just deserts when he reveals the truth to her and she resolves to let nothing more pass her lips, this somewhat ambiguous retribution is passed over by Konrad, who concludes the poem, rather echoing Gottfried, by speaking in more general terms of the way in which love is misused today.

Konrad's poem is a version, told with characteristic pungency, of a popular story, which made its appearance very early in the 12th century and was then told with variations throughout the Middle Ages and into the modern period, culminating in Uhland's ballad "Der Kastellan von Coucy" (1814). In some versions, the husband actually arranges the death of the lover, a feature which Konrad avoids, with some regard perhaps for conventional morality.

The impact of Konrad's story is increased by his mastery of the short verse narrative. Here, as in *Der Welt Lohn* and *Heinrich von Kempten*, he shows himself at his best when he is concentrating on a single-stranded account, unmarred by the digressions which sometimes weaken his other works.

*Heinrich von Kempten*, sometimes called *Otte mit dem Barte*, belongs to the same period and, broadly, to the same category of *mære* as the two preceding poems. The disparity of theme, however, is evidence of the variety which characterizes Konrad's works as a whole.

Here he turns to vaguely historical material, though more anecdotal than factually attested. The poem is a glorification of chivalry and an exhortation to knights to follow the path of courage and resolve exemplified by the central character that, says Konrad, is so rare nowadays (748-749). The Emperor who is known for his temper and keeps any oath which he swears by his fine long beard (1-7) is probably an echo of Otto II ("the Red") who reigned from 973 to 983 and had a reputation for violent over-reaction. Once more, Konrad was dependent on a Latin source.

The poem really contains two separate anecdotes, linked by the vigorous personality of Heinrich von Kempten. The vivid scene of the first part of the poem, after the Prologue that introduces Otto and his formidable reputation, has Heinrich von Kempten at the emperor's court, which he is visiting with his protégé, the young son of the duke of Swabia. When the boy commits the faux pas of taking a piece of bread from the imperial table, he is brutally struck by the steward, who, in turn, receives a fatal blow from the sword of Heinrich. Otto swears vengeance, and Heinrich, recklessly, since he knows that he is doomed, seizes his beard and hurls him to the ground, threatening to cut his throat. He spares him only on condition that he himself can go free, but the emperor banishes him for life. He returns to his native Swabia (383).

Ten years later the emperor is campaigning in Italy and, requiring reinforcements, sends to the abbot of Kempten who prepares to join him himself and to engage the service of his ministeriales, among them Heinrich von Kempten. The latter protests in vain that it will cost him his life and offers, also in vain, his own sons instead of himself. Since it must be so, he goes with the abbot and performs with great courage but takes care to keep out of the emperor's sight, until one day, sitting in his bath in his encampment, he glimpses some treacherous citizens from the next town preparing to ambush the emperor who is unarmed and under the impression that he is meeting them for a discussion of tactics. Heinrich leaps out of the bath and bravely fights with them before returning to his bath as though nothing had happened. The emperor goes back safely to his nobles, who know what he does not know: that his life has been saved by the man whom he has sworn to kill.

The two "parts" of the poem are linked by the picture of the naked knight fighting to save the emperor and the same knight, all those years before, leaping across the table and seizing that same emperor by his precious beard (666-673). Otto acknowledges the courage of the man and agrees to forgive him his earlier deed, retracting his usually resolute oath. Kisses of reconciliation and rich rewards follow for Heinrich, together with enduring fame (743), and Konrad's Epilogue underlines this example to all knights.

The humor of this poem can hardly be denied, despite the serious message, and it thus adds further to the variety of Konrad's short narrative, with its robust, almost burlesque tone. As with several of the other shorter works, the relative abundance of manuscripts suggests that this work, with its undeniable reference to an earlier age, was well received by Konrad's audience.

## The Legends: *Silvester, Alexius, Pantaleon*

This group of verse narratives based on the lives of saints may belong to a slightly later period than the works just treated, probably during the 1270s—though some critics place *Silvester* much earlier—and almost certainly they were composed in Basel. The order of composition is generally agreed to be that indicated above. Konrad has followed his Latin sources fairly closely, and these legends are not imaginative narratives of saintly figures (like Hartmann's *Gregorius* or his *Armer Heinrich*, or the *Barlaam und Josephat* of Rudolf von Ems) but straightforward and relatively brief factual accounts. Their purpose is to extol the virtues of the saints by reference to their lives, or significant parts of their lives, to honor God and to urge the listeners to pay heed to these examples and to try to emulate them. They belong in a long tradition of lives of the saints, but within Konrad's work they indicate the diversity of his interests and his talents. As elsewhere in his work, it is evident that Konrad is greatly interested in form and style, and this has given rise to the question, with regard to the legends, of whether aesthetic considerations are at least as important as religious ones.

Although the actual events of the life of the saint in each case are, of course, important, it could reasonably be argued that these are in fact merely the means to convey the higher truth of the power of God Himself, and to this higher truth Konrad devotes his prologues, epilogues and central passages throughout the poems. He is not concerned with character or individual traits, but rather with the sharp contrast between belief and unbelief, and the way in which faith affects the behavior of the central figures.

*Silvester* is by far the longest of Konrad's legends (5222 lines). The closing lines refer to the patron as Liuthold von Roeteln, a cleric closely associated with Basel cathedral. Equally important, perhaps, is his close association with the guilds, for St. Silvester was the patron saint of builders.

The subject of this legend is Pope Silvester I (314-335), and its theme is essentially the triumph of Christianity over heathendom and Judaism. Its basis is the popular story of the conversion of Rome which followed upon the baptism of the Emperor Constantine by Pope Silvester. Silvester has freed the city from a dragon and then effected a cure through baptism for the leprosy which afflicts the emperor and for which the only remedy known to the Roman doctors is the blood of many thousands of innocent children. Constantine's refusal to allow this sacrifice leads to Silvester's conversion of him (1860). The compassion which Konrad has advocated as a prime human virtue (1159-1162) has been rewarded.

The second part of the legend represents an assertion of the Christian faith against Judaism. Constantine arranges a disputation between Pope Silvester and twelve learned Jewish teachers. Although Silvester's arguments prevail, the ultimate proof comes when he raises to life in the name of Jesus Christ a stag which has been killed in the name of Judaism.

Judging from the proliferation of manuscripts, *Alexius*, a strange little story, was the most popular of Konrad's legends. St. Alexius was honored as the patron saint of beggars and pilgrims, and the legend, based again on a Latin source but with its roots in the East, tells of a life of suffering and self-imposed privation and a death accompanied by miracles which proclaim his sanctity.

> Alexius is the young son of wealthy parents in Rome but he abandons his home and his new bride, without consummating the marriage. After years of wandering, mainly in the East, he comes, seemingly by chance but in reality by the will of God, back to Rome, where he persuades his own father, who fails to recognize him, to allow him to live in his house. Uncomplainingly he endures torment and torture from the servants, until, informed by God of the approach of death, he writes a letter to his parents revealing his true identity. This letter comes into the hands of the pope after his death, and the grieving parents and the young widow are left to mourn their loss and to reproach themselves for having failed to recognize him. The beauty of the corpse and the fragrance which it emits are signs of his saintliness.

What seems like a rather insubstantial story and even rather dubious claims to sanctity may well have appealed to Konrad's audience for its emphasis on modesty and self-degradation, while the features of non-recognition and belated revelation of identity were, of course, favorite ones in the courtly romances. In these respects, and in matters of style and language, the model of Hartmann von Aue, and particularly of his *Gregorius*, comes most readily to mind.

According to Konrad himself, the work was commissioned by two well-known citizens of Strasbourg, further evidence of the growing influence of the higher middle classes on literary production.

*Pantaleon*, the third of Konrad's legends, belongs, artistically, to a somewhat different category. Here Konrad is composing more independently, though again with a Latin source, and the work has more in common, from the stylistic point of view, with the works of his maturity. However, like *Silvester*, it does not appear to have been particularly well received perhaps beyond the limited sphere of Basel, where Pantaleon was a popular saint, and the man who commissioned the work, Johannes von Arguel, had some local political significance.

> As the prologue makes clear, the story of St. Pantaleon is a glorification of martyrdom. Pantaleon is the son of a heathen father and a Christian mother. Having been baptized himself, he persuades his father to be converted. Then, as a doctor, he uses his skills to effect remarkable cures, and he converts a great many people, who witness his extraordinary powers. The conclusion of the work, however, describes the terrible suffering inflicted on him by the Emperor Maximian, culminating in his being beheaded. The descriptions are stark, and the whole poem is single stranded, to an even greater extent than the other two legends. Particularly impressive is Pantaleon's prayer before his execution and the response of God to it (2016 ff.).

### The Longer Narrative Works:
### *Engelhard, Partonopier und Meliur, Trojanerkrieg*

Turning from these historically based legends, we come now to three works which, possibly from different periods of Konrad's career, nevertheless belong together from the generic point of view though they are very different in substance.

***Engelhard***, generically somewhere between a short story and a novel, is fairly highly regarded in modern scholarship. The fact that the poem has come down to us only in a printed version of 1573 should not necessarily lead to the conclusion that it was not popular in its own time. It is assumed that this version will have had as its basis a manuscript of the 13th or 14th century.

Controversy still surrounds the chronological position of *Engelhard* within Konrad's oeuvre. The absence of an explicit reference to a patron and the uncertainty about how early one may place Konrad's arrival in Basel are factors which make it difficult to say with certainty when the work was composed, but on the whole the weight of opinion seems to point to an early work of considerable quality, superior to the later longer narratives which suffered from being too long.

Artistic considerations apart, however, there are obvious problems of evaluating *Engelhard* as the piece of moral teaching Konrad clearly intended it to be. It is a poem in praise of *triuwe*, that much lauded loving devotion which is a prime virtue in courtly literature. Konrad, in his artistically complex and stylized prologue, makes his purpose as clear as Gottfried does in the prologue to *Tristan*, which probably was Konrad's model. Gottfried had elevated his ideal of love between a man and a woman to the point where it defied convention and socially accepted morality, and Konrad's poem is likewise a demonstration of the unassailable worth of *triuwe* in the form of the friendship between two men, Engelhard and Dieterich.

Although Konrad refers to a Latin source (6493), what that source was has not been established nor do we know how closely he adhered to it. It is generally accepted, however, that the poem belongs in a tradition of friendship tales, and that it is specifically related to the story of *Amicus and Amelius*, which was popular throughout Europe in the Middle Ages. However, since Konrad gives his two central characters such unambiguously German names, he may have had access to another, German, version of the tale.

> The story tells of two friends, so alike as to be indistinguishable. The king's daughter, Engeltrût, falls in love with both of them and is torn between them, until she eventually chooses Engelhard, because of the similarity of his name and hers, and because she finds the name pleasant to the ear (1196 ff.). Yet still she does not reveal her feelings for him. Dieterich is summoned back to Brabant, to take up his inheritance on the death of his father. He tries to persuade Engelhard to come with him but he declines. When Engelhard falls in love with Engeltrût, she at first rejects him, until, moved by his almost fatal lovesickness, she agrees to return his love if he will become a knight and fight for her. This he does, but a secret tryst is discovered and Engelhard, having denied the charge, must defend his honor in combat. Now in great danger, he seeks advice from his friend Dieterich who offers to stand in for him in the combat, while Engelhard remains in Dieterich's stead in Brabant. The substitution is detected by no one. Engelhard, posing as Dieterich, places a sword between himself and Dieterich's wife.
>
> Meanwhile, Dieterich, taking Engelhard's place, is victorious in the combat and pronounced innocent by the king, who gives him his daughter in marriage (4992). Engeltrût is oblivious to the deception, and Dieterich also places a sword between himself and his friend's bride. He then announces that he is going on a pilgrimage, returns instead to Brabant and resumes his life there, while Engelhard returns to his bride, Engeltrut.

Some time later (5142 ff.), Dieterich falls ill with leprosy and goes to live in isolation on an island. There he is informed by an angel that there is a cure for his affliction, namely, the blood of Engelhard's children. He journeys to his friend's land and lives in a house built specially for him by Engelhard. When eventually Engelhard discovers that there is a cure for the leprosy and what exactly that cure is, he is in a terrible dilemma, but, remembering their friendship and what Dieterich has done for him, he beheads his children while his wife is in church. Dieterich recovers immediately, and when the nurse goes to find the children, they are alive and well (6381), miraculously restored to life by God in recognition of the devotion of the two men. The poem ends, as it began, with praise of loyalty.

The story would seem to afford considerable scope for the analysis of emotions and psychological insights, but such matters are not among the strengths of Konrad von Würzburg. One is left, moreover, with misgivings about the morality of the whole poem, although in no way does Konrad invite one to pursue them. Like Gottfried von Straßburg he establishes his own level of ideal behavior in this poem, but, needless to say, the poem comes nowhere near to *Tristan* in artistry. The echoes of Hartmann von Aue, too, though striking, are incidental in a poem which is relatively lacking in depth. That said, one must concede that *Engelhard* is an effective tale, told, like Konrad's shorter works with some pungency and that it has an important place among all his works.

At line 21784, ***Partonopier und Meliur*** comes to an abrupt end, in the middle of the narrative and without the epilogue which one might reasonably assume would have balanced the lengthy prologue to this work. The scribe who produced the only substantial manuscript names himself as H. Winklar, and he adds a brief concluding prayer. The date and place of the manuscript, 1471 in Hall am Inn, are also supplied.

It is assumed that Konrad von Würzburg did not complete the narrative because the French source to which he refers, though not specifically, in his prologue was also incomplete. The story of Partonopeus de Blois was a popular one in the Middle Ages, existing in many languages, but with an impact on French literature which has been compared with that of the Tristan material and the Grail legend. Konrad's poem does not appear to have been well received, and various explanations have been put forward: that it came either too early or too late, that it was too obviously identifiable with a specific family, that there were too many similar works around at the time. One can only speculate.

The material is a mixture of historical and political elements, but what dominates in the tone of the poem is the fairy tale. Partonopier, son of the Count of Blois, finds himself in a strange town where he encounters an invisible woman who tells him that she will marry him in two years' time, but that in the meantime, although they will be lovers, he will not see her. After a year he returns to his family home in France, where he acquits himself splendidly in combat with the heathen king Sornagiur. Persuaded by his mother and the archbishop of Paris that he has become embroiled in the work of the devil, he goes against the conditions imposed on him by his beloved and takes a magic lantern one night in order to be able to see her as she lies beside him. She banishes him and his happiness is at an end. In despair he wanders off into the wilderness and leads the life of a recluse. Meanwhile, his beloved, whose name is Meliur and who is the daughter of the emperor of Constantinople, is under pressure to marry. In a tournament arranged to determine the best knight who will become her bridegroom, Partonopier is victorious and their marriage follows, now that he has won her properly, by means of chivalry. However, one of her defeated suitors amasses an army to take her from him, and it is in the middle of this battle that the work breaks off.

Even a synopsis shows the extent to which Konrad's work gathers together familiar motifs: a mysterious place to which the hero comes seemingly by chance but in reality drawn by some magic force; the lavish hospitality he receives there; the candles borne by unseen hands (1115-1119); the love between a human and a fairy; the breaking of a condition which results in separation (as in *Der Schwanritter*); the mother who tries first to arrange a love match for her son by means of a potion (6957), then makes the magic lantern which will lead to his betrayal of the bond with his true love (7759 ff.); the role played by non-recognition. The figure of Irekel, the sister of Meliur, who tries to help Partonopier on several occasions, attempts to mediate with her sister on his behalf, and eventually brings about the happy reunion by arranging for his participation in the tournament, reminds one of Hartmann's Lunete; indeed, the influence of *Iwein* is strong in this story of the man banished by his beloved, who accuses him of betrayal, and then finding his way back to her through acts of valor which prove his true worth.

The elevation of the ideals of chivalry harks back to an earlier age, but the poem is usually described as the first chivalrous romance composed, not for a courtly audience, but for townspeople, albeit of the higher classes. We know from the prologue that the work was composed for Peter Schaler, a Basel citizen of some standing, to whom Konrad attributes artistic sensibility and taste, in a climate, he maintains, which did not always favor art. Yet, equally, he addresses himself to an audience of the nobility, listeners concerned with courtly manners and ideals. Along with the lengthy descriptions of fighting, there are descriptions of beautiful natural settings and lavish celebrations. The detailed description of Meliur, seen for the first time by Partonopier in the light of the magic lantern (7863), recalls the emphatically sensual description of Isolde, seen in the Love Grotto through the eyes of her prying husband. Konrad's debt to Gottfried von Straßburg is apparent throughout his oeuvre, and it takes many different forms.

Although the society which Konrad describes in his poem is an elevated one, like the one for which he was composing, he does include rogues like Mareis and Phares who are motivated by greed and jealousy and who ultimately have no place in his social scheme of things in which good must triumph over evil.

The lengthy prologue makes a significant contribution to the views of Konrad von Würzburg on art, and in particular on his own art, that special gift to which he devotes other substantial passages, and the whole of *Die Klage der Kunst*. Returning to the question of the relative lack of response to this work in the Middle Ages and, indeed, the relative neglect of it by modern scholars, one might concede that it is structurally less than perfect, with some passages excessively drawn out, and, of course, the lack of a conclusion. There is emotion in it, but again this is described at length rather than in any depth. It is an interesting work for the further dimension that it gives to a prolific and varied poet, whose own obvious sense of vocation, as much as the tastes of his patrons, seems to have led him to try his hand in areas beyond his artistic reach.

***Der Trojanerkrieg***, an enormous work (40424 lines), remains unfinished, and it is usually assumed that Konrad died in the course of writing it (1287). As was the fate of other massive yet unfinished works of the Middle Ages, another much less competent successor, an anonymous continuator, saw fit to attempt to complete it, adding a further 9000 lines or so. Quite unlike the very different *Partonopier und Meliur*, the work was both highly appreciated in its day and had a substantial impact on later literature, finding its way into collections of *Weltchroniken* (world histories).

The basis of Konrad's work was the *Estoire de Troie* of Benoît de Sainte-Maure, a very popular work of about 1160, but he appears to have used also a number of other sources, Ovid and Virgil, the *Achilleis* of Statius, the *Excidium Troiae* and the *Ilias latina*.

This is a work conceived on a vast scale and possibly doomed to remain incomplete. In the prologue Konrad himself shows his awareness of how ambitious this undertaking is. The material, of course, was popular in the Middle Ages. In Germany in the last decade of the 12th century, Hermann von Thüringen had commissioned both the *Liet von Troya* of Herbort von Fritzlar and Heinrich von Veldeke's *Eneit* (see p. 122 ff.).

Konrad von Würzburg's poem encompasses much more material than any of his predecessors, and, even when it breaks off at line 40424, he has covered only one third of the material of his principal source. He devotes 23,000 lines to the pre-history of the Trojan wars, going right back to the birth of Paris to provide their extensive context.

The poem is a mass of separate episodes, with much intertwining, numerous parallels, and frequent recapitulation. This, together with the unfinished state of the poem, makes it difficult to speak of a unifying idea, although Konrad himself makes it clear in his prologue that he will be telling about love and warfare, and the inextricable linking of the two. His claims for his projected work are ambitious: this is *allen mæren . . . ein her* (a lord over all tales, 235). He is going to tell of a battle such as has never been known before (291-293), and he defers to the eyewitness report of Dares, who was himself engaged in the fighting at Troy and who gave his account in Greek (296-298). He himself has had the story passed on to him in Latin and French and is now about to tell it in German (302-307). Undoubtedly, Konrad is conscious of being part of a tradition, the transmitter of world events. He is equally concerned with the famous people of whom he will tell, the foremost of them Helen, the source of so many deaths (314-315).

The work is pervaded by the sense of catastrophe to come, the juxtaposition of positive and negative in which the negative prevails. When he begins with Hecuba's dream of the torch that grows out of her breast and sets fire to Troy, he founds the story in the disaster to come. God intervenes to save her unborn child whom King Priam would kill in the attempt to prevent the realization of her prophetic dream (473), and Paris lives to become the lover of Helen and so precipitate the catastrophe which is thus interpreted as divinely intended. Konrad is scrupulously conscientious in the detail he provides of the complex train of events which leads to this culmination; indeed some of the events are more peripheral than central.

Konrad shows an awareness of the relationship between the lives, the actions and the fates of individuals, and the course of history. There are many individuals in the poem and their stories are told in detail, yet, probably not surprisingly from all we know about Konrad von Würzburg, they do not show much depth or individuality and are often endowed with exemplary qualities.

Scholars see the main problem of the work in the tension between the lack of organic wholeness and the highly polished style. It is easy to see style as important in its own right, a conscious playing with the artistry of narrative, discernible in most of Konrad's works, but even more apparent in the *Trojanerkrieg*, which seems to possess a quality evident in final works of other prolific writers: not a decline in powers but a last attempt to rise to an enormous tour de force to which the poet gives his all.

### Two Individual Works: *Die Klage der Kunst, Die goldene Schmiede*
Turning from Konrad von Würzburg's last work which may justly be described as "great" from many standpoints, it seems appropriate to look at a small work from an earlier period. ***Die Klage der Kunst*** (The Complaint of Art) might be seen to belong more correctly within the consideration of Konrad's lyric poetry, although the melody is lost to us. However, as is the case with so many of his works, it defies precise generic categorization and is therefore considered here in isolation as an important statement of a matter which has already been raised so often: Konrad's awareness of his own artistry and of the value of art in general.

There is only one manuscript of this work, and that is the *Hausbuch* of Michael de Leone which has already been mentioned. Its inclusion there, along with *Das Turnier von Nantes* and *Die goldene Schmiede*, has led to the now uncontested opinion that this poem is indeed the work of Konrad von Würzburg. It shows him again trying his hand at another kind of literary creation, an allegorical work for which he uses a distinctive poetic form, 32 strophes of 8 lines each, rhyming ab ab ab ab, and closer to his *Sprüche* to which we shall come later.

The central idea of the poem is the trial. The poet is led by *Vrou wildekeit* (Lady Wildness) into a meadow where a court of law is being held. Present are twelve women personifying twelve virtues; the plaintiff is *die kunst* (art herself), who is accusing *Milde* (Generosity) of having wasted her gifts on worthless people who do not appreciate art. The judgment is that anyone who does not love art, even if he pretends to be generous, should be avoided. The poet is a witness and has the responsibility of passing on this verdict to the mighty lords.

The question that obviously arises is: who is this hazy figure *Vrou wildekeit*, and what is her relationship with art?

It has been suggested that this was an experiment on the part of Konrad and that it did not find much favor, hence the dearth of manuscripts. Certainly it seems to have been an act of daring on his part, given that he was a professional poet, dependent on the support of his patrons, to appear to be standing in judgment on those who misplace their generosity.

The poem would seem to relate to the prevailing mood of pessimism about the taste of the day and to the kind of gloom expressed much earlier by Walther von der Vogelweide in his laments for the decline in values and in particular the failure to appreciate good art. Certainly it is consistent with the other passages in Konrad's works which are devoted to his concern for his profession and his sense of his special vocation. The trial is deliberately set in delightful natural surroundings, and he expends some care on this description (1-4). It has also been observed that Konrad has elsewhere—in *Der Schwanritter, Heinrich von Kempten* and *Engelhard*—displayed his interest in and some knowledge of the processes of the law, which here constitute the central motif.

Whether or not the work was received with enthusiasm by those who heard it, it may have played a role in introducing the idea of the allegory as an independent poetic form into medieval German literature, and it has been generally accepted that it served as a direct model for the disputation *Von den zwei Sanct Johansen* of Heinzelin von Konstanz (dated somewhere between 1320 and 1340) which appeared in the same manuscript. The crux of the argument is very different, but there is a similarity in the conception of the work. However, this influence, like others which have been suggested, must remain a matter of some speculation, and the chief interest of the *Klage der Kunst* lies in its effectiveness in its own right, and its contribution to the remarkably varied works of Konrad von Würzburg himself.

*Die goldene Schmiede* (The Golden Smithy), too, belongs on its own within the oeuvre, although it also belongs within the tradition of poems in praise of the Virgin Mary (see p. 422 f.). In its own day it was clearly a popular work, with more extant manuscripts, not all of them complete, than any other work by Konrad von Würzburg. Although it does stand in isolation in many ways from his other compositions, there are many respects in which it links with them. The concentration on a religious theme suggests comparisons with the legends and with some of the songs, while the mastery of the chosen form and the ornate style comes as no surprise from one who shows a preoccupation with the techniques of poetic composition throughout his work. It is probably for this command of form, of language and imagery, that the poem has provoked much attention, if not always undiluted admiration, from modern critics, who see it as the ultimate expression of Konrad's artistic virtuosity. The suggestion that the work was commissioned, perhaps by Bishop Konrad von Lichtenberg, to coincide with the resumption of work on Strasbourg cathedral, is attractive but hard to prove: thus the date of 1275, though entirely feasible, has no real evidence to support it.

In 2000 lines, in rhyming couplets, Konrad expresses the traditional adoration of the Virgin Mary, in images which are also to a large extent traditional but supplemented by some all his own. Indeed, the whole poem is conceived as an image: it opens with Konrad proclaiming his intention of creating in the smithy of his heart a poem of gold and precious stones in honor of the Empress of Heaven. A little later in the prologue he declares that Gottfried von Straßburg, the master smith, could have praised her better (97-101), a significant expression of humility in a poem which, in the eyes of some critics, is Konrad's attempt to out-Gottfried Gottfried.

With its abundance of vivid but sometimes unconnected images, the poem has brought forth a variety of responses from scholars, ranging from those who dismiss it as "tasteless" and "mere intellectual play," to those who describe it, anachronistically, as "Gothic" or "Baroque." Attempts have been made to discern a structure to it. The impression of the poem is well conveyed in the words of Max Wehrli (*Geschichte*, 555):

"Es ist ein kostbarer Wortschleier, eine Wortkaskade, die vielleicht die angeredete Gottesmutter mehr verhüllt als offenbart—dennoch ist hier der Ort, wo das sprachliche Kunstgewerbe Konrads zauberhaft und hinreißend wird und eine echte Legitimität bekommt" (It is a precious veil of words, a verbal cascade, which rather conceals than reveals the Mother of God addressed—nevertheless, this is the place where Konrad's artistic skill with words becomes magical and rapturous and attains genuine legitimacy).

## The Lyric Poetry

To complete the picture of Konrad von Würzburg's immense literary production, we come now, though not chronologically, to his contribution in the field of the lyric. Like his narrative and other work his lyric poetry is wide ranging, covering what may be described as conventional Minnesang, songs with religious and didactic content, and two *leiche*, one religious and the other secular. Nor is it surprising that, here too, he shows himself to be a master of form, demonstrating his command of a wide range of metrical patterns. Though formally accomplished, his contribution as a lyric poet is much less remarkable than his other work, but it was nevertheless appreciated by his contemporaries and his successors, many of whom composed under his influence, and he was lauded by the Meistersänger as one of the twelve masters (see p. 302 f.).

Minnesang in the town has been considered a contradiction in terms, since the relationship treated presupposes a courtly context. Yet Konrad von Würzburg contributed substantially to this type of poetry, often associating love with a natural setting, praising women above the season and pointing to the edifying nature of love. His love songs contain a strong didactic element, and sometimes there is only a very fine dividing line between poems which can be said to be love songs and those which belong more properly in the category of *Sprüche*, strophes which treat of serious issues, sometimes religious, sometimes social or political.

The two *leiche* treat very distinct subject matter. The *leich*, a narrative poem in unequal strophes, was intended to be accompanied by a melody played on the harp or some other instrument. With its roots in the Old High German period, the *leich* was cultivated in Germany throughout the 13th century and into the 14th, with Frauenlob (see p. 299 f.) as the last to produce this kind of poetry. There are two separate though related types of *leich*, the one religious, the other secular, and Konrad von Würzburg is the only representative of both. The religious *leich* (1 in the edition by E. Schröder) celebrates the wonders of God, the mystery of the Trinity and the Incarnation. The adoration of the Virgin recalls the thought, though not the language, of *Die goldene Schmiede*. His secular *leich* (2) describes the triumph of Mars over Venus, the ousting of love and virtue by warfare. It contains a mass of mythological allusions and references to epic events.

Lyric poetry is frequently difficult to date, and it is assumed that Konrad composed his songs at intervals throughout his career. Only the *Sprüche* which have obvious historical connections can be dated with any certainty: *Spruch* 32,316 (E. Schröder's edition), for example, refers to the subjugation of the Bohemian lion to the Roman eagle and is taken to refer to the oath of allegiance to Rudolf von Habsburg taken by Ottakar in 1276.

Texts:

Bartsch, Karl, ed. *Partonopier und Meliur.* Vienna: Braumüller, 1871. (Contains also *Das Turnier von Nantes,* the probably not authentic *Sant Nicholaus,* and the *Lieder und Sprüche*).

Gereke, Paul, ed. *Konrad von Würzburg. Die Legenden.* Halle: Niemeyer, 1925, 1926, 1927 (= ATB, 19, 20, 21: *Silvester, Alexius, Pantaleon*).

―――, ed. *Engelhard.* Halle: Niemeyer, 1912. Rev. ed. by Ingo Reiffenstein, Tübingen: Niemeyer, [2]1963 (= ATB, 17).

Gernentz, Hans Joachim, ed. and trans. *Der Schwanritter.* Berlin: Rütten & Loening, 1972. (MHG text with mod. Ger. trans. of: *Klage der Kunst, Herzmære, Der Welt Lohn, Heinrich von Kempten*).

Grimm. Wilhelm, ed. *Die Goldene Schmiede.* Berlin: K.J.Klemann, 1840.

von Keller, Adelbert, ed. *Der Trojanische Krieg.* Bibliothek des literarischen Vereins: Stuttgart. Repr. Amsterdam, 1965.

Schröder, Edward, ed. *Kleinere Dichtungen Konrads von Würzburg.* 3 Vols. Berlin: Weidmann, 1924, 1925 and 1926, frequently reprinted, more recently with an afterword by Ludwig Wolff. Vol. I: *Der Welt Lohn, Das Herzmære, Heinrich von Kempten.* Vol. II: *Der Schwanritter, Das Turnier von Nantes.* Vol. III: *Die Klage der Kunst; Leiche, Lieder und Sprüche.*

―――, ed. *Die Goldene Schmiede des Konrad von Würzburg.* Göttingen: Vandenhoeck & Ruprecht, 1926. Repr. 1969.

Translation:

Rölleke, Heinz, trans. *Konrad von Würzburg: Heinrich von Kempten, Der Welt Lohn, Daz Herzmære.* MHG text of E. Schröder, with mod. Ger. trans., notes, and afterword. Stuttgart: Reclam, 1987 (= UB, 2855).

See also Gernentz (above).

## Konrad von Würzburg—Bibliography

Blamires, D. M. "Konrad von Würzburg's Verse Novellen." In: *Medieval Miscellany, presented to Eugène Vinaver.* Manchester: Manchester UP; New York: Barnes and Noble, 1965. Pp. 28-44.

de Boor, Helmut. "Die Chronologie der Werke Konrads von Würzburg, insbesondere die Stellung des Turniers von Nantes." *PBB* (Tübingen) 89 (1967): 210-269.

Brandt, Rüdiger. *Konrad von Würzburg.* Darmstadt: Wiss. Buchges., 1987 (= Erträge der Forschung, 249).

A very useful Forschungsbericht covering the research from the beginning of the 19th century to 1984. Excellent bibliography and evaluative synthesis of the then-current state of research, with description of on-going projects.

Ganz, Peter. "Nur eine schöne Kunstfigur. Zur Goldenen Schmiede Konrads von Würzburg." *GRM* 60, N.F. 29 (1979): 27-45.

Jackson, Timothy J. *The Legends of Konrad von Würzburg. Form, Content, Function.* Erlangen: Palm & Enke, 1983.

Lienert, Elisabeth. "Konrad von Würzburg: *Trojanerkrieg.*" In: Horst Brunner, ed. *Mittelhochdeutsche Romane und Heldenepen.* Stuttgart: Reclam, 1993 (= UB, 8914, Interpretationen). Pp. 391-411.

Oettli, Peter H. *Tradition and Creativity. The "Engelhard" of Konrad von Würzburg. Its Structure and Its Sources.* New York, Bern: Peter Lang, 1986.

_____. "Konrad von Würzburg: *Engelhard*." In: Horst Brunner, ed. *Mittelhochdeutsche Romane und Heldenepen*. Stuttgart: Reclam, 1993 (= UB, 8914, Interpretationen). Pp. 373-390.

Rupp, Heinz. "Rudolf von Ems und Konrad von Würzburg. Das Problem des Epigonentums." *Deutschunterricht* 17 (1965): 5-17.

A stimulating article linking the two poets, considering them as individuals, and in their literary context.

See also Olive Sayce (1982) for a useful account of the lyric poetry.

## SECONDARY ARTHURIAN ROMANCES

### Heinrich von dem Türlin: *Diu Crône*

Although critical assessments of Heinrich von dem Türlin, based on the major work attributed to him, are almost uniformly negative, he occupies a place all his own in the immediate aftermath of the poets of the classical courtly period, and the interest of this unique poem is undeniable. *Diu Crône* is usually dated somewhere between 1220 and 1230. The very length and detail of this romance speak for the apparently barely satiable appetite of the public for more tales of Arthur and his knights as well as, it must be admitted, for the self-confidence of Heinrich himself in presenting his audience with a work which, at 30,000 lines, exceeds any of its predecessors. His own conception of the task he has set himself is conveyed in his image of the work as a crown set with precious stones and offered to the honor of ladies. This somewhat extravagant claim was subsequently supported by Rudolf von Ems, who spoke of the poem as "aller aventiure krône" (the crown of all romances) and seemed to accord it an admiration not shared by the contemporary public.

There is only one complete manuscript of the poem (P) dating from the 15th century, and that is itself far from satisfactory. There are, in addition, six fragments. Doubt has been cast on the authenticity of the closing lines of P, with their reference to Heinrich's eighty-year-old wife and his hope that God will permit her to die before him, or, if not, that she should marry a Swabian after his death. The lines have no relationship to the rest of the poem and may well have been added, for some reason, by a mischievous scribe.

Lines 182-216 of *Diu Crône* contain an acrostic of the name Heinrich von dem Türlin, and he names himself on three further occasions within the work, but who exactly he was and what his status was remains unknown. He was almost certainly not a knight; speculation suggests that he stemmed from a bourgeois family in St. Veit, at that time the capital of Carinthia, that he may have been an official of the chancellery or a ministerialis at the Court of Duke Bernhard von Kärnten. The poor manuscript provides no precise guide to his dialect.

The only complete edition of *Diu Crône* remains that by Gottlob Heinrich Friedrich Scholl, painstakingly produced in 1852 (repr. 1966) from a copy made in Heidelberg and handed on to him, he informs us, by Professor Keller, supplemented by the 14th century Vienna manuscript(V), which contains only the first 12,281 lines. This latter was known to Scholl also only in a copy. The dedication implied in seeing that the poem saw the light of day is further manifested in the detailed synopsis which Scholl supplies and which itself occupies 32 pages of his preface. He appears to have had the same kind of stamina as Heinrich von dem Türlin himself, who pursues his subject with a thoroughness not always matched by his narrative skill.

The criticisms leveled at *Diu Crône* concern its inordinate length, its shapelessness, and its somewhat ill-defined sense of purpose. It professes early on to be about to tell the history of King Arthur, but in fact that intention soon falls by the wayside, and the work is first and foremost about Gawein, who now for the first time assumes a central position—the earlier Arthurian romances have always cast him in a supporting role. Some of the adventures related are familiar from earlier accounts of this favorite among Arthurian knights, and some appear to be the product of Heinrich's admittedly vivid powers of invention.

Heinrich displays considerable learning and had an acquaintance with the language and literature of France and Germany as well as a knowledge of Latin and Italian. He speaks of an *exemplar* out of which he extracted his material (970), and he refers on three occasions to Chrétien de Troyes as his source. In reality the work would seem to be an amalgam of French and German sources with additions of his own. Perhaps one of the chief interests of the poem lies in the awareness that it embraces a great many sources, some of them lost to us. He attributes adventures to Gawein which are elsewhere accomplished by other heroes, even to the extent of giving to Gawein the honor of pursuing and finding the Grail. He asks *the* question of his host at the Grail Castle: "What is the meaning of these marvelous things?" This is the question which releases the Grail family, and, once he has asked it, the Grail disappears forever. The preoccupation of the Middle Ages with the Grail has its place in this work, yet Heinrich divests it of its mystery and declines to pursue the spiritual potential so recently exploited by Wolfram.

Those critics who have spoken of Heinrich's misunderstanding of Wolfram have probably missed the point, however, for it is much more likely that he is deliberately rejecting the path of his great predecessor and that it is nearer the mark to view the work, as some have done, as an anti-*Parzival*.

Gawein's quest for the Grail is just one of the myriad of adventures which constitute the complex substance of this narrative, in which conventional exploits and familiar motifs (chastity tests, abductions, rescues, wastelands, and islands inhabited by unidentified women) combine with fantastic and sometimes even grotesque elements. At times Heinrich appears to be tied to the traditions of the Arthurian romance with something approaching deference, at others one is tempted to think rather in terms of burlesque or parody. Although, for example, hideously malformed creatures suggest imitations of Hartmann's *waltman* or Wolfram's Cundrie, Heinrich outdoes even these predecessors in his descriptions. Indeed, outdoing his predecessors seems to be one of his aims in this poem. For all its reminiscences of the works on which it is at least in part based, it stands on its own in length, extravagance and perhaps even in the purpose which some critics have glimpsed in it. Joachim Heinzle suggests that, for the audience, it was a kind of literature quiz, into which the author has packed a vast amount of knowledge of other works in a somewhat incoherent way, creating a collage whose overall structure and purpose are not altogether clear (*Litgesch.*,II,II, 137-138).

The idea of *vrou sælde*, Lady Fortune with her Wheel, had, of course been present in Wirnt von Gravenberg's *Wigalois* (see p. 314 ff.), and is indeed central to that earlier romance, but her function here is almost certainly a different one. Gawein, the darling of Fortune, is subject to her, but this is not a status that he attains, as one might expect from the pattern of Hartmann's works, for example. *Diu Crône* lacks completely that progression to a higher state which dominates the earlier romances. The Court of Arthur is very much in the foreground, not, as previously, a significant background which itself develops as the central figures progress. The notion of the chivalrous adventure as the goal of the knight has receded, to the extent that some have seen the work as a satire on the earlier literature. Certainly there is comedy here, and sometimes a surprising perception in the presentation of characters though not, in general, of emotion. The overwhelming impression of a mass of detail dominates and a shapelessness which has defeated even the most well-meaning attempts to see any coherent structure in the work.

There is good reason to think of it as a poem that falls into two parts or even to view it as two distinct though obviously related works, breaking at 13,901. The first part, or poem, is considerably better than the second, where the tendency to prolixity is even more evident, and the charge of repetition, disconnectedness and errors of chronology is harder to refute. When Heinrich says that he will not tell *all* the stories which relate to the credit of Gawein, we can only utter a sigh of relief. The paucity of manuscripts suggests that the work did not receive the acclaim apparently hoped for by its author.

He can hardly have hoped that his work would attain the reputation of "the most tedious, superficial and ill-constructed" of the German Arthurian romances of the period before 1250. This is how Rosemary Wallbank summarizes the assessments of past critics at the beginning of her own measured and illuminating examination of the composition of the poem. Hermann Schneider's dismissal of it as the nadir of courtly literature in Germany, demonstrating a new level of brutalization in both form and content ("ein Symptom formaler und inhaltlicher Verrohung," 309) is typical of the tone of older critics, though later scholars have been somewhat gentler in expressing their distaste for a poem which suffers, like so many of its generation, from comparison with precisely those predecessors which gave it its existence.

Ulrich Wyss, in one of the most recent attempts to make sense of the phenomenon of *Diu Crône*, has gone a long way in his well-argued interpretation of the poem on the basis of its allegorical significance. Moreover, he emphasizes that Heinrich himself sees his work as an artifact and is thus able to arrive at the view of it as "der erste Literatenroman in deutscher Sprache" (291). Whether this rescues it from its own reputation is not clear.

In the case of a work like *Diu Crône*, the question naturally arises of the extent to which one can rightly talk of plagiarism, although the purpose of the poem, inasmuch as we can discern it, seems to contradict the view of it as mere imitation. Other works of this period raise similar questions.

Only one other work is now fairly conclusively attributed to Heinrich von dem Türlin: the fragment (a mere 994 lines!) which is given the title *Der Mantel* and which precedes Hartmann's *Erec* in the *Ambraser Heldenbuch*. It tells of a chastity test by means of a magic cloak, and the strongest argument for attributing it to Heinrich von dem Türlin, apart from the reappearance of a motif familiar from *Diu Crône*, is his own reference in that work to his having told elsewhere of a cloak (23502-23505).

Text:
Scholl, Gottlob Heinrich Friedrich, ed. *Heinrich von dem Türlin. Diu Crône.* Stuttgart: Bibliothek des literarischen Vereins, 1852. Repr. Amsterdam: Rodopi, 1966.

Translation:
Thomas, J. Wesley, trans. *The Crown. A Tale of Sir Gawein and King Arthur's Court by Heinrich von dem Türlin.* Lincoln: Univ. of Nebraska Press 1989.

## Heinrich von dem Türlin—Bibliography

The first five works listed here are recommended as studies in English which all in their different ways throw light on this quite taxing work.

Heller, E. K. "A Vindication of Heinrich von dem Türlin, based on a Survey of his Sources." *MLQ* 3 (1942): 67-82.

Jillings, Lewis. *Diu Crône of Heinrich von dem Türlin: The Attempted Emancipation of Secular Literature.* Göppingen: Kümmerle, 1980 (= GAG, 258).

Thomas, Neil. "*Diu Crône*: An Arthurian Fantasy." In: *The Defence of Camelot.* Bern: Peter Lang, 1992. Pp. 97-111.

Wallbank, Rosemary. "The Composition of *Diu Crône*." In: *Medieval Miscellany, presented to Eugène Vinaver.* Manchester: Manchester UP; New York: Barnes and Noble, 1965. Pp. 300-320.

Walshe, Maurice O'C. "Heinrich von dem Türlin, Chrétien and Wolfram." In: *Mediaeval German Studies presented to Frederick Norman.* London: Institute of Germanic Studies, 1965. Pp. 204-218.

Worstbrock, Franz Josef. "Über den Titel der *Krone* Heinrichs von dem Türlin." *ZfdA* 95 (1966): 182-186.

Wyss, Ulrich. "Heinrich von dem Türlin: *Diu Krône*." In: *Mittelhochdeutsche Romane und Heldenepen.* Stuttgart: Reclam 1993 (= UB, 8914, Interpretationen). Pp. 271-291.

## Der Stricker: *Daniel von dem blühenden Tal, Karl der Grosse*

The poet who gives himself this rather puzzling name was probably active during the years 1215-1250, beginning to compose at a time when the literary scene in Germany was dominated by the great poets of the classical period. He was doubtless influenced by them in his early works: the full-length romance very much in the traditional manner, *Daniel von dem blühenden Tal*, and his lengthy adaptation of the *Rolandslied*, *Karl der Grosse*. It would seem that he moved thereafter to another quite different area in which he became prolific, achieving his lasting fame as a writer of short stories, pungent cautionary tales and humorous sketches in the manner of the *Schwank*. This was breaking new ground in German literature and represented an important trend away from the conventional works of the *Blütezeit*. Whether all the many examples attributed to him were in fact his own or by imitators of his is not conclusively established, but it is clear that he was the first to introduce a kind of narrative which was to become very popular in the 13th century and beyond.

Little is known about him. The meaning of his name has attracted discussion, with the suggestion that it may not be a real surname ("rope-maker" may but need not denote his actual craft) but that he may be referring to himself as an itinerant (a "stroller") or, more metaphorically, that he is thinking of himself as a "twiner" of tales. On the whole, the consensus seems to be in favor of the last of these possibilities, although he probably was an itinerant poet, dependent on the generosity of the noble lords but describing a world and a way of life quite different from theirs. The earliest assumption was that Der Stricker was an Austrian, but such linguistic evidence as can be adduced from the manuscripts points rather towards Franconia as his place of origin, although he may well have spent substantial periods in Austria.

Rudolf von Ems, who so often supplies valuable clues about the literature of the period (see p. 340) refers to Der Stricker in both his literary passages. The lines in his *Alexander* (3257-8):

> swenn er wil der Strickære,
> so macht er guotiu mære

tell us two things: that Der Stricker was still active at this point (c.1250) and that his fame, then as now, rested on his story-telling, on the *mære* (a fairly general term denoting a short story) which constitute the greater part of his output. However, the reference in Rudolf's *Willehalm von Orlens* (2230-2233) singles out *Daniel von dem blühenden Tal*.

*Daniel von dem blühenden Tal.* Skill in sheer story-telling is indeed a dominant feature of Der Stricker's early work. It owes much to Hartmann von Aue, in particular to his *Iwein*, but it also goes off on its own, exploiting traditional Arthurian material, to produce a romance which is notable for its use of the fantastic and for its exuberant style. From the start, Der Stricker's relationship with his material is telling: in his prologue he says that Master Alberich von Besançon brought him the story from France and that he has translated it into German. Scholars have failed to find corroboration of this statement. As far as we know, Alberich did not compose any such work, though the passage itself is very reminiscent of the passage in the *Alexanderlied* (see p. 93), where Pfaffe Lamprecht acknowledges his debt to Alberich. Indeed, no trace has been found at all of a source for *Daniel von dem blühenden Tal*, which is now generally believed to be the product of Der Stricker's own powers of invention. Thus we can immediately make two observations: that Der Stricker was able to invent quite independently and that he was sufficiently close to the traditions of his age to feel the need to claim a source, however spurious.

The very name Daniel represents a departure: presumably Der Stricker took it, not from Arthurian literature but from the Bible. Yet, of course, the Arthurian motifs in the poem are undeniable, even though they are used for a purpose very distinct, for to a considerable extent the poem can be seen as a humorous reworking of some familiar ideas, a kind of skit on the courtly romances of his predecessors. To this end, the poet deploys a range of material and methods gleaned from a diversity of sources, not just the works of Hartmann and Wolfram, but the *Wigalois* of Wirnt von Gravenberg (see p. 314 ff.) and Ulrich von Zatzikhoven's *Lanzelet* (see p. 328 ff.), and even, further back than these, the "Spielmannsepen" (see p. 106 ff.), and classical mythology. This is not to suggest, however, that *Daniel von dem blühenden Tal* is a rag-bag: far from it. The work is coherent in structure and conception, and though it may not deserve the extensive serious analysis to which some modern critics have subjected it, it probably does not warrant, either, the dismissive treatment of earlier scholars.

*Daniel* is different from the traditional Arthurian romance in important respects: the descriptions of large-scale warfare and the emphasis on cunning as a means to outwit opposition and the absence of *minne* as a motivating force or indeed as any force at all in the poem. The flavor of the poem is very different then, and therein lies much of its interest. Its blatant divergence from the literary norms of its own day probably accounts for its relative lack of popularity at the time. If one reads it, not as a failed imitation of much better works, but as an attempt to use those works in order to achieve something very different, then one can see it in its proper relationship to the literary context and, perhaps more important, in its relationship to Der Stricker's more obviously significant achievements.

The heart of the work is a series of adventures accomplished by Daniel, a knight of the Round Table, in the attempt to defeat, first of all, King Matur of Cluse, the declared enemy of King Arthur—who actually kills Matur himself—and then his vast armies, before he marries the widow and becomes lord of Cluse. Thus far, the content of the poem sounds fairly familiar, but the nature of these adventures is different, with the emphasis on the grotesque and the supernatural, the recurrence of superhuman tests, and the part played by monstrous creatures. Moreover, the ethical nature of the progress of the heroes in the classical romances is absent here. Daniel succeeds because he is bold and cunning and because he harnesses magic forces, but there is no suggestion that he is undergoing any kind of learning process. Early critics suggested that Der Stricker had simply misunderstood the deeper meanings of the Arthurian romances, but there is good reason to argue, given the high degree of originality that characterizes his work as a whole, that he was actually setting out to do something quite distinct.

***Karl der Grosse.*** Although there is little doubt that the two long epics are Der Stricker's earliest works, the order of the two is not so certain. Indeed the only "firm" dating for *Karl* is that it was composed after Wolfram's *Willehalm*, a conclusion reached largely on the basis of lines 12192-12199. That would suggest a date of 1220-1230 for *Karl der Grosse*, and recent research inclines to place *Daniel von dem blühenden Tal* just a few years earlier. In the absence of firm evidence, however, it must be admitted that the sequence of the two epics could be reversed.

The single most important source for the work is Pfaffe Konrad's *Rolandslied*, itself a reworking of the Old French *Chanson de Roland* (see p. 94), but there is good reason to think that he may have had other French source material at hand, since his work expands on Konrad's version and adds some significant new episodes. This may have emanated from *chanson de geste* material which Der Stricker may have received only orally. Most notable is the style of the work, for Der Stricker was presenting familiar material to a new, courtly audience, and, under the influence of the elegant diction and narrative style of Hartmann von Aue, he has achieved a much more polished work. Judging by the large number of manuscripts of this fairly long work (12206 lines) it seems to have appealed greatly to his audience. The meter, too, shows greater elegance and seems to reflect a deliberate attempt at modernization in this respect too.

The central interest of the poem is in the figure of Charlemagne himself. Der Stricker was composing at a time when the great Emperor was being increasingly honored: it was not long, after all, since the re-interment of his remains in Aachen in 1215, an occasion of immense celebration in the presence of the newly crowned Frederick II, and Charlemagne represented a glorious past which was recalled at this time which anticipated a glorious future. However, it is not easy to assess the extent to which the poem may be seen as having political intentions. Der Stricker nowhere names a patron, and his allegiances are not apparent.

Der Stricker supplies an introduction which speaks of his subject, the special nature of Karl, selected by God from birth, and his own privileged task of retelling this old tale. He goes back further than Pfaffe Konrad and tells of the birth of Karl and his youth, possibly prompted to do so by the practice of the courtly narrative poets of presenting the parentage of their heroes. There can be little doubt, from the start then, that it is Karl himself, rather than Roland, who is the true focus of this poem, although the familiar events relating to the deeds of Roland and his death are conscientiously told as before.

For some critics the poem loses the impact of its model precisely because, in achieving his avowed intention of pleasing a courtly audience (115-118), the poet has deprived his material of the heroic ruggedness which characterized his source. In this respect, the poem is significant, of course, belonging to its own age though telling of the deeds of another.

### The Shorter Works: *Pfaffe Amis*

The bulk of Der Stricker's oeuvre and really the cornerstone of his reputation are the short works which themselves show considerable diversity of type and substance. It is virtually impossible to establish a satisfactory chronological sequence.

Another difficulty attaching to these short works is their designation within a specific genre, and here there is a certain amount of overlap and room for scholarly dispute. The terms used to distinguish these poems, which are often described collectively as Der Stricker's "kleinere Gedichte," are *mære*, *bîspel* (an example, a kind of parable, an essentially didactic, cautionary tale, Latin: *exemplum*), fable (a story, again with a message of some kind, in which animals play the central roles), *Schwank* (a humorous anecdote, often aimed at satirizing human foibles), *rede* (a more theoretical treatment of a particular subject, notably love and religion). In all these areas Der Stricker tried his hand with considerable success, and in many respects he can be seen as an innovator who paved the way for much imitation during the decades, and indeed centuries, which followed him.

The nature of the humor is not subtle, but it is pungent in its effect, and the messages are unmistakable, often precisely because of the absurd terms in which they are couched and the blatant ridicule of human behavior. Unlike many of those who came after him, Der Stricker manages to avoid the coarseness which sometimes seems to be inherent in his material.

*Pfaffe Amis* is the name given to a cycle of stories about the antics of the English priest Amis. Its precise origins are unknown: no evidence has been found for earlier assumptions that it was based on a collection of French fabliaux, and it may be that the actual idea of a group of stories with a single common character came from Latin sources. The tone of the work is humorous but pointing eventually to a serious moral: its didactic purpose is apparent, as is the case with the individual short stories (*mære* and *bîspel*) of Der Stricker.

*Pfaffe Amis* is sometimes described by modern scholars as a *Schwankroman*, a term which really has no literary tradition to support it but which conveys an accurate impression of this group of comical stories, linked together by a central figure and forming, with a prologue and an epilogue, a coherent, if somewhat unbalanced, whole. The work begins with a fairly familiar lament of the day for the passing of proper courtly standards, a list of those values which were once prized and which have now been supplanted by their opposites. Where joy prevailed there is now sorrow; greed has taken the place of generosity, injustice of justice, and so on. Now Der Stricker is about to tell of the man who caused this sorry state by bringing lies and deceit into the world. The central part of the work is then devoted to a series of anecdotes with the clever but cunning and self-seeking Pfaffe Amis as their common character, as he goes about the world playing on the weaknesses of others to further his own material ends. His grotesque deceptions are comical, but they are also deeply harmful and thought provoking.

Critics have pointed to the ambivalence of this poem which ends very suddenly with the conversion of Amis to a pious way of life and his elevation to the position of Abbot of the monastery he has entered. The promise of eternal bliss for him has a somewhat hollow ring, when one recalls the trail of human suffering and exploitation that he has left in the thirty years of his reprobate life. The double edge of Der Stricker's thrust must also be considered, for, though he cannot excuse the behavior of Amis, he does not deny the weakness and misbehavior of his victims which make it all possible. Amis succeeds in his deceptions because he seeks out and easily finds the weak points in his fellow men, their avarice, their pride, and their sexual infidelities.

Although Der Stricker will have been composing for an audience of the nobility, the nature of his characters, mostly very ordinary people of the lower class, is universal, and he will not have failed to make his point. His work is remarkably divorced from the political events of the day, which makes it difficult to date individual parts of it with any certainty, although he gives way on a number of occasions to expressions of regret and disapproval at the general decline he observes around him (see, for example, *Die Klage*). He is concerned about more timeless issues of a social and sometimes spiritual nature. A preoccupation of many of his anecdotes is marriage, represented for the most part as an abrasive situation, with the two partners emerging as comic figures with larger-than-life characteristics engaged in forthright debate. Such stories often begin with the words "ein man sprach ze sînem wîbe," or sometimes it is the woman who begins the conversation.

These are not the knights and ladies of the courtly romance conversing about elevated matters, but ordinary people against a simple domestic background grappling with everyday issues.

His works, however, are not restricted in the picture they offer of medieval life. They are peopled with knights and merchants, peasants and clergy, but, as elsewhere in medieval literature, he is dealing with types rather than individuals, and his understanding of human behavior, though acute, is fairly basic. One is not looking for psychological insights. His main concern is the point that he is making, and this he does with considerable spirit. It is not surprising, then, that the fable is one of his favored forms, for there the moral issues emerge clearly, without the distraction of any human dimensions. In this area he is following much more obviously in the path of some notable predecessors— above all Aesop—who employed the animal kingdom to demonstrate human weaknesses.

The overt didacticism of Der Stricker's short narratives is well expressed in the *bîspel*, where he directs his attention to a wide range of concerns, some relatively trivial and everyday, and others of a more far-reaching, religious or philosophical nature, such as the perils attaching to an over-preoccupation with worldly matters or the need for repentance and atonement. It is the universality of his subject matter which accounts for the popularity of Der Stricker's shorter works, in his own day and in the later Middle Ages as well as for his relative popularity today. Although a man of apparently considerable learning, he speaks not primarily to scholars but to a range of listeners. Scholarly interest has turned in recent years to Der Stricker in the recognition of his works not just as entertaining stories told with an urbane awareness of human frailty but as an important body of literary works, which raise important issues of source and genre.

Texts:
Bartsch, Karl, ed. *Karl der Grosse von dem Stricker*. Quedlinburg und Leipzig: Gottfr. Basse, 1857. Repr. with an afterword by Dieter Kartschoke, Berlin: de Gruyter, 1965.
Ehrismann, Otfrid, ed. and trans. *Der Stricker. Erzählungen, Fabeln, Reden*. Stuttgart: Reclam, 1992 (= UB, 8797). With mod. Ger. trans. and commentary.
Fischer, Hanns, ed. *Der Stricker. Verserzählungen I*. Tübingen: Niemeyer, 1960 (= ATB, 53).
Hahn, Karl August, ed. *Kleinere Gedichte von dem Stricker*. Quedlinburg und Leipzig: Gottfried Basse, 1839 (= Bibliothek der gesammten deutschen National-Literatur, 18).
Henne, H., ed. and trans. *Der Pfaffe Amis von dem Stricker. Ein Schwankroman aus dem 13. Jahrhundert in zwölf Episoden*. Göppingen: Kümmerle, 1991 (= GAG, 530).
_____, ed. *Der Stricker. Verserzählungen II*. Tübingen: Niemeyer, 1967 (= ATB, 68).
Kamihara, K., ed. *Des Strickers Pfaffe Amis*. Göppingen: Kümmerle 1978, [2]1993 (= GAG, 233).
Mettke, Heinz, ed. *Fabeln und Mären von dem Stricker*. Halle/Saale: Niemeyer, 1959 (= ATB, 35).
Moelleken, Wolfgang et al., eds. *Die Kleindichtung des Strickers*. 5 vols. Göppingen: Kümmerle, 1973-1978 (= GAG, 107, I-V). The most comprehensive edition of the shorter works, but some reservations have been expressed about it. Other smaller collections of Der Stricker's narratives may be found easier to use and fairly readily available, at least in libraries.

Resler, Michael, ed. *Der Stricker: Daniel von dem Blühenden Tal.* Tübingen: Niemeyer, 1983 (= ATB, 92).

Rosenhagen, Gustav, ed. *Daniel von dem blühenden Tal: ein Artusroman von dem Stricker.* Breslau: Koebner, 1894 (= Germanistische Abhandlungen, 9). Repr. Hildesheim and New York: Georg Olms, 1976.

Rosenhagen, Gustav, ed. *Mären von dem Stricker.* Halle/Saale: Niemeyer, 1934.

Schilling, Michael, ed. and trans. *Der Stricker. Der Pfaffe Amis.* Stuttgart: Reclam, 1994 (= UB 658). From Heidelberg Ms. cpg 341, with mod. Ger. trans. and commentary.

Schwab, Ute, ed. *Der Stricker. Tierbîspel.* Tübingen: Niemeyer, [3]1983 (= ATB, 54).

Translations:
Resler, Michael, trans. *Der Stricker. "Daniel of the Blossoming Valley" ("Daniel von dem blühenden Tal").* New York: Garland, 1990 (= GLML, B 58).

See also H. Henne, M. Schilling, and O. Ehrismann (above).

## Der Stricker—Bibliography

For a general introduction to Der Stricker and a commentary on *Daniel*, see M. Resler's translation (above); for a very accessible introduction to *Pfaffe Amis* and some of the short narratives, see resp. M. Schilling's and O. Ehrismann's editions, translations, and commentaries (above).

Brall, Helmut. "Strickers *Daniel von dem blühenden Tal.* Zur politischen Funktion späthöfischer Artusepik im Territorialisierungsprozeß." *Euph.* 70 (1976) 222-257.

Brandt, Rüdiger. *erniuwet. Studien zu Art, Grad und Aussagefolgen der Rolandsliedbearbeitung in Strickers Karl.* Göppingen: Kümmerle, 1981 (= GAG, 327).

Hahn, Ingrid. "Das Ethos der *kraft.* Zur Bedeutung der Massenschlachten in Strickers *Daniel von dem blühenden Tal.*" *DVjs* 59 (1985): 173-194.

Margetts, John. "Non-feudal Attitudes in Der Stricker's Short Narrative Works." *Neuphil. Mitt.* 73 (1972): 754-774.

Wailes, Stephen L. "Der Stricker." In: *Dictionary of the Middle Ages.* Ed. by Joseph R. Strayer. Vol II. New York: Charles Scribner's Sons, 1988. Pp. 492-494.
Excellent, concise introduction to Der Stricker.

_____. *"Studien zur Kleindichtung der Strickers.* Berlin: Erich Schmidt, 1981.
One of the fullest studies available; a detailed scholarly analysis of the short narratives, particularly in the light of contemporary theology.

## Der Pleier: *Garel von dem blühenden Tal, Tandareis und Flordibel, Meleranz*

Though less well known than some of his contemporaries and difficult of access to non-German readers, this poet merits treatment as the author of three substantial works in the Arthurian tradition. Indeed, his rather strange name, which literally means "blower," and perhaps more precisely "blower of glass" has been interpreted as referring to his skill in melting down old material and fashioning it into new works. The name did exist in the Middle Ages to designate the master glass-blower and is recorded as a surname in the region of Salzburg. His language indicates an Austrian poet, and his works are usually dated around the middle of the 13th century. Otherwise little can be deduced about his identity.

Readers may not find it easy to locate the texts, which exist in very early and not very satisfactory editions or in reprints of those editions or, in the case of *Garel von dem blühenden Tal*, a copy of the manuscript. The manuscript tradition itself is poor. The most comprehensive account of Der Pleier's work is contained in the detailed study by Peter Kern (1981). Readers of English may find of considerable assistance a much earlier article by John Lancaster Riordan (1948), entitled, rather significantly, "A Vindication of the Pleier." It succeeds in rebutting the commonly held view of Der Pleier as "a shameless plagiarist, utterly devoid of originality" (p. 29).

There can be no doubt that **Garel von dem blühenden Tal** is the first of the three romances which bear Der Pleier's name. As the title suggests, the poem is a response to Der Stricker's *Daniel von dem blühenden Tal* (see p. 362 ff.), as indeed a reaction to that work which could be seen to some extent as a burlesque on the Arthurian romance, for in his work Der Pleier extols more traditional values and presents a hero who, unlike Daniel, espouses the high courtly ideals of the exemplary knight. As in *Daniel*, there is a mixture here of warfare and personal exploits in search of adventure, but, unlike Daniel who wins by means of the ruthless exercise of force and blatant cunning, Garel progresses through a series of adventures much more in the manner of the heroes of Hartmann von Aue.

Garel is known already, from Hartmann, Wolfram, and from Wirnt's *Wigalois* (Chandler, *Catalogue of Names*, pp. 98-99). He is the nephew of King Arthur who, in Der Pleier's work, rides off alone towards the land of Kanadic, whose king, Ekunaver, has declared war on Arthur for the following year. While Arthur and his troops are preparing for war, Garel becomes embroiled in adventures of a very different kind. These correspond more closely to those of the traditional Arthurian romance: freeing a damsel in distress, achieving the release of a dwarf king from a giant, releasing a noble knight who holds his defeated opponents captive against the day when he is himself defeated, and so on. The echoes, particularly of Hartmann, are many and not disguised. Der Pleier seems to have seen himself very much as a follower of Hartmann, Wolfram, and Wirnt, but equally he may have wished to rectify a situation created by Der Stricker in *Daniel* which threatened accepted courtly values and harmed the very foundations of courtly literature. Although he probably lacked the skill to reverse a process already very much in train, his work seems to have found resonances. There is only one manuscript of *Garel*, and one fragment, but the work is immortalized in the frescoes at Runkelstein, where abundant attention is paid to it, alongside that given to *Wigalois*. Illustrations of the relevant frescoes were included in the first edition of the poem by M. Walz (Freiburg, 1892). The fact that the work achieved such lasting fame suggests a popularity greater than modern critics might be inclined to attribute to it.

Der Pleier's borrowings in this work from Der Stricker's *Daniel* are not evidence of the paucity of his own creative talent (de Boor, *Litgesch.*, III, 78) but indicate a quite distinct purpose: to reverse the impression of that earlier "anti-hero" and rehabilitate the central figure in accordance with the model of Hartmann.

Even de Boor, however, cannot elevate Der Pleier's other two works above the level of mere imitation (p. 79): **Tandareis und Flordibel** and **Meleranz** are at best a compilation from a number of sources, identifiably German ones, although the author himself claims to have had French sources. The stories tell of familiar events, manipulated to create the impression of originality, and occasionally featuring characters plucked from unconnected stories in his models. Sometimes he takes it upon himself to supply stories lacking in earlier narratives. The focus is always Arthur and his court; events proceed through a series of adventures, occasionally over obstacles and complications, but inevitably to a happy end with a proper recognition of true virtue.

The audience for which the works were intended must have enjoyed this spectacle of traditional characters and episodes from an age of literature now some time past, and J. L. Riordan, at the conclusion of his article, points to the circulation of the romances throughout the later Middle Ages, albeit in a relatively confined geographical area. Possibly the attraction of the element of a revival will have outweighed the less-than-remarkable artistic skill of one who was, nevertheless, a competent story-teller.

Texts:
Bartsch, Karl, ed. *Meleranz*. Stuttgart, 1861. Repr. with an afterword by A. Hildebrand. Hildesheim: Olms, 1974. Herles, Wolfgang, ed. *Garel von dem blüenden Tal*. Vienna: Halosar, 1981.
Khull, Ferdinand, ed. *Tandareis und Flordibel: Ein höfischer Roman*. Graz, 1885.

### Der Pleier—Bibliography

Kern, Peter. *Die Artusromane des Pleier*. Berlin: Erich Schmidt, 1981.

Comprehensive, detailed study.

Riordan, John Lancaster. "A Vindication of the Pleier." *JEGP* 47 (1948): 29-43.

Schröder, Werner. "Das *Willehalm*-Plagiat im *Garel* des Pleier oder die vergeblich geleugnete Epigonalität." *ZfdA* 114 (1985) 119-131.

A useful article which demonstrates Der Pleier's debt to Wolfram in his *Garel* but goes beyond that to a wider consideration of him as an epigone, which leads Schröder to a confrontation with Peter Kern's findings.

Tax, Petrus. "Der Pleier." In: *The Arthurian Encyclopedia*. Ed. by Norris J. Lacy. New York: Garland, 1986. Pp. 427-429, or *The New Arthurian Encyclopedia*. Ed. by Norris J. Lacy. New York: Garland, 1991. Pp. 362-363.

A balanced, fairly detailed summary.

See also the chapter on Der Pleier in Neil Thomas's *The Defence of Camelot*. Bern: Peter Lang, 1992. Pp. 44-69.

### Konrad von Stoffeln: *Gauriel von Muntabel*

This relatively short romance (4172 lines in the longer of the two extant manuscripts) is, as far as we know, the only work by Konrad von Stoffeln. He lays claim to it in one of the manuscripts, but his identity remains obscure. In all probability he came from the noble family of Hohenstoffeln, to the northwest of Lake Constance. Certainly his language supports that suggestion. The occurrence of the names Garel and Meleranz, known already as central characters of Der Pleier, argues for a dating of about 1280. Konrad's own reference to a source from Spain is regarded as spurious, and the likelihood is that his work is based on French stories, although one does not need to look far for resemblances to the great masters of German medieval literature whom he honors early on in his poem as "getihtes meisterschaft" (the corporate masters of poetry). Above all the echoes of *Iwein* abound in a work which has been largely dismissed by scholarship as a tedious recital of borrowed motifs, eked out in a romance that would have been more suited to a shorter narrative form.

The core of the work is the story of the knight Gauriel who goes against the condition imposed on his relationship with his fairy mistress when he betrays her identity. His punishment is exile from her, and he undertakes numerous adventures with his appearance hideously distorted by her magic powers and accompanied by a he-goat in the hope of regaining her favor. On the way he encounters Iwein and Gawein and Erec, and he achieves victory upon victory until, at last, he has proved himself worthy of the favor of his lady, who restores to him his former handsome features. The poem culminates in the return to Arthur's court and his reunion with his lady amid great rejoicing.

The accusations of imitation appear justified, and the suspicion that Konrad might be parodying earlier accounts, particularly *Iwein*, meet with the objection that he lacks the skill to carry it through. More recently Neil Thomas has argued for some revision of the prevailing negative view of the poem, seeing Konrad von Stoffeln not as a blatant plagiarist more or less devoid of talent but as one who has effected "a creative confrontation" with Hartmann's *Iwein* (*Arthuriad*, 91-103), presenting a solution to a problem left unsolved by Hartmann. One may feel that Thomas attributes too much deliberation to Konrad, but this section of his book is well worth reading for the challenge it offers to accepted views of these late romances as trivial imitations, often excessively drawn out by their artistically limited authors.

Text:
Khull, Ferdinand, ed. *Gauriel von Muntabel.* Graz: Leuschner & Lubensky, 1885, repr. with a preface and notes, Osnabrück, 1969.

## Konrad von Stoffeln—Bibliography

Thomas, Neil. *The Medieval German Arthuriad: Some Contemporary Revaluations of the Canon.* Bern: Peter Lang, 1989 (= Euro. Hochschulschr., Reihe I, Dt. Spr. u. Lit., 153). See pp. 91-103.
For description see last paragraph of section above.

## Berthold von Holle: *Crâne, Demantin, Darifant*

Standing somewhat alone, both geographically and in the nature of his works, is the Lower Saxon Berthold von Holle, whose three known works are usually dated a little after the middle of the 13th century. None of these is handed down in a complete form, and *Darifant* is so fragmentary as to be ignored in many literary histories. There is evidence to suggest that Berthold was a member of a family of ministeriales from the region of Hildesheim. He names Duke Johann von Braunschweig as the source of the material of his *Crâne,* and it is assumed that his other poem *Demantin* was probably also composed for the court of Brunswick.

For all their obvious debt to the traditional Arthurian romance, in particular to Hartmann von Aue, both works are clearly rooted in the political environment of the mid-13th century. There is no sign of Arthur or his court, although chivalry constitutes one aspect of the poems. The focus of *Demantin*, like that of the *Willehalm von Orlens* of Rudolf von Ems (see p. 338 ff.), is the English court, which, through its connection with the Welfs and in particular through the recent support given by them to Richard of Cornwall, would have had a special significance. The background to the *Crâne* is similarly a real place, the imperial court. The hero and two companions arrive at the court where they conceal their real identities and take the names of birds: Crâne, Valke, and Stare ("crane," "falcon," "starling"), hence the title. There they start out as pages and rise to become knights. In both *Demantin* and *Crâne* the action ranges far and wide geographically, and the central figures engage in adventures of a familiar nature in their pursuit of fame and the hands of their lovely ladies, though the element of *minne* is not handled with any depth or fervor. Familiar motifs occur; festivals, partings and reunions are described with all due regard for ceremony; combats and tournaments have their place side by side with large-scale battles more reminiscent of Wolfram's *Willehalm*. Markedly absent is the element of the supernatural and the extravagant. Although success is crowned for the young knight in each case when he becomes the ruler of a land, the works lack the sense of progress through adversity and the explicit pattern of that progress. The tenor of the classical courtly romance is no longer present, yet the poems cannot compete in their originality or artistry with Konrad von Würzburg, the most remarkable narrative poet of the post-classical period.

In line with the rejection of the extravagant in favor of a more sober style is Berthold's rather simple, direct language which is, in itself, a feature of his contribution to the narrative diversity of the age. His basic language is a unique mixture of his native Low German with the literary language of his antecedents and superimposed on that are occasional echoes of Wolfram von Eschenbach and of the language of the heroic epic and even of the "Spielmannsepen." The suggestion that the *Crâne* in particular was appreciated by his contemporaries, albeit within his immediate locality—and it *is* a good story—is supported by the fact that it was retold in a prose version in the fifteenth century and performed in Lübeck as a "Fastnachtspiel" in 1444.

Texts:
Bartsch, Karl, ed. *Berthold von Holle: Werke*. Tübingen, 1875. Repr. 1967. Separate editions of 'Demantin' (Tübingen, 1875) and 'Crâne' (Nürnberg, 1858), both by Bartsch may be available.

### Berthold von Holle—Bibliography

Fromm, Hans. "Berthold von Holle." In: $VL^2$ 1 (1978) 813-816.

A basic introduction with somewhat grudging literary comment.

Von Malsen-Tilborch, Gabriele. *Representation und Reduktion*. Munich: Beck, 1973 (= MTU, 44).

See also de Boor, *Litgesch*. II, 211-213, for a fuller appraisal.

# THE CONTINUATIONS

An important area of post-courtly literature is composed of continuations of works left unfinished or deemed to be in need of continuation or supplementation. A number of factors can be postulated to account for this phenomenon: the very fact that Gottfried's *Tristan*, Wolfram's *Willehalm*, and Wolfram's *Titurel* were handed down in a state which contemporary audiences would almost certainly have found incomplete; the delight of the medieval listeners in a "good" story which meant one in which the ends of the narrative were neatly tied up and which had a recognizable structure, a beginning, a middle, and an end; the veneration which later poets obviously felt for their predecessors, who were their models, and the dedication which they must have applied to the completion of their works. The motivation was there, but the continuators in general lacked the artistic skill to fulfill their worthy self-imposed tasks. Nevertheless, the most important of these continuations warrant our attention, because they are a significant dimension of the literary activity of the day, important in their own right but even more because they show the extent to which the *Blütezeit* continued to exert an influence over succeeding decades.

## Continuations of Gottfried's *Tristan*

Although questions have been raised about whether Gottfried's *Tristan* is in fact as complete as he meant it to be (see p. 157 ff.), these are generally dismissed as invalid. We can speculate at length about the reason his narrative breaks off so abruptly and probably arrive at the most likely, if rather unexciting, conclusion that he died. Nevertheless, there can be little doubt that the Middle Ages viewed his story as incomplete, and we can base this assumption on fairly firm indications: the predilection of the medieval audience for a nicely rounded story, Gottfried's own assertion that he is following the only version he regards as correct, and the unlikelihood that he would therefore not pursue it to the end, and, most tangible of all, the existence of at least two continuations in the later 13th century. Both of these, by Ulrich von Türheim and Heinrich von Freiberg, base their conclusions, not on Gottfried's declared source, Thomas von Britanje, but on the native German version of Eilhart von Oberg (see p. 118 ff.).

### Ulrich von Türheim

Ulrich von Türheim's *Tristan* was composed before 1243, the date of the death of Konrad von Winterstetten, the seneschal at the Hohenstaufen court who commissioned this continuation, as a favor to himself and in honor of his lady (25-32). Konrad is known as a prominent figure in the promotion of literature (*Bumke Mäzene* 251, 276 f.), remembered first and foremost as the patron of Rudolf von Ems. It is likely that the distinctly moral tone of Ulrich's work is attributable to his instigation of it, and it is a morality which owes nothing to Gottfried's own conception of a love which transcends conventional standards. Indeed, although it is true to say that Ulrich has completed Gottfried's work in that he has supplied an ending, he has not continued its ethos or its artistry. That the Middle Ages may have been concerned more with the tale than its style is suggested by the obvious popularity of this work, which, an amalgam of Gottfried, Eilhart and Ulrich himself, is more harshly judged by modern critics. Probably the principal mistake the detractors make is to compare Ulrich with Gottfried and discover, not surprisingly, that he does not match his predecessor.

Ulrich himself appears to have been more circumspect about his ability when he declares his objective of bringing the story to its end as best he can (21-24), a task made necessary by the lamentable death of Gottfried before he had managed to complete it (15-20). Rarely in the course of the 3730 lines of Ulrich's text does one discern any pretense at emulating the great master of poetic language, although he just occasionally attempts a clumsy playing with words which might be construed as an effort to copy one of Gottfried's characteristic stylistic devices.

The fact that Ulrich von Türheim takes his material, not from Gottfried's declared source but from the pre-courtly version by Eilhart, may be explained as a conscious turning away from Gottfried, despite his admiration for him, or, more mundanely, it may be because he had no access to the version of Thomas. It is also possible that the audience at the Hohenstaufen court was not acquainted with Eilhart's poem and that his ending was therefore as good as any other if the only criterion were the completion of the story. There is indeed the sense of a speedy dispatch about Ulrich's work which suggests that a prime concern was to finish the story as quickly as possible. Yet in doing so he has brought down upon himself the disdain of many modern critics who often appear to think that he simply did not understand Gottfried's poem.

It is hardly surprising that W. T. H. Jackson, with his boundless admiration for Gottfried, sees Ulrich as falling far short of his predecessor, linking Ulrich with the later Heinrich von Freiberg (see below) and maintaining that neither had any conception of Gottfried's true stature (in Loomis, *Arthurian Literature*, p. 156). Marianne Kalinke, (in *The Arthurian Encyclopedia*, p. 587-588) also compares Ulrich with Heinrich von Freiberg and finds him "pedestrian and uninspired." Burghart Wachinger is less dismissive of Ulrich, though fully aware of his limitations. In his article on the reception of Gottfried in the later Middle Ages (1985), he suggests that Ulrich was actually attempting something very different from Gottfried and that his failure to continue along the same lines is not a failure of comprehension but a deliberate remolding of the theme of love and its function, to the extent that Wachinger can postulate a lost source side by side with, or even in the place of, that of Eilhart von Oberge, an opinion not generally accepted. William C. McDonald, who makes every effort to be fair to Ulrich, to the extent perhaps of overvaluing the poem, succeeds in demonstrating that, far from continuing in the spirit of Gottfried, Ulrich has branched off in a direction all his own, in what McDonald describes as this "paean to fidelity" (1990, p. 7). In McDonald's eyes, the emphasis on *triuwe* means that this poem challenges conventional morality but in a different way from Gottfried: the adulterous pair are exalted, not as Gottfried would have his noble listeners believe, by the unique perfection of their love, but by their constant fidelity to one another which can survive even the marriage of Tristan to the second Ysolde and constitute their passport into a heaven presided over by a recognizable Christian God.

The incongruity of the prayer at the end of this work with Gottfried's *Tristan*, which it explicitly sets out to complete, serves to demonstrate how inappropriate it is to describe Ulrich as a continuator and to condemn him for having failed in that role. Thomas Kerth, in an article which demonstrates how much there is that is worth considering in Ulrich's version, ponders what he calls Ulrich's "dilemma" and concludes that Ulrich, when faced with the impossibility of reconciling love and honor within the confines of his courtly narrative, ultimately "places the problem in the hands of a Higher Authority" (Kerth, 1981, p. 91). Like other post-courtly poets, Ulrich seems to have been possessed of an over-zealous admiration for his predecessors and a mind of his own. These two ingredients may not have been matched by a remarkable literary talent, but they were sufficient to satisfy their contemporaries, left in the lurch by the original poet and eager for more. In most cases, modern critics have been less ready to accept their achievements in such simple terms, and they range between those who dismiss them as worthless and those who seek to endow them with more sophistication than they in fact have. Even Thomas Kerth, who accords Ulrich more respect than most critics, seems to detect a kind of compromise in a work which, "compatible with both its models, is curiously inferior to each" (p. 91).

Although one may not agree with William McDonald's overall evaluation of Ulrich's *Tristan*, this chapter of his book on the post-Gottfried German versions of the Tristan story (1990) can hardly fail to prompt a re-reading of the work, particularly when it is juxtaposed to his chapter on Heinrich von Freiberg's *Tristan*. Both chapters represent significant analyses of two works which have only really become easily accessible during the last fifteen years, via the editions of Thomas Kerth and Danielle Buschinger, respectively. For the English reader, William McDonald's two books convey a very full picture of the impact of the Tristan legend on German literature.

Whether it is true to assume, as Max Wehrli does (*Litgesch.* 477), that the very existence of Heinrich von Freiberg's *Tristan* suggests that Ulrich von Türheim's version had not satisfied its public, is possibly open to question. Heinrich von Freiberg was, after all, composing for a later generation, at some distance from the *Blütezeit* and, no doubt encouraged by the products of the intervening decades, inclined to a new view of the old material and in particular to look for greater stylistic refinement. As Joachim Bumke puts it (*Litgesch.* 195), the later work does not so much replace the earlier one as compete with it. This may have been the case for the Middle Ages, and, in the eyes of modern critics, as we have seen, there is little doubt as to who won the competition, but it also represents an injustice, probably to Ulrich von Türheim, but almost certainly to Heinrich von Freiberg, whose work deserves more independent status.

### Heinrich von Freiberg

Heinrich von Freiberg's **Tristan** was composed probably a little before 1290, at the behest of Raimund von Lichtenburg, a member of one of the most powerful houses of Bohemia (*Bumke Mäzene*, 277). In an elegant tribute at the beginning of the poem, Heinrich extols the youth and nobility of his patron, his chivalry and his manifold virtues (53-84). He is the one who has prompted him to his task of completing the work of Gottfried, a task which he approaches with traditional expressions of inadequacy, combined with the hope that God will grant him time enough to complete it. He makes no mention of Ulrich von Türheim, an omission which is hardly surprising and may not, in fact, be at all significant. The language of the opening points to one who is well acquainted with Gottfried and capable of emulating him, and, as the work proceeds, Heinrich emerges as a not inconsiderable poet in his own right, with a wide range of poetic and narrative skills which seem to reflect the impact also of Hartmann and Wolfram.

Little is known about Heinrich. In addition to his *Tristan*, he is believed to have composed two smaller works: *Die Legende vom Kreuzholz*, based on a Latin legend telling of the origin of the Cross in three seeds from the apple plucked by Eve in the Garden of Paradise, and a panegyric *Die Ritterfahrt des Johann von Michelsberg*, in honor of the victory of Johann I of Michelsberg over two French knights. These two works are included along with the *Tristan* in the 1906 edition by Alois Bernt, together with a fourth work, the authenticity of which is disputed and now generally rejected, a little story in the manner of the *Schwank*, *Das Schrätel und der Wasserbär*. Until the recent work by Danielle Buschinger, who has done much to illuminate the later fate of the Tristan legend in Germany and in particular to focus attention on Heinrich von Freiberg, Bernt's volume, which contains the four texts and detailed introductions, was the only substantial work on the poet. It is still the most comprehensive account.

As far as the *Tristan* is concerned, the work of William C. McDonald is likely to prove most valuable for the reader of English wishing to look closely at the poem, even though his distinctive interpretation may not be entirely unassailable. He sees it as a poem that is more than a mere and unsatisfactory conclusion to a greater predecessor. Indeed, the whole tenor of Heinrich's work is at odds with that of Gottfried's. Like Ulrich von Türheim, Heinrich has a moral purpose, and, like Gottfried too, he indicates how his audience should understand his poem. Yet, in total opposition to Gottfried, he makes no attempt to excuse the lovers, whose behavior is seen as an affront to courtly society and, ultimately, to heaven itself.

The society which is allowed to dominate in Heinrich von Freiberg's *Tristan* is a courtly society represented to a large extent by the realm of Arthur, a dimension which occupies a large proportion of the poem and which serves to show Tristan himself in a different light, as hero among heroes, rather than as struggling lover in an alien world. The Arthurian ingredient of Eilhart's poem is extended in Heinrich's, which owes much to the Arthurian literature represented in the works of Hartmann and Wolfram. Thus Heinrich's *Tristan* goes beyond Gottfried's and away from it, and the "conclusion" in the deaths of the lovers in consequence of the treachery of the second Isolde diverges from the spirit of Gottfried's poem. Following Eilhart and much more in line with his own instincts for a statement within the confines of conventional morality, Heinrich has Marke learn of the love potion from Kurvenal (6707 ff.). Marke expresses his regret at the secrecy which has enshrouded the love and led to this tragic outcome and seeks to make amends by founding a monastery, to which he himself withdraws and where he allows the rose and the vine to entwine above the tombs which he has had made for the lovers. This grandiose gesture, echoing similar acts in Eilhart and Ulrich, sits ill with Gottfried's own picture of Marke, but it is particularly appropriate in a poem that is essentially a cautionary tale. The love of Heinrich's Tristan and Isolde is not idealized, and Christians must take note of its *swachez ende* (base, ignoble end, 6855) and turn their thoughts to that true love which knows no end. In a startling final statement, Heinrich employs the image of the rose and the vine to underline his message: Christian people, like the vine, should entwine themselves with the Son of God, the true, blossoming rose. The love between Tristan and Isolde, far from being paramount, is shown as essentially earthbound, and, as such, prone to error and catastrophe. The prospect of salvation remains, however, but this is on an entirely different plane.

Thus the impact of Heinrich von Freiberg's *Tristan* exists less in his doubtful success in completing Gottfried's work than in his achievement in creating a work which borrows heavily from Gottfried when it comes to individual episodes and in his sometimes impressive use of language, but which is, in the final analysis, a powerful and independent creation by a poet of some quality. To describe it, as Max Wehrli does (*Litgesch.* 478) as "sehr hübsch und liebenswert" (very nice and pleasant), is to underestimate it. As Wehrli himself clearly recognizes, the work has distinctive qualities all its own, with regard to its style, and William C. McDonald has opened the way to discussion of its content and meaning. Its place in late 13th-century German literature has yet to be defined more fully.

Chronologically earlier than Heinrich, conceivably much earlier, is the little work **Tristan als Mönch.** It does not belong strictly speaking with the continuations, but it clearly owes much to Gottfried's *Tristan*. Indeed, it is placed after Gottfried's poem and before Ulrich von Türheim's in the only two manuscripts which record it. Although no one is likely to claim that it has any literary stature, it is interesting as a contribution to our understanding of the interest in and the reception of the Tristan material in the 13th century. Moreover, with its distinct tendency towards the *Schwank*, it shows the movement away from the courtly romance towards the shorter episodic narrative for which the designation "novella" seems the most fitting, even at this early period. Whether the author had a separate French source which told of Tristan disguised as a monk and able to pursue his love for Isolde unidentified at Marke's court, or whether the germ of the idea came from a single hint in the version of Thomas, when Isolde of the White Hands expresses her fear that Tristan might become a monk, is impossible to say. Certainly Tristan's capacity for disguise is familiar from all the versions of the story, and the idea that he might become a monk coincides with the tradition in the *chansons de geste* of the hero's withdrawing into a monastery at the end of his life. Such issues are set out in the volume by Betty C. Bushey which contains an edition of this work which had been largely neglected by scholarship, and perhaps not unjustifiably. Again, the chapter devoted to it by William C. McDonald (1990, 104-132) opens up the work as an area for serious scholarly consideration, although, again, one is left wondering if this essentially slight work has not been given a status it barely merits. Nevertheless, McDonald's work is an invaluable companion to the serious study of the impact of the Tristan story in Germany in the Middle Ages and beyond.

Texts:
Bernt, Alois, ed. *Heinrich von Freiberg: Dichtungen mit Einleitungen über Stil, Sprache, Metrik, Quellen und die Persönlichkeit des Dichters.* Halle: Niemeyer, 1906.

Buschinger, Danielle, ed. *Heinrich von Freiberg: Tristan.* Göppingen: Kümmerle, 1982 (= GAG, 270).

Bushey, Betty C., ed. *Tristan als Mönch: Untersuchungen und kritische Edition.* Göppingen: Kümmerle, 1974 (= GAG, 119).

Kerth, Thomas, ed. *Ulrich von Türheim: Tristan.* Tübingen: Niemeyer, 1979.

### *Tristan* Continuations—Bibliography

Kerth, Thomas. "The Dénouement of the Tristan *"Minne"*: Türheim's Dilemma." *Neophil.* 65 (1981): 79-93.

McDonald, William C. *The Tristan Story in German Literature of the Late Middle Ages and Early Renaissance: Tradition and Innovation.* Lewiston: Edwin Mellen, 1990.

____. *Arthur and Tristan: On the Intersection of Legends in German Medieval Literature.* Lewiston: Edwin Mellen, 1991.

## Continuations of Wolfram's *Willehalm*

There are a number of manuscripts in which Wolfram's *Willehalm* is preceded by Ulrich von dem Türlin's *Willehalm* (sometimes called *Arabel*, for greater clarity) and followed by the *Rennewart* of Ulrich von Türheim (also called somewhat confusingly *Willehalm* in the older literature on the subject). That they were seen in this way, as a kind of trilogy, is quite understandable: Ulrich von dem Türlin's *Willehalm/Arabel* deals with events leading up to those in Wolfram's *Willehalm*, and Ulrich von Türheim's *Rennewart/ Willehalm* describes what happened after the action in Wolfram's *Willehalm* breaks off. It probably also speaks for the need which the medieval public had to know the *whole* story, a need obviously recognized by the two Ulrichs and abundantly satisfied by them, to judge by the large number of manuscripts of their work, both in trilogy form with Wolfram's poem and separate from it.

It is clear that Wolfram's *Willehalm* could not be deemed to be complete in the eyes of his audience. The work breaks off with far too much left untold, and in particular the fate of Rennewart needed to be known. It is not surprising, then, that the next generation brought forth an admirer of Wolfram who was ready, if not altogether able, to fulfill this need. Moreover, however rigorously one may criticize the *Rennewart* of Ulrich von Türheim, one must concede that he possessed considerable stamina and dedication to produce his enormously long (36518 lines) work which does rather more than simply provide an ending to Wolfram's unfinished masterpiece. The continuators of the great classical poets of Middle High German had a number of features in common with one another, and these included a veneration for their predecessors, a sense of their own inferior talent, and a refusal to let that stand in their way.

### Ulrich von Türheim: *Rennewart*

Ulrich von Türheim's *Rennewart* was almost certainly completed shortly before 1250, and, although he does not actually name a patron, his lament for the many friends he has lost (25756 ff.) includes names associated with the Hohenstaufen court (*Bumke Mäzene*, 274). His name is attested in the region of Augsburg. He is known to have composed a *Clîes*, a version of the *Cligès* of Chrétien de Troyes, but surviving only in a single slight fragment. His greater "fame" stems from his continuation of two great fragments of the

*Blütezeit*, Gottfried's *Tristan* (see above) and, more prominently, Wolfram's *Willehalm*. It is evident that his *Rennewart* was more kindly received by its first audiences than by modern scholars. In 1809 Jacob Grimm dismissed the work as "ein unbeschreiblich langweiliges Gedicht" (an indescribably boring poem), complaining that it was long and rambling and did not merit an edition. Karl Lachmann apparently did not quite share that view since he devoted considerable effort to the text, before turning his attention to more obviously significant editorial work. However, an initial reaction by Lachmann to the poem, quoted by Christa Westphal-Schmidt in her 1979 study, sums up his response and goes to the heart of the quality of Ulrich's narrative: "Ulrich von Türheim gefällt mir wenig, auch die Fabel nicht, aber er hat eine Unzahl von Sprichwörtern" (I don't really like Ulrich von Türheim very much, nor the story either, but he has an enormous number of proverbs, Westphal-Schmidt, p. 10). As so often, Lachmann's authority was enough to condemn a work to decades of neglect, yet towards the end of the 19th century other scholars contributed important investigations which were eventually taken up in the only existing edition of the whole poem, that by Alfred Hübner, originally published in 1938.

Like so much of the literature of this period, the work is important to modern scholars as a phenomenon which reflects the taste of its age and the demands of the post-classical audiences. Gerhard Eis describes Ulrich von Türheim as "ein ausgesprochener Epigone" (a pronounced epigone, *VL* IV, 1964, 608), and the term is unambiguously detractive. In taking up where Wolfram left off, he is fulfilling a need, first and foremost to tell the story of Rennewart to its conclusion, but he also makes no pretense of emulating Wolfram stylistically, aware as he is that he lacks the art of the "künsterîcher Wolfram" (skillful Wolfram) whose death he so laments (21711-21715). Moreover, as far as content is concerned, he moves beyond his great master when, using other *chansons de geste* as well as the *Bataille d'Aliscans*, he tells of the withdrawal of both Rennewart and Willehalm into monasteries. He concludes his story by emphasizing the elements of the saintliness of his two central male characters, possibly drawing on Latin lives of saints to do so. This is not to suggest, of course, that the germ of such an emphasis is not already present in Wolfram, in his conception of the saintly intercessor Willehalm and the *heilec vrouwe* Gyburc, as well as in his handling of the figure of Vivianz, but Ulrich does demonstrate a degree of narrative independence, though sadly unsupported by his style, which remains at best pedestrian, and generally turgid and totally lacking in anything which could be described as distinction.

Ehrismann points to the discrepancy between the narrative style and the potentially lively content (*Litgesch. Schlußband*, 68), and one cannot but agree that, in the hands of a greater artist, this powerful story of love and conflict might have been a worthy successor to the poem which inspired it. As it is, one must concede that Ulrich certainly satisfies the desire of his audience to know what became of Rennewart after his disappearance on the field of Alischanz. His baptism and investiture are spelled out in a way that may well not have matched Wolfram's intentions, but these, together with his marriage to Alize and the birth of their child, the giant-like Maleser, whose abduction, coming soon after the death in childbirth of his beloved wife, prompts Rennewart to enter a monastery, are all very much the substance of enthralling narrative. The later events, the story of

Maleser and his marriage with the Amazon queen Penteselie, takes the story into the East and widens the whole perspective of the poem in a way that demonstrates Ulrich's appreciation of the scale of Wolfram's works, even if he lacks the talent to handle it effectively. The close of the work shows Willehalm, widowed now and a hermit, but still ready to rise to the challenge of a new heathen threat to Christendom under the leadership of Terramer's son, and then withdrawing again, to build the monastery where he dies.

If content were the only criterion, Ulrich von Türheim has achieved enough to earn him the place which the manuscripts often accord him, side by side with Wolfram, but the judgment of the modern critic is in general a harsh one. Christa Westphal-Schmidt's book is the only recent comprehensive account of the poem. It is factual and informative, examining aspects of Ulrich's narrative in its own right and delineating the position that the work occupies within the later development of medieval German narrative.

### Ulrich von dem Türlin: *Arabel*

With the work of Ulrich von Türheim, Wolfram's *Willehalm* may have been considered well and truly completed, but about a decade later another devotee, Ulrich von dem Türlin, took it upon himself to fill in the details of the background to the situation which pertains as Wolfram's work opens. He proceeds in a different way from Ulrich von Türheim, taking up details from Wolfram himself and eking these out to form a narrative which actually contributes little to the overall understanding and represents a crass contrast to the tone of Wolfram's poem. Again, however, to judge by the number of manuscripts, the work seems to have been devoured by an eager public. However, one pointer to the possibility that even that voracious appetite may have had its limits, exists in the suggestion that Ulrich von dem Türlin himself revised his own work of about 10,000 lines and slimmed it down to less than a third, as contained in the Heidelberg manuscript A. The reduction is achieved, not by excising the substance but by removing the repetitions and refining the account.

The work begins with the story of the young Willehalm's early life, when, as we know from Wolfram, he was disinherited by his father, along with his six younger brothers. Growing up at the court of the Emperor Charlemagne, he becomes a knight and fights against the heathens. He is instrumental in bringing Charlemagne's son Louis to the throne upon the death of the emperor (a bond which accounts for the bitterness of Wolfram's Willehalm when Louis is so reluctant to help him). Following the defeat of Terramer at Ronceval by the Christian forces under Louis, Willehalm is captured and imprisoned in Todjerne, where, during his eight-year captivity, he comes to know and love Arabel, wife of King Tybalt. They flee together, she is baptized by the Pope himself, and their marriage follows.

Here, after almost 10,000 lines, most of the manuscripts end, at a point where one might say that Wolfram's poem begins, but a further 930 lines appended to one of the leading manuscripts tells of the upbringing of Vivianz by Willehalm and Gyburc and of his investiture (taking up the idea of the important bond that Wolfram stresses) and then leads more directly into the first battle of Alischanz when the news comes of the approach of Tybalt.

The echoes of Wolfram's poem are very much in evidence, and Ulrich even actually incorporates two substantial and highly recognizable passages of Wolfram's text into his own. He adds little to the events already known, though he does linger on frankly erotic scenes in a way that would have been alien to Wolfram, and he seems to enjoy descriptions of material luxury, though, again, in a much cruder way than Wolfram. He is conscious, as anyone acquainted with Wolfram's poem would be, of the dilemma of Arabel and the depth of the love which takes her from her blameless heathen husband, but he does not explore the implications.

There is no reason to think that Ulrich based his work on any source other than Wolfram's own work, which he appears to have known very well. As far as we know, this was the only work of one who, like his namesake and possible kinsman, Heinrich von dem Türlin, author of *Diu Crône* (see p. 358 ff.), was an Austrian, from the region of Kärnten. Where Heinrich appears to have taken Hartmann von Aue as his model, Ulrich clearly saw it as his special task to try to emulate Wolfram, an ambition that was obviously well beyond his reach. Straightforward narrative does not elude him, and he can tell a story in a satisfactory, if somewhat pedestrian way, but he engages in much repetition, of individual phrases and even of whole passages, and in his case repetition is not a stylistic device but a weakness. For all his admiration for Wolfram, he can simply not approach him. Hans Friedrich Rosenfeld, in his generally lukewarm appraisal (*VL*, 1964, 610), has diagnosed the problem well when he says that Wolfram is actually the source of Ulrich's downfall.

Once more, then, we have the phenomenon of the epigone: the devotee who no doubt appreciated all the virtues of his model, yet who, in trying to imitate them, succeeded only in demonstrating his own inadequacy. It is, however, an interesting phenomenon, in the Middle Ages as later in the post-Goethe decades, and, in the massive products inspired by the great masters of the *Blütezeit*, it is an ingredient of the literature of the age which should not be ignored. In the case of Ulrich von dem Türlin, the ability of this phenomenon to command attention is demonstrated by the fact that no less an authority on Wolfram von Eschenbach than Werner Schröder who describes Ulrich as "ein dürftiger und umständlicher Erzähler, der vom Geborgten, Angelesenem und Ausgeschriebenem lebt" (a feeble and laborious narrator, who lives materially and stylistically from what he has borrowed, acquired by reading, and written out in full, *Texte und Untersuchungen zur "Willehalm"-Rezeption*, I, p. XII) can devote himself to producing volumes of analysis of the *Arabel* continuation. His massive work largely supersedes the only other existing edition of the poem, that by Samuel Singer, published in 1893 under the title *Willehalm* and now very difficult to find.

Texts:
Hübner, Alfred, ed. *Ulrich von Türheim: Rennewart, aus der Berliner und Heidelberger Handschrift*. Berlin, 1938 (= *DTM* 39), repr. Berlin: Weidmann, 1964.
Schröder, Werner, ed. *Texte und Untersuchungen zur "Willehalm"-Rezeption, Band 1: Eine alemannische Bearbeitung der "Arabel" Ulrichs von dem Türlin*. Berlin: de Gruyter, 1981.
Schröder, Werner, ed. *Arabel Studien* (6 vols.). Wiesbaden: Franz Steiner, 1982-1993 (= Akademie der Wiss. u. d. Lit., Mainz. Abh. d. Geistes- und Sozialwiss. Kl., Jgg. 1982,6; 1983,4; 1984,9; 1988,6; 1988,7; 1993,4).

Singer, Samuel, ed. *"Willehalm". Ein Rittergedicht aus der zweiten Hälfte des dreizehnten Jahrhunderts von Meister Ulrich von dem Türlin.* Prag: np, 1893. Repr. Hildesheim: G. Olms, 1968.

### *Willihalm*-Continuations—Bibliography

Rosenfeld, Hans Friedrich. "Ulrich von dem Türlin." *VL* 4 (1963): 608-612.

Westphal-Schmidt, Christa. *Studien zum "Rennewart" Ulrichs von Türheim.* Frankfurt/M: Haag und Herchen, 1979.

Factual, informative, comprehensive account.

## Continuation of Wolfram's *Titurel*: Albrecht's *Jüngerer Titurel*

Among the continuations, this huge work stands out as the most remarkable in a number of ways. The poet who eventually names himself as Albrecht in stanza 5883 has set himself an immense task, to tell the story of Sigune and Schionatulander left tantalizingly incomplete by Wolfram von Eschenbach and to supplement it with other adjacent matter (the adventures of Gahmuret in the Orient, the whole history of Schionatulander, which embraces also much of the story of Orilus and includes the grief of Sigune and her meetings with Parzival, and the death of Orilus at the hand of Ekunat). Albrecht supplies more information about the Grail (the early life of Titurel, his marriage, his children, his abdication; Parzival's release of Anfortas and his kingship of the Grail, and the future of the dynasty and of the Grail company, taken to India and linked with the rule of Prester John, whose place is eventually taken by Parzival himself) and does all this in the manner of Wolfram, taking even the powerful metrical form of the *Titurel*-fragments (see p. 190 ff.) as his model but making it, if anything, even more complex. It is hardly surprising that out of this vast concept there emerges a poem of well over 6,000 strophes (24,000 lines), which borrows liberally from both *Parzival* and *Willehalm* in language and subject matter. Embedded in it almost intact are the mysterious two fragments known as Wolfram's *Titurel*, that tender love-story which is now barely recognizable in the material that swamps it.

Hardly less remarkable than Albrecht's own ambition are the fluctuations of critical opinion about his achievement. The later Middle Ages appears to have had a high regard for the work and even to have accepted without question the fiction that this was the product of Wolfram himself, although its original audience, hearing the work some fifty years after the death of Wolfram, can hardly have been deceived. Its rediscovery in the late eighteenth century was greeted with enthusiasm, and it was even proclaimed as a masterpiece superior to *Parzival*, though the work of the same hand. It was Karl Lachmann himself, the great Wolfram scholar, who exposed the impersonation and condemned the poem to decades of neglect and disdain by his contemptuous characterization of it as "ein langweiliges, todtes und geziertes Werk" (a boring, dead, and affected work). Not until the second half of the present century has the work received more kindly judgments and been viewed more favorably once Albrecht's own subterfuge was removed and the real achievement could be assessed as an important phenomenon. Although the edition by Wolf, interrupted by his death and then completed by Nyholm, may be controversial in some respects, it represents a huge advance in research on a very significant product of the later 13th century and doubtless paves the way for further scholarly work. *Der jüngere Titurel* is not just a dreary leftover from a bygone age but very much a product of its own time, which honored the accomplishments of the *Blütezeit* but also had its own path.

For all his allegiance to Wolfram, Albrecht seems to have wanted to do more than complete the narrative of his great predecessor. He certainly does this, supplementing what Wolfram has related even in areas where he might have been thought to have said all there was to say. When one has taken into account the many and often substantial additions to the narrative itself, one is left with the essential difference in the tone, and this can be swiftly defined as the emphasis in Albrecht on overt didacticism. One of the most recent (1993) essays on the *Jüngerer Titurel*, that by Alfred Ebenbauer, describes the work as "ein Dokument der Laiengelehrsamkeit und der enzyklopädischen Weltsicht des 13. Jahrhunderts" (a document of lay erudition and the encyclopedic world-view of the 13th century, p. 363). This may perhaps be going rather too far, but it helps to highlight the important new dimension that Albrecht has given to the familiar material. It also makes one wonder even more at the success of Albrecht's masquerade over such a long period, for the wisdom of Wolfram von Eschenbach seldom intrudes upon his storytelling. At the same time, it is mistaken to see the poem as no more than a pedantic handbook, for Albrecht has set out to compose a romance and has to a large extent fulfilled this objective with his accounts of human stories, of vast battles, and the extension of the Arthurian material. How successful he has been is a matter of opinion—and the question provokes vehement responses—but the genre of the work should not be brought into doubt.

Perhaps one can usefully weigh up Albrecht's achievement in terms of the two distinct attitudes contained in Werner Schröder's subtitle to his 1982 book: was it devotion or arrogance which motivated Albrecht in his composition of this remarkable work? Early in his poem, Albrecht expresses his intention of straightening out that which is bent ("ich wil die krumb an allen orten slichten" 20,3), a possible reference to Wolfram's own use of the bow metaphor to describe his narrative technique (*Parz.* 241,1-30). However, there is nothing straightforward about Albrecht's language, and, here too, he shows a clear sense of purpose, when he refers to his intention to clothe his words *mit geblümter kunst* (with ornate artistry 1632,3). The deliberately elaborate style which prompted Lachmann to describe the work, not unjustly but with pejorative intention, as *geziert* (affected) corresponds to Albrecht's ideal of poetic art. As Linda Parshall puts it in her excellent, balanced comparison of Wolfram and Albrecht as narrators, which can serve as a lucid introduction to this puzzling poem, "Albrecht's achievement can be understood on its own terms as a glorification of language, especially written language, and what it can attain" (15). It is helpful, too, in studying *Der Jüngere Titurel*, to bear in mind her premise that "Albrecht is not composing just for the transitory experience of listening but primarily for the more leisurely contemplative activity of reading" (16), although the complex findings of D. H. Green suggest that one must be cautious in accepting such an adamant conclusion in relation to any work of the period (*Listening and Reading*, 1994).

The contemporary appeal of *Der Jüngere Titurel* is attested by the large number of manuscripts, of which 11 are complete and 45 fragments. Among the latter is the so-called *Verfasserfragment* (lit. author-fragment), a single sheet containing 23 strophes and apparently belonging to none of the other manuscripts. The provenance of this fragment is unclear. It was reportedly seen attached to the Heidelberg manuscript H in 1817, subsequently seems to have disappeared and did not come to light again until the turn of the century. Since then it has been published on several occasions and it affords some important clues in the complicated history of the poem as well as some insights into Albrecht's view of his task. The usually accepted opinion is that this fragment is the work of Albrecht, who names himself in it, and that he composed it when, far advanced in the composition of the poem, he was abandoned by his original patrons, the three princes to whom he refers in his prologue (64), and was hoping to gain support from another. The identity of the original patrons has not been conclusively established, but it seems clear that he directed the *Verfasserfragment* to Duke Ludwig II of Bavaria, the "duc loys et palatinus" of strophe 20. When this appeal failed, it is believed, he will have completed the poem rather hastily, without support. The combination of evidence points to a dating of 1270-1275 for the whole poem.

There is now considerable doubt as to the identity of Albrecht, who was earlier thought to be the Albrecht von Scharfenberg to whom Ulrich Füetrer attributes, along with the *Titurel*, two further epic poems, a *Merlin* and a *Seifrid von Ardemont*, neither of them extant in their original form. Similarly, there was previously a fair degree of unanimity about his standing as a knight, although more recently this has also been brought into question, and the more commonly held view is that he was a man of clerical background, possibly a monk or a priest. There is no doubt that he was a man of considerable learning: his work reveals a wide knowledge of Latin and Old French, of classical poets, philosophy, theology, and ancient history. He is informed on a range of subjects, and at ease in handling debate and exegesis. The "Wolfram" who speaks in the *Jüngerer Titurel* is a far-cry from the "illiterate" author of *Parzival* and *Willehalm*. For all his admiration for Wolfram, he shows little lack of confidence in approaching his self-imposed task, and it is really in this light that we should view his achievement.

Again the *Verfasserfragment* is helpful. Early on in it Albrecht likens his ambition of completing Wolfram's work to builders who took up the task of finishing a temple in Venice left incomplete when the initiators of it died. Clearly any sense he has of being a lesser master is overridden by his conception of a special function, an almost sacred duty to his art. His poem is thus to be interpreted, not as a tying-up of ends of a narrative but as a great edifice which fulfills its own artistic purpose. It is directed at devotees of Wolfram who, in the original audience, no doubt enjoyed the frequent echoes of the master in terms of language and turn of phrase, while being privy to the masquerade which subsequently eluded their successors. Modern devotees of Wolfram tend to treat the poem as a grotesque travesty, something approaching sacrilege. Werner Schröder, in his entertaining but somewhat intemperate onslaught on the work, talks of *das monströse opus* (the monstrous opus, *Wolfram-Nachfolge* 19), but perhaps, in his admiration for Wolfram, he fails to take account of the deliberately different tenor of the two poems.

Thinking of Albrecht's heavy-handed treatment as a re-working of Wolfram's delicate elegy leads to accusations of vandalism, it is true, but Linda Parshall's more measured comparison of Wolfram and Albrecht as narrators, based largely on *Parzival*, arrives at some fruitful conclusions which accord Albrecht his just place in the German narrative of the 13th century. Nevertheless, one might just agree with Werner Schröder's view that Albrecht has taken rather too much on himself, or to put it in Schröder's more colorful way: "Der Anzug, den er sich angezogen hat, war ihm je nachdem zu eng oder zu weit, jedenfalls nicht angemessen" (the suit he has put on is either too big or too small, but, whichever it is, it does not fit him, *Wolfram-Nachfolge* 134).

Text:
Hahn, K. A., ed. *Der Jüngere Titurel*. Quedlinburg and Leipzig, 1842.
Wolf, Werner, ed. *Albrechts von Scharfenberg Jüngerer Titurel*. Berlin: Akademie Verlag, 1955, Vol. 1; 1964, Vol. 2,1; 1968, Vol. 2,2. (= DTM 45, 55, 61). Continued by Kurt Nyholm, Berlin: Akademie Verlag, 1985 and 1992 (2 vols.). Vol. 1 contains a lengthy preface and descriptions of the manuscripts. Last vol. includes index of names.

## Albrecht's *Jüngerer Titurel*—Bibliography

Ebenbauer, Alfred. "Albrecht: 'Jüngerer Titurel.' " In: *Mittelhochdeutsche Romane und Heldenepen*. Stuttgart: Reclam, 1993 (= UB, Interpretationen, 8914). Pp. 353-372.

A straightforward analysis of the work and some of its problems, in the context of some of the scholarly work which surrounds it. It contains a useful summary of the contents.

Fromm, Hans. "Der jüngere Titurel. Das Werk und sein Dichter." In: *Wolfram-Studien*, Vol. 8. Ed. by Werner Schröder. Berlin: Erich Schmidt, 1984. Pp. 11-33.

This volume was largely devoted to *Der Jüngere Titurel*. Fromm's contribution is a helpful introduction to the poem.

Huschenbett, Dietrich. *Albrechts 'Jüngerer Titurel'. Zu Stil und Komposition*. Munich: Wilhelm Fink, 1979 (= Medium Aevum. Philologische Studien, 35).

Uses strophes 1-2297 as basis for his study.

_____. "Der *jüngere Titurel* als literaturgeschichtliches Problem." In: *Wolfram Studien*, Vol. 8. Ed. by Werner Schröder. Berlin: Erich Schmidt, 1984. Pp. 153-176.

This article includes a substantial bibliography on the *Jüngerer Titurel*.

Parshall, Linda B. *The Art of Narration in Wolfram's 'Parzival' and Albrecht's 'Jüngerer Titurel.'*, Cambridge: Cambridge UP, 1981 (= Anglica Germanica, Series 2).

See remarks on Schröder (below).

Ragotzky, Hedda. *Studien zur Wolfram-Rezeption. Die Entstehung und Verwandlung der Wolfram-Rolle in der deutschen Literatur des 13. Jahrhunderts*. Stuttgart: Kohlhammer, 1971 (= Studien zur Poetik und Geschichte der Literatur, 20).

This study deals with how Wolfram was received during the 13th century and includes a chapter on the 'Jüngerer Titurel,' pp. 93-141.

Schröder, Werner. *Wolfram-Nachfolge im 'Jüngeren Titurel'. Devotion oder Arroganz*. Frankfurt/M: Klostermann, 1982 (= Frankfurter wiss. Beitr., Kulturwiss. Reihe, 15).

This book and Parshall's book (above), published at about the same time, do not (were not able to?) take account of one another. Taken together, they represent opposing attitudes and methods and, as such, provide stimulating reading.

## *Lohengrin*

Not strictly to be regarded as a continuation but inextricable in its origins as far as we are able to judge from Wolfram's *Parzival*, is this fairly problematic work, which most critics now date somewhere in the 1280s. Wolfram's great poem was actually in no need of a continuation, in the way that we can say that Gottfried's *Tristan*, or Wolfram's other two poems were. Yet in making Parzival's son Lohengrin the Swan Knight and giving a shadowy account of his doomed marriage, Wolfram had perhaps unintentionally held out a key to future poets eager to tell a story. Not many years before the composition of *Lohengrin*, Konrad von Würzburg had used the legend, without naming the Swan Knight or relating him to the Grail, so that there is no reason to think that Konrad was inspired by Wolfram in his version of a favorite legend of the Middle Ages (see p. 344 f.). The situation is different in the case of the unknown author of *Lohengrin*, for here the shadow of Wolfram is much in evidence. Indeed, the whole story is put into the mouth of Wolfram von Eschenbach, not as a masquerade in the manner of *Der Jüngere Titurel* (see p. 381 ff.), but emerging from the debate with the magician Klingzor which opens the poem. The confrontation between the poet and his own creation had already found its way into the essentially fictitious *Wartburgkrieg*, a compilation dating from somewhere in the middle of the 13th century and purporting to tell of the (unhistorical) contest of Minnesänger at the court of Hermann von Thüringen, a work which clearly also echoes in *Lohengrin*. The metrical form, the ten-line strophe more reminiscent of the *Spruch* than the courtly romance, is borrowed from the debate between Wolfram and Klingsor in the *Wartburgkrieg*, where Wolfram's artistry is more than a match for the dark powers of the magician. The passing mention of Lohengrin there, too, no doubt prompted this account of his story which forms the core of this work, though by no means the whole of it.

The 768 strophes of the poem are thus probably more fascinating for their literary relationships than significant in their own right. However, the work is an interesting if not entirely successful example of the way in which traditional material and sometimes literary models fused with historical and pseudo-historical matter at this period. Lohengrin is a member of the Grail family, but his mission in this poem is a broad political one: to support the Empire, and to fight on the Christian side for the great imperial order under the historical Heinrich I in a fictional battle against the heathens. There is no denying the resemblance to Wolfram's *Willehalm* in the two parallel battles, and, form apart, one senses the impact of Wolfram in the language and presentation of the material, though hardly, it must be said, in the overall achievement. When the author speaks, in strophe 764, of the elegant style of "der von Eschenbach," who adorns his words with abundant wit, one wonders if he is thinking of the Wolfram of *Parzival* and *Willehalm*, or the spurious Wolfram of *Der Jüngere Titurel*. Like many of his contemporaries, it seems, he may not have been able to distinguish between them (see p. 381 ff.).

The lengthy account of imperial history which runs from strophe 731 to 762, with the recital of the names of the German kings, owes more to the earnest tone of Albrecht than to the fantasy of Wolfram von Eschenbach. The culmination of the list in the name of Heinrich II, the last emperor to come from the House of Wittelsbach (1002-1024), supports the view that the poem was composed for the Bavarian court in Munich. It is more than likely that its patron was the Bavarian duke who had prompted the composition of *Der Jüngere Titurel* and then unaccountably withdrew his support when the work was well advanced. Thomas Cramer, who more than anyone has worked on *Lohengrin* and is responsible for the modern edition, argues that Ludwig II of Bavaria (Ludwig der Strenge) is indeed the patron (p. 179). This is an opinion widely accepted, even by those who would dispute Cramer's dating of the poem (see *Bumke Mäzene*, p. 396, note 96), and it argues for the entirely realistic view of the Wittelsbach court as a stronghold of Wolfram admiration and emulation. It also emphasizes the impression that *Lohengrin* is as much a political statement as a romance. Lohengrin is, after all, the friend and ally of the emperor, and his success stems from that relationship as well as from his own personal qualities. Although not particularly elegant, the poem is a tribute to a royal household, united now through the marriage of Ludwig to Mathilde, daughter of Rudolf, to the reigning house of Habsburg.

For all its literary connections and its political aspirations, *Lohengrin* is probably one of the least successful products of the period, precisely because it is attempting too much and lacks cohesion. The somewhat unwieldy form, sustained throughout by an author not notable for his poetic skill, fails to unite its disparate parts, and, like other works of the period, it is interesting as a phenomenon rather than for any intrinsic qualities. There is some support for the view that the work represents the end of the Arthurian romance as a genre. It cannot be said to have had any tangible impact on later generations, though a version does appear in Ulrich Füetrer's *Buch der Abenteuer* (1473-78). The related fragment *Lorengel* is further evidence of the survival of the story into the 15th Century.

Text:
Cramer, Thomas, ed. *Lohengrin*. Munich: W. Fink, 1971.
Rückert, Heinrich, ed. *Lohengrin, zum erstenmale kritisch herausgegeben und mit Anmerkungen versehen*. Quedlinburg: Basse, 1858.

## *Lohengrin*—Bibliography

See de Boor, *Literaturgesch*. 3,1, pp. 108-115, for some useful comments on the poem.

Cramer, Thomas, "Lohengrin." $VL^2$ 5 (1985) 899-904.

Excellent summary, with bibliography.

Ragotzky, Hedda. "Die Umbildung der Wolfram-Rolle in die Fiktion einer Wolfram-Verfasserschaft im *Lohengrin*: die Demonstration des Leitbilds eines *wîsen meisters* in der Praxis des Erzählvorgangs." In: *Studien zur Wolfram-Rezeption*. Stuttgart: Kohlhammer, 1971. Pp. 83-90.

### Ulrich von Etzenbach: *Alexander* and *Wilhelm von Wenden*

In the earlier critical literature, this author appears as Ulrich von Eschenbach, and, although no relative of Wolfram's, he was almost certainly an admirer of the earlier poet, whose style he approaches more closely than that of his actual contemporaries. Where precisely he came from remains unknown, but it is possible to place him in the general region of northern Bohemia and to pinpoint his activity to the court of Prague in the last quarter of the 13th century. Indeed, both his works can be closely linked with historical figures and circumstances in a way that is not always possible in other cases. Both are substantial poems which appear to have enjoyed a fair degree of popularity in their day, the one a lengthy history, *Alexander,* which goes considerably beyond the version of Rudolf von Ems (see p. 340 ff.), although it seems to have had the same source for its early portions, and the other *Wilhelm von Wenden*, a work in the manner of the legend—and thus also to be viewed perhaps as following in the path of Rudolf von Ems and Konrad von Würzburg—but linked with contemporary events in Bohemia.

*Alexander.* At 28,000 lines, Ulrich von Etzenbach's version of the story of Alexander the Great is the longest work on the subject in German. Although of course the basis is the historical figure of Alexander and the events surrounding his life, as is true for the version by Rudolf von Ems, the inclusion here of descriptions of knightly combat and courtly celebrations, and the greater emphasis on love give it a very different flavor. Supernatural elements play a significant role too, but primarily the work should probably be seen in relation to actual circumstances of its own age. Ulrich himself tells how he was prompted to compose the work by Archbishop Friedrich II of Salzburg, and it was intended to honor the great King Ottokar II who died in 1278. In any event, the poem was not completed until about 1287 and is dedicated to Ottokar's son Wenzel II. Alexander is presented as the great ruler against the background of a glorious court, but increasingly the negative side of his character and, in particular, his insatiable lust for power and his arrogant self-confidence are emphasized, together with familiar expressions of regret at the transient nature of human life and fame. The poem ends with a lament for Alexander which is linked with something much closer to a sermon on the downfall of a man through pride and excess. It is more than likely that one should see here the regret of the poet for the collapse of Ottokar's ambitions and his sudden death.

Similarly closely linked to the court of Prague, where Ulrich seems to have enjoyed considerable respect, is his second poem, *Wilhelm von Wenden*. This is also dedicated to Wenzel II and his wife, Guta, daughter of Rudolf von Habsburg, who arrived in Prague after the marriage in 1287 and died there in 1297. We can thus date the poem to the last decade of the century and see in it quite clearly a very close relationship with actual events. The central figures are an unhistorical ancestor of Wenzel, the heathen Wilhelm, and his wife, whose name, Bene, is the author's version of the name of Queen Guta. As Guta did, so in this legendary tale does Bene bear twin sons. The essential feature of the story is the conversion of Wilhelm and his eventual benevolent rule in Wenden, converted under his influence to Christianity. Clearly, then, the work contained the ingredients to fulfill its intention of honoring the royal pair and the reigning house. The author's reference to "Meister Heinrich der Walsch," who made the story known to him, links it even more closely with the court of Prague, where one Henricus de Iserna, otherwise known as Henricus Italicus, was a very influential figure and may even have commissioned the poem (*Bumke Mäzene*, p. 264).

The events of the story itself contain some of the familiar elements of lives of the saints. Wilhelm sells his twin sons to Christian merchants and leaves his wife, in order to journey to Jerusalem, having heard by chance of Christianity from a group of pilgrims. During the twenty-four years of their separation, the virtuous Bene remains faithful to him and achieves renown as a ruler. When Wilhelm returns in the clothing of a pilgrim, she fails to recognize him but is eager to hear from him about Christian teaching. Meanwhile, their twin sons have grown up and, anxious to find out more about their origins, have come into their mother's land, where, also unrecognized, they have pursued the life of robbers. The poem ends with recognition all round, Wilhelm's accession to the throne, the conversion of the whole country, and, finally, the withdrawal of the royal couple into a monastery.

The poem combines the elevation of the court and its inhabitants with an exhortation to a pious life. The events of the story are interesting, if largely derivative, but the work is unremarkable as a piece of literature. Ulrich was no great poet, though the sincerity of his intention is evident. The interest of both his works lies rather in their relationship with contemporary events. However, a work of the scope of his *Alexander* can hardly be ignored, particularly since it clearly enjoyed a fair degree of popularity, and *Wilhelm von Wenden* is important within a tradition which includes *Die gute Frau*—an anonymous work of the first half of the 13th century which likewise praises piety and chastity and proposes a vision of perfect sovereignty based on exemplary Christian values—but also works as significant as Konrad von Würzburg's *Engelhard* and *Der gute Gerhard* of Rudolf von Ems (see p. 350 ff. and 334 ff.).

Texts:
Toischer, Wendelin, ed. *Alexander*. Tübingen, 1888 (= Bibliothek des Literarischen Vereins in Stuttgart, 183).
Rosenfeld, Hans-Friedrich, ed. *Wilhelm von Wenden* Berlin: Akademie Verlag, 1957 (= DTM, 49).
Sommer, Emil, ed. "*Die gute Frau.*" *ZfdA* 2 (1842): 385-481.

### Ulrich von Etzenbach—Bibliography

Huehne, Margot. *Die Alexanderepen Rudolfs von Ems und Ulrichs von Eschenbach*. Würzburg, 1939.
Rosenfeld, Hans-Friedrich. "Zum Willehalm von Wenden Ulrichs von Eschenbach." *Neophil.* 12 (1927): 173-186.
____. "Zum Alexander-Anhang Ulrichs von Eschenbach." *ZfdA* 68 (1931): 275-283.
Mackinder-Savage, Dennis J. B. "Die gute Frau." *VL*[2] 3 (1981): 328-330.

### *Mai und Beaflor*

Although this poem can hardly be called a "continuation," it is included here because it has some of the legendary traits of *Wilhelm von Wenden* and *Die gute Frau* mentioned above.It is probably from Upper Germany in the latter half of the 13th century and is fairly swiftly dismissed in most of the references. Ehrismann describes it as a courtly legend, pointing to the fact that it is different in structure and tone from the courtly romance: *Den Grundton bildet die heiligende, den Menschen mit Gott vereinende Frömmigkeit* (Sanctifying piety that unites man with God forms the basic tone, *Schlußband* p. 62). In many respects it appears to be a modest successor to *Der arme Heinrich* and *Gregorius*, in thought and language, but there are also distinct echoes of Hartmann's other works and of Wolfram and Gottfried. The poem tells of the suffering of the wrongly accused princess, Beaflor, who belongs in the tradition of Genoveva and Crescentia, whose piety and devotion in the face of injustice are immortalized in legend. Unlike these two women, Beaflor occurs only in this work, based on a story passed on, according to its unknown author, by a knight who had read it in a prose chronicle (3, 15-17).

No source has been discovered for this work which has made little impact on scholarship and is available only in the edition in the series *Dichtungen des deutschen Mittelalters*. Uncertainty has even surrounded the identity of the editor, since no name appears on the title page and the edition was attributed to Franz Pfeiffer who was explicitly responsible for the two preceding editions of *Barlaam und Josaphat* and of *Wigalois*. It is now thought to be the work of Alois J. Vollmer, possibly with Pfeiffer as the author of the preface.

The moralizing tone dominates from the prologue on, when the author makes it clear that his intention is a didactic one, to the happy-ever-after ending which shows good triumphing over evil and the firm assurance of the mercy of God in this life and beyond. Above all it is the humility of Beaflor that is extolled, together with her capacity to endure seemingly intolerable suffering: the intended violation by her father; the jealousy of her mother-in-law who tricks her son into believing that his wife has been unfaithful to him; the years of isolation with her child after her mother-in-law, replacing letters from her son to his young wife, makes a thwarted attempt to have her killed. There is much that is familiar in the narrative: the young innocent setting out to sea in order to avoid the shame of incest; her arrival in a strange land where she marries the handsome young Mai; the devoted guardians; the joyful reunion after years of separation. When Mai realizes the injustice which has been perpetrated in his name, he resolves to atone as a pilgrim and eventually comes to Rome to seek absolution from the pope. Beaflor's faithful guardian effects a reunion of the husband with his devoted wife and the son he has never seen. Mai is elevated to the position of emperor.

Much of this sounds as though it emanates from a mind deeply versed in the courtly literature of many decades before, while the wicked mother-in-law, her mind twisted by jealousy, reminds one of Gerlint in *Kudrun*, who comes to a similarly violent end (see p. 399 ff.). The use of the word *vâlandinne* to describe this monstrous woman is likely to have been borrowed from the *Nibelungenlied* (see p. 205 ff.). Indeed, this is a poet who borrows liberally, to the extent that one doubts whether much of the work can be attributed to his own originality. Clearly such a question cannot be resolved without knowledge of the source, but there are features of the poem which one might view more positively. The poet does seem to have some understanding of human emotions, although the expression of them, like so much of his description, is often prolonged.

There is also something excessive in the geography, which ranges far and wide and lacks coherence. He drops in names of people and places, often picking them up, or so it seems, from his predecessors. He often uses biblical references to support this moral tale and incorporates them wholesale into his narrative.

All that said, it must be stressed that the story itself is a good one, which might have flourished in the hands of a better craftsman. Even as it stands, the poem probably merits closer attention than it has so far received. In particular, perhaps, it might be worthwhile pursuing the comment by Joachim Bumke about the implied criticism of contemporary nobility in it (*Geschichte*, p. 248). For all its debt to the literature of the early part of the century, the poem probably belongs to a much later period, possibly 1270-80, and it is strangely isolated there.

Text:
Vollmer, Alois J., ed. *Mai und Beaflor, eine Erzählung aus dem dreizehnten Jahrhundert.* Leipzig: Göschen, 1848. (The first and only edition of the poem).

## *Mai und Beaflor*—Bibliography

de Boor, Helmut. *Literaturgesch.* 3,1, pp. 103-105.

One of the fullest mentions of the poem in literary histories.

Fechter, Werner. "Mai und Beaflor." In *VL*[2] 5 (1985): 1163-1166.

Leitzmann, Albert. "Mai und Beaflor." *ZfdA* 67 (1930): 283-284.

This brief article, one of the few devoted to the work, concerns the edition and the identification of the editor.

## HEROIC LITERATURE AFTER THE *NIBELUNGENLIED*

The greatest heroic poem of the German Middle Ages is, of course, the *Nibelungenlied* (see p. 205 ff.), but literature in the heroic tradition continued to exist throughout the 13th century, finding its most significant and in many respects puzzling expression in *Kudrun* (see below p. 399 ff.), but also in the proliferation of epics, for the most part anonymous, many of them centering on the figure of Dietrich von Bern and emanating primarily from South Germany. The impact of the *Nibelungenlied* is evident in the language and often in the strophic form of these works, but, in content and ethos, they often also reflect the courtly literature of the early 13th century, and, going back further than that, some of the elements of the *Spielmannsepik* (see p. 106 ff.). They are thus a unique conglomeration of a mixture of influences, yet they belong essentially to this later period. Since they come from a time of transition between oral and written transmission, some of these works exist in a number of versions, often widely divergent.

### Dietrich Epics

The phenomenon of the Dietrich epics probably emerges most clearly if one considers the works as a whole, yet the distinctive qualities of individual works demand their separate treatment. Although there is some substantial scholarly work in this field, there is only a limited amount in English and there are few translations.

For an introduction in English to medieval German heroic poetry, see the all-too-brief but characteristically stimulating chapter by A.T.Hatto in *Traditions of Heroic and Epic Poetry*, Vol. 1. Unfortunately, his treatment of the later developments is relatively slight. The most authoritative and comprehensive survey of the Dietrich literature will be found in the volume by Roswitha Wisniewski in the Metzler Series, while Werner Hoffmann's study of heroic literature is a vital complement to this. The work by Joachim Heinzle in this field is also very important.

Dietrich von Bern, who had found his way as an almost peripheral figure into the *Nibelungenlied*, was a popular hero in the German Middle Ages. The historical source was Theoderic, king of the Ostrogoths from 493 until his death in 526. The one firm fact about his reign is his conquest of Italy, yet this very fact is reversed in popular legend, which has him defeated and fleeing to the Huns. In a further contortion of history, he is made a contemporary of the much earlier Ermanarich and Attila, who were not contemporaries of one another either.

Central to the reputation of the literary figure of Dietrich is his enormous skill in fighting and his courage, coupled with his disposition, peaceful until roused to action. There is also something of an ambivalence in his achievements, since often he seems to fail in spite of his best efforts. The cluster of stories which surround Dietrich link him with his doughty retainer, Hildebrand, the central figure of the great OHG poem (see p. 34 ff.), and Dietrich's stalwart companion in the closing stages of the *Nibelungenlied*. It has been thought that there must have been a single large-scale epic centered on Dietrich, that it is inconceivable that there should not have been, yet none has been found. As it is, a huge collection of Dietrich stories exists in the Old Norse *Thidrekssaga*, compiled in Bergen in about 1250 and apparently embracing all the known German material. There is some support for the view that the very existence of this compilation speaks for an earlier work, or perhaps two earlier works, offering a complete biography of Dietrich in German.

Dietrich scholarship traditionally divides the individual extant works into two groups: the historical epics and the mythical or legendary epics. The first group is based on his battles in pursuit of Italy; the second tells of his trials of strength in other adventures, notably in combat with a variety of subhuman creatures, and, absorbing as it does a wide range of influences, covers a much greater diversity of themes.

### The Historical Epics: *Dietrichs Flucht, Die Rabenschlacht, Alpharts Tod, Dietrich und Wenezlan*

*Dietrichs Flucht* is one of the most substantial works in its group. Otherwise known as *Buch von Bern*, in accordance with its own designation of itself at the end of the poem, it is composed, unlike most of the others, in rhymed couplets, totalling 10,152 lines. It differs in another respect from most of the others by naming an author, one Heinrich der Vogler, an unidentified poet, believed to be Tyrolean and probably from the last decades of the 13th century.

The beginning of the work is devoted to a lengthy account of the genealogy of Dietrich, the central character. His uncle Ermanrich plots to destroy him, along with his other relatives, and forces him into exile from Bern (Verona). Together with his good friend Hildebrand, Dietrich goes to the court of Etzel the Hun, where he receives the support to take Bern back by force. He allies himself with the Hunnish court through marriage with a relative of Etzel's own wife, Helche. A second campaign is launched when Raben (Ravenna) comes under attack from Ermanrich. Once again Dietrich is victorious, but he suffers immense losses, not least of which are some of his personal friends. The work closes with his return to Etzel's court.

This brief summary of the plot can give no idea of the details of this long and rather tedious work, but it emphasizes some of the essential features, in particular the attempt to create a parallel structure, possibly in accordance with the structure of the courtly romance. The lengthy account of Dietrich's antecedents suggests at least as great an interest in this more legendary material, which embraces the slaying of a dragon, wooing expeditions, and Dietrich's father's living for 340 years, as in the more historical matter which succeeds it. The conflict between good and bad, and specifically between loyalty and treachery, is highlighted, although there is no real sense in which good ultimately triumphs.

*Die Rabenschlacht* follows *Dietrichs Flucht* in all four of the complete manuscripts and appears to have been conceived as a companion poem to it. It is unlikely that it is by the same person, and it may even have been composed earlier. In the absence of convincing evidence, the best one can say is that it, too, belongs in the latter half of the 13th century.

The distinctive quality of the poem is evident already in its metrical form, a unique mixture of long and short lines, reminiscent simultaneously of the *Nibelungenlied* and of *Kudrun*. With this complex form, which he does not succeed in maintaining throughout, the poet appears to be making some kind of statement: on the one hand, he is composing very much within the heroic tradition, and on the other hand he stands alone.

Essentially, this work tells of Dietrich's attempt to recover his territory in Italy. Its focus is that same battle of Ravenna at which he had defeated Ermanrich in *Dietrichs Flucht*. He is accompanied by Etzel's two sons, who perish when they go against his express orders and ride off alone. Thus, when he returns victorious to Etzel's court, he must contend with his own grief and the bitter reproaches of Queen Helche. The place of such human interest and emotion in the poem lifts it out of the normal framework of these heroic works, but the poet is in general not skilled enough to handle his quite original conception of his material, any more than he is capable of sustaining his metrical form.

*Alpharts Tod.* Both *Dietrichs Flucht* and *Die Rabenschlacht* allude to the death of Alphart, the first telling of his death and the revenge taken for it by Dietrich himself, and the second of Dietrich's lament for him. This poem has the gallant young Alphart at the core of the first part of the narrative, which relates his death at the hand—in this version—of Witege and Heime. The second part of the work, which follows after a gap in the manuscript, has Hildebrand as the central figure, as he amasses forces on behalf of Dietrich. Alphart is recalled in the lamentation at his grave.

The interest of this poem, which benefits, despite its incomplete state, from the hand of a more accomplished poet, lies in the juxtaposition of the two central characters, the impetuous young Alphart who perishes in consequence of the less-than-heroic behavior of his adversaries, and the circumspect Hildebrand. The "whole" poem stands between two ages, with Alphart the representative of the new age of chivalry, albeit one whose ethos is brought into question, and Hildebrand deeply rooted in the older heroic tradition. In accordance with this blending of literary and cultural traditions is the mixture within the poem of the forms of the *Nibelungenlied* and the *Hildebrandslied*. The early opinion that the work belonged to the very early 13th century, although understandable in view of its essentially transitional qualities, is now generally disregarded, and *Alpharts Tod* is assigned, like the other works treated, to the second half of the century.

*Dietrich und Wenezlan* is extant in just one manuscript, in which the beginning and end of the poem are missing and there is a gap in the middle. It is thus not very easy to reconstruct the narrative, but the action clearly belongs within the story of Dietrich's flight and exile at the court of Etzel. Dietrich is challenged to combat with King Wenezlan of Poland and accepts, in the hope of securing the release of two of his trusted men, Hildebrand and Wolfhart, who have been taken captive by Wenezlan. Accompanied by Etzel himself, Dietrich rides out to participate in this event which evolves into something much closer to a courtly tournament, with the ladies watching the men fighting.

The suggestion that the Wenezlan of this fragment was to be identified with King Wenzel II of Bohemia and later of Poland was rendered invalid when a much earlier date was accepted for it. If, as is now generally believed, the fragment belongs to the first half of the 13th century, it is likely that King Wenzel I of Bohemia was the model for Dietrich's opponent here and that the work emanated from his court (see *Bumke Mäzene*, p. 186 ff.).

Texts:
Martin, Ernst, ed. *Dietrichs Flucht*. In: *Deutsches Heldenbuch*, Vol. 2. Berlin: Weidmann, 1866. Pp. 55-215.
____, ed. *Rabenschlacht*. op. cit. pp. 217-264.
Zimmer, Uwe, ed. *Alpharts Tod. Studien zu Alpharts Tod nebst einem verbesserten Abdruck der Handschrift*. Göppingen: Kümmerle, 1972 (= GAG, 67).
Zupitza, Julius, ed. *Dietrich und Wenezlan*. In: *Deutsches Heldenbuch*, Vol. 5. Berlin: Weidmann, 1870. Pp. 265-274.

## The Mythical/Legendary Epics: *Eckenlied, Sigenot, Goldemar, Virginal, Laurin, Der Rosengarten zu Worms, Biterolf und Dietleib*

Apparently enjoying a much greater popularity than the "historical" Dietrich epics in the Middle Ages is the other group, described in English as "mythical" or "legendary," in German as *märchenhaft* or sometimes *aventiurenhaft*. All these designations convey the essential spirit of these works, which celebrate the figure of Dietrich, as do the others, for his strength and courage but emphasize also his larger-than-life qualities which often lead him into exaggerated situations and sometimes comic escapades. In this respect they bear more resemblance to some of the adventures described in the later courtly romances, with possibly some influence from the *chansons de geste*. Undoubtedly behind them lies a tradition which saw Dietrich as a superhuman figure with mythical origins, a tradition which may have had its source in very old stories of the young Dietrich's being freed from the clutches of monstrous creatures, his defeat of dragons, his acquisition of strange powers and magic accessories. In some traditions, the negative aspects of his nature were attributed to the influence of the devil.

The *Eckenlied* is the oldest example of this category of Dietrich epic, probably dating from the early 13th century and enjoying considerable popularity throughout the Middle Ages and right up to the 16th century, when it was printed. The fact that the work was at one time attributed to Konrad von Würzburg speaks for the skill of its execution, although the suggestion has long since been dismissed. The form is a characteristic 13-line strophe, quite complicated in its detail, and known as the *Bernerton*, or sometimes more specifically, as the *Eckenweise*.

There are a number of versions of this work, varying in length, but the essential details are the same. The young giant Ecke goes out in search of Dietrich on behalf of three princesses who have heard of him and wish to meet him. In the fierce combat that ensues between Ecke and Dietrich, Ecke is slain, and Dietrich brings his head back to the princesses. Beyond this basic plot, the versions vary considerably, but the poem in all its MHG forms raises important questions about the substance and its intention. It contains courtly elements certainly, but these exist side by side with older features which belong not so much to the heroic tradition as to the darker and more obscure realm of legend.

*Sigenot*, composed in the same meter as the *Eckenlied*, is closely linked to it and was apparently conceived as an introduction to it. This tells a similar story, of Dietrich's encounter with the giant Sigenot who strikes him down and hurls him into a rocky cave in the mountains, intending to claim Bern for himself. On the way he meets Hildebrand, who believes his master is dead. They fight and Sigenot is killed. Hildebrand manages to free Dietrich, but only with the help of a dwarf who supplies a ladder, and not until Hildebrand has upbraided his master for his foolhardiness. They journey together back to Bern, and the poet concludes with a trailer to the *Eckenlied*. Like the *Eckenlied*, the *Sigenot* must have aroused considerable interest, although there is only one extant manuscript of this early version: its content was considerably expanded in the so-called *Jüngerer Sigenot*, a much longer version of the same story (200 strophes as compared with 40), and by 1661 this poem had been printed 20 times.

*Goldemar*. The heroic tradition is linked not surprisingly with the courtly ideal of love in the Dietrich poems. This is the case with the tiny fragment *Goldemar* which has Dietrich in the role of knight rescuing, or attempting to rescue, a lady in distress. She has been abducted by dwarfs, the leader of whom, Goldemar, declines to fight with Dietrich. The outcome of the encounter is lost to us. The fragment is frustrating on other counts, too, since it would appear that its author, who names himself as *von kemmenaten Albreht*, a name which appears in the two literary lists of Rudolf von Ems (see p. 340), was a gifted poet, who, by the time Rudolf was writing, had achieved a high degree of recognition. This has led to the suggestion that the author of *Goldemar* was also the author of the other three Siegfried poems composed in the Bernerton (*Sigenot, Eckenlied, Vir-*

*ginal*), and that this fragment was indeed his first attempt at a very complex strophic form. Against this suggestion is the very marked difference in tone between *Goldemar* and the other three poems, and the significant fact that, contrary to all custom, the poet names himself here but not in the other three. Thus the fragment raises issues out of proportion to its intrinsic significance.

*Virginal*. Despite some of the arguments which were once put forward to link *Goldemar* with *Virginal*, it is now agreed that they cannot have been by the same person and that *Virginal* is considerably later and almost certainly composed under the influence of Konrad von Würzburg, though not, as was also once suggested, by him. That the two poems have in common the appearance of Dietrich von Bern as a knight, albeit in *Virginal* a knight only just beginning to learn his craft and unconvinced by the validity of *âventiure*, is undeniable. The poem is also sometimes called *Dietrichs erste Ausfahrt* (Dietrich's first excursion), for in it Dietrich does indeed go out for the first time, in search of the *âventiure* he has only just heard about. The central adventure concerns his rescue of Queen Virginal from a giant, and in one of the two versions, he marries her and takes her back with him to Bern. In the other, he returns to Bern alone. In both cases he has demonstrated his worth as a knight by means of a complicated series of adventures. This is a different Dietrich from the Dietrich of some of the other poems, coming to grips with different issues, learning the meaning of *âventiure*, and comprehending the role of love-service in his progress towards his goal which nevertheless remains essentially that of the heroic leader.

*Laurin* enjoyed exceptional popularity in the Middle Ages, it seems, and it also has echoes in the modern period, with the reference to the rose garden in Gerhart Hauptmann's poem "Die blaue Blume," and in Peter Hacks's novella, *Geschichte vom König Laurin*. The anonymous author is thought to have been Tyrolean, and the dating of the poem, though controversial and ranging between 1170 and 1250, tends now towards a later rather than an earlier composition, with the suggestion that there may have been an earlier, oral version of the tale.

Although the poem is usually classed within the legendary Dietrich cycle, it differs in some important aspects from most of the other examples. For one thing, it is composed in rhymed couplets, while, as we have seen, the strophic form was favored by the other poets. For another, the central figure is the dwarf Laurin, rather than Dietrich. With the exception of Laurin himself, and his "bride" Künhilde, the characters in the poem—figures like Witege, Wolfhart, Hildebrand, Dietleib, and of course Dietrich himself—would have needed no introduction and the bravery of their exploits would have been part and parcel of their reputation, but central to the action this time is Laurin, an ambivalent figure who wavers between the positive and the negative.

The poem relates essentially two episodes which are separate yet linked, the invasion of the garden and the abduction of Künhilde, sister of Dietleib. After much action, some of it quite violent, the poem is resolved by the baptism of Laurin and his pledge of lasting friendship with Dietrich. Magic elements dominate: the magic ring which reveals the enemy, the magic cloak which renders the wearer invisible; and the whole idea of the lovely rose garden, surrounded by a boundary which is broken by the outsider and the peace of the garden invaded.

The obvious heroic elements mingle with features of the courtly: the treatment of the ladies and the description of festivities are among the more obvious examples. There are marked literary echoes, particularly of Hartmann's *Iwein*, with the description of the tranquillity of the garden, and the disturbance from outside which provokes a violent response, reminiscent of Kalogrenant's story. The dwarf-king may have been prompted by Guivreiz in *Erec*. At times there are distinct verbal echoes of Hartmann's work, which speak, of course, for the later dating.

The origin of the idea of the rose garden has been explained as an attempt to account for a natural phenomenon, the effect of the evening sun on the limestone of the Dolomites. In essence, then, the idea may go back way beyond the 13th century, with this work the first literary expression of an established idea.

*Der Rosengarten zu Worms* is traditionally included among these mythical Dietrich poems. It is a story which appears in a number of versions of very variable length and which clearly also has links with the theme of the magic rose garden of *Laurin*. Once more the role of Dietrich is not really the central one, although again his activity is central to the progress of the plot. This time it is Kriemhild, or in one version her father, who is the principal instigator of events, when she issues a challenge to Dietrich to prove whether he or Siegfried is the superior warrior. In the combats which ensue between the men from Worms on the one hand and the men from Bern on the other, Dietrich's men are all victorious, until in the ultimate combat between Siegfried and Dietrich, the latter wins by virtue of his fiery breath, which penetrates even the famous horny skin.

Clearly, then, the *Nibelungen* tradition and the Dietrich legends collide in this group of versions of essentially the same story, in which version A and version D are the most significant, composed possibly three decades apart, between about 1250 and 1280. The Kriemhild of this story is the *vâlandinne* (she-devil) of the *Nibelungenlied*, ruthless in her arrogance and her readiness to sacrifice human lives on the basis of a whim. That a woman can issue this challenge, not, as her pretext implies, in order to bestow her roses and her kisses on the victors but out of sheer enjoyment at seeing men do her bidding is a crucial ingredient of this poem. The men react with anger and indignation rather than accept the prize offered by a beautiful woman. As if to intensify this impression of ruthless blood lust and perhaps also to offer an element of burlesque comedy, the poet has introduced the bizarre figure of the monk Islan, Hildebrand's brother, who is summoned from his monastery to join the expedition to the rose garden and who returns having received fifty-two of Kriemhild's kisses and bringing with him fifty-two of her roses, one each for his fellow monks, on whose heads he presses them until they bleed. This grotesque conclusion matches the earlier moment when the monk receives her kiss and scratches her face with his stubbly beard, drawing blood. After all this, the attempt by the poet to suggest some kind of remorse and conversion on the part of Kriemhild rings rather hollow.

***Biterolf und Dietleib*** is a lengthy epic, probably of about the same period, and equally mixed in tone. It also cedes the central position to characters other than Dietrich, whose role is more that of mediator than of instigator or active participant. This time it is Biterolf, king of Toledo, who goes to Etzel's court in search of adventure. In an encounter which links motifs from the courtly romance and the tragic tradition best exemplified in the *Hildebrandslied* (see p. 34 ff.), his son Dietleib grows up and sets out to find his father but, not recognizing him when he meets him at Etzel's court, launches into combat with him. Only the intervention of Dietrich prevents the imminent tragedy. There follows a somewhat unconnected second part of the poem, in which Etzel amasses a revenging army against King Gunther in Worms. This campaign necessitates a series of combats which includes an inconclusive one between Dietrich and, here too, Siegfried. The lengthy closing stages of the poem bring into action characters familiar above all from the *Nibelungenlied* as well as motifs seemingly borrowed from that poem, like the accusation of cowardice leveled at Dietrich by none other than Hildebrand, who is lucky to escape with his life. Unlike the *Nibelungenlied*, the poem dissolves eventually into peace and reconciliation but not before mass conflict and slaughter have taken place.

The poem is structurally unsatisfactory, with the theme of revenge ill motivated. The whole poem is a mass of somewhat discordant motifs, with courtly and heroic mixed together, and a final political message seeming to be its ultimate intention: the praise of Steiermark which comes close to the end of the poem and is underlined when Biterolf and Dietleib are given Steiermark in fief.

### *Ortnit* and *Wolfdietrich*

It is appropriate to attach to our consideration of the Dietrich poems two other works, which do not strictly speaking belong to the Dietrich cycle but were juxtaposed with one another in the manuscripts and often even placed at the head of the Dietrich stories. *Ortnit* and *Wolfdietrich* both belong to the first half of the 13th century, and they appear to be the surviving remnants of a cycle which may have been comparable to that of Dietrich von Bern. Indeed, the story of Wolfdietrich is linked with that of Dietrich inasmuch as the former is identified as the ancestor of the latter. *Ortnit* and *Wolfdietrich* overlap in content to some extent: Ortnit is slain by a dragon in the work which essentially tells his history, and Wolfdietrich, in the poem, or rather the various versions of the poem, devoted to him, avenges Ortnit and marries his widow. Both works abound in elements taken from a wide spectrum of literary sources, mingling heroic and courtly elements with motifs from legend and fairy-tale type stories in a way that seems to have appealed to the public for which they were intended.

*Ortnit* tells of a young Christian prince who sets his heart on winning a beautiful heathen princess whose father protects his daughter from all suitors by killing any man who approaches her. Ortnit discovers that he is the son of the dwarf Alberich, who supplies him with a sword and a fine suit of armor and, having rendered himself invisible, aids his son in his wooing expedition. The marriage of Ortnit with his now-baptized princess is short lived, however. Her father tricks them into thinking that he is well disposed to them and sends them two dragons' eggs as choice gifts. When they hatch out, the dragons prowl the land causing chaos until Ortnit himself resolves to slay them but dies in the attempt.

The unheroic death of Ortnit was presumably acceptable only if the poem could be seen in relation to *Wolfdietrich*, and it is likely that at least part of the latter poem, in its oldest form known as *Wolfdietrich A*, was composed by the same person, using the same strophic form, the *Hildebrandston*. This version is not complete, but the ending can be supplied by other, later versions. The story is a much more complicated one in detail, but essentially it tells of the third son of Hugdietrich, king of Constantinople. When the idea is put into the king's head that this boy is the child of the devil, he orders him to be killed, but the child is saved from his fate and escapes the hazards of the forest, where he is brought up with the name of Wolfdietrich. When, on the death of his father, he is deprived of his inheritance by his two brothers, both called Dietrich, he seeks help from Ortnit, only to discover that he has just been slain by the dragons. He kills them and marries Ortnit's widow and returns to Constantinople where he has his brothers put to death. The versions which contain an ending tell of his subsequent withdrawal into a monastery, his kingdom being given into the custody of the sons of the man who saved him from death as a child.

### Walther und Hildegund

Before attempting to draw any conclusions about the survival of heroic poetry in the mid-13th century in Germany, we should mention this quite unconnected fragment, the 57 strophes in the manner of the *Nibelungenlied* which survive of what may well have been a considerable epic about the Walther of the *Waltharius* (see p. 55 ff.). The theme of the exile is a favorite one in heroic literature, and the story of Walther's love for Hildegund and their elopement from the land of the Huns, together with the accounts of his bravery in combat with Gunther and his companions in Worms, was obviously popular. The name of Walther occurs on a number of occasions in the heroic poetry of the 13th century, but it is above all a playful mention by Walther von der Vogelweide which appears to contravene the convention that the lady's name in the Minnesang is kept strictly secret (74,19) which recalls the relationship in the 13th century. The fragment known as *Walther und Hildegund* is tantalizingly slight and gives little away about how this story was told in epic form in the MHG period. That it existed at all is further evidence of the range of material in what one can broadly term heroic literature at this time.

Texts:
Amelung, Arthur, ed. *Ortnit*. In: *Deutsches Heldenbuch*. Vol. 3. Berlin: Weidmann, 1871. Pp. 1-77.
Holz, Georg, ed. *Die Gedichte vom Rosengarten zu Worms*. Halle: Niemeyer, 1893. Repr. Hildesheim/New York, 1982.
_____, ed. *Laurin*. Halle: Niemeyer, 1897.
Schneider, Hermann, ed. *Wolfdietrich A*. Halle: Niemeyer, 1931 (= ATB, 28).
Schnyder, André, ed. *Biterolf und Dietleib*. Bern: Haupt, 1980 (= Sprache und Dichtung, 31).
Strecker, Karl, ed. "Walther und Hildegund." In: *Ekkehard, Waltharius*. 1907. Pp. 100-109.
Zupitza, Julius, ed. *Eckenlied*. In: *Deutsches Heldenbuch*, Vol. 5. Pp. 217-264.
_____, ed. *Goldemar*. op. cit., pp. 201-204.

_____, ed. *Virginal.* op. cit., pp. 1-200.

_____, ed. *Sigenot.* op. cit., pp. 205-215.

Translations:

Thomas, J. Wesley, trans. *'Ortnit' and 'Wolfdietrich:' Two Medieval Romances.* Columbia, SC: Camden House, 1986 (Engl. trans. with useful introduction).

Facsimile:

Heinzle, Joachim, ed. *Heldenbuch. Nach dem ältesten Druck hrsg. von J. H.* Göppingen: Kümmerle, 1981 (= Litterae 75).

### Dietrich Epics—Bibliography

de Boor, Helmut. *Literaturgesch.*, 3,1. Chapter 4, pp. 136-186.

Contains a detailed survey of the heroic poetry.

Hatto, Arthur T. "Medieval German." In: *Traditions of Heroic and Epic Poetry*, Vol. 1, under the general editorship of A.T. Hatto. London: The Modern Humanities Research Association, 1980. Pp. 166-195.

Heinzle, Joachim. *Mittelhochdeutsche Dietrichepik. Untersuchungen zur Tradierungsweise, Überlieferungskritik und Gattungsgeschichte später Heldendichtung.* Munich: Artemis, 1978.

A very thorough, useful basic study of the genre.

_____. "Dietrich von Bern." In: *Epische Stoffe des Mittelalters.* Ed. by Volker Mertens and Ulrich Müller. Stuttgart: Kröner, 1984. Pp. 141-155.

Hoffmann, Werner. *Mittelhochdeutsche Heldendichtung.* Berlin: Erich Schmidt, 1974 (= GLG, 14).

Wisniewski, Roswitha. *Mittelalterliche Dietrichdichtung.* Stuttgart: Metzler, 1986 (= Sammlung Metzler, 205).

Excellent concise exposition of the genre with good bibliography.

## *Kudrun*

The reasons for the decline of German heroic literature and, coupled with this, the poor transmission of so much of what did exist remain as problems. In many ways this kind of literature was out of tune with its age, something which could already be discerned in the attempts of the poet of the *Nibelungenlied* to clothe his work in the superficial trappings of the court (see p. 205 ff.). In doing so he had created a work of towering stature which had its roots in the distant past, yet was clearly popular with its contemporary audiences and even managed to transcend chronology by confronting issues which are more human than historical. However, the hand that pieced together the disparate components of the *Nibelungenlied* belonged to a master of narrative, who employed technical skills and imaginative genius in a way that was not to be repeated. The authors of the works just considered did not belong in the same class, although occasionally one glimpses gifts which either remained unfulfilled or were not handed down in any tangible form. The figure of Dietrich von Bern apparently continued to exercise a fascination throughout the 13th century, yet his exploits are recorded in a diffuse and somewhat contradictory way. Literary expectations had moved on, as is clear from the study of other works of the century, and the significant achievements in Germany in the decades which followed the *Nibelungenlied* are of a very different nature and aimed to please an expanding and changing public. Heroic literature, even dressed up to satisfy a courtly audience, had become even more of an anachronism than the *Nibelungenlied* in its own day. A more appropriate question than why German heroic literature declined might be how it came to survive for so long.

Such speculation leads us to the single most significant post-*Nibelungenlied* example of heroic literature, the isolated and in many ways very puzzling *Kudrun*. Yet even this initial designation is controversial, and some critics have declined to put it into the category of "heroic literature" emphasizing those qualities which link it more closely to the romance. However, there are those who would question the desirability of applying the term to the *Nibelungenlied* itself (see p. 205 f.), and probably one must concede that, if a single description is required, then "heroic epic" comes closest to characterizing both poems. Immediately we are engaging in one of the most frequent activities of *Kudrun* scholarship, juxtaposing it to its great predecessor and running the risk of comparing it unfavorably. Although it is probably right to conjecture that *Kudrun* owes its existence to the existence of the *Nibelungenlied* and that there is some force to the argument that it was conceived as a kind of anti-*Nibelungenlied*, close study of the work reveals its intrinsic interest and individuality. That this is so may perhaps be suggested by the fact that, quite by coincidence, three translations into English appeared recently within five years, each with its distinctive introduction (see: Translations).

On the other hand, there is evidence to suggest that the poem was not well received in its own time. The only manuscript is that contained in the *Ambraser Heldenbuch* (see p. 135), where the work appears together with the *Nibelungenlied, Dietrichs Flucht, Rabenschlacht, Biterolf, Ortnit* and *Wolfdietrich A*, firm evidence of how it was classified in the mind of the late Middle Ages. The text is legible enough, but it presents considerable problems which have been resolved by the decisions of successive editors to emend, transpose strophes, and even supply phrases from elsewhere, notably from the *Nibelungenlied*. Our reading of the poem today may thus be some way from its original conception, believed to have been by a Bavarian or Austrian poet, probably about 1230-1240. Always bearing in mind the difficulties attached to this text, there are some excellent editions of the poem, as indicated in our bibliography, and anyone intent on the serious study of *Kudrun* should also use the painstakingly produced diplomatic text by Franz Bäuml.

At first sight, *Kudrun* resembles the *Nibelungenlied*, but closer examination of its strophic form reveals a more complex pattern, in which the first two long-lines do indeed match those of the *Nibelungenlied*, with the third and fourth lines resembling the first two lines of Wolfram's *Titurel*-strophe (see p. 192 f.). The effect of the *Kudrun* meter, with its more lingering final line, is thus gentler than that of the *Nibelungenlied*, a feature which accords well with its overall tone. That is not to say, however, that *Kudrun* is lacking in vigor. It, too, is a poem that tells of the passions of human beings, of deep-rooted emotions of love and hatred, jealousy and revenge. It can be read as a political poem, which handles issues of authority and subjugation, or as a statement about the relationships among generations of the same family. Some critics see it first and foremost as a *Frauenroman*, a work which, way ahead of its time, brings women into the forefront of the action and in which the women appear not only as the more dominant sex, but as the more clearly delineated characters. It may be protested that such dominance had already been achieved by Kriemhild, but the difference is that it is not just Kudrun who is the instigator but her mother and grandmother before her in their respective parts of the work. Moreover, the minor women characters are also vividly drawn: the faithful Hildeburc, who suffers alongside Kudrun, the treacherous Hergart who finds it easier to wheedle her way into the heart of one of the enemy and, of course, Gerlint, whose evil behavior earns her the descriptions of *tiuvelinne* (she-devil) and *wülpinne* (she-wolf), possibly in imitation of the abuse hurled at Kriemhild.

Perhaps it is when one finds the echoes of the *Nibelungenlied* in *Kudrun* and senses the extent to which the later author was influenced by the earlier one, that one recognizes the essential differences between the two poems. Above all it is a difference of ethos, and the ethos dictates the outcome in each case. Although the heroic spirit which pervades the adventures of the young Hagen, grandfather of Kudrun, is maintained and handed down to his daughter and thence to her daughter, the validity of that heroic spirit is tempered, perhaps because it is handed down on the female side, with a gentler spirit of reconciliation, and something which, in the last resort, can best be described as Christianity. That does not mean that the men are not heroes in the true sense of the word. They fight with great valor and determination—and the splendid battle scenes are among the most memorable in a poem which is rich in colorful and varied descriptions—but the message of the poem is ultimately of peaceful reconciliation, not the defeatist acceptance of superior power but the conviction that superior strength can afford to be magnanimous, especially when it can best promote its own interests in that way.

Whether contemporary listeners, still very much under the thrall of the *Nibelungenlied*, failed to be impressed by this message or whether, as has been suggested, they failed to respond to a work which lacked a single dominant male hero, it is impossible to conjecture. Nevertheless, *Kudrun* is a work of considerable subtlety, which, at its best, produces some brilliant moments of perceptive description and, ultimately, betrays a clear sense of direction. At times, however, the emphasis on parallels, with the successive generations of the dynasty of Hagen, one battle balancing another, the succession of suitors for the hand of Kudrun, and so on, leads to the impression of repetition in a poet who perhaps lacked the technical skill to fulfill his vision. To say that *Kudrun* takes its lead from the *Nibelungenlied* is a truism which has been amply demonstrated on many levels, of motif and language as well as of thought, but there is evidence of other influences. In the manner of the classical hero, Hagen is abducted by griffins and grows up in the wild. The abduction of the young bride, the pursuit by the father, warriors disguised as merchants, the motif of non-recognition: these elements have their forerunners in the *Spielmannsepik* and in the courtly romance. It is inconceivable that the author of *Kudrun* was not thoroughly familiar with the works of Hartmann and Gottfried, while the impact of Wolfram is very evident, perhaps most particularly of *Willehalm*, in the depiction of a powerful woman, suffering for love and ready to urge an alternative

response to anger and wrong, and in the two parallel battles which constitute a significant structural element in both poems.

Texts:

Bäuml, Franz H. ed. *Kudrun. Die Handschrift.* Berlin: de Gruyter, 1969 (diplomatic edition of the manuscript in the *Ambraser Heldenbuch*).

Stackmann, Karl, ed. *Kudrun, hrsg. von Karl Bartsch.* 5. Auflage, überarbeitet und neu eingeleitet von K. S. Wiesbaden: Brockhaus, 1965. Repr. 1980 (with very useful notes to the text and a detailed introduction).

Symons, B., and Bruno Boesch, eds. *Kudrun, hrsg. von B. Symons.* 4. Auflage bearbeitet von B. B. Tübingen: Niemeyer, 1964 (another modern edition of the text, with notes which refer more to textual variants than Stackmann's edition does).

Translations:

Gibbs, Marion E., and Sidney M. Johnson, trans. *Kudrun.* New York: Garland, 1992 (= GLML, 79,B). Engl. trans. based on Stackmann's text, with extensive introduction and notes.

McConnell, Winder, trans. *Kudrun.* Columbia: Camden House 1992. Engl. transl. following the text in the Ambraser Heldenbuch.

Murdoch, Brian O., trans. *Kudrun.* London: Dent, 1987. Engl. trans. with very helpful introduction and notes.

Neumann, Friedrich, trans. *Kudrun.* Stuttgart: Reclam, 1958 (= UB, 465). MHG text with modern German trans., reworked version of the old verse transl. by Karl Simrock of 1843.

## *Kudrun*—Bibliography

Campbell, Ian R. *Kudrun. A Critical Approach.* Cambridge: Cambridge UP, 1978.

A challenging, controversial interpretation of the poem but well worth reading.

Hoffmann, Werner. *'Kudrun'. Ein Beitrag zur Deutung der nachnibelungischen Heldendichtung.* Stuttgart: Metzler, 1967 (= Germanistische Abhandlungen, 17).

An exhaustive discussion of the characters, followed by discussion of specific prob-
lems, e.g. relationship to *Nibelungenlied.* This was one of the first complete studies of the poem and full of detailed analysis.

McConnell, Winder. *The Epic of Kudrun: A Critical Commentary.* Göppingen: Kümmerle, 1988 (= GAG, 463).

One of the most recent interpretations of the poem, this emphasizes the social aspects of the work and, in particular, the role of women.

Wailes, Stephen L. "The Romance of Kudrun." *Speculum* 58 (1983): 347-367.

A very readable article on the question of the genre of 'Kudrun' and attempting to show that the poem is really a medieval romance by stressing the courtly elements in it. Not totally convincing but well argued.

Wisniewski, Roswitha. *Heldendichtung III: Kudrun.* Stuttgart: Metzler, 1963, rev. ed. 1969 (= Sammlung Metzler, 32).

Excellent, concise introduction to *Kudrun* and concise orientation in the scholarship but only to 1969.

For further bibliography, see K. Stackmann, $VL^2$ 5 (1984) 410-426, and the introductions to any of the translations.

## Wernher der Gartenære: *(Meier) Helmbrecht*

Even though one may be tempted to retain the shorthand terms of "courtly" and "heroic" to describe some of the narratives of the 13th century, what emerges is how ambivalent these designations are and how varied the literature of this period. Within the broad oeuvre of Rudolf von Ems and Konrad von Würzburg, we saw a great deal of variety and a certain amount of experimentation. We now continue in this ambivalence with a work which stands generically very much on its own and is also very much a product of the prevailing social upheaval: *Meier Helmbrecht* by Wernher der Gartenære.

For a number of reasons this poem, only 1934 lines long, commands a great deal of interest among scholars, and it is often used to introduce more general readers to the literature of the period. Indeed, it may be that it arouses greater enthusiasm among modern readers than it did within the possibly rather restricted public for which it was intended, and the reasons for this discrepancy are not hard to find. This is an absorbing story brilliantly told, but Wernher does not mince his words and he drives a hard message home.

There are only two manuscripts surviving, and both are very much later than the original composition, somewhere in the second half of the 13th century. Early editors assumed that both manuscripts were based on a common source, but this assumption has been dismissed more recently, notably by Kurt Ruh in his revision of the frequently reprinted edition by Friedrich Panzer and, quite adamantly, by the poem's most recent editor, Ulrich Seelbach. Once again, we have to thank the Emperor Maximilian for the survival of the poem in the *Ambraser Heldenbuch* (Ms. A), but it survives also in the early 15th century Leombach Manuscript (B), along with Albrecht's *Jüngerer Titurel* (see p. 381 f.). Although the principal editors have agreed in regarding A as the leading manuscript, they have also taken account of B, bearing in mind that the methods of the two copyists were different. Hans Ried, the scribe of the *Ambraser Heldenbuch*, was little more than a conscientious copyist, but the Leombach scribe was much more inclined to think about what he was copying and to take liberties from time to time as he saw fit. The closing lines (1923-1934) are contained only in A, and 1923-1930 are usually attributed to a scribe rather than to Wernher himself. However, precisely because Hans Ried was not given to inventing, it is assumed that they must have been present in his model. They do little more than repeat in rather clumsy fashion the warning which Wernher has just given to young people to avoid the fate of Helmbrecht. The last four lines in A name Wernher and contain a brief conventional plea for God's mercy on him and whoever recites the poem.

If we begin with the end of the poem, we are faced with one of the central issues, the problem of the identity of Wernher der Gartenære. Was he, as some earlier critics thought, really a gardener, perhaps a prelate entrusted with the upkeep of the monastery garden? This colorful idea has been dismissed in more recent research, which is more inclined to think of him as a layman, with education which could have been acquired in the church by the later 13th century by one who was neither destined to be a cleric nor of the higher nobility, a status which he himself actually denies (864-866). He talks about travelling from place to place, and he envies Helmbrecht for the reception which he is given when he returns to his home on the first occasion, unlike, he says, any reception *he* has ever received. Some have taken such passages as evidence that he may have been a wandering minstrel, though they do not necessarily point to this conclusion since, like his relationship to his audience and his assertion of the truth of what he is saying, such personal comments are part of a tradition of narrative.

Recent research by Ulrich Seelbach has focused on the idea that the poem was performed before a select audience at the court of Duke Heinrich XIII of Lower Bavaria, in Burghausen, and this location, together with the suggestion that Wernher had some kind of position as an occasional poet there, has been convincingly argued also by Linda Parshall. The findings are important, because, precisely in the case of *Helmbrecht*, the question of the intended original audience cannot be divorced from the interpretation of the substance of the work. Whether one can go so far as to date the poem to the summer of 1268, as Linda Parshall does, following Ulrich Seelbach, and base the specific dating on the known fact that Ludwig of Bavaria was visiting his brother Heinrich at Burghausen at that time, is less sure, although probably no one would now argue against a date of about 1260-1270.

There was almost certainly no title on the original manuscript, but both A and B bear a title, in each case of a later date than the manuscript itself. A describes the work which follows as "the book of farmer Helmbrecht," while B says that it is about to tell "the story of the fool and cheat Helmbrecht." Although traditionally the poem has been called *Meier Helmbrecht*, it probably makes better sense to call it simply *Helmbrecht*, as modern editors tend to do. It is actually the story of *both* Helmbrechts, but, although the father, Farmer Helmbrecht, has a central role to play, not least in drawing the moral, the antics and the dreadful end of young Helmbrecht constitute the true action of the poem.

Wernher begins his poem without ado: this is to be the account of a personal experience, something which he saw with his own eyes. In the absence of any literary model for the poem, it has been suggested that it may well be based on a true happening, although it is generally accepted that the inspiration for Helmbrecht himself was a song by Neidhart (see p. 280), in which he told of a young peasant with ideas above his station, whose foppish ways and social aspirations are expressed in the showy cap which crowns his golden locks. The fate of the cap in each case is symbolic of the downfall of the peasant who has forsaken his true station in life, but Neidhart's thirty-two lines (85,38-86,30) are characterized by light-hearted mockery, very different from the sense of doom which pervades Wernher's work and culminates in the grisly account of the terrible outcome that awaits young Helmbrecht. In no way can the song be regarded as a source in any usual sense of the term, although it may well have provided this germ of an idea to illustrate a much larger issue.

Wernher's poem is quite clearly a cautionary tale, and when he focuses immediately on the cap, he emphasizes the importance of this symbol of Helmbrecht's inappropriate aspirations: "Alas," he says, "that ever any peasant should have worn such a cap!" (54-55). Initially he is described as "a fool," "a simpleton," "an idiot." It is totally incongruous that a peasant should parade himself in this richly decorated head-gear on flowing curls. It was, moreover, against the law in a society which was very conscious of social divisions. The perils attendant upon stepping outside one's proper station are already signalled: the cap was sewn by a nun who had deserted her vocation, lured by the attractions of the court but now reduced to sewing for her supper. Depicted on it are scenes from courtly life, details from tales of the past ranging from the siege of Troy to the exploits of Charlemagne: they have as little place upon the head of a peasant as in the hands of the runaway nun.

Helmbrecht's sartorial excesses do not stop at his cap, of course. No expense is spared as his mother and his sister deck him out in the richest and most elaborate of clothing, significantly the kind of clothing which would grace any knight but which clearly does not suit him at all. The malleable women are contrasted with the father who, with his feet firmly on the ground, foresees disaster if his son persists in his ambition of going to court: "Give this idea up," he urges him, "the ways of the court are hard for those who have not been brought up to it" (242-246). Yet, even so, he provides him with a horse, making considerable personal sacrifices to do so.

Wernher draws a sharp contrast between the flippant, self-centered son and the loving father whose honor consists in remaining in his rightful place in society. Much of the poem is taken up with the conversations between these two, and there are strong dramatic elements in these scenes, as they adopt diametrically opposed attitudes and show themselves increasingly as they are. Although Wernher does not refer to any literary antecedents, beyond what sounds like a traditional tribute to Neidhart (217-220), it is not difficult to discern the traces of Hartmann's *Gregorius*, in the debate between the young man and the wise advisor who wishes to restrain him from setting out on a potentially hazardous, because inappropriate, pathway, or of Wolfram's Parzival, who received very different treatment at the hands of his mother when he wished to become a knight. In Parzival's case, the clothing of a fool barely conceals his natural courtesy, while in Helmbrecht's, the fool beneath the knightly trappings is the true nature which will lead him to his premature and terrible end.

The word *tump* is used to describe Helmbrecht (106), but it lacks the deeper connotation associated with the young Parzival, who is also *tump,* young and inexperienced, but who will learn. Helmbrecht rejects the advice of his father, and his "mentors" will be robbers and ruffians who will guide him to his doom. Like Gregorius and like Parzival, Helmbrecht sees the acquisition of a horse as being the vital next step towards the fulfillment of his ambition to go to court. The language is often reminiscent of those predecessors, but it is used with grim irony and linked with the language associated with the life which he is rejecting. When his legs and feet are finely clad (*gezieret*, 320), no one will guess that his previous work has been driving oxen or putting up fences. When he scoffs at the prospect of marrying the daughter of the neighboring farmer, he does so in language which must surely have struck a chord with the listeners: he is not going to laze around wasting his time, as Hartmann's Erec did, for the sake of a woman (328).

For all these echoes, however, *Helmbrecht* stands very much on its own, and the difficulty of assigning it to any known genre has taxed critics who like to give works a label. It has been called, somewhat anachronistically, a *Dorfgeschichte* (country tale) and a novella; some see it as a kind of exemplum; it does not really fall into the category of epic, even if one modifies the term with the adjective "short." The German term *Märe* probably suits it as well as most: it is a short tale with a didactic intention. Yet it verges at times on drama, for which, at that period in German literary history, there were no prototypes.

However, elusive though the work may be when it comes to defining it generically, the quality of the narrative is not a matter for any dispute. Wernher tells his story with considerable power, moving easily between humor, albeit mostly black humor, and a serious, didactic tone, with occasional echoes of a sermon. Above all through the figure of the father, he pushes his message home: no good will come of young Helmbrecht's ill-judged ambitions, and, when the boy returns blind and maimed, the father turns him away, sending him away from the home which he has so despised and out into a world where he will be strung up by his own kind, the peasants whom he has rejected and abused. This is no story of the Prodigal Son, though at one time it may seem to be heading that way. There is no sanctuary for a ruthless young man who can mock at his worthy parents and walk out on their way of life and even lead his sister—not entirely against her will—into a catastrophic marriage with one of his robber friends.

The harsh message has been uttered all along in the predictions of the desperate father, recounting his terrible dreams which come true one by one, and in his ominous words to his son, that he should take care of his cap and the silk doves on it (429-430). This symbol of his arrogance will be hacked to pieces by the avenging peasants at the end of the poem, and those same doves will lie strewn on the road, along with all the other birds which adorned the cap, and with the remnants of Helmbrecht's lovely hair (1886-1891). Once more, the old father's words return to accentuate the fulfillment of the inevitable, for the peasants cry out to him, too, to take care of his cap, but now it is too late.

The central message seems unambiguous enough. "Good rarely comes to him who strives against his proper station: your status is the plow," the father tells the son, when he is desperately trying to dissuade him from his foolhardy enterprise (289-291). Helmbrecht comes to his grisly end because he has stepped outside the limits, but it is not as simple as that, and the numerous scholarly studies of the poem demonstrate its subtlety.

Father Helmbrecht knows, even as he muses about the courtly standards of bygone days, that things are not the same any more (913 ff.): the contrast between past and present can be summed up in his assertion that the wise man is the one who knows how to lie and cheat, for such a man is honored at the court today (974-980). The "court" at which Helmbrecht finds a place is the household of a robber knight, and he becomes a member of a disreputable gang which goes about the country on marauding expeditions. His confederates bear hideous names, comic in his recital of them, but all expressing the violence and rapacity which is their ethos: his own new name is Slintezgeu (gobbler up of land), a far cry from his real name, Helmbrecht, handed down from his father and grandfather before him and symbolizing the solid family traditions which he throws away. The gifts that he brings to impress his family are clearly selected from his loot. When he arrives home again after a year spent rampaging through the land, his family fails to recognize this visitor who aims to impress them with garbled greetings in unknown languages. It is only when he is able to name the four family oxen that he identifies himself to them, and at that their hospitality knows no bounds.

All this is told with a fine sense of detail and considerable comic effect, but the somber meaning is not concealed. When Helmbrecht leaves his home a second time, against the advice of his father, he severs all bonds with home and family, and confirms his adherence to his assumed lifestyle. That there is no going back for him now is underlined when he persuades his sister to accompany him to become the bride of his friend, the robber who rejoices in the name of Lemberslint (swallower of lambs). There ensues a riotous wedding celebration, full of broad humor but with an underlying sense of threat. Wernher peoples the congregation with the traditional officers of the court, the marshall and the steward and the cupbearer, and the bridal pair may shoot glances at one another with the ardor of true lovers, described in language which some critics have seen as mimicking Gottfried von Straßburg (1493 ff.), but, too late, Gotelint experiences a frisson of apprehension and wishes that she were back in the parental home (1576 ff.). The end is approaching in the form of a judge and four companions, who succeed, despite the number of the robbers, in overpowering them and bringing them to justice. We recall how his father had warned him that when the time was right, the band of robbers would not be able to escape the single judge appointed by God to apprehend them (1260-1264).

What becomes of Gotelint is left untold, for Wernher's concern is to tell of the end of Helmbrecht, saved from the summary execution which befalls his companions to lead the life of a blind beggar, maimed by the loss of one hand and one foot. His gruesome lot is interpreted as his specific punishment for his ill-treatment of his parents, to whom he now returns for a second time. With this final juxtaposition of father and son, the equation is completed. There is no room for compassion in the older man, for whom young Helmbrecht is now the embodiment of evil, despised even by the sun itself (1801), and, as he goes on his way, the blind thief is scorned by all the peasants he meets, who see his wretched state as his just deserts for the affliction they have suffered at his hands. Significantly, it is the peasants who turn on him and mete out his final terrible punishment, fulfilling the prophecy of the father's fourth and final dream.

The careful structure of the poem has frequently been admired, but it is important to recognize that structure is not, of course, Wernher's prime concern. Events balance one another: Helmbrecht leaves home on three occasions, once when he goes off to seek the courtly life, against the advice of his father, the second time when he rejects his father's offer to remain at home in idleness rather than return to his criminal way of life, and the last time when his father turns him away. He spends a year as a robber knight, harassing the peasants, and a year as a blind cripple at the mercy of the peasants. When Father Helmbrecht greets the blind cripple, whom he pretends not to recognize, in French, we must recall the more protracted charade played out by Helmbrecht on his first return home, when he showed off his "knowledge" of various languages. More sinister is the echo, in Father Helmbrecht's address to him as *"her blindekîn"* ("little Mister Blind-man," 1716) of Helmbrecht's insolent dismissal of his father as *"ir gebûrekîn"* ("you little peasant," 764).

The cap itself frames the poem, as we have seen, with its fate as it lies in pieces at the end reminding us of its exaggerated splendor, the tangible symbol of the arrogance which causes Helmbrecht's downfall. Some have seen the lengthy description of the cap as excessive, pointing out that it does, indeed, occupy a very large proportion of the whole, fairly short poem, but it has, of course, a very real function as the focus of the moral of the tale. That, however, begs the question, for there is almost certainly more than one moral to Wernher's poem, and it may well be that beneath the obvious message is another, more complex one. The poem belongs very much to its time, and the times were politically and socially turbulent. It is no exaggeration to say that this short work contains a mass of detailed information about daily life at that time—laws and customs, food and clothing, farming and economic matters—but it also reflects an age of social upheaval on a larger scale. When Father Helmbrecht speaks of an age gone by, when standards were very different at court, he is almost certainly striking a chord with his listeners, who must have been aware of the erosion of stability contingent upon the grad- ual decline of the feudal system. The work must have added to the unease of a nobility already fully aware of the increasing power of the peasantry. In this instance the object of the revenge of the peasants is one of their own number, but the circumstances which make this possible are the prevailing unrest of the age and the breakdown of order.

Texts:
Brackert, Helmut, et al., eds. and trans. *Helmbrecht*. Frankfurt/M: Fischer Taschenbuch Ver- lag, 1972. Repr. 1990 (= Bücher des Wissens, 6024). MHG text with mod. Ger. trans., valu- able afterword and notes.
Gough, Charles E., ed. *Meier Helmbrecht. A Poem by Wernher der Gartenære*. Oxford: Blackwell, 1942, [2]1947 (= Blackwell's German Texts). Long the standard edition for English readers, with introduction and notes but now dated.
Panzer, Friedrich, ed. *Meier Helmbrecht von Wernher der Gartenære*. Halle: Niemeyer, 1902. 6th-9th editions revised by Kurt Ruh. 9th revised edition: *Helmbrecht*. Tübingen: Niemeyer, 1974. (= ATB, 11). Standard edition of the text, still relatively dated .
Parshall, Linda trans. *Wernher der Gartenære: Helmbrecht*. MHG text by Ulrich Seelbach. New York: Garland, 1987 (= GLML, 28A). MHG text and Engl. trans. with introduction, bibliography, and notes.
Speckenbach, Klaus, ed. *Helmbrecht: Text, Nacherzählung, Begriffserklärungen*. Darmstadt: Wiss. Buchges., 1974. MHG text with mod. Ger. re-telling.

Translations:
Bell, Clair Hayden, trans. *Peasant Life in Old German Epics: 'Meier Helmbrecht' and 'Der arme Heinrich.'* New York: Octagon Books, 1965 (orig. publ. 1931).
See Brackert, et al.; Parshall; and Speckenbach above.

## *Helmbrecht*—Bibliography

Banta, Frank G. "The Arch of Action in *Meier Helmbrecht*." *JEGP* 63 (1964): 696-711. A helpful discussion of the structure of the poem, though, as Banta himself says, there are many ways of looking at this aspect of the poem.
Jackson, W. T. H. "The Composition of *Meier Helmbrecht*." *MLQ* 18 (1957): 44-58.

Essentially an examination of how Wernher composed his poem, with particular reference to apparent inconsistencies. Also addresses some interesting points of interpretation.

Kolb, Herbert. "Der *Meier Helmbrecht* zwischen Epos und Drama." *ZfdPh* 81 (1962): 1-23.

A very detailed analysis of some passages of the poem departing from the problem of genre and possible antecedents.

Seelbach, Ulrich. *Bibliographie zu Wernher der Gartenære*. Berlin: Erich Schmidt, 1981 (= Biblio. z. dt. Lit. d. Mas., 8).

____. *Späthöfische Literatur und Rezeption. Studien zum Publikum des 'Helmbrecht' von Wernher der Gartenære*. Berlin: Erich Schmidt, 1987.

This volume and the bibliography (above) are indispensable to the further serious study of *Helmbrecht*. They present some of the most up-to-date scholarship on the subject.

Sowinski, Bernhard. *Wernher der Gartenære: 'Helmbrecht'. Interpretation*. Munich: Oldenbourg, 1971.

Helpful discussion of a wide range of significant issues.

## Other Shorter Works of the Period

Although *Helmbrecht* is probably the outstanding short narrative of the later 13th century, remarkable for its form and for the issues which it treats with such pungency, there are other less well known short works which are worth looking at. Many of them are to be found in the collections of short stories in the older editions and in modern translations mentioned in our bibliography below. We have simply selected some of the most interesting representative examples.

### Rüedeger von Hünchoven: *Der Schlegel*

This appears to be the only significant literary work extant by Rüedeger von Hünchoven, or Rüedeger der Hunchover, although his name is attached to one version of *Die Heidin* (see below). The name occurs as the author of an undated document in Regensburg and in other documents towards the end of the 13th century. Such evidence is accepted as establishing both the approximate time and region of this little story, which belongs within the growing tradition of short narratives with something of the quality of drama already present. This one is particularly effective, with its didactic message clothed in a ready humor and an ironic, even cynical, view of human nature. The narrator displays a brilliant sense of structure and timing which make this a powerful little work. It could belong to a much later age or perhaps to none at all.

The essential theme is a timeless one, selected, as Rüedeger tells us early on, to illustrate the Fourth Commandment. The old father, now widowed, shares out his considerable wealth among his five children in the forlorn hope that they will care for him in his declining years. He is shunted from one to another, as in turn they soon weary of his presence in their comfortable, hedonistic lives. An old friend, recently returned from the Holy Land, suggests a solution, and the old father allows it to be known that he has a huge chest with five keys, one of which he wears for all to see, though apparently surreptitiously, on an ostentatious silver chain about his waist. The transformation is dramatic, and the children are now eager to heap their care and hospitality upon him, vying with one another to do so. When he dies, in the kind of comfort to which he always felt entitled, the children cannot get to the chest quickly enough. When it is opened they see only a big hammer (*schlegel*) with a message attached to it: anyone who is so foolish as to give his possessions to his children should have his skull smashed in to his very tongue with this hammer.

This admittedly not very subtle tale is full of inspired little touches, details which above all display the bitter truth about human nature. One son is deep in a game of chess when his old father arrives and can hardly bother to get up to greet him. One of his daughters presents him with a bowl of very thin broth, with the spoon already in it. With masterly economy, the author tells a tale which involves much repetition, as he proceeds through the reactions, in differing circumstances, of the five children, yet he does not repeat himself. The suspense builds up, as the father describes several times over how the chest will remain locked until after his death and how the children will all have to assemble round it together with the five keys in order to open it. We can hardly doubt that a rude awakening is in store for them, yet the element of suspense is there, for the narrator has deliberately held back the title of his work, he tells us, until the end. The inverted demonstration of the Fourth Commandment is linked with another message, also revealed at the end: one may do better to trust one's friends and neighbors than one's blood relatives.

Hardly a great work of literature—and it does not set out to be one—*Der Schlegel* merits attention in its own right, as a clever little story very well told but also as an indicator of the way medieval literature was progressing at this point, away from the long courtly narratives and the lengthy works based on historical and heroic tradition, towards something much more domestic and timeless, and, in terms of genre, opening up the way increasingly to the *Schwank* and the growth of drama (see p. 430 ff.).

### Die halbe Decke

Closely linked with *Der Schlegel* is another story which treats a similar theme: *Die halbe Decke* (also called *Der Kozze* or *Kotzenmære*). Although what is probably the earliest version of this tale may stem from about the same time as *Der Schlegel*, towards the end of the 13th century, it underwent a number of reworkings in the course of its complex development.

At the heart of this rather touching tale is again the observation—or, rather, non-observation—of the Fourth Commandment. Again, an old father, unwisely as it turns out, gives away his considerable wealth and is then ill treated by his son, reduced to poverty and extreme discomfort, consigned to a life under the stairs, alongside the pigs and with only his little grandson showing any concern for him. Pressed by a particularly hard winter, he asks for a blanket and very grudgingly the son cuts one in half and gives the smaller portion to his own son to deliver. When the old man receives this paltry solace with gratitude, the little boy goes to his father to ask for the other half. It is the simple compassion of the small boy, who reminds his father that he will one day be old and in need and dependent upon his son, that prompts the man to make belated retribution and restore his father to his rightful place. It is not just remorse which moves him, however, but the simple statement by the small boy that he will treat his father in his old age in accordance with the example which he has been set. The cynicism again lurking in this story is countered, perhaps, by the narrator's epilogue, which speaks of the ultimate fatherhood of God and the judgment to be made in the next life.

The essence of the story remains in its various transformations: what changes is the emphasis on human responses and the way in which the various characters are brought forward. The tale is another example of the effective use of the short narrative to point a moral and to exploit the dramatic potential of this form.

### Die Heidin

This much longer work, which must nevertheless be assigned to the short narratives of the period, is very different in tone and purpose. Again there are several versions of the really quite daring tale of the love between a married heathen lady and the Christian count who sets his heart on winning her when he first learns of her existence. The third character in a work which is again quite dramatic in its impact is the devoted heathen king who tries to protect his wife from all outsiders and who in the end is betrayed by her. At the core of a relationship that is surrounded by the trappings of courtly love is the erotic question which had been raised already by Andreas Capellanus in his *De arte honeste amore* in the mid-12th century about the relative desirability of the two parts of the lady's person. The lady gives in to the pleas of her suitor after he has dedicated years to showing her his commitment to her service and offers him the choice between her upper and lower half, cunningly calculating that this way he will gain the whole person he so desires.

The four versions of the poem end in three distinct ways: with the count returning alone to his own land, or with the elopement of the pair and the baptism of the lady, or, third, with the heathen king seeking revenge but accepting reconciliation. The evolution of this story probably extends from the mid-13th century probably just into the 14th, and the versions vary considerably in length. One of these was at one point attributed to the same Rüedeger who composed *Der Schlegel*, but this is no longer accepted. The version known as *Heidin IV*, at 1902 lines the second shortest, is regarded as the finest. Here particular emphasis is placed on the eloquent debates between the count and the heathen lady, in which she emerges as the more skillful participant. Aside from these more passive portions of the poem, there is considerable color in the depiction of the chivalrous activities of the would-be lover who embarks on his journey to the East and his enthusiastic career with the sole purpose of winning her favor. Some elements are reminiscent of portions of the courtly romance, while others reflect the dialogue of the Minnesang, or, at times, the more basic human relationships of the *Schwank*. In the extended versions of the story, the erotic qualities are emphasized to the point of crudity.

### Der Schüler von (zu) Paris

This is another of the stories which exists in a number of versions as Sarah Westphal makes clear in her book on "textual poetics" (see BIBLIOGRAPHY, below). The oldest version probably dates from the end of the 13th century.

Essentially a tale of tragic love, the poem in all its versions seems to be pointing to the danger of immoderation. The student falls in love with the daughter of his landlord and, evading the surveillance of her father, satisfies his longing for her in a blissful fulfillment which leads to his dying of sheer joy. At his funeral, the girl betrays her love for him by dying of grief. This skeleton of the plot is varied in the three versions by the manner of the subterfuge which enables the young couple to outwit her possessive father, by clandestine meetings, the young man's disguising himself as a monk (perhaps with a backward glance to the Tristan story?) and, in the latest of the versions, the desperate act of the girl in hauling her lover up on a rope to the tower where her father has imprisoned her.

Helmut de Boor (*Litgesch.*, 3/1, p. 235 f.) draws attention to the elements of the *Schwank* in the two later versions of the story. He also points out some of the ways in which the poem uses the motifs of the courtly romance but applies them to the new context of the bourgeois narrative with its basis in the town.

### Die Frauentreue

This fusion of the courtly overtones and the bourgeois, town-based action is evident in another short love story from about the same period. *Die Frauentreue* is also a more complicated account of a similar tragic love. This time the lady is married and devoted to her husband, but a knight seeks to prove his love by fighting for her without his armor (as Wolfram's Isenhart did for Belakane decades before). When he is wounded, she removes the spear and saves his life, prompted to do so by her husband, who has no inkling of the desire of the man for her. More obsessed by her now than ever, the knight makes his way to her at night and, with her husband sleeping beside her, embraces her with such force that the recent wound bursts open and he falls into a faint and dies. Terrified lest her husband wake up and discover him there, the lady drags him back to his own bed, where he is found next morning by his servants. Meanwhile, but too late, she has realized the depth of his feeling for her, and she begs her husband to allow her to make a sacrifice on behalf of the dead man. She divests herself of all her outer garments and prepares to lay them on the body; overwhelmed with grief at the sight of the corpse, she falls dead herself. Whether she dies of grief or shame is not clear, but she is mourned and venerated by all, especially her husband who recognizes her great loyalty and has her united with the knight in the grave.

There is something unsatisfactory and unconvincing about this ending, it must be admitted. The excessive display of grief by the woman and the indulgence of the husband are incongruous in view of their previous mutual devotion. The poet seems to have overstepped the boundaries of the acceptable in his praise for womanly loyalty. Alternatively, it may be interpreted, as it is by Sarah Westphal as evidence of "the absolute and unforeseen power of minne to intervene in normal life" (121-122).

Ulrich Pretzel's selection of the shorter narratives of the German Middle Ages in modern German (see BIBLIOGRAPHY below) affords a useful insight into the way in which literature was developing and broadening. As has already become clear, many of these tales were told and retold in different versions, with slight and sometimes not so slight variations. What they have in common is the concentration of their form and the sometimes poignant concentration on events and the behavior of human beings involved in those events. In this respect they are often quite dramatic in their impact, and, often displaying a sharp and sometimes quite satirical view of human nature, they sometimes, though obviously not always, achieve a comic effect. It is likely, one feels, that they were popular entertainment, hence their frequent transmission, and that their frequently didactic purpose will not have been missed by the listeners.

A designation which has already been mentioned is that of the *Schwank*, for very often these brief anecdotes anticipate this kind of writing which was to become increasingly popular in the late Middle Ages and beyond. Indeed, a great deal of scholarly controversy surrounds the question of genre, and sometimes it is not possible, or even desirable, to assign a work to a precise genre.

### Herrand von Wildonie: *Der verkêrte wirt, Die getriuwe kone,* *Von dem blôzen keiser, Diu katze*

Within the group of works currently under consideration, one author stands out as representing four distinct but related types of short narrative, the knight from Styria Herrand von Wildonie who appears in the Manesse Manuscript as a Minnesänger, albeit a not very distinguished one, and whose four short narrative works occur only in the *Ambraser Heldenbuch.*

One of these, ***Der verkêrte wirt***, has all the earmarks of a *Schwank*, in its relentless exposure of adultery, albeit in a courtly context. The "lady," the wife of the knight, is not only unfaithful to her older husband but succeeds in making him into the wrongdoer, manipulating the situation to her own ends by a series of blatant tricks. If, as Herrand maintains, he was given the original as a true story by his father-in-law, none other than Ulrich von Lichtenstein (see p. 311 ff.), he has molded it to his purpose in this mixture of the courtly and the frankly vulgar.

Very different in tone is the story by Herrand which may have been based on an earlier anonymous tale which is usually called *Das Auge*. This is his account of the faithful wife, ***Die getriuwe kone***, who stabs out her eye with a pair of scissors in order to preserve the marriage with her husband, who, ugly enough already, has lost an eye in battle. Helmut de Boor *Litgesch.* 3/1, p. 249) points out that, far from being an affirmation of the courtly ideal of beauty, this is a powerful demonstration of true loyalty on an "everyday" level. Put like that, one can see these two anecdotes as counterpart pieces.

The parable of the naked emperor, ***Von dem blôzen keiser,*** points the moral of humility through the story of the proud and conceited emperor whose clothes are removed by an angel while he is in his bath. While the angel performs the rightful deeds of his imperial function, he must endure humiliation, until the situation is restored and he reigns henceforth in proper fashion. The message is clear: that all men are equal in the eyes of God. The same story is told in the very popular ***König im Bad***, once attributed to Der Stricker but now accepted as being by an unknown poet.

The fourth of Herrand's tales is ***Diu katze***, his story of the tomcat, who, like the emperor, gets above himself and has to be brought down to a realization of his proper place and to true humility. Thinking himself too good for his place by the fire and above all tired of his modest partner, he goes off in search of a grander destiny and on the way encounters a series of inanimates, each of which directs him to another which seems superior to it. Thus the sun directs him to the mist, the mist to the wind, the wind to the wall, the wall to the mouse: each has been defeated by the next. Thus the mouse directs him to none other than the cat, his partner back at home, and, coming full circle, he comes face to face with the truth of his rightful position in the order of things. Like the emperor, he has learned a lasting lesson. A pleasant enough fable, it would seem, but the signs are that the message is a political one: he addresses himself to the fickle knights who think they can do better for themselves but are forced to realize that they are best off with their original lords. There is evidence to suggest that Herrand and his family were politically engaged at the time of the Interregnum, and this is a surviving comment on the prevailing uncertainty. Herrand von Wildonie is no great literary figure, but he is a powerful enough story-teller in his own way.

Texts:

*Der Schlegel:*
Pfannmüller, Ludwig, ed. *Mittelhochdeutsche Novellen.* Bonn, 1912. Vol. 1, pp. 7-63.
*Die halbe Decke:*
von der Hagen, Friedrich Heinrich, ed. *Gesamtabenteuer. Hundert altdeutsche Erzählungen.* 3 vols. Stuttgart and Tübingen, 1850. Repr. Darmstadt: Wiss. Buchges., 1961. Pp. 391-399.
Rörich, Lutz, ed. *Erzählungen des späten Mittelalters und ihr Weiterleben in Literatur und Volksdichtung bis zur Gegenwart.* Vol. 1. Bern: Francke, 1962. Pp. 93-97.
de Boor, *Texte u. Zeugnisse* I/2, pp. 1434-1438.
*Die Heidin*
Henschel, Erich, and Ulrich Pretzel. *Die Heidin.* Leipzig: Niemeyer, 1957.
*Der Schüler von Paris:*
von der Hagen, *Gesamtabenteuer* 1, pp. 277-311.
Rosenfeld, Hans-Friedrich, ed. *Mittelhochdeutsche Novellenstudien.* Leipzig: Mayer und Müller, 1927. Pp. 163-470 (= Palaestra, 153).
*Die Frauentreue:*
de Boor, *Texte u. Zeugnisse* I/2, pp. 1428-1433.
von der Hagen, *Gesamtabenteuer* 1, pp. 257-276.
*Der verkêrte Wirt, Die getriuwe kone, Von dem blôzen keiser, Diu Katze:*
Fischer, Hanns, ed. *Herrand von Wildonie. Vier Erzählungen.* 3rd edition ed. by Paul Sappler. Tübingen: Niemeyer, 1984 (= ATB, 51).

Translations:

Fischer, Hanns. *Schwankerzählungen des deutschen Mittelalters.* Munich: Hanser, 1967.
Pretzel, Ulrich, trans. *Deutsche Erzählungen des Mittelalters.* Munich: Beck, 1971. Contains: *Der Schlegel* (84-103); *Die Heidin* (135-136); *Frauentreue* (128-134).
Thomas, J. Wesley, trans. *The Tales and Songs of Herrand von Wildonie.* Lexington: UP of Kentucky, 1972 (= Kentucky Univ. Studies in the Germanic Langs. and Lits., 4).

## Other Shorter Works—Bibliography

Curschmann, Michael. "Herrand von Wildonie." *VL*[2] 3 (1981): 1144-1147.

Kully, Rolf Max. "Der Schüler von Paris." *VL*[2] 8 (1992): 867-869.

Margetts, John. "Scenic Significance in the Work of Herrand von Wildonie." *Neophil.* 54 (1970): 142-148.

Actually an interpretation of the social significance of *Der verkêrte wirt.*

Müller, Hermann-Josef. *Überlieferungs- und Wirkungsgeschichte der Pseudo-Strickerschen Erzählung 'Der König im Bade'.* Berlin: Erich Schmidt, 1983.

Ruh, Kurt. "Die Frauentreue." *VL*[2] 2 (1980): 880-882.

Schirmer, Karl-Heinz. "Die Heidin." *VL*$^2$ 3 (1981): 612-615.

Westphal, Sarah. *Textual Poetics of German Manuscripts 1300-1500*. Columbia, SC: Camden House, 1993.

Williams, Ulla. "Rüedeger von Hünchoven." *VL*$^2$ 8 (1991): 307-310.

# Literature of the Late Middle Ages: Innovations and Continuing Trends

## INTRODUCTION

The vexed question of when the late Middle Ages begins in relation to German literature need not detain us, although the existence of this controversy is obviously of interest to anyone engaged in studying the period particularly in connection with the secondary literature surrounding it which tends to imply certain divisions. Attention is drawn to an article by Joachim Heinzle, "Wann beginnt das Spätmittelalter?" (*ZfdA* 112 [1983]: 207-223), that examines some of the principal standpoints, though conceding that it is impossible to be adamant on the subject and that there is bound to be an element of circularity in attempting to establish firm divisions on the basis of genre.

In our book as a whole we have set out to outline some of the main trends in German literature which led up to and followed from the period traditionally referred to as the *Blütezeit*, since few would question that the brief period around 1200 must be the focus of attention for the student of MHG literature. By contrast, however, German literature of the later Middle Ages contains few immediately recognizable names, and we are likely to be dealing more with isolated works or groups of works. Instead of concentrating on specific authors or works as we have generally done heretofore, we shall now place more emphasis on some of the principal trends in the later literature, indicating works of particular interest as they arise. In doing so we shall also be able to demonstrate that, although new genres and movements begin to dominate and proliferate in the post-courtly period, very frequently their origins are much earlier: in other words, we discover that MHG literature of the *Blütezeit* is perhaps less isolated and certainly far less homogeneous than at first seems the case.

If we sum up what we have so far covered, we can identify three important areas of literary development which go far beyond the early 13th century and represent a continuum through that century and beyond, in some cases well beyond. The courtly narrative occupied a very firm place, with the most important works being copied, often many times over, while the narrative itself developed and went off in new directions, especially through the works of Rudolf von Ems and Konrad von Würzburg. Heroic themes apparently continued to fascinate the public well beyond the *Nibelungenlied* and even *Kudrun*. A strong lyric tradition exists long after the so-called "classical" Minnesang, and, taking its cue in differing ways from Walther von der Vogelweide and from Neidhart, it flourishes right through to the colorful poetry of Oswald von Wolkenstein. Increasingly a tradition of didactic poetry exists side by side with the pure lyric. Some of the most important manuscripts date from the 14th century and suggest a keen interest in the literature of the *Blütezeit* and a conscientious desire to see it survive.

The fact that there are no really significant narrative works dating actually from the 14th century may have several explanations. Not least among these is probably that, while the works of Hartmann and Gottfried and Wolfram were perpetuated in performance and so did not need replacing, the actual environment that had produced them was no longer dominant. The courtly code and the courtly background had been replaced by a broader context, and the period of the Hohenstaufens was now obscured, at least as far as literature was concerned, in a rosy glow of remembrance. It is also true to say that, even though the great narrative works of the German Middle Ages were rooted in the early 13th century, they possessed that quality of mature reflection on the bigger issues of life which made them ahead of their time and thus ensured their survival for centuries to come.

Yet the 14th century itself was no time for passive reminiscence, characterized as it was by instability and change, a sense of the overturning of established values and a teetering on the brink of new ideas. Fritz Martini expresses the sense of the age in his discussion of the literature of the later Middle Ages in Germany (*Lit.Gesch.* 84): "Noch blieb alles dem Chaotischen nahe, voll Widerspruch bis in das einzelne Werk hinein, reich an Spannungen und auch Steigerungen. Man schwankte zwischen einer bewunderten, aber verlorenen Vergangenheit und einer noch ungewissen Zukunft." (Everything was poised on the very edge of chaos, full of contradictions, even in terms of individual works, rich in exhilaration and tension. One was hovering between an admired but lost past and a still uncertain future).

## NONFICTIONAL WRITING: *SACH-, FACHLITERATUR*

With the shift of power from the court to the town, the rise of the "middle classes," the spread of literacy, the increase in trade, and the need to communicate on the basic things of life, "literature" ceased to be the somewhat limited possession of the élite. A substantial dimension of the body of writing in German during the Middle Ages can thus be considered under the general heading of *Sachliteratur*, a term which embraces a wide variety of nonfictional writing (chronicles, historical and geographical accounts, legal writings) and works relating to specialized areas of knowledge (*Fachliteratur*). These works, significant and numerous though they are, need little attention here, since their nature can be fairly quickly described and they are for the most part not available in translation. Moreover, there are some full accounts which provide details for those wishing to pursue specific areas within these general categories.

Excellent accounts of this aspect of medieval German literature will be found in Bumke (*Geschichte* 343-369) and, more fully, in Chapters 7, 8, and 9 of de Boor/Newald, 3:2, ed. Glier (pp. 371-454). The single most comprehensive account of specialist literature remains the volume by Gerhard Eis (1962). In English, a certain amount of material will be found in M. O'C. Walshe's chapter on "The Beginnings of Prose Writing" (p. 304 ff.) and, very briefly, in Paul Salmon (p. 155 ff.).

Intimately linked with any consideration of the prose writing for utilitarian purposes in Germany from the 13th century on must be its effect on the growth of the language itself. Inevitably, once the possibility, in fact the necessity, existed of replacing the traditional Latin with the vernacular, the German language and, particularly, its vocabulary, had to expand and develop. A convenient approach to this area of the subject may be found in the concise but very interesting accounts contained in C. J. Wells, *German. A Linguistic History to 1945* (see in particular pp. 103-108; 125-130).

## Legal Writings

One of the principal areas in which German was used for the first time in place of Latin, or sometimes side by side with it, was jurisprudence, where, although traditionally professional lawyers communicated in Latin, the need to convey issues directly to a lay public demanded the use of the vernacular. Indeed, the work most frequently cited in this connection, and certainly one of the earliest codifications of German law in the German language is *Der Sachsenspiegel* by Eike von Repgouwe, a work which falls into two parts, treating the law of the free people in general on the one hand (*Landrecht*) and on the other the law relating to the disposition and tenure of fiefs (*Lehnrecht*). Originally written in a Latin version now lost to us, it was translated by its author into Low German in about 1222 and proved so successful that not only was it disseminated in numerous manuscripts, of which several hundred survive, but it seems to have constituted the inspiration for a great many similar compilations of German law: the *Magdeburger Weichbild, Das Rechtbild von der Gerichtsfassung*, the *Magdeburger Schöffenrecht*, all belong to the same general area geographically and to the later 13th century. The *Augsburger Sachsenspiegel* (ca. 1270) almost certainly arose indirectly from the work of Eike von Repgouwe, as did the so-called *Deutschenspiegel* (ca. 1274/5) and the *Schwabenspiegel* (ca. 1275/6), which is sometimes called *Das Lehenrechtsbuch* or *Das Kaiserrecht*, in recognition of the fact that it is not at all limited to Swabian law.

> The *Sachsenspiegel* is available in a two-volume edition by Karl A. Eckhardt. Göttingen, 1955-56 (= MGH Fontes iuris germanici antiqui, N.S.I,1 and 2) and in translation into German by Ruth Schmidt-Wiegand and Clausdieter Schott. Zürich: 1984.
> See also Ruth Schmidt-Wiegand in $VL^2$ 2 (1980): 400-409. The *Augsburger Sachsenspiegel* and the *Deutschenspiegel* are edited by Karl A. Eckhardt and Alfred Hübner. Hannover: Hahn, 1933. The *Schwabenspiegel* may be found in an old edition by Friedrich L. A., Freiherr von Lassberg. Tübingen, 1840. 3rd ed. by Karl A. Eckhardt. Aalen: Scientia, 1971.

Linked with these books of jurisprudence are the *Landfrieden*, the decrees prohibiting feuding among the nobles or at least stipulating certain limitations, which were issued for specific regions and made valid for appointed periods of time. The oldest of these is the *Reichslandfriede* issued by Heinrich IV in 1103, and another similar document of significance, the *Mühlhäuser Reichsrechtsbuch*, probably dates from the third decade of the 13th century and is thus contemporary with the *Sachsenspiegel*. The most famous is the *Mainzerlandfriede* of Friedrich II (1235), which was originally drawn up in both Latin and German but later disseminated in German and elevated to imperial law by Rudolf von Habsburg in 1281. Originally, however, these documents were intended to be strictly local in their applicability, with a proliferation of works based on these early models and arising not only in the central German cities but extending also to less prominent towns and cities throughout the land and even over into the eastern territories of Poland and Hungary.

> For details of this whole subject, see de Boor/Newald 3:2, ed. Glier: "Achtes Kapitel: Rechtsschrifttum."
>
> See also, on this general topic: Gernhuber, Joachim. *Die Landfriedensbewegung in Deutschland bis zum Mainzer Reichslandfrieden von 1235.* Bonn: Rohrscheid, 1952.

## Chronicles

A further important dimension of writing in German in the 13th and 14th centuries and one which is actually closely linked to the preceding one of legal documentation is that of historical accounts, and of these there is a great abundance. Again, too, this development had its source in the much earlier period, when the monks and the clergy had written their accounts in Latin prose. Only gradually did German become acceptable as the language for such works, and with that development came sometimes also the use of verse rather than prose, possibly because verse was deemed to have a special elegance. Such works were in all likelihood commissioned by noble families and rich merchants, and they were very often ambitious in their scope and conception.

We have already mentioned one of the most important of these histories, the *Weltchronik* of Rudolf von Ems, the final and uncompleted work of one of the foremost literary figures of the period (see p. 340 f.). This was an enormously influential work, even though the original conception of its scope remained unfulfilled, and it constituted a model for later medieval chronicles in German. It was not, however, the first of its kind, and for earlier attempts at historical writing in German one needs to go back to the early 13th century and specifically to the *Gandersheimer Reimchronik* of a priest called Eberhard (1216). This work is in itself not very remarkable, although its metrical form— rhyming couplets of four beats each—is distinctive. The substance is fairly parochial: the founding of the convent at Gandersheim near Hildesheim in Lower Saxony and praise of the Abbess Mechthild von Wöltingerode for her courage and political expertise in securing the freedom of the convent from its ties to the bishopric of Hildesheim and replacing these with direct allegiance to Rome. Apart from its interest as a very early effort at historical writing in German verse, the work is important for the use made of it by a much more distinguished chronicler, the anonymous author of the *Braunschweigische Reimchronik*, which belongs to the last decade of the 13th century. This substantial work (9339 lines) is first and foremost a eulogy of Duke Albrecht I of Brunswick, whose death is lamented at the close of the work, and a history of the city of Brunswick. The author declares his debt to the *Gandersheimer Reimchronik* and to another Low German work, this time in prose, the *Sächsische Weltchronik* sometimes attributed to Eike von Repgouwe. This is a large history of the world from its creation, with the central portion the history of the (Holy Roman) Empire. The work poses problems of dating, not least because the various versions contain different and obviously later material which actually makes the attribution to Eike von Repgouwe unlikely. It is probable that this work was the inspiration to a chronicle of a slightly different kind (ca.1270-80), the *Buoch der künege alter und niuwer ê* (Book of Kings of the Old and the New Law), which traces the history of the world from biblical times through to the reign of Konrad III. The second part of the work owes much to the *Kaiserchronik* (see p. 92 ff.).

The tradition of chronicle writing continued to flourish throughout the 14th century, and it constitutes one of the most abundant areas of vernacular writing in both prose and verse and sometimes in a mixture of the two. Historical accounts were undertaken, it would seem, less for their intrinsic value in committing the past to posterity than in order to demonstrate the Hand of God at work and the relationship between the individual at any point in time and the almighty Plan. Many of these works are very long and sometimes quite tortuous, with many insertions from apparently unconnected areas—biblical references, anecdotes and fictitious material, sometimes even borrowed from the literary works of earlier decades. Containing as they do a high proportion of fiction, they should not be regarded as entirely reliable history, nor was that their intention. On the other hand, the past could be used as a kind of barometer for the future, and the element of the cautionary tale is sometimes evident.

Although they often set out to embrace the history of the world, these chronicles were also frequently very local in their provenance and their concerns. Some of them emanated from regions; some from individual towns and cities. The quality is obviously not uniform, but some individual examples—the *Weltchronik* of Heinrich von München and the *Österreichische Reimchronik* of Ottokar von Steiermark could perhaps be mentioned here or the *Limburger Chronik* of Tilemann Ehlen, whose work is not remarkable as a town chronicle but includes some unusual material in his references to such matters as literature and music and fashion—stand out for their distinctive contribution to a significant branch of writing during the 14th century which was to lay the foundations for a tradition of considerable status during the 15th and 16th centuries in Germany.

> The very clear account by Ingeborg Glier (de Boor-Newald, 3:2, Kapitel 9: "Geschichtsschreibung") shows the geographical distribution of chronicles during the 14th century. Other relevant further reading: *Gandersheimer Reimchronik*, ed. by Ludwig Wolff. Tübingen: Niemeyer, 1969 (= ATB, 25). See also Volker Honemann, *VL*[2] 2 (1980) 277-282. *Braunschweigische Reimchronik*, ed. by Ludwig Weiland. Hannover: Hahn, 1877 (= MGH, 2). Pp. 430-574. Also: Thomas Sandfuchs, *VL*[2] 1 (1978) 1007-1010. *Sächsische Weltchronik*, ed. by Ludwig Weiland. Hannover: Hahn, 1877 (= MGH, 2). Pp. 1-384.

### Specialist Literature (*Fachliteratur*)

Mention must be made, albeit briefly, to the mass of prose writing in German during the second half of the 13th century and throughout the fourteenth on areas of knowledge such as science and nature, medicine and geography, with individual works on specific subjects as diverse as herbs and cooking, precious stones, and veterinary medicine. The most comprehensive account of this material remains the book by Gerhard Eis (1962) who begins by considering the much earlier encyclopedic works in Latin which were the inspiration for the originally Low German *Lucidarius* compiled by two chaplains at the behest of Henry the Lion in 1190/95. The structure of the work is based on question and answer between master and pupil, and its range is great, encompassing the major preoccupations of medieval learning: the Creation, and, in relationship to that, geography, astronomy and human physiology; theology and the Church; the Last Judgment, heaven and hell. Although based on Latin sources, the work is an important turning point in the writing of German: it was copied many times over, translated and expanded, and it was frequently referred to throughout the Middle Ages, being elevated to the status of *Volksbuch*.

> Edition: Heidlauf, F., ed. *Der große Lucidarius, aus der Berliner Handschrift.* Berlin: Weidmann, 1915 (= DTM 28). Repr. Dublin: Weidmann, 1970. See also: Glogner, Gunther. *Der mittelhochdeutsche Lucidarius, eine mittelalterliche Summa.* Münster: Aschendorffsche Verlagsbuchhandlung, 1937 (= Forsch. z. dt. Spr. u. Dicht., 8).

Although the *Lucidarius* retained its popularity for so long, more specialist works were produced during the late 13th and 14th centuries. To the turn of the century belongs a work which, despite its quality, appears to have had little impact. This is the so-called *Mainauer Naturlehre* which concerns itself more specifically with geography and the related subjects of astronomy and medicine. Its provenance and attribution to Hugo von Langenstein are unsupported, but it is worth noting the description of it by Karl Stackmann in the *VL*[2]: he calls it "ein Kabinettstück früher deutscher Prosa" (a tour de force of early German prose) and with that he accords it a special place in an otherwise undistinguished category of German writing in this period. It can be read in a very early edition by W. Wackernagel (Bibliothek des literarischen Vereins Stuttgart, 22, 1857).

More important is a later work (1349/50), the *Buch der Natur* by the scholar Konrad von Megenburg. This was arranged as a more systematic presentation of natural phenomena, and it became an influential work, although—or possibly because—the purely scientific analysis is mixed with a more literary approach and an overt desire to edify his public.

> Edition: Pfeiffer, Fritz, ed. *Konrad von Megenburg: Das Buch der Natur. Die erste Naturgeschichte in deutscher Sprache.* Stuttgart, 1861. Reprinted Hildesheim, 1971. Most of this specialist material is available only in older editions, but very clear and detailed accounts by Peter Assion will be found in Chapter 7 of de Boor/Newald 3:2 (ed. I. Glier, 1987). See also Bumke (*Geschichte*, 364-369) and Cramer (*Geschichte*, 121-132), and G. Eis, *Mittelalterliche Fachliteratur.* Stuttgart: Metzler, 1962, [2]1967 (= Sammlung Metzler, 14).

## DIDACTIC LITERATURE

The use of the German language for essentially utilitarian purposes leads reasonably to another whole area of "didactic literature," something that is by no means an innovation of the later period but constitutes quite a large proportion of the material to be taken into account during the later 13th and 14th centuries. Some of the most significant and readily available items are discussed below, but anyone wishing to pursue the subject will find the following very helpful: Sowinski, Bernhard. *Lehrhafte Dichtung des Mittelalters*. Stuttgart: Metzler, 1971 (= Sammlung Metzler, 103). This defines didactic literature and traces its origins back to Classical literature, before considering the didactic literature of the early Germanic period and the various types in the German Middle Ages.

## Religious Works

Within the category of "didactic literature" it is usual to consider works of a generally religious nature. As early as the beginning of the 13th century—though some would put it perhaps as late as 1220—a knight from the Danube region had composed a little religious epic known as the *Kindheit Jesu*. Konrad von Fußesbrunnen appears to have composed his work for a courtly audience, and the influence of Hartmann von Aue is particularly apparent. Moreover, the work was often placed in manuscripts alongside courtly epics. Certainly it was a popular work which appears to have influenced later writers, who used it as the inspiration for works on the life of the Virgin Mary and the childhood of Christ.

The adoration of the Virgin Mary had been expressed in German literature since the *Driu liet von der maget of Priester* Wernher of the late 12th century (see p. 77 ff.). One of the most significant later works on Mary is the *Passional* (ca. 1280-1300), an enormously long collection of legends of the saints. It contains as a large part of it the account of miracles attributed to the Virgin. This work shows considerable skill in its narrative and in the linking of its component tales and was apparently very popular. It is likely that the material dealing with the Virgin Mary in particular was highly regarded and accorded a special place within the other Marian literature of the Middle Ages.

> See: Fromm, Hans, and Klaus Grubmüller, eds. *Konrad von Fußesbrunnen: Kindheit Jesu*. Berlin: de Gruyter, 1973.
> Also: Hans Fromm in $VL^2$ 5 (1985) 172-175. *Passional*. Vols. I-II, ed. by Karl A Hahn. Frankfurt/M, 1845; vol. III, ed. by Karl Köpke. Quedlinburg & Leipzig, 1852.

Although the taste of the end of the 12th century may have intervened to give prominence to other writers and to very different forms of literature, there is a consistent flow of poems and legends on the life of the Virgin throughout the 13th century. A work such as the *Kindheit Jesu* shows the merging of two very different traditions, and it may have been influential beyond its intrinsic value. Certainly another Konrad, a priest from the village of Heimesfurt near Nördlingen, went a little further a decade or so later when he combined early models, notably in Latin, of hymns to the Virgin with the narrative skills gleaned from the great narrative masters of the MHG *Blütezeit*. The resulting two poems are *Unser frouwen hinvart* (The Assumption of the Virgin Mary) and *Diu Urstende* (The Resurrection).

> See: Gärtner, Kurt, and Werner Hoffmann, eds. *Konrad von Heimesfurt*. Tübingen: Niemeyer, 1989 (= ATB 99).
> Werner Fechter: $VL^2$ 5 (1985) 198-202.

The *Marienleben* of Brother Philipp (1270-1345) is likewise undoubtedly influenced by the *Kindheit Jesu*. It combines biblical accounts with legend into a work that is essentially didactic in tone as is the work by Walther von Rheinau, the longest poem on the life of the Virgin of the 13th century (ca.1300). This too shows the influence of the courtly romance, and its overt didacticism is tempered by some poetic skill. Other anonymous poems in praise of Mary exist, and, towards the end of our period, another Wernher, the Swiss Wernher, produced a lengthy poem of considerable literary merit.

Although the Virgin Mary was the favorite subject for religious works of this kind at this period, there were other subjects as well: other saints, such as St. George and St. Christopher and St. Nicholas, while St. Francis of Assisi found his way at a very early stage into the realm of legend and literature. A close link with the glorious cultural past is forged in the life of Elisabeth, the wife of the Landgrave Ludwig of Thuringia, who, after his death on the Crusade, endured much persecution as she devoted herself to the life of piety which earned her canonization in 1235. Apart from its significance to our immediate context here, this *vita*, which was taken up in later collections, including the *Passional*, is interesting for its evocation of the past glories at the court of Hermann, her father-in-law and the renowned patron of literature.

Old Testament figures also provided the material for works of literature, sometimes seeming to compete with the traditional heroes and heroines of courtly literature. Much of this writing comes very close to translation, and favored subjects are the story of Adam and Eve, of Daniel, Job and Judith, and other biblical accounts where the opportunity to expound a moral message is evident.

At its best, of course as we have seen in our consideration of Konrad von Würzburg (see his legends and the *Goldene Schmiede*, p. 355 f.), material of this kind could be used by a writer of stature, but the greater part of it is interesting rather for what it tells us about general trends at the time. Comprehensive accounts and bibliographical details will be found in Bumke (*Geschichte* 369 ff.) for the earlier period, and Cramer (*Geschichte* 199 ff.) for the 14th century, and in Sowinski.

## Allegories of Love

We should perhaps draw attention in passing to a specific category of didactic literature which is only relatively recently receiving closer attention from scholars of the period. The analysis of the nature of love and of the problems relating to wooing found its most emphatic expression in the treatise *De amore* of Andreas Capellanus (ca. 1185), but this was not actually translated into German until 1402. Meanwhile, however, the *Büchlein* of Hartmann von Aue (see p. 154 ff.) had introduced into German literature the idea of instructing in the art of loving by means of allegory. It was almost a century later, however, that this kind of writing became really fashionable, exemplified in works like *Die Klage der Minne* and *Das Herz* of Meister Egen von Bamberg (ca. 1330), the *Konstanzer Minnelehre*, which was probably composed at the end of the 13th century. The most famous of all is *Die Jagd* by the nobleman Hadamar von Laber (c.1340), a lengthy work which deliberately uses the complex form of the *Jüngerer Titurel* (see p. 381 ff.) and thus explicitly states its relationship to courtly literature. Quite simply, the pursuit of the beloved is seen as a hunt (*Jagd*), in which the animal pursued, a doe, is hunted by her lover in the company of hounds who bear the names of abstract virtues seen as desirable in the lover:joy and desire, constancy and loyalty, good fortune and determination, and so on. Despite every effort, however, the pursuit remains unsuccessful and the lover is left with a wounded hound, his heart, and lamentation mingled still with hope.

The works appear to have been popular among their medieval audiences, but they do not really appeal to modern taste. A very full scholarly treatment of treatises on love and love allegories is available.

See: Glier, Ingeborg, *Artes Amandi. Untersuchungen zu Geschichte, Überlieferung und Typologie der deutschen Minnerede*. Munich: Beck, 1971 (= MTU, 34).
A helpful description of the genre in English is contained in Walshe, *Medieval German Literature* 290-293.


## OTHER DIDACTIC WORKS

Possibly more interesting for our purposes are some individual works which need to be considered for their specific contribution to medieval German literature. These are often didactic in a more literal sense, in that they explicitly set out to teach a particular lesson. Sowinski calls them *Moral- und Verhaltenslehren* (lessons in morality and in behavior).

### Thomasin von Zerklære: *Der Welsche Gast*

This lengthy work (14,752 lines) by the cleric Thomasin von Zerklære ranks as one of the most important pieces of didactic writing of the German Middle Ages. Its purpose is to preach the morality of chivalry and to instruct knights in proper behavior within the world. The author was an Italian writing in German, one of the clerics in the retinue of Wolfger, known as the Bishop of Passau and the one-time patron of Walther von der Vogelweide. In 1204 Wolfger had become Patriarch of Aquileia, and Thomasin himself is the stranger of the title of his work, sent across the Alps into Germany. His German is excellent, and he tells how he composed the work in ten months in 1215-16, with the express purpose of counteracting the decline of the German nobility by this lengthy piece of instruction to young people and to knights in particular.

He castigates those fools (*tôren*) who transgress the ideals of proper behavior as he sees it. When he commends his young pupils to learn from the morals expressed in the heroes of courtly literature—Gawein and Iwein, Erec and Parzival, and even, somewhat surprisingly, Tristan—this is because he recognizes their value as models of chivalry, rather than because he admires the literature in which they occur, romances which, as he says, are not true. Moreover, the edifying qualities of these fictional characters are valid only in the initial stages of a young person's development. Once they have come *ze sinne* (to an age of reason, presumably), profounder teaching is appropriate, and Thomasin, very much the preacher, refers them then to serious didactic matter.

The work was obviously a great success in the 13th century, prompting even in its own day at least two reworkings. There are 24 manuscripts, some of them illustrated.

Editions:

Rückert, H., ed. *Thomasin von Zerclare: Der Welsche Gast*, Quedlinburg: Basse, 1852. Repr. 1965.

von Kries, F. W., ed. *Der Welsche Gast*. (4 vols. of text and analysis, with commentary on the illustrations in vol. 4). Göppingen: Kümmerle, 1985 (= GAG 425).

## Der Winsbeke (Die Winsbekin)

In the early 13th century (perhaps 1210/1220) a fellow-countryman of Wolfram von Eschenbach's composed a work comprising fifty-six stanzas of ten lines each which probably took some of its inspiration, in thought if not in any way in form, from Wolfram. In the Manesse manuscript, the heading is *Der Winsbeke*, but whether this is a family name or whether the author was given the name of the little town of Windsbach to the south-west of Nuremberg is not clear, and in other manuscripts the work is ascribed to *der tugenthafte schrîber* (the worthy scribe) or left anonymous.

The content is a series of pieces of advice from an old knight to his son and it treats the question of chivalry and of love, the behavior towards one's fellow men, towards the ladies and the clergy. It advocates loyalty and compassion, truth and generosity in one's bearing towards others. Chivalry, the father contends, is a game of chance (*topelspil*), in direct echo of Wolfram (*Parz.* 289,24), and, like Gurnemanz, he emphasizes the pain and hazards of knighthood, while urging the dual service of the world and of God.

A counterpart work, in which the son responds to the father, is almost certainly the work of a cleric, with its more obviously religious tone and the ultimate suggestion from the son that his father found a hospital and withdraw from the world, renouncing the things of this life in favor of a more spiritual existence. This is almost certainly of later date, possibly as late as the 14th century, while another related work of the earlier period—*Winsbekin*—has the mother instructing her daughter in similar fashion, stressing matters of love and the dangers of the world and advocating an honorable way of life.

These positive instructions are turned on their heads by a 14th century parody, in which the advice is negative.

Editions:

Leitzmann, Albert, ed. *Winsbecke, Winsbeckin und Winsbeckenparodie*. Tübingen: Niemeyer, [3]1962 Rev. by Ingo Reiffenstein (= ATB, 9).

*Der Winsbeke und die Winsbekin*, with commentary by Moriz Haupt. Leipzig: Weidmann 1845.

Cf. also *Der Magezoge* (The Tutor), which is dated about 1250 and also contains instructions from father to son. Text: In: Rosenhagen, Gustav, ed. *Die Heidelberger Handschrift Cod. Pal. Germ. 341*. Berlin, 1909. Pp. 21-29.

## Tirol und Fridebrant

The Manesse manuscript gives this title to two pieces, one a puzzle (*Rätselgedicht*) and the other, like the *Winsbeke* poems, a passage of instruction (*Lehrgedicht*), this time from King Tirol to his son Fridebrant, a name borrowed presumably from *Parzival* though with no other obvious relationship to Wolfram. This time the advice centers on the role and obligations of a ruler. The existence of a group of fragments in the same metrical form and also treating of Tirol and Fridebrant raises the question of whether there was in fact an epic, possibly of the mid-13th century and now lost, of which these are the surviving pieces.

Text: In: Leitzmann/Reiffenstein, ATB, 9 (above).

## Konrad von Haslau: *Der Jüngling* (The Young Man)

This is likewise a *Lehrgedicht* (1264 lines), which provides instructions to young noblemen. Emanating from Konrad von Haslau and dated about 1270, it differs from the above works in that the emphasis is on the more superficial aspects of proper behavior (clothing, table manners, restraint in matters of eating and drinking). The repeated exhortation to reward the poet marks it as the work of a professional travelling poet.

Text: Tauber, Walter, ed. *Konrad von Haslau: Der Jüngling*. Tübingen: Niemeyer, 1984 (= ATB, 97).

## *Diu Mâze* (Moderation)

This little poem of 218 lines praises moderation as the ultimate virtue. Moderation is desirable in young people and is relevant to men and women alike, though in different ways. Although an early date has been suggested (1180), the influence of Walther von der Vogelweide and his personification of Moderation, together with his famous advocacy of Honor and God's Grace in his *Reichston* poem (see p. 273) seem to favor a later dating, and some critics have even put it as late as 1300.

Text: In: Meyer-Benfey, Heinrich, ed. *Mhd. Übungsstücke*. Halle, [2]1920. Pp. 24-30.

## Freidank: *Bescheidenheit*

An important didactic work of the 13th century (ca.1230) is this collection of gnomic verses by a certain Frîdanc, who is praised for his "hübsche deutsche gedichte" in a mention in Alsace in about 1300. Here he is referred to as a *vagus*, a travelling poet, but whether the name Frîdanc (or Frîgedanc) was a genuine surname or an assumed penname is not known. He appears to have been of Swabian origin, and, though not a poet of any great talent or a particularly original thinker, his epigrams are characterized by a sharpness of formulation that often gives them a touch of the proverbial.

The subject matter is fairly far ranging but essentially provides instruction on how a human being should live within the world but in relationship to the divine order. *Bescheidenheit* means "proper behavior" or perhaps rather "knowledge/understanding of how to behave properly," and in most cases the point is made in two brief lines, a single couplet. Sometimes the reference is to a specific contemporary situation, perhaps of social or political significance, and, like Walther von der Vogelweide who used the *Spruch* so powerfully, Freidank does not shrink from quite sharp criticism, as he treats the relationship between the emperor and the pope, for example, or attacks the Church for its obsession with power and material wealth. Thus he ranges from the small foibles to which human beings readily succumb to the important issues which can corrupt a nation.

There are a great many manuscripts of Freidank's verses, though they vary in what they contain and in the ordering of individual verses. Whether there was indeed any original order or whether they could be delivered more or less randomly within certain groupings is not clear. What is evident is that their impact was considerable, to the extent that they were not only disseminated widely in their own day or shortly after their composition, but that some were actually translated into Latin during the 14th century. This side-by-side version was printed in 1500. In the course of the 16th century, many editions were made on the basis of Sebastian Brant's rendering of Freidank, while epigrammatists of that later period very often derived their own verses from *Bescheidenheit*.

Editions:
Bezzenberger, H. E., ed. *Freidank: Bescheidenheit*. Halle 1872. Repr. 1962.
Spiewok, Wolfgang, ed. and trans. *Freidank: Bescheidenheit*. Leipzig: Reclam, 1985. Repr. 1991 (= UB, 1105). Sel. with mod. Ger. trans., some illus.
See also:
Neumann, Friedrich, in *VL*[2] 2 (1980) 897-903.
Eifler, G. *Die ethischen Anschauungen in Freidanks Bescheidenheit*. Tübingen: Niemeyer, 1969 (= Hermaea, NS 25).

## Hugo von Trimberg: *Der Renner*

This work is probably comparable in importance to Freidank's *Bescheidenheit*, but it dates from the early 14th century and is very different in form and tone. It is a lengthy allegory comprising in all close to 25,000 lines, and as such it can claim to be the longest didactic work of the German Middle Ages. Departing from an account of the seven deadly sins, the work develops into a discourse on contemporary knowledge treated under the headings of the seven liberal arts. These are expounded, however, less for their intrinsic value than as a means to the apprehension of God.

The work, which has the not altogether justified reputation of a tedious encyclopedia, is actually interspersed with anecdotes and illustrations which enliven it, while the sermonizing tone has occasional touches of humor. However, it must be admitted that it is not the most entertaining work of its period, although it is an important document of its age, and certainly it was appreciated and copied until the 16th century.

The title needs some elucidation: some would say that the "runner" is the work itself, making its way through many lands, and others that the verb "rennen" refers to the manner of Hugo's writing, as he races from one subject to the other. In fact the title usually given to the work comes not from Hugo von Trimberg himself but from Michael de Leone who included it in his *Hausbuch* (see p. 343) and provided the explanatory heading "*Renner ist diz buoch genant, Wann es sol rennen durch diu lant*" (This book shall be called *The Runner*, for it is supposed to run through many lands.) The idea that the verb "rennen" is in some way Hugo's own description of his style derives from his frequent use of it in phrases like *wir suln ein wênic vürbaz rennen* (let's go on a bit further, l. 855) and *nun sül wir aber vürbaz rennen* (but now we must go on, l. 2887). G. Schweikle, in his article in the *VL*[2], goes even further in his interpretation of the movement conveyed in the verb, which, he maintains, not only denotes the way Hugo sweeps from one theme to the next but also his striving to understand the nature of God.

An interesting piece of autobiographical detail is provided by Hugo when he tells how, after thirty years writing in Latin, he had almost forgotten his German. There are indeed a number of other surviving works of his, in Latin, and in Latin and German, but *Der Renner*, evidently his last work, is his most important one. It is known that he was born about 1230 in Franconia and worked as a schoolmaster in Bamberg. He says that he completed his *Renner* in 1300 but he continued to add to it until his death, probably some time after 1313.

Edition:
Ehrismann, Gustav, ed. *Der Renner von Hugo von Trimberg*. 1908-1911. 4 vols. (= Bibliothek des literarischen Vereins Stuttgart, 247, 248, 252, 156). Repr. with afterword and additions by G. Schweikle, 1970-71.
See also:
Goheen, Jutta. *Mensch und Moral im Mittelalter: Geschichte und Fiktion in Hugo von Trimbergs "Der Renner"*. Darmstadt: Wiss. Buchges., 1990.
Schweikle, G. "Hugo von Trimberg." $VL^2$ 4 (1982/3) 268-282.

## THE COURTLY ROMANCE IN THE 14TH CENTURY

It is clear that much of the emphasis in the writing of the later Middle Ages in Germany was on factual material or material with some distinct purpose other than entertainment, and one may well ask what had become of the tradition of fiction which had been so dominant a short time earlier. We have already suggested one possible explanation, but another is well argued by Thomas Cramer in his consideration "Neue höfische Romane" (*Geschichte* 27). In attempting to explain the gap of some hundred years in the produc- tion of courtly romances, he cites the inordinate cost of commissioning such a work (equal, he tells us, to the cost of three or four substantial houses in Strasbourg) and con- cludes that potential patrons may have considered their money better spent on more ostentatious objects, such as a fine manuscript of an existing text or fine regalia.

Thus, only a handful of new romances arose during the later period and they need to be mentioned here as much for their value as curiosities as for their intrinsic literary merit. In any case they should not be too abruptly dismissed, and indeed for the earliest of them, Johann von Würzburg's **Wilhelm von Österreich**, a convincing claim has been made that it is deserving of serious analysis in a recent article by Dietrich Huschenbett (Brunner, *Interpretationen* 412-433). This *Minneroman* belongs in the tradition of romances of the 12th and 13th centuries and displays its links with the works of Hartmann and Wolfram and Gottfried's story of the love of Rivalin and Blanscheflur as well as the influence of Rudolf von Ems, but it also looks forward to the romances of adventure of the 16th century, exemplified above all in **Fortunatus**. There is a high degree of originality in the execution of the work, which was finished in 1314, according to its author, and stands somewhat isolated if one bears in mind the time that had elapsed since the heyday of the courtly romance and even since the works of Rudolf von Ems and Konrad von Würzburg. In some respects, *Wilhelm von Österreich* represents these latter works more closely. It is the story of a dynasty, the dukes of Austria, beginning with Duke Leopold, whose son Wilhelm falls in love as a small child with Agyle, daughter of the heathen king Agrant of Zyzya: their child is Friedrich, who inherits the duchy while still a minor when his father is treacherously murdered and his mother dies of grief. The material sounds fairly familiar, and the ill-fated lovers were joined with Tristan and Isolde and Wilhelm von Orléans and Amelie (see p. 338 ff.) on the frescoes at the Castle of Runkelstein, a tribute to their appeal to the Middle Ages, which is also demonstrated in the large number of manuscripts. History and fiction merge in a work that names Duke Friedrich of Austria and his brother Duke Leopold as its patrons. Established literary material is the childhood love, the generational structure, and the conflict between Christian and heathen which constitutes a large portion of the poem.

Text:
Regel, Ernst, ed. *Johann von Würzburg: Wilhelm von Österreich*. Berlin, 1906. Repr. Zürich: Weidmann, 1970 (= DTM, 3).
See: Huschenbett (above) for good bibliography.
See also: Glier, Ingeborg. $VL^2$ 2 (1983) 824-827, and Huschenbett, Dietrich. "Tradition und Theorie im Minneroman. Zum *Wilhelm von Österreich* des Johann von Würzburg." In: Haug, Walter, et al. eds. *Zur deutschen Literatur des 14. Jahrhunderts*. 1983. Pp. 202-220.

Possibly inspired by this work is another dynastic romance which refers to *Wilhelm von Österreich* and tells the story of the dukes of Swabia: this is the somewhat diffuse **Friedrich von Schwaben**, which incorporated fairy-tale motifs possibly not particularly congenial to the audience of its day (after 1314) and seems to have been very much less popular.

Text:
Jellinek, M. J., ed. *Friedrich von Schwaben*. Berlin, 1904 (= DTM 1).

**Peter von Staufenberg** is a little work which is similarly concerned with the question of genealogy but which belongs to the category of short story (*mære*) rather than romance. Its author, Egenolf von Staufenberg, from a noble Strasbourg family, professes to tell the tragic story of his forebear who fell in love with a fairy who made it a condition that he should never marry. For a time he remained true to his word but died, as prophesied, three days after he was forced into a marriage with the daughter of the emperor. The interest of the poem is twofold: this is one of the first German versions of the Melusine story, but it also has socio-historical interest in the picture it gives of the pressures exerted on the lesser nobility by the emperor himself.

(The Melusine story, French in its origins, was to receive its most significant medieval German form in the prose romance of Thüring von Ringoltingen in 1456, where the lovely water sprite brings misfortune on the entire dynasty of Lusignan.)

Text:
Schröder, E., ed. *Zwei deutsche Rittermären*. 1894, Berlin: Weidmann, [2]1913, [4]1929.
See: Walker, Richard Ernest. *Peter von Staufenberg. Its Origin, Development and Later Adaptation*. Göppingen: Kümmerle, 1980 (= GAG, 284); Grunewald, E. ed. *Egenolf von Staufenberg: Peter von Staufenberg. Abbildungen zur Text-und Illustrationsgeschichte*. Göppingen: Kümmerle, 1978 (= Litterae, 53).

This account of the relics of the tradition of romance in the 14th century cannot fail to mention a work which is largely scorned by literary histories, but which nevertheless has something to contribute, if only by its very existence, to the picture. *Der niuwe Parzifal*, sometimes called the *Rappoltsteiner Parzifal*, was composed between 1331 and 1336 by Claus Wisse and Philipp Colin, at the behest of a member of the noble family of Rappoltstein, who is named in the poem as Ulrich. This is an enormously long (36,426 lines) piece meant for insertion between Books 14 and 15 of Wolfram's poem, in order to complete it (!). Based on the French continuation of Chrétien's fragment, it tells of the fruitless search for the Grail of Gawain, the central hero of this interpolation. In the course of numerous and convoluted adventures, he comes upon his long-lost son.

The language is clumsy, the narrative rambling, but the work pays tribute to its great predecessor, albeit inappropriately, and it bears witness to the continuing preoccupation with *Parzival* itself, whose popularity was evinced time and time again in the manuscripts produced during the 14th century.

Edition:
Schorbach, K., ed. *Parzifal von Claus Wisse und Philipp Colin, eine Ergänzung der Dichtung Wolframs von Eschenbach*. Straßburg: Karl J. Trübner, 1888 Repr. 1974.
See also: Wittmann-Klemm, Dorothee. *Studien zum "Rappoltsteiner Parzifal"*. Göppingen: Kümmerle, 1977 (= GAG, 224).
See: Cramer, Thomas. "Aspekte des höfischen Romans im 14. Jahrhundert." In: *Zur deutschen Literatur und Sprache des 14. Jahrhunderts* Ed. by Walter Haug et al. Heidelberg: Winter, 1983, on the whole subject of the courtly romance in the 14th century.


## MEDIEVAL GERMAN DRAMA

Drama as it is usually defined is conspicuous by its absence in medieval Germany, as is largely the case throughout Europe during this period. The reasons are not hard to find. The survival of epic traditions and of lyric poetry intended for public performance probably filled a comparable need, while the absence of an obvious venue apart from the Church and the court meant that there was little opportunity for drama as we understand it to thrive. In that great period of German literature which we call the *Blütezeit*, there is no sign of anything that could be described as "courtly drama," although other genres which flourished at that time contained elements of the dramatic within them.

The development of medieval drama in German is a lengthy process and not easy to trace precisely. Max Wehrli, in his excellent account of the subject, conveys the arbitrary nature of this development when he says (*Geschichte* 586): "Die allgemeine Richtung geht vom Lateinischen zur Volksprache, von der liturgischen Feier zum Spiel und Drama, vom geistlichen zum bürgerlichen Träger, vom Kircheninneren zum städtischen Platz, vom musikalischen zum gesprochenen Vortrag, von Frömmigkeit zur Moral und Unterhaltung, vom kurzen zum langen Spiel—wobei aber diese Übergänge keineswegs gleichzeitig oder gar identisch sind und im einzelnen auch reversibel sein können." (The general direction passes from Latin to the vernacular, from liturgical celebration to play and drama, from clerical to bourgeois actors, from the interior of the church to the market-place, from musical to spoken delivery, from piety to moralizing and entertainment, from short play to long play, but these transitions are by no means simultaneous or in any way identical and individual ones can even be reversible).

As in other European countries, origins of drama in Germany are quite divorced from the classical drama which we tend to use as a yardstick for our conception of drama as a literary form. We must regard medieval drama as an entirely new phenomenon, deeply rooted in the ceremonies of the Church and gradually, in fact only very gradually, becoming secularized. At the same time, the "characters" central to the Christian story do not offer the tragic potential which is a prerequisite of high drama as a literary genre, while the external features which we have become accustomed to regard as prerequisites of drama—features of structure and the unifying factors essential in classical drama—are absent. Again, Max Wehrli puts it in an illuminating way (580): "Wir befinden uns am Rande der Literaturgeschichte und oft jenseits ihrer Grenze: im Bereich der Liturgie, des Brauchs, der Musik, der Pantomime." (We find ourselves on the periphery of literary history and often beyond its frontier: in the realm of liturgy, of custom, of music, of pantomime). It is only relatively late in the Middle Ages that we can begin to speak of drama as a literary form, and by then it is completely divorced from the environment which produced the classic literature of the earlier period. Medieval German drama proper belongs not to the court or the social élite of that earlier age but to the people.

## Hroswitha von Gandersheim

The origins of medieval German drama actually lie many centuries earlier, however unrecognizable they may be. The Latin comedies of Terence, in particular, were widely known in the early Middle Ages, but they were simply read, not performed, more for their language than for their content, which did not meet with much approval in a society dominated by the clergy. It is all the more interesting, then, that it was a religious woman who became eminent precisely in the sphere of drama and is sometimes referred to as the first German woman of letters. This is the nun **Hroswitha von Gandersheim** who, writing in Latin in the 10th century, imitated the form of Terence's drama but replaced the often immoral content with religious or quasi-religious matter. The form is not "plays," but a brief preface which relates the plot, followed by dialogue. Development of character and the other qualities, such as confrontation between human beings, which later centuries found to be the essence of drama, are absent, yet there is evidence that these plays were meant to be performed. Some controversy surrounds the question of whether they were indeed performed during her lifetime, but on the whole it is considered that this is more than likely. Although there are no "stage directions" as we know them, there are indications of living performance in the references to facial expressions and gestures, for example, and to costumes. The didactic qualities do not, moreover, exclude the element of comedy, in which disguise and mimicry play their part.

## Religious Drama

The true origins of medieval German drama, as of most European drama, lie in the Church services which afforded ready-made dramatic potential, particularly in the case of those linked with significant occasions in the Church calendar. Thus the festivals of Christmas and Easter and all the associated occasions provided the material for presentation in church from the 9th and 10th centuries on and gradually accrued fresh details which made for a lively performance, supported by readings and, above all, by music. We can be fairly sure that these performances were in Latin until well into the 12th century, and it was left to the audience to follow as much as they could. Inevitably, however, the lay members of the audience came to expect at least part of the performance to be in the vernacular. A further stage was that members of the laity assumed active roles in the performances, and gradually the material broadened to encompass worldly matters and even elements of comedy. Thus it is possible, indeed desirable, to speak of religious and secular drama as separate categories in the German Middle Ages, while always accepting that there was considerable overlap, at least in the early stages. Members of the clergy may well have looked with great disapproval at these, particularly since the actual church was the most obvious venue and the altar the focus of the performance. It is not far from the religious processions which frequently formed an important part of the early "dramas" to the often exuberant processions of the populace, accompanied by dancing and miming and sometimes demanding that the performers appear in masks. Thus, by the 14th century, there was established in Germany a tradition of Shrove-tide plays which has endured to the present day in the characteristic celebrations of *Fasching*.

Wolfgang Michael, in his study of the development of German drama from the early Middle Ages through the 16th century, asserts that, despite the gifted practitioners of whom he writes, German medieval drama remains essentially "naive," in Schiller's sense of the term. This is hardly surprising, given its origins and its background, but it is worth bearing in mind in assessing the weight which one should give it in the whole picture of medieval German literature. Again and again, in our examination of the narrative literature of the *Blütezeit* and the decades that followed, we have referred to the essentially dramatic qualities within the tradition of epic and romance. The *Nibelungenlied* comes very much closer to our idea of what constitutes drama than what we are now considering, while the lyric poems of Wolfram von Eschenbach and Walther von der Vogelweide, for example, often have more obviously "dramatic" moments that evoke a vivid background and depend on the juxtaposition of people in a highly charged situation. The work of Der Stricker, in the later period, contains much of the potential and sometimes the reality of drama, as he exploits often quite credible human situations (see pp. 364 ff.).

In any assessment of the so-called drama of the Middle Ages, however, we encounter a major disadvantage, since our perception of it must be one-sided, lacking as we mostly do the knowledge of how the works will have been performed. We can only guess at the impact on the audience. Moreover, our only evidence for the existence of the plays is the manuscripts which are frequently unreliable and very difficult to date. We hope therefore to suggest the variety and nature of this material by description and to attempt to indicate the principal characteristics. There is something to be said for following the practice of dividing the material into the two broad categories of "religious drama" and "secular drama," though it must be emphasized that the two merged, with liberal borrowing between the two areas and adaptation of the material of the one to the mood and purpose of the other.

The origins of what can be described as religious drama lie in Germany, as elsewhere in Europe, in the *tropes*, the passages of text inserted into the mass and other church services. These usually took the form of dialogues placed at strategic points in the liturgy and thus containing an embryonic sense of the dramatic. One of the earliest examples is contained in the 10th-century St. Gallen manuscript, the frequently quoted *Quem quaeritis in sepulchro, Christicolae*, which takes as its basis the question of the angel to the three women at the empty tomb. The dramatic scene, which is a principal focus of Christianity, marks the beginning of European drama, and it found its way, in extended form, into many versions throughout Europe in the Middle Ages. Gradually other figures were added—Christ Himself appearing as the Gardener and the Apostles Peter and John racing to the empty tomb—and other material relating to the Easter story. It is well-nigh impossible to draw a line between liturgy and dramatic performance in such "plays," the intention of which was not to effect a theatrical performance, to create the illusion of an historical event through imitation, but to convey a religious truth by means of a sensual experience. Central to the performances must have been the detachment of the actors, the stylized presentations, and the emphasis on symbolism.

Judging from the surviving manuscripts—and this is really our only criterion, and possibly not an entirely reliable one—the vast majority of plays written in German were concerned with the Easter story in its broadest sense. Thus there were predominantly Passion plays, Easter and Resurrection plays, so-called *Marienklagen* which treat the grieving Virgin beneath the Cross, and Corpus Christi plays, while individual examples survive of less popular subjects such as the account of the life of Mary Magdalene, the Last Supper, the Ascension, and the Assumption of the Virgin Mary.

Perhaps rather surprisingly, plays relating to the Christmas season appear to have been much less frequent, though there is evidence of episodic depictions of the central events associated with the story of the Nativity from the announcement to the shepherds to the flight into Egypt. Some of the German examples include a characteristic feature known as the *Kindelwiegen*, which entailed singing and even dancing round the cradle (*Wiege*) of the Christ child.

There are other plays of religious content, and these could presumably be performed at almost any time in the year. Some of these are saint plays, with Theophilus and "Pope Joan" (Frau Jutta) the most popular, while others were based on legends such as the discovery of the Holy Cross. Plays on the theme of the Last Judgment were evidently popular, and there were some attempts at dramatizing Old Testament stories. The distribution and survival of manuscripts means that we must remain fairly cautious in asserting the existence or lack of certain forms: only fairly recently have some morality plays been discovered where previous scholarship had maintained that there were no such plays in German, compared with their existence as a popular feature of the English Middle Ages, for example. The so-called Erfurt Morality Play (*Erfurter Moralität*) is in fact the longest (almost 18,000 lines) and most complex German play known to exist. Indeed, its very length and complexity suggested to some critics that this was a play to be read and not performed, but the very recent (1986) discovery of another fragment textually related to it has led to the view that morality plays were indeed performed and disseminated for performance. Probably the most accessible account of the distribution of the texts, chronologically and geographically, is contained in the long article by Rolf Bergmann in the *Reallexikon der deutschen Literatur* (2nd edition, 64-100).

The first play in which we can be sure that Latin and German were both used is the **Benediktbeuern Passionsspiel** (Benediktbeuern Passion Play) of about 1200. This is preserved in the same manuscript as the *Carmina Burana* (see p. 225 ff.). Probably three or four decades later is the **Osterspiel von Muri** (Easter Play from Muri in the Aargau), which is usually held to be the first play completely in German. The content is not surprising, corresponding as it does largely to the treatments of the Easter story in Latin, but what is remarkable is the use of the courtly couplet of the medieval German romance and the effective exploitation of the dramatic potential of the scenes portrayed through a deepening of the characters and the sense that they are placed in a "real" human context. However, the possibility that this play might have ushered in an age of courtly drama of high quality in Germany was not to be fulfilled: the work remains strangely isolated and appears to have had little impact on the Easter plays which succeeded it. Critics usually point to only one other play which may reflect its influence: the much less effective St. Gallen play which relates the childhood of Christ and belongs to the same general geographical region, though considerably later in the 13th century.

These two examples of plays exclusively in German stand out from the many dramas of the same period which use Latin and German side by side, and sometimes with considerable effect, often juxtaposing the familiar Latin with a homely use of the vernacular. The mixture sometimes achieves a purpose which verges on the comic, as when Jesus, in the guise of the Gardener, addresses to Mary Magdalene the question "*Mulier, quid ploras, quem quaeris?*" before launching into German to tease her about being in the garden so early in the morning, perhaps waiting for a young man (**Trierer Osterspiel** [Trier Easter Play], in the edition by Froning, vol. 1). In this way, it would appear, the use of both languages was in itself a dramatic device and not simply an expedient to please the audience and to cater to the increasing use of lay actors alongside the clergy.

As the scope of the plays became greater and the numbers of "actors" increased, the need arose to move the performances from the church and its environs to the market place. This shift of location probably served as an invitation to the general public to participate and led increasingly to the secularization of the plays and even to the introduction of material which could be regarded as profane and verging on the obscene. In the later Middle Ages, a certain amount of detail of staging and costumes, for example, can be obtained from the working manuscripts and sometimes from information gleaned in municipal archives.

## Secular Drama

It is impossible to prove the existence of what can properly be described as "secular drama" in German before the middle of the 14th century, the dates of the earliest texts, yet we can be sure that something of the kind did exist, though probably not before the middle of the 13th century. We are not dealing here with what might be called "literary drama" which could be committed to parchment, but with improvisation and mimicry, accompanied by dancing and often doubtless taking the form of a procession, which in itself could be seen to derive from a central feature of the church services.

The vast majority of the secular "plays" are Carnival entertainments, and from the earliest occurrences of these there arose a tradition during the 14th century of *Fastnachtsspiele*, of which many examples survive in texts dating from the 15th century. These are mostly very short texts deriving from the performances of small groups of players, and, although most are anonymous, it is possible to point to distinguishing features. These small groups apparently moved from town to town, particularly in South Germany, requiring nothing more sophisticated in the way of staging than the local market place or inn. There will surely have been a certain amount of robust audience participation in the performances. It would be reasonable to assume, too, that local references will have played a part. The language and style of the surviving plays lack refinement, to say the least, and yet there is evidence of a range of subject matter, deriving not just from the everyday life of the audience but also from the social and even political environment of the day. Satire was sometimes present in attacks on individual professions or groups within the community. With this trend which led out of the late Middle Ages and into the 16th century, we are nearing the much more consolidated oeuvre of Hans Sachs and the beginnings of what may justly be described as German comedy.

Only a few individual plays are capable of being dated. One of these is *Des Entkrist Vasnacht*, whose very title, with its sharp paradox, points to its satirical intention. This "Shrovetide Play of the Antichrist," a crude but unambiguous attempt at a political drama, seems to arise from the events of 1353-54 in Zürich, when the Emperor Charles IV tried to intervene in the conflict between Zürich and Austria. Other contemporary figures appear to be portrayed in this somewhat confused play, notably, some critics would maintain, the Roman tribune Cola di Rienzo, who, banished by the Pope, had taken refuge at the court of Charles. If it is true that this highly ambiguous player in the Church politics of the day lies behind the figure of the Antichrist, holding out false hopes to the Emperor, then this is indeed a powerful departure from the innocuous performances of the travelling players.

Another identifiable play which probably dates from the early 14th century is based on the familiar medieval idea of a debate, in this case the conflict between Autumn and Spring. It centers on the lovely Gotelind, daughter of Lord Maytime, who is abducted, without much resistance on her part, by Lord Autumn. Twelve knights on either side fight for her, and the victory comes to Autumn. Each of the knights speaks a strophe in turn, and their comic names, and indeed the whole conception of the conflict between the seasons, echoes the earlier medieval period, in particular *Helmbrecht* (see p. 403 ff.) and the songs of Neidhart (see p. 279 ff.).

It is in fact Neidhart, with his predilection for dancing songs and his emphasis on the natural background, who most commends himself to these early attempts at dramatic portrayal, and a small group of extant texts points to a separate tradition within the category usually called rather loosely *Fastnachtsspiele*. The so-called *St. Paul Neidhartspiel* is probably of about the same date as the battle between Autumn and May, and these are the oldest surviving texts in German of secular plays. The little play (a *Schwank*) is based on the rather insubstantial anecdote of how Neidhart finds the first violet of the season and covers it with his hat while he goes off to inform the Duchess of Austria. On his return with her he discovers that a peasant has played a prank on him and removed the violet, to the irritation of the Duchess and the fury of Neidhart, the traditional enemy of the peasantry, who swears to take his revenge. Unlikely though it may seem, this scrap of dramatic action came to constitute the core of a series of Neidhart plays, contained in three extant collections of a rather later period (15th century), and again eventually finding their way into the repertoire of Hans Sachs.

The development of medieval German drama, perhaps more than of any other genre of the period, needs to be viewed within a European context. There are, as indicated, characteristic German trends, but much of the material, in terms of content and form and presentation, can, and probably should, be seen in a broader context. The preceding outline is no more than a sketch of some of the principal trends in a development which was more than usually complex and made all the more hazy by the nature of the transmission of the material.

Hroswitha von Gandersheim:
Bannhauer, Otto, et al., eds. and trans. *Hrotsvit von Gandersheim: Sämtliche Dichtungen. Vollständige Ausgabe. Aus dem Mittellateinischen übertragen. Mit einer Einführung von Bert Nagel.* Munich, 1966.
Nagel, Bert. *Hrotsvit von Gandersheim.* Stuttgart: Metzler, 1965 (= Sammlung Metzler, 44).
Rädle, Fidel. *VL*[2] 4 (1983) 196-210.
Wilson, Katharina M., trans. *The Plays of Hrotsvit of Gandersheim.* New York: Garland, 1989 (= GLML, B, 62).

Texts of German plays:
Froning, Richard, ed. *Das Drama des Mittelalters.* Stuttgart, 1891-92 (= DNL, 14). Repr. Darmstadt: Wiss. Buchges., 1964. (3 vols.).
Mone, F. J., ed. *Schauspiele des Mittelalters.* Aus Handschriften herausgegeben und erklärt von F.J. Mone. Karlsruhe: Macklot, 1846. (These two volumes, which may not be easily found, contain some very interesting texts with some illustrations, while the commentary, despite the very early date, contains much material which has really not been superseded and remains very valuable.)
____. ed. *Altdeutsche Schauspiele.* Quedlinburg and Leipzig: Basse, 1841.
(For specific plays, it is probably increasingly preferable to use individual editions which are now appearing: details will be found in the recent works referred to below [e.g. Linke]. There is very little material in English translation.)

## Medieval German Drama—Bibliography

Axton, Richard. *European Drama of the Early Middle Ages.* London: Hutchinson University Library, 1974.

Not specifically concerned with German examples, but containing some illuminating material, particularly on general background issues and matters of presentation.

Brett-Evans, David. *Von Hrotsvit bis Folz und Gengenbach. Eine Geschichte des mittelalterlichen deutschen Dramas.* Berlin: Erich Schmidt, 1975 (= GLG, 15 & 18).

Vol. I: *Von der liturgischen Feier zum volksprachigen Spiel*, treats the period covered here; Vol II: *Religiöse und weltliche Spiele des Spätmittelalters*, takes the subject to the mid-17th century.

Linke, Hansjürgen. "Drama und Theater." In: de Boor/Newald, 3:2, *Literaturges.* ed. by I. Glier, Chapter 4 (153-233).

Some very solid material, covering the religious plays and the secular plays. Particularly helpful summary: "Frühgeschichte des Dramas und Theaters im Überblick." Pp. 230-233.

____. "Germany and German-speaking Central Europe." In: *The Theatre of Medieval Europe. New Research in Early Drama.* Ed. by Eckehard Simon. Cambridge: Cambridge UP, 1991. Pp. 207-224.

____. "A Survey of Medieval Drama and Theater in Germany." In: *Medieval Drama on the Continent of Europe.* Ed. by Clifford Davidson and John H. Stroupe. Kalamazoo: Medieval Institute Publications, 1993. Pp. 17-53.

This and the article above by Linke are trans. into Engl. The two volumes are useful collections of articles on the broader subject.

Michael, Wolfgang F. *Das deutsche Drama des Mittelalters.* Berlin: de Gruyter, 1971.

A very full account of the subject.

____. "Tradition and Originality in the Medieval Drama in Germany." In: *The Medieval Drama.* Papers of the third annual conference of the Center for Medieval and Early Renaissance Studies, SUNY Binghamton, 3-4 May 1969. Ed. by Sandro Sticca. Albany: SUNY Press, 1972. Pp. 23-37.

See also Wehrli *Geschichte* 580-608 and Walshe *Med. Ger. Lit.* 296-303.

For detailed information on specific texts and collections, see: Bergmann, Rolf, "Spiele, Mittelalterliche geistliche," and Bauer, Werner M., "Spiele, Mittelalterliche weltliche." In: *Reallexikon der deutschen Literaturgeschichte.* Berlin: de Gruyter, [2]1979. Vol. IV. Pp. 64-100 and 100-105 resp. (The first is by far the more valuable).


## MYSTICISM

An important phenomenon in the later 13th and throughout the 14th century is the growth of mysticism, which finds expression in German, notably in the works of Mechthild von Magdeburg, Meister Eckhart, Johann Tauler, and Heinrich Suso (or Seuse). The origins of mysticism lie further back, however, in the writings of St. Bernard of Clairvaux (1090-1153) and Hugh of St. Victor (1096-1141), two of the most influential theologians and teachers of their day.

The development of mysticism is a complex subject, and the manifestations of mysticism in medieval Germany are varied and somewhat elusive. What follows is thus a necessarily simplified account of a vast subject, and one may do well to begin with a necessarily simplified definition of mysticism itself. Indeed, one can hardly do better than take the definition proffered by Alois Haas in his book *Geistliches Mittelalter* (p. 185): "Der Mystiker ist einer, der Gott in besonders intensiver Weise erfahren und kennenlernen darf." (The mystic is one to whom it is vouchsafed to experience God and to become acquainted with Him in a particularly intensive manner). Haas continues: "Mystik ist existentielles Erfahren Gottes, ist nach einer alten Formel *cognitio Dei experimentalis*, ein durch Erfahrung geprägtes Wahrnehmen Gottes meist in Form einer spürbaren Vereinigung mit ihm." (Mysticism is the existential experience of God; in accordance with the ancient formula *cognitio Dei experimentalis*, it is the perception of God characterized by personal experience and usually takes the form of a palpable union with Him.)

Already in the German *St. Trudperter Hohes Lied*, composed in about 1140, possibly by a nun, the influence of St. Bernard was evident (see p. 74 f.). The work combines learning and lyrical outpourings of emotion as it urges an abandonment of worldly things in pursuit of the union with God which is the essence of mysticism. Such mystical experiences were recorded for the first time in the Latin work by Hildegard, the famous German Benedictine nun who founded the convent at Bingen on the Rhine and is usually identified as the first German mystic (1098-1179). Her most important work is *Scivias* (Know the ways [of the Lord]), which is an account of the visions experienced by this saintly woman from her childhood on and it is illustrated by Hildegard herself.

## Mechthild von Magdeburg

Hildegard's example was followed by other nuns, also writing in Latin, and it was not until a century later that another devout woman, who was originally attached to no specific order (a "Beguine") but subsequently joined the Cistercians, composed a remarkable work in German. This is *Das fließende Licht der Gottheit* by **Mechthild von Magdeburg**, a work which, with its abundant use of the language and imagery of the Minnesang, expresses in striking terms a deeply personal relationship of the soul with God. Mechthild herself manages to control the frankly erotic elements in her statement, but this was not always to be the case with some of those who sought to imitate her and who were less restrained in their outpourings of ecstasy. The convent at Helfta, near Eisleben in her native Saxony, became a center of mysticism, with Mechthild as the focus as she worked, possibly until close to her death in about 1282, on this major product of German mysticism, which, at that time, was largely represented by women.

Mechthild's original Low German text does not survive, but a translation into High German dating from 1344 is extant, together with an earlier translation into Latin. We are thus well able to assess the qualities of this unique work which is a strange amalgam of verse and prose, encompassing personal accounts of mystical experiences, some in diary form, hymns, prayers, dialogues and anecdotes. It would appear that the work was intended first and foremost to be read by her "geistliche swester" (spiritual sisters), as she calls them, and, although she admits herself that she was in any case not versed in Latin, her use of the vernacular, quite a daring departure, coincided with her intention of making these thoughts known among a specific audience which was also quite separate from the usual recipients of theological debate. The tone ranges from ecstasy to earnest admonition. The goal is the *unio mystica*: the core of mysticism. Yet the intimacy of the soul with God is juxtaposed to the experience of the alienation from God, and the work contains dire warnings about the separation from the Divine which can come from a life lived in accordance with worldly matters, particularly by those of the nobility who place their social position above their relationship with God. It is the seriousness of this message that redresses the eager seizing of the desired union. The accounts of visions make explicit use of the language of mysticism which speaks, for example, of the soul naked before the divine bridegroom and relates the union of the soul with God in the bed of love. Central images are those of flowing and fusion which express the core of her relationship with God, in which union and mutual possession dominate. In order to know this perfect love, the soul must be prepared to endure suffering and hardship, isolation and loneliness, but the love, when it is realized, is suffused with a warmth and depth that afford full compensation for hardships experienced. In her introduction, Mechthild speaks of her sense of having been inspired by God: "This book is to be welcomed with joy for God Himself speaks in it" (*Dis buch sol man gerne enpfan, wan got sprichet selber die wort*: P. Gall Morel edition, p. 3).

In terms of artistry, Mechthild's work remains an isolated peak of its kind at this point of German literature, anticipating in some of its language and thought, though less in its intention, the lyric outpourings of the Baroque. Mechthild, like some of her less famous sisters, represents a spiritual literature centered in women writers at a time when, in France, secular writings by women were gaining prominence in the form of the love lyric. The whole issue of the growing religiosity among women that found expression in the foundation of convents and then, following the decree issued in 1198 by Pope Innocent III which curtailed the further expansion of such formal institutions, in the Beguine movement, has been the subject of some important scholarship in recent years, as the selection in our bibliography suggests. Some critics would question the validity of a category of women's mystical writings (*Frauenmystik*), but most would concede that the writings of women do constitute a separate division with recognizable characteristics. Interestingly, Mechthild herself noted the astonishment of her "editor," Meister Heinrich, at the *masculine* way in which she wrote (Morel 5,12: "Meister Heinrich, uch wundert sin menlicher worten, die in disem buche geschriben sin"). In the simplest terms, the women mystics tend to write of their personal experiences, of visions and revelations, while, if one may generalize, the men often write with the authority of the Church which was indeed accorded to them in medieval society.

## Eckhart, Tauler, and Suso

In many respects and for a variety of reasons, the single remarkable work of Mechthild is in sharp contrast to the other major products of German mysticism, represented by three names: **Meister Eckhart, Johannes Tauler,** and **Heinrich Suso** or (**Seuse**). In turning now to these figures, it may be helpful to bear in mind the characterizations of the three implied by Joseph Quint in his *Textbuch der deutschen Mystik* (p. 135): "Wenn Eckhart der spekulative Kopf der deutschen Mystik, Tauler ihr energievoller Ethiker und Lehrer der mystischen Praxis ist, so ist Seuse ihr großer Lyriker, der Mystiker ganz aus dem Grunde eines tiefen und starken Gefühls." (If Eckhart is the speculative thinker of German mysticism, Tauler its energetic moralist and teacher of the mystical practice, then Seuse is its great lyricist, the mystic from the very depths of a profound and powerful feeling). Like any attempt at a brief characterization, this has its limitations but it is a useful starting point for anyone trying to unravel the nature of this complex trio.

## Meister Eckhart

Meister Eckhart was born at Hochheim in Thuringia about 1260. He entered the Dominican order in Erfurt and was subsequently sent to study in Paris, following in the footsteps of Thomas Aquinas. He may indeed have studied under Thomas, or at least almost certainly under Albert the Great (died 1280) during the last years of the latter's life, in the Dominican house of theology in Cologne. After a further period lecturing in Paris, Eckhart returned to Erfurt as prior of the Dominican house there and Vicar of Thuringia. Clearly his administrative skills were appreciated, and he held successively the posts of Provincial of Saxony (1303) and Vicar-General of Bohemia (1307), before being nominated to the office of Provincial of Alemannia (1310), a post which in the event was not confirmed. Instead he went again to Paris and thence to Strasbourg, which was by that time (ca.1314) an important center of religious activity and, in particular, a focus of German mysticism. His increasing scholarly reputation which was expressed in his attainment of the title *magister* led at some point (ca. 1322) to his appointment to the chair previously held by Albert the Great, at the *Studium Generale* in Cologne. Here he came into conflict with the Archbishop of Cologne, who initiated the charges of heresy which were to lead to lengthy proceedings against him and culminated, after his death, in his condemnation by Pope John XXII.

The basis of the charges was that Eckhart had spread dangerous doctrines among the ordinary people, and they had their roots in the distortion or misunderstanding, whether deliberate or otherwise, of the mystical writings for which Eckhart is justly renowned. At the heart of the conflict was doubtless the rivalry between the Dominicans and the Franciscans, and Eckhart's translation to the prominent chair in Cologne almost certainly provoked the action against him. The intervention of the Pope pronounced the disapproval of the Church on him, albeit posthumously, and ensured that his influence was relatively limited, though the abundance of his writings bears witness to an impact which could not be suppressed. Nevertheless, although the prominent 17th-century mystic Johannes Scheffler (usually known as Angelus Silesius) reflects his influence in his poetry, Eckhart did not emerge as a significant figure again until the 19th century. Our own age, with its appreciation for less conventional attitudes and its predilection for personal religions, has shown a new enthusiasm for his works as the spate of translations and accounts reflected in our bibliography suggests. That said, however, it is generally agreed that Eckhart was actually not out of step with the thinking of the Church, but that, as he himself conceded, his expression, complex and subtle as it often was, and beset with repetition and paradox, was capable of being misunderstood by the less educated among whom he had become so popular and by the envious who deliberately sought to pervert his teachings.

By birth a nobleman, Eckhart is inextricable by education and inclination from the principal scholarly trends of his day. As a doctor of the University of Paris, he inherited the traditions of learning of Albert the Great and Thomas Aquinas, and his name is significantly linked with two other great cities of the Middle Ages: Strasbourg, where he wrote and preached and became the outstanding figure in the prevailing mystical thought, and Cologne, where he probably studied in his youth and attained his important though controversial reputation in his mature years. It is evident, too, that he travelled widely in Germany and into Switzerland, preaching in friaries and convents, as well as to the laity. Since one of his functions was to instruct the religious sisters under the Dominican authority, he may be held responsible to a substantial extent for the growth of women's mystical writings. In his own writings, as in his sermons, he combined learning with more speculative theology. It is thus possible to speak of Eckhart the theologian and philosopher, and Eckhart the mystic, but it is important also to understand that his work is the fusion of the intellectual and the intuitive in the sense that he attempts to put into intellectual terms that which he has experienced mystically. Although much of his work was in Latin, the abundance of writings in the vernacular means that, in common with the other great mystics writing in German, he also had a powerful impact on the language (see below).

Eckhart's Latin works were obviously intended for the educated, specifically for those learned in theology and ecclesiastical matters. Of these the most important is his *Opus Tripartitum* (ca. 1314), an enormous work of which only very little survives. In addition he wrote sermons in Latin as well as the documents which relate to the charges brought against him, his defense, and his reply to the accusations. It is the German writings which constitute the major part of Eckhart's surviving oeuvre, and these are mostly sermons, preached in the Beguine houses and nunneries that lay within his purview.

We shall not attempt to analyze the often very complex thought of Meister Eckhart. There are many routes to gain an insight into this very important and in many ways very puzzling figure. Our intention is merely to suggest his position within German mysticism and the place of that mysticism within the development of German literature. It is clearly a significant aspect of German writing during the later Middle Ages. Although undoubtedly more restricted, its impact on thought is akin to the impact of chivalry in the earlier period, and there is good reason to suggest that the impact on the German language was if anything greater. New words, particularly abstract nouns, had to be invented, often using Latin models, in order to express ideas which had no predecessors. The mystics were, after all, attempting to express the inexpressible, and, however impossible their task, they had to find the means to perform it.

Mystical thinking places man in a new relationship with God. This is no longer the relationship dependent on love and service which characterized the thought of the courtly poets, and it is far removed from the humanistic viewpoint that was to value man for his own sake within an order which might include God but in which He was no longer the prime motivating force.

A central concept simple in its expression but hardly simple to comprehend is Eckhart's notion of "living without a why" (*sunder warumbe*), and this defines a new way of living in the world which he advocates. In attaining the state of living without a why, the soul is able to find God in all things, and the consequence of this is that activity within the world has a validity: the contemplative way of life is not necessarily the superior one, and man should seek to make holy that which he does rather than to aspire to holiness by his deeds. The soul which lives without a why can remain untouched by the troubles which afflict those who have not attained this state, which is, moreover, akin to the state of detachment (*abgeschiedenheit*) which Eckhart advocates elsewhere. In the "letting go" (*gelâzenheit*), man achieves this detachment which unites him with God. The love that Eckhart talks about is a mutual love which enables the soul to become one with God and God to become one with the soul. Unlike Mechthild von Magdeburg, Eckhart on the whole avoids using the language of human love to describe the state of the soul in its relationship with the Divine, though he welcomes this goal with no less enthusiasm. The process is less the ecstatic fusing of the soul with the godly bridegroom than a deliberate movement towards the point where man, divorced from worldly concerns, can attain to the higher state from which there is no turning aside.

No one will deny that Eckhart is difficult to comprehend, and any comparison of the existing translations will demonstrate how amenable he is to differing interpretations. It is small wonder, then, that his works were open to misunderstanding, whether innocent or contrived to effect his downfall. Even his defense and his so-called "retraction" reflect some complex and even ambiguous thinking. One of the 14th-century sermons mistakenly attributed to him is headed "This is Meister Eckhart from whom God hid nothing," yet any attentive reading of him will reveal that this cannot be his own claim, for the absolute mystery of God is central to his thought. At the same time, however, the assertion reflects—albeit with some irony, given that he had recently been condemned by papal decree—the power of his reputation in his own day and indeed in the present age, when he is rightly assessed as a central thinker, a focus of German mysticism and a pivotal contributor in the consideration of the progress of German literature.

The authoritative edition of Eckhart's works is that published by Kohlhammer (Stuttgart, 1936 ff.), with J. Quint responsible for the German works and J. Koch for the Latin works. This edition forms the basis for the many translations of Eckhart.

### Johannes Tauler

Although not a great deal is known about the details of Johannes Tauler's life, it is certain that he was born in Strasbourg, probably about 1300. He speaks of a distinct religious calling, and it is likely that, when he entered the convent in Strasbourg, he will have met Meister Eckhart who was already installed there as prior in about 1314. The family figures in documents of the city in the early 14th century, and it appears that they were quite important members of the Strasbourg community, of substantial means. His theological studies continued at the *studium generale* in Cologne. Thus the pattern of his early career closely followed that of Eckhart, whose teachings he clearly respected, even if he was not precisely under his tutelage at any point. It cannot be established for sure whether he was ever in Paris, although some critics would maintain that he was.

What we do know is that he lived for a period in Basel, when the conflict between the Emperor and the Pope forced the Dominican friars into exile in 1339. Tauler returned to Strasbourg in 1343 and died there in 1361. There is fairly reliable evidence that he spent a period later in his life in Cologne, at a time when additional building work was in progress on the great cathedral. The few details we have about Tauler's life have been supplemented by other information, not all very reliable and some of it verging on the legendary.

All of Tauler's works are in German: eighty-four sermons, all composed for specific occasions in the Church calendar and each one based on the reading for the day from the Scriptures. The basis of his teaching is what may be termed everyday morality, and there is something altogether traditional about his advocacy of a life devoted to God, freed from worldly things and devoted to charitable works. Put like that, his teaching would appear to be somewhat homespun, yet he relates these simple precepts to mystical themes. In demanding that man remain passive in his submission to the will of God, he urges that detachment from worldly matters which is central to Eckhart's teaching but which, in Tauler, is related also to the theme of suffering. He draws a contrast between *wirken* (acting, working) and *leiden* (suffering or being passive, which in its ultimate form is acceptance of God's working through one). The idea is linked to his juxtaposition of speech and silence: in silence man can await the speech of God, patiently biding one's time until God reveals His purpose. Man must remain alert to the fact that his actions are dependent upon God's will.

The question of suffering is embraced in the double meaning of the verb *leiden*: in suffering, one can submit to God's will and wait patiently for it to be shown to us. Thus, all suffering is intended by God, the product of His love, to be received by us with love. Acceptance of suffering is the means we have to imitate Christ.

Tauler's message of passive submission must be seen in relation to his advocacy of action, though such action may be interpreted as the spiritual action of fasts and vigils as well as of pilgrimages and charitable acts. Such "actions" are the outward manifestations of inward disposition. One should not be distracted by outward actions from the cultivation of one's spiritual life, and if the former threatens to impair the latter, then one should set it aside until the proper spiritual state is restored or achieved.

From these few examples, it is apparent that Tauler's teaching is relatively simple, and he often takes his examples from ordinary human life, stressing his message by sometimes quite homely language and imagery and thus adjusting to a far greater extent than Eckhart to a congregation going about its everyday occupations and not necessarily attuned to mystical language and experiences. Indeed, when difficulties in textual matters do occur, these are often precisely in the more obviously mystical passages, where they may be due to a lack of understanding on the part of the scribe.

It may be that the relative accessibility of the works of Tauler accounts for the fact that they had a more enduring effect than his master Eckhart who was undoubtedly actually a much more powerful mind, or it may be attributable to the suppression of Eckhart's works following his trial and condemnation. Some critics have questioned the applicability of the term "mystic" to him, so little does he speak of his own inner life, but the same is true of Eckhart himself, who, unlike the women writers of the age, refrains from outpourings of personal experience and defines his concept of mysticism in much more abstract and less intimate terms. It would be misleading to imply that Tauler is totally devoid of lyrical qualities. His popularity with the German Romantics bears witness to his impact on the imagination.

## Heinrich Suso

It is Heinrich Suso who most emphatically evokes the world of the emotion and whose works attain heights of lyricism more akin to the language of the women mystics of medieval Germany. Indeed, there are qualities in Suso's work which link it with the world of medieval chivalry, once very much alive in his native Swabia, but well into its decline by the time he came to write, in the first half of the 14th century. Surprisingly, one finds in his work reminders of medieval German epic and lyric poetry, in the rhythmic style and even in the substance, the references to the beauty of nature, for example. Frank Tobin, in his authoritative translation and introduction to the work of Suso, sums up his quality when he says: "The expression of spiritual truths in literary form was Suso's ultimate goal." This characterization, together with that of Joseph Quint quoted above, serves to demonstrate the distinctive nature of Suso's contribution.

Central to Suso's mysticism is the Passion of Christ and the attempt to enter into the suffering of God through His Son. In this respect he is an innovator in German, although he almost certainly studied in Cologne under Eckhart and was a close contemporary of Johann Tauler. His style is very different from the latter's, however, and his early dependence on the teaching of Meister Eckhart gave way increasingly, as he produced his most characteristic works and subsequently edited them for posterity, to highly individualized writings which are also remarkably varied.

The volume which resulted from this later editing and addition is the *Exemplar*, which comprises the *Life of the Servant*, the *Little Book of Eternal Wisdom*, the *Little Book of Truth*, and the *Little Book of Letters*. Also extant are sermons in the vernacular, though not all of these are considered authentic.

Suso's *Life of the Servant* is sometimes seen as "the first German autobiography," although the description is somewhat misleading. The origin of the work is known to us: it is based on the notes which his protégée, the saintly Elsbeth Stagel, took of their conversations, in the course of which he answered her questions on spiritual matters and also imparted to her details of his own, sometimes anguished, spiritual journey. He tells how he confiscated these notes when he discovered their existence but subsequently refrained from destroying them in response to an instruction from God while he was in the very act of burning them. The result is a superb work of sometimes quite poetic prose, which moves between pure narrative and sermonizing, interspersed with vivid anecdotes and characterized by a remarkable simplicity of language and revelation. Of course, given the genesis of the work, we cannot be entirely sure how much is by Suso and how much by Elsbeth Stagel, and to what extent the work was edited by him. The work, which is incredibly moving in the excellent translation by Frank Tobin, concludes with the account of the death of Elsbeth and her appearance in a vision to the man who had become her spiritual father. The chapter headings give some idea of how the work goes to the heart of spiritual experience and questioning: for example, "The right distinction between true and false detachment" (chapter 48), "A sensible introduction for the Outer Man to his Inwardness" (chapter 49), "Instruction concerning where God is and how God is" (chapter 51).

It is usually held that the earliest of these individual works was the *Little Book of Truth*, dated by the reference to the death of Meister Eckhart to about 1326-28. The work takes the form of the dialogue that emerges as a favorite form of Suso's, although in this respect he was not original: Mechthild von Magdeburg had used the device to a limited extent, but probably a more important model was *The Consolation of Philosophy* of Boethius. Between the *Little Book of Truth* and the *Little Book of Eternal Wisdom*, probably his next work, Suso develops the device, endowing the two central speakers, by now the Servant (himself) and Eternal Wisdom (Christ), with considerable psychological depth. In some chapters it is the Virgin Mary who replies, in one (Chapter 21), some of the answers are given by the man dying unprepared. This Book is usually regarded as Suso's most important piece and it was described by the prominent 19th-century scholar of mysticism, H. S. Denifle, as "the finest fruit of German mysticism." The central theme is that of St. Bernard: *per Christum hominem ad Christum Deum*. Man can come to know God only through the story of Jesus Christ and his Passion. The core of the Book is the third part, which contains one hundred meditations consisting of a single sentence and grouped in tens and fives, each group followed by a prayer.

This is a highly imaginative work of great beauty, evoking the suffering of Christ and of the Virgin Mary, and pointing to suffering as the certain way to the perfection of heaven which is also evoked with considerable poetic skill and contrasted with the anguish of hell. The second part of the work which is essentially concerned with the need to live in a way that prepares one for heaven, not least through the devout acceptance of the sacraments, culminates in a chapter that advocates the praise of God. The tone and language of the first part of the final speech of this section, in the mouth of the Servant, may serve as a demonstration of the way in which Suso combines his considerable literary skills with his overriding concern to convey a spiritual lesson. It is also a characteristic example of the language of the mystical writing at this period:

> Minneklicher herr, min zartu, Ewigu Wisheit, ich beger, swenne minu ogen des morgens erst uf gant, daz och min herz uf gange, und von ime uf breche ein ufflammendu vurinu minnevackel dins lobes mit der lieplichsten minne des minndesten herzen, daz in zit ist, nach der hizigosten minne des hohsten geistes von Seraphin in ewigkeit, und der grundlosen minne, als du, himelscher vatter, din gemintes kint minnest in der usblikenden minne uwer beider geistes, und das lob als suzklich erklinge in dinem vaterlichen herzen, als in zit in siner achte kein suz gedone aller minneklichen seitenspil in keinem vrien gemut ie gedonde, und in der minnevackel uf tringe ein als suzer smake des lobes. . . . (Bihlmeyer, 313)

> (Beloved Lord, my tender, everlasting Wisdom, I ask of you that when my eyes first open in the morning, my heart should open up as well and that from it there should burst forth a flaming fiery torch of love praising you with the dearest love of the most loving heart that exists, like the most burning love of the most sublime spirit in all eternity and the boundless love with which, heavenly Father, you love your beloved child in the radiating love of the spirit of both of you, and that this praise should resound as sweetly in your fatherly heart as any sweetly sounding melody of its kind ever did from any lovely stringed instrument resounding in a free spirit, and that in the torch of love such a sweet fragrance of praise should penetrate that. . . .)

Not for nothing has Suso been called the "Minnesinger of Jesus," and he reflects the way in which the language of Middle High German was being adapted for a new purpose at this period, when the dominance of courtly poetry was giving way to new dimensions of thought and expression. The special prominence of mysticism in medieval Germany may have many explanations, historical and social as well as strictly religious, but not least among them must be the capacity of the language itself at this point in its development to express new ideas which were being grafted upon the established ones.

## Mysticism—Bibliography

### General Introductions to Mysticism:

Davies, Oliver. *The Mystical Tradition of Northern Europe*. London: Darton, Longman and Todd, 1988.

McGinn, Bernard. *The Presence of God: A History of Christian Mysticism*. Vol. II: The Growth of Mysticism. London: SCM, 1995.

An authoritative study of the subject.

Szarmach, Paul, ed. *An Introduction to the Medieval Mystics of Europe*. Albany: SUNY Press, 1984.

This is a helpful volume of essays on some of the major figures in European mysticism by specialists in the field. Particular attention is drawn to the contribution by Bernard McGinn on Meister Eckhart (pp. 237-257) and on Johannes Tauler by Richard Kieckhefer (pp. 259-272), but the entire selection, and the introduction by the editor, provide detailed insight into the place of mysticism in the cultural and social life of the Middle Ages.

Texts:
Lanczkowski, Johanna, ed. *Erhebe dich, meine Seele: mystische Texte des Mittelalters*. Stuttgart: Reclam, 1988 (= UB, 8456). Convenient little anthology.

### Women Mystics:

Bowie, Fiona, ed. *Beguine Spirituality. An Anthology*. Trans. by Oliver Davies. London: Society for the Propagation of Christian Knowledge, 1989.

A very useful little paperback, with a lucid introduction to the Beguine movement against the background which produced it, particularly in relation to the position of women in later medieval society. Translations into modern English of the works of three significant women writers: Mechthild of Magdeburg, Hadewijch of Brabant, and Beatrice of Nazareth. Provides an excellent introduction to the essence of mysticism.

Dinzelbacher, Peter, and Dieter R. Bauer, eds. *Frauenmystik im Mittelalter*. Ostfildern bei Stuttgart: Schwabenverlag, 1985.

Series of papers from a meeting sponsored by the Akademie der Diözese Rottenburg-Stuttgart. 1984.

Lagario, Valerie M. "The Medieval Continental Women Mystics." In Szarmach, 161-193 (above).

Pp. 163-174 are devoted to the German mystics.

Phillips, Dayton. *Beguines in Medieval Strasburg: A Study of the Social Aspects of Beguine Life.* Ann Arbor: Beck, 1963.

Stoudt, Debra L. " 'ich súndig wîp mus schriben': Religious Women and Literary Traditions." In: *Women as Protagonists and Poets in the German Middle Ages. An Anthology of Feminist Approaches to Middle High German Literature.* Ed. by Albrecht Classen. Göppingen: Kümmerle, 1991 (= GAG, 528). Pp. 147-168.

**Hildegard von Bingen:**

Hart, Columba, and Jane Bishop, trans. *Hildegard von Bingen: Scivias.* New York: Paulist Press, 1990 (= Classics of Western Spirituality).

Bowie, Fiona, and Oliver Davies, eds. *Hildegard von Bingen: An Anthology* with a new translation by Robert Carver. London: SPCK, 1990.

**Mechthild von Magdeburg:**

Morel, P. Gall, ed. *Offenbarungen der Schwester Mechthild von Magdeburg oder das Fließende Licht der Gottheit, aus der einzigen Schrift des Stiftes Einsiedeln* Darmstadt: Wiss. Buchges., 1980.

The standard edition of her works, a photographic reprint of the original, 1869, edition.

Menzies, Lucy, trans. *The Revelations of Mechthild of Magdeburg.* New York: Longmans, Green & Co., 1953.

The introduction is helpful if now somewhat old-fashioned in its tone.

Tobin, Frank J. *Mechthild von Magdeburg: A Medieval Mystic in Modern Eyes.* Columbia, SC: Camden House, 1995.

A very full and thoroughly readable introduction to the woman and her work with an interesting account of its reception through to the modern period.

**German Mysticism:**

Bundschuh, Adeltrud. *Die Bedeutung von "gelassen" und die Bedeutung der "Gelassenheit" in den deutschen Werken Meister Eckharts unter Berücksichtigung seiner lateinischen Schriften.* Frankfurt/M: Lang, 1990 (= Europäische Hochschulschriften, Reihe 20, Philos., 302).

Specific study of a central concept in Meister Eckhart.

Clark, James M. *The Great German Mystics. Eckhart, Tauler and Suso.* Oxford: Blackwell, 1949.

A fairly brief but still highly regarded early study of the subject.

Campbell, Karen J., ed. *German Mystical Writings.* New York: Continuum, 1991 (= The German Library, Vol.5).

Trans. into Engl. from the works of Hildegard von Bingen, Mechthild von Magdeburg, Meister Eckhart, Heinrich Seuse, Johannes Tauler, Jacob Boehme and Angelus Silesius, with a Foreword by Carol Zaleski.

Davies, Oliver. *Meister Eckhart: Mystical Theologian.* London: SPCK, 1991.

Haas, Alois M. *Geistliches Mittelalter.* Freiburg, Schweiz: Universitätsverlag, 1984 (= Dokimion, 8).

A substantial volume on religious writing in MHG, thus of broader interest. Focus on mysticism.

Pfeiffer, Franz, ed. *Deutsche Mystiker des 14. Jahrhunderts.* Göttingen: Vandenhoek, 1907-1914.

Quint, Joseph, ed. *Textbuch zur Mystik des deutschen Mittelalters: Meister Eckhart, Johannes Tauler, Heinrich Seuse.* Halle: Niemeyer, 1952.

A standard work.

Schürmann, Reiner. *Meister Eckhart. Mystic and Philosopher.* Bloomington: Indiana UP, 1978.

Tobin, Frank. *Meister Eckhart: Thought and Language.* Philadelphia: Univ. of Pennsylvania Press, 1986.

Wehr, Gerhard, ed. *Meister Eckhart in Selbstzeugnissen und Bilddokumenten.* Hamburg: Rowohlt, 1989 (= Rowohlts Monographien).

A popular, but useful, miscellany of information.

Wentzlaff-Eggebert, Friedrich-Wilhelm. *Deutsche Mystik zwischen Mittelalter und Neuzeit: Einheit und Wandlung ihrer Erscheinungsform.* Tübingen: Mohr, $^2$1947.

One of the classic studies of the subject.

Texts & Trans.:
Meister Eckhart:
Colledge, Edmund, and Bernhard McGinn, trans. *Meister Eckhart: The Essential Sermons, Commentaries, Treatises, and Defense.* Preface by Huston Smith. New York: Paulist Press, 1981 (= Classics of Western Spirituality).
Fox, Matthew, trans. *Breakthrough: Meister Eckhart's Creation Spirituality in New Translation.* Garden City, New York: Doubleday, 1980.
McGinn, Bernard, et al., eds. *Meister Eckhart—Teacher and Preacher.* Preface by Kenneth Northcott. New York, Mahwah, Toronto: Paulist Press, 1986 (= Classics of Western Spirituality). (A second substantial vol. in this series, it provides an authoritative introduction: of particular interest and use may be the "Glossary of Eckhartian Terms" pp. 388-405).
Quint, Josef, ed. *Meister Eckhart, Deutsche Predigten und Traktate.* Zürich: Diogenes, 1979. (= Diogenes Taschenbuch. 202). Orig. publ. Munich: Hanser, 1963.
Walshe, Maurice O'C., ed. and trans. *Meister Eckhart. Sermons and Treatises.* Shaftesbury, Dorset: Element Books, 1979. $^2$1987. 3 vols. (Paperback edition of the Ger. writings by Eckhart, preface to each vol., and detailed notes).

Heinrich Suso:
Bihlmeyer, Karl, ed. *Heinrich Seuse. Deutsche Schriften im Auftrag der Württembergischen Kommission der Landesgeschichte* Stuttgart: Kohlhammer 1907. Repr. Frankfurt/M: Minerva, 1961.
Hofmann, Georg. *Deutsche mystische Schriften von Heinrich Seuse.* Darmstadt: Wiss. Buchges., 1966. (MHG text with mod. Ger. trans.)
Jaspert, Bernd, ed., and Winfried Zeller, sel. *Mystische Schriften: Heinrich Suso und Johannes Tauler.* Munich: Eugen Deiderichs, 1988. (A convenient selection of both writers).
Sturlese, Loris, and Rüdiger Blumrich, eds. and trans. *Heinrich Seuse: Das Buch der Wahrheit.* Hamburg: F. Meiner Verlag, 1993. (MHG text with mod. Ger. trans. on adjacent pages).
Tobin, Frank, ed. and trans. *Henry Suso. The Exemplar, with two German Sermons.* Preface by Bernard McGinn. New York, Mahwah: Paulist Press, 1989. (= Classics of Western Spirituality). (A very informative introduction by Tobin, set in the broader context of German mysticism. Excellent translation).
See also: Karen Campbell (1991, above).

Johannes Tauler:

Corin, Adolphe Léon, ed. *Sermons de J. Tauler*. Liège & Paris: Bibliothèque de la Faculté de Philosophie et Lettres de l'Université de Liège, 1929. (Another standard edition).

Gnädinger, Louise, ed. and trans. *Johannes Tauler*. Olten: Walter, 1983. (MHG text with intro. and mod. Ger. transl.).

Kelley, C. F., ed. and trans. *The Book of the Poor in Spirit: A Guide to Rhineland Mysticism*. London: Longmans, Green, 1954. (MHG text with intro. and Engl. trans.).

Morrell, J. R., trans. *Johannes Tauler: The Following of Christ*. London: Unwin, 1910.

Shady, Maria, trans. *Johannes Tauler, Sermons*. New York: Paulist Press, 1985 (= Classics of Western Spirituality). (Intro. by Josef Schmidt and preface by Alois Haas).

Vetter, Ferdinand, ed. *Die Predigten Taulers*. Berlin, 1910 (= Texte des Mas.). Repr. Frankfurt/M: Weidmann, 1968. (Standard edition).

See also: James Clark (1949) under "German Mysticism" and Bernd Jaspert and Winfried Zeller (1988) under "Heinrich Seuse" above.


## JOHANNES VON SAAZ (TEPL): *DER ACKERMANN (AUS BÖHMEN)*

We have chosen to draw our introduction to the study of MHG literature to a conclusion with this small but in many ways very significant work. Historically, the year 1400 is unremarkable: the deposition of the Emperor Wenzel cannot be seen as a turning point of any moment in itself (see p. 307), but, as far as the progress of German literature is concerned, it ushers in a century of significant changes in language and thought, a movement away from the Middle Ages into the beginnings of the European Renaissance. In 1400 the impact of printing lay half a century away, still further away the overwhelming revolution produced by Martin Luther, but in many respects the *Ackermann* anticipates distant developments and has a remarkable ring of modernity about it, though it is simultaneously deeply rooted in the Middle Ages.

By now the German language was established as a medium for prose writing, for works of factual information, as we have seen, and increasingly for conveying religious thought, from the sermons of the Franciscan Berthold von Regensburg in the mid-13th century to the great writings of the mystics which can justly be considered one of the most significant aspects of German literature of the later Middle Ages. Notably absent is a considerable work of fiction in prose: the *Prosa-Lancelot* remains a strange and isolated phenomenon (see p. 331 f.), and it was not until well into the 15th century that anything approaching prose fiction in German emerged in the works of Elisabeth von Nassau-Saarbrucken and Eleanore von Österreich, who both produced substantial "novels," which took their material from actual or quasi-historical events.

German prose was, however, the medium for the *Ackermann*, and it is no exaggeration to say that the work represents a modest pinnacle in the literary landscape of the later Middle Ages in Germany. Moreover, it is not too strained to think of the work in relation to some of the diffuse threads of the late 13th century and the 14th century which we have been considering. Its author is no mystic, yet he may well have had some acquaintance with the writings of the mystics: his own exploration of the relationship between Man and God is fresh and original, his faith ultimately made more solid by the questioning and the doubt. The form of the work is a simple dialogue, yet it is imbued with dramatic qualities greater than most of the drama of the time. He uses the German language with great skill, demonstrating his training in Latin language and rhetoric, possibly at the University of Prague where he may have gained the degree of Master of Arts which he appends to his name in the acrostic of the final prayer. Johannes von Tepl was a scholar of the new age, a teacher and notary in the region of Prague at a time when the humanistic ideas born in the Italy of Dante, and even more of Petrarch and Boccaccio, were taking hold in Bohemia. His work shows in general the influence of the *De consolatione Philosophiae* of Boethius and, more explicitly, of Petrarch's *De remediis* and, in the lament for the human condition contained in Death's final speech, of the famous treatise by Pope Innocent III. The self-confidence of the humanist is shattered, however, by the impact of a personal loss, and, for all the bold effort at attack and self-defense of the Ploughman, it is the thinking of the Middle Ages which emerges intact.

A further factor in our attempt to relate the literature of Germany to its broader context is that the year 1400 is attested as the year of the death of Chaucer. It would appear, then, that one of the great figures of medieval Europe died in the same year as the young woman Margaretha, whose claim to fame, regardless of scholarly attempts to dispute the autobiographical basis of the work, lies in the effect of her death on her husband and the literary immortality which she achieves in the moving debate between the distraught survivor and Death itself. It provides an interesting perspective on the literature of the German medieval classical period to remind ourselves how apart it is in time from what is traditionally regarded as the focus of English medieval literature.

The *Ackermann* is usually dated very soon after the death of Margaretha, and its author has been established as Johannes von Tepl, sometimes called Johannes von Saaz, after the town in which he occupied the function of Imperial Notary, or even Johannes von Schüttwa, the small village in the north-west of Bohemia where he was born.

The popularity of the work in its day is suggested by the relative abundance of manuscripts, though the earliest of these (A) dates from almost fifty years after the original composition. A further fifteen manuscripts, not all of them complete, belong likewise to the second half of the 15th century. In addition, the work exists in seventeen printed versions of the second half of the 15th century and the first half of the 16th. Despite this early popularity, the work, like so much of the literature of the German Middle Ages, disappeared from view until it was rediscovered in the 18th century by Gottsched who planned an edition based on his painstaking copying of an early printed version. In fact it was not edited until 1824, when Friedrich von der Hagen produced an edition based on Gottsched's copy. More important than the edition itself, which, with its modernizations and many inconsistencies, was actually rather unsatisfactory, is the evident awareness which von der Hagen demonstrates of the special qualities of this unique work.

An important turning point in the understanding of the *Ackermann* came as relatively recently as 1933, when a letter was discovered in the University library in Freiburg in Breisgau. This letter, sent by Johannes von Tepl to his old friend Peter von Tepl in Prague, was explicitly written to accompany the little book which he calls the *Ackermann* and which, he says, he has recently written. The letter is a vital aid to our understanding of the author's intention, not so much with the content, which is self-evidently an attack on inescapable death, as with the manner of his presentation, his deliberate use of language in a varied and powerful way. Although Johannes appears to be lamenting the limitations of the German language, he nevertheless displays a consciousness of what he has achieved and guides us in our analysis of the highly deliberate style of this extraordinary work. In particular, he points to the paradoxes in style which are so striking and so much a part of his purpose, aware as he is, for example, that it is possible to praise and blame the same thing, and to juxtapose humor with seriousness.

The essence of the work is summed up in his statement *arenga inuehitur et demollitur* (the spokesman inveighs and is brought to submission). Yet the submission to which the Ploughman is brought is ultimately a willing one, and the message of the work is gentle. The bereaved husband who attacks Death with such venom in the opening onslaught: "Grimmiger tilger aller lande, schedlicher echter aller werlte, freissamer mörder aller leute, ir Tot, euch sei verfluchet!" ("Death, you grim annihilator of all lands, you ruinous persecutor of the whole world, hideous murderer of all people, curses be upon you!") arrives at a calm acceptance of the progression of human life in which death has its place.

The work is divided into thirty-four chapters. Of these, the majority forms a dialogue between the Ploughman, the representative of Man, and Death. Only in Chapter XXXIII does God intervene to pronounce judgment, according the victory to Death but honor to the Ploughman, who concludes the work with a tranquil acceptance of the will of God and the commendation of the soul of his wife to Him.

The whole work is remarkable for its fluctuations in mood and tempo, as the debate passes between the two protagonists, reflecting anger and bitterness, exasperation and indignation, contempt and resentment, yet also understanding and deep sadness. Despite the limitations which, according to the dedicatory letter to Peter von Tepl, he perceives as inherent in the German language, the author shows considerable flexibility and range, employing a variety of rhetorical devices to great effect and with unique panache. Such linguistic virtuosity probably stems from his close familiarity with Latin: the name of Johannes von Tepl is recorded as the director of the Latin school in Saaz, and the only other works attributable to him are in fact Latin verses. Nevertheless, it is his manipulation of the German language for his purpose which is so remarkable.

The work belongs in the tradition of the *disputatio*, the debate between two opposing forces in which each in turn puts forward his point of view. The structure is based on this legalistic presentation of a case, the one protagonist the plaintiff, the other the defendant. However, it is not that clear cut, for the work is characterized by movement, with the apparently irreconcilable opponents not so much shifting their ground as varying their manner of attack and rebuttal. In this way the work attains the quality of drama, at a time when, as we have seen, drama as we understand it was virtually unknown in Germany. Moreover, as the debate proceeds, the purely personal gives way to the universal, as Death comes to see that the Ploughman, initially consumed by grief for his lost wife, is also the spokesman for all mankind and begins to place his defense into a broader context, assuring him that all living things are destined to die and that joy has no part in man's physical existence.

Against Death's contempt for human achievement and his rejection of the higher aspirations of Man, the Ploughman, the representative of the humanistic view which sees Man in a positive light, begins to assert a standpoint that is ultimately more optimistic. In a central passage (Chapter 25), he eulogizes the human head for its exquisiteness of form and as the repository of such fine senses. This is in direct response to the immediately preceding attack by Death, who had heaped upon the human body a string of abuse, reducing it to crude physical terms, and linking with this onslaught a brief dismissal of woman who is nothing but a wretched doll, a flower that quickly withers.

Despite the fluctuations within the argument, the essential opposition remains, and the debate can be resolved only by the intervention of a Higher Power, to whom, as God reminds them, they are both subject. He enters on the scene with the parable of the four seasons, warring among themselves and forgetting that the power of each of them emanates from Him. His measured allocation of responsibility and achievement moves the argument to a higher plane and leaves the way clear for the Ploughman's calm statement of his recognition of a Higher Authority, to Whom he is now prepared to entrust all things, even the soul of his wife.

*Der Ackermann aus Böhmen* has evoked some diametrically opposed views in those who have devoted their time to it, often to the point of obsession. Of the earliest scholars, some adhered to the view of Konrad Burdach (1926 and 1932) who saw it as an early product of Humanism, a rejection of the attitudes of the Middle Ages and an affirmation of the spirit of Man, contained in a piece of writing essentially confessional in its nature. Others were inclined to accept Arthur Hübner's emphasis on the derivative elements which root it deeply in medieval tradition (1935 and 1937). Hübner's opinion that the work was first and foremost a rhetorical exercise seemed to be vindicated, certainly for Hübner himself, by the discovery of the letter of dedication by the author, who makes no reference to an underlying personal experience which may have inspired it. Probably none of these extreme views of the work is exclusively right, and one cannot help feeling that the more appropriate assessment is the one which takes the middle pathway, the route of compromise and reconciliation, and which accords to the poem its place as a significant document of an age of progress and change, of movement forward on the basis of firm traditions.

Certainly for us the work marks something of a goal, combining as it does much that is present in the literature preceding it, yet pointing the way forward into areas as yet untouched. Linguistically it demonstrates the capacity of the German language to express itself in new and vibrant ways. In form, it stands out as the first major work of literature in prose. Thematically, it treads new ground in its presentation of a world in which God ultimately retains His central position but where Man can assert his right to challenge and to question.

Texts:
Hämmerich, L. L., and G. Jungbluth, eds. *Johannes von Saaz, "Der Ackermann aus Böhmen." Textausgabe*. Heidelberg: Winter, 1951.
Jungbluth, Gunther, ed. *Johannes von Saaz: Der Ackermann aus Böhmen*. Vol. I: Edition. Heidelberg: Winter, 1969 (This contains a very full bibliography). Vol. II: *Kommentar aus dem Nachlaß von G. Jungbluth*. Heidelberg: Winter, 1983.

Krogmann, Willy, ed. *Johannes von Tepl: Der Ackermann. Auf Grund der deutschen Überlieferung und der tschechischen Bearbeitung kritisch herausgegeben.* Wiesbaden: Brockhaus, 1954 (= Deutsche Klassiker des Mas, N.F., 1 ).

Walshe, M. O'C., ed. *Johannes von Tepl, "Der Ackermann aus Böhmen."* London: Duckworth, 1951.

____, ed. *Johannes von Tepl. Der Ackermann aus Böhmen. A Working Edition with Introduction, Notes and Glossary and the Full Text of MSS E and H.* Hull: New German Studies, 1982. (A very useful contribution which deserves a more convenient form. It discusses the manuscripts and contains a more recent bibliography than Jungbluth).

Translations:

Genzmer, F., ed. and trans. *Johannes von Tepl. Der Ackermann und der Tod.* Stuttgart: Reclam, 1951 (= UB, 7666). (MHG text with mod. Ger. trans., notes, and afterword).

Krogmann, Willy, trans. *Der Ackermann und der Tod. Ein Streitgespräch von Johannes von Tepl. Ins Neuhochdeutsche Ubertragen von Willy Krogmann. Mit einem Nachwort von Reinhold Schneider und den fünf Holzschnitten der Bamberger Frühdrucke.* Frankfurt/M: Insel, 1957 Repr. 1985. (The woodcuts are an interesting addition to this little book).

Maurer, K. W., trans. *Death and the Ploughman: An Argument and a Consolation from the Year 1400 by Johann von Tepl.* London: Euston Press, 1947. (Also contains a commentary in English).

## *Ackermann*—Bibliography

Hahn, Gerhard. *Der Ackermann aus Böhmen des Johannes von Tepl.* Darmstadt: Wiss. Buchges., 1984 (= Erträge der Forschung, 215).

A full and readily accessible commentary by a leading authority on the work.

Natt, Rosemarie. *Der Ackermann aus Böhmen des Johannes von Tepl, ein Beitrag zur Interpretation.* Göppingen: Kümmerle, 1978 (= GAG, 235).

Schwarz, E., ed. *Der Ackermann aus Böhmen.* Darmstadt: Wiss. Buchges., 1968 (= WdF, 143). (Important articles to 1968 collected and reprinted).

See also: Hahn, Gerhard, $VL^2$ (1983) 763-774.

# CHRONOLOGICAL TABLE I

| 700AD | 800AD | 900AD | 1000AD |
|---|---|---|---|
| | *Heliand* [39] | | *Merigarto* [80] |
| | *OHG Tatian* [30] | | |
| *Abrogans* [27] | *Muspilli* [37] | *Waltharius* [55] | *Physiologus* [80] |
| *OHG Isidor* [29] | *Merseburg Charms* [33] | *Hroswitha von Gandersheim* [431] | *Ruodlieb* [56] |
| | *Otfrid* [42] | | *Memento mori* [85] |
| *Hildebrandslied* [34] | *Ludwigslied* [52] | *Notker* [31] | *Ezzolied* [81] |
| | *Wessobrunn Prayer* [36] | | *Annolied* [92] |

## AUTHORS/WORKS FROM OTHER PARTS OF EUROPE

| 700AD | 800AD | 900AD | 1000AD |
|---|---|---|---|
| *Beowulf* (? c.725) | | | *Battle of Maldon* (post 991) |
| | | *Anglo-Saxon Chronicle* → | |

## HISTORIC EVENTS & FAMOUS PEOPLE

| 700AD | 800AD | 900AD | 1000AD |
|---|---|---|---|
| | Treaty of Verdun (843) Treaty of Meersen (870) Battle of Saucourt (881) | | First Crusade (1096-1099) |
| Charles the Great (768-814) | | Otto I (936-973) | Otto III (983-1002) |
| | | Otto II (973-983) | Henry II (1002-1024) |
| ← CAROLINGIAN DYNASTY | | SAXON AND SALIAN DYNASTIES → | |

Note: Numbers in the upper section refer to pages in the text.

# CHRONOLOGICAL TABLE II

## 1100AD

König Rother
[106]

Der von Kürenberc
[239]

Herzog Ernst
[109]

Dietmar von Aist
[241]

Oswald
[111]

Salman und Morolf
[113]

Albrecht von Johannsdorf
[250]

Graf Rudolf
[115]

Orendel
[112]

Friedrich von Hûsen
[247]

Alexanderlied
[93]

Heinrich von Melk
[87]

Rolandslied
[94]

Hildegard von Bingen
[71]

Heinrich von Veldeke
[122/245]

Eilhart von Oberg
[118]

Kaiserchronik
[92]

Priester Wernher
[77]

Hartmann von Aue
[132/257]

## AUTHORS/WORKS FROM OTHER PARTS OF EUROPE

Chanson de Roland
(c.1100/1130)

Béroul

Andreas Capellanus:
De arte honeste amandi

Thomas of Britain
(fl. c.1160)

Marie de France

Anglo-Saxon Chronicle

Chrétien de Troyes
(fl. c. 1170)

## HISTORIC EVENTS & FAMOUS PEOPLE

St. Bernard of Clairvaux
(1090-1153)

Murder of Thomas à Becket
(1170)

Peter Abelard
(1079-1142)

Hugh of St. Victor
(1140-1200)

Concordat of Worms
(1122)

University of Oxford
(c.1160)

Worms Cathedral
(c.1192)

University of Bologna
(c.1120)

Court Festival at Mainz
(1184)

University of Paris
(c.1120)

Second Crusade
(1147-1149)

Third Crusade
(1189-1192)

Frederick I ('Barbarossa')
(1152-1190)

### HOHENSTAUFEN AND WELF DYNASTIES

Note: Numbers in the upper section refer to pages in the text.

# CHRONOLOGICAL TABLE III

## 1200AD

Walther von der Vogelweide [267]  Ulrich von Liechtenstein [311]  Steinmar [294]

Eike von Repgouwe [418]  Der Pleier [367]

Reinmar von Hagenau [260]

Hadlaub [295]

Neidhart [279]  Mechthild von Magdeburg [438]

Heinrich von Morungen [252]  Der Stricker [361]  Frauenlob [299]

Moriz von Craûn [322]

Lanzelet [328]  Wigamur [319]  Meister Eckhart [440]

Prosa-Lancelot [331]

Wigalois [314]  Kudrun [399]  Jüngerer Titurel [381]  Passional [422]

Nibelungenlied [205]  Rudolf von Ems [333]  Konrad von Würzburg [342]  Lohengrin [385]

Wolfram von Eschenbach [174]  Diu Crône [358]  Freidank [426]  Heinrich von Freiberg [374]

Gottfried von Straßburg [157]  Ulrich von Türheim [372/377]  Meier Helmbrecht [403]

## AUTHORS/WORKS FROM OTHER PARTS OF EUROPE

Njal's Saga (c. 1280)

Le Roman de la Rose (c. 1250-1300)

## HISTORIC EVENTS & FAMOUS PEOPLE

St. Francis of Assisi (1181-1226)  Thomas Aquinas (1225-1274)

Magna Carta (1215)  Stifterfiguren in Naumburg Cathedral (1260/1270)

Cologne Cathedral (begun 1248)

Hermann von Thüringen (died 1217)  Westminster Abbey (1245)  Strasbourg Cathedral (nave completed 1275)

Dietrick von Meissen (died 1221)  Crusades of Louis IX (1248-1269)

Philip of Swabia (1198-1208)  Frederick II (1215-1250)  Rudolf of Habsburg (1273-1291)

Otto IV (1198-1215)  Interregnum (1254-1273)

HOHENSTAUFEN AND WELF

Note: Numbers in the upper section refer to pages in the text.

# CHRONOLOGICAL TABLE IV

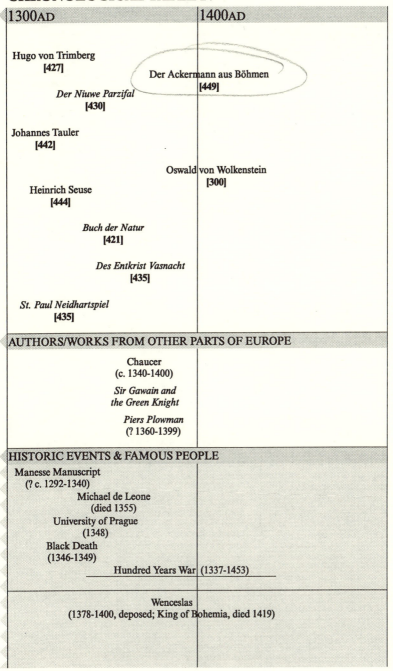

| 1300AD | 1400AD |
|---|---|
| Hugo von Trimberg [427] | Der Ackermann aus Böhmen [449] |
| *Der Niuwe Parzifal* [430] | |
| Johannes Tauler [442] | |
| | Oswald von Wolkenstein [300] |
| Heinrich Seuse [444] | |
| *Buch der Natur* [421] | |
| *Des Entkrist Vasnacht* [435] | |
| *St. Paul Neidhartspiel* [435] | |

## AUTHORS/WORKS FROM OTHER PARTS OF EUROPE

| | |
|---|---|
| Chaucer (c. 1340-1400) | |
| *Sir Gawain and the Green Knight* | |
| *Piers Plowman* (? 1360-1399) | |

## HISTORIC EVENTS & FAMOUS PEOPLE

| | |
|---|---|
| Manesse Manuscript (? c. 1292-1340) | |
| Michael de Leone (died 1355) | |
| University of Prague (1348) | |
| Black Death (1346-1349) | |
| Hundred Years War (1337-1453) | |
| Wenceslas (1378-1400, deposed; King of Bohemia, died 1419) | |

Note: Numbers in the upper section refer to pages in the text.